A SOCIAL AND RELIGIOUS HISTORY OF THE JEWS

High Middle Ages, 500–1200: Volumes III–VIII

VOLUME VI

LAWS, HOMILIES, AND THE BIBLE

A SOCIAL AND RELIGIOUS HISTORY OF THE JEWS

By SALO WITTMAYER BARON

Second Edition, Revised and Enlarged

High Middle Ages, 500–1200: Volumes III–VIII

VOLUME VI

LAWS, HOMILIES, AND THE BIBLE

Columbia University Press
New York and London
The Jewish Publication Society of America
Philadelphia

ISBN 0-231-08843-4
LIBRARY OF CONGRESS CATALOG CARD NUMBER: 52-404

PRINTED IN THE UNITED STATES OF AMERICA
10 9 8 7 6 5 4

CONTENTS

A SOCIAL AND RELIGIOUS HISTORY OF THE JEWS

LAWS, HOMILIES, AND THE BIBLE

XXVII

REIGN OF LAW

NOTWITHSTANDING unceasing sectarian clashes and the growing organizational dissolution into provincial and local communal groups, the main body of the Jewish people preserved its world unity primarily through the unbroken continuity of its legal structure. Basic integrity was maintained regardless of numerous modifications imposed by changing environmental conditions, the growing urbanization of both the Jews and their neighbors, the intensification of agricultural and industrial production, and the rapid exchange of goods. It was upheld against all forces of disintegration, both external and internal, by the people's great law-consciousness, the overwhelming power of tradition, and the tenacity as well as pliability of leaders utilizing the well-established techniques of talmudic learning. Ever since the days of ancient Pharisaism the sages had combined conservative adherence to traditional ideals and modes of living with great adaptability to changing social needs and environmental conditions.

Rabbinic leadership found considerable support in the general climate of opinion prevailing among the Near Eastern peoples of the pre-Islamic period, and even more so after the rise of the new civilization. The antinomianism of the early Church had long been submerged in a flood of new laws and regulations and in perennial sectarian disputes about minutiae of ceremonies and observances. True, the Byzantine Empire had inherited from its pagan predecessor a division between *jus* and *fas,* as well as between civil and religious law. The latter distinction was now the more clearly defined, as the state had to strain its resources to stave off the growing encroachments of the clergy. But no such lines of demarcation were ever recognized in the Sassanian Empire, now the focal center of Jewish legal studies as well. There religion and law formed an inseparable entity among both the Zoroastrians and the religious minorities.

Among the Nestorian Christians, for example, the interlocking of religious and legal provisions and sanctions was so intimate that it created striking resemblances with the religio-juridical evolution in Judaism—a resemblance further heightened by the recourse of both faiths to biblical law. Only where Roman patterns had invited direct emulation did the parallels with Jewish law diminish in size and intensity. As observed by Viktor Aptowitzer, a keen student of Nestorian-Jewish legal interrelations, the so-called Syro-Roman Code incorporates relatively few Jewish ingredients, obviously because its compiler stressed the Roman rather than the natively Syrian elements. Moreover, it now appears likely that the entire treatise, used chiefly for educational purposes, had originated in the West and was merely translated into Syriac with relatively minor modifications. But other collections, including the laws of inheritance compiled by Patriarch Mar Abba (about 500) and the more general code of laws summarized from older sources by Archbishop Yeshubokht (after 750), furnish many manifest similarities with talmudic law. The same holds true also for the Armenian Code. In addition, there circulated outright epitomes of Mosaic law, or of what the contemporary ecclesiastical leaders considered a still valid Mosaic heritage, in which the Judeo-Christian relationships were perfectly obvious. We need not unreservedly follow Aptowitzer's theory and assume far-reaching direct indebtedness of the Syrian and Armenian churchmen to Jewish teachings, yet we must concede the all-pervading similarity, even identity, of many general approaches and detailed provisions. In Babylonia, the heartland of both faiths and the main scene of the great scholastic efforts in their schools of jurisprudence, both religions were also nurtured by immemorial traditions of the ancient Babylonian civilization and its long-enduring legal institutions. Similar social needs, moreover, would in any case have generated similar answers in legal practice. Nonetheless the presence of a strong and influential Jewish minority, which had long faced similar problems and developed an effective technique of meeting them, must have served as an additional incentive and model. Reciprocally, the great Christian interest in biblical law in all its ramifications, as well as the parallel juridical emphases among the Zoroastrian *mobedhs,* doubtless strengthened the rabbinic controls and enhanced the prestige of legal studies among the Jews of Babylonia and the other Persian provinces.[1]

Nor were developments in Palestine and other Byzantine possessions antagonistic to Jewish law-mindedness. True, the original Latin sources of Byzantine law, less and less understandable without Greek translations even to non-Jews in the Balkans and western Asia, had never appealed to Jewish sages. The relatively few similarities between Roman and Jewish law, as we recall, were probably owing more to their common heritage from Hellenistic institutions than to any direct borrowings from either side. Certainly, neither the underlying humanistic, not theistic, approaches of the great Roman jurists before 313 nor their cosmopolitanism and transcendence of denominational boundaries could find much response in a minority struggling to maintain its traditional heritage behind the ramparts of its national law. A concept like that of a *jus gentium* common to all subjects of a heterogeneous empire, or of a "natural law" obligatory for all men regardless of race and creed, was necessarily alien to Jews who saw in their legal structure a peculiar divine endowment and their main claim to being the chosen among nations. Other peoples, the rabbis insisted, had had their chance to accept the Torah, but had rejected it. The Jews alone undertook to carry the burden and, despite all hardships, would continue to carry it to the messianic age, when it would be adopted in its totality by all nations. The farthest the Jewish jurists were able to go in recognizing "natural law" was to formulate six or seven "Noahide commandments," to which all peoples must submit and which were to be enforced on all subjects of a Jewish state. Otherwise Jewish law was to be an exclusively Jewish possession.[2]

At the same time, the open struggle between the orthodox Byzantine regime and its sectarian provincials was conducted far more on the plane of dogmatic disputes about Christ's nature and divine rank in the Trinity than on that of individual rituals and ceremonies. These conceptual controversies were of no direct Jewish concern. Nevertheless they may have stimulated the interest of Palestinian Jews, too, in the aggadic rather than legal aspects of talmudic lore. That predilection, noticed already by a third-century rabbi and explained by him through the economic decline of Palestinian Jewry, now received new stimuli from the sectarian controversies among the Christians of the Holy Land, Syria, and Egypt. Most of these disputants sought justifications for their particular points of view in the hermeneutic reinterpretation of Scripture through methods which their ancestors had long before taken over from the rabbis and the Hellenistic savants. The aggadic midrash thus gained easy ascendancy over juridical hermeneutics.

On the other hand, beneath the surface most sectarian controversies were accompanied, if not actually preceded, by ceremonial differences which also necessitated constant hermeneutic rationales. Before long the Syriac Christians, even under Byzantine rule, began sharing with their coreligionists across the Sassanian border a healthy respect for law and observance. Certainly, in daily practice the struggle of the religious minorities for toleration by the imperial authorities was directed more at the maintenance of existing ceremonies and observances than at the freedom to profess certain dogmatic variants whose complexities must have eluded the understanding of the masses. It was also in the area of local customs and mores inherited from forefathers that the ancient Roman Empire and its Byzantine successors were traditionally least intractable. All of this tended to reinforce the interest of the Jews in their own legal heritage and its elaboration down to minutest details.[3]

INTERRELATIONS OF JEWISH AND MUSLIM LAW

The expansion of Islam likewise strengthened rather than weakened the grip of the Law upon the life of Jewry. Islam, like Judaism, is a pronouncedly nomistic religion; nomistic in the widest sense, to be sure, including ritual, moral, civil, and criminal law. The early Semitic conception of God as the great judge of the tribe, the heavenly sheikh, was transposed now by the builders of the vast empire into that of Lord and Judge of the whole world. That is one reason why the new rulers found such easy acceptance among the Semitic Christians of Asia, to whom the new religion appeared as but a slightly different version of resuscitated Arianism. It was not altogether without reason that the Qur'anic revelation styled itself "a law of liberty, an act of mercy vouchsafed by God to mankind, in order to soften the rigidity of the preceding revelations." That it was a *law,* and as such not antinomian in principle, made it very palatable to the Christianized Syrians, to whom the Pauline idea of liberty as freedom from the law had long become meaningless. In fact, in comparison with the legal technicalities in the controversies of the Syriac sectarians, the discussions of the Pharisaic contemporaries of Paul appear as those of juridical amateurs. As time went on, however, this "liberal" Islamic movement developed a new orthodoxy of its own, for whom religion became primarily *din,* an expression which—whether borrowed from the Persians or not—conveyed to the Arab, as it did to the Jew, the idea of justice in its full inflexibility.

Under these circumstances, the interpenetration of Jewish and Islamic constituents largely contributed to shaping the destinies of both religious groups. The influence of Judaism on Islam during the lifetime of Mohammed has found numerous investigators. But the subsequent developments, during the first two or three centuries of the Muslim era, so vital in the evolution of the new religion, have been treated less adequately. The enormous mass of the *sunna* and *ḥadith,* that accumulation of Muslim traditions in an age paralleling to a certain extent the apostolic and patristic periods in Christianity, reveals close similarities to some of the most fundamental teachings of the contemporary Jewish *halakhah.* The resemblance is so striking, not only in generalities but frequently also in minutest detail, that to assume parallel development, rather than influence, seems hardly justified. The present stage of scholarship in respect to the early geonic period is such that no definite conclusions can be drawn on this question. Our whole estimate of the age may be revolutionized when the new knowledge contained in the many documents unearthed in the last two or three decades (and those yet to be unearthed in the near future) has been adequately assimilated. Istanbul alone possesses scores of thousands of precious manuscripts, still hidden away in its eighty mosques. A definitive synthesis will have to wait until many more sources, Jewish as well as Arab, are available for further study.[4]

In matters of principle, Islam is no less indebted to Judaism than is Christianity. Although neither the founder nor the first leaders came of Jewish stock, the import of Jewish law and legend in Islam's formative period cannot easily be exaggerated. True, there was no lack of recrimination on either side. Some anti-Jewish biases constituted from the outset an integral part of Islam's religious outlook. In view of Mohammed's purported intent to restore the ancient Hebrew faith of Abraham, the common Arab and Jewish patriarch, Jews were accused, as we recall, of falsifying their religious tradition; indeed, of consciously tampering with the text of their Scripture—an accusation which had long before played such an important role in Samaritan and Christian-Jewish polemics. As a matter of fact, however, many early Muslims, beginning with Mohammed himself, frequently consulted Jews in matters of law. On the whole, Islam assimilated more elements from later Pharisaism than from the Old Testament itself. One need but consider the formula of the official creed, without which no Muslim is regarded as a pious follower of the Messenger: "I believe in Allah, in his angels, in his scriptures, in his prophets, in the future life, in the divine decree [concerning] the good as well as the evil, and in the resurrection of the dead." Most of these confessions obviously represent postbiblical Judaism. All of them, however, are unrestrictedly Jewish, and could have been recited by a medieval Jew in almost the same phraseology.[5]

The similarities between Islam and Judaism go far beyond these dogmatic elements. Law was the core of both religions, and both Jews and Muslims believed it to be of divine origin, transmitted through a revelation to *one* great prophet. Orthodox Muslims always adhered faithfully to, even suffered martyrdom for, the originally aggadic tenet of the preexistence of the Law. Many a legal prescription later emanating from the changing necessities of life was put back into the age of the founder himself, much like the numerous Jewish *halakhot le-Mosheh mi-Sinai* (traditions from Moses on Sinai). There is an old talmudic legend that Moses' Torah contains whatever ingenious students may discover in all future ages. "What is in agreement with the Qur'an is from me, whether I have actually said it or not," states a similar injunction of Mohammed. So far-reaching has been this affinity between Islam and Judaism that in both faiths the judge and legal expert, rather than the priest, were the pillars of the entire social order. "The spiritual authority in catholic Islam," observed C. Snouck Hurgronje, one of its most authoritative Western interpreters, "reposes in the legists, who in this respect are called in a tradition the 'heirs of the prophets.' " This had long been the regnant theory of rabbinic Judaism. If it be true that the 'Umayyad dynasty consciously developed the office of *qadhi* (judge) as the main "bearer of its organizational policies for the Muslim state," this would have been a doubly striking adoption of Jewish patterns, in contrast to the two priest-ridden civilizations of Byzantium and Persia which Islam had inherited. Even in regard to the priestly specialty of conducting divine services, most Muslim teachers might have echoed the reply of a gaon. When questioned as to whether a scholar or a less informed person endowed with a pleasant voice should be asked to lead the congregation in prayer, Yehudai Gaon unhesitatingly answered: "Certainly the scholar, for he knows what he is saying." Sherira sharpened it further by prohibiting congregational services conducted by a permanent reader "who fails to comprehend the intent of the prayer." [6]

Conversely, the example set by the 'Umayyad caliphs undoubtedly stimulated the central Jewish authorities to a new appreciation of the permanent local judge and the need of more effectively controlling him. In the talmudic period, we recall, judges had found it increasingly advisable to secure an "authorization" from the exilarch in order to escape personal liability in cases of mistaken judgments. Now, however, they were directly appointed, and deposed, by exilarchs and geonim in their respective regions and converted into general administrative and fiscal agents as well. In a responsum dated in 1011, Hai Gaon informed the scholars of Kairuwan of "the custom in Babylonia" for the high court [of the academy] to appoint judges in each district. Only as a result of such an appointment could a judge force a party to appear before him, even if it meant breaking a vow. Finally, against the specific talmudic statements, repeated by Maimonides, that "ordination" was limited to Palestine whereas Babylonia had merely the right of "authorization," Samuel ben 'Ali insisted that

Babylonian chiefs could also "ordain," although such ordination enabled the judge only to adjudicate litigations without imposing the biblically prescribed fines. Since courts had long learned to inflict similar financial penalties under other names, this distinction was largely academic.[7]

Islam, to be sure, had sacerdotal groups far transcending in importance both the professional "readers" of the synagogue and the hereditary, but purely honorary, Jewish "priests" and "levites." In the early Middle Ages the latter were still collecting tithes and *ḥallah* offerings and hence were expected to produce evidence of their descent. For the sake of peace they were also rigidly given precedence in summons to the weekly scriptural lessons. Otherwise they had no official status in the communal bureaucracy. Islam, on the other hand, developed a variety of religious orders, as well as groups of dervishes and other religious enthusiasts, apart from the ordinary mosque officials, particularly *imams* and *muezzins*. Such Jewish associations as the "Mourners for Zion" were but a pale approximation of corresponding Muslim leagues. Certainly Judaism never had anything like the *futuwwa,* para-military organizations resembling Christian knightly orders. Stimulated by the religious fanaticism engendered by the Crusades and the growth of Near Eastern feudalism, the *futuwwa* played a great role during the later Middle Ages. But even then, the legal expert remained the leading figure in both religions.[8]

Accepting from the Jewish tradition also the concept that the king was under the law and on the whole, except for its Shi'ah wing, equally averse to the extreme Western doctrine of the "divine right of kings," Islam was forced to strike some tenuous compromises between the legitimate legislative authority of temporary rulers and the perennial validity of the fundamentals of traditional law. Side by side with the more or less uniform and universally valid "Muslim law," thus evolved many local variations in the "law of Islam" intended to meet local needs of a more or less transitory nature. But was not Judaism, too, long used to the distinction between local custom and general legal doctrine? The deep-rooted differences between Babylonian and Palestinian practices had long shown the way, though on a lesser scale, to the reconciliation of general uniformity and local variation.

The great reverence for the law animating even the most powerful caliphs also found expression in the frequent inquiries they addressed to their doctors and jurists (*'ulama* and *fuqaha*). They were often saved from an embarrassing breach of the law only by choosing between two contradictory opinions, since Islam, in contrast to geonic Judaism, did not possess two official arbiters of controversial issues. Even the Mongol conqueror of Baghdad in 1258, Hulagu, is said to have tried to legitimize his conquest by a favorable reply from Baghdad's Muslim academy. Similarly, we recall Hai Gaon's reference to the purely juridical presumption "that no one cohabits illicitly [if he can help it], and certainly a prince would not do so" to defend the legitimacy of Bustanai's offspring by the Persian princess. If this presumption lent itself to abuse and elicited protests by Maimonides and others, the sage of Fusṭaṭ himself served as an excellent illustration of that hegemony of the expert legist. Although still apparently but a private citizen and extremely busy with his medical practice, he nevertheless informed his translator, Samuel ibn Tibbon, that on every Sabbath after the services the whole Fusṭaṭ congregation foregathered at his home, "and I instruct the community what it should do during the week." [9]

Because of this extraordinary prestige of the juridical experts, Islam, as well as Judaism, was averse to teaching Scripture to members of other faiths. The Malikite school even prohibited, partly on this score, the translation of the Qur'an into other languages. According to Bukhari, on the other hand, Ibn 'Abbas had reproached his coreligionists for inquiring from *dhimmis* about the meaning of their Scriptures. "By Allah, we have never seen one of them asking you about what had been revealed to you." When asked about R. Johanan's prohibition for a Gentile to study the Torah, Maimonides drew a characteristic distinction between Christians, who admitted the correctness of the biblical text and only erred in its interpretation, and Muslims, who denied its authenticity according to revelation. "That is why they [the Muslims] hate all strangers dwelling among them, and from it [their study of the Law] would arise a stumbling-block for Israel who, on account of their sins, live in captivity among them." The geonim tried even to tighten up the talmudic prohibition of instructing slaves. When informed that a Jew had taken to school an unfree child born in his household, Sherira tersely replied, "The master acted wrongly in providing instruction for the child." The progressive sharpening of the pertinent prohibitions is the less surprising, as the rabbis had learned with chagrin of the growing use made by converts from Judaism of their biblical and talmudic learning for strident denunciations of their former faith. Slaves, too, were more likely to join the dominant religion than were free Jews. Of course, the master was entitled, though not encouraged, to liberate his slave and open to him free access to Jewish learning.[10]

As a matter of fact, the parallels between the two religions go so far that simply to list them would be an enormous task. From the purely formal similarity between the six principal collections of Muslim traditional law and the six divisions of the Mishnah and Talmud, to the more intrinsic nexus between the term *shari'ah* (the straight way) as the totality of Muslim law and the Hebrew *halakhah,* and to the numerous detailed affinities in worship, laws of purity, and prohibited food, everywhere one finds the same basic attitude to life. There are often striking resemblances even in minute details, while the divergences are frequently but differences in form arising out of different social conditions. It would be, of course, too much to assert that all similarities represent direct influence. Much in early Islam is derived so directly from pre-Islamic Arabia, as well as from the new social life in the Caliphate, that many supposedly Jewish elements would certainly have been developed had there been no Jews left in the world. The presence in all these countries of numerous Jews, however, some of whom had been converted to the new creed and had brought into it their age-old heritage, greatly facilitated this evolution. The dynastic-sectarian faction of the 'Alides, for example, would have found a rationale of its own in any case. But the purported counsel of 'Ali's Jewish adviser 'Abdallah ibn Saba, who, perhaps referring to Jeremiah and Baruch, suggested that 'Ali was a supreme executor (*wasi*) of Mohammed's will, undoubtedly helped to infuse a new doctrinal, semi-messianic ingredient into Islam.[11]

Conversely, the *halakhah* appears to follow the lead of Muslim legists in many ways. To be sure, talmudic law, which even in its formative stages had been little affected by the laws of either Rome or Persia, could now in its fully developed form effectively resist the incursion of Islamic concepts. Nevertheless, Islam's overpowering dynamic force has left a distinct mark, be it only through its emphases and nuances. The evolution of both legal systems depended far more on successive interpretations than on legislative enactments. Not the will of the caliph, nor that of the exilarch, created new law, but the changing viewpoints of the juristic expert. In both faiths, therefore, the constant interplay of their legal traditions, in themselves far from dissimilar, and changing social conditions confronting both groups with essentially the same problems of adjustment, was reflected in the ever new precedent-setting legal decisions of the great jurists of each generation.

One illustration may suffice here: the changing attitude toward prayer. The pre-Islamic Arabs ridiculed prayer, and many resisted this innovation even in the days of Mohammed—the very term *ṣalat* had been but a recent Aramaic loan word. But now prayer became, to quote Muḥammad Ali, an orthodox Muslim of our day, "the first and foremost duty of a Muslim." In Arabic "to recite prayers" has almost become synonymous with being a Muslim. One of the caliph's most distinguished titles was that of *imam,* or leader of the congregation in worship. It has been convincingly demonstrated that Judaism and, to a lesser extent, Christianity were the main sources of inspiration for this transformation. The very name "mosque" is apparently derived from the Aramaic *masgeda,* first mentioned in the Elephantine papyri, while the early Islamic teachers were usually called *rabbaniyun,* evidently a Jewish or Syriac Christian term. Abu Huraira's exclamation that prayer in the midst of a congregation stands twenty-five degrees higher than the prayer one performs at home or in the market place, is reminiscent of the reiterated talmudic emphasis on congregational worship. The great appeal exercised by the democratic simplicity and egalitarian austerity of the Jewish prayerful assemblies became a source of strength for expanding Islam, just as it had been for the early Christian mission. Much as the Muslims protested against such indebtedness, scorned allegedly Jewish gestures, and actually outlawed public lamentations for the dead not only for themselves but even for the *dhimmis,* they could not shake off these far-reaching influences. Nor could they escape the impact of Jewish rituals on the related requirement of fasting, which loomed, next to prayer, as the highest ceremonial duty of a pious Muslim. The very concept of the fast's expiatory function was a clear Muslim borrowing from a popular Jewish Aggadah.[12]

Once prayer had become a dominant feature of Islam, however, it began in turn to influence Jewish ritual. Judaism had long required washing of hands before prayers (apart from demanding general physical cleanliness in honor of the Creator in whose image man was formed), and this practice was taken over by Islam. But the latter went much further and required the washing of feet as well, at least preliminary to morning prayers. After a period of hesitation Near Eastern Jewry followed suit, occasional protests by traditionalists notwithstanding. Similarly, ablutions before prayers after a nightly pollution were now accepted as a binding requirement. Maimonides, when asked about the latter custom, admitted that it was not practiced among Jews of Christian lands who, on the contrary, taunted their Eastern coreligionists that they "had learned cleanliness from the Arabs." He nevertheless accepted the new practice, being generally convinced of the superiority of the Eastern standards of cleanliness—a remarkable study in contrasts with both the actual conditions and the racial preconceptions of our time. In fact, Maimonides found therein a proper rationale for the Muslim as well as Jewish rejection of pork, for if it "be permitted for consumption, the market places and the houses would be dirtier than privies, as you may see it today in the Frankish countries." So impressed was the sage of Fusṭaṭ with the decorum of Arab services and the ridicule heaped by Muslims on Jewish chatting and disrespectful turning away from the prescribed orientation toward Jerusalem, that he undertook a major liturgical reform. Instead of having the reader, in accord with a long-hallowed tradition, repeat aloud the *'Amidah* after its silent recitation by the congregants, a practice often found boring and conducive to inattentiveness, he introduced a single joint recitation aloud by reader and congregation. On Maimonides' authority this reform, though running counter to both talmudic law and age-old custom, was widely accepted in Egypt and Palestine, until it was abrogated three centuries later by David ibn abi Zimra, who pointed out the futility of all such measures to mitigate Arab fault-finding with Jews and Judaism.[13]

Under the impact of the overwhelming Muslim emphasis on prayer, medieval Jewry also elevated it to a position it had never held before. Utterances such as Naṭronai Gaon's, who declared that a man sick for thirty days is obliged to make up thereafter all the prayers he had missed, or that one who omits the midrashic sections in the Passover Haggadah is a heretic and should be excommunicated, would have sounded strange in the days of the Talmud. Close attention was paid to the prayer book, and many geonim themselves (Naṭronai [!], Amram or his associate Ṣemaḥ, and Saadiah) compiled authoritative manuals. The most famous of these was that of Amram Gaon, which soon was generally accepted in Babylonia and in Spain, and which has ever since remained in force among Sephardic Jewry. Saadiah's compilation, on the other hand, despite the author's great prestige and his intention to produce a popular work, was too philosophic to be permanently attractive to the masses. Certainly the gaon's main purpose of unifying dispersed Jewry ritualistically was no more fulfilled than his effort at communal centralization. But this very resistance to unification and conservative adherence to local ritualistic customs demonstrated that growing reverence for the liturgical factor in Jewish observance.[14]

Differences between Jewish and Muslim prayers were as pronounced, however, as were the similarities. From the outset Muslim jurists tried to differentiate between Islamic and Jewish devotions in such externals as raising one's hands or swaying one's body in prayer, which early *ḥadith* condemned as "Jewish" gestures. Jewish liturgy for the Sabbath, in particular, was, like the Sabbath itself, in many ways unique. While the Muslim Friday did not radically differ from any weekday, Saadiah waxed eloquent in describing the Jewish Sabbath and its services.

For about half a day [he wrote] we stay in the synagogue, devoting ourselves to prayer, reading the Torah, and discussing matters pertaining to that day. The rest of the time we eat and drink, but do not cease remembering the Lord and his Torah. It is permitted to visit the sick, to comfort mourners, and to pay heed to matters of public concern, but under no circumstances must we engage in private affairs with respect to forthcoming developments, although we may relate what happened to us in the past.

Saadiah's opponents objected even to the inclusion of public affairs, and attacked him personally for violating the Sabbath through his negotiations with Gentile authorities. Prompted by anti-Karaite feelings, Saadiah apparently wrote a special treatise on the Sabbath lights. Some geonim permitted fasting on the Sabbath of Repentance (between the New Year and the Day of Atonement) because, if aimed at expiation rather than self-mortification, even fasting might be pleasurable. On the other hand, Maimonides and others prohibited the recitation of prayers of petition "so that the Sabbaths be dedicated to rest, and holidays to joy, and they not be days of fasting, lamenting, or shouting." With an obvious polemical slant against prevailing Muslim notions, Halevi exclaimed, "The contrition on a fast-day does nothing to bring one nearer to God than does joy on Sabbaths and holidays, if it is the outcome of a devout heart." [15]

CONSOLIDATION OF TRADITIONS

Preeminence of individual scholars was not without danger to the unity of both legal systems. If every jurist were entitled to reach his own conclusions in regard to fundamentals, as well as details, of the law, there would have been as many differing interpretations as there were men, or at least groups of like-minded men. The creative ferment of the first two centuries produced, in fact, four major schools of jurisprudence which have ever since divided the "world of Islam." In later centuries the Near East largely followed the liberal Ḥanafite or the moderate Shafi'ite school, while Spain and most of North Africa accepted the more orthodox Malikite tradition. The extremely orthodox Ḥanbalite school, though less permanently entrenched in any distinct area, served as an explosive force to inspire such extremist groups as the modern Wahabis.

Judaism escaped this danger by virtue of the overwhelming control long exercised by the Babylonian academies and the voluntary submission to it of the dispersed communities. Even in its decline, as we recall, the Baghdad academy in 1191 empowered its messenger, Zechariah ben Berekhel, "to expound the Torah in public . . . appoint interpreters . . . scribes, *ḥazzanim,* leaders in services, and heads of communities." The great peril of two rivaling Talmudim was obviated for a long time by their limited circulation and by the early teachers' studious avoidance of direct references to the Palestinian compilation which diverged from its Babylonian counterpart not only with respect to numerous legal minutiae, but even in regard to the very text of the Mishnah. When later growing literacy and the general increase of literary output made a clear-cut decision imperative, the rule was adopted, to cite Hai Gaon's responsum, "We rely on our Talmud, and in matters decided here we pay no attention to what is written there. Only when the Palestinian Talmud reveals data which are neither stated clearly in the Babylonian Talmud, nor contradicted by it, may we rely on the former, or else use it for purposes of interpretation." [16]

Before thus insisting upon the exclusive authority of the Babylonian Talmud, the academies of Sura and Pumbedita had to make sure that they had at their disposal a complete and authentic text of that tremendous compendium. True, the work on the "redaction" had already begun under the presidency of R. Ashi (before 427). It was largely completed by the following two generations of Amoraim before the end of the fifth century. Yet there remained many questions left open, while some readings, if not altogether contradictory, called for further elucidation. This was indeed the task of some four generations of so-called Saboraim (reasoners or disciples) during the sixth and early seventh centuries. The transition from one group to the other was so gradual that only in retrospect could the geonim somewhat arbitrarily set the demise of Rabina the Younger, son of R. Huna (500 C.E.), as the terminal date of the amoraic age. They quoted to this effect a mystical "Book of Adam," in which Mar Samuel (3d cent.) had allegedly read a prophecy that "Rabbi [Judah the Patriarch] and R. Nathan mark the end of the Mishnah [tannaitic age], Ashi and Rabina that of *hora'ah* [amoraic age]." Probably only the first part was originally attributed to Mar Samuel, but a later supplement, perhaps first added orally or in a marginal note, brought the prediction more up to date.[17]

Because of that imperceptible transition from the amoraic to the saboraic age, and from that to the geonic age, it is almost impossible to fix the exact date for that important middle period. The setting of the conclusion of the amoraic age with the death of Rabina in 500 is justified, if at all, only from the standpoint of the academy of Sura, which in the fifth century had, indeed, been the main center of the editorial work on the Babylonian Talmud. But, viewed from the Pumbeditan angle, the head of its academy R. Yose, or Abba Yose, Rabina's collaborator in that work, survived his Sura colleague by fourteen years. Sherira, who had accepted the long-established Suranic version, but also wished as usual to claim credit for his own academy, somewhat equivocally asserted that "in his [R. Yose's] days was the end of *hora'ah,* and the Talmud was concluded" (*Iggeret,* ed. by Lewin, p. 97).

Even more blurred was the transition from the Saboraim to the geonim, since the early geonim continued cultivating the ancestral lore in approximately the same way as had their saboraic predecessors. The only major difference apparently was administrative, rather than intellectual. Under the new Muslim regime, the exilarchate and its allied institutions regained their former authority over the Jewish communities; in fact, they extended it to communities which had never before been under their jurisdiction. In time this administrative transformation, combined with the intellectual *élan* characteristic of the new civilization, brought about major changes also in the inner workings of the two academies, and particularly caused them to become far more articulate in the literary sphere. The struggle with the heterodox trends, and to a lesser extent the defense of Judaism before Muslim public opinion, likewise forced the academic leaders to rethink the fundamentals of their faith and law, and to modify some parts, and elaborate many others, of their talmudic tradition. All this ultimately turned the geonim into a novel and distinct school in the evolution of talmudic learning, although down to the middle of the eighth century these changes appeared to be slow and intangible. For this reason, it may indeed be convenient to begin the geonic age with the Islamic conquest of Babylonia and the ensuing reorganization of the Jewish communities under the vigorous leadership of Exilarch Bustanai, about 650 C.E. The preceding century and a half, roughly covering four or five generations, may therefore be well assigned to the saboraic age, the age of the final completion of the Babylonian Talmud.[18]

The Saboraim could the more readily perform that major editorial function, as even the latest Amoraim had apparently not committed to writing the fruits of their endeavors, but allowed them to be preserved at the central academies through the careful recording of specially trained "memorizers" (*tanna'im*). We recall how much greater reliance the ancients had generally placed in the oral transmission by faithful human recorders than in written copies which, they felt, were bound to perpetuate scribal errors and unauthorized alterations and could thus become the source of endless dissensions. Although not completely safeguarded against occasional disagreements about a particular saying or decision, the oral transmission by a few "memorizers" could be far more effectively controlled by the outstanding leaders of each generation, whose names and institutions would serve as the ultimate guarantors of its authenticity. This ancient attitude must have been greatly reinforced in Babylonia by the Zoroastrian example. As is well known, the ruling classes of the Persian Empire for many centuries refused to commit to writing the very "sacred scriptures" of their faith. If H. S. Nyberg is right, this resistance was not completely broken until after the Muslim conquest of Persia. At that time the quest for sheer self-preservation forced the priests' hands and made them "publish" these ancient classics so as to persuade the new rulers that the Zoroastrians, too, were a "people of the book."

Consolidation of the heritage was now the watchword of the age. Beset by tremendous difficulties in both the Byzantine and the Persian empires, the Jewish people sought shelter behind the walls of its ancestral lore as epitomized in the Talmud. A later chronicler thought of bestowing upon them the highest praise when he wrote that the Saboraim "had neither added to the Talmud nor subtracted anything from it." In fact, they had to add a great deal. Since the Talmud contained but a fraction of earlier traditions, all subjected to constant and intensive study at the academies, ever new insights would have emerged from the discussions, even if the first compilers themselves had not left certain matters in doubt. True, like their contemporary counterparts in the schools of Masorites, the Saboraim saw their major task in the faithful recension of traditions handed down by predecessors. But by continuing to mull over that material in lengthy academic debates, later crystallized in so-called *sugyot* (lessons), essentially as their predecessors had reviewed the earlier traditions, they clarified many a moot point. They were also able to answer some older questions, raise new problems and offer solutions for them, decide matters of law left undecided by the last Amoraim, suggest certain general rules such as which of two Amoraim was to be followed in cases of conflicting opinions, and to insert many editorial hints to facilitate the students' orientation in the still very baffling "sea of the Talmud." With predilection they placed summaries of the academic discussions at the beginning of talmudic tractates, but occasionally wove them into other relevant debates. "Generally speaking," observes H. Klein, "the more complicated a *sugya* is, the greater is the part the Sabara has played in its construction and the greater the advantage of isolating the two elements and studying them separately." Many *sugyot* seem, in their entirety, to be of saboraic origin. These "editors" also liked to repeat in another context a lesson, of their own or of their predecessors, previously incorporated in another tractate; to insert for the sake of clarity references to older sources; and to buttress a specific decision by further arguments. They generally revised the traditional texts with far greater freedom than has hitherto been assumed. Even with these aids much of the talmudic literature was to remain a sealed letter to many scholars as yet unable to consult the later exegetical literature. This final editorial performance appeared so vital to later generations that, according to an otherwise restrained ninth-century chronicler, only for the sake of these scholars "were the heavens stretched out and the earth spread forth." [19]

The Saboraim performed all these tasks with much anonymity. Only occasionally did the name of a particular scholar like R. Aḥa find its way into the Talmud. Otherwise we owe the very record of their existence to such later chroniclers as Sherira Gaon or the author of the *Seder tanna'im va-amora'im*. But no more than eleven names in all and but a few flimsy biographical data have been recovered from the debris of ages. Only a small portion of the saboraic work was incorporated in the Talmud itself, the rest was carried down in oral form to fructify the thinking of the early geonim and their successors. Abraham Weiss may indeed not have indulged in a serious overstatement when he claimed that this intermediate saboraic age "was no less productive than either the preceding or the following periods" of Amoraim and geonim.[20]

After a century and a half of such intensive efforts at editing and revising its text, the Talmud was ready for circulation in the early Muslim period. If Maimonides correctly estimated the age of some old talmudic scrolls he had seen in Egypt as having been written some five hundred years before his time (about 700 C.E.), this must have been one of the very first sets made available in written form. We recall that several decades later (771) the deposed exilarch Naṭronai bar Ḥabibai (Ḥakhinai), arriving as an exile in Spain, did not have at his disposal a copy of the Talmud, but had to rely on his memory in communicating it to eager students in his adoptive fatherland. It seems that for another century or more copies of that voluminous compendium still were extremely scarce. The mere parchment or leather used in its reproduction must have made its price well-nigh prohibitive. It became readily available in many communities only after paper had come into more common use during the tenth century. Even then the task of preparing an exact copy was not only arduous and time-consuming for the scribe, but also required from him expert familiarity with the text. That is why Samuel ibn Nagrela was extolled as a great patron of learning because he had employed "scribes to transcribe the Mishnah and Talmud and gave copies to students unable to afford them both in the Spanish academies and in those of other lands [Morocco, Ifriqiya, Egypt, Sicily, and even the academies of Babylonia and the Holy City]." [21]

For a long time the geonim thus were in almost exclusive possession of the revised text of the Babylonian Talmud and many of its supplementary traditions. They could now undertake the task of unifying world Jewry under its aegis. They encountered little difficulty in Babylonia and the other formerly Sassanian provinces which had long been inured to follow the lead of the two academies, now revived under the leadership of the resuscitated exilarchate. Just as the prince of captivity represented all of imperial Jewry before the government, the heads of the two academies claimed spiritual and juridical control over the Jews of all Muslim lands and beyond. We recall Pirqoi ben Baboi's climactic attempt to deny even the right of the Palestinians to cultivate their divergent customs under the excuse that these had originated only in periods of persecution. He demanded that now, with the passing of these emergencies, the provisions of the Babylonian Talmud alone should enjoy uncontested validity. If this vigorous campaign encountered the hostility of heterodox groups, some of which denied the validity of the Oral Law, the very spread of such dissent, even if it was more vocal than effective, made the adoption of a single standard for orthodox practice doubly imperative. For this reason, and also in recognition of the historic reality that their own Talmud had been left in an unfinished and unrevised state, the Palestinians themselves ultimately bowed in reverence before the Babylonian Talmud, which now became the universally recognized canon of the unwritten "second law."

In the meantime, however, even experts were not always certain whether a particular tradition, known to them through oral communication, had been incorporated by the redactors in either talmudic text. That is why even such luminaries as Aḥai of Shabḥa, Yehudai Gaon, and Simon Qayyara at times independently cited an older statement verbatim as it is found in the Palestinian Talmud, giving rise to doubts whether they were altogether familiar with that compendium. Much of that confusion, however, was owing to the exclusively *literary* approach of the nineteenth-century savants who paid no heed to the parallel transmission at the Babylonian academies of oral records, only partially taken over into the major compilations.[22]

Inheriting from their saboraic predecessors both an edited text of the Talmud and a vast number of authoritative interpretations thereof, the early geonim added some finishing touches to the text. They also offered further explanations of their own. Occasionally they had at their disposal written records of earlier academic discussions, jotted down for their private benefit by student participants. Such a notebook, not intended for general circulation, was cited centuries later by Hai Gaon as a "secret scroll." Its general accuracy is attested by the independent verbatim appearance of Hai's quotation therefrom in the much older *Halakhot gedolot*. More frequently, the saboraic traditions circulated orally. On another occasion Hai cited a Pumbeditan oral tradition which had appeared in exactly the same form in Aḥai of Shabḥa's *She'eltot* and in the book *Ve-hizhir*. He solemnly enjoined the recipients of his reply carefully to guard these "words which are a tradition with us from our fathers and grandfathers for many generations." Of course, the closer these traditions were to the writer's own time, the fuller was the available information. After the reorganization of the academies in the early Muslim period, each kept archives containing copies of replies sent out to various lands and other pertinent documents. These records now effectively supplemented the older oral traditions and interpretations. The same careful Sherira Gaon, who had candidly admitted that he possessed only fragmentary information about the sister academy of Sura until the end of the first millennium Sel. era (689 C.E.), emphatically asserted that from then on his data were absolutely reliable. More, defending the talmudic story about R. 'Aqiba invoking in the name of R. Dosa the testimony of heaven and earth that the prophet Haggai had made a certain statement in a particular spot, he furnished the following illustration:

> We are positively certain about much that happened in the days of the geonim, Palṭoi, Aḥai, and Mattathias of blessed memory [more than a century before]; we know the place of each, and his seat, as well as many of their conversations and the daily sequence of their lessons. [We know] how each of them sat and delivered his discourse, and what was said in the academy. . . . Some of these laws and traditions are so firmly imbedded in our hearts that they seem as if we saw and heard them ourselves. It would actually be possible for us to invoke the testimony of heaven and earth that, for instance, R. Ṣemaḥ had said something or had hermeneutically derived a particular lesson.[23]

Nor did the transmission of such personal minutiae appear trivial to Sherira's contemporaries. Many of them knew that a great mass of legal material in the contemporary Muslim *fiqh* had been derived from traditions about the personal behavior of Mohammed and his companions, since it was assumed that these pious founders of the new faith could not possibly have lived in contravention of the will of God. Hence that strongly biographical coloring of the entire body of the *ḥadith,* which the more strongly appealed to all Near Eastern peoples, as behavioral anecdotes had from time immemorial been put to extensive use in conveying moral and juridical lessons. Was not the Talmud itself filled with such biographical narratives recorded for no other reason than to set an example in model behavior or to convey a fine point of law?

Not that the two academies themselves always were of one mind. Even with respect to Palestinian customs there had existed serious differences of opinion already in the talmudic age. From its foundation in 219 by Rab, we recollect, Sura had cultivated Palestinian traditions brought along by the founder from Judah the Patriarch's academy, whereas Pumbedita, which had inherited the mantle of ancient Nehardea, prided itself on being the direct heir of the ancient Babylonian exiles from the days of Jehoiachin and Ezra. With an overdose of local patriotism Sherira even claimed that not only Hillel, but also the majority of the other leaders of the Palestinian Sanhedrin during the Second Commonwealth (the so-called *zuggot*) had been recruited from Babylonia. It is small wonder, then, that Sherira and other Pumbeditans looked askance at any other than Palestinian Jews following Palestinian customs. A Moroccan community once informed Sherira about its local practice to insert into marriage contracts a phrase indicating that the marriage settlement was due the bride in accordance with *biblical* law. Thereupon the gaon irately replied that this matter had been the subject of debate of long standing between the sages of Babylonia and Palestine, the former claiming that the settlement had owed its origin only to a *rabbinic* enactment. "We still find it [that local practice] reprehensible," he added, "and you who in all your actions follow our customs and our Talmud, ought to do this too" in the Babylonian way. More emphatically than their colleagues of Sura, therefore, the Pumbeditans proclaimed the unrestricted supremacy of the Babylonian over the Palestinian Talmud. By historic coincidence the greatest expansion of rabbinic learning to Kairuwan, Spain, and the Franco-German territories took place during the latter part of the tenth and the early eleventh centuries, when Sura was in relative eclipse, while Pumbedita's light shone the more brightly under the vigorous leadership of Sherira and Hai. This preeminence clinched the victory of the Babylonian patterns in world Jewry, Sura itself ultimately surrendering some of its observances in favor of those current at the sister academy.[24]

Although the Palestinians did not entirely surrender their right to cultivate their ancestral mores, the hegemony of the Babylonian academies converted the Palestinian Talmud into but a secondary, subsidiary source of authority in the vast expanses of the Diaspora. Not going quite to Hai Gaon's extremes, his younger contemporary Isaac Alfasi of Spanish Lucena advanced a more moderate argument for the supremacy of the Babylonian Talmud, which became the standard reasoning of the medieval rabbinate. "We have to rely on our Talmud," Alfasi taught, "for it is the younger one. They [the Babylonian sages] were more familiar with the western [Palestinian] Talmud than we are, and they would not have rejected any of its statements, unless they were sure that it was not dependable." In time, the Palestinian compilation was altogether neglected in scholarly circles, and many a European, as well as Eastern, jurist overlooked it entirely while weighing in his mind the pros and cons of a case submitted for his legal decision. Even if, through Byzantium and Italy, the Palestinians succeeded in perpetuating some of their outlook and observances in Christian lands, they never brought about any such permanent legal divisions in the Jewish world as existed under Islam. True, the ever-widening breach between Ashkenazim and Sephardim led to many differences in ritualistic and legal minutiae, some of which may indeed be traced back to the Palestino-Babylonian dichotomies. But the inherent legal unity of all Jews remained unaffected, and works written by eminent authors of either group circulated freely and enjoyed great authority in both. In fact, the final great code of laws, prepared by the Spanish savant Joseph Karo, required only some supplementation and correction by the Polish scholar, Moses Isserles, to prove acceptable and binding on Ashkenazic Jewry as well.[25]

So great was, in fact, the authority of the early geonim that Hai had already voiced objections to some of Saadiah's innovations as contrary to the decisions of the "ancients." Ḥananel ben Ḥushiel of Kairuwan, Hai's contemporary, constantly apologized whenever he had to deviate from the opinion of any gaon because of a strong local tradition. The more independent Maimonides registered in his major code but twenty-two divergent decisions, while in forty-six other passages he quoted the geonim approvingly, and in innumerable details tacitly presupposed their ideas. Naḥmanides was sufficiently aroused by the few mild reservations concerning geonic teachings in the Maimonidean *Book of Commandments* to devote the bulk of his pertinent polemical treatise to the defense of the views held by Simon Qayyara.[26]

The authority of the Palestino-Babylonian academies and their leading scholars during the millennium of tannaitic, amoraic, saboraic, and geonic leadership deeply and enduringly impressed itself upon the minds of Jewry. Even after their disappearance as the supreme unifying force in the course of the eleventh century, the Jewish people continued to look to heads of newer academies and other expounders of the law for authoritative guidance. From the talmudic age it had inherited both the record of numerous disputes and differences of opinion and the method of adjusting them through assigning to each great teacher a specific position in the hierarchy of authorities. This method, in part employed also by Syriac Christians and others, was followed by Islam, where a particular tradition's acceptance or rejection by the public depended entirely on the personal authority of its real or alleged originators. In the style of the Mishnaic "Sayings of the Fathers," many a Muslim writer also grouped the existing body of traditions in accordance with successive authorities. One such enormous collection (*musnad*) of some 30,000 traditions ascribed to seven hundred of Mohammed's "companions" was compiled by Aḥmad ibn Ḥanbal (died in Baghdad, 855) in a manuscript of 2,885 closely written pages. After 1040 the Jewish people, too, deprived of any universally recognized central organs, learned to choose with perfect informality some outstanding scholar and vest in him the power of leadership. Even those who objected to, or had never heard of, the extremes of Saadiah's doctrine of the God-given sage and leader of each generation, reverently bowed before the authority of such great masters as Gershom of Mayence, before long styled the "Light of the Exile," Isaac Alfasi of Morocco and Spain, soon revered as the author of the "Little Talmud," or Maimonides.[27]

TERMS AND METHODS

Once the Talmud became available to readers throughout the dispersion, its difficult, even then partly archaic, terminology puzzled many students. From the outset it was not easy to make the vast talmudic-midrashic library, written in its peculiar mixture of Hebrew and Aramaic, understandable to persons living outside the Aramaic-speaking Near Eastern countries. Neither the Byzantine possessions, retained by the Eastern Empire after the Arab conquests, nor the western lands ever spoke Aramaic, while those which came under the sway of Islam were rather speedily converted to the use of the Arabic medium. Only the Babylonian countryside, as we shall see, held out until the eleventh century. Long before the rise of Islam, moreover, the eastern Aramaic dialect used by the Babylonian sages must have caused some difficulty in the Palestinian academies, just as, conversely, the western dialect in which the Palestinian Talmud was largely composed offered many a puzzle to Babylonian students.

Explanation of numerous technical terms and of names of certain less common objects now became a major desideratum. Many inquiries were addressed on this score to the Babylonian academies. This may also have been the primary concern of the earliest recorded geonic commentaries. According to a letter written in 953 by a leading member of the Pumbedita academy (apparently Hezekiah bar Samuel, a great grandson of Ṣemaḥ bar Palṭoi Gaon) to a Spanish grandee (probably Ḥisdai ibn Shapruṭ), the Spanish sages had asked Palṭoi Gaon of Pumbedita (842–58) "to write for them the Talmud and its explanation." Undoubtedly, the gaon merely secured for them a copy of the Talmud, one of the few to circulate outside Babylonia, and added some brief notes explaining certain complex terms.[28]

A good example of such explanations of difficult terms is offered by a relatively well preserved geonic commentary on the last section of the Mishnah (*Ṭeharot*) which apparently is but a revised paraphrase of a similar work by Saadiah Gaon. Except for the introduction, in which the author tried to give some substantive interpretations, the commentary is limited to brief identifications of words, only here and there adding a juristic aside. To make his meaning clear, the writer employed at times Arabic, Persian, and Greek glosses, the latter particularly astonishing in the case of a Babylonian sage, but less surprising in Saadiah's underlying text since the gaon may well have picked up some such references in both his Egyptian homeland and in Palestine. Indebtedness to Saadiah may also account for the occasional references to Palestinian conditions, and even a note taken from a tradition current in Egypt. This important work in talmudic philology subsequently served as an aid to scholars locally removed from the talmudic habitat, and it was speedily put to extensive use by the Kairuwan savants, Ḥananel and Nissim, and even more so by Nathan ben Yeḥiel of Rome, who incorporated almost all its renditions into his comprehensive dictionary.[29]

From these explanatory notes in the sequence of the Mishnaic or talmudic tractates, incorporated in both responsa and commentaries, it was but one step to regular lexicographical treatises. Tradition has it that a first regular dictionary to the Talmud, under the later common title of *'Arukh,* was compiled by Ṣemaḥ bar Palṭoi of Pumbedita (served as gaon in 872–90). Unfortunately, not a single fragment of that work has been preserved, and even possible quotations therefrom are so equivocal that some modern scholars have altogther denied its existence. But biblical-talmudic lexicography soon made tremendous strides, reaching great heights of achievement in the eleventh-century works by the Karaite David ben Abraham al-Fasi and the Rabbanites Jonah ibn Janaḥ and Nathan ben Yeḥiel. These works and their antecedents will be more fully considered in connection with the general developments of Hebrew and Aramaic linguistic studies.[30]

Linguistic barriers could more easily be overcome than the

substantive difficulties inherent in the talmudic texts, with their agglomeration of pithy, often enigmatic sayings and brief highlights of debates extending over many centuries. Students and practitioners of Jewish law knew generally the distinctions between tannaitic and amoraic sages, of whom the former enjoyed superior authority, although the Talmud itself had assigned to leading Amoraim of the first generation (Rab, Johanan and others) an intermediary status allowing them to reject tannaitic views. Similarly, the Talmud had occasionally indicated whom one was to follow in practical decisions when two sages disagreed. At the same time, it often stated that the law follows the latest authority (*halakhah ke-batra'i*), since one may assume that the later sage knew what his predecessor had said and yet had strong reasons to repudiate it. These bare essentials, recorded in the Talmud itself, whetted the interest of students; first, in the historic succession of talmudic sages, and secondly, in additional rules stating which of two contemporary rabbis or schools of thought one was to follow. In their quest for brevity, the redactors of the Talmud had indicated their final decision by using certain complex technical terms whose significance was still debated by the geonic and postgeonic leaders. How much more puzzled must have been the lesser scholars, and particularly local judges forced to adjudicate cases on the basis of these ambiguous hints!

Out of this curiosity, both scholarly and practical, grew a new type of historical literature, furnishing authoritative data on the chronology of ancient sages, as well as methodological handbooks analyzing the rules of talmudic jurisprudence. Some of these works were produced in answer to inquiries and hence appeared in the form of responsa. On other occasions, too, authors of responsa liked incidentally to expatiate on general principles and methods, influencing later generations of rabbis to no lesser an extent than if they had formulated them in specific handbooks. Some rules were universally accepted, others remained controversial among the geonim themselves. If most of the formulas now known stem from responsa by Hai and Sherira, this numerical preponderance may be owing only in part to their greater availability (nearly one half of all geonic responsa are attributed to these two writers). In part they undoubtedly reflect the growing awareness of leaders that general rules had become an urgent need for students in many lands. Apparently even before assuming the presidency of resurrected Sura, Samuel ben Ḥofni, too, wrote a lengthy letter answering numerous chronological and methodical questions. The most important work of this genre is Sherira's well-known "Epistle." These historical responsa were preceded, apparently without a preliminary inquiry, by the *Seder tanna'im va-amora'im* (Order of Tannaitic and Amoraic Sages), probably written by a Sura scholar in 884–86. On the other hand, in his *Sefer ha-Qabbalah* Abraham ibn Daud avowedly pursued apologetical anti-Karaite purposes. These and similar other works of the period will be more fully analyzed in connection with the general evolution of historical studies during the High Middle Ages.[31]

While Sherira and Ibn Daud occasionally inserted methodological hints in their presentation, only the author of the *Seder tanna'im* set aside a large section of his treatise to state, with remarkable brevity, the rules concerning the juridical determination of talmudic debates. He amplified the talmudic regulations concerning cases of conflict (for instance, between the schools of Hillel and Shammai), with specific exceptions. He formulated new rules, such as that in differences of opinion between teacher and disciple we generally follow the teacher, except after the generation of Raba of fourth-century Pumbedita, when the decision always rests with the latest authority. He also discussed the relative merits of decisions recorded in the Mishnah versus those mentioned in another tannaitic source, and the handling of such quotations in the Talmud. He further advised to follow these rules:

> Wherever it is written, "At first they ordained thus and thus" without mentioning the [ordaining] sage, this is the law. Whenever our Mishnah states, *Ba-meh debarim amurim, Ematai, Bi-zeman, Be-emet* [qualifying clauses relating to certain conditions], this is a tradition from Moses on Sinai. Every unnamed Mishnah states the valid law. If a division of opinions between sages is followed by an anonymous statement, the law agrees with that statement, but not if it precedes the record of divided opinions. If an anonymous statement in the Mishnah contrasts with a divided opinion in a Baraita [another tannaitic source] the law follows that statement, but not if it occurs in a Baraita, while the Mishnah records a divided opinion. . . . Wherever the Talmud

expressly leaves open the decision between conflicting opinions, one may act in accordance with either view. After each talmudic objection to an opinion without subsequent decision, one may [likewise] adopt either that opinion or the tenor of the objection. . . . Every *tequ* [a query officially left unanswered] ought to be decided in the more rigid vein if it relates to ritual prohibitions, and more liberally if it concerns monetary matters. Similarly, if the same rule is stated in two conflicting versions, one must follow the more rigid line in cases of biblical law and take a more lenient view with respect to a rabbinic regulation.

This sample should suffice to give an idea of the complexities plaguing a Jewish judge who had to reach a speedy decision in a litigation, or had to pass judgment on a ritualistic matter on the basis of some talmudic discussion, if indeed a full copy of the Talmud was available to him at that time. He had to master, moreover, the whole range of the talmudic and early extratalmudic letters, because many a problem only briefly stated in one context appeared fully elucidated in another passage of the Talmud itself or of some tannaitic collection.[32]

Not that all the rules formulated in our manual enjoyed universal acceptance. Many of them were still heatedly debated in the North African, Spanish, and Franco-German academies. For example, the talmudic formula that whenever a tannaitic record mentions R. Judah the Patriarch as opposed only by one sage Judah's opinion was to prevail, still left the question unanswered as to what was to be done if that opponent had been Judah's own father and teacher, R. Simon ben Gamaliel. Here one might act in accordance with another rule giving general precedence to the teacher. The author of the *Seder tanna'im,* an early gaon, Jacob bar Mordecai, as well as Ḥananel and Alfasi, decided in favor of the father, whereas Naṭronai Gaon (by implication), Rashi, and other Franco-German scholars adhered to the general primacy of R. Judah. Similarly, the old talmudic decision in favor of R. Judah bar 'Ilai in his differences of opinion with R. Meir was expanded by Ṣemaḥ bar Palṭoi Gaon to include instances where an unnamed Mishnah had adopted R. Meir's view. This extension was controverted, however, by both Sherira and Alfasi. Such divergent views even with respect to general rules, however, far from hurting the evolution of Jewish law, proved a real blessing. They not only saved Jewish jurisprudence from crystallization around a generally recognized set of principles from which there could be no deviation, but also enabled judges and students to choose between conflicting opinions, and thus more readily to adjust the law to the social needs of each moment.[33]

With the growth of systematic training in philosophy and science, problems of juristic methodology likewise assumed new significance. In this area, too, Saadiah Gaon performed a pioneering service. Apart from writing a comprehensive commentary on the Mishnah, still extensively used in the Near Eastern schools two and a half centuries later, according to the traveler Petaḥiah of Ratisbon, but no longer extant today, the gaon composed a special methodological treatise, probably in Arabic, though later cited only under its Hebrew title, *Darkhe ha-talmud* (Talmudic Methods). The few passages quoted therefrom by Bezalel Ashkenazi, a distinguished sixteenth-century student of talmudic methods, give us only a bare inkling of its nature; they are enough, however, to make us deplore the loss of the rest. Saadiah also had much to say about talmudic methods and approaches in many of his exegetical and juridical monographs, especially in his "Commentary on the Thirteen Hermeneutic Modes" formulated in the ancient school of R. Ishmael. This important tannaitic classification had been incorporated into the daily prayers of the synagogue, perhaps in order to emphasize the importance of the Oral Law to worshipers subjected to a variety of antitalmudic attacks. With his customary lucidity, the gaon tried to define each of these basic rules and to demonstrate its application to legal doctrines. At the same time he insisted, with his characteristic daring, that all these hermeneutic modes were intended also for purely theoretical research in the meaning of biblical passages, and taught that they could still be used by posttalmudic scholars. Even with respect to the most complex mode, the so-called *gezerah shavah* (parallel determination), which the talmudic sages themselves had handled very gingerly and used only in conjunction with certain clearly superfluous words, the gaon intimated that he "would only mention a few main instances, as an example for others [to be used] in comparing passages to one another." [34]

Saadiah's example was followed by the other philosophically

trained gaon of Sura, Samuel ben Ḥofni. The latter's "Introduction to the Talmud" was drawn on a very broad canvas, and contained one hundred and fifty chapters, of which only a few small fragments have survived. This Arabic work seems to have served as a basis for, and may actually have been paraphrased with minor additions by, Samuel ibn Nagrela in his *Mebo ha-talmud* (Introduction to the Talmud), of which, too, despite its relative popularity, only small portions have come down to us. By being incorporated in many editions (including the well-known Vilna edition) of the Babylonian Talmud, however, these excerpts have become the most influential direct heritage of the geonic and early postgeonic age to enrich the methodical thinking of modern students of the Talmud.[35]

No more fortunate was Samuel's North African compeer, Nissim bar Jacob ibn Shahin, whose *Mafteaḥ le-man'ole ha-talmud* (Key to the Locks of the Talmud), a work of extraordinary erudition in the whole range of ancient rabbinic letters, though often quoted by subsequent grateful generations, has likewise survived only in a few fragments, partially published in recent years. This work, whose fifty-chapter plan is detailed in the author's general introduction, was to be combined with a commentary on the entire Talmud. Both parts were intended to guide the student by supplying relevant cross references to other talmudic tractates.

> I have seen [Nissim added] many students in our time who failed to take cognizance of that factor and in vain looked for the demonstration [of each statement in its place]. Hence they could not comprehend the law which remained a puzzle to them. I have decided, therefore, to assemble all these puzzling passages in a book which would serve like a key to them, so that each student in need of finding further references should be able to locate them without effort.

Doubtless in preparation for this ambitious program, Nissim kept a vast notebook, called by some successors a "secret scroll" (*megillat setarim*), into which he entered observations of all kinds, as they came to his mind after reading and reflection. This was evidently but raw material for further work, never intended for publication in that form. Later generations, however, often mistook the author's intention, and quoted statements from this notebook, lengthy parts of which enjoyed wide circulation.[36]

One does not have to search too far for reasons for the nearly total disappearance of all these geonic and early postgeonic works in talmudic methodology, except the *Seder tanna'im,* which was personally copied by no less a French authority than Joseph Bonfils (Tob 'Elem). The general lack of interest in such discussions of generalities in the influential schools of Rashi and the Tosafists stifled their circulation in the Franco-German areas. At the same time they were replaced by similar, but more systematic and pedagogically more useful, handbooks throughout the Sephardic world. The relative indifference of the great Ashkenazic schools, moreover, may also have stemmed from the semiconscious suspicion that rules, once rigidly defined, might militate against the dynamism of Jewish law. Since rabbinic tradition dominated all Jewish life and thought there, the disciples of Gershom and Rashi, as well as their successors in medieval Germany and early modern Poland, cared much less for the formalization of general rules than for their dynamic application in the constant flux of legal study and practice.

Pedagogic considerations must indeed have played an increasing role in this entire branch of literature. As long as the Talmud was more or less the private possession of a few academicians assembled at leading Eastern schools, the teachers could readily impart to their pupils orally all the necessary explanations, with respect to principles as well as details. But when copies of the Talmud spread to ever wider circles, the need for educational aids became more imperative. This demand could the less be resisted, as the rise of antitalmudic heterodoxies forced the geonim themselves to try to make talmudic learning a common possession of the whole people. Characteristic of the new attitude is the explanation offered by Naṭronai Gaon, and echoed by Jacob Tam, as to why contemporary education had failed to follow the talmudic injunction that every man should devote a third of his time to the study of Scripture, a third to that of the Mishnah and another third to that of the "Talmud." The present impoverished generation, the gaon taught, devotes all its time to the Babylonian Talmud, because it is a composite containing biblical, mishnaic, and amoraic ingredients. Incidentally, by "Talmud" everyone now understood the particular Babylonian or Palestinian compendium, rather than a student's independent research, which alone could have been in the mind of the originator of that threefold educational division, R. Joshua ben Ḥananiah, a sage of the first century. However, such independent research and reaching one's own conclusions on the basis of the canonical sources, somewhat akin to the Muslim method of *idjtihad,* was never neglected. It remained an essential ingredient of the training of students and judges.[37]

Since concentration on talmudic studies now became the main educational goal of leaders interested in Jewish survival in both East and West, they themselves began promoting pedagogic handbooks. In fact, the assistance extended to eager students by talmudic glossaries, even full-fledged dictionaries, as well as treatises on methodology, now proved inadequate. Not only the pupils, but even most teachers in the far-flung dispersion now required the aid of outright commentaries, explaining the more difficult talmudic texts passage by passage.

INTERPRETATION AND REINTERPRETATION

Explaining sacred texts to interested students and the public at large was a time-honored practice in Judaism even more than in its surrounding civilizations. We recall Philo's description of a synagogue service during which a learned member discoursed on the weekly scriptural lesson. Much of Philo's own literary output, as well as the work of the Palestinian sages, was centered around such exegetical efforts. Simple interpretation of scriptural texts was probably relegated to ordinary schools, while the higher exegesis in both synagogue and academy aimed at expanding the horizons of knowledge by elaborating on their moral and legal contents. In its objectives, Philo's allegorical interpretation of Scripture did not differ from the hermeneutic interpretation of the rabbis; both were intended to build around the scriptural texts certain significant ethical or juristic conclusions. In time, the same procedures began to be applied also to other writings of great authority, especially the Mishnah, and finally to the Talmud. In this slow evolution, the original concentration on the biblical text was never abandoned, but the hermeneutic derivations from Scripture were now combined with the reinterpretations of tannaitic and amoraic passages. Together they formed the hallowed triad of "Scripture, Mishnah, and Talmud."

In the next chapter we shall see how important the hermeneutic sermon was for the development of the aggadic lore of Judaism. It was no less significant for the evolution of *halakhah*. According to the long prevailing practice, the preacher combined both ingredients so as to make even the juristic lesson, by its nature relatively dry and complex, more palatable to broader audiences. At the academy, too, where in the ordinary course of instruction the two elements were undoubtedly kept apart, the old custom of delivering combined aggadic-halakhic sermons during Sabbath and holiday services seems to have been long maintained. On state occasions it was the head of the academy, or even the exilarch, who personally delivered such orations, just as most caliphs, too, felt it incumbent upon themselves to preach in public. In his famous description of an exilarchic election, Nathan the Babylonian mentioned that after the vote the new "exilarch opens [the homily] and delivers a discourse on the subject of that day's lesson. . . . When he finishes, he raises a [juridical] problem and says, 'Indeed, one ought to learn' [thus and thus about it]. Thereupon arises an elder, wise, understanding and experienced, and addresses himself to that problem." This tenth-century procedure seems to have been somewhat abbreviated, for in the earlier periods the proceedings apparently followed a fairly standardized quadripartite division: (1) The leader began by citing a passage from the weekly lesson and indicated certain hints of a legal or ethical nature contained in it; (2) then he, or someone else, raised a pertinent juridical question which required a fairly elaborate answer; (3) subsequently some preacher, often different from the former, took the floor and delivered a discourse but loosely connected with that query and covering a large range of legal and ethical problems; and (4) the first leader then reverted to the query and summarized the upshot of the preceding discussion for legal practice. If we may take a clue from the unfortunate experience of an ancient preacher, Levi bar Sissai, in the small Palestinian community of Simonias, any member of the audience was free to raise legal questions and expect the homilist to furnish an improvised but adequate answer.[38]

Contents of more important discourses and some of their characteristic sentences were carried down to posterity by effective memorizers. Major findings or pithy sayings by celebrated teachers at the main academies were thus incorporated in the living tradition of the people. At times older discourses were repeated and elaborated by new data and insights, thus snowballing into an ever growing body of traditions. Handed down orally from generation to generation, they represented that perennial flow of talmudic learning which during those centuries dominated the creative thinking of the Jewish élite.

Out of such complicated ethico-legal discourses emerged the first extraordinary product of geonic jurisprudence: Aḥai of Shabḥa's *She'eltot* (Propositions). Like its oral prototypes, this work is a combination of homiletical and juridical elements, arranged in the sequence of weekly lessons in accordance with Babylonia's annual cycle. We know little about the circumstances which induced the author to commit this work to writing, or about the date of its composition. It seems to have been drafted before Aḥai's departure from Babylonia after he had been passed over in the appointment to the gaonate of Pumbedita in favor of his assistant, Naṭroi (or Naṭronai) bar Emunah (748). According to a persistent tradition, recorded by the thirteenth-century author Menahem Me'iri, Aḥai first prepared his tract for the benefit of his son, to whom he thus wished to impart the knowledge of law and ethics in connection with the recitation of the weekly lessons. Possibly, however, he had only carried with him to Palestine the memory of these oral discourses together with more or less extensive notes, but decided to record them in book form for the benefit of his new compatriots during the few remaining years of his life (according to Me'iri, he died in 752). This unusual origin of the book may indeed account for its numerous repetitions and inconsistencies, its largely unfinished state, its many lacunae, and some Palestinian linguistic ingredients—all of which have puzzled investigators. Of course, some of these deficiencies may be attributed to copyists who, because of carelessness or specifically personal interests, omitted sections which they considered unimportant, especially lengthy quotations from talmudic sources which had since become accessible to the general public.

They have thus caused irreparable damage to efforts at reconstructing the original talmudic texts which, in the absence of older manuscripts largely destroyed by medieval inquisitors, can only be secured through a careful scrutiny of quotations therefrom by early rabbinic writers. Nor is there any way of ascertaining how much of Aḥai's work represented his personal contribution, and how much was merely a restatement of older discourses, delivered in more or less the same form by his predecessors. Although the form of his tract is unique in medieval letters, Aḥai probably was not at all conscious of reintroducing into Hebrew literature the ancient patterns of the "halakhic midrashim," which had organized the rabbinic hermeneutics of their time in the sequence of scriptural lessons. He may merely have wished to record for his Palestinian confreres, and indirectly for posterity, a number of the discourses he himself or other Babylonian teachers had delivered in the academy.[39]

It being not yet customary at that time to preface one's work with a programmatic introduction, we would probably not have been informed about the author's intentions even if the work had come down to us in its original form. Modern scholars have often classified it as a legal code which allegedly summarized the main precepts of Jewish law by analyzing the fundamental six hundred and thirteen biblical commandments and showing their ramifications in later theory and practice. This theory is unfounded. The *She'eltot*'s inadequacy as a recodification of all biblical precepts is evidenced not only by its coverage of less than a quarter (145) of their total number, but also by its inclusion, on a par with them, of forty-three commandments clearly stemming from postbiblical ordinances. The frequent explanation that the copies now extant are incomplete does not account for the failure of later medieval authorities to refer to Aḥai's interpretation of more than a few additional commandments. Similarly, his association of no less than thirty-seven legal discussions with the book of Genesis is totally at variance with any later attempt at reconstructing that canonical total of six hundred and thirteen, most of which assign to Genesis but three commandments in all. Surely, this unique interpretation of the First Book of Moses could not be due exclusively to the state of flux in which that enumeration still was in Aḥai's time. He apparently took over from earlier homilists the habit of relating almost any commandment to a biblical passage which, through some mental association, seemed relevant to him during the delivery of his sermon. For example, God's statement to Noah announcing the flood, "for the earth is filled with violence" (Gen. 6:13), appropriately enough recalled to the preacher's mind the biblical laws against robbery. The story of Abraham's and Lot's migration to Palestine together with "the souls that they had gotten in Haran" (Gen. 12:5) had long been interpreted in the rabbinic Aggadah as referring to Abraham's successful missionary efforts. It was easy to think in this connection of the duty of every Jew to teach the Torah to one's own sons and those of fellow Jews. In neither case did Aḥai intimate that he considered those passages as the main sources of these commandments. He merely preached on their legal, and even more their moral, import as part of a customary homily on a biblical narration.[40]

Because these were public addresses, the preacher understandably tried to drive home moral even more than legal lessons. Within the legal sphere he also chose with preference aspects with strong moral implications. For this reason he omitted altogether any reference to the laws of sacrifices or of purity and impurity, except for the "plagues" attached to persons and houses. The latter gave him the opportunity to describe blemishes in man's conduct which, according to the Talmud, caused these plagues to appear. Certainly, if his primary objective had been to enumerate the six hundred and thirteen commandments, he could not possibly have glossed over some such entire sections of the biblical law. As a preacher Aḥai could also freely indulge in repetitions. Jewish education, for example, was so close to any homilist's heart, that he, too, reverted to that theme in a later pericope. Sometimes an entire discourse is repeated in another context, as when he analyzes the commandment of circumcision and explains why, for its sake, even the Sabbath rest commandment must be broken. Human proneness to make rash vows appears to have bothered our preacher sufficiently for him to devote to that problem no less than six out of a total of one hundred and seventy-one pericopes.[41]

Aḥai of Shabḥa's work was far from typical, however, of the geonic writings in the field of Jewish law. Its nearest approximations are the midrashic works *Tanḥuma* and *Yelamdenu*. But where these *midrashim* share with the rest of that literary genre a strong emphasis on homiletics, and contain but relatively few juridical lessons (though more than are usually included in rabbinic homilies), the *She'eltot* place the reverse emphasis on the law. Both kinds were but a prolongation of the academic recitations developed during the talmudic age, and doubtless often reproduced oral traditions going back to talmudic and saboraic times. In method, approach, and probably also in his primary purposes, Aḥai was but a homilist of the old order, who more fully than most of his fellow preachers included traditions and lessons derived from the legal doctrines of the ancient sages. For this reason alone he was often quoted as a legal authority by later generations, though far less frequently by his immediate successors in the geonic age. In many respects his work appears as but the last offshoot of the school of Saboraim who, through their hermeneutic-homiletical elaboration, helped reinterpret the ancient amoraic sayings.[42]

Even in the geonic age, we are told, there was no lack of scholars willing to pay Aḥai the great compliment of direct imitation. In fact, a distinguished teacher of the following generation, Raba (or R. Abba), a pupil of Yehudai Gaon, and possibly of Aḥai as well, wrote a juridical tract in the same vein and apparently studded it with quotations from the master. Somewhat later, the anonymous *Midrash hashkem,* so styled because it begins with a homily on God's order to Moses, "Rise up early [*hashkem*] in the morning" (Exod. 8:16), and another midrash, with strong halakhic content, usually called *Ve-hizhir* because its pericopes start with the phrase, "And the Holy One Blessed be He warned [*hizhir*] Israel," closely followed the same patterns. Neither work is fully extant today. But, to judge from later quotations, they are so similar to one another that some scholars actually believe that the two titles refer to the same work. Those who consider them separate products of the geonic age still are inconclusively debating as to which was prior in time. But all agree on their great indebtedness to Aḥai's work. Even this assumption may have to be qualified, however. If Aḥai often reproduced homilies and discourses long current in oral form, much of what Raba had allegedly borrowed from Aḥai may have been taken from such common sources. This may in part be true also of the two midrashim of somewhat later vintage, which not only contain many data lacking in Aḥai's compilation, but also show in both substance and quantity significant variations from their alleged prototype.[43]

Despite his generally popular tone, aimed at the edification of synagogue audiences, R. Aḥai's objective was to go beyond the talmudic text in conveying certain new legal and moral lessons. His work certainly could not satisfy the newly arising demand for commentaries which would open up the vast recesses of the Talmud to wider circles of students. True, this distinction must not be pushed too far. Even commentaries often pursued practical-juridical as well as theoretical-exegetical aims. Conversely, outright codes were often used to interpret crucial passages in the Talmud. But there now began circulating at least some explanatory comments on the Talmud which could be utilized for purely pedagogic purposes on a par with the glossaries and essays in talmudic methodology.

Like most of the early treatises on words and methods, the first talmudic commentaries owed their origin to inquiries addressed to leading scholars. The very first comments, combining explanations of difficult terms with succinct interpretations of legally relevant passages in the talmudic tractate Shabbat, were probably included in two replies addressed to Spain by Naṭronai bar Hilai of Sura (853–58). Neither reply is preserved in full. Both beginnings and endings, which might shed more light on author and inquirers, are missing. We can nevertheless see that the gaon took pains to offer more than a mere glossary of objects and an analysis of concepts. For instance, he explained Rab's quotation from the "secret scroll" of the school of R. Ḥiyya (Shabbat 6b) as relating to "a scroll containing brief decisions of the kind included in a book of *halakhot*. It is not like the Talmud which is available to all." Rab's statement referring to the prophetic selection (*hafṭarah*) following the afternoon recitation of Scripture (Shabbat 24a) also called for an explanation, since that practice had been known in neither the questioner's nor the gaon's locality. Using the old shibboleth of blaming liturgical changes on anti-Jewish persecutions, Naṭronai declared that "the Persians had issued an intolerant decree suppressing the *hafṭarah* and, once removed, it was never restored." Of course, the gaon supplied no evidence for such persecution, nor any explanation why the Persians should have resented the recitation of prophetic passages in the afternoons more than in the mornings. In fact, as pointed out by Ginzberg, the Persian as well as some Byzantine communities unperturbedly continued such recitations during the Middle Ages. Naṭronai's inquirers also seem to have been puzzled by the meaning of the penalty *makkat mardut* (flagellation for insubordination) discussed in the Talmud in connection with the sin of cooking on the Sabbath with the warm waters of Tiberias (Shabbat 40b). Here the gaon explained the difference between the regular biblically prescribed flagellation which could only be inflicted on transgressors of a biblical prohibition after due warning, and the wholly discretionary rabbinic flagellation. Its name was derived from the culprit's rebellion "against the words of the Torah and the [scribes]." In all these interpretations the gaon took full cognizance of the existing law, but also made clear the meaning of its talmudic source.[44]

Naṭronai's *Commentary* was followed by similar works by Naḥshon Gaon (871–79) on several tractates (B.Q., B.B., Sanhedrin, and 'A.Z.). More comprehensive were the commentaries on the Mishnah and parts of the Talmud by Saadiah. For the most part apparently written before Saadiah's ascension to the gaonate, they owed their origin to their author's intellectual propensities rather than to direct inquiries. They must have included, therefore, many illuminating observations on general principles, as well as on philological and legal details. Regrettably, only small segments of these commentaries can be reconstructed from later quotations, or from such subsequent paraphrases as the aforementioned geonic commentary on Ṭeharot. The same holds true for Saadiah's equally prolific successor in the gaonate of Sura, Samuel ben Ḥofni. In a remarkable letter of 985, probably written while he still resided in Pumbedita as head of the anti-Sherira faction, Samuel invited his correspondents to send him regular inquiries.

"Please write us," he added, "about all your uncertainties concerning Scripture, Mishnah, and Talmud. A reply will reach you to your full satisfaction. . . . In this way you will know our strength and the difference between us and the others [Sherira]." Yet we learn, mainly from book lists, that there had at one time existed commentaries on a few tractates (such as Yebamot and Ketubot) written by him.[45]

We are more fortunate with respect to similar works by Sherira and Hai. From subsequent quotations we learn that, apart from a glossary on the first and last orders of the Mishnah, Sherira wrote some sort of commentaries on several talmudic tractates (Berakhot, Shabbat, and B.B.; only a fragment of the latter, apparently written in 972, has come to light). Collaborating in part with his aged father and in part working independently, Hai composed commentaries on at least seven tractates (Berakhot, Shabbat, 'Erubin, Ḥagigah, Beṣah, 'A.Z., and Ḥullin). While none of these is preserved in its entirety, substantial portions are known from either Genizah fragments or quotations by later authorities. Through these and their other writings Hai and his father greatly influenced the entire exegetical, as well as juridical, work of later sages, especially in Western lands.[46]

So preponderant was the juridical interest in all these commentaries that Hai usually skipped entirely the Talmud's aggadic passages, although these too were in need of explanation. This marked a complete reversal from Aḥai of Shabḥa's approach. We shall see how, under the impact of the newer philosophic concepts, Samuel ben Ḥofni and Hai generally tried to reduce the authority of the Aggadah as compared with the really binding halakhic doctrines. But there were innumerable bridges connecting these two lines of talmudic learning which could not safely be separated.

Law students, on the other hand, were frequently puzzled by the differences of opinion among the geonim themselves which came to the fore not only in their juristic works but also in their talmudic commentaries. We need but quote here one characteristic example: The old query of what was to be done "if someone was in doubt whether he had already prayed or not," had been answered in the Talmud by a majority opinion that such a man better not pray on that occasion, while R. Johanan exclaimed, "One wished that this man should pray all day" (Berakhot 21a). Some unnamed geonim, quoted by later authorities, explained this amoraic controversy as based on the assumption that, in so far as prayers were recited in fulfillment of a commandment, any extra prayer might fall under the generic prohibition of "adding" to the existing commandments. R. Johanan, however, taught that one was entitled to add supplementary offerings of a voluntary kind. These geonim decided, therefore, that the doubting worshiper should recite the prayer, announcing in advance that he wished to pray in fulfillment of the commandment if he had missed his prayer before, but that it be considered a voluntary offering if he had already performed his duty. Other geonim limited such option to individual worshipers, whereas congregational services could not be held in such dubious cases, for they stood for the ancient sacrifices which could not be repeated as voluntary offerings. For the same reason still other teachers outlawed additional prayers on Sabbaths and holidays, for no voluntary sacrifices had been permitted on those days in the ancient Temple. We shall see that this factor played a certain role in the opposition, however futile, of many geonim to the recitation of additional liturgical compositions (*piyyuṭim*) on those days. In the long run, however, these differences of opinion, like those recorded in the Talmud itself, only served to enrich the juristic thinking of later generations and enabled them to follow their own intellectual or practical preferences. At times great scholars of the rank of Samuel ibn Nagrela or Alfasi ventured to disregard altogether the geonic comments, if, as they believed, "none had done justice" to a particularly difficult talmudic discussion.[47]

NEWER EXEGESIS

None of the geonim, except perhaps Saadiah, felt the need to compose a comprehensive commentary on the entire Mishnah or Talmud. Saadiah was a non-Babylonian who may have begun writing his commentaries before his arrival in the Euphrates valley. Almost all the geonic commentaries hitherto mentioned had been evoked by inquiries, for the most part sent from other lands.

Evidently the interested Babylonian students, familiar with the local idiom and living in the proximity of the great academies, felt little need of such handbooks.

It is small wonder, therefore, that the first large and influential exegetical works in the talmudic field emanated from the newly awakened cultural center of Kairuwan. While in his *Mafteaḥ* Nissim bar Jacob still pursued primarily juristic aims and, hence, was quite selective in the passages he chose to interpret, he also felt the need of composing more strictly exegetical works. Only a few excerpts from his commentaries on several talmudic tractates (Berakhot, 'Erubin, Sanhedrin, Ḥullin, and parts of R.H.) are extant today, but they reveal the new pedagogic concerns of the rabbinic scholars and their efforts to meet a rising demand.[48]

With greater *élan,* Nissim's colleague, Ḥananel bar Ḥushiel (*ca.* 980–1056), undertook to provide the whole Babylonian Talmud with succinct and lucid comments which would guide any moderately informed student toward a better understanding of the text. Though not addressing himself to pure beginners, and frequently failing to comment on certain passages which he considered simple or "self-evident," he did not take too much for granted in regard to the reader's linguistic and even talmudic equipment. Adopting, therefore, the technique long used by compilers of legal decisions, he briefly and enlighteningly restated lengthy talmudic debates in clear and simple summaries, pointing up the main items under discussion, and in many cases also the juridical conclusions to be derived from them. Only occasionally did he indulge in lengthy excursuses which, however, were usually abbreviated by later copyists.

In exceptional cases, when he was touched to the quick in his theological convictions, Ḥananel even allowed himself to wax rhetorical, as when he tried to explain the strange talmudic story of R. Qeṭina's visit with a necromancer. His explanation of the meaning of earthquakes revealed both his deep-seated loyalty to his people and his abhorrence of Divine corporeality in any form:

> At the time when the Holy One blessed be He sees Israel's suffering caused by the nations' excessive oppression, He contemplates producing another deluge, and sheds two tears—that is no real tears from an eye, God forbid, but drops resembling tears. But the Holy One blessed be He reconsiders because He does not wish to destroy

His world, whereupon [the drops] flow into the Great Sea [the Mediterranean] with a noise audible from one end of the world to the other. This is the quake. All this is to show Israel that the Holy One blessed be He has not abandoned or forgotten them, but will some day restore them. In this way their heart will be strengthened lest they despair of redemption, and they will suffer all inflictions until the fulfillment of the time set by the Lord for their life in Exile, just as He announced in advance about their first exile [in Egypt], "And they shall afflict them four hundred years" [Gen. 15:13]. While the duration of that exile was thus known, that of the present exile is not known, but is nevertheless definitely set. That is why the Lord gives certain signs in His world to demonstrate that He encounters some difficulty because of Israel's living a migratory life under foreign domination, but that His mercy has not abandoned them and that some day He will restore them to their pristine glory.

Except for his repudiation of all anthropomorphic implications of the ancient legend—an attitude imposed upon all enlightened leaders by the combined attacks of Muslim and Karaite apologists—this was as pietistic an exclamation as could have come from any member of the Franco-German Ḥasidic circles. More surprisingly, Ḥananel paid no heed to contemporary science whenever it controverted rabbinic views. Trying to explain the talmudic discussion of the earth's size extending to only six thousand parasangs, he concluded, "Although astronomers of our time contradict this doctrine, we disregard their opinion. We rigidly adhere to the words of our masters, and pay no heed to other views." In law, too, he often took the more stringent position. We recall that the author of *Seder tanna'im* had restated the prevailing rabbinic opinion that in matters left open (*tequ*) by the Talmud, one ought to decide in the more rigid vein in the case of a biblical prohibition, but take the more lenient view with respect to a rabbinic ordinance. Ḥananel, however, followed by many Western rabbis, decided that this rule applied only to doubts in practical cases, but in legal theory one must always more stringently interpret any ritualistic prohibition, even if it be of rabbinic provenance. Perhaps the then prevailing overemphasis on the binding nature of all rabbinic enactments, produced by the intellectual debate with Karaite and other antitalmudic spokesmen, accounts for these extremes.[49]

No mere pedagogue, Ḥananel always remained awake to the

legal implications of the talmudic debates. At times he apologized for commenting on a very simple passage merely because he wished to decide a legal issue. Nevertheless, his primary objective, unlike that of his predecessors, was exegetical, rather than juridical. For that purpose he utilized materials accumulated by the geonim, from whose decisions, as we recall, he reluctantly deviated. But he also had at his disposal much of the wisdom transmitted by earlier generations of Western scholars, particularly in his father Ḥushiel's Italian homeland. Since Italian observances had been greatly influenced by Palestinian customs, he leaned on the Palestinian Talmud more heavily than did his geonic prototypes. Occasionally, he even decided an issue in favor of the Palestinian version, especially when it recorded an actual practice which always had the force of a legal precedent or was supported by an analogous doctrine of the pro-Palestinian academy of Sura. Like many of his confreres, he cited with particular relish the "custom of all Israel," reminiscent of the Muslim *idjma'*, as with respect to the prolonged blowing of the horn during public fasts. At times he did not hesitate to give the talmudic text an unusual twist, or even to emend it, if the improved reading stated the law more accurately. For instance, at the beginning of Berakhot he replaced the widely accepted reading concerning the recitation of the evening *Shema'* (Hear, O Israel!) until the worshiper "gets up from his evening meal" by "gets up to go to bed." Somewhat less radically, he interpreted the well-known rabbinic injunction against those who speak ill "after the casket [*miṭṭatan*] of scholars," as aimed at talking ill about their "deviation" (from *haṭṭayah)* from the righteous way. By this slight twist he conveyed the idea that gossip about a living scholar was equally outlawed.[50]

Although Ḥananel spent a lifetime in writing and rewriting his vast work, he apparently never completed it. If we may assume, as is likely, that he wrote his *Commentary* in the sequence of the Talmud, two dates incidentally recorded in two tractates (1038 in B.Q. and 1053 in 'A.Z.), may convey the idea of the years of hard work which went into its preparation. From fragments published in recent years, as well as from quotations in older letters, we are now able to reconstruct a substantial portion of the *Commentary*. These quotations also attest to its early and widespread popularity; among the distinguished Spanish and Italian authorities of the next generation who used it extensively were no lesser figures than Alfasi and Nathan ben Yeḥiel.[51]

It took some time, however, before Ḥananel's *Commentary* came into wider use in northern France and the Rhinelands. Such regions as Lotharingia were a particularly fertile ground for that upsurge of Jewish learning as they were open even to the incursion of Arabic scientific teachings, probably in part transmitted by Jewish arrivals from Muslim lands. Western Europe's Jewish exegetical tradition started in the days of Yehudah bar Meir ha-Kohen (Leontin; 10th cent.) and his pupil, Gershom bar Yehudah of Mayence (*ca.* 960–1028). Gershom, in particular, evinced considerable care in securing exact copies of important Eastern works. Tradition has it that for many years he labored over copying with his own hand and revising the text of the entire Talmud, just as soon thereafter Joseph bar Samuel Bonfils (Tob 'Elem) personally copied the methodological *Seder tanna'im,* as well as a collection of geonic responsa. Probably disgruntled by his experience, Gershom "cursed" scribes who were not exactingly accurate in transcribing older texts. He also urged them not to omit the introductory materials, which usually enabled readers to identify the authors and become familiar with their objectives. At the same time Gershom and his disciples, particularly in the two growing centers of Mayence and Worms, began interpreting the talmudic texts for the benefit of younger scholars. Although from the outset some comments were recorded by faithful pupils, no comprehensive commentary circulated in the Rhenish schools for many years to come. Each academy apparently possessed but a single master text, constantly supplemented by additional observations distilled from the academic debates in the course of years. It was such a composite work which ultimately made its appearance, and was later attributed to the outstanding leader, Gershom, "the Light of the Exile." While Gershom's individual contribution was undoubtedly very substantial, no one can really tell how much stems from his collaborators and immediate successors. None of them was familiar with the works of the great North African scholars, and yet their comments reveal many similarities in both fundamental approaches and significant details. These affinities are readily explainable by the indebtedness of them all to the Eastern geonim (uncritical posterity actually believed that Gershom had been a pupil of Hai Gaon or Ḥananel) and also by the specific Palestino-Italian heritage of both the Franco-German and the North African cultural centers.[52]

All these endeavors were soon eclipsed by the superlative exegetical work of Rashi (Solomon bar Isaac, or Yiṣḥaqi, 1040–1105). A native of Troyes, the important commercial city in the Champagne, Rashi spent his younger years studying in both Worms and Mayence. Posterity readily ascribed to Rashi the erection of, or at least worship in, the so-called Rashi Chapel in Worms, which was not built until several centuries later. True, it did not thus name the Worms Jewish bath dating from the middle of the twelfth century, or about half a century after Rashi's death. Clearly, contemporaries saw nothing particularly spectacular in that bath, whose significance rests only with its monumental value for modern research. But there is no question about the benefits Rashi derived from his prolonged studies at the German academies. Such living contacts with contemporary bearers of tradition in various localities, recorded already during R. Judah the Patriarch's preparation of the Mishnah and widely indulged in especially by early Muslim students of the law, were considered no less indispensable in eleventh-century France and Germany. Only later did the written word, widely distributed in moderately priced copies, make literary journeys less imperative.[53]

From Germany Rashi brought back to Troyes a vast mass of traditions and specific interpretations of the talmudic text. He was even allowed to copy for his own use some of the accumulated records kept in a *quntres* (handbook, probably derived from the Latin *commentarius*) in each of the two academies. Through correspondence he also retained lively contacts with the scholars there and in other communities. Thus equipped, Rashi began teaching in his own rather small academy of Troyes, although, since he made his living through the cultivation of vineyards, he could not devote all his time to instruction. He concentrated on explaining the talmudic text to his pupils, who included his sons-in-law and soon also his grandson Samuel bar Meir. In the course of years he succeeded in going over many tractates more than once. Writing down or dictating his comments, and constantly revising them, he produced three recensions of some parts, unwittingly creating much confusion in later literature when students consulted different autograph versions. We have the testimony of Isaac Or Zaru'a that he had seen such an autograph, in which words were deleted and replaced by others over the line while many supplementary comments appeared in the margins.[54]

Out of these oral as well as literary labors grew one of the great masterpieces in the world's exegetical literature: Rashi's *Commentary* on the Talmud. It was one of those rare, almost definitive accomplishments which has never been superseded. Immediately accepted as the authoritative text in the West, and soon also in the East, it has ever since accompanied most texts of the Talmud, as if it were an integral part thereof. It was printed as one of the first Hebrew incunabula in the fifteenth century (on Berakhot in Soncino, 1483) and in the first complete edition of the Babylonian Talmud (1520–22), as well as in practically all other editions which have since seen the light of day. It was exalted by such medieval authors as the fourteenth-century Spaniard, Menaḥem ibn Zeraḥ, who wrote that "the Holy Spirit has rested upon R. Solomon, and he mastered the Talmud. He composed commentaries on the Babylonian Talmud in a lucid and succinct style, the like of which had not been known before. Without him the ways of the Talmud might have been forgotten in Israel." Rashi's successors paid him the highest homage by constantly working on his commentary, clarifying and improving it, reconciling its apparent contradictions, and bringing its decisions up to date. In fact, several generations of Franco-German scholars spent their best intellectual energies on writing supplements (*Tosafot*) to Rashi's great work.[55]

So impressed were later generations with Rashi's towering personality that each ascribed to him heroic features according to its own taste. With the growth of kabbalistic preconceptions, in particular, they tried to find in Rashi's commentaries hidden mystic doctrines. No less an authority than the sixteenth-century jurist Mordecai Jaffe roundly declared that Rashi's commentaries "contain both overt and hidden meanings and both are right." The biographer Azulai unhesitatingly recorded as true the legends that Rashi had appeared in a dream to his grandson Samuel bar

Meir in order to teach him the pronunciation of the Ineffable Name, and that before writing his biblical commentaries the master had fasted on six hundred and thirteen days. Discounting these folkloristic tales, the fact remains that Rashi never questioned views expressed by the ancient sages whose words he interpreted entirely in their spirit. Unconcernedly, he repeated even some of their glaringly anthropomorphic statements. Of course, living in a Christian environment with its emphatic assertion of the doctrine of Incarnation, he was far less subject to those polemical pressures to which Ḥananel and most of the geonim had readily yielded. At times he even added some supranaturalistic explanations of his own, as when he contended that R. Ishmael, together with the four well-known entrants into the mystic orchard, had gone up to heaven by the use of the divine name.[56]

Rashi's mastery was not merely stylistic, although in an extraordinary way he combined brevity with lucidity, great erudition with judicious weighing of conflicting opinions. What ultimately mattered to him, as to most of his readers, was to ascertain the fine points of law. In fact, he saw the main purposes of Bible and Talmud in their guiding the Jew in proper behavior and teaching him the norms under which he was to live. Rashi's *Commentary* on the Pentateuch opens with the characteristic query, "The Torah did not have to begin before the verse, 'This month shall be unto you the beginning of months' [Exod. 12:2], which is the first commandment imposed upon Israel. Why did it open with, 'In the beginning God created' . . . ?" In his answer Rashi declared that the entire book of Genesis and the first eleven chapters of Exodus were but an introduction to the essential legal part of the Bible, mainly intended to explain why God, as Creator of the universe, felt free to confer upon Israel the possession of the Holy Land with all the commandments attached to it. It was for legalistic as much as for exegetical reasons that he evinced great solicitude for the accuracy of the talmudic text and painstakingly sought out the best manuscripts. With his expert knowledge of readings in other rabbinic sources and his almost unerring intuition about the intentions of the ancient sages he was able greatly to improve upon the existing versions. At times he relied on his own reasoning and understanding of the context as much as on manuscript readings or traditions handed down by his teachers. In a remarkable responsum to his son-in-law, Meir bar Samuel, he dismissed his teachers' objections as superficial. With candor he added: "I invoke, to be sure, the great authority of R. Jacob bar Yaqar [his eminent teacher]. Although I have not heard him say so, yet my reasoning and understanding stem from his teachings. Moreover, they [the objectors], too, judge not on the basis of tradition or talmudic proofs, but from personal opinion. If they could advance persuasive arguments, I should reverse myself. But I find it difficult to waste Jewish money in a case which seems to me clearly and demonstrably permissible." Of course, Rashi reached such independent conclusions only after mature deliberation. Occasionally he mentioned that he had "labored from his youth" on the understanding of a particular passage, especially if it meant departing from a talmudic reading found in Gershom's autograph copy and accepted by his teachers. Ironically, we are today no longer in a position to gauge the full extent of Rashi's textual emendations, because most of his suggestions, particularly in the third and final recension of his *Commentary,* have long since been incorporated in almost all editions of the text itself.[57]

Among Rashi's major concerns was the clarification of the vocabulary and *realia* of the talmudic age; he often appended to his explanation their contemporary French equivalents. He followed therein Gershom's example, who in turn had imitated his geonic predecessors with their numerous Arabic glosses. These French *la'azim* (foreign words) in Rashi, more than three thousand in all, have long served as an important source of information for the French language, and especially its Champagne dialect during the eleventh century. To make certain objects or customs clearer to the reader, Rashi also frequently referred to French usages, although he sometimes sensed, more instinctively than from direct knowledge, that there also existed great differences between the two epochs. For example, to explain the talmudic reference to a woman wearing a dress "split open from both sides" as a sufficient ground for divorce, he observed, "This is similar to the way of Christian women in France whose flesh [above the elbows] is visible from their sides." He also evinced great interest in the Talmud's methodological rules and the chronological sequence of ancient sages. Curiously, he rarely repeated verbatim the same explanation of parallel passages, because his main purpose was to make each passage understandable in its particular context. Finally, he also often indicated the legal decisions emerging from some lengthy debates.[58]

Rashi thus combined in his work the best approaches and interpretations of the geonim and the North African scholars. He presented these findings in a manner so simple and unobtrusive as to become the most effective guide to relative beginners. At the same time he was also the most authoritative expounder of the talmudic text for experts. This extraordinary combination proved inimitable even for his closest associates. There is an entry in the middle of the tractate Makkot (19b) which, playing on the words of the last comment relating to the consumption of the levitical tithe with a pure body, states, "Here our master of pure body, his soul expiring in purity, ceased commenting. From here on it is the language of his pupil, R. Yehudah bar Nathan." As Rashi's disciple and son-in-law, R. Yehudah carried on in the master's spirit. The commentary on Baba Batra was similarly interrupted by Rashi's death (at fol. 29a) and had to be completed by his grandson Samuel bar Meir, while that on Nedarim, apparently not genuine to begin with, was replaced (from fol. 22b on) by the older commentary attributed to Gershom. Although both son-in-law and grandson grew up under the impact of Rashi's personality and teachings, and although both men were distinguished commentators in their own right, these continuations, obviously extracted from their authors' independent commentaries, never reached the high level of the original masterpiece. Ironically, several commentaries on talmudic tractates, whose origin from Rashi's unnamed disciples rather than his own pen has been successfully argued by Zunz, J. Reifmann, and others, have proved to be more felicitous imitations.[59]

Yehudah, Samuel, and other disciples of Rashi such as Shemayah and Simḥah of Vitry, laid the foundations for the school of Tosafists whose work extended over more than two centuries after Rashi's death. Its name was taken from the ancient custom of "adding" materials to an existing official collection, like the ancient Tosefta which allegedly contained only tannaitic supplements to the Mishnah. Unlike these old additions to substantive laws, however, the medieval *Tosafot,* like Rashi's own *Commentary* to which they were appended, pursued primarily exegetical aims. By bringing together materials from the vast range of talmudic letters, and by dialectically raising serious problems and then ingeniously solving them, they sometimes deviated from Rashi's interpretation, but more frequently they merely amplified the master's views with novel applications. The same is largely true also of their independent commentaries, except perhaps when Simson bar Abraham of Sens (*ca.* 1050–1115) undertook to interpret anew the much neglected sections of the first and last orders of the Mishnah, not provided for with a Babylonian *gemara.* The Tosafists' discussions were carried on entirely in the spirit of the ancient Babylonian academies. Indeed, the "dialectics of Abbaye and Raba" never had more genuine and faithful devotees than these scholars residing in the Champagne, Lotharingia, and the Rhinelands. Immersed in talmudic studies with almost total exclusion of all other intellectual interests, the Tosafists recreated on western European soil the entire atmosphere of academic learning characteristic of the Jewish schools in Sassanian Persia.[60]

Behind this exclusive concentration loomed the Church-imposed, as well as self-chosen, Jewish segregation from the Christian world, a circumstance which was constantly increasing in the twelfth and thirteenth centuries. True, some rabbis were keenly aware of what was happening outside their ghettos. They continued speaking the language of their environment, and Simson of Sens, emulating Gershom and Rashi, inserted a considerable number of French translations of technical terms into his commentaries on the Mishnah and the *Sifra.* Consciously or unconsciously, they also revealed certain basic links to the intellectual currents among contemporary Christian scholars. Even outwardly there were basic similarities, though hardly any mutual imitation, between the Tosafists and the famous "glossators" of the *Corpus* of Justinian at the University of Bologna and elsewhere, whose work served as the major instrumentality of adjusting that ancient codification to contemporary needs. Yet these were more formal than substantive resemblances, stemming from the common indebtedness of the original tannaitic and Roman laws to

Hellenistic prototypes rather than from direct interrelations during the Middle Ages. To all intents and purposes Jacob Tam and his associates might have lived in Sassanian Babylonia and participated there in the academic debates. Their basic approaches, indeed their very categories of thinking, were different from those of a Guarnerius or an Accursius, just as those of their ancestors had differed from the approaches and categories employed by a Gallus or an Ulpian.[61]

Even a man of Jacob Tam's extraordinary brilliance sought his laurels exclusively in carrying on the grand debates of the Babylonian academies entirely in their spirit and according to their method. The fifteenth-century Spanish-Algerian scholar Isaac bar Sheshet was not guilty of an overstatement when he described Tam as a man "unmatched by anyone else in talmudic dialectics since the conclusion of the Talmud. Before him the entire Talmud is spread out. He is both erudite and ingenious, 'uprooting mountains and grinding them against one another'; his sharp dialectics, depth of understanding, and breadth of knowledge inspire fear in every wise man." Only incidentally, and yet even more significantly than Rashi, did the Tosafists point up problems of a legal nature. Not surprisingly, it was possible for a later author (Asher ben Yeḥiel, his son Jacob, or someone else) to compile so-called *Pisqe Tosafot* (Legal Decisions of the Tosafot), which summarized the legal findings indirectly emerging from this dialectical exegesis. Long before that compilation, however, nearly all students of the law, especially in the Ashkenazic areas, took cognizance of the legal decisions by Tam, his associates, and his successors, on a par with those found in codes or responsa.[62]

Under their collective name the Tosafists included the cream of Franco-German scholarship of the twelfth and thirteenth centuries. Among their more famous members were the aforementioned martyrs, Jacob of Orléans and Yom Ṭob of Joigny; Eliezer bar Samuel of Metz, Eliezer bar Nathan of Mayence, Isaac bar Samuel of Dampierre (generally known under the abbreviation RI), his pupil Isaac bar Abraham, the latter's brother Simson of Sens, and later on Yeḥiel of Paris, Isaac bar Moses of Vienna, Meir bar Baruch of Rothenburg, and Asher ben Yeḥiel who, by moving to Toledo, helped transplant their teachings to the Iberian Peninsula. Most of these scholars had academies of their own and boasted of distinguished disciples and associates. Some wrote independent juridical tracts which have been, or will be, quoted here in various contexts. Even the Spanish-Provençal jurists, who sometimes looked down on their northern coreligionists as deficient in secular learning and systematic thinking, gradually had to submit to the juristic hegemony of these sharp-witted northern glossators. In the twelfth century the independent and ingenious Abraham ben David of Posquières could still speak sarcastically of "the Frenchmen who consider themselves the world's heroes." But the outstanding Spanish teacher of the thirteenth century, Naḥmanides, called the Tosafists "the teachers and masters, who reveal to us all hidden matters." True, in Muslim lands the resistance to the incursion of the Tosafists' dialectical findings continued much longer. There Naḥmanides' contemporary Yehudah ben Samuel ibn 'Abbas sharply condemned these speculations, "all of which merely waste man's time with vanity and futility." But nothing could in the long run check the steamroller effect of the Tosafists' teachings, in method even more than in content, throughout the Jewish world of letters.[63]

MISHNAIC REVIVAL

Curiously, Palestine participated but slightly in this exegetical effort. The academy of Tiberias-Jerusalem and other schools undoubtedly cultivated the Palestinian Talmud alongside the Babylonian, but there probably was too little practical interest in the former for anyone to write an extensive commentary on it until the modern period. As to the Babylonian compendium, the Palestinians left it entirely to their better equipped colleagues of Sura and Pumbedita to offer authoritative interpretations. In fact, combined with the general decline of the Aramaic speech, both talmudic texts became less and less familiar to the average Palestinian student, and an effort had to be made to translate parts of them into the current Hebrew language. This at least seems to have been the purpose of a translation of the tractate 'Erubin, a small fragment of which (on fol. 54) has come to light.

This interesting document (*Difter,* published in Ginzberg's *Ginze Schechter,* II, 375 ff.) is signed in 1093 by the otherwise unknown Abraham bar R. Shabbetai and is particularly noteworthy because of its numerous variants from the accepted text.

About the same time, on the very eve of its eclipse by the Crusaders, Palestinian Jewry produced a fairly significant *Commentary* on the Mishnah, common to both Talmudim, from the pen of Nathan ben Abraham (died before 1102). Serving as vice-chairman of the main Palestinian academy under Abiathar Gaon, Nathan wrote his comprehensive commentary in Arabic. Parts of it were subsequently incorporated with selections from other sources by an anonymous compiler, approximately sixty years after Nathan's death. It seems never to have enjoyed great popularity, however, even in countries following Palestine's spiritual lead, and its contents have become known only in recent years through a Yemenite manuscript. Remarkably, this Palestinian author was so exclusively under the domination of the Babylonian Talmud and Babylonia's geonic literature that he rarely referred to the Talmud or any posttalmudic writings of his own country, but quoted rather extensively from Saadiah, Samuel ben Ḥofni, Hai, and Ḥefeṣ ben Yaṣliaḥ, as well as from Nissim's *Mafteaḥ.* Our author may not have been typical of his Palestinian compatriots, however. Probably a grandson of the gaon Nathan ben Abraham, who had spent some years in Kairuwan studying at Ḥushiel's academy, he was undoubtedly imbued with special reverence for the Babylonian Talmud as the ultimate authority. Hence, rather than comment on the Palestinian Talmud, he chose to write his observations on the Mishnah, utilizing preeminently the materials of the Babylonian *gemara* and geonic letters and, like Ḥananel, consciously omitting comments on simple passages.[64]

Perhaps the major effect of that *Commentary* was its possible influence on the similar work by Maimonides, if indeed the then youthful exile from Cordova had used it in his Spanish-Moroccan residence or revised in its light the parts of his commentary already written at his arrival in the Holy Land (1165). In a lengthy introduction, Maimonides explained the objectives of his work, which he called *Kitab as-Siraj* (Book of Light). Having found, he declared, that none of the geonim had succeeded in completing a commentary on the whole Talmud, he had decided instead to explain the Mishnah directly for the benefit of busy students and those unequipped for dealing with the intricacies of the talmudic debates. For this purpose he had started in his early years to collect traditions current in his Spanish homeland, especially in the circle of his own scholarly father Maimon and the latter's teacher, Joseph ibn Megas.

What induced me to compose this work [he added] was the recognition that the Talmud explains the Mishnah in a way no one could guess through mere reasoning. Basing itself on general principles, it asserts that one Mishnah attests a specific thing [not mentioned therein], that another lacks certain words or must be amended in a certain way, and that still another voices a particular sage's opinion which is thus and thus. At times it adds words to the Mishnah, or removes some words, and explains its underlying reasons. I have decided, therefore, to write this book on the entire Mishnah. If written the way I shall explain it, it ought to prove useful from four angles: First, we shall explain the meaning of the Mishnah and the significance of its words. For were you to ask the greatest scholar for an interpretation of the law of a Mishnah he could not do so unless he remembered by heart the talmudic comments on it, or else looked them up. No one can learn the whole Talmud by heart. Particularly, since any law in the Mishnah may require explanations through discussion, queries, and answers in the Talmud which extend over four or five folios, none but a well-experienced student can decide what has thus become clear in the meaning of the Mishnah. But what shall even he do if the explanation and the law derived from it hinge on additional data from two or three other tractates? The second advantage will accrue from my stating in the interpretation of every legal dispute which opinion has become law. The third advantage is that [the book] will serve as an introduction to advanced speculation for any beginner, so that he may learn therefrom the method of investigating the sayings [of the sages] and their interpretation. In this way he may embrace in his mind [the ways] of all talmudic discussions, which will aid him greatly with respect to the entire Talmud. The fourth advantage is that he who has already studied the Mishnah and understood what he read, will remember it [for a long time] as if it stood before his eyes, and he will fluently recite both his Mishnah and his Talmud.

Not allowing the perils of his journey from Spain to Morocco and thence to Palestine and Egypt seriously to interfere with his work, Maimonides completed the first version of his *Commentary* in

1168, at the age of thirty-three, after ten years of concentrated effort. But he did not desist at this point. His later studies made him often revise his opinion on some point of law or interpretation, and he unhesitatingly corrected his *Commentary*. Asked in later years about a contradiction between certain statements in his *Code* and his *Commentary,* he expostulated that in the first edition of the latter he had sometimes followed a geonic authority (in that particular case Ḥefeṣ ben Yaṣliaḥ's "Book of Commandments"), but that on further reflection he had realized the untenability of that view and accordingly had revised the early text.[65]

Not that Maimonides blindly followed the older authorities. He was a great admirer of Alfasi's law book, which, during his work on the *Commentary,* he considered almost errorless and wrong only in "at most ten points." But he dared freely to controvert Alfasi and even the earlier geonim with what must have appeared to most contemporaries the recklessness of youth. Having acquired in Morocco considerable medical knowledge, he was particularly prone, in the manner of brash young scientists, to ride roughshod over the older physiological tenets. For example, discussing the bridegroom's accusation on the morrow of the wedding that he had not found the requisite signs of virginity in his bride, Maimonides stated bluntly, "Thus have taught all the geonim whose opinions we know, yet I have come to the conclusion that the opposite is true." Occasionally he ventured to defy the very talmudic interpretation of the Mishnah, even when legal decisions were involved. He also indulged in outspoken excursuses, especially on contemporary superstitions, popular misconceptions of religious and scientific fundamentals, the professionalization of learning, or the current mania for titles. On the other hand, as he expostulated later in the introduction to his *Book of Commandments,* he had planned in the *Commentary* only "to explain briefly each law in the Mishnah. But it was not our intention to elaborate on the laws of each commandment and to state all one needs to know about what is forbidden or allowed, obligatory or free." [66]

More significant than interpretations of individual passages were Maimonides' enlightening general observations. He always liked to analyze first the basic issues in each set of regulations, and often he succeeded thus in succinctly summarizing the lengthy debates in the Talmud. His introductions to some Mishnaic orders, tractates, or even chapters, have long enjoyed deserved recognition. His general introduction to the *Commentary,* from which the above lengthy quotation was taken, was paralleled by a similar introduction to the last order of Ṭeharot. Here he tried to convey to readers no longer familiar with the ancient laws of purity the fundamentals of these laws as viewed from the standpoint of the biblical-talmudic legislation. Some introductions, resembling independent essays, were studied quite apart from the Maimonidean *Commentary* itself. The introduction to the Sayings of the Fathers, especially, divided into eight sections, soon circulated widely as an independent ethical treatise under the title of "Eight Chapters." In this form it became one of the classics of the medieval Jewish ethical literature. The introduction, on the other hand, to the tenth chapter of Sanhedrin, in which the young thinker endeavored to define the Jewish credo, served as the foundation for the so-called "Thirteen Principles." Prefaced by the personal declaration, "I believe," these principles were incorporated into the daily prayers of orthodox Jewry in the West. They have been recited in a more elaborate form in a solemn monthly service among Sephardic Jews. The fame of some of these introductory essays spread beyond the confines of the Jewish community. As early as 1655, the Oxford Hebraist, Edward Pococke reissued them with a Latin translation in his *Porta Mosis.*[67]

Greeted with almost immediate acclaim, although also with some grumbling, the Maimonidean *Commentary* quickly displaced the older works of this kind, including that by Saadiah. Even in its author's lifetime, its renown spread to western Europe. Before long the community of Marseilles commissioned the distinguished poet Yehudah al-Ḥarizi, to translate it into Hebrew for the use of Western students. After translating five tractates of the first order, however, the somewhat erratic poet tired of this undertaking (1194–97), and it took another century and the efforts of several other translators before the task was completed. In its Hebrew garb the work quickly became a classic in both East and West. It so speedily displaced the Arabic original, even in thirteenth-century Spain where the Arabic language was still widely used, that, according to Solomon ben Joseph ibn Ya'qub, one of the latest translators, a messenger of the Roman community had been unable in 1296 to locate a single copy in Catalonia and the Provence. The envoy was more fortunate in Huesca, where he found the text of the second and third orders. Only in Saragossa did he get hold of a fairly complete set with the exception of the last order, Ṭeharot. Even in the Near East the Hebrew version largely displaced the original in scholarly use, although Joseph Karo still found the Jews of Egypt and Yemen following a halakhic decision of Maimonides' Arabic text. Of course, the Maimonidean *Book of Light* could not compare in either popularity or influence with Rashi's *Commentary* on the Talmud; even in the East it was consulted primarily by scholars, rather than the general run of students. But everywhere it distinctly facilitated direct study of the Mishnah, and in more recent editions of the latter it has usually accompanied the text of that fountainhead of all Jewish Oral Law.[68]

Rashi's and Maimonides' superlative exegetical achievements relegated many older and contemporary works to limbo, or at least confined them to a few narrow scholarly circles. In the second section of his major philosophic-apologetic work, *Magen Abot* (Shield of Fathers), devoted to a commentary on the Mishnah tractate Abot, Simon bar Ṣemaḥ Duran observed: "We have placed before us the commentary of R. Solomon [Rashi] of blessed memory, who is unmatched in explaining statements according to the intentions of their authors; the commentary of R. Moses of blessed memory who is unrivaled in bringing them closer to the dictates of reason; as well as the commentary of R. Jonah [ben Abraham Gerondi] the Pious of blessed memory who has had none like him in speaking of the fear of the Lord and attracting the hearts of men to life of piety." The fame of these works committed to total oblivion an indubitably noteworthy work by the great scholar and poet Joseph ibn Abitur, who, according to Ibn Daud, had "interpreted the entire Talmud in Arabic" for the Muslim Caliph Al-Ḥakim of Cordova (d. 962). And, not even the greatest of the Spanish masters before Maimonides, such as Isaac ben Yehudah ibn Gayyat (*ca.* 1030–89), Isaac ben Baruch ibn al-Balia (1035–94), and Joseph ben Meir ha-Levi ibn Megas (1077–1141) wholly escaped that fate. Admiring successors may have spoken about Ibn Megas with bated breath and contended that "even in the generation of Moses there was none like him" (Ibn Daud). Yet they failed to preserve for posterity more than some brief comments by him on two talmudic tractates (B.B. and Shebu'ot). That perennial fighter, Abraham ben David of Posquières, likewise left behind some expository comments, including one on Baba Qamah but recently published. An interesting commentary on the tractate Mashqin (Mo'ed qaṭan), written by the otherwise unknown Solomon ben ha-Yatom (the Orphan), probably a twelfth-century southern Italian scholar, suddenly appeared in a private manuscript and was published half a century ago. Another exegete of the same region, Isaac ben Melchizedek of Siponto, Apulia (later of Salerno), wrote a lucid commentary on the Mishnah, of which only parts have thus far been published. Not undeservedly he was styled "the great rabbi" by Benjamin of Tudela, who met him on his journey.[69]

Probably the fact that, unlike these Italian scholars, the celebrated Spanish jurists preferred to write commentaries devoted not to the comprehensive interpretation of entire texts, but rather to observations on what their authors considered either *cruces interpretum* or sources of some new laws, discouraged all but the most expert or dedicated students. Of course, knowledgeable persons derived much new information from such *ḥiddushim* (*novellae*), and often used their findings with or without acknowledgment. In time, when the remnants of these works have been more fully published, we may yet learn much about the history of rabbinic exegesis. But they are not likely to contribute to the understanding of the ancient classics more than a few important insights, as well as some improved readings and quotations from still older authorities. Probably the best fruits of this learning have since been absorbed in later exegetical works and other branches of halakhic lore, and thus have been incorporated into the living heritage of the people.

HALAKHIC MONOGRAPHS AND MISCELLANIES

A similar fate befell most halakhic works dealing with specific phases of Jewish law. Most of them, particularly those of early vintage, were so completely absorbed by later comprehensive codes that sometimes their very titles could be recovered only by the slow and painstaking research of modern scholars. Yet their aggregate contribution to Jewish jurisprudence was enormous. Without them the famous medieval codes of law probably would never have seen the light of day.

Palestine seems to have been the cradle of such monographs summarizing the existing law in special areas of interest either to the public at large or to certain professional groups like the scribes. Perhaps the very fact that the Palestinian Talmud had been left in a rather unfinished state, combined with the inroads of what had become known of the Babylonian Talmud, added to the legal uncertainties. The gradual decline of the Aramaic language, too, must have enhanced the quest for Hebrew texts going beyond the Mishnah.

Some juridical-ethical collections seem to have made their appearance already in talmudic times. The Babylonian Talmud itself refers to compilations of "Laws concerning Proper Conduct" (*Derekh Ereṣ*) and others relating to mourning (*Ebel rabbati*). These treatises, apparently comparable to the later "minor" tractates, *Derekh Ereṣ* and *Semaḥot* (Joys; euphemism for mourning), were doubtless revised in the early posttalmudic period and so became part of the general category of *Massekhtot qeṭanot* (Minor Tractates), in contradistinction to the sixty (or sixty-three, if one counts the three Babot and Makkot separately) tractates of the Mishnah. This category included summaries of the laws of *Kallah* (The Bride; on marital and sexual problems); dealt with the socially significant problems of Samaritans, proselytes, and slaves (*Kutim, Gerim,* and *'Abadim*); and reviewed the regulations affecting the scribal profession, especially in the preparation of scrolls of law, phylacteries, and doorpost inscriptions (*Soferim,* including *Sefer Torah; Tefillin,* and *Mezuzah,* as well as *Ṣiṣit*). Although these texts consist primarily of tannaitic sayings, they betray their posttalmudic origins by outright quotations from the two Talmudim. They also reveal unusual concern for methodological problems, as when the compiler of *Soferim* generalizes: "Wherever there is a difference of opinion between two Tannaim or Amoraim, and it is uncertain whom the law follows, we act according to the more stringent view." If, in some passages, their authors pay special attention to conditions in the dispersion, such as the regular observance of two holidays, such consideration for world Jewry need not shake our confidence in their Palestinian provenance, strong traces of which are noticeable in their language and thought patterns. They stress above all the binding force of custom—at that time a pronouncedly Palestinian bias. Not surprisingly, therefore, these tractates exercised but limited influence on the legal evolution during the geonic age. In fact, most of them were unknown to such leading jurists as Aḥai, and came in vogue only through the influence of the Western schools. Jacob Tam treated them on a par with geonic writings and declared: "One ought to rely on them in matters in which they do not controvert, but merely add to, our Talmud. We observe many customs in accordance with their views." [70]

Another significant Palestinian product of the late Byzantine or early Muslim era was the so-called *Sefer ha-Ma'asim li-bene Ereṣ Yisrael* (Book of Precedents for the Population of Palestine). Judging from the few fragments recovered during the last three decades, it consisted principally of court decisions, probably rendered in Tiberias. Hence the juxtaposition of frequently unrelated subjects, probably so found in the original court records of that crucial period of transition, with its accompanying manifestations of social and communal disintegration. We have already quoted some passages revealing feminine libertarianism such as had been recorded among Jews neither before nor in the later Middle Ages. Perhaps for that reason the few extant fragments betray so much concern for family relations. One characteristic decision reads: "If a woman says to her husband: 'Divorce me or else write down that you will not inherit my estate,' her words have no validity. If he writes her [a writ of divorce or hereditary renunciation] under duress, this document is null and void." One sees here a reflection of the same social turmoil which induced the early Babylonian geonim to issue their so-called "Ordinance concerning the Obstreperous Woman," ordering husbands to give immediate divorces to wives demanding them under threats (about 670). Apparently the Palestinian decision was either reached before that Babylonian enactment or was the latter's pointed denial. Other sections dealt with the "Laws of *Me'un*" (the right of a minor girl betrothed by her mother and brother to reject her husband upon reaching maturity), and the "Laws of *Ḥaliṣah*" (the biblical substitution for the prescribed levirate marriage). Some of these "precedents" were taken over bodily into the early Western law books known as *Ma'ase ha-geonim* (Geonic Precedents) and *Sefer ha-Pardes* (Book of the Orchard). Not surprisingly, however, their impact upon the development of Babylonian, and through it also of North African and Spanish, juridical studies was quite insignificant. While Yehudai Gaon and Simon Qayyara still used this Palestinian tract to good advantage, it all but disappeared in the later geonic age. In one of his responsa Hai Gaon pleaded ignorance of the source of a certain decision by Simon and added, "But we have *heard* that these matters were found in the Book of Precedents of the Palestinians." [71]

Equally obscure is the origin of a small monograph on the laws of phylacteries, probably part of a larger work written in Babylonia. Long known from quotations by medieval jurists, it was appended to Asher ben Yeḥiel's own restatement of the laws governing phylacteries. Asher mentions its title, *Shimmusha Raba* (Raba's Legal Practice), and calls it the work of a gaon. It may well have been written by Raba, the disciple of Yehudai Gaon in the eighth century, or else summarized from his lectures by one of his pupils, perhaps Pirqoi ben Baboi. In any case, he was not the famous fourth-century Amora. As noted by Yehudah bar Barzillai, many of his utterances actually run counter to talmudic regulations. Also, the use of such formal devices as the term *tenan* for introducing an Amoraic quotation sounded strange to the Spanish scholar. He attributed these irregularities to errors by pupils or copyists, whereas they may really have stemmed from oral traditions current in the Babylonian academies before the final revision of the talmudic text.[72]

Once again a significant step forward was made by Saadiah Gaon. Just as he pioneered in talmudic methodology and exegesis, Saadiah also evinced deep interest in a new systematic analysis of existing laws. In a series of monographs he reviewed important branches of both ritual and civil law, classifying them by major divisions and subdivisions. At times he supplied general rationales or decided certain practical issues in the light of the Babylonian Talmud, but also with some consideration of the Palestinian sources. Perhaps because he wrote most of these works before he became gaon, his doctrines appeared to most contemporaries and successors as based on purely individual decisions, not necessarily representing the official position of the academy of Sura. Hence they were copied less extensively and quoted less fully than they deserved. Their practical utility, too, was diminished by their excessive systematization, so that any judge wishing to find a particular legal decision had to wade through much "irrelevant" circumlocution. Moreover, most students of Jewish law, trained on talmudic sources, doubtless found it easier to handle legal handbooks arranged in the accustomed talmudic order rather than in this novel sequence. Nevertheless, Saadiah's monographs found emulators among the later, more systematically trained geonim, and they influenced the legal thinking of even the most tradition-minded jurists.[73]

Such influence emanated from Saadiah's earliest monograph, known as the Book of Deeds (*Sefer ha-Sheṭarot*) or, under its broader Arabic title, *Kitab ash-Shahada wal-Wataiq* (Book of Testimony and Deeds). Rules of evidence, whether derived from the oral testimony of witnesses or from documents, always posed perplexing problems to conscientious judges. Much ingenuity had been expended by the ancient sages on defining these rules and formalizing certain deeds to make their meaning unmistakably clear. Since the discovery of the Elephantine papyri it has also become evident that the ancient Jewish scribes were very careful in writing marriage contracts and other deeds so as to meet the ever more stringent legal requirements.

Saadiah considered it, therefore, a great help to scribes, students, and judges to review the vast talmudic legislation on this subject, as well as to produce significant samples and forms of various deeds. As he wrote in his preface, "The whole of this [treatise] is one of the chapters on jurisprudence which I am prepared to discuss. I have, however, decided to take this chapter first, because I have realized the urgent want of it on the part of the people, as well as its great usefulness." He untiringly emphasized the need of extreme care in the formulation of deeds. As an example he pointed out that, according to talmudic provisions, a difference in the use of a letter *B* instead of *L* in the testamentary provision for a daughter might cost the latter a great deal of money, dependent on differing local customs. Similarly, if one writes in the deed of sale "I have sold thee one half of the field I have" in lieu of "one half I have of the field," the purchaser acquires only, say, a quarter of the field jointly owned by the seller with someone else, instead of his entire half. The gaon realized, of course, that "deeds are, like the cases they deal with, infinite in number. Hence the specific details of their textual formulation are likewise infinite in number. But they all follow certain basic principles which serve as their mothers [roots]." In furnishing examples he could limit himself, therefore, to a representative selection of fifty-four deeds (divided into three sections of eighteen each) dealing with private business, and to ten more devoted to transactions under public law. As a preamble, for example, to a testamentary disposition, he suggested the following formula: "We, the undersigned witnesses, attest that we have come to John Doe and found him sick in bed but in full control of his reason and able to speak clearly and to transact business by saying yes or no like any person walking in the market. In our presence he provided in his will as follows. . . ." Among the "public" documents Saadiah's formula for the writ of appointment by a court of a legal guardian for orphans is of special interest.[74]

A far better preserved monograph by Saadiah dealt with the laws of inheritance. This *Kitab al-Mawarit,* written in the style of contemporary Arabic books on the same subject, included both a legal and a mathematical section showing how to subdivide among heirs estates including fields. This book was to be part of a trilogy, the other portions of which were to have been devoted to sales and gifts. Saadiah's *Sefer ha-Mattanot* (Book of Gifts) is indeed quoted by Naḥmanides. Probably the gaon's most important monograph dealt with the laws of sales and purchases; its existence is attested by Hai Gaon's chance remark referring to "good things on sales, especially sales of land" appended to Saadiah's Book of Inheritance. Saadiah's penchant for subdividing his subjects comes to the fore also in the latter tract's four major divisions, dealing respectively with the inheritance rights of descendants, ascendants, siblings, and other relatives. These are in turn subdivided into sections dealing with the rights of male and female heirs, males alone, and females alone, treated with reference to the size of the estates, and so forth. A separate section discusses questionable family relationships, which, as the gaon emphasized, could only arise from some defiance of existing laws, such as premature remarriage of a pregnant widow. Saadiah's attempt at furnishing clear-cut rules may be illustrated by the following regulations governing the inheritance rights of female heirs:

> We have to explain here two matters: First, if some of the daughters are minors and others adults, the minors may not suggest that they be maintained to maturity, foregoing their portions in the estate. Although in the case of an estate shared by both sons and daughters the minor girls may insist on their claim for maintenance, in the case of all the heirs being daughters this law does not apply, but they all share equally. Secondly, if some of the daughters had already been married in their father's lifetime and the others are still unmarried, the latter may not demand 'Give us first the amount needed for our marriage, and then let us divide the rest,' but they all share equally. This law applies, however, only to daughters previously married off by the father; if they married after their father's death, the unmarried ones may demand that their [marriage] portion be first set aside.

In formulating these rules the gaon did not refer directly to any talmudic authority, as he had in some cases in his "Book of Deeds." But his utilization of the whole range of talmudic law is evident from every line. At times, however, he overlooked, or consciously departed from, the ancient regulations. In one case brought to Sherira's attention, Saadiah's decision appeared so overtly at variance with a statement in the Mishnah that Sherira attributed that "slip" to a copyist's error, for Saadiah "was a great scholar and an entire Mishnah could not have escaped him." [75]

Saadiah wrote also on other branches of civil and ritual law. We may regret the loss of his *Kitab Aḥkam al-wadia* (*Sefer ha-Piqqadon,* or Laws of Pledges). If published, this treatise doubtless would shed significant light on the new trade in deposits which played so great a role in the evolution of Jewish and Muslim banking. Perhaps related thereto was the gaon's tract on the laws of usury, of which not even a lengthy quotation is now extant. Here Saadiah took cognizance of the secret nature of contemporary deposits to evade the vigilance or cupidity of government officials. Because of the ensuing inability of many depositors to submit unequivocal proof of their claims, the gaon leaned over backward in relaxing on their behalf the usual rules of evidence. A century later, under changed conditions in Spain, both an inquirer and Alfasi were unable to reconcile his decisions with the talmudic sources. Apparently not in a position to review Saadiah's own text, Alfasi curtly replied, "I have studied the four possibilities quoted by you from the 'Book of Pledges.' Not one of them is correct. You need not bother to examine them further, for you are right in everything you say." Other essays by Saadiah were devoted to such significant subjects as an "Interpretation of the Laws of Incest," a topic then heatedly debated because of the 'Ananite doctrine of *Rikkub* (Catenation). Nor was the gaon's treatise on the "Laws of Purity and Impurity" devoid of contemporary implications, as it probably also dealt with the laws affecting the menstruating woman, which section was sometimes quoted in later literature under the independent title of *Hilkhot Niddah*. Not even the treatise "On Priestly Gifts," attributed to him, was purely theoretical, since Palestinian priests were still collecting such dues at that time. Possibly Saadiah wrote it during his prolonged sojourn in the Holy Land. In some respects, his most important halakhic monograph was the *Siddur* (Prayer Book), which combined an extensive summary of the laws governing prayers with the text of many liturgical compositions, both old and new. Like the similar work by his predecessor Amram, this volume, now available in print, can be fully evaluated only in connection with the general liturgical evolution of the High Middle Ages.[76]

Here, too, Saadiah's example was followed and even exceeded by Samuel ben Ḥofni and Hai. Regrettably, Samuel's great creativity in this field has been subjected to even greater ravages of time than was Saadiah's. Of the list, still incomplete, of his twenty-seven monographs compiled by S. Assaf on the basis of an ancient list and other sources, sixteen are known to us by title only. Three more exist in manuscript fragments; of the other eight relatively small portions have thus far been published. This neglect is doubly regrettable, as the gaon was wont to cover his subjects with great thoroughness, and he might have salvaged for us many older sources since lost. Samuel's monographs were devoted to such ritualistic problems as prayers, showfringes, and the examination of ritually permissible meat, as well as to the socially significant subjects of divorce, alimony, gifts, and the duties of judges, the latter an urgent topic indeed because of temptations for Jewish judges arising from the prevailing corruption in the Muslim judiciary. A very extensive treatise dealt with the laws governing guaranties and sureties, the fourth chapter analyzing the differences between the Jewish and Muslim legal institutions, but only its introduction and the first five (of thirty-one) chapters have thus far appeared in print.[77]

In all these works, Samuel tried to systematize the diffuse talmudic materials and to offer rational justifications. In his *Sha'are Berakhot* (Chapters on Prayers), relatively one of his best preserved tracts, he devoted the second chapter to the classification of all required benedictions into seven groups relating to "food, drink, smell, sight, hearing, as well as over the performance of a commandment and other actions. [The first of] these are derived from the five senses with which our Creator has endowed us for our benefit." Understandably, later jurists often quoted only the juridically relevant gist of his lengthy discourses. The numerous succinct quotations from Samuel's *Sha'are Sheḥitah* (Chapters on Ritual Slaughtering) in Eliezer bar Joel ha-Levi's *Sefer Rabiah* are thus devoid of the particular "scientific" flavor of the gaon's discussions. For example, the statement attributed to Samuel, "The slaughtering of animals by a slave, woman, eunuch, mourner, a sick person, and an old man over eighty is disqualified," doubtless is but the quintessence of a more elaborate analysis of the background of each disqualification. From the standpoint of legal reasoning, therefore, and still more from that of the historical evolution of legal thinking and the underlying social conditions, the loss of most of Samuel's tracts is truly grievous.[78]

Hai Gaon was more fortunate than his father-in-law—in fact, than any other gaon. Several of his halakhic monographs are preserved in Arabic fragments, Hebrew translations, or both; some have been published, commented on, and frequently quoted. His great reputation in the Western lands, now fully awakened to independent literary creativity, accounted largely for that continuous popularity. Not surprisingly, Hai, too, evinced great interest in those areas of civil law where far-reaching adjustments had to be made to meet the requirements of an ever expanding economy. Among his major works was another "Book of Deeds," published about a quarter of a century ago; a comprehensive "Book of Purchases and Sales" (including a summary of Hai's separate tract on the "Laws of Loans"), long ago published in a Hebrew translation and provided with an extensive commentary; and treatises on "Deposits," the preemptive "Rights of Neighbors," and the laws governing "Conditions." He omitted entirely such ancient regulations as those relating to the acquisition of houses in fortified Palestinian cities, since they apply only "when Israelites live [as masters] in their own country." Connected with these aspects of business laws were such procedural tracts as the comprehensive "Book of Oaths" and a "Book of Conduct of Judges," the latter, regrettably, known mainly from a few quotations. This area required particularly delicate treatment, and in his monograph on oaths Hai inserted the following characteristic warning:

> God knows that I have compiled this study only for the purpose of enabling the man without sagacity to comprehend it, the man without learning to study it, and the ignorant man to know it, for I have realized the paucity of understanding to be found among most students of the Talmud today. Should, however, a party to a litigation learn therefrom some new arguments [such aid in legal chicaneries had long been prohibited by the Talmud], . . . I shall be innocent before my Creator, for I have prepared this study only for the benefit of those walking in the paths of righteousness, so that they may comprehend and teach it.

Compared with these major works, Hai's contributions to ritualistic law were relatively slight and less frequently cited by later authorities. In fact, we possess only a few fragments of his main work in this field, the "Book of the Forbidden and the Permitted," while his specialized essays on "Phylacteries," and the "Laws of Slaughtering" have but sporadically been mentioned in later literature. Since few of these texts are available in full, we cannot tell whether they had been evoked by inquiries from other countries and hence shared the fate of the numerous responsa wrongly attributed to Hai, nor do we know the extent to which they have been altered in their transmission to posterity. Enough has remained of the gaon's authentic work for us to judge that the seeds planted by Saadiah had borne rich fruit, and that a new discipline of halakhic writings was thenceforth to enable scholars to explore the ramifications and hidden nooks of many legal branches on a scale transcending the bounds of either commentaries or all-embracing codes.[79]

Juridical monographs mirrored the growing specialization of learning characteristic of Near Eastern civilization in the tenth and eleventh centuries. "He who would be a savant," observed Ibn Qutaiba, "should cultivate a particular branch of learning, but he who would be a littérateur, let him range over the entire domain of learning" (cited in Mez, *Renaissance,* p. 170). Like Muslim jurisprudence, to be sure, the Halakhah had to be mastered as a whole. However, there was room for greater or lesser concentration on some of its phases, a particularly frequent distinction being drawn between laws applying to contemporary conditions and those which had become obsolete in the course of ages.

The newly awakened Western lands, on the other hand, developed a special interest in halakhic miscellanies, which in subject matter resembled collections of monographs, without the latter's searching qualities. Here the author could select certain areas of special interest to him and his disciples, without attempting to review other branches of the law as well. There was no fundamental difference between the treatment of such materials in these juridical *collectanea* and that of the comprehensive commentaries by Ḥananel or Nissim, except that the purpose here was exclusively juridical, not exegetical. Among the outstanding writers of this kind was the statesman-poet, Samuel ibn Nagrela, whose work bearing the remarkable title *Hilkhata Gibrata* (Mighty Laws) has thus far been known only from a few minor surviving fragments and brief quotations by later authorities. But the forthcoming edition of substantial fragments ingeniously assembled by Mordecai Margulies will finally place at the disposal of scholars large parts of this forgotten major classic of Jewish jurisprudence. Much better known has been the work by his compeer Isaac ben Yehudah ibn Gayyat, bearing the equally ambitious title of *Halakhot Kelulot* (Comprehensive Laws). However, this book was not in fact concerned with civil law, but was primarily devoted to the ritualistic problems of holiday observance and prayers. At least only these aspects are included in the two published volumes and in various quotations by later jurists. Ibn Nagrela's and Ibn Gayyat's works are important not only in their own right, but also because of their numerous citations from geonic sources no longer extant.[80]

Far more comprehensive was an encyclopedic work undertaken by Yehudah bar Barzillai al-Barceloni (about 1100). Following in Ibn Nagrela's footsteps, he tried to survey, on the basis of the latest as well as the ancient sources, all those branches of Jewish law which were of contemporary actuality. By giving lengthy quotations from geonic responsa, Al-Barceloni salvaged many of these sources for posterity and helped fructify the whole range of juridical thinking among his European compatriots. Apparently he never completed this gigantic work, which seems to have consisted of three main sections devoted respectively to ritualistic, family, and civil laws. The second section is totally lost, while a portion of the first, called *Sefer ha-'Ittim* (Book of Times, dealing with holidays and related subjects), and a part of the third, called *Sefer ha-Sheṭarot* (Book of Deeds), are now available in critical editions. The very bulk of that work discouraged copyists, which helps explain both the disappearance of most of the original text and its numerous abridgments circulating in the later Middle Ages. The distinguished law book *Sefer ha-Eshkol* (Cluster of Grapes), by the Provençal author Abraham ben Isaac of Narbonne, Father of the Court (d. 1158), was largely but an epitome from the work of the Catalan scholar.[81]

On the other hand, his brilliant and independent son-in-law Abraham ben David of Posquières composed a remarkably original juridical monograph on the laws of menstruation, ritual ablutions, and related subjects, which, not surprisingly, evoked a controversial tract by his perennial friendly opponent, Zeraḥiah ha-Levi. The distinguished jurist of Posquières gave his booklet the unusual title of *Ba'ale ha-nefesh* (Masters of the Soul) to indicate, as he explained, that it contained regulations "for those who master their [lustful] souls, rather than allow the latter to master them." For this reason Abraham did not limit himself to the exposition of formal laws, but added a number of purely ethical injunctions. In a passage quoted by Aaron ben Jacob ha-Kohen of Lunel, he insisted:

It is customary for man not to give much money to his daughter. He who is very particular and quarrelsome about his wife's possessions is not successful and their marriage is bound to fail. One ought rather to accept joyously whatever his father-in-law, or mother-in-law, gives him, for money received together with a wife is not righteous money. . . . This is the proverbial saying: "He who marries for money, not for Heaven's sake, builds himself wings [commandments to break]."

Perhaps the most influential juridical miscellany of that period was the *Sefer 'Iṭṭur soferim* (Word Separation of Scribes), or more briefly *'Iṭṭur,* by Isaac ben Abba Mari of Marseilles (1122–93). This comprehensive work, amounting almost to a complete code of laws, is even more noteworthy for its numerous citations from geonic letters, which it helped to salvage, than for the author's own decisions.[82]

French and German jurists cultivated with even greater zest such halakhic miscellanies. Being less addicted to systematic thinking than their Spanish coreligionists, they often preferred, more in keeping with the original talmudic method, to roam over a vast range of subjects, often related to one another merely by some chance mental association. In their lectures delivered at the Rhenish academies the teachers not only interpreted the talmudic texts, but also summarized for the benefit of students the legal decisions handed down by tradition or newly recorded in responsa and other letters reaching the West from the Eastern centers. Some pupils collected such information in special handbooks which served as starting points for further juristic deliberations.

One of the earliest compilations of this kind apparently stemmed from the school of Makhir bar Yehudah, a brother of Gershom the "Light of the Exile." At his Mayence academy, Makhir and his four sons reviewed a large body of laws and customs and summarized it in a book titled *Ma'aseh ha-Makhir.* This book, since lost, served as a fountainhead for many similar collections, especially those emanating from the school of Rashi. Perhaps the earliest of those is the so-called *Ma'aseh ha-geonim* (Geonic Precedents). In the parts now extant, this volume covers a variety of subjects. Beginning with ritual food and holiday observances, including those relating to Passover and Ḥanukkah, it discusses prayers and other liturgical problems and concludes with laws relating to ritualistic slaughtering. Apart from quoting at considerable length geonic and Franco-German responsa, it often refers to local customs and as such serves as an important source of information for Jewish life in that culturally formative period of the Ashkenazic communities. It reports, for instance, the story of two bridegrooms, both *kohanim* (priests), who appeared in the Mayence synagogue (apparently the only one in existence in 1093), each demanding that he be summoned to the Torah for the same first lesson reserved to men of priestly descent. From a reply by Nathan, one of Makhir's sons, we also learn about the seven-day wedding celebrations customary at that time in the Rhinelands. The author frequently quotes Rashi, whom he calls "Rabbi" without further identification, while the title "Rabbenu" (our master, or our great master) is for the most part reserved for R. Isaac bar Yehudah, the chief teacher of the sons of Makhir.[83]

More directly connected with Rashi's academy, and often indebted to notes collected from the master's oral discourses by such faithful disciples as Shemayah, were the well-known collections, long attributed to Rashi himself, entitled *Siddur* (Prayer Book), *Sefer ha-Pardes* (Book of the Orchard), and *Sefer ha-Orah* (Book of Light) or *Sefer ha-Oreh* (Book of the Plucker). The latter work, an attempt to synthesize the juristic findings of the school of Rashi with the vast legal research condensed in Yehudah bar Barzillai's encyclopedic work, seems to have been compiled in the Provence at the crossroads of French and Spanish learning. Another classic of Rashi's school, known as the *Maḥzor Vitry* (The Vitry Prayer Book for Holidays), was prepared by Simḥah bar Samuel of Vitry. The outstanding characteristic of all these works is their great reliance on local traditions and customs, as well as on Rashi's oral teachings and his actual performance of certain rituals. Because their compilers worked independently of one another, they frequently repeat the same statements from the original sources; on many other points they disagree sharply while yet invoking the same older authority. Rather than annoying later students, however, such duplications served as useful controls for the correctness of their transmission. Wherever opinions diverged, they stimulated further independent juristic thinking.[84]

RECODIFICATION OF TALMUDIC LAW

Quite early, however, the need was felt for more comprehensive summaries of the existing regulations and observances, cutting across the complex talmudic discussions and furnishing legal guidance to both students and judges. Such guidance became doubly imperative when the continued debates at the Babylonian and Palestinian academies and the growth of legal learning and letters elsewhere increased the mass of available legal data almost beyond the control of individual scholars. The considerations which had once compelled the sages from R. 'Aqiba to Judah the Patriarch to organize the main body of traditions in the Mishnah, and had prompted other members of those ancient schools to compile the Tosefta and the halakhic midrashim, centuries later induced R. Ashi and his disciples to review the enormous accumulation of amoraic lore and to subsume it all in the form of comments on the Mishnah. The same factors operated now with even greater intensity. The number of diverse traditions and their interpretations, as well as of local customs and observances, had grown into a formidable mass. With the increasing diffusion of the Jewish people and the establishment of new and independent centers of learning, the very knowledge of these regional achievements became a taxing responsibility for leading experts. It offered an often insurmountable obstacle to ordinary scholars and administrators of justice.

Increasing availability of exegetical writings, which, in connection with their interpretation of specific mishnaic or talmudic passages, communicated the results of these manifold researches, was of great help. So were the numerous monographs dealing with certain aspects of the law, as well as the halakhic miscellanies which covered a variety of subjects in up-to-date discussions. But all these works merely whetted the appetite for some constructive single summaries which in a lucid and authoritative fashion would present to informed readers the entire body of Jewish law, or at least that part of it which was still of practical concern. The effective operation of such legal handbooks among Muslims and Christians must have served as an additional incentive, just as the jurists of these faiths were, in turn, influenced by the Jewish example.

Of great significance to all these legal systems was the problem of invalidation of laws which had either become totally obsolete or else been greatly modified in their practical application. Notwithstanding its compass, the Talmud itself is but a residuum of several centuries of juridical discussions which were distilled by its redactors into comparatively few traditional decisions (the original meaning of the term *gemara*) for practical use. This process of elimination was further facilitated by the talmudic distinction between purely theoretical and practical laws, the former often being singled out as being *halakhot ve-lo le-ma'aseh* or *ve-en morim ken* (laws not to be applied in life). This distinction was to find still wider application under the rapidly changing conditions of the geonic age.

By proclaiming the general principle, "We do not rely on the Aggadah," and yet reserving the right of picking out from the large body of talmudic legend legal and ethical norms, practices, and customs which suited the contemporary needs, the geonim and their successors secured for themselves a wide range of discretion in validating or disregarding traditional views. If such selectivity sounded rather arbitrary, they sought to safeguard its uniform acceptance by sharply discouraging individual dissent from the decision of the two academies. "He who attacks anything they say," succinctly states a responsum attributed to Sherira Gaon, "is like one assailing the Lord and His Torah." Similarly, Simon Qayyara, author of the most widely read early code, prefaced his large compilation by a rhetorical introduction extolling the virtues of study and law observance. One of its highlights is his restatement of the old tannaitic injunction which had already replaced the priests by sages in the old Deuteronomic appeal, "Thou shalt not turn aside from the sentence which they shall declare unto thee, to the right hand, nor to the left" (17:11). This means, the homily added, that "if they tell you that right is left and that left is right, thou must obey them." Muslim law likewise developed its jurisprudence, the so-called *fiqh,* which went beyond and often disregarded older traditions more or less faithfully preserved by the experts in tradition, the *'ilm.* In the very first generation of Islam, we are told by Ibn Sa'd, there were persons "bringing traditions and reports, but no one, not even from among their closest associates, paid any heed to them." Bukhari is said to have assembled 6,000,000 traditions, of which he incorporated in his legal compilation only 7,275. Among the Jews, Karaite sectarians like Jephet ben 'Ali adopted that distinction between the *ahl al-'ilm w'al-fiqh* (men of tradition and of independent legal judgment). Yet even the most orthodox Rabbanite traditionalist had to use his discretion in selecting traditions for further study and practical utility.[85]

Codification certainly was an even greater necessity for the Jew with his much older tradition. Jewish sectarians of all ages, particularly, had found it imperative to lay down their heterodox legal systems in definitive codes; and there courses a strange line from the recorded *Sefer Gezerata* of the Sadducees, the code of the New Covenanters of Damascus, and the Manual of Discipline of the Qumran sectarians to the numerous legal compilations of the Karaite leaders.[86]

Rabbanite Judaism followed suit. Building upon the foundations laid down by the ancient Jewish codifiers from the author of the biblical Book of the Covenant to the redactors of the Babylonian Talmud, the rabbis under the domination of Islam developed the three fundamental methods of Jewish codification: the juridical summary of the extensive and complex talmudic discussions; the enumeration and analysis of the basic commandments of Judaism in their manifold ramifications; and, finally, the systematic code of the entire law.

Apparently the first to sense the need for recodification of Jewish law was Yehudai bar Naḥman Gaon, who seems to have served only during the last three (or possibly thirteen) years of his long life as head of the academy of Sura (760 or 750 to 763). He was prompted by the growing realization in geonic circles of the uncertainties existing in Jewish communities concerning the operation of many talmudic provisions. He was one of the first geonim on record to be approached from various quarters with inquiries, some relating to simple matters clearly settled in the Talmud itself. Most of the one hundred and thirty-one responsa written by him and still extant today are but laconic replies. For instance, he was once asked whether a creditor, whose debtor was about to remove to an overseas locality before the due date, was entitled to demand immediate payment or at least the naming of a local guarantor. Yehudai answered both questions with a simple "No." He came to the conclusion, therefore, that placing in the hands of interested readers a concise epitome of the talmudic legislation would enable them to ascertain the law, even if they could not consult the Talmud itself, texts of which still were extremely rare in the mid-eighth century. Otherwise he was quite averse to innovations. The same Pirqoi ben Baboi, a pupil of his pupil Raba, who was to extol his extraordinary piety and learning unmatched for many generations, also quoted Yehudai as saying, "You have never asked me a question to which I have not replied on the basis of both a demonstration from the Talmud and a tradition from my teacher, which he had received from his teacher, concerning the application of that law in practice." This emphatic assertion probably reflected not only the gaon's aversion to the individualistic "search in the Torah" by sectarian leaders, but also the heated contemporary Muslim debates on the legitimacy and limitations of the use of the subjective *ra'y* (discretion) to supplement tradition.[87]

In these terms he composed his *Halakhot pesuqot* (Legal Decisions), sometimes called *Halakhot qeṭu'ot* (Set Laws) or *Halakhot qeṭanot* (Small Laws), in contrast to the *gedolot* (Large Laws) by Simon Qayyara. Although its Aramaic original was first published in 1950, its author's basic approaches have been known for some seventy years through the publication of its Hebrew paraphrase, the *Hilkhot Re'u* (Laws of "See"; from its *incipit,* "See that the Lord hath given you the Sabbath," Exod. 16:29). It had, moreover, been widely quoted in the medieval juridical literature and extensively debated by modern scholars even before the publication of either text. Regrettably, both versions reveal much tampering by copyists and revisers, which may in part explain their serious divergences.

Yehudai attempted to present to his readers a brief restatement of the talmudic debates in the language of the Talmud itself but without its argumentation. He also omitted most of the legendary sections which had no bearing on legal decisions. To make the talmudic discussions more comprehensible, he rearranged their sequence by starting with more general summaries and then taking up specific aspects. At the very beginning, for example, he combined the laws of the tractates 'Erubin and Shabbat by discussing first the prohibition of walking on the Sabbath beyond the stated bounds of two thousand ells without the use of an *'erub* (a symbolical act establishing continuity of residence beyond those confines); followed by the problem of kindling lights, significant in itself and also because of the old attacks on this Jewish practice antedating the Karaite schism; and, finally, by the other laws governing the Sabbath rest. Here the Aramaic original breaks off in the middle; the Hebrew version, though fuller, likewise seems incomplete. Both versions continue with a discussion of the laws concerning other holidays, pointing up certain differences from the Sabbath observance. But only the Hebrew version has small additional paragraphs relating to the laws of circumcision and the Ḥanukkah lights, which through mental associations had incidentally been treated within the talmudic tractate Shabbat. Possibly these paragraphs represent later additions in emulation of a similar arrangement in Simon Qayyara's code. On the other hand, the Hebrew version omits many passages extant in the Aramaic, and it lacks whole sections, such as those devoted to the laws of prayers or "the Palestinian laws of *ṭerefot* [maimed animals]," the latter of very dubious authenticity. In short, Yehudai's work is more important for its pioneering attempt to restate the talmudic law in a concise rearrangement than for any substantive innovations or novel interpretations.[88]

Some of that code's shortcomings may be accounted for, however, by Yehudai's inability, because of his blindness, personally to compose his juridical selection; he had to dictate it to his disciples. Among these pupils was Raba, who may have followed Yehudai's example in his aforementioned *Shimmusha Raba* on phylacteries and other subjects, just as he imitated Aḥai of Shabḥa by writing *Halakhot* in the sequence of the weekly lessons (see the excerpts published by J. N. Epstein in *Madda'e ha-yahadut,* II, 147–63). Raba's pupil Pirqoi ben Baboi, in turn, tried to impose upon the Palestinians the regime adopted in Babylonia. His booklet, too, had some of the characteristics of a juridical tract. None of these works represented innovations from the standpoint of accepted Babylonian usage. They only varied in their emphases upon one or another doctrine or practice.

Essentially the same may be said about Simon Qayyara's more comprehensive and influential code, the *Halakhot gedolot,* probably written about 825. As a private citizen of Baṣra, the great center of Arab juridical and philological studies, Simon did not enjoy Yehudai Gaon's great reputation. In fact, later geonim often haughtily disregarded his teachings as stemming from an unauthorized source. He shared therein the rough treatment extended to Aḥai of Shabḥa, whose equally unofficial *She'eltot* he himself still frequently cited, but which was largely ignored by the heads of the two academies. In his *Epistle* Sherira briefly mentioned Aḥai, but he passed over Simon's contribution in complete silence. His son Hai once nonchalantly dismissed an inquirer's quotation from Simon's work with "It is not according to law and do not rely on it." [89]

Simon followed the talmudic text more consistently than Yehudai, as a rule departing only from the sequence of chapters in the same tractate. When the subject demanded it, he segregated certain topics and assigned to them separate chapters. He treated, for example, the laws of Ḥanukkah and circumcision in connection with the laws of Sabbath, prefacing the former with the general observation: "The house of Israel are obliged to thank and praise before Heaven whenever a miracle occurs to them . . . for example, on Ḥanukkah over the candlestick, and on Purim over the Scroll [of Esther]." Otherwise he so slavishly adhered to the talmudic models that he discussed, for instance, at great length the laws governing levirate marriage, slaves, and the prohibited degrees of marriage, all included in the tractate Yebamot, and followed them up by an analysis of the laws of divorce before he summarized very briefly, as if by afterthought, the laws of betrothal. All this merely because such had been the order of the talmudic tractates. Although generally eliminating laws no longer applicable in his day, he dealt with ancient agricultural laws and those pertaining to sacrifices, most of which were purely theoretical in his time even in Palestine. It is possible that these concluding chapters were added by a later hand. In fact, this important juridical classic suffered from so many alterations in the following generations that two substantially different recensions circulated in the West during the eleventh century. We who now possess both the "Spanish" and the "German" recensions, though neither in a truly critical edition, are often puzzled by their substantial variations in content as well as in form, and we can but rarely determine which version is more authentic. In both forms, however, together with its prefatory exaltation of the Oral Law and, as we shall presently see, its pioneering endeavor to enumerate the basic laws of Judaism, Simon's work exerted great influence on the subsequent development of Jewish jurisprudence.[90]

Despite its official neglect on the part of the Pumbedita leaders, the immediate impact of Simon's code is well illustrated by its numerous imitations in various lands. In Palestine, or possibly in southern Italy or the Balkans where Palestinian influences had predominated ever since their joint Byzantine occupation, a collection called *Halakhot qeṣubot* (Adjudicated Laws) made its appearance perhaps as early as the mid-ninth century. Basically it follows in the footsteps of both codifiers Yehudai and Simon, except that its language is purely Hebraic. Its title is obviously derived from the compiler's extensive use of court decisions. He even goes so far as to subsume an entire range of laws, relating to marriage and divorce, inheritances, sales, deposits, and oaths, under the general category of "judicial practice [*shimmush*]." His generally succinct style and the absence of any precise order in his work, although not quite so pronounced as in the Palestinian Book of Precedents, likewise favor this judicial origin. In many instances the author clearly deviates from the laws of the Babylonian Talmud and geonic decisions and often follows the Palestinian observances. Some local customs may actually have been of Byzantine or Italian origin, although we know too little about the cultural life of these Jewries during that early period to draw any definite conclusions.[91]

More directly mediating between Palestine and Babylonia was the position taken by another similar compilation bearing the nondescript title of *Metibot* (Subjects). Probably composed by a Palestinian scholar of the tenth century, it may have been alluded to by the eleventh-century Karaite Yeshu'a ben Yehudah when he wrote, "I have seen among the Rabbanite scholars one who has epitomized the two Talmudim of Palestine and Babylonia." The author also followed to a large extent the pro-Palestinian geonim of Sura, rather than those of Pumbedita. He allowed, for instance, a creditor's utilization of a mortgaged farm or house, provided the debtor received credit from that revenue—a practice which Simon Qayyara had declared as being a daily occurrence but which the Pumbeditans, including Sherira and Hai, condemned as outright usury. Although rarely quoted in the East, *Metibot* was sufficiently popular in the West for Isaac ben Abba Mari of twelfth-century Provence to cite it more than three-score times. In fact, that scholar knew it in two recensions, one older and one newer. Some writers believed that it had been written by no less an authority than Ḥananel.[92]

Ḥananel allegedly was also the author of a similar compilation entitled *Sefer ha-Miqṣo'ot* (Book of Legal Decisions). This literary mystery is juridically quite remarkable, for it often mentions decisions unencountered elsewhere in contemporary letters. For one example, in explaining the talmudic statement that when a scholar dies the entire population should mourn for him as if for a relative, our author is quoted as adding the following observation:

> He who is slain for the sanctification of the name or the profession of the unity of the Name of the Blessed One, whether in a period of general persecution or any other time; for instance if Gentiles ordered him, "Worship the idol, or else we shall kill you!" but he resisted to death and was slain [by the sword], crucified or burned for the sanctification of the Name, such an one [requires even more exceptional treatment]. Because he had sanctified the Name with his body and soul, all of Israel are obliged to tear their garments for him, to mourn and eulogize him in their synagogues and houses of learning. His wife must never remarry for the honor of Heaven and his honor.

Curiously, this work seems to have remained unknown to the Spanish scholars, although it is frequently quoted by French and German rabbis. Like its predecessors following predominantly the arrangement of the talmudic tractates, but more frequently switching toward systematic analyses of related subjects, this comprehensive work seems to have included lengthy quotations from geonic letters. Its method is well illustrated by a fairly long excerpt recovered by the editor from an Antonin MS in Leningrad. In this discussion of the laws of slavery the compiler cited extensive amoraic sayings, mainly from the tractate Giṭṭin though not in the order of the Talmud, and interspersed them with citations from geonic responsa, including those by Hai, the *She'eltot,* the *Halakhot pesuqot* and *gedolot* (evidently taken from a text underlying both the shorter "German" and the "Spanish" versions). The preservation of but a few small fragments and scattered quotations is doubly to be regretted, therefore, as its lengthy excerpts from geonic writings, including entire pages from Simon Qayyara's Code, might have proved very helpful for the reconstruction of the original texts of these important sources.[93]

ALFASI

All these works were soon superseded by the *Halakhot* (Laws) of Isaac ben Jacob Alfasi (*ca.* 1013–1103). A native of Kalat al-Ḥammad (Kalaa of the Beni Ḥammad), Algeria, Isaac presided for many years over the academy of Fez (hence his name Alfasi, abbreviated RIF); because of a political denunciation he had to leave for Spain at the age of seventy-five. Before long he took over the great academy of Lucena, long headed by his opponent, Isaac ibn Gayyat. As in Fez, Alfasi was surrounded here by a multitude of distinguished pupils, including one Ephraim, a former compatriot from Kalat al-Ḥammad; Joseph ibn Megas, his successor at the Lucena academy; and Yehudah Halevi, who wrote a remarkable elegy on his death. With the customary exuberance of that period, the great poet sang:

> As in Sinai's ancient days, before thee mountains trembled,
> For the Lord's angelic hosts around thee have assembled.
> They engraved the Torah's lore on the tables of thy heart,
> And her glory's shining crowns to thy mind they did impart.
> The strength of the wisest men gave out in hesitation,
> Unless from thy wisdom's springs they drew their inspiration.[94]

Generally following the example of the previous authors of juristic epitomes, especially Simon Qayyara, whom he frequently quotes, Alfasi went beyond them all in summarizing not only the ultimate decisions emerging from the talmudic discussions, but also the relevant reasonings behind them. More than his predecessors he also restated the legendary portions of the Talmud, in so far as they imparted juridical lessons as well. He usually succeeded in explaining lengthy and complicated debates by skillfully inserting a few words, written so clearly in the talmudic idiom that they can be detected only through comparison with the talmudic text itself. By reviewing in a single discussion matters debated in various talmudic tractates, he placed them in their most appropriate contexts; sometimes he summarized the talmudic teachings fully in one tractate and but briefly restated them in others. Only exceptionally did he expatiate on some point by adding a paragraph of arguments pro and con, motivating his own decision. He himself felt that such digressions tended to spoil the architectonic symmetry of his work, and he often apologized for them. At times he replaced them by special excursuses at the end of a tractate. Curiously, these lengthy notes are usually written in Arabic, although obviously they could be of little use to students not thoroughly familiar with the talmudic blend of Hebrew and Aramaic in which his main work was composed. For example, he deviated from the mediating position of Hai Gaon and other authorities with respect to a complicated discussion in Mishnah and Talmud relating to the equitable distribution of an estate's insufficient assets among three widows who had been promised different amounts in their marriage contracts.

We have examined this matter carefully [he asserted] and it became clear to us with the help of Heaven. We have interpreted the Mishnah and the *gemara* thereon and clarified its principle from the words of our teachers of blessed memory with a good explanation and lucid words of which there is no doubt. When you weigh them carefully, you will see clearly that this unquestionably is the opinion of the Tannaim and Amoraim. One need not fear its reversal, for it is the law of truth and a tradition from Moses on Sinai. We have explained it [more fully] in Arabic and appended it [our interpretation] at the end of this tractate, together with an explanation of two other talmudic discussions.

With self-assurance he often departed from the teachings of his geonic predecessors, although he did it usually with some words of apology. He also disregarded many decisions of the Palestinian Talmud, not only where it was clearly controverted by its Babylonian counterpart, but also in cases derived from mere inference of the latter's intent.[95]

Like his predecessors, Alfasi was basically interested only in laws of contemporary relevance. For this reason he summarized only the talmudic tractates of the second, third, and fourth orders, as well as Berakhot and Ḥullin. He also selected a few relevant laws from the last several tractates and grouped them together at the end of his work under the generic title of "Small Halakhot" (on the impurity of priests, scrolls of law, doorpost inscriptions, phylacteries, and showfringes). Not wishing to assign a separate section to the laws of menstruation, he attached them to the tractate on oaths (Shebu'ot), because of an incidental reference thereto in the first Mishnah of that tractate. On the other hand, he adhered more rigidly than Simon Qayyara to the sequence of the talmudic tractates, not changing the position of individual chapters even where logic demanded it. He did not hesitate, however, to omit entire chapters having little bearing on contemporary problems. For example, he summarized the last chapter of Yoma, dealing with the laws of fasting on the Day of Atonement, but omitted all the preceding descriptions of that holiday's order of services at the ancient Temple. Similarly, he omitted Chapters V–IX in Pesaḥim, because they merely debated the ancient Passover sacrifices. In short, he presented an effective, practical epitome of the Talmud, giving not only general conclusions but also the main reasonings behind them, and thus enabling students and judges to reexamine each particular problem with full realization of the motivations of the ancient sages. Not unjustly, therefore, Alfasi's distinguished law book came to be known as the "Little Talmud."[96]

Alfasi's ill fortune turned out to be a blessing in disguise, for it caused him to spend the last fifteen years of his life in Spain, then in the midst of its greatest intellectual expansion. With their zest for knowledge and intellectual daring, Alfasi's disciples began using his work as a fountainhead for new talmudic studies. They realized, of course, that Ibn Gayyat and Al-Balia, Alfasi's Spanish contemporaries, had often sharply combated his decisions. One of Alfasi's own disciples, Ephraim, wrote a book of strictures on, and supplements to, the teacher's law book. When some of these observations came to Alfasi's attention, probably through earlier oral exchanges, he was honest enough often to reverse himself, and in the constant revisions of his work to delete or alter many sections. Unfortunately, as in the case of many other medieval authors, the later recensions did not altogether displace the earlier formulations, which often continued to circulate among students and thus became the source of much confusion.[97]

In the Provence, the border country between Sephardic and Ashkenazic Jewry, the great scholarly achievements of the schools of Gershom and Rashi invited constant comparisons with Alfasi's work. In fact, the very talmudic text, on which the northern masters had lavished so much care, often differed from that used by Alfasi. Naturally, the ensuing legal decisions diverged greatly. It was this observation, rather than any personal animus, which induced the Provençal scholar Zeraḥiah ben Isaac ha-Levi (d. 1186) at the age of nineteen to embark upon his *Sefer ha-Ma'or* (Book of Light), which was to appear in two installments entitled the "Great" and "Small" Books of Light. Apart from being a fairly standardized name for commentaries, this title reminded the young author of both his resplendent first name and the name of his residence at Lunel. This work is entirely devoted to corrections of, and objections to, Alfasi's work. Although often using sharp language, especially in the "Great Book of Light," written with youthful exuberance, Zeraḥiah explained that he had found that "no such beautiful work has been composed on the Talmud since its completion." Hence he had written his strictures "only in order to honor, adorn, sanctify, purify, and cleanse it [of mistakes] to the extent of his ability."[98]

A similarly admiring objector to Alfasi was the generally sharp-tongued, as well as sharp-witted, Abraham ben David of Posquières (1120–98), Zeraḥiah's colleague, who humbly apologized for writing a book of "objections" to the work of a great master. On the other hand, Abraham wrote a polemical work on Zeraḥiah's *Book of Light,* defending Alfasi. Curiously, his tone is sharpest when Zeraḥiah's is mild, and vice versa, perhaps because he revised the sections on the third and fourth orders after his friend's demise. "This Light does not shine!" reads one of his typical exclamations. "He merely weaves a spider's web," Abraham declared in another context, "for all this is vanity and things wherein there is no profit." On one occasion he actually intimated that Zeraḥiah had merely plagiarized his own opinion. Abraham also attacked his friend for too readily yielding to Rashi's and the Tosafists' purportedly superior knowledge of talmudic lore. A remarkable correspondence, concerning the interpretation of a difficult talmudic passage, which took place between these two friends likewise sheds much light on their personal relations and scholarly attitudes. This collection of five letters by Zeraḥiah and four by Abraham was circulated, with an introduction by the former, under the characteristic title *Dibre ha-ribot* (Words of Contention). In this particular controversy Zeraḥiah retained the upper hand against Abraham, who was otherwise recognized as one of the greatest Jewish jurists of the Middle Ages. Alfasi found another equally eloquent and well-informed defender in Naḥmanides (*ca.* 1194–1270), whose *Milḥamot Adonai* (Wars of the Lord), together with the main object of its attacks, Zeraḥiah's *Book of Light,* became classics of the polemical literature in the field of Jewish law. Among many others who wrote commentaries on Alfasi were Isaac ben Abba Mari, in his "Hundred Chapters," and Jonathan bar David of Lunel, Maimonides' great admirer.[99]

A different type of supplementation to Alfasi's work was offered by Maimonides himself. We recall that while writing the introduction to his *Commentary* on the Mishnah this Spanish refugee in Fusṭaṭ still deeply admired the greatest jurist of his Spanish homeland. At that time he could detect only ten mistakes in the entire voluminous code of the grand old man of Lucena. Even in his later more critical years, when he had had occasion to make innumerable corrections and retractions in his own works, he raised the number of inaccuracies in Alfasi's *Halakhot* to but "more than thirty." Not surprisingly, therefore, the young jurist not only composed direct scholia on Alfasi, but also prepared for it a remarkable supplement in his *Hilkhot ha-Yerushalmi* (Laws of the Palestinian Talmud), parts of which, apparently written in

Maimonides' own hand, have recently been published. Here the younger scholar endeavored to round out Alfasi's juridical work by summarizing, in exactly the same vein, the discussions of the Palestinian Talmud. Of course, in the eyes of both authors the Babylonians enjoyed uncontested primacy. Hence, wherever there was a clear conflict between the two Talmudim, not only Alfasi, but also Maimonides felt free to disregard the Palestinian doctrine. Where no such conflict existed, the Palestinian teachings could be quoted to good advantage both with respect to uncontested legal decisions, and to the more correct interpretation of the Babylonian views. Maimonides pursued this objective, even if he did not intend to circulate his own treatise but merely to use it in preparation of his future work. In retrospect, we may well agree that this preliminary effort served him in good stead when he finally proceeded to the preparation of his legal codes.[100]

Apart from these commentaries, apologias, and indirect supplements, there appeared tracts whose main aim was to fill in lacunae in Alfasi's work. We recall that Alfasi's pupil Ephraim may have already endeavored to write such a supplement. The famous legal miscellanies by Yehudah bar Barzillai and, following him, by Isaac ben Abraham of Narbonne may initially have been juridical supplements, especially from geonic sources, to Alfasi's code. A more direct attempt to round out Alfasi's law book was made early in the thirteenth century by Meshullam ben Moses of Béziers (d. 1238) in a work designated the *Sefer ha-Hashlamah* (Book of Supplementation). Several parts of this treatise, covering five talmudic tractates, are still extant. With all his modest disclaimers, Meshullam found it necessary at times to differ from Alfasi's decisions. Occasionally he even evinced preference for statements by the master's chief opponent, Zeraḥiah. But he disavowed such "betrayals" by saying that he had not borrowed his theses from Zeraḥiah, but rather from his own father, Moses ben Yehudah, who had personally debated these issues with the latter at the Lunel academy. By that time, moreover, the impact of Rashi and the Tosafists forced all Provençal scholars to check Alfasi's decisions against the textual readings and the reasoned arguments of these northern authorities. But all these corrections and revisions left Alfasi's prestige undiminished.[101]

These early disciples and admirers found many followers in the subsequent generations. Thus Alfasi's work, which in some respects originated from a mere commentary on the Talmud, gave rise to a whole literature of supercommentaries—a branch of learning which began to proliferate among Jews, particularly in the later Middle Ages, as it did among Muslims and Christians. In Alfasi's case the need for such exegetical and elaborative works increased with the growing acceptance of the "Little Talmud," especially after the middle of the thirteenth century, when the burning of the real Talmud and its growing suppression by ecclesiastical censorship turned Alfasi's summary into an ever more indispensable manual of talmudic learning and practical jurisprudence. But long before that time even the generally independent northern schools had felt its full impact. Samuel bar Meir composed "Supplements" to it, while the great Tosafist, Isaac bar Samuel of Dampierre, tersely observed, "The divine presence surely rested on him [Alfasi] while he wrote his law book." [102]

SYSTEMATIC CODES

Codes following closely the talmudic order fulfilled only some expectations of the interested public. Assiduous students of the Talmud, who had spent a lifetime in immersing themselves in its "sea," found that arrangement most familiar. But the ever growing scientifically trained intelligentsia, deeply engrossed in the pursuit of other disciplines as well, now demanded a new reassessment of the entire body of Jewish law in accordance with some logical order which would readily impress itself on the minds of students. The same factors which induced Saadiah or Samuel ben Ḥofni to reclassify particular legal branches in a series of juristic monographs also created the demand for similar, but more comprehensive, systematic restatements of the entire traditional law.

Understandably, the first hesitant efforts to meet this requirement, too, were made with an eye to established traditions. Talmudic scholars were ever mindful of the statement by R. Simlai, a Palestinian Amora of the third century, that "six hundred and thirteen commandments had been revealed to Moses: three hundred and sixty-five prohibitions, a number equal to that of days in the solar year, and two hundred forty-eight positive injunctions, corresponding to the number of human limbs." This computation was reinforced by R. Hamnuna's homily on the verse, "Moses commanded us a law [*torah*], an inheritance of the congregation of Jacob" (Deut. 33:4). This means, explained Hamnuna, that Moses had transmitted to Israel six hundred and eleven commandments, the numerical equivalent of *torah,* in addition to the first two of the Ten Commandments which, according to an old rabbinic tradition, had been revealed by God directly to the people assembled at Sinai. These homilies, intended to impress upon the minds of listeners the permanence and immutability of Jewish law then strongly attacked by Christian and gnostic antinomians, had its much older roots in tannaitic teachings. Yet no talmudic sage ever tried to enumerate these commandments in detail. In fact, so averse was ancient Judaism to any static system that other rabbis tried to whittle down the essentials of the faith to a few general principles (eleven, six, three, two, or even one) formulated by various prophets and psalmists. But the total number of six hundred and thirteen persisted in the popular figure of speech of the Torah's *taryag miṣvot.* It was quite tempting, therefore, to conceive of their detailed classification, under which one could subsume the whole structure of Jewish law. Something of that kind must have occurred to Aḥai of Shabḥa in his collection of weekly homilies, in so far as he envisaged his work to serve also as a law book.[103]

More incisive was the brief summary included by Simon Qayyara in the introduction to his *Halakhot gedolot.* After the aforementioned pietistic homily on the value of Torah, both written and oral, the author tried to reformulate Jewish law under some general headings. To begin with, he enumerated the Torah's seven methods of physical punishment, namely the four ancient methods of execution, two forms of death imposed from Heaven without human intermediaries, and flagellation. He then counted the seventy-one biblical prohibitions under the sanction of capital punishment, and two hundred and seventy-seven violations punished by flagellation only. Subsequently he described the positive commandments, whose lack of fulfillment was not subject to direct penalties. Curiously, the latter's total number amounted to only two hundred, to which Simon added sixty-five laws addressed to the community at large. These totals added up to six hundred and thirteen commandments, but contrary to the talmudic adage they amounted to three hundred and forty-eight prohibitions and two hundred and sixty-five positive injunctions. Satisfied with these general hints, Simon proceeded to summarize the talmudic law in the traditional talmudic sequence. Whether this division had originated with him or, as is more likely, was taken over from some older computation, even his unusual figure of two hundred positive commandments was later repeated by Saadiah. The great gaon not only used this computation in his juristic works, but also, following the example of earlier poets and yielding to an insistent popular demand, restated it in two liturgical poems, one of them called *Azharot* (Warnings). Many other liturgical pieces of this kind were composed in both Hebrew and Arabic, including an impressive poem by Solomon ibn Gabirol which found wide acceptance in the synagogue liturgy and is frequently recited by Sephardic congregations today. Its very popularity led to much tampering with its text, the poet himself praying for forgiveness for the inaccuracies of his enumeration. Jurists like Maimonides looked askance at these popularizing efforts, censuring their inescapable lack of precision but finding mitigating circumstances in the fact that, after all, their authors "were poets, not rabbis." [104]

Saadiah was, of course, a rabbi as well as a poet. He felt that in his Prayer Book he had to apologize for indulging in these poetic creations:

> I have found that men of our generation are wont to recite during the *Musaf* prayers [of the Festival of Weeks] the principal *taryag* [six hundred and thirteen] commandments which the Lord ordained to the children of Israel. . . . I have examined them [these prayers] and found that they did not contain the complete *taryag* commandments; I have also noted much repetition and wordiness in them on which I need not expatiate in this book. I have decided, therefore, to replace them by another prayer, not because it is obligatory to have such a recitation, but rather because I noticed that people had set their hearts on it.

With unmistakable reference to the enumeration by Simon Qayyara, which he rejected, the gaon explained his own division into positive and negative commandments applying to all times and places, and others of but a temporary nature. These would be followed by regulations pertaining to criminal and public law—six divisions in all. The gaon also started his enumeration with the positive commandments of the fear of God and the obligation to pray to Him, followed by the more detailed commandments of the recitation of *Shema'* twice a day, the wearing of phylacteries on one's head and arm, showfringes, and doorpost inscriptions. Of these eight commandments, Simon Qayyara had counted only four, omitting the first two and concentrating the *Shema'* and phylacteries into one commandment each. Similarly, in the negative commandments, Saadiah assigned the first place to the prohibition of worshiping other gods, perhaps following a precedent established by earlier poets. In any case, while differing in many details, his poetic classification appeared as but a modification of that suggested by Simon. On the other hand, Saadiah's own *Book of Commandments* (quoted under slightly different Arabic titles) initiated an entirely new division, arranged according to purely logical categories. Here the division was apparently increased to some twenty-four or twenty-five categories (the extant fragment of their summary, prepared by Samuel ben Ḥofni, gives us an inkling of only twenty-one of these), some of them admittedly repetitious. With his penchant for systematization, noticeable also in his halakhic monographs, Saadiah set up a few, rather artificial, categories which were hardly conducive to either deeper penetration or greater facility in memorization. Nevertheless he adhered substantially to the principles underlying this enumeration in his philosophic classification of the commandments which, as we shall see, played a considerable role in his general legal philosophy.[105]

The first truly comprehensive attempt to recast all Jewish laws in terms of this ancient classification was made by Ḥefeṣ ben Yaṣliaḥ (probably about 980–85). A native of Mosul, Ḥefeṣ resembled Saadiah in being a "foreigner" in Babylonia and yet reaching there the high academic position of *alluf,* unless this was but an honorary title given to an academy's distinguished friend who presided over a school of higher learning in his own locality. It is possible, but unlikely, that Ḥefeṣ had first tried his hand in summarizing large segments of Jewish law along the more customary lines initiated by Yehudai Gaon. A *Sefer Ḥefeṣ* (Book

Ḥefeṣ) is indeed frequently quoted by later Franco-German authorities. These quotations so greatly resemble the aforementioned *Metibot* that a long and inconclusive debate has been conducted by modern scholars about the mutual relationships between the two compilations. Probably we deal here with independent works, whose startling similarities are derived from their reliance on the same talmudic and geonic sources, including the Palestinian Talmud. Both books seem originally to have been written in Hebrew, rather than Arabic. Hence, the "Book Ḥefeṣ" hardly stems from the rationalist and well-disciplined scholar of Mosul; it may have been written by another scholar named Ḥefeṣ, or it may have been symbolically named for the "satisfaction" which readers would derive from perusing it. In that case, its title might be translated by "Book of Satisfaction," after the fashion of the many picturesque titles current among the disciples of Rashi.[106]

Of an entirely different brand was the *Kitab ash-Shara'i'* (Book of Precepts) by Ḥefeṣ ben Yaṣliaḥ, written in Arabic, although at least parts of it were later accessible to European scholars in a Hebrew translation. In this large work, probably covering a thousand closely written pages, Ḥefeṣ tried to reformulate the entire body of Jewish law by linking it directly to the reputed biblical computation of six hundred and thirteen commandments. These he reconstructed anew on the basis of his own reasoning and by supplying philosophic moorings to both the general computation and each particular group of commandments. Much of that bulk, however, was owing to the author's verbosity and frequent repetitions, probably intended to drive home his lessons more effectively —a shortcoming Ḥefeṣ shared with most Muslim and Judeo-Arabic jurists of the period. In their Arabic monographs, Saadiah and, still more, Samuel ben Ḥofni likewise indulged the same repetitious circumlocutions and casuistic divisions and subdivisions which characterized most contemporary Arabic books of jurisprudence. One need but compare the oldest extant Muslim classic, Malik ibn Anas' *Muwaṭṭa* (Paved Path), with the more or less contemporary works by Yehudai and Simon to notice both the extreme prolixity and casuistry of the Muslim writer. Ḥefeṣ' treatment, too, contrasted rather sharply with the conciseness of most of the contemporary Hebrew-Aramaic codes.

Ḥefeṣ departed further from the older Jewish models by starting his series with two commandments relating to the belief in the existence of God and His oneness. This section, more philosophical than juridical, inspired philosophers and Bible commentators like Baḥya ibn Paquda and Ibn Bal'am much more than jurists, other than Maimonides, who, despite numerous disagreements in detail, was Ḥefeṣ' most kindred soul among the Jewish codifiers. It certainly went far beyond Saadiah's poem and probably also his *Book of Commandments,* where the gaon still adhered to the activist traditions of earlier jurists and counted the fear and worship of God, both involving actions, as the first two commandments. Even in his philosophic treatise Saadiah devoted the first two chapters to a discussion of Creation and the doctrine of God, and only then turned to the problem of commands and prohibitions. Ḥefeṣ, however, followed by Maimonides, declared the two *beliefs* in the existence and uniqueness of God to be true commandments, for which he could quote Hamnuna's aforementioned statement as his talmudic authority.[107]

If we may judge from the few extant fragments covering some fifty complete and two incomplete commandments, or about a sixth of the total, Ḥefeṣ combined a topical arrangement with some of the sequences of the biblical books. He dealt successively with commandments occurring in Genesis, Exodus, and so forth. But once he started treating a certain subject, he covered all related commandments, even if the relevant passages appeared in a later biblical book. Such division necessarily resulted in much duplication. For example, because he devoted the first of his books to man's relation to his Deity, he included here also the laws relating to the first fruits, heave-offerings, and vows. The latter topic appears again, however, in Book IV, the only one fully preserved, which deals with the laws of sacrifices, and hence also includes voluntary offerings and pledges. A fairly typical section enumerates here three commandments related to the fulfillment of vows. After describing the positive commandment of keeping one's vows, Ḥefeṣ continues:

The second commandment [in this group] is that if a man vows unto the Lord or takes an oath to bind his soul with a bond, he shall not violate his word, but rather do exactly as his lips had uttered, as it is written, "When a man voweth . . ." [Num. 30:3]. A sensible man is obliged to fulfill his vow even if he be but twelve years and a day old at the time of his vow. But if he did not know what he had vowed, or is not of a sensible mind, the vow does not apply to him. If his age is below twelve years and a day, even if he be of sensible mind and able to fulfill the vow, he is not obliged to do so. But if he was at the time of his vow more than thirteen years and a day old, of sensible mind, and able to fulfill his vow, but he claims, 'I have no understanding nor any notion unto whom I have vowed,' he must keep his vow, as the sages have said: . . . .

Ḥefeṣ concludes with a lengthy discourse on the various qualifications of vows, and the circumstances which invalidate them according to rabbinic law.[108]

Although we do not possess Ḥefeṣ' introduction, in which he undoubtedly explained his method of selecting the commandments and their grouping, we may nevertheless assume that he pursued his new course without the backing of previous tradition. He never quotes any geonic sources, not even under such customary general designations as the "geonim" or "our teachers." As a pioneering effort Ḥefeṣ' work decidedly deserved far greater recognition than it received from later jurists. However, he shared that fate with Saadiah himself, whose great fame in other branches of learning did not prevent most of his juridical works, except his Prayer Book, from being practically forgotten by the general public after two or three generations. If the gaon exercised considerable influence on the monographic literature from the days of Samuel ben Ḥofni and Hai, Ḥefeṣ' impact was no less strongly felt in the parallel work by Maimonides and, through him, also in all later attempts at reclassification of the six hundred and thirteen commandments. But the sage of Fusṭaṭ himself spoke less kindly about Ḥefeṣ' achievement. In the introduction to his *Book of Commandments* he dismissed nearly all his predecessors for basically subscribing to Simon's enumeration. Finally, Maimonides added, "the famous author of the Book of Precepts [Ḥefeṣ] realized a small part of the mistakes of the author of *Halakhot gedolot,* and declined to count [among the biblical commandments] the duties of visiting the sick or of comforting the mourners. But he has included even more remote matters, and followed that author in more objectionable things, as will become evident to anyone closely examining the present study." [109]

Maimonides decided, therefore, to make a fresh start. In his methodical way, he began his *Book of Commandments,* or, more fully, *Book concerning the Number of Commandments,* by laying down fourteen principles which guided him in his selection and arrangement. The first and foremost of these principles was that "it is inappropriate to count in that total [of 613] commandments ordained by the rabbis." Similarly, one must exclude laws but hermeneutically derived from Scripture, and those not enacted for perpetuity. After laying down eleven more principles, which he explained at some length, Maimonides turned to the enumeration of the commandments. He disregarded altogether the biblical and talmudic sequences. Following his own philosophic predilections he started with the positive duties of (1) believing in the existence of God and (2) in His oneness, (3) of loving Him, (4) of fearing Him, and (5) of worshiping Him. In support of each precept he cited an appropriate biblical verse, such as the first of the Ten Commandments, or the "Hear O Israel!" Like Simon Qayyara, he emphasized that many positive commandments apply to the community rather than to individuals; for example, the duty to erect a Temple or choose a king. Many persons, moreover, may never have occasion to fulfill even commandments addressed to individuals. For instance, the regulations governing slaves or the payment of tithes do not affect persons owning no slaves nor property subject to tithes. But sixty commandments, in his opinion, apply to all men at all times. After an equally detailed enumeration of the three hundred and sixty-five prohibitions, Maimonides explains that every commandment has its good and definite reason, but that God preferred not to divulge it, lest people believe that they need not fulfill a particular commandment if they can meet its fundamental objective in some other way. This happened, for example, to King Solomon, who violated the Deuteronomic prohibition for a king to multiply horses, wives, and gold (17:16–17) because he thought that he knew how to avoid the dire effects of such actions predicted in Scripture. If the wisest of kings could thus be misled, how much more do we have to fear from such argumentation on the part of the ignorant and foolish populace! All in all, while this Maimonidean work represented an enlightening new summary, its selection of commandments and their arrangement were fundamentally no less arbitrary and dependent on individual preferences than had been the previous experiments.[110]

Equally significant were the methodological difficulties of the Maimonidean classification. Maimonides was not always consistent in his exclusion of rabbinic enactments. He was challenged on this score by his friend, Phinehas ben Meshullam, an Alexandrian judge, who asked him why, even in his Code, he had distinguished between the three forms of betrothal cited in the first Mishnah of Qiddushin, and declared that the betrothal through money stemmed only from a rabbinic ordinance. In his reply, Maimonides insisted that he had clearly demonstrated the error of the *Halakhot gedolot* and shown that neither a conclusion derived by the sages through one of the thirteen modes of interpretation, nor even a "tradition from Moses on Sinai," is to be construed as a biblical law unless the Talmud expressly designates it as such. Despite this reiteration, we have the testimony of his son Abraham that in his autograph copy the revised text expressly classified all three methods of betrothal as belonging to biblical commandments.[111]

No wonder, then, that the Maimonidean attempt encountered considerable opposition and ultimately evoked Naḥmanides' detailed refutation through point by point "objections." The Gerona rabbi agreed with the sage of Fusṭaṭ in regard to the legitimate differentiation between commandments derived from the Torah and those enacted by the rabbis, but he noted that in the detailed application of this distinction Maimonides had allowed himself numerous liberties. He insisted that laws deduced by the rabbis through hermeneutic rules be treated as biblical enactments, unless the opposite is clearly stated. Later jurists (for example Simon bar Ṣemaḥ Duran) tried in vain to bridge the gap between the two great halakhists. In practice, however, the distinction between these two categories of laws narrowed down principally to cases of doubt, which in purely rabbinic enactments could be resolved by a lenient interpretation. Otherwise, all commandments, rabbinic as well as biblical, appeared equally binding to a pious Jew.[112]

From the outset, however, Maimonides himself must have realized the artificiality of separating the positive from the negative precepts. At the beginning of his second section he dealt with the prohibition of worshiping other gods, which was but an obvious counterpart to the first two positive commandments of the belief in the existence and oneness of the God of Israel. Nor could he, by merely discussing the ramifications of these commandments, fulfill his basic program of composing "a treatise which would embrace all the laws of the Torah and its norms so that nothing would be omitted therefrom," as he had announced in the introduction. Not that he ever disavowed this work. Even in later years he spoke of it with considerable elation. When challenged by inquirers from the community of Tyre, then the main seat of Palestinian learning, he referred them to his *Book of Commandments,* "in which I have explained the computation of all commandments, and where for every questionable aspect of each law I have adduced evidence from the *Sifra, Sifre,* the *Toseftot* and all places in the Talmud." In the introduction thereto he had also laid down the principles of his counting, so that students might not be misled into false computations, the result of the previous haphazard method. "Many copies of that book," he added with pride, "have reached Babylonia, the extreme West, and the cities of Edom [Christendom] . . . and I have already regretted having written it in Arabic, since all ought to read it. I now await the opportunity of translating it into Hebrew with God's help." [113]

MAIMONIDES' "SECOND TORAH"

Whatever merits this book may have had in properly classifying the commandments, it clearly did not supply the necessary answers to students wishing speedily and reliably to ascertain the law. Maimonides decided, therefore, to accomplish his aim in a new and, except for Judah the Patriarch's Mishnah, unprecedented way in the history of Jewish codification. After having completed his comprehensive *Commentary* on the Mishnah and the *Book of Commandments,* and largely for his own benefit having also tried his hand in commenting on several talmudic tractates and summarizing the laws of the Palestinian Talmud, he felt justified in attempting his revolutionary restatement of the whole Jewish law. In arduous labors extending over an additional ten years, he succeeded in completing the first draft of his great code (about

1176). But he continued working on it to the end of his life, entering corrections and revising his views, especially in the light of numerous inquiries addressed to him by critics, both friendly and hostile.[114]

The codifier spelled out his main objectives in his introduction. True, because of their utter brevity, these prefatory statements, like many others in the body of the book, were subject to a variety of interpretations, even willful misinterpretation. After stating that "all the laws given to Moses on Sinai were given in their explanation" through Oral Law which, therefore, is an integral part of the written law as well, he described briefly the transmission of these oral traditions through the ages. In the vein of a typical Muslim traditionalist, he counted the forty generations which had allegedly elapsed from Moses to R. Ashi and in which the original oral Revelation had been faithfully handed down from one leading authority to another. For this reason "all matters stated in the Babylonian Talmud are obligatory for all Israel, and one forces cities and countries everywhere to observe all the customs adhered to by the talmudic sages. One must follow their decisions and obey their ordinances, for with respect to all matters stated in the Talmud there is universal agreement among all Israel." In contrast to these talmudic regulations thus supported by both an authentic historical *isnad* and Israel's universal consent, the *idjma'*, later teachings and ordinances had but limited validity.

Further to explain this great difference between the talmudic and posttalmudic traditions, Maimonides unhesitatingly subscribed to the prevailing historical notion that, after R. Ashi, there had been an almost total hiatus in rabbinic learning. After the days of R. Ashi and Rabina, he wrote, "Israel's dispersion was greatly increased and they reached to the distant corners and islands; wars ravaged the world, armed bands obstructed the roads, and the study of the Torah diminished. No longer did Jews enter their academies in thousands and myriads, as they used to do before, but a small remnant of individuals, with God's call in their hearts, gathered in every city and country to expound the Torah." In his own time the knowledge of Torah had sunk to another low level in most countries of the dispersion. These historical rationales, however erroneous they may appear to us today, reflected such widely accepted opinions that even Abraham ben David, who raised objections to certain historical details, had nothing to say in opposition to this general reconstruction.[115]

Yet the enormous mass of juridical learning accumulated in the posttalmudic responsa, commentaries, and books of legal decisions had tremendously complicated the task of scholars. Especially in times of great trial for the Jewish people, only few could marshal the necessary "breadth of knowledge, wise understanding, and long-time endurance" to master the intricacies of the ramified rabbinic lore. That is why Maimonides decided to prepare a code summarizing the entire body of the law emerging from both ancient and more recent letters, so that all of it might become familiar to both the small and the great.

In short, none will be required to study any further book concerning the laws of Israel, for the present treatise will assemble the whole Oral Law, together with the ordinances, customs, and enactments which had been issued from the days of Moses to the completion of the Talmud, as they have been interpreted by the authorities in all writings composed after the Talmud. For this reason I have called this treatise *Mishneh Torah* [the Second Torah], for one need but read the written Torah first, and then study this book, to learn the entire Oral Law without being required to peruse any intervening tract.

This self-confident assertion shocked a great many rabbinic scholars even before they began studying the first pages of the code itself.

Their sense of wonder must have increased when they turned to the first book entitled the *Sefer ha-Madda'* (Book of [Religious] Knowledge). Before Maimonides, few Jews cared to define the fundamentals of their faith in rigorous legal terms. Some metaphysical doctrines belonged, in fact, in the category of subjects on which speculation had been discouraged by the talmudic sages. Others were left to preachers to elaborate in their sermons, rather than to jurists to formulate in normative terms. Maimonides, philosopher of religion that he was, had not been satisfied with this juridical vagueness. Even in his youthful work on the Mishnah, we recall, he had formulated the thirteen basic doctrines of Judaism as part and parcel of Jewish law. Similarly, in his *Book of Commandments* he had begun both series of laws with norms pertaining to basic beliefs. He assigned, therefore, also the first section of his Code to creedal matters, calling the respective subdivisions the "Principles of the Torah," "Concepts" (relating to ethical doctrines and behavior), "Study of Torah," "Idolatry," and "Repentance." In the first of these subdivisions alone, he taught, were included six positive and four negative commandments. These ten precepts well illustrate the general duplication in the Maimonidean and all other computations of the six hundred and thirteen commandments. They are: (1) to know that God exists; (2) not to perceive the idea that there exists another god; (3) to believe that He is One in a uniqueness of its own kind; (4) to love Him; (5) to fear Him; (6) to sanctify His name; (7) not to desecrate His name (that is, to suffer active and passive martyrdom); (8) not to destroy anything containing one of His holy names; (9) to listen to a prophet bearing His message; and (10) not to try Him. Although all these beliefs had long been accepted by professing Jews, in this form they appeared as a decidedly alien philosophic incursion into the domain of law.[116]

All his life, moreover, the jurist-philosopher was concerned with the reasons of the various commandments. Although he had previously explained why the Torah itself had refrained from stating their objectives, he himself felt free to search for such ultimate motivations. This quest was to lead him later, in his *Guide,* to classify all Jewish laws under fourteen headings, just as he had divided his great Code into fourteen similar though not identical books—a division which caused the "Second Torah" to be known also under the title *Yad ḥazaqah* (Strong Hand). In subdividing these books into chapters and paragraphs he also followed his own sense of proportion and logical relationships, rather than the traditional divisions of Mishnah or Talmud. Maimonides always gave much thought to problems of structure. Not without reason have later commentators drawn important conclusions from the very arrangement of his work. In the introduction to his *Commentary* on the Mishnah, he himself had searched for the reasons behind Judah the Patriarch's choice and sequence of orders, tractates, and even chapters. With full awareness of its importance he now tried to rearrange his legal materials in a new logical order. Much ingenuity has, indeed, been expended by both medieval and modern scholars in finding the reasons for each sequence in the Code, although Maimonides himself sometimes yielded to the temptation to follow the traditional order, or else he combined somewhat heterogeneous matters merely because they had thus been associated in the Torah or rabbinic literature. But, on the whole, his approach was altogether novel, and as such it was doubly suspicious to conservatives.[117]

Of course, the halakhic monographs by Saadiah, Samuel ben Ḥofni, and Hai and the various juridical miscellanies had long paved the way for the rearrangement of traditional laws. But it was one thing to collect scattered talmudic references for the purpose of reviewing a small segment of the law, and another to present the entire system in a novel order. In his restatement of the laws of circumcision, for example, Maimonides combined data spread over fourteen talmudic tractates, while in his brief subsection devoted to the laws of the study of Torah he used materials found in thirty-two tractates, or more than half the Talmud. Most disconcerting to informed readers was his frequent personal decision as to which talmudic statement was to be considered official doctrine, and which but the personal opinion of a single sage and therefore to be safely disregarded. Such "arbitrariness" was particularly painful when it sprang from scientific or philosophic convictions. True, in his treatment of the talmudic laws concerning animals whose life-endangering illnesses made them unfit for human consumption (the so-called *ṭerefot*), he specifically discarded medical findings and declared that one must not add to the categories adopted by the ancient sages and agreed upon in Jewish courts. For other blemishes need not necessarily cause the animal's death, "even if we know from the study of medicine that it cannot survive." But Maimonides allowed his mathematical and astronomic studies to color many decisions relating to the calendar. More significantly, because his own scientific outlook ran counter to any belief in the existence of demons and the power of magic he had to interpret away certain talmudic regulations and the ancient motivations of many others. Even his antianthropomorphic bias, which was widely shared in the Near East, did not enjoy unanimous acceptance in the Christian West, with its belief in the doctrine of Incarnation.[118]

Most grievous to students of Jewish jurisprudence, then and later, was the semioracular style of the Maimonidean pronunciamentos. Accustomed as all had been to the airing of every problem in its pros and cons with constant reference to talmudic and posttalmudic debates, they looked askance at a work which, going far beyond the Mishnah whose example it invoked, merely stated the law as the author saw it. Only occasionally did he add a reference to some scriptural verse—frequently different from that cited in the same context in the traditional sources—but he entirely ignored the complex talmudic discussions. According to a report, recorded in Abraham Maimuni's name, a visitor from Cairo at his father's academy in Fusṭaṭ once raised a question about the meaning of a passage in the Code by reference to the division of opinion in its underlying talmudic source. Maimonides is said to have replied, "If I had wished to explain my work through the Talmud, I should not have written it." Of course, any really informed student could see that each and every statement had been the result of prolonged study and reflection, based on the consummate mastery of all authoritative sources. But, so long as these were not spelled out, they left a considerable residuum of doubt in the minds of readers. They certainly could often mislead tyros unable to detect in these terse formulations all the fine nuances which were often decisive in practical application.[119]

During the following centuries, to be sure, numerous commentators made it their business to supply the sources of most Maimonidean decisions. But on occasion even they could not locate the source, partly because of the author's frequent use of texts no longer accessible to them. We recall how delighted Maimonides had been when he was able to consult a copy of the Talmud, then some five hundred years old. His very readings may have seriously differed, therefore, from those known to his commentators, whose talmudic texts had largely undergone the revisions adopted by the school of Rashi. Even Abraham ben David had noted Maimonides' great reliance on the Palestinian Talmud; here, too, his text doubtless varied in many significant details from those later current in the Western schools. Maimonides had also derived much information from the then generally neglected tannaitic sources preserved in the Tosefta and halakhic midrashim;

often these were in recensions unfamiliar to his Western exegetes and, in part, no longer available today. But precisely because of these textual uncertainties, more exact data on the reasoning behind, and the sources of, any controversial decision appeared doubly urgent for use at academies and courts of justice.[120]

It was this juridical weakness of the new code which, though a pedagogic strength, served as the main target for growing attacks in both East and West. The Baghdad academicians, grouped around Samuel ben 'Ali Gaon, had long resented the growing independence of Jewish scholars. They now assailed with relish particularly some of Maimonides' overt inconsistencies. They had at their disposal revisions of the Maimonidean *Commentary* on the Mishnah, and they used them to demonstrate glaring errors in that work without mentioning that the author himself had made the necessary corrections. In the West it was particularly the profound halakhist Abraham ben David of Posquières who took up the cudgels in behalf of the traditional methods of talmudic learning against this dangerous Egyptian innovator, and he was the more dangerous as his beautiful Hebrew style—in itself a major contribution to Jewish studies—made his work doubly attractive to students. An old fighter, who had dared to controvert the very authority of Alfasi whose mastery of Jewish law he fully recognized, Abraham was even less ready to condone the pecadillos of a man his junior by ten or twenty years. He therefore provided the Maimonidean Code, which seems to have reached him in installments, with a number of marginal *Hassagot* (Objections). In one of his first strictures on Maimonides' aforementioned programmatic statement he argued that the author "thought that he had improved matters, but he did not, for he had abandoned the road traveled by all writers before him who had always cited proofs for their statements and named their authorites." With unusual acerbity, exceeding that of his former colleague Zeraḥiah's attack on Alfasi (which, however, had its author's extreme youth as an excuse), he pounced on every point, big or small, in which he sensed weakness. One cannot help but sympathize with this old, learned talmudist, whose sensibilities were deeply wounded by the younger man's brilliant act of daring. In his special pleadings Abraham often failed to examine more closely Maimonides' intent or his explanation in another context. A considerable number of strictures also stemmed from differing local traditions or variations in the talmudic texts, for Maimonides, very careful in his own textual apparatus, did not have at his disposal the great achievements of textual purification by the schools of Gershom and Rashi.[121]

For whatever reason, there was enough substance in Abraham's "Objections" to keep ingenious students busy for many generations, indeed until the present day. We possess, moreover, at least some replies, indirectly issued by Maimonides himself. Abraham apparently discussed some of his strictures with his learned colleagues of the great academy of Lunel, so glowingly described by Benjamin of Tudela. These academicians included numerous friends and admirers of Maimonides such as Jonathan ben David ha-Kohen. Both opponents and friends decided, therefore, to address inquiries directly to the author in Egypt, requesting elucidation on numerous points of law and method. In his replies to these scholars and others, who evinced a similar curiosity, Maimonides seized the opportunity to defend his general and specific positions. He candidly admitted certain errors in the original draft, many of which he had already corrected in subsequent recensions. Most significantly, he conceded that perhaps his failure to mention his authorities was a serious mistake, and expressed the hope that he might some day reissue his Code with fuller documentation.[122]

Nonetheless this whole debate was a clear demonstration of the Code's instantaneous impact on the legal thinking and practice of that generation—an impact which increased in the course of years. Few persons, in fact, have impressed themselves so deeply on the folk psyche of the Jewish people in both East and West, and as late as the nineteenth century many Jewish homes were adorned with an alleged portrait of the great jurist-philosopher. His personality often assumed heroic proportions in Jewish folklore, without thereby being deprived of its truly human qualities.[123]

In retrospect, all minor flaws mattered little when compared with the monumental achievement of the great Code. True, the codifier himself once allegedly conceded, "I have never been vanquished except by a specialist in a single field." But even if that apocryphal admission had indeed been addressed to Abraham ben

David, we must remember that the latter was able to develop his greatest talents only in his marginal "objections" to the works of Maimonides, Zeraḥiah, or Alfasi. By himself he was far less creative. It took a master architect of Maimonides' vision and grandeur to conceive the gigantic structure of a new, all-embracing Code. The sage of Fusṭaṭ could calmly leave it to lesser minds, including a great many pygmies, to replace some of the weaker bricks and remove mere flyspecks from his marvelous edifice.

INSTRUMENTS OF LEGAL PROGRESS

Opposition to the Maimonidean Code went far deeper, however. Quite apart from its alleged technical deficiencies, the idea of a code of laws as such appeared objectionable to many students of the law. Its author's overambitious program merely deepened the ancient aversion to anything that might impede the untrammeled progress of Jewish law.

At this juncture one perceives, indeed, a noteworthy difference between Islam and Judaism. In Jewish, much more than in Muslim, law the codes had to remain merely practical reference books, to be disregarded as soon as the scholar or judge found that his own interpretation of the talmudic sources differed from that of the codifier. True, Abu Ḥanifa, one of Muslim law's founding fathers, had allegedly declared that "it is not permissible for the one who gives a *fatwa* from my books to give it until he learns the grounds on which I have said what I have said." Caliph Harun ar-Rashid is reputed to have objected altogether to the codification of Muslim law because it might put an end to those differences of opinion which a *ḥadith* attributed to Mohammed had viewed as an act of grace. But it was in Judaism, rather than in Islam, that ever new voices protested against the very principle of substituting a legal code, nonobligatory though it be, for the living flow of independent derivation from the sources themselves. As early as the days of R. Joshua, even before R. 'Aqiba's first compilation of tannaitic law, a warning had been sounded against those teachers and judges who merely quoted a legal enactment without its underlying reasons. Such proceedings appeared all the more dangerous when the vast "sea of the Talmud" had become a source of deep perplexity to hurried administrators of justice who readily grasped the opportunity offered them by the "adjudicated halakhot." It was against such "aberrations" that Ṣemaḥ Gaon raised his voice, and his father Palṭoi Gaon rebuked the uncritical followers of such outlines as "causing the Torah to be forgotten." Rabbis were so greatly encouraged to defy even established authorities that, as we recall, Ḥananel repeatedly asserted, "Our teachers, the geonim, gave here a different explanation, but we wrote what we have learned from our own teachers." [124]

On the other hand, the principle of following clear-cut statements by later authorities found an influential champion in Joseph ibn Megas (see his *Responsa,* No. 114); and even Hai, the head of the previously most antagonistic Pumbedita academy, warmly defended codification. The ever present cloud of sectarian controversies also strengthened the forces of conformity best symbolized by simplified legal compilations. Since the eternal debates in the rabbinic schools of jurisprudence were grist for the mill of Karaite assailants of the Oral Law's purported roots in reliably transmitted traditions, a lucid restatement of that law without the encumbrance of antecedent dialectics seemed to present a far more solidly united Rabbanite front. Even without exaggerating the extent of the Karaite "menace," we can readily see that legal uniformity, such as advocated by Pirqoi ben Baboi, appeared to many leaders a powerful dam against the spread of heterodoxies. With the weakening of central controls in the tenth and eleventh centuries, the unity of the people seemed doubly to demand some such vehicles of legal conformity.

Opponents again became vociferous, however, when the Maimonidean Code was received with tremendous acclaim by students from Yemen to southern France. To be sure, the anti-Maimonidean controversy transcended that issue and became involved in the perennial dilemma of relations between faith and reason. In fact, most Western defenders of Maimonides were prepared to condone his more disputed metaphysical doctrines for the sake of his signal juristic achievements. But the two areas could not be strictly separated, since the codifier himself had injected his philosophic biases into his Code. The full story of that remarkable controversy must, on chronological grounds, be postponed to a later volume. But from the outset many anxious voices were heard about the danger looming for the future of all Jewish learning if students were to take literally the codifier's advice and study only his work together with the written Torah. What the author had intended merely as a pedagogic convenience to scholars, and a practical aid to judges, could indeed be abused by overly timid or lazy pupils and practitioners.

Unquestionably, the danger was greatly exaggerated by vociferous opponents. The very multiplicity of codes, none enjoying final and undisputed authority, and the differences of opinion between them kept students on the alert. The strictures which Abraham ben David appended to the Maimonidean Code reopened the debate on many points, just as the negative observations on Alfasi's work by his colleague Zeraḥiah had greatly expanded the horizons of knowledge even for those who deeply admired the sage of Lucena. Moreover, in addition to codes, there existed the vast literature of legal monographs and miscellanies, methodological handbooks, and particularly of commentaries and supercommentaries, which vouchsafed constant reinterpretation of the traditional body of material to suit the needs of various generations and localities. It certainly prevented even gullible individuals from blindly following recognized authorities. For this reason codes, rather than obstructing legal progress, actually represented brief pauses, enabling generations of students to take stock of earlier achievements before embarking on newer intellectual ventures.

GEONIC RESPONSA

If there remained any residuum of doubt about the possible "petrification" of Jewish law at a particular stage of its evolution, such fears must have been dispelled by the dominant role played by the rabbinic responsa—that most eminent means of adjustment of law to life. More than any neighboring civilization, Judaism developed in these legal exchanges a major instrument of legal progress, appropriate to both its dynamic, history-oriented—if not always history-conscious—spirit and the needs of its far-flung dispersion. True, this institution had already been developed by

Roman jurists, to whom we owe its designation. It soon was also cultivated with much fervor by the Muslims, whose vast territorial expansion, combined with the lack of a universally recognized judicial authority, likewise helped to establish the *fatwa* as an important vehicle of juridical thinking. But the priority of the Jewish responsum is indubitable. Already in the talmudic age we hear of inquiries addressed, for example by the community of Nineveh (!), to R. Judah the Patriarch. Zacharias Frankel has even suggested that the "messenger to Zion," mentioned in a talmudic passage, was a permanent official in charge of inquiries regularly arriving in Palestine from Babylonia and other lands. Nonetheless, once established and widely used, the *fatwa* may well have exercised a reciprocal influence on the rabbinic responsum beyond the occasional borrowings of Arabic phrases in an otherwise Hebrew-Aramaic context. In fact, beginning with Saadiah, many geonim used the Arabic language as the main medium of communication in their replies, at least to inquirers who had used that language in their letters. With the linguistic unavoidably came terminological and conceptual borrowings, which imperceptibly built further bridges between these related legal systems.[125]

Even the geonic responsa, however, had a rather slow start. Not only in the saboraic period, but also under the early geonim, there persisted a lingering suspicion against written communications in matters of vital legal importance. As late as the ninth century Sar Shalom (or Ṣemaḥ) and Amram complained of their inability to communicate orally with their correspondents. Asked about a difficult problem concerning the "wine of ablution" handled by idolaters, the gaon replied:

> All these problems are complicated and highly obscure. If it were possible for you to be with us, we might be able to explain them to you and to distinguish one from the other with the necessary clarity. For when a pupil sits before his teacher and discusses a legal problem the teacher notices where his attention is focused and what escapes him, or what is clear or puzzling to him. The teacher can then interpret for him, enlighten him and settle for him that legal question. But how much can one write? At best a small part. Nevertheless we have ordered that the general principles governing the "wine of ablution" be described to you.

In Babylonia itself the *kallah* gatherings long obviated the necessity of written replies. During these sessions the leading academicians reviewed orally questions submitted to them during the preceding months, discussed their more complex aspects with their associates, and answered them publicly for the benefit of both the questioners and other interested persons. Because of their contemporary relevance, such debates must have been memorable as living experiences to many students and visitors. As the questions increased in number and urgency, it was no longer possible to keep the inquirers waiting until that semiannual convocation, and answers were more or less immediately dispatched. Even then, it appears, the heads of academies reserved a number of either more recent, less urgent, or particularly complicated questions for such public airing during the *kallah* sessions.[126]

With the incessant growth of the Jewish dispersion, the increase in commercial and intellectual exchanges, and the greater availability of travelers who could reliably transmit letters to and from Babylonia, the written responsum established itself as a vital link between the various communities. It often took a year for a letter from Spain or southern France to reach Sura or Pumbedita, and another year for the reply to be delivered to the original questioners. Undoubtedly a great many letters were lost in transit. As a precautionary measure, the geonim entrusted their representatives in Fusṭaṭ with the task of preparing complete copies of the responsa and depositing them in their own archives before sending them on to Kairuwan or Spain. For this reason the Cairo Genizah has become such an inexhaustible mine of information in this field. This was not an altogether selfless performance, since the Eastern academies had increasingly become financially dependent on the contributions of foreign communities. Most of the hard-pressed latter-day geonim, as we recall, actually solicited inquiries and the accompanying donations. Immediately upon his accession to office, Saadiah assured his Egyptian disciples with considerable verbal felicity, "Please let us regularly know about your welfare, for it is also our welfare. Where there is no army there is no king, and without pupils there is no splendor to scholars." [127]

Some queries were purely academic. In the early period, in particular, when copies of the Talmud were extremely scarce and its interpretation outside the two academies still in its infancy, many inquiries pertained merely to the meaning of certain talmudic texts. Later on they became more learned and exacting. At times the questioners sought information about scattered talmudic passages or interrelated legal problems. In such cases the geonim usually lumped their answers, too, in a series of replies consecutively numbered. Some such series were handed down in later collections and still constitute distinct segments within the published volumes of responsa. Nor were the questions limited to strictly legal problems, for transitions from *aggadah* to jurisprudence were very fluid. Ultimately, Maimonides devoted an entire lengthy responsum to the analysis of rabbinic views on each person's expected life-span, whose predetermined duration, taught by some Muslim thinkers, he sharply repudiated. On other occasions the questions were so comprehensive that they stimulated the heads of academies to compose regular monographs. The most famous of these, Amram's *Seder* and Sherira's *Epistle,* have since become classics in medieval Jewish liturgy and historiography. The same is true of such important works of Muslim jurisprudence as Abu Yusuf's *Kitab al-Kharaj,* a lawyer's memorandum for the benefit of Harun ar-Rashid, from which we derive most of our information about the taxation of "protected" subjects. Many halakhic monographs, too, were written in response to such outside queries, although in view of their generally poor state of preservation we rarely have an inkling of the particular circumstances and personalities involved in these exchanges.[128]

Regrettably, the original archives of the two academies are irretrievably lost. At times the geonim themselves referred to earlier decisions recorded in these repositories, although on other occasions they had to admit their inability to locate precedents. Probably their filing system was no better than that of many modern institutions. The mere transfer of the academies from Pumbedita and later Sura to Baghdad must in itself have caused the loss of many records, according to the common saying among modern archivists that moving an archive twice is worse than a fire. Especially in the chaotic tenth century, when the capital was a difficult place to live in and inhospitable to records because of frequent conflagrations and the ravages of unruly bands of soldiers, many earlier accumulations must have been destroyed. On the other hand, under Sherira and Hai in Pumbedita and Samuel ben Ḥofni in Sura the volume of correspondence doubtless swelled to unprecedented proportions, thus creating new difficulties for the recorders. Hai Gaon must have found it particularly trying to keep up his far-flung correspondence during the last two or three decades of his almost centennial life.[129]

Posterity has sustained its greatest and most irreplaceable losses in the geonic correspondence with communities located east of Babylonia. With their intellectual *élan* rather quickly exhausted, they were unable to perpetuate the record of their own achievements or that of whatever intellectual stimuli they had received from the great academic centers. In the earlier years inquiries from the Iranian Plateau and adjoining lands must have vastly exceeded in volume and intensity those reaching Babylonia from the western Mediterranean. But no eastern Genizah has survived to salvage for us transcripts of that correspondence, nor was there enough intellectual creativity to preserve that Babylonian heritage through extensive quotations of the kind accomplished by Western scholars from Ḥananel to Simḥah of Vitry.

Later historical, rather than contemporary, factors thus account for the overwhelming share of the western countries among the recipients of geonic responsa now known. Needless to say that here, too, time played havoc with the preservation of more than a small fraction of these replies. Apparently transcripts of geonic responsa, arranged according to some plan, began circulating in Kairuwan already in Hai's lifetime. Somewhat later one Isaac *ha-ḥazzan ha-gadol* al-Lusani (Chief Reader of Lucena) and Joseph Tob 'Elem (Bonfils) of France instituted their own collections. Works of this kind were already available to Samuel ibn Nagrela, Isaac ibn Gayyat, and Yehudah bar Barzillai. Some of these medieval compilations have since served as a basis for many modern publications as well.[130]

The underlying inquiries, which in so far as they recorded actual events may be historically at least as important as the answers, have suffered almost total eclipse. On their passage to Babylonia they were not treated with the same reverence as the geonic replies and hence were forwarded untranscribed to their destination, where they were speedily lost. Many may indeed not have deserved a better fate. The following generations of copyists and scholars were likewise far more interested in the replies and their precedent-setting decisions than in the inquiries which had provoked them. At best we possess, therefore, but the gist of questions, sufficient to point up the legal or exegetical problems, but not to identify the authors or detail the facts.

Nor were these later generations particularly interested in the authors of responsa, so long as they knew that they had the academy's authority behind them. Frequently they merely quoted a decision as rendered by "geonim" without further identification—a practice seriously aggravated by the widespread Western predilection for attaching that distinguished title to Ḥananel or Alfasi. Although experts early realized that it made a difference whether a reply was sent by Sura or Pumbedita, and that by knowing a particular gaon's name one could consult his other responsa or literary works, the majority was rather negligent in keeping the record straight. Frequently the same responsum is attributed to different writers in different collections, or in subsequent quotations. Even where names are given one must entertain reasonable doubts with respect to their authenticity. Sherira bluntly denounced a responsum ascribed to Saadiah as a forgery, because Saadiah "was a great scholar," and hence he could not possibly have overlooked a plain Mishnah. In the eleventh century, Joseph ibn Megas knew that many responsa were ascribed "to other than the real authors." It was natural that, particularly, the best known and most revered geonim should be made responsible for utterances of their less famous colleagues. Nor are the names always exactly identifiable. We must bear in mind, observed Louis Ginzberg, "that there were six Josephs and six Ḥaninas, four Ṣemaḥs, two Kohen Ṣedeqs and two Hilas, three Naṭronais, and three Jacobs among the Geonim." If during the half century since these words were written some of these questions were solved by additional finds and researches, the new materials have raised as many or more novel problems.[131]

Frequently we are uncertain as to whether we are dealing with actual responsa. Just as many commentaries and halakhic monographs originated from inquiries, some original literary works, or excerpts therefrom, were converted by later compilers into responsa by the insertion of a prefatory phrase such as *Ve-she-she'altem* (As to your question). The most flagrant instance was that of the compiler of the second printed collection of geonic responsa, published in Constantinople in 1575. Wishing to round out the total number to four hundred, he incorporated at the end of his volume fifty decisions from the then recently published code of laws by Joseph Karo and gave them the form of replies. On a lesser scale such conversions from code or commentary into a responsum or vice versa had been going on for centuries, consciously or unconsciously. At times the authors themselves unconcernedly cited verbatim in their replies a statement from one of their previous works, or else incorporated in a later work word for word quotations from a responsum. The same Hai Gaon who in one responsum expressly referred to his commentary on Berakhot, in another reply failed to indicate that his lengthy discourse had appeared almost verbatim also in the commentary. Later copyists and scholars citing geonic passages cared little for the literary genre of their sources, and many quoted more or less indiscriminately a particular decision as stemming from either a responsum or a book. Still more blurred is the line of demarcation between a letter and a responsum, since the former, too, sometimes dealt with a legal problem.[132]

In their replies the geonim acted as if they were a legally recognized supreme court issuing decisions against which there was no demurrer. Whatever backing the caliphal government extended to them, either directly or through the exilarchic office, certainly did not extend to independent areas like Kairuwan, Spain, or non-Muslim countries. And yet, as we recollect, the geonim were wont to insert phrases into their replies intimating that their decisions brooked no contradiction. No one seemed to object to these peremptory commands, except some Palestinian resisters to the general encroachments of such Babylonian spokesmen as Pirqoi and Saadiah. In other countries Jews reverently listened to these orders and often publicly recited them in synagogues, even if they failed to execute them when they ran counter to established local customs. Asked about judges unqualified to study the Talmud but relying on geonic responsa despite their well-known deficiencies, Joseph ibn Megas stated that "he who decides a case on the basis of geonic responsa and relies on them, although he may not be able to understand the Talmud itself, is decidedly preferable to one who thinks that he knows the Talmud and relies on his own deductions" (*Resp.*, No. 114). Fortunately, the majority of scholars did not share that view, but allowed each judge and student to reach his own conclusions.

So great was the prestige of the heads of the two academies that few of their successors cared to preserve transcripts of decisions rendered by the exilarchic court, although from the standpoint of governmental law enforcement they could even more readily be executed, at least within the Caliphate's shifting area of authority. One of the few extant letters of this kind, written by Exilarch Hezekiah ben David in 1036 two years before his assumption of the geonic office as well, has recently been published (Assaf, *Tequfat,* pp. 285 ff.). In this Arabic letter to a distinguished scholar, perhaps not wholly typical because written in the period of waning exilarchic power, Hezekiah extended greetings also in behalf of the two academies, and assured the recipient, "You will also make me rejoice by writing to me the news of what has happened to you, your needs and your business dealings; also about whatever may occur to you with respect to the books of prophecy [Scripture] or the words of our sages of blessed memory relating to commandments, laws, or any new events as they happen." Very likely the exilarchs corresponded more frequently with the eastern communities than with those of Egypt, Kairuwan or Spain. All of the latter were under the domination of rival caliphs who doubtless viewed with a jaundiced eye direct appeals to Jewish chiefs formally invested by the Commanders of the Faithful in Baghdad. Interstate exchanges between academicians, customary also in the Muslim world, appeared much less suspect. The correspondence emanating from the exilarchic court thus doubly suffered from the general oblivion into which had fallen all exchanges between Babylonia and the countries to the East.

LATER CORRESPONDENCE

No such unquestioning obedience was expected by later rabbinic authors. More like the Muslim *fuqaha,* they merely expressed their legal opinions, leaving the implementation to the questioners. Nevertheless, the later rabbis, too, effectively used this vehicle for both the constant reinforcement of basic talmudic laws and their modification in the light of intervening precedents or changing local conditions. Over-all uniformity, combined with great flexibility in detail, became the imperative need of an ever pioneering people in contact with a variety of older and newer civilizations.

While formerly even scholars great in their own right, such as Nissim bar Jacob and Samuel ibn Nagrela, had sent their questions to Hai, after the latter's death, the growingly independent provincial centers relied more and more on the expert opinions of their own authorities. Several hundred responsa by Alfasi written in Fez or Lucena have been published, partly in their Arabic original—doubtless but a small part of his juridical correspondence. His pupil and successor, Joseph ibn Megas, also wrote numerous responsa, a selection of which, for the most part likewise in a Hebrew rendition from the Arabic, is available in a published volume.[133]

Western individualism, especially characteristic of the Spanish-Jewish Golden Age, made itself felt also in this domain. Collections assembled in eleventh-century Kairuwan and elsewhere usually lumped together responsa written by various heads of academies and arranged them according to subjects, if not entirely at random. Only when the original reply consisted of a series of answers to interrelated questions or a succession of talmudic passages did many compilers maintain that unity in their volumes. There seems never to have existed a special collection of Naṭronai's, Sherira's, or Hai's responsa alone. Alfasi marks the transition, inasmuch as some of his replies are included in general collections of geonic answers such as underlay Harkavy's edition, while others seem to have circulated early in independent codices under his name. Beginning with Ibn Megas, individual volumes became the accepted procedure in the Spanish schools.

Among the earliest Western writers of responsa was Alfasi's Italian contemporary, Meshullam bar Kalonymus of Lucca (end of the 10th cent.). A member of the famous Kalonymide family, the reputed fountainhead of all Franco-German rabbinic learning, Meshullam was in correspondence with Sherira and Hai, as well as with Palestinian geonim, and was sometimes himself called gaon (for instance, by Rashi). He answered a number of legal inquiries, probably addressed to him from other Italian communities. Because of their polemical intent, these responsa were extensively quoted in the Middle Ages and found an early compiler. Perhaps Meshullam himself had arranged such a collection to be used as an apologetic pamphlet in staving off the inroads of heresies. Karaite propaganda must have been quite familiar to any Italian scholar in contact with the Jewish leaders of Palestine, then the great intellectual center of the Karaite movement.[134]

North of the Pyrenees the older system continued to operate for a long time. Even responsa by such outstanding authorities as Gershom and Rashi were, as a rule, included in broader juridical works, particularly the halakhic miscellanies from Rashi's school. Fortunately, later medieval French and German writers were in the habit of quoting older sources at great length. From the legal compendia by Eliezer bar Nathan, Eliezer bar Joel ha-Levi, Isaac Or Zaru'a, Mordecai bar Hillel ha-Kohen, and others modern scholars were able to piece together many such replies by the early northern authorities. Some identifications are necessarily doubtful. From the outset copyists were not careful in distinguishing between actual replies to inquiries and decisions rendered at the scholars' courts; a responsum attributed to an author in one compilation is often ascribed elsewhere to another writer. But through the maze of conflicting traditions and copyists' corruptions we note that quite early the Franco-German centers of learning were forced to rely on their own resources. Only rarely did they appeal to the Eastern academies, Babylonian or Palestinian. Somewhat more frequently they exchanged ideas with the older Italian communities, especially that of Rome, the matrix of all northern Jewish learning.[135]

Of the later collections of northern responsa that by Jacob bar Meir Tam is highly significant, both because of its enormous prestige and because it essentially stems from his own and his pupils' compilations. Some of these replies were early incorporated in Jacob's major juridical work, the *Sefer ha-Yashar*. This volume includes Tam's acrimonious correspondence with Meshullam bar Nathan of Melun, which, together with the contemporary sharp exchanges between Zeraḥiah and Abraham ben David, provides the most remarkable illustration of medieval legal polemics. Tam's responsa also show that, even in his lifetime, his fame had spread far and wide. Among the inquirers were rabbis residing in Bari and Otranto in southern Italy who had long cherished the conviction that "the Torah will go forth from Bari and the Lord's word from Otranto." That they nevertheless recognized Tam's great learning and addressed their inquiries to him was among the highest tributes which contemporaries could pay to a foreign savant. If, in his great self-confidence, Abraham ben David repudiated the incursion of these foreign teachings, his colleague Zeraḥiah cited Tam with admiration. In fact, later folklore made Abraham himself visit Tam's academy in disguise. From Naḥmanides on, all Spaniards bowed to the Frenchman's superior learning.[136]

Query and responsum were so firmly established in the twelfth century that almost immediately upon his settlement in Egypt Maimonides began to be approached with legal inquiries. As his fame spread, these questions multiplied, and they came from many lands extending from Yemen to southern France. Reference has already been made to his correspondence with Jonathan of Lunel. In this particular instance we are fortunate in possessing the text of Jonathan's letter, which, notwithstanding its excessive verbiage, offers some insights into the inquirer's motivations. Curiously, one of Maimonides' correspondents was Abraham ha-Kohen, member of the Baghdad academy, a fact which reflects the intervening decline of the Babylonian schools. To be sure, this inquiry may have been inspired by the gaon Samuel ben 'Ali himself, who wished thus to expose an alleged mistake in the Maimonidean Code. The gaon, who had already quarreled with the Maimonidean teachings concerning resurrection, now disagreed with the tenor of the responsum shown to him by Abraham. He formulated his objections in an epistle to the latter which, reproduced in Abraham's second letter to Maimonides, evoked a courteous but firm reply from the sage of Fusṭaṭ. Maimonides pointed out that in his earlier responsum he could not embrace all aspects of the problem (pertaining to traveling on ships on Sabbath), but had addressed himself only to those facets which seemed of particular concern to the questioner. His general views on the subject were on record in his published works, readily available in Baghdad. Remarkably, despite their author's enormous reputation, the Maimonidean responsa were not collected and used extensively as sources of Jewish law until a much later age. Even Abraham Maimuni, who frequently cited his father's other works and at times adduced a practice observed in his father's house as a valid precedent, apparently did not have such a collection before him.[137]

Postgeonic rabbis, too, occasionally consulted their academic colleagues, but their replies were decidedly individual. Gershom bar Yehudah, who did not hesitate to issue formal enactments (*taqqanot*) deeply affecting the lives of individuals and communities, used a very moderate tone in his answers, and these often contained such clauses as "What I have learned and is indicated in my opinion, I have written and signed." Even where, to reinforce his decision, he concluded by stating "And this is the law," he realized that it was but the expression of personal judgment. True, such expressions of humility had become the fashion of the age. Even Jacob Tam, as self-assertive a scholar as any, considered it necessary to comply with this literary usage. In his reply to R. Joseph bar Moses the Elder about the permissibility of a couple getting married during the thirty-day period of mourning for a close relative, Tam stated, "I am not worthy of your sending me that inquiry, but I am inclined to believe that such an immediate union is allowed." That fashion, long before set by Gershom and Rashi, was so much taken for granted that copyists frequently omitted these references to personal inadequacy as irrelevant to the legal decision. But behind these stereotyped formulas loomed the recognition of these rabbis themselves that they did not possess the power vested in the geonim by virtue of their high office.[138]

Some scholars were more resentful of criticisms than others. In his reply to Samuel ben 'Ali's strictures, Maimonides assured his correspondent:

> The Creator of the world knows that even if the youngest of his pupils or any student would have raised a legitimate objection, we would rejoice over it. We would be happy over his turning our attention to a matter which had escaped us. Even where we notice that an

objector is in error, we do not hate him nor alienate him, God forbid . . . for anybody approves or disapproves of a particular view according to his own examination of the facts, be it correct or erroneous.

The sage of Fusṭaṭ often acknowledged his mistakes, and he kept on revising his published works to the end of his life. Others were less forbearing, and some differences of opinion were aired in bitter exchanges. Such temperamentally intolerant scholars as Abraham ben David or Jacob Tam often upheld their views with excessive vigor. In the aforementioned correspondence between Tam and Meshullam bar Nathan of Melun, Meshullam addressed Jacob reverently and treated him almost as his teacher. But, impatient of any criticism, Tam replied with venom. "Those who correct in vain," runs one of his characteristic exclamations, "appear to me to deserve by law to be committed to hell. . . . Even if that were a textual version current in your province it must stem from robbers like yourself, particularly since I am certain that it is not so." Tam quoted in his support a version included in Ḥananel's *Commentary* and the "Spanish" *Halakhot gedolot.* He actually threatened to excommunicate all those who would follow his adversary's decision, and even tried to appeal to the community of Melun over the head of its constituted spiritual authority. But apparently Meshullam was not too seriously disturbed by either the threats or the appeal to his constituents. All this sound and fury notwithstanding, Tam himself would have admitted that the final decision should rest with the general community of scholars, who would either back him up or else accept the views of his opponent.[139]

LOCAL AND REGIONAL CUSTOMS

Another major corrective to the untrammeled imposition of views held by individual rabbis consisted in the general reverence for local customs. Rather than serving as an impediment to legal progress, such reverence actually promoted the constant adjustment of law to changing social needs. Already in antiquity it made possible the organic growth of law in the lesser Palestinian townships and throughout the ever expanding dispersion. As a direct continuation of the ancient Palestinian municipal courts foregathering at the city gates and publicly administering justice, the medieval communities continued to entrust to their local organs the passing of judgments in individual cases. Such democratic cooperation of the public in law finding and developing local observances was but slightly interfered with by the central appointment of judges by exilarchs and geonim in certain districts of Babylonia and its vicinity. Even there such appointees were recruited in consultation with local leaders, and mainly from among local citizens. Upon the latter's complaints they were removed from office. Even strangers, therefore, undoubtedly made it their business to acquaint themselves with the local usages, lest they antagonize their new constituents.

Customs in family relations, consumption of food, table manners, prayers, and other rituals, as well as in business, usually showed the greatest diversity and commanded the most tenacious adherence. Many such local differences between Palestine and Babylonia, and even between various regions in Palestine, have already been mentioned. This was also the tenor of Ṣemaḥ Gaon's reply to the community of Kairuwan, reassuring it that the customs reported by Eldad ha-Dani, though often at variance with accepted laws, need not be considered heretical. Time and again, when asked for advice by outside communities, the geonim could do no better than mention a custom prevailing at their academies, intimating that the questioners might wish to follow that example but not ordering them to do so. Only in exceptional cases did one or another gaon feel obliged to intervene against local mores. Hai once censured his questioners for allowing a bridegroom to pronounce the formula of marriage without simultaneously giving his bride a marriage or betrothal contract, a practice unheard of in Babylonia. "But in Khorasan for more than a hundred years there has existed the custom of wedding a wife by a ring at a festive meal or the like. The result was that there arose many quarrels, contentions, and even denials of the marriage." For this reason Hai's great-grandfather, Yehudah, had already ordained that they follow the Babylonian procedure and declared marriages without the simultaneous signing of a marriage contract null and void. Hai advised, therefore, that this system be adopted also in the questioners' locality. The geonim did not mind that, from ancient times, Palestinian Jewry preferred to marry on Wednesdays, while the Babylonians preferred Thursdays. But they sharply opposed a custom, prevalent in a Christian country (Edom, probably Byzantium), that allowed the weddings to take place on any weekday and be repeated on the Sabbath. Such proceedings invoked, a gaon insisted, the pronunciation of a superfluous blessing and taking of the name of the Lord in vain, as well as the imitation of Gentile customs, which is outlawed by the injunction "Neither shall ye walk in their statutes" (Lev. 18:3). It is much worse, he added, if they also break a cup on the Sabbath.[140]

As a rule, however, the talmudic sages had already learned to be tolerant of local diversities. Echoing a talmudic homily, Aḥai of Shabḥa glorified adherence to ancient customs by quoting Rab, or more likely Rabbi (Judah the Patriarch), who stressed the ancient proverb "Hear, my son, the instruction of thy father, and forsake not the teaching of thy mother" (1:8). Especially if a ritualistic act of supererogation struck the fancy of a pietistic observer, he liked to invoke it as a precedent to be followed. For example, in expressing preference for the recitation of the Sabbath *quiddush* blessing over wine rather than bread, Hai Gaon emphasized that former generations had toiled over securing the necessary wine. He admitted, however, that bread was preferable to other alcoholic beverages, because it was part of a meal. For this reason the geonim agreed that the *habdalah* ceremony on Saturday night could not be performed over bread, except when it was part of a holiday recitation connected with a meal. In their anxiety to find historic precedents, some geonim adduced traditions unsupported by any independent historic evidence. Naṭronai, for instance, was once asked about the propriety of worshipers gathering in synagogues on Sabbaths and holidays, studying and reciting Psalms for several hours, and only then starting with the regular services. Such preliminaries necessarily delayed the recitation of the morning *Shema'* beyond the prescribed period. The gaon decided that this was a good custom. He construed an historical hypothesis that, when the first Babylonian exiles had found themselves devoid of learning and busy with making a living, their prophets and teachers ordained that they foregather in their synagogues at early hours on Sabbaths and holidays and devote themselves to study. Apparently unfamiliar with this geonic decision, Rabbi Isaac bar Yehudah reported a homily which he had allegedly heard from Hai Gaon in the city of Rome (Hai is nowhere else recorded to have visited either Rome or Constantinople) to justify the "general" custom of people arising early on weekdays to go to synagogue for both study and prayer, as against the Sabbath, when they lingered in their beds much longer. Such contradictions were, of course, but rationalizations of different regional mores, so firmly rooted that even lesser authorities could easily invoke them. The geonim were cognizant, in particular, of the perennial divergences between Palestine and Babylonia, and even between the two academies themselves. Despite Pirqoi ben Baboi and others, who sought to attribute most of these differences to emergency measures occasioned by anti-Jewish persecutions, the geonim learned to accept them gracefully, so long as they did not affect any fundamentals of their faith and law.[141]

Some of these differences in customs reached back to remote antiquity and caused enduring cleavages among the geonim themselves. Even in such simple matters as a widow's support there had already existed a basic difference between ancient Jerusalem and Galilee, on the one hand, where husbands provided in their marriage contracts for their widows' permanent maintenance by the heirs, and the Judean countryside, where the heirs were given the alternative of paying a lump sum to the surviving spouses. This difference continued through the geonic ages in Babylonia where the areas under Sura's control accepted Rab's decision to follow the Judean custom, while Nehardea under Samuel's leadership generally adopted the Galilean usage. The growingly influential community of Baṣra, however, claimed that it did not necessarily follow the customs of either academy. Without resolving its quandary, Naḥshon Gaon argued that generally Nehardea's geographic limits were clearly defined, and hence its customs were restricted to that area alone, but the rest of Babylonia, embracing Baṣra, must act in accordance with the usage of Sura. At the same time he admitted that, according to a talmudic rule, in the domain of civil law we generally follow Samuel against Rab; doubly so in this case when an unnamed Mishnah had decided in favor of the

Jerusalem procedure. Baṣra was entitled, therefore, to accept either system. On the other hand, Sherira and Hai, while admitting the existence of such differences, argued with vigor for the adoption, in localities without a clearly defined local custom, of the Galilean-Nehardean-Pumbeditan usage. In Spain, on the contrary, Samuel ibn Nagrela decided to follow Rab and Sura.[142]

Generally, it required much self-restraint on the part of these authoritarian leaders to extend that modicum of recognition to local usages. They reluctantly approved even such strange observances as the *kapparot* ceremony before the Day of Atonement, a vestige of the old expiatory substitution of sacrificial animals for sinful individuals. A somewhat less obvious survival was a similar use of wrappers filled with plants some twenty or fifteen days before the New Year, a usage recorded only for the benefit of minors. Neither did the generally moderate Naṭronai Gaon wish to forbid the recitation of the *Kol Nidre* (All Vows) prayer on the Day of Atonement in those countries where it was practiced. He merely wrote in reply to an inquiry, "It is not customary at the two academies or any other place [in Babylonia] to dissolve vows on either the New Year's Day or the Day of Atonement. But we have heard that in other countries they recite 'All Vows and Abnegations.' Yet we have neither seen nor heard from our ancestors" about it. Such an answer clearly intimated disapproval without urging the recipients to desist. On rare occasions, however, especially when he wished to combat heretical trends, Naṭronai wielded the practice of the two academies as a weapon to overrule contrary usages elsewhere. He concluded, for instance, his aforementioned anti-Karaite responsum with the injunction to banish the opponents, "for anyone who does not observe our custom, does not fulfill his duty." [143]

A temperamentally less forbearing leader like Saadiah, engaged in a major drive to unify the Jewish people under the spiritual leadership of the Babylonian schools, was less kindly disposed toward the bewildering variety of ritualistic customs. After describing how, on his peregrinations through many lands, he had observed the great divergences in prayers and ceremonies, he condemned them as the result of "neglect, additions to, and omissions from" standard practice. To restore the pristine unity he wrote his great prayer book combining both prayers and ritualistic regulations. True, in his attack on Ben Meir, Saadiah himself did not hesitate to cite the usage accepted "by all the children of Israel in East and West, in the North and the islands of the sea," which had favored his point of view. But when an accepted ritual did not suit his philosophic preconceptions, he readily denounced it, as in the case of the conclusion of the prayer reading, *Ve-or ḥadash* (And a New Light Let Shine over Zion). The gaon objected to this formulation because the prayer refers to thanksgiving for the ordinary light shining daily, rather than for the new miraculous light of the messianic age. We shall see that even the great gaon's prestige failed to overcome the inveterate habits of the dispersed communities.[144]

In historic retrospect it appears that, apart from differences in personal temperaments, the changing status of the gaonate greatly affected its attitude to local customs. In the early period the main stress is laid on the "custom of the two academies," frequently invoked merely in order to abrogate one or another divergent local custom. Instead of thus expressing respect for local usages, this appeal to precedent became merely another vehicle for geonic hegemony over Jewish life everywhere. In the days of Hai, on the contrary, his genuine recognition of the autonomous validity of local customs clearly reflected the decline in central controls and the rise of independent cultural centers throughout the dispersion. Time and again this last of the great geonim insisted that "it is appropriate for each locality to adhere to its own custom." He frequently cited with approval Iranian usages clearly at variance with those of Babylonia. Understandably, statements like these were quoted with much relish by Ibn Gayyat and other rabbis who thus wished to reinforce adherence to their local customs.[145]

Postgeonic leaders had to be the more tolerant, as their own authority largely rested on the recognition of local diversity. Born and bred into particular sets of observances, they were also less likely to notice divergences from geonic norms and more prone to rationalize even customs running counter to talmudic laws. With the growing concentration on local, rather than international, trade imposed upon Jewish merchants by untoward outside developments in the eleventh and twelfth centuries, local business usages, too, had to be given fuller recognition. In his remarkable correspondence with Abraham of Baghdad, Maimonides defended the proposition that "one ought to permit people to do things as much as possible, and not to burden them with [unnecessary] prohibitions." He also believed that individuals imposing upon themselves restrictions because they erroneously thought them to be required by law ought to be taught that these were unnecessary acts of supererogation.

In general, the sage of Fusṭaṭ was an outspoken champion of ritualistic self-determination by communities and regions. Among the significant sources of law enumerated in his Code he included "the customs and ordinances which they [the sages] have issued or observed in each generation." At the same time he did not hesitate to invoke the Spanish or "Western" customs as guides for the proper behavior also of the Eastern communities. On some occasions, as we shall see, he was sufficiently provoked by the local practices to induce the communal leaders to issue remedial ordinances. When a custom touched one of his sensitive theological beliefs he unhesitatingly condemned it. Asked, for example, about standing during the recitation of the Ten Commandments, a custom frowned upon by the questioner himself as a mere survival of the Babylonian etiquette requiring congregations to rise in honor of heads of the academies, Maimonides confirmed these compunctions and added:

> It is indeed appropriate to hinder people from thus standing up wherever they are accustomed to do so. For from it may arise a detriment to the faith, as they may believe that one section of the Torah is superior to another, which is a very grave matter indeed. All gates leading to this corrupt belief ought to be shut. The argument of the other scholar [who was in favor of that custom] that the Babylonians are in the habit of doing it, is meaningless. For if we see sick people, we shall not on their account turn healthy people sick so that they be equal to one another, but rather try to make the sick equally healthy.

Not surprisingly, his son Abraham went further in this effort to outlaw "erroneous customs." Not having his father's wide experience and being formally invested with the office of Egyptian *nagid*, this mystically minded jurist insisted on the supremacy of the existing written norms. In one responsum, concerning the minimum marriage settlement for a wife, he rejected the combined authority of geonic decisions and local custom because he considered them at variance with the talmudic regulations. "We must not adhere to ancient customs," he declared, "if they are clearly built on air, but we must abrogate them and restore the people to the true path." Abraham was not quite aware of the irony of his own statements when on the one hand he gloried in the changes he or his father had introduced into the Egyptian observances, and on the other hand blamed some mistaken customs on recent "innovations." [146]

Such ambivalence toward established local mores is characteristic of the entire evolution of the *halakhah*. In the perennial conflict between the authoritative sources of tradition and the demands of a life subjected to varying environmental pressures, much flexibility had to be left to leaders in deciding which custom they wished to uphold, and which they deemed necessary to suppress. Occasionally they went to the extreme of recognizing the old principle that "custom uproots [formal] law." This was most frequently the case in Western lands whose novel ways of life could not readily be subsumed under the system of talmudic laws formulated under totally different conditions. The slowness and difficulties of communication, which converted most Western regions into self-sufficing units, as well as the corresponding growth of diverse customs and their legal recognition among the Christian neighbors, instilled there a healthy respect for local observances with which even the more self-assertive rabbis rarely dared to interfere.

Rashi was quite outspoken on this score. On one occasion he rejected a postulated aggravation in existing mourning customs by arguing, "The Jews are sages, sons of sages, and if they are not prophets they are sons of prophets. Hence their customs which they had learned from their fathers are parts of Torah, additions to, or subtractions from which are forbidden." On the other hand, he censured, for example, the newly arisen but ever more widely spreading custom of accepting payment in wine from Gentile debtors. This custom, meeting a growing demand of French-Jewish moneylenders, was justified by its protagonists because

Christians were not idolaters putting wine to sacrificial uses. Rashi, otherwise rather liberal in these matters, could not countenance such flagrant deviation from regnant law, since "that prohibition had spread throughout the world." But this exception merely confirmed his general rule of extending, wherever possible, full recognition to local usages. This was, indeed, one of the pillars of his school's entire approach. Most of the juridical monographs emanating from it are replete with records of local observances which, along with the interpretations of geonim and other authorities, were considered coequal sources of the law.[147]

Neither could Jacob Tam, despite his personal authoritarian proclivities, escape the impact of that trend. In his violent attacks on Meshullam he merely denied the existence of the customs cited by his adversary. At times he himself invoked opposing precedents, as when he wrote, "The custom observed by R. Hai was accepted by Gershom the Light of the Exile and our teachers in Bari and Lotharingia. This was indeed R. Solomon's [Rashi's] usage, and we rely upon these men." To be sure, in his major effort to unify at least all of Western Jewry under the aegis of the school of Rashi, he found himself often stymied by the perseverance of local divergences. While appealing to the communal elders of Melun over Meshullam's head, he implored them not to "turn our kingdom into separatist cliques [*agudot*], for all of us are nurtured from R. Solomon's waters." But he realized that such unification could be achieved only after properly balancing the fundamental unity of the universal rabbinic law in its reinterpretation by Rashi's school with the great diversity and richness of minutiae established by local customs. This quest for unity amidst diversity was, indeed, the all-pervading passion of Tam's life.[148]

Before long scholars felt the need of a fuller record of these regional diversities than could be included in comprehensive juridical works, where the literary sources unavoidably predominated. The great era of European custumals, both Jewish and non-Jewish, was to come in the later Middle Ages. But an early work of this genre was prepared by Abraham bar Nathan ha-Yarḥi ("of Lunel"), who lived at the turn from the twelfth to the thirteenth century. After extensive wanderings from his native

Provence to northern France and Spain, Abraham decided to record for the benefit of students of Jewish law the various customs he had observed. Unlike Saadiah, he considered them "all built on truth and stemming from the same living God." He therefore proceeded to register them and to try to find the reasons behind them.[149]

Abraham was a well-read, as well as a widely traveled, author. He quoted extensively from geonic and postgeonic letters; on one occasion he even translated a responsum by Saadiah from Arabic into Hebrew. But he combined the fruits of his readings with direct observation and folktales to exhort his readers to live a pious life, promising them heavenly and earthly rewards. To explain why worshipers repeat "Amen" after many benedictions, he quoted first Samuel bar Meir's reasoning that Amen stands for the two divine names of YHWH and Adonai, whose combined *gemaṭria* has the same numerical value of 91. "But I have found that each benediction resembles a signed deed which had not been certified at court, and hence can be denied. But once it is confirmed and certified [by Amen], one can neither add to, nor subtract from it." He also offered an interesting explanation for the custom of betrothing women with rings without stones, because otherwise the bride's acceptance might depend on her erroneous overestimate of the value of the stone. While mentioning the old custom not to marry between Passover and the Festival of Weeks, he made clear that this was not an outright prohibition, and that in northern France and the Provence one could marry during the last seventeen days (after *Lag be-'omer*). On his wanderings he had to rely on memory, and he often quoted his sources inaccurately; sometimes he even reported the same custom with considerable divergence in detail. He stated, for example, that it was "a custom not to pray with a bare head because of fear of the divine Presence," but soon thereafter quoted a would-be tannaitic source that one was in duty bound to cover one's head all day. Despite these deficiencies he presented to the reading public a well-written popular account of many customs and observances. With some justice he gave his book the rather ambitious title of *Manhig ha-'olam* (World's Guide), usually quoted in the abbreviated form *Manhig*.[150]

ORDINANCES

Notwithstanding the universal reverence for both custom and literary tradition, communities could make significant changes by way of new enactments. Even Ibn Daud, who in his Chronicle aimed at Karaite subversion stressed the unbroken chain of Jewish tradition, admitted that the ancient sages had also "enacted ordinances with universal consent [the *idjma'*] to build a fence around the Torah." The distinction between these sources of law are not to be drawn too sharply. Many customs undoubtedly had originated from local innovations by the conscious resolve of leaders whose names were no longer remembered. Asked about a benediction preceding the nightly recitation of *Shema'* recommended by the highly respected Joseph ben Yehudah, Abraham Maimuni condemned this usage. "These are recent innovations," he declared, "and in this way mistakes originate. They then become customs, which are upheld and defended by men of little wisdom." Abraham may have been wrong in this particular case, since such a blessing is recorded in geonic writings. But the fact that some communal ordinances turned into local customs as soon as their originators were forgotten, which often happened after but two or three generations, is indubitably true. The geonim unconcernedly spoke of "a custom introduced by a gaon"; for instance, by Zadok who, in lieu of imposing a fine, forced an assailant to seek an equitable compromise with his victim. Conversely, much that had started as a local observance was later attributed to a well-known figure. Even formal ordinances, enacted in the full light of history by some outstanding leaders acting in a public convention, often merely confirmed under superior sanctions what had long been practiced as a mere custom, sometimes one accepted by Jews from their non-Jewish neighbors. Nevertheless, the availability of this major instrumentality to alter existing regulations greatly added to the elasticity and dynamism of Jewish law.[151]

By virtue of their unique position in world Jewish life, the geonim sometimes issued ordinances which they expected to be universally followed. An early illustration is offered by a geonic responsum, preserved by Isaac ben Abba Mari. The expanding economy of the Caliphate had accelerated the process of Jewish urbanization and caused the gradual decline of Jewish farming. Under these circumstances, the talmudic regulations, which had made debts arising from commercial transactions or marriage contracts collectible only from the immovable property of deceased debtors, worked great hardships on lenders and widows. According to a responsum by Naṭronai, therefore, eighty-two years earlier (in 787)

> the judges of the exilarch and the two academies (the chief judges and the heads of the academies all) introduced the custom of collecting from the movable property [of orphans] the debts owed to creditors, as well as the marriage settlement and alimony provided in marriage contracts. They dispatched to all Jewish communities letters provided with the seal of the exilarch and the four seals of the authorities, ordering the removal of any judge who would fail to collect from movable property. They also issued the [requisite] blanket decree of removal. Thenceforth immovable and movable possessions were to be treated alike, precedence being given to respective claimants according to the same law.

This ordinance so clearly corresponded to social needs that it was widely adopted without demurrer, although the right of geonim to issue such binding regulations did not remain unchallenged. Maimonides recognized that this procedure had spread to most countries, but on legalistic grounds he praised the "Western" custom of inserting into the loan and marriage contracts special clauses authorizing the satisfaction of claims from both movables and immovables. For, he emphasized, a geonic ordinance had no power to abrogate a system introduced by the ancient Sanhedrin, and a debtor familiar only with the talmudic regulations might indeed object to such a change, unless he specifically committed himself to it in his own contract.[152]

Universality and duration of other geonic ordinances, too, depended on their relation to the existing social structure. Perhaps the earliest general ordinance was that enacted some time during the third quarter of the seventh century by Mar Rab Raba and Mar Rab Huna. It reflected the state of dissolution of the existing order after the rapid Islamic conquests. Formerly, a Jewish wife could not demand divorce from her husband, except in certain cases specified in talmudic law. Now, however, some women obtained the dissolution of their marriage vows with the aid of Gentiles, placing in doubt the validity of such "enforced writs of divorce." Moreover, some women left their husbands without being divorced, or even converted themselves to Islam. The two geonim decided, therefore, to force husbands through local courts to issue writs of divorce on their wives' demand after a brief waiting period, variously given as of one to four weeks. These "obstreperous women" were to receive, moreover, all that they had brought into the marriage, including compensation for property already expended, as well as the legal minimum of their marriage settlement, though not the extra payments promised them individually in the marriage contracts.

Although enacted as a generic ordinance without any expiration date, this new regulation was but an emergency measure intended to meet a particularly pressing problem. So profound was the reverence for the early heads of academies and an established practice of several generations that, according to Sherira, Hai, and Samuel ben 'Ali, the Babylonian courts still applied it half a millennium after its enactment. Many Western rabbis, too, including Gershom bar Yehudah, Samuel bar Meir and Isaiah of Trani, accepted it on geonic authority as binding law. More independent minds, however, severely objected. In a letter to his brother Samuel and the sages of Paris, Jacob Tam argued that there was a difference between this innovation and the geonic ordinance concerning the collectibility of debts from movables. "The geonim may indeed," he declared, "extend the rights provided in marriage contracts over movable property, be it on the basis of law or out of their own reasoning, because this is merely a financial matter. But from the days of R. Ashi to those of the Messiah we have no power to legitimize a legally void writ of divorce." Maimonides, too, merely restated the older talmudic law and added, "The geonim have reported that they have different customs in Babylonia concerning the obstreperous woman. But these customs have not spread to most Jewish communities, and many distinguished men in most localities have combated their views. One ought, therefore, to act and judge in accordance with talmudic law." [153]

Of course, in the perennial debates of the schools of higher learning the juristic technique as such likewise exercised considerable influence. We recall, for example, the differences of opinion between the two academies and among the rabbis of various lands with respect to the use of each Jew's ideal claim to four ells in the land of Israel as a means of transferring property. Even less uniform was the treatment of men condemned for capital crimes. While a geonic ordinance, indicated by Naṭronai and Sherira, demanded that murderers be subjected to rabbinic flogging and perpetual excommunication, a decision accepted by Maimonides and others, the geonim themselves were reluctant to adopt that procedure in the case of violations of the Sabbath rest commandment, a major capital crime in Jewish law. On the other hand, cases of actual execution of criminals, as in Spain, or of some form of lynching, were extremely rare and almost exclusively limited to such socially dangerous individuals as informers. On the whole, the distinguished jurists of the postgeonic generations never were at a loss to find arguments in favor of either adoption or rejection of geonic innovations in their own communities.[154]

Without the universal authority claimed by the geonim, the later rabbis, as a rule, issued proclamations of but local or, at best, regional scope. More overtly than their predecessors, they also sought the cooperation of other communal leaders. In most cases, to be sure, we do not possess the original enactments themselves, but merely some more or less brief summaries by later jurists. Only the ordinance, issued by Maimonides and nine associates in 1176, has come down to us in a fairly complete Arabic text and in a somewhat abridged and corrupted Hebrew version. Many Egyptian Jewesses of that period followed Karaite rituals in their postmenstrual ablutions and otherwise violated Rabbanite marital laws, often in concurrence with their husbands. The ten leaders enacted, therefore, a sharp ordinance demanding that such wives be instantly divorced without payment of the marriage settlement, and threatening cooperating or complacent husbands with the severe excommunication and confiscation of property. Although starting in an almost apologetic tone and mentioning how each member had long individually pondered over the best means to stem those abuses, they waxed eloquent about the dangers resulting from them for the entire Jewish community. But with perfect self-confidence they "proclaimed the major ban upon any court functioning in the whole land of Egypt which might not judge, and upon any scholar or student who might not teach, in accordance with this ordinance until the days of the Messiah." This self-assertiveness of Egyptian leadership may not be typical of all such enactments, however. It bears the earmarks of Maimonides' exceptionally strong personality. It also was a reaction to the serious sectarian inroads into the Rabbanite community, which had resulted in cases of intermarriage between the two sects, with the Karaite wife often reserving to herself the right of continuing to live according to the requirements of her own faith. Even the ordinances subsequently issued on Maimonides' initiative (1187) seem to have been written in a more moderate vein.[155]

Maimonides and the other elders knew, of course, that the ancient laws had not required the assistance of any specially qualified officials at weddings, and that even writs of divorce could be issued by any person familiar with the required textual minutiae. Yet they effectively threatened with excommunication all those who allowed unqualified persons to function on such occasions, although they would have been hard put to declare either a marriage or a writ of divorce null and void merely because it had run counter to their ordinance. Certainly, one of their main concerns was to maintain Jewish judicial autonomy and to forestall appeals to Gentile courts. Understandably, the local elders were not always sure how far they could go in enforcing these new enactments; some approached Maimonides himself for relaxation of the stringent rules. But the jurist-philosopher remained adamant and, on one occasion, enlisted the cooperation of two cosigners to enhance the force of his reply (*Resp.*, pp. 266 f. Nos. 295–96).

Curiously, the most important and enduring ordinance issued during our period is nowhere recorded in full, nor even in any direct quotation. Known as the main *taqqanah* of Gershom, the Light of the Exile, it peremptorily outlawed polygamy. Perhaps in the same connection Gershom also forbade divorces against a wife's will. Because the medieval rabbinate could not abrogate an unequivocal biblical-talmudic law, Gershom, too, had to use the roundabout way of placing all plural marriages under a ban. In the absence of detailed records, we know nothing about the date and particular circumstances of that proclamation, although the Mayence leader probably acted in collaboration with the community of Worms and perhaps also some of the other nascent centers in northern France and Germany. From the outset there may have been an escape clause for exceptional cases. In fact, our oldest records mention the previous outlawing of polygamy merely as an introduction to the provision that the excommunication "may not be suspended except by one hundred men from three countries and three communities. These men shall not agree to suspend the ban unless a cogent reason is given for the request, and unless the payment of the marriage settlement is assured either by cash or other guarantee." Among these urgent cases undoubtedly were those involving a wife's insanity or her conversion to another faith, when the husband was allowed by the concurrent action of a hundred men—later interpreted to refer to a hundred rabbis—to remarry without formal divorce.[156]

There are, however, some significant contradictions in the various reports, including those relating to the alleged expiration of that decree. According to a responsum attributed to Solomon ibn Adret but not extant among the several thousand of his known letters, published and unpublished, Gershom himself had set a terminal date for his ordinance at the end of the fifth millennium (1240 C.E.). If this report is at all true, Gershom may have included in his proclamation a phrase resembling that of the "perpetual" ordinance enacted by Maimonides, which demanded adherence "until the days of the Messiah." Such a formula is indeed quoted, in the name of Yeḥiel Ashkenazi, by the sixteenth-century Salonican rabbi Samuel di Medina in connection with Gershom's decree as well. Someone in Germany, believing that the sixth millennium would usher in the messianic era, may have interpreted this phrase to mean that the year 5000 A.M. was to be the terminal date, and so informed Ibn Adret. Be this as it may, none of the rabbis living closer to Mayence ever mentioned such a limitation. On the contrary, Asher ben Yeḥiel, who settled in Spain in 1303 a few years before Ibn Adret's death, admiringly spoke of the ordinances issued by Gershom as being "permanent and deeply rooted as if they had been given on Sinai." [157]

In itself Gershom's ordinance was no innovation in European Jewish life. Even in talmudic antiquity plural marriages were quite exceptional. They must have disappeared entirely in the later Roman and Byzantine possessions, where the law of the country specifically forbade all subjects to marry more than one wife. This system doubtless continued under Western Rome's successor states through the Carolingian era. Under the impact of Islam, however, some wealthy Eastern Jews may have wished to indulge, if not in regular harems or the permissible Islamic quota of four wives, at least in marrying another wife if the first mate was ill or barren. With the increase of Eastern Jewish immigration into Western lands and the spread of the Eastern literary sources clearly showing the permissibility of plural marriages, some individuals may have begun clamoring for their reintroduction into the Western communities as well. This demand now appeared more feasible as segregation between Jews and Christians grew tighter and Jewish leaders were given ever greater leeway in the management of Jewish affairs. Gershom and his associates may well have been prompted by such demands to reinforce the existing Western order and to threaten banishment of all would-be bigamists. While this situation can merely be conjectured, it appears that, mainly because it confirmed a long-existing practice, Gershom's ordinance encountered little, if any, opposition and was speedily accepted far beyond the range of his direct authority. Nor did his Western successors ever feel the need of renewing it. They were merely concerned with defining those exceptional circumstances under which it could be revoked by interterritorial Jewish action. Perhaps for this reason Eliezer bar Nathan, one of the earliest northern scholars to mention it (*Eben ha-'Ezer,* fol. 121a), does not call it by Gershom's name but merely speaks vaguely of "the ordinance of the communities."

In fact, Gershom himself may already have been mainly concerned about regulating these exceptions. Certainly, conversions to Christianity constituted a serious problem in his time, as he learned from personal experience with his son. Some married levirs may have wished to marry their deceased brothers' widows, while others doubtless wanted to secure offspring from other mates without divorcing their first wives. When the latter case was brought before Gershom himself, apparently because the first wife demanded divorce and the full payment of the marriage settlement, Gershom sided with the husband. He merely conceded that if the wife strenuously insisted upon divorce she must be granted one in terms of an "obstreperous woman." [158]

With the growth of ascetic trends in medieval Jewry, these monogamous postulates became ever more stringent. Eliezer bar Joel ha-Levi and several associates went much further than Gershom himself, and even denied some petitioners the remedial quest for an exemption by a hundred men. According to Eliezer, one Samuel bar 'Azriel of Mayence, whose childless wife had gone insane, appealed to an assembly of rabbis and laymen and on several occasions interrupted prayers in the synagogue seeking to force the communal leaders to release him from Gershom's ban. Eliezer and his associates consistently refused.[159]

Despite the ever provocative Muslim example, Eastern Jewries, too, succeeded in reducing polygamy to a minimum. They had to use, however, more indirect ways of making each husband insert into the marriage contract a pledge not to marry another wife during the bride's lifetime. An Egyptian marriage contract of this kind, issued in 1221 under the authority of Nagid Abraham Maimuni, is still extant. Of course, there was a major difference between such a voluntary contract and Gershom's ordinance, since in the former case, violation carried with it only the monetary penalties stipulated in the contract itself. Moreover, these were collectible only at the wife's demand, and necessarily resulted in the dissolution of marriage. Very likely many wives acquiesced in their husbands' actions rather than seek divorce in their old age. That is why an extension of Gershom's ban to the Eastern lands, in so far as it was voluntarily accepted by communities, offered more effective protection. Communal action was also involved in the ordinance issued by Maimonides for the protection of Egyptian Jewesses marrying foreign Jews. Invoking the old talmudic prohibition of marrying wives in different countries, which might ultimately lead to incestuous unions between children ignorant of their blood relationship, the sage of Fusṭaṭ and three associates ordained that thenceforth each foreigner wishing to marry an Egyptian woman must submit proof, or testify under oath, that he had no wife or else that he was divorcing her. Similarly, a foreigner leaving the country even with his wife's consent was to hand her a conditional writ of divorce, providing a time limit of up to three years for his return. After the expiration of that period his wife would automatically be treated as a divorcée and allowed to remarry.[160]

Other communal ordinances enacted by Gershom, though less spectacular, represented greater departures from existing norms. To favor local merchants Gershom provided that visitors, even those attending fairs and usually treated as a privileged class, must appear before local courts. They could also be subjected to the payment of local charitable dues around the Purim festival. Owners of lost objects could force officials to proclaim bans on anyone refusing to divulge information which might lead to the latter's detection. In still other ordinances Gershom forbade reminding repentant sinners of their former transgressions, "cursed" those who tampered with ancient texts, and delimited direct appeals to public opinion through the "interruption of prayers." More questionable is Gershom's authorship of the much-quoted regulation safeguarding the privacy of correspondence by forbidding anyone to read letters without the writer's or the addressee's permission. This regulation, often invoked by modern letter writers through a five-letter abbreviation on the envelope, is attested in an earlier geonic source. Possibly Gershom and his associates merely renewed the provision in terms of a ban, as the safeguards for the secrecy of the business exchanges under the Caliphate now loomed large also in the mercantile Western communities. Certainly the arbitrary fiscal policies in both areas made the unauthorized revelation of private transactions a grave menace to Jewish bankers and their clients. Gershom's generation also found it necessary to reinforce some old injunctions recorded only in the Palestinian Talmud, familiarity with which still was limited at best to small circles of scholars. (Even Eliezer bar Joel did not always have a copy at his disposal.) Worshipers were enjoined, for instance, not to leave the synagogue before the completion of services, a practice which must often have depleted the necessary quorum in the small Western communities.[161]

Besides these general ordinances, there was a plethora of local enactments intended to meet purely local needs. Some of these have been mentioned here as illustrations of Jewish self-governmental operations. A noteworthy local ordinance was adopted in Baghdad in 810, but half a century after the establishment of this great 'Abbasid capital. To assure proper wedding rites among Jews streaming into the new metropolis from various provinces, the exilarch and local elders of Baghdad, without the cooperation of the two academies which still were in Sura and Pumbedita, resolved that thenceforth all bridegrooms should recite the formula of betrothal close to the marriage ceremony. In cases of contravention, they threatened "to fine and punish the bridegroom, as well as the witnesses to the wedding, and the fathers of bridegroom and bride, to whatever extent will be necessary." [162]

One of the most remarkable communal ordinances relating to Jewish education seems to have been formulated late in the twelfth or early thirteenth century, but probably it was never enacted. It is preserved in an early copy written in 1309, and consists of statutory provisions concerning teachers, schools, their maintenance and curricula. Long known under the title of *Ḥuqqe ha-torah* (Laws of the Torah), it doubtless originated in one of the northern communities under the impact of Provençal mysticism or of German-Jewish pietism of the school of Yehudah the Pious and Eleazar of Worms. Among its remarkable postulates were the demands that every *kohen* and levite should consecrate one of his sons to the study and teaching of Jewish lore, and that each community should establish an academy for devotees who would spend all their time on study. "For just as one appoints synagogue readers to enable the congregation to fulfill its liturgical obligations, so one must provide for a permanent group of students dedicated to study without interruption, so that the congregation may fulfill through them its educational obligations." These devotees were to spend seven full years in residence at the academy. "There they shall eat and sleep, and not talk about irrelevant matters." To maintain such an establishment, all communal members were to pay 12 deniers annually, in lieu of the half shekel their ancestors had paid to the ancient Temple. Since we have no record of such a practice in any Jewish community, we must assume that these statutes were but the expression of pious wishes formulated in one or another pietistic conventicle, but never formally enacted by any communal authority.[163]

PHILOSOPHY OF LAW

Equipped with these various instruments of both legal progress and legal conservatism, the Jewish people continued to develop its traditional legal system in its ever more complex ramifications. Using various methods, the leaders reinforced the ramparts behind which the dispersed communities could freely cultivate their ancestral mores, as well as adjust themselves to the new conditions. Since even more than any other legal system Jewish law penetrated all nooks and corners of Jewish living, any review of Jewish socioreligious history must constantly refer to the legal sources of the period, the most numerous, detailed, and reliable records of Jewish experience during the High Middle Ages.

In most respects, medieval Jewry merely amplified and spelled out in detail the legal principles laid down by the talmudic sages. But, by using the new implements of systematization, classification, interterritorial correspondence, local and regional ordinances, and more modern methodology, it had to come to grips with fundamental logical categories and especially with the law's underlying rationalizations, which the ancient sages had unreflectingly taken in their stride. The general concepts indirectly emerging from the halakhic debates in the Talmud had for the most part been but the result of empirical law-finding according to well circumscribed juridical techniques. With the awakened scientific curiosity of the Islamic and "twelfth-century" European renaissance, however, and the progressively deepening quest for philosophic answers to the riddles of human existence, the very justification of law came under close scrutiny. This was particularly true of Jewish law, that core of Jewish life, for it had long been a major battleground in all debates with Christians and to a lesser extent with Muslims. While the attacks on the nomistic principle as such were now greatly diminished in virulence and frequency, many specific aspects of

Jewish law remained a permanent feature of religious controversy with non-Jews and Jewish sectarians alike.

Some basic answers were supplied by the great jurist-philosopher of Fusṭaṭ.

The general object of the law [Maimonides wrote] is twofold: the well-being of the soul, and the well-being of the body. The well-being of the soul is promoted by correct opinions communicated to the people according to their capacity. Some of these opinions are therefore imparted in a plain form, others allegorically; because certain opinions are in their plain form too strong for the capacity of the common people. The well-being of the body is established by a proper management of the relations in which we live one to another. This we can attain in two ways: first by removing all violence from our midst; that is to say, that we do not do every one as he pleases, desires, and is able to do; but every one of us does that which contributes towards the common welfare. Secondly, by teaching every one of us such good morals as must produce a good social state. Of these two objects, the one, the well-being of the soul, or the communication of correct opinions, comes undoubtedly first in rank, but the other, the well-being of the body, the government of the state, and the establishment of the best possible relations among men, is anterior in nature and time.

Halevi, too, considered the rational law "the basis and preamble of the divine law, preceding it in character and time," for it is indispensable even to a society of robbers. But only both laws together, as summarized in the Torah, could furnish true guidance for the pious man. Biblical-talmudic law was distinguished by its comprehensive nature, and because it regulated opinions as well as actions and thus safeguarded also the salvation of the soul. For this reason, Halevi declared, and because of its divine origin which removes it from the realm of human error and perdition, the Torah is far superior to any man-made constitution, however ideal, and ranks high above the Platonic "Laws" or "Republic." Even divine law, however, is essentially rational, according to Maimonides and most other thinkers, and hence one ought to try persistently to search for the inner meaning of each commandment. At the same time unreasoned obedience, especially on the part of the uneducated masses, was in itself a virtue. Ibn Daud actually saw the main value of the entire ceremonial law in that it offered an opportunity for such unreasoned submission to the divine will.[164]

Ibn Daud alone ventured to draw from this distinction the radical conclusion that the various parts of the Torah "are not equal in rank." In his opinion there was a definite difference between those relating to (1) faith, (2) morals and social life without which no society could endure, and (3) on the lowest level, certain ceremonies which even Israelitic prophets mentioned in disparaging terms. Needless to say that Ibn Daud did not suggest that the latter might be disobeyed with impunity. No such suggestion ever came from any medieval Jewish thinker. Writing with the exuberance of youth, Maimonides grew quite vehement in denouncing those who distinguished between "important" and "unimportant" matters in Scripture and drew a line between its "core and shell." In another context he defined the main sin of King Manasseh as having consisted precisely in that line of demarcation between "severe" and "light" commandments. According to the sage of Fusṭaṭ, "every one of the six hundred and thirteen precepts serves to inculcate some truth, to remove some erroneous opinion, to establish proper relations in society, to diminish evil, to train in good manners, or to warn against bad habits. All this depends on three things: opinions, morals, and social conduct." Even Baḥya and Abraham Maimonides, who most strongly felt the impact of Ṣufism's antinomian tendencies, never for a moment wavered in their staunch adherence to every tittle of the law of Scripture and tradition. By insisting on the "duties of the heart" they merely wished to counteract the widespread religious hypocrisy. They doubtless knew some Jews, of whom one could say what a Muslim slavegirl told about the Arab historian, Al-Haitham ibn 'Adi (d. 825), that he prayed all night and lied all day—and prayer was as much a duty of the heart as of the limb. Baḥya himself claimed that he had merely tried to restore the balance between the overt and the hidden behavior, so "that the testimony of heart, tongue, and the other bodily organs shall be alike, and that they shall support and confirm, not contradict or differ from, one another." He also advised the readers tirelessly to study the Torah, Prophets, liturgy, and words of the sages so as to find in them ever new insights. Abraham Maimuni reminisced that the Deuteronomic constitution (17:18–20) had enjoined the kings to immerse themselves in the study of Torah, which would both counteract their natural conceit and make them remember the laws.[165]

Intensive study of Torah appeared equally indispensable to Halevi, who insisted that the very "rational" laws could be detected by human reason only in their general framework, not in detail. If left to his own devices, every man would reach divergent conclusions. Only one who approaches God through the medium of His commands "knows their comprehensiveness, division, time, places, and consequences." Maimonides altogether repudiated the distinction between rational and irrational laws—a distinction first introduced into Jewish debates by Saadiah, though never consistently carried through by him. To the sage of Fusṭaṭ the assumption that God would enact irrational laws was the symptom of a diseased mind, although he admitted that in a few cases he was unable to supply their rationale. If he divided the commandments into fourteen classes and placed at their head the "fundamental principles," this classification may have faintly intimated, but it certainly did not spell out, any gradation in importance similar to that suggested by Ibn Daud. This basic equivalence of all commandments left little room for the sharp distinction between "natural" and "positive" laws, which was to play such an enormous role in medieval Christian scholasticism and in early modern political theory. Bearing in mind the old Greek doctrine, already adapted to Jewish needs by Philo, Maimonides declared pointedly, "The Law, though not a product of Nature, is nevertheless not entirely foreign to Nature." [166]

The idea of "natural law," though not altogether absent from the Jewish philosophy of Arab lands, did not become commonplace except later under the impact of Western scholasticism. It is barely hinted at in Maimonides' *Guide,* where the philosopher discusses the natural or innate sentiment prohibiting injustice. Characteristically, in his *Commentary* on the *Guide,* Don Isaac Abravanel endeavored to withdraw the distinction of good and evil from the realm of purely conventional and to subsume it under the "rational" laws. But this "Western" reinterpretation clearly went beyond the intention of Maimonides himself. Halevi, who, as we recall, distinguished between rational and divine laws, came closer to identifying the rational laws with natural law. However, even he could not escape the impact of the Jewish belief in the permanent validity of all laws only because of their revealed character.[167]

Not even the old rabbinic concept of Noahide commandments, which bears some resemblance to the idea of natural law, really fits that juristic category. In Halevi's opinion, if the Israelites in Egypt had possessed only a few laws "inherited" from Adam and Noah, these laws, too, had been revealed by God to the first men and were not discovered by them through their own reason or because of some natural compulsion. Moreover, Halevi added, "these laws were not abrogated by Moses, but rather increased by him." Maimonides stated it even more bluntly. "Everyone," he wrote, "who accepts the seven commandments and observes them carefully is one of the 'pious of the Gentile nations' and has a share in the world to come. But he must accept and observe them because the Holy blessed be He ordered them and announced through our teacher Moses that the children of Noah had previously been enjoined concerning them. If, however, he did it only on the basis of his own reasoning, he is not a *ger toshab* [semi-proselyte], nor one of the 'pious of the Gentile nations' or of their sages." [168]

Halevi's concluding remark was, of course, a dig at the Muslim and Christian contentions of the "abrogation" of Mosaic law. Although bent far more on internal apologetics, the medieval Jewish philosophers advanced ever new proofs for the immutability of Jewish law. Curiously, the argument that the divine will cannot be subject to change enjoyed little vogue among the Jewish thinkers, and it was expressly rejected by Ibn Daud. Similarly, Saadiah's contention that the Torah's perfection attests its immutability, for any change would indicate its imperfection before the alteration, attracted little following. Evidently, pressing such arguments to their logical conclusion would have imposed too many static shackles on the evolution of man and of Israel, and would have run counter to the indubitable historic fact of Judaism's progressive adjustments via interpretation of the written through the oral law. Nor did Ibn Daud's plea, that had Ezra introduced a new law, it would neither have been accepted by the people nor been preserved in substantially the same texts throughout the Jewish world, carry full conviction. It sounded too much like the Muslim doctrine of *idjma'*, which presupposed that universal consent of the masses was in itself proof of veracity—a doctrine dangerous, indeed, to a people in exile, staunchly adhering to its minority position. The best resolution of this inherent conflict was, therefore, to insist upon the immutability of the revealed text while admitting the feasibility of ever new discoveries in it of hidden truths.[169]

Such a compromise, however, did not quite lend itself to purely philosophic motivation. In the face of equally convincing philosophic arguments to the contrary, the Jewish thinkers had to fall back on dogmatic proofs, namely statements of the Torah itself concerning its eternal validity. In trying to dispose of no less than seven arguments in favor of abrogation, advanced even by some Jews claiming to have found in the Bible itself evidence for partial revocation, Saadiah resorted to a historic, rather than philosophic, demonstration. Long before Halevi he exclaimed, "Our nation of the children of Israel is a nation only by virtue of its laws. Since, then, the Creator has stated that the Jewish nation was destined to exist as long as heaven and earth would exist, its laws would, of necessity, have to endure as long as would heaven and earth." While the gaon invoked here the testimony of Jeremiah (31:35–36), Maimonides quoted Isaiah (66:22) to prove that "our religion, which gives us our special name, will remain permanently." Characteristically, this statement is imbedded in the Maimonidean discussion of the eternality of the Universe. Otherwise agreeing with Aristotle that the Universe is permanent and indestructible, the jurist-philosopher disagreed with respect to its beginning through an act of Creation. He had to admit, therefore, that the Creator also "has the power to change the whole Universe, to annihilate it, or to remove any of its properties." But he believed, on the basis of Jewish tradition, that divine wisdom had decreed that the Universe would forever retain all its properties "except in some instances." It was, therefore, in the ultimate sense, on account of tradition alone that Maimonides included the belief in the absolute immutability of the Torah in his thirteen principles of Judaism.[170]

Some inconsistencies, nevertheless, crept in. Obviously neither Maimonides nor his contemporaries were sufficiently history-minded to realize the numerous subtle changes gradually introduced into the whole fabric of Jewish law by changing social conditions. They noticed only the few outright innovations introduced by public ordinances. For example, the great transformation in Jewish life from ancient to medieval times, which arose from the conversion of a preeminently agricultural population into an overwhelmingly urban community, entirely escaped their attention. Believing that the social order familiar to him had always existed, Maimonides thus tried to explain the biblical differentiation between a robber, who was merely obliged to restore the property plus one fifth of its value in expiation for his sin, and a thief who, dependent on the stolen object, was forced to pay back two to five times its value. Instead of recognizing the historical difference between primitive law, which in ancient Israel, as in many other semiprimitive civilizations, sought to penalize cowardly stealthiness more severely than overt hold-ups, he argued that the biblical lawgiver had been guided only by the relative frequency of the two crimes. "Theft can be committed everywhere; robbery is not possible in towns except with difficulty." Following Alfasi's and Rashi's interpretation of talmudic law, Maimonides also favored a purchaser of land who wished to use that parcel for building a house, over a competitor who wanted to put it under cultivation. Jacob Tam went even further and, on the basis of the same talmudic passage, suggested that urban real estate be entirely removed from the restrictions imposed upon owners by the preemptive rights of neighbors. To such an extent did their predominantly urban orientation insinuate itself into the minds of the leading medieval jurists.[171]

More significantly, Maimonides himself could no longer defend the institution of sacrifices on rational grounds. Among Saadiah's contemporaries there had been some Jews—not only Ḥivi—who questioned the biblical legislation concerning sacrifices, the Tabernacle, or the contrary effects of the red heifer. The gaon took pains to explain these regulations in rational terms. Since "God does not require anything, but all things, rather, have need of God," the real objective of sacrifices was only to demonstrate man's submissiveness to the divine will, by his offering some of his most precious possessions. Here Maimonides took refuge in the simple historical explanation that sacrifices had been necessary for a time because, in the early stages of its development and in the face of the prevailing customs of surrounding nations, Israel had not been ripe for non-sacrificial worship. Though ignoring the specific problem of sacrifices, Baḥya had advanced similar purely historical reasons for the biblical enactment of ceremonial laws on a par with rational laws, as well as for the silence of Scripture concerning reward and punishment after death. These unusually modernistic explanations, quite in line, especially, with Maimonides' fine insight into the historic stages of the Mosaic religion, understandably did not gain universal acceptance. With all his deep reverence for Maimonides, Naḥmanides sharply rebuked his theory of sacrifices as "sheer nonsense." Halevi, in turn, looked for another historical explanation, namely, that sacrifices had served Israel as a means of ascertaining God's approval of its actions, through the visible sign of God's fire descending upon the altar. Even Maimonides, however, in codifying Jewish law, by no means eliminated the regulations concerning the sacrificial cult. If judged by his legal writings, one might even expect its restoration in the messianic age.[172]

In this way the eternality of Jewish law was subtly intertwined with the eternal existence of the Jewish people. Saadiah's contention that the Jewish people was a people only because of its adherence to the Torah had old and venerable antecedents in the talmudic and midrashic letters. But now this doctrine assumed new meaning for a people exposed to the strong assimilatory pressures of the Islamic Renaissance as well as to the powerful conversionist forces under Christendom, both Byzantine and Western.

FREEDOM OR "SURRENDER"

During the High Middle Ages Jewish culture became ever richer and more multicolored. Nevertheless the core of Jewish life and thought still was the traditional law in its theoretical and practical forms. Under its reign, the people weathered all sectarian onslaughts and maintained its unity and solidarity amidst diverse civilizations. A geonic responsum addressed to a Persian or Spanish community was cited as a valid precedent by judges administering Jewish law in Egypt or France. The daily life of any individual at home or in the synagogue, even in the market place, was largely controlled by that basic uniformity transcending all local variations, which, however, were allowed to persist. On the whole Judaism remained, therefore, the same monolithic entity it had become in the talmudic age, and its law served as both the most effective reflection of contemporary socioreligious realities and the main vehicle of historic continuity.

Not surprisingly, Jewish intellectual leadership was largely recruited from among the leading jurists of each age. The greatest exponents of other intellectual disciplines, apart from being also themselves students of Jewish law, bowed their heads in reverence before the outstanding halakhists of their generation. Yehudah Halevi, one of the greatest Hebrew poets of all ages, wrote some of his most eloquent poems in honor of the great Lucena teachers Alfasi and Ibn Megas, the latter his own younger colleague at Alfasi's academy. He showered upon them the then customary fulsome praise with far greater conviction than when he extolled some wealthy patron of arts. The greatest Jewish mathematician and astronomer of the Middle Ages, Abraham bar Ḥiyya (Savasorda), meekly reassured the Barcelona jurist Yehudah bar Barzillai that his astrological interpretations and predictions did not run counter to any accepted legal doctrine. True, in the latter case, Abraham may have feared reprisals on the part of communal organs represented by this Barcelona leader. In general, the combination of teaching of the law with authority in law enforcement, often vouchsafed by both the community's autonomous will and the provisions of public law, lent the jurists much political power. At times, indeed, such power could corrupt and develop in its administrators traits of intolerance and arbitrary rule. But, on the whole, the vast expanses of the Jewish dispersion and the declining central controls led to increasing democratization of the Jewish communities and the ability of the rabbis and elders to govern only with the consent of the governed. It evidently was wholehearted inner approval, rather than fear or quest of personal advancement, which dictated the appeasing tone of Abraham bar Ḥiyya's letter.

Outwardly this predominance of Jewish law did not seem essentially different from the analogous reign of law over all phases of Muslim life. Yet in both scope and application the two legal systems necessarily reflected the crucial differences between

Judaism and Islam. Islam is also an historical creed. It, too, is based upon the dynamic element of history's progress against nature. Like Christianity, however, Islam claims finality. No Jewish prophet (not even the Second Zechariah) has ever declared himself to be the last, because the greatest, of all prophets, as Jesus was the final Messiah and Mohammed the seal of all prophecy. This static element was increased by the political orientation of Islam, its predominant state idea. To be sure, its eternal—in fact unachievable—goal, the universal state, was anything but static. Before long there emerged, therefore, a sharp dichotomy between the ideal requirements of Muslim law and the practical needs of the state, which were often given precedence. Since, unlike the Jewish state, those under Muslim domination were an indisputable reality, the contrast between the ideal public law, as expounded by Al-Mawardi and others, and the existing legislations was often staggering. Even in civil law, the chasm between its ideal postulates and practical compromises caused, as we recall, many conscientious jurists to decline appointment to a judgeship. On the other hand, Jewish constitutional law was considered so purely academic, at least until the messianic age, that, though himself residing in Egypt while reformulating the "laws of the kings," Maimonides could unblushingly repeat the old provision that a Jew "is entitled to live anywhere in the world except in the land of Egypt" and cite three biblical prohibitions to this effect (*M.T.* Melakhim v.7–8). His readers were hardly pacified by the *tour de force* in his reasoning that residence in Egypt was at least not punishable by public flagellation. Few Muslims could so readily shrug off so obvious a discrepancy between their religious and constitutional law.

So long as the sword of believers conquered one country after another, the dynamic force in the Muslim religion triumphed over the static. As soon, however, as political expansion ceased and Islam had to struggle to hold its ground, the crystallized political organization at any given moment made the static element of statehood and space prevail again. The influence of the conquered territories, although Christianized by that time, added strength to the static principle, because so many ingredients of ancient Hellas and Rome had been carried over from the former age.

This political undercurrent found its expression also in the recognition of the Muslim's political duties as identical with his religious obligations. Controversial though it may be with respect to its origins, the term "Islam" essentially connoted to most of its followers something like "surrender," that is full unrestrained obedience to a superior power. God appeared here as the absolute monarch of an oriental state, only more absolute than any human monarch could possibly be. A Muslim's primary duty was to wield the sword in the service of God and his "Messenger." In Abu Bakr's famous proclamation, the entire Muslim community was rightly defined as "brethren in faith, partners in sharing booty, allies against the common foe." Fatalism became another fundamental principle of Muslim theology. Fatalism with its conviction of finality was but another sign of the dynamic yielding ground to the static. In contrast thereto, Judaism, by adhering to, and constantly modifying its traditional law, and submitting to its ever flexible controls by processes increasingly based on democratic cooperation, safeguarded the fundamental dynamism of its uninterrupted historic progression.

XXVIII

HOMILIES AND HISTORIES

NEITHER Western Jewry nor that under Islam ever limited its intellectual interests exclusively to the domain of law. Although because of its all-embracing character rabbinic law appealed to a variety of human needs and temperaments, the "imaginative faculty" of men, of which the medieval philosophers so frequently spoke, often sought an outlet in the realm of fancy. Interest in human behavior likewise extended beyond the realm of law, however broadly conceived. As in ancient times, the great rabbis themselves gave free reign to their homiletical and ethical propensities and cultivated the variegated and uncontrolled, but rich and multicolored, domain of Aggadah.

Social and environmental factors further stimulated interest in aggadic studies. Already in the late third century Isaac Nappaḥa, a Palestinian teacher, had attributed the increasing preference of the masses for discourses on Bible and Aggadah to the growing economic scarcities and governmental oppression. These factors had cumulative effects. Even in the more quiescent fourth century, when economic stability replaced the inflationary trends of the preceding century and the hostility of the newly Christianized Roman regime had only begun to unfold, the homiletical interests were gaining ground. Long before the conclusion of the Palestinian Talmud, the jurists of the Holy Land began playing a role that was secondary only by comparison with the shining legal lights of the Euphrates Valley. Leaving the field more and more to their Babylonian confreres, the Palestinian teachers now concentrated on those homiletical and biblical studies which so greatly appealed to the masses.

Nor must one minimize the impact of the Christian environment. The very circles which repudiated the Christian attacks on Jewish "legalism"—these attacks diminished in frequency and virulence as the Eastern Christians developed strong legalistic tendencies of their own—could not fail to be impressed by the

Christian emphases upon the dogmatic ingredients of religion. The dichotomy between the preeminently secular law of the Byzantine Empire, dealt with in secular courts and academies and deeply affecting the life of the average citizen, and the restricted canon law, which was of real concern only to churchmen, further limited discussions of legal problems in congregational assemblies. The more accustomed the general population thus became to listening to ecclesiastical sermons, embroidered with poetic imagery and based upon peculiar hermeneutic derivations from Scripture, the more did Jewish audiences, too, clamor for similarly appealing imaginative expositions of the Bible. The reverse was also true. Frequently Christian auditors felt attracted to Jewish preachers expounding the same Scriptures in a different vein; they evoked the ire of such ecclesiastics as Chrysostom of Antioch and Constantinople, and Agobard of Lyons. When subsequently Justinian altogether forbade the Jews to cultivate their "second lore" and thus outlawed all study of *halakhah,* he left enough loopholes open for the cultivation of the aggadic branches of the Oral Law, in both prose and poetry. It is small wonder, then, that Byzantine Palestine became the main center of aggadic studies, and that, for centuries after Mohammed, homiletical interests continued to dominate Jewish thinking in the Byzantine possessions in the Balkans and Italy.

The rise and expansion of law-centered Islam, to be sure, helped stem that trend. Now legal research, never equally neglected in Babylonia under the law-minded Persian civilization, reasserted itself as the supreme concern of the Jewish intellectual leaders. Yet even under Islam homilies remained a permanent feature of divine worship of all three faiths, and they entered manifold combinations with juristic explorations. In Baṣra, the newly evolving center of Arab learning and piety, preachers were expected to deliver sermons daily. The caliphs themselves felt obliged regularly to hold forth from the pulpit. A typical story is told about Caliph 'Abd al-Malik (685–705): Asked about the reasons for his premature aging, the monarch is said to have explained, "No wonder, every Friday night I have to match my wits with those of the people." Under the Faṭimid caliphs, especially, the royal sermon became a major affair of the state. Prepared by the official drafting department, the sermon was read or recited from memory by the ruler in person.

Byzantine emperors, too, occasionally occupied the pulpit. We possess, for example, eighteen published sermons by Leo VI, surnamed the Philosopher (886–911). An admirer of the "golden-mouthed" preacher of Antioch, the imperial homilist also echoed some of Chrysostom's attacks on Jews and Judaism. Before that time (692) the universal Council of Trullo (the so-called *Quinisextum*) had formally enjoined clerics to preach to the people every day, but particularly on Sundays, and ordered them to follow closely the patristic tradition and the exegesis of the Church luminaries and doctors. Unlike the Church, moreover, both the synagogue and the mosque also served as centers of secular life. Hence many a "secular" storyteller (*qaṣṣ*) usually found there attentive listeners outside the stated hours for services. In short, now that the pagan rhetor had given way to the Christian preacher and the Muslim *imam* and *qaṣṣ,* all speaking essentially the same jargon and utilizing basically the same hermeneutic arguments from Scripture, the Jewish homilists, too, found widely receptive, indeed eager, audiences for their sermons, as well as for the literary compilations of older and newer aggadot. At times itinerant preaching could be combined with salesmanship. From a story told, with minor variations, in several midrashim we learn that the third-century sage, R. Yannai, once heard a peddler, visiting the villages around Sepphoris, announce loudly, "Let anyone who needs it come and buy the elixir of life!" Summoned by the rabbi, the peddler at first refused to come, claiming that neither the sage nor any of his disciples required that elixir. On Yannai's insistence, he finally appeared and explained that he was merely trying to sell psalters, which he considered an elixir of life, for it is written, "Who is the man that desireth life? . . . Keep thy tongue from evil" (Ps. 34:13–14). Yannai paid handsomely for this illuminating explanation, admitting that all his life he had failed to comprehend the connection between the two verses until he was taught their meaning by the peddler-homilist.[1]

The fifth to the ninth centuries, far from being, as is often alleged, an era of intellectual sterility, were the heyday of midrashic literature. The same unruly but creative forces of the people which found an outlet in the sectarian religious quests also produced constant reformulations of the traditional teachings within the framework of orthodox Judaism. This growing popular interest also stimulated ever new compilations of sayings transmitted orally for untold generations. As in the juristic domain, there soon emerged more specialized interests which ultimately led to the flowering of several literary branches, all of them having their common ancestry in the talmudic Aggadah.

HERMENEUTIC ELABORATION

In contrast to the spokesmen of other faiths, the Jewish preacher often remained anonymous. From the outset the missionary and expansive Church invested the sermon, that most important vehicle of Christian mission, with a dignity second to none in its intellectual pursuits. Some of its greatest apostles, fathers, and saints were celebrated preachers, often remembered best for their homiletical works. No such recognition was granted to Jewish homilists.

True, from ancient times the rabbis, particularly the aggadists among them, praised the educational and liturgical values of the sermon. Even the author of Abot de-R. Nathan had interpreted the well-known dictum of R. Simon the Pious about the Torah being one of three mainstays of the universe to mean that "Scripture places a sage sitting and preaching before the public on a par with one who offers fat and blood on the altar." The compiler of a midrash on the Song of Songs reproduced several complimentary sayings about preachers. Almost at the outset, he quoted R. Judan's homily on Canticles 1:1 which "teaches you that he who expounds the Torah in public achieves that the Holy Spirit rests upon him." He also emphasized the sermon's missionary value. "When the old man sits and preaches," he declared, "many proselytes join the Jewish faith." Nonetheless, even such celebrated preachers of the talmudic era as R. Meir and R. Abbahu were revered principally as heads of academies devoted to the study of the law. Other rabbis, less gifted for, and perhaps also less interested in, preaching, were accorded no less public recognition. In the Muslim era, we hear less and less about a gaon or exilarch addressing public audiences. When they spoke, as during the *Kallah* months, they seem to have concentrated more on imparting legal information. Maimonides held the art of preaching in high esteem and, in one of his epistles, stated that a preacher should rehearse his speech at least four times before its delivery. But he himself seemingly never addressed public audiences. It is no mere coincidence that the first collection of weekly addresses compiled by a well-known rabbi, namely the *She'eltot* of R. Aḥai of Shabḥa (not formally the head of a leading academy), was devoted to the elucidation of the law in its all-embracing sense, including individual and communal behavior, as much as to aggadic problems.[2]

Halakhic exercises, however, could naturally satisfy only the legally trained élite. The masses of the population flocked to sermons of a theological and moralistic content, increasingly interspersed with parables and stories, which greatly enriched the ever more lengthy and cumbersome divine services. Before long there seems to have developed, from antecedents reaching back to remote antiquity, a class of itinerant preachers who, even if in command of but a limited repertoire, could cater to the appetites of diverse audiences throughout the vast expanse of the dispersion. One such itinerant Palestinian scholar, "profoundly learned in the law of God, a master of wisdom," was allowed, upon his arrival in Venosa, Italy, to address the local synagogue audience. "Every Sabbath," we are told, "he would give instruction and expound the Law before the community of the people of God. The master would lead with a discourse (on the selected portion of the Law), and R. Silano would follow with his elucidation." The preacher fell victim to a prank played upon him by jealous Silano, a poet in his own right. In retribution Silano was excommunicated by the Jerusalem elders, and he was not forgiven until Aḥimaaz, a local scholar and philanthropist, personally intervened in his behalf with the Jerusalem authorities. Such private preachers (one might call them lay preachers if the distinction between laity and clergy had been more sharply drawn in Judaism) and storytellers must have been particularly popular in the Near Eastern communities.[3]

Few, if any, of these discourses were fully recorded for posterity by the speakers or their disciples. Even in the highly literate twelfth century, Maimonides drew a sharp line of demarcation between a public discourse, for which he advised four rehearsals, and a book, which, he insisted, the author ought to review a thousand times before publication. The same reasons which had made the talmudic sages suspicious of committing to writing their legal interpretations operated with increased force in the vast and uncontrollable domain of aggadic folklore. Greek orators, both pagan and Christian, usually employed shorthand writers (*tachygraphoi*); Origen, for example, was provided by a wealthy friend with nine permanent assistants. In contrast thereto, the talmudic rabbis apparently refrained from writing down even the gist of their sermons before or after delivery and circulating such transcripts among interested readers. We possess nothing in the rabbinic literature even faintly resembling the large collection of sermons delivered by Chrysostom in fifth-century Antioch. Nor are individual sermons of some two to seven thousand words in length, the size of Chrysostom's homilies, recorded in any ancient or early medieval Jewish letters. At best we have a few incomplete epitomes of such discourses included in Aḥai's work or some exceptional midrashic compilations, but even these have suffered greatly in their transmission by rather careless scribes. Usually only one or another salient point, or particularly felicitous turn given to a biblical passage, was considered in academic circles worthy of literal transmission through the customary channels of effective memorizing.

A good case, to be sure, has been made for the use by some talmudic sages of written compilations of sayings by predecessors. Explaining his failure to show due respect to an elder colleague, R. Ḥiyya told R. Judah the Patriarch, "I was looking then at the Aggadah of the book of Psalms." Though himself a prominent aggadist, R. Joshua ben Levi had condemned the written Aggadah and declared, "He who writes it down, has no share in the world to come, he who preaches it gets burned [is excommunicated], and he who listens to it receives no reward." Yet he admitted that, after first consulting a "book of Aggadah," he found therein a worth-while interpretation which he proceeded to quote at length. Curiously, that particular homily betrayed the preachers' keen interest in both Masorah and numerical symbolism and stressed the parallelism between the number of Pentateuchal sections, psalms, and *halleluiahs* and the respective ages of Abraham, Jacob, and Aaron. R. Johanan and R. Simon ben Laqish finally yielded to popular pressure and authorized the writing and circulation of such works. From that time on, and still more in the posttalmudic period, midrashic letters, poetry as well as prose, grew by leaps and bounds and soon outnumbered all other literary productions.[4]

After a lengthy debate initiated by Zvi Chajes, Zacharias Frankel, and others, there has emerged something like a consensus of scholarly opinion that the early objections to "books of Aggadah" were aimed only at heretical writings. Since, however, the talmudic sources, otherwise quite vocal wherever they suspect heresy, are completely silent on this score, it is more probable that the rabbis basically objected to the uncontrolled perpetuation of possibly erroneous teachings. Their fears that cumulative mistakes in written compilations might lead to sharp disagreements and internal splits were fully borne out by the ultimate anarchical variety of inaccurate, contradictory, and even completely false aggadic traditions. Nevertheless, in time, the need for recording both the legal and aggadic discussions became overwhelming. Remembering the general rabbinic interpretation of the psalmist's verse "It is time for the Lord to work; they have made void Thy law" (119:126) as tantamount to an injunction to alter the law whenever it conflicted with the urgent needs of the people, the Palestinian Amoraim of the third century and their successors gave up their opposition to written midrashim.

On the whole, these written summaries may have referred to aggadic annotations by students of the Bible as frequently as to teachings originating from public discourses. In the case of R. Meir, we are expressly told that his copy of the Pentateuch contained a number of brief aggadic notes, from which later rabbis quoted some telling passages. His famous pessimistic pronunciamento, "It was very good [*me'od*], that is death [*mot*]," came from such a scribal pun on Genesis 1:31. Not only was the borderline between midrash and commentary never sharply drawn, but ancient Jewry had already developed an intermediary form called *pesher,* as in the Dead Sea Scroll of Habakkuk, which was rightly defined as an inspired commentary relating the biblical text to contemporary events.[5]

Although this entire literary output was too small to arouse the professional interest of booksellers such as greatly aided in the distribution of pagan and Christian oratorical works, Jewish audiences were not spared the attribution of recent works to ancient and revered authors, that most vicious by-product of ancient and early medieval book trade promotion. With its deeply ingrained reverence for tradition, the Jewish people had long created an extensive apocryphal literature, parts of which had allegedly been fathered at the dawn of human history by such "authors" as Enoch or the Israelitic patriarchs. Some of the newer works of popular fancy, too, written in the later geonic period, were called by the names of biblical heroes, such as the "Book of Shem, son of Noah," the "Death of Moses," the "Book of Zerubbabel," or "Mordecai's Dream." There also existed, as we shall see, a "Scroll of Hasmoneans" (or "of Antiochus"), as well as an "Alphabet of Ben Sira" and other compilations relating to events and personalities of the Second Commonwealth. With the growing popularity of the talmudic sages, however, more and more writings of this genre were now attributed to well-known tannaitic authorities. Significant Jewish reactions to the Muslim conquest of western Asia were reflected in aggadic works ascribed to R. Eliezer ben Hyrcanus and R. Ishmael. Other rabbinic grandees like R. 'Aqiba or R. Simon ben Yoḥai, as well as such distinguished ancient homilists as R. Joshua ben Levi, were claimed as authors of many later and often more obviously spurious works.[6]

Sometimes attributions of this kind sprang from simple mistakes. For example, an ancient rabbi's utterance opening a particular collection often sufficed to persuade uncritical and more than willing readers and copyists that that rabbi was the author of the entire product. At times, however, such mistaken identities were fruits of conscious fabrication. Even without the stimulus of the aforementioned canon 19 of the Council of Trullo, which enjoined Christian preachers to follow the homilies of Church Fathers rather than to invent their own sermons, Jewish writers likewise preferred to hide behind the cloak of some great name, rather than appear suspect of unorthodox "innovations."

Nor was outright invention of ancient heroes necessarily absent from Jewish literature, any more than it was from contemporary pagan and Christian letters. Just as "Eusebius" of Alexandria was to become the subject of heated debates among modern students of patristic literature, so did, for example, the significant midrash *Seder Eliyahu,* known under a variety of names all referring to the authorship by one Elijah, cause much controversy among modern historians of the Aggadah. To make matters worse, a *Seder Eliyahu rabbah* and a *Seder Eliyahu zuṭa* are mentioned in genuine talmudic sources (they were allegedly taught to R. 'Anan, a pupil of Rab, by the prophet Elijah himself), while our text of that midrash expressly refers to nine centuries since the destruction of the Temple (968) and to the world's existence theretofore during ninety-four jubilees and forty-four years, or 4744 A.M. (984). Elijah is, moreover, occasionally spoken of in the third person in the text of that midrash—and not by virtue of a literary device akin to Caesar's. Yet it is at least possible that parts of the midrash included in the present compilation go back to an ancient author named Elijah and that only later readers confused him with the great prophet.[7]

Less doubtful is the pseudepigraphic nature of *Midrash Agur.* Apparently at first connoting merely a midrashic anthology, this compilation was soon attributed to an author named Agur ben Jakeh mentioned in Proverbs 30:1. This writer had long been identified with King Solomon (the alleged author of the whole book of Proverbs) and Kohelet, since all three names could indicate the idea of gathering stray items and, more remotely, the idea of peace.[8]

Many of these compilations are arranged as running homiletical commentaries on biblical books. Most radical was the procedure of some authors of the Palestinian Targum who, under the guise of a translation, gave an entirely new and vastly expanded midrashic paraphrase. Such an allegorical "version" is the sixth- or seventh-century Targum of the Song of Songs, which, accepting the rabbinic view of this immortal love song, converted it into a paean on the history of the Jews from Moses to the messianic age. Regular midrashim could be somewhat more selective and comment only on individual passages of their choice. Next to the Pentateuch, the liturgically significant Psalms and Five Scrolls lent themselves most effectively to hermeneutic elaboration, not only because of their content, but also because they offered quotations directly relevant to sermons on certain holidays.[9]

Jews living in Christian countries found themselves under curious restraints. According to Origen and Clement of Alexandria, contemporary Hebrew teachers refused to instruct their pupils in the story of creation at the beginning of Genesis, the vision of the Chariot at the beginning of Ezekiel, and the concluding chapters of that book and of the Song of Songs. The former two subjects, constituting the core of Jewish cosmogony and cosmology, had indeed long been restricted by rabbinic legislation. But the two sections dealing with Ezekiel's blueprint for the Temple and the exaltation of love became difficult subjects to teach only because they had begun to be interpreted by both the Synagogue and the Church as relating to the mystical Jerusalem on high and the love between God and Israel, or the new Israel (the Church), respectively. We have a curious confirmation of the reluctance of Jewish homilists to elaborate on the allegorical theme of the Song of Songs in a homily reproduced by a thirteenth-century Judeo-Arabic commentator on that biblical book. According to this writer, one ancient rabbi (Isaac Nappaḥa) had compared the reading of the Song with bearing false witness, while another sage (Zedekiah) had explained the prohibition by the parable of a slave girl who killed her queen and, clad in royal vestments, tried to convince the king that she was his legitimate spouse. All these were, of course, but veiled polemical allusions to the Judeo-Christian controversy in regard to the Song. In general, rabbinic opinion permitted the ordinary study and recitation of that immortal poem, but discouraged the homiletical elaboration of its mystical content.[10]

Other biblical books were not entirely neglected, however. Ultimately a twelfth- or early thirteenth-century German author (Simon Qara?) was able to compile, from older sources, a running midrash on the entire Hebrew Bible called the *Yalquṭ Shime'oni* (Simon's Anthology). We may discount Marcus Horovitz's exaggerated comparison of this vast aggadic collection with the Maimonidean codification of the law, and yet admire its comprehensiveness and discernment which rightly made it one of the most popular works of the period. Identifying our author with

R. Simon an der Pfort (perhaps so designated because of the location of his house near the fish gate of Frankfort), Horovitz also applies to him the popular adage, "Rabbi Simon an der Pfort kann die ganze Thora auf ein Wort." However, Qara's authorship has often been disputed. The compiler's remarkable erudition is attested by his quotations from more than fifty aggadic works, some of which are no longer extant. He also often had better recensions than are now available. In fact, it is a testimony to both the assiduity of the German book collectors of that time and to "Simon's" prolonged quest for all pertinent primary sources that he was able to assemble these rich materials. That he refrained from citing the Targumim is not surprising. Since he largely followed the scriptural sequence, interested readers were able to consult any of these translations and paraphrases. More astonishing is his extremely parsimonious use of the mystical midrashim, including the renowned *Hekhalot* literature. Perhaps this was his way of protesting against the great influence of the pietistic circles on the German Jewish public. On the other hand, this very aloofness may have been coresponsible for the relative neglect of his work by scholars of the next several generations. In subsequent more quiescent periods, however, his book often became a *vade mecum* for both students and homilists.[11]

While this entire literature retained much of the character of homiletical commentaries on Scripture, there was no lack of collections which more directly mirrored their origin from sermons delivered on special Sabbaths and holidays. This practice, doubtless going back to remote antiquity, influenced the Church, which greatly elaborated the solemn orations delivered by high ecclesiastics on holidays and other festive occasions. The Church's example may well have reciprocally influenced the medieval Jewish audiences. The *Pesiqta de-R. Kahana* (extant in two different versions) and the *Pesiqta rabbati,* the two outstanding literary summaries of these addresses, follow the order of the holidays and the intervening Sabbaths with their respective lessons from the Pentateuch. The original arrangement probably began with the New Year, but subsequent copyists often rearranged the sequence to suit their own needs. Buber's edition of the older *Pesiqta,* for instance, begins with summaries of sermons related to the Sabbath of the Ḥanukkah week, the preachers taking their cue from the Scriptural passage that Moses had "made an end of setting up the tabernacle" (Num. 7:1 ff.). This passage was perfectly appropriate for the celebration of the Maccabean rededication of the Temple. The sermon itself could be more or less loosely connected either with that crucial passage or with the main theme of the holiday. At times Moses' building of the tabernacle could even assume cosmic significance, as it did, according to Kahana, in the mind of the famous homilist R. Isaac.

It is written [R. Isaac taught], "The righteous shall inherit the land" [Ps. 37:29], but where will the evildoers be? They will be suspended in the air. But what is the meaning of "And dwell [*Ve-yishkenu*] therein for ever" [*ibid.*]? It means that they will cause the *Shekhinah* [divine presence] to dwell [*Ve-yashkinu*] in the land. For the original locale of *Shekhinah* had been among the lower beings, but when Adam sinned, it moved up to the first heaven; when the generation of Enosh arose and sinned, it moved further to the second heaven [and so forth to the seventh heaven as a result of the sins of the subsequent generations]. Against these men arose seven righteous men [Abraham, Isaac, Jacob, Levi, Kehat, Amram, and Moses] and brought it back to earth. That is why it is written, "And . . . Moses had made an end of setting up the tabernacle."

Only rarely, however, is the author of the homily mentioned by name. Even when the name of Tanḥuma precedes a homily, as it frequently does, it is merely an indication that the passage was quoted from an earlier collection by the renowned compiler of agadic works bearing that name.[12]

LITERARY RAMIFICATIONS

Since most of the present collections merely epitomize sayings on particular biblical passages attributed to various authors, it is difficult to reconstruct the original spoken and literary form of the old rabbinic sermon. Nevertheless, some summaries betray essential similarities with the threefold division of the Graeco-Roman oration and the Christian homily. Even in the talmudic age Greek orators, carrying on the traditions of the great masters of ancient Greek rhetoric, must have impressed their immediate Jewish neighbors in Palestine or Babylonia, and still more so in the

Hellenistic dispersion. Many rabbinic homilies do, indeed, contain vestiges of an introduction (*prooemion*), a main theme (*diegesis,* often through broad elaboration, the so-called *diaskeué*), and an epilogue. The latter usually is very brief and consists merely of a eulogy of the divine government of the world, or a reference to the messianic future. In most midrashic collections, to be sure, the proems, and still more frequently the epilogues, were omitted or independently summarized by later compilers who, as a rule, were interested only in the gist of the homily or some pithy excerpt. The obviously loose, often wholly artificial, connection between these appendages and the main body of the sermon greatly facilitated their elimination from most subsequent anthologies.

Nonetheless this threefold division of Greek rhetoric and Jewish sermons in turn greatly influenced the evolution of Christian homiletics. If, as has long been recognized, Byzantine preachers followed patterns developed by the "ingenious Syrian," Ephraem, we must not lose sight of the latter's great indebtedness to Jewish prototypes. We possess some lengthy proems (*petiḥot*) lending a characteristic hue to certain posttalmudic midrashim. For example, the relatively old midrash on Lamentations called *Ekhah rabbati* (probably completed in the fifth or sixth century, though containing some later interpolations), opens with thirty-four (originally probably thirty-six, the numerical equivalent of *Ekhah*) introductions quoting numerous talmudic sages from R. Eleazar ben Azariah to R. Tanḥum bar Ḥanilai (first to third centuries and beyond). Each proem begins with an ancient scholar's interpretation of some biblical phrase or other, but invariably leads up, directly or indirectly, to the main theme of Lamentations. This literary form became so popular that it seems to have been used even in purely academic discussions. Some proems may indeed have been but opening remarks for a hermeneutic debate at the seat of the academy.[13]

On the other hand, some public discourses were entirely devoted to the hermeneutic elaboration of biblical verses as such, the speaker often suggesting a long series of alternate interpretations of the same verse or phrase. These interpretations may have been culled from predecessors, whether or not mentioned by name, or they may have been original with the preacher. While we have no record of a Jewish exegete paralleling the eighth-century Muslim lecturer who, according to Jaḥiẓ, had spent several weeks in explaining a single verse in the Qur'an and required forty-six years to go over the whole book, there undoubtedly were learned Jews who could equal that feat. Certainly many could match 'Ubaid-Allah al-Azdi's achievement of compiling one hundred and twenty different interpretations of the well-known Qur'anic adage, "In the name of God the merciful and compassionate." Most of the older midrashim, beginning with *Genesis rabbah,* are to a large extent but summaries of some such ambitious exegetical efforts. This method, although apparently less popular among Greek rhetoricians (despite their equally unbounded reverence for Homeric texts), remained the mainstay of Jewish homiletics before and after the rise of Islam.[14]

None of the extant midrashim reproduces fully a discourse of either kind. That is why exhortations to the audience, the usual purpose of sermons, are often implied rather than recorded verbatim. Even the *Pesiqta rabbati,* which more than any other early midrash has preserved lengthy excerpts from the original sermons (for this reason it is recommended by its editor, Meir Friedmann, to the special attention of modern preachers), includes but few hortatory passages like the following based on an ingenious exposition of Hosea 14:2, and Deuteronomy 4:30–31:

> "Return, O Israel, unto the Lord thy God." [Five things bring forth] the redemption: Because of his *distress* man is saved [as it is written] "in thy distress, when all these things are come upon thee." Also because of the [predetermined] *end,* that is "in the end of days." Also because of *repentance,* for "thou wilt return to the Lord thy God." Also because of [the divine] *mercy,* "for the Lord thy God is a merciful God." Also because of the *merit of the fathers,* [for God will not] "forget the covenant of thy fathers." Repentance is indeed the source of both mercy and the merit of the fathers. That is why Scripture says, "Thou wilt return to the Lord thy God," immediately followed by, "For the Lord thy God is a merciful God." Well then, let us return to Him, for there is no God like Him who takes us back whenever we repent from sin [XLIV, fol. 184b].

This exhortation was, appropriately, delivered on the Sabbath of Repentance before the Day of Atonement.

These hermeneutic elaborations were by no means intended to replace, or in any way to deprecate, the ordinary meaning of the Bible. Long before Origen contrasted the body of Scripture with its soul and spirit and recognized the independent value of each, the rabbinic sages believed in the essentially complementary function of their three parallel approaches to the ordinary meaning of the text (*peshaṭ*), the hermeneutic derivative (*derash*), and the hidden mystery (*sod* or *remez*), often hinted at by a single letter or another minutia. Among the accepted thirty-two (or rather thirty-three) modes of aggadic interpretation, the last eight consisted of (1) parable, (2) (allegorical) intimation, (3) correspondence with some other idea, (4) *gemaṭria,* (5) transposition of letters, (6) *noṭariqon,* (7) unusual sequence in the same context, (8) unusual sequence in scriptural sections. The posttalmudic era, especially, became extremely creative in the production of midrashim and, as we shall see in a later chapter, of esoteric writings as well.[15]

Methodologically, the newer midrashim differed little from the patterns developed in the tannaitic era. Notwithstanding the growing uniformity of biblical texts and their official translations, preachers still suggested alternate spellings or pronounciations of scriptural words in order to draw certain conclusions from the new readings. Of course, by using the formula *al tiqri* (thou shalt not read thus, but thus), they did not intend to impugn the authenticity of the accepted version or to propose emendations along the lines followed with relish by modern critics. They merely toyed with the richness of Hebrew vocabulary, which, by a slight turn, could yield entirely new implications. They, and especially the mystics among them, also interpreted certain words or phrases as if they were abbreviations, each letter representing an independent word. By using such a *noṭariqon* the preacher could easily read into the text unsuspected new meanings. Time-honored folk etymologies, sometimes based on rather remote but like-sounding words in a foreign language, and conceptual analogies derived by ingenious *gemaṭrias* from coincidental numerical values of Hebrew letters, continued and even increased in vogue during the Middle Ages.[16]

Medieval preachers made equally extensive use of parables and proverbs. *Mashal le-mah ha-dabar domeh* (a parable which illustrates our subject) became a standard tool in the equipment of Jewish homilists. Storytelling was, of course, an ancient art, reaching back to prehistoric times. With the growing literacy of the Graeco-Roman world, however, its influence and pecuniary rewards greatly declined, at least in the more advanced communities. During the early Middle Ages, on the other hand, it revived again in ratio to the diminishing literary output and the increasing concentration on religious topics. To satisfy the public's craving for picturesque narrations, Christian authors developed an ever more popular hagiographic literature devoted to eulogistic biographies of saints and martyrs. Preachers, too, made extensive use of these dramatic sagas, especially in sermons delivered on days commemorating individual saints. This ritualistic stimulus was largely absent from the ancient and early medieval synagogues, and was replaced in part by national days of mourning or rejoicing. The Ninth of Ab and Ḥanukkah, in particular, lent themselves to effective dramatization. Judah the Patriarch had already developed twenty-four homiletical themes on the destruction of the Temple. He was surpassed by R. Johanan, who produced sixty variations of this mournful subject. Later homilists greatly expanded these themes, and before the end of the first millenium produced two independent collections, called *Midrash Ekhah rabbati* and *Midrash Ekhah zuṭa*. The latter clearly originated from some synagogue recitals. Its first twenty-eight chapters give the impression of a connected sermon delivered on that fast day, ranking second only to the Day of Atonement.[17]

Exaltation of the Maccabean dynasty had long given way to that of the Maccabean martyrs, and hence became more appropriate for a fast day than for a week of rejoicing. Before long the entire martyrology was transferred from the days of the Maccabean revolt to those of the fall of Jerusalem, or even of Bethar. The *Megillat Bene Ḥashmona'i* (Scroll of the Hasmoneans), though puny in comparison with the compilations on the book of Lamentations, is, like the *Ḥalom Mordekhai* (Mordecai's Dream), extant in a vocalized text, evidently because both were used in synagogue services. Recitation of the former is, indeed, expressly mentioned by the eleventh-century Italian jurist Isaiah ben Mali of Trani.

In all these cases the preachers had to strain their imagination to embellish the stray biographical data of Jewish heroes recorded in Bible or Talmud by a multitude of dramatic details.[18]

FREE FLIGHTS OF FANCY

If Christian martyrologies and eulogies of saints thus stimulated also among Jews the spinning of ever new yarns on exalted biblical figures or celebrated Tannaim, the expansion of Islam resuscitated the ordinary, secular narration, buttressed by the growing glorification of the Arabic language and poetry of the ancient Bedouins. Although Jewish storytelling could hardly become as lucrative a profession as that of the Muslim *quṣṣas,* dramatic narratives increasingly crept also into the newer aggadic midrashim.

With the age-old Jewish proclivities for glorifying biblical personalities, it was natural for storytellers, too, to weave many of their tales around some well-known person or incident recorded in Scripture. This old practice, reinforced by Mohammed's frequent encounters with Jews embellished in the *ḥadith,* led to the development of a new branch of Muslim literature, the so-called *isra'iliyat.* Before long the talmudic sages themselves attained the stature of national heroes. Already the *Ekhah rabbati* is filled with many figments of popular imagination, some of which have been much too seriously treated by modern scholars. Apparently inspired by the reading of a *hafṭarah,* a later preacher elaborated the biblical story of Elisha's good deed for the impoverished widow (II Kings 4:1–7) into a regular storiette of "rags to riches," via the miraculously inexhaustible flow of oil from a pitcher. Similarly, the fact that a collection of rabbinic sayings began with a quotation from a proem by R. Eliezer sufficed for an aggadic compiler to designate the entire midrash the *Pirqe* (Chapters of) *R. Eliezer.* He prefaced it with two chapters describing the allegedly bitter struggle of this scion of one of the wealthiest Jewish families of the first century to secure good rabbinic training, which is but tangentially hinted at in the older, more authentic biographical records. Finally, some midrashim consisted exclusively of more or less edifying or amusing tales. For example, the so-called "Story of R. Meir," describing in vivid detail the hero's seduction in a state of inebriation by the second wife of his host and the subsequent penance imposed upon him by the "head of the academy in Babylonia," would have been a most fitting subject for Boccaccio.[19]

Very frequently an ancient tale or saying served as a peg for elaborate narratives. The memory of Sirach's pithy epigrams, for example, was sufficiently alive in the early Muslim period for an unknown compiler to assemble some twoscore newer popular sayings and proverbs, to arrange them alphabetically, and to spin around them lengthy stories. This concoction, known as the "Alphabet of Ben Sira," bore but the remotest resemblance to its famous prototype of the second pre-Christian century. In the introduction, the story of Sirach's birth from Jeremiah's daughter is told in a strangely syncretistic vein, combining the Christian belief in immaculate conception with Parsee exaltation of incestuous unions. The name of Ben Sira was evidently used to increase the prestige of these rather vulgar and uninspired tales among gullible readers. Even Maimonides was prepared to condemn, on this score, the works of Ben Sira together with many others "which neither possess wisdom nor yield profit for the body, but are a sheer waste of time." Such authoritative disavowals, incidentally, did not prevent Peter of Cluny from citing this storybook as an example of the inferiority of talmudic letters.[20]

Besides parable and story, the midrashim had an extremely varied content. Unlike the Christians of the patristic period and after, talmudic and early posttalmudic Jewry developed no specialized literature devoted to dogmatic and ethical subjects. The Aggadah absorbed practically all the intellectual energies of the Jewish people, outside the domains of law and Masorah, until the rise of the rich and variegated scientific literature of the ninth and tenth centuries. Even the new poetry, as we shall see, was largely an elongation, in poetic form, of the midrashic prose writings.

For this reason practically no aspect of human life—political, social or scientific, theological or ritualistic—totally escaped the attention of homilists. Even the sermon often started with an intricate legal problem, at times stimulated by an inquiry from the floor, a procedure well reflected in Aḥai's *She'eltot.* We also have vestiges of such queries in the *Yelamdenu* midrashim, which invariably begin with the formula "May our master teach us," with respect to such and such a problem. However, the discourse soon veered off into some ethical, historical, or theological questions but loosely related to the original inquiry.[21]

Like their confreres of other faith, few of these preachers or street-corner orators dared to plead ignorance of any subject. They certainly had to know the names of any person and locality connected with outstanding biblical events. Where the scriptural record left them in the dark, they invented names which, before long, achieved wide circulation and were incorporated into the stream of tradition. True, Jewish interpreters did not display the same proclivity for anonym hunting and the identification of every obscure detail which had become such a favorite sport with their Muslim colleagues that it elicited serious misgivings among Qur'an commentators like Ṭabari. Nor do we have any recorded Jewish counterpart to that Muslim soapbox orator who identified the wolf which devoured Joseph. When interrupted by a listener who said that Joseph had never been eaten by a wolf, the speaker unperturbedly answered, "Well, then this must be the name of the wolf which did not devour Joseph." Nevertheless, at some time or other Jewish homilists "found out" the names of Abraham's mother, and of his children by Keturah. The author of *Pirqe de-R. Eliezer* "knew" the names of Lot's wife and daughter. Even before the Christian era aggadists had "discovered" rich biographical data about Potiphar's daughter Asenath, and they knew a great many intimate details concerning her attempt to seduce Joseph—a story which readily kindled the imagination of erotically minded readers in all ages. The "Chronicle of Yeraḥmeel" did not hesitate to enumerate eleven sons and eight daughters of Adam. The messianic theme, too, and the people's undying hope of redemption, inspired many a homilist to describe in resplendent colors mankind's ultimate catastrophe and rebirth. Emulating the ancient apocalypses, medieval Jewish writers, particularly in darker moments of their people's history, often lent forceful expression to their belief in its ultimate indestructibility. Sometimes an emotional speaker's imagination completely ran away with him. We recollect the numerous apocalyptic midrashim, where fantastic exaggerations, even utter nonsense, were often perpetuated by faithful disciples as part of a living tradition.[22]

Many orators, often through mere oversight, incorporated in their presentation teachings stemming from gnostic and other heretical circles. Quite unbeknown to its originators, many a heterodox doctrine thus insinuated itself into widely accepted Jewish letters. This was particularly true of periods of weakened communal controls during the fifth to the eighth centuries and, again, after the decline of gaonate and exilarchate in the eleventh century, both periods of greatest aggadic creativity. In Narbonne, Moses the Preacher (*ha-Darshan*) reproduced many aggadic sayings which stemmed from extrarabbinic, even heterodox, groups and often went back to such outwardly long-forgotten teachings as are known to us only from either the apocryphal book of Jubilees or Philo. The Narbonne homilist probably had no direct access to those ancient letters, but he may have been familiar with their derivatives still circulating orally or in writing throughout the Mediterranean world. Manichaeism in its various permutations was to prove, after all, a sufficiently powerful trend to help nurture some of the great Christian "heresies" in Moses' southern French fatherland two centuries later.[23]

Understandably, some unorthodox legends and homilies lent themselves to anti-Jewish interpretation. They were to furnish weapons to Christian controversialists, especially in Spain, during the growingly heated debates in the later Middle Ages. Raymond Martini, an informed student of rabbinic letters, assembled many aggadic sayings which seemed to prove both the purported knowledge of the Jews themselves that Jesus had been their Messiah and their obstinacy in refusing to admit that "fact" publicly. Since few manuscript works by Moses ha-Darshan and other early Western aggadists have reached us, we cannot tell with assurance whether Martini accurately quoted his Hebrew sources. These were readily accessible to him as a member of a royal commission to which, by royal order, the Aragonese communities had delivered thousands of rabbinic manuscripts for examination of their possibly "subversive" anti-Christian content. Some of Martini's alterations and reformulations may have been previously introduced by unwary, clandestinely heterodox, or Christian scribes. But some may well have been modified by Martini himself, the better to suit his polemical purposes. Absolute accuracy in quotation could certainly not be expected from any medieval polemist defending his faith. So convinced was Martini of his ability to prove Christian beliefs from Jewish sources that he was prepared to uphold the very Talmud as a useful armory of Christian apologetics. His *Pugio fidei* (Poniard of the Faith) became, therefore, a major source of information for Christian controversialists and played a particularly significant role during the fateful debate at Tortosa in 1413–14. Don Isaac Abravanel, though several times admitting that he had been unable to secure a copy of the original midrash by Moses ha-Darshan, roundly condemned Martini as an outright forger, an accusation frequently echoed, but also often denied, by modern scholars.[24]

Among compilers of aggadic collections Moses the Preacher is extraordinary, however, in that we know at least something about the man, his time, and his environment. Narbonne, long a major center of Jewish life and learning at the crossroads between Western Islam and Christendom, had retained many ancient traditions in direct continuity from the Roman and Visigothic periods. With its Jewish "king" and extended self-government in Carolingian times, the community enjoyed considerable intellectual independence from the Eastern rabbinic centers until the influx of Eastern settlers and the successful geonic drive for world supremacy set in motion the great talmudic renaissance associated with the names of Gershom, Rashi, and the Tosafists. Before that time, however, and particularly in the aggadic domain, the divergent local traditions had preserved much of their inner vitality, notwithstanding the heterodox tinge some of them received through their sheer deviation from the regnant Eastern doctrines.

Ultimately, some preachers began deriding the very foundations of rabbinic learning and its main representatives, the scholars. This was a remarkable reversal, since early posttalmudic homilists had continued to exhort the populace to pay unbounded homage to students of the law. As a rule, the third Sabbath after the Feast of Tabernacles and its weekly lesson *Lekh lekha* (Get Thee Out of Thy Country; Gen. 12:1), long set aside for celebrations in honor of the exilarch (possibly earlier also of the Palestinian patriarch), lent themselves particularly well to such glorification of scholarship. A preacher, describing at some lengths the virtues of charity, became lyrical in extolling the rewards for extending hospitality to a scholarly traveler. He also harped on the theme of assistance to scholars which, he reiterated, was superior even to the very study of Torah. In time, however, there appeared some anti-intellectual rebels who not only attacked the elementary teachers enjoying little recognition in academic circles, but parodied the very talmudic scholars under the guise of "donkeys." [25]

Such criticisms appeared the more dangerous as aggadic literature was often very popular with the masses and enjoyed wide circulation in many lands. The easy transmission of aggadic learning is well illustrated by the works of Tobiah ben Eliezer. A native of Castoria in Bulgaria, though possibly of German-Jewish parentage, Tobiah lived for a time in Salonica, where he may have become involved in some messianic movements. The Balkan Jews, long in direct contact with Palestine with which they had shared subjection to Byzantine rule, had fewer independent memories and folkways than their southern French coreligionists. At the same time the growing Karaite threat in Constantinople forced the orthodox leaders to hew more closely to the regnant talmudic line. That is why Tobiah ben Eliezer, to be distinguished from his Karaite compatriot and namesake Tobiah ben Moses, represented in Byzantine Jewry the same predominance of talmudic-geonic learning as did his elder contemporary, Rashi, in the Western countries.

Ever awake to the contemporary situation of their people, both Rashi and Tobiah also indulged occasional polemical asides, but with a major difference in their targets. In eleventh-century France, where the Judeo-Christian tension was steadily mounting, Rashi constantly had the Christian challenge in mind. Byzantium, on the other hand, beset in Tobiah's days by great perils from both its Islamic neighbors and Western Crusaders, allowed the Judeo-Christian debate to become calmly routinized. At the same time the Karaite propaganda was making serious inroads in the Rabbanite camp. For this reason Tobiah aimed his shafts mainly at these sectarians, on whose divisive agitation he even blamed in part the empire's increased fiscal exploitation of its Jewish subjects.[26]

Beyond their fundamental similarities in theological and juridical approaches, Rashi and Tobiah demonstrated the same remarkable ability to fuse in their works the Halakhah and Aggadah with the more recent achievements of Hebrew philology. Much more wordy, but also more selective in his comments on scriptural passages, Tobiah wrote a *Commentary* on the Pentateuch and the Five Scrolls, employing a remarkable combination of rational exegesis and detailed attention to grammar with the homiletical elaborations transmitted by generations of aggadic teachers. On more than one occasion he emphasized that "although the interpretation of Scripture must not abandon its ordinary meaning, hermeneutics is a beautiful discipline enabling us to make one thing intelligible through another and to penetrate more deeply the significance of the context." Residing in a region where Aramaic had never been spoken, Tobiah took special pains to translate all Aramaic quotations into a smooth and lucid Hebrew. In his observations on the legal section of the Mosaic books he frequently restated lengthy juristic debates, including some which had previously been reformulated in R. Aḥai's and Simon Qayyara's law books. He also had a sense for history. In the introduction to his *Commentary* on Lamentations, for example, he drew illuminating comparisons between Jeremiah, the assumed author of that biblical book (acting under divine inspiration the prophet was supposed to have dictated the Lamentations to Baruch in the fourth year of Jehoiakim's reign, that is before the fall of Jerusalem), and Job, who, Tobiah believed, had lived more than eight centuries before Jeremiah. To show the similarities between these two tragic figures, Tobiah cited passages from both Job and Jeremiah, often giving them interesting homiletical twists; in some cases, it appears, these were quite original with him. Midrashic thinking so deeply permeated all his reactions that, when on one occasion he had to write a letter of introduction for a prospective pilgrim to the Holy Land, he turned that epistle into a regular homily on the charitable obligations of communities and individuals. The charity here envisaged was not to be limited to financial assistance, since this particular Russian-Jewish visitor knew neither Hebrew, Greek nor Arabic, but only the Slavonic speech of his native land. For such a man to undertake a journey to the Holy Land via Egypt (hence the presence of this letter in the Cairo Genizah) certainly was an act of great daring.[27]

Tobiah's *Leqaḥ ṭob* (Good Lesson, a pun on his name; wrongly called by its first printer *Pesiqta zuṭrata*) enjoyed almost immediate acceptance. Many leading scholars in France, Germany, and Italy soon quoted passages from this work, with or without acknowledgement. Only the more sophisticated Spanish intellectuals showed a certain aloofness, even disdain, for this homiletical exegete who did not pointedly separate the allegorical and homiletical superstructure from the ordinary meaning of Scripture. Abraham ibn Ezra, in particular, in the oft-quoted introduction to his *Commentary* on Genesis sharply censuring earlier commentators, also attacked the "fourth" group, consisting of homiletical interpreters, particularly common "among the scholars of Greek and Latin countries, who pay no heed to the grammatical forms, but rely on hermeneutics; for instance, the author of *Leqaḥ ṭob*." Other rationalist exegetes were particularly irked by Tobiah's high appreciation of the mystical *Hekhalot* literature despite its obvious anthropomorphisms and other "sins" against reason. Ultimately, however, when kabbalistic preoccupations largely displaced the early rationalism of the Spanish intelligentsia, Spanish students of Bible and Midrash likewise acknowledged Tobiah as a master exegete and homilist.[28]

MIXED REACTIONS

Lack of unanimity in the appreciation of aggadic works was not limited to certain individuals or countries. Not only occasional antirabbinic utterances, but also perfectly orthodox homilies often created problems for the authoritative expounders of rabbinic law. On the one hand, the aggadists quoted sayings by the same outstanding talmudic sages on whose legal decisions largely rested the whole structure of Jewish law. Like their contemporaries of other faiths, moreover, most medieval Jewish scholars were historically gullible and rarely applied to historical problems their great critical acumen in the domains of law, linguistics, science, or philosophy. They were in no position, therefore, to sift the spurious from the authentic sayings attributed to the ancient masters. On the other hand, even some of the most genuine aggadic traditions no longer squared with their convictions. They therefore invoked with relish the old talmudic saying, "One does not derive any [binding] conclusions from *aggadot*" (j. Pe'ah II.6, 17a), whereby the ancient sages themselves had safeguarded the integrity of their legal teachings against the incursion of uncontrollable, folkloristic "misconceptions."

Such ambivalence is most clearly noticeable in the attitude of Hai Gaon, generally an exponent of a middle-of-the-road philosophy. Hai was just as far apart from the unquestioning faith in the Aggadah of some of his geonic predecessors as he was from the more radical skepticism expressed by his father-in-law, Samuel ben Ḥofni. He was prepared to reject many *aggadot* as "mere words not to be taken literally," to discard the ancient sages' medical advice as no longer up-to-date, and particularly to repudiate the grossly anthropomorphic descriptions of God in the current mystic writings. At the same time he profoundly revered the Talmud.

Everything written in the Talmud [he replied to well intentioned inquirers] is more correct than what is not included in it. Although *aggadot* written in the Talmud, if they prove untrue or distorted, need not be considered authoritative, because of the general rule that one does not rely on *aggadah,* yet we are obliged to remove wherever possible the distortion of any statement included in the Talmud. For if that statement had not contained some [worth-while] hermeneutic interpretation, it would never have been incorporated in the Talmud. But if unable to remove the distortion, we shall treat it like any of the rejected laws. Statements not included in the Talmud, however, require no such exertion on our part. If one is correct and beautiful, we preach on it and teach it to pupils; if not, we simply disregard it.

In another responsum concerning the well-known report about the four sages who had "entered the orchard," Hai warned his correspondents not to deviate from historic truth: "We are wont to explain the opinion of a Tanna and its essential import in the way he had really thought, without assuming any responsibility for his view being the accepted norm. There certainly are many Mishnayot which fail to reflect accepted norms, and yet we attempt to understand them in their authors' spirit." In this very responsum, however, the gaon insisted, in contrast to Samuel ben Ḥofni, that God performed miracles through the mediation of rabbinic scholars, as well as of prophets. He also generally believed in angels and demons, whose powers were controlled by the ancient sages and were still subject to influence through talismans or the proper use of the divine name.[29]

Even Samuel ben Ḥofni merely preached discrimination in the use of ancient homilies and tales, not their outright repudiation. He realized that the Aggadah contained an accumulated store of ancient interpretations of Scripture which could be used to excellent advantage in his rational Bible exegesis as well. In his methodical way he tried, therefore, to sift and classify these traditional approaches. With full understanding of the differences, as well as the basic similarities, between the juristic and aggadic hermeneutics, he even grouped together the thirteen long-accepted modes of halakhic interpretation of the school of R. Ishmael with the newer compilation of thirty-six (or the more widely used enumeration of thirty-two) modes applied to aggadic derivations from Scripture. Whether or not he had initiated the latter computation, he analyzed a total of forty-nine modes used in both domains of ancient hermeneutics. While in the extant portions of Samuel's Bible commentaries we possess only a few brief references to this analysis, he probably pursued this methodological classification to all its logical divisions and subdivisions and illustrated it with a profusion of detail. Perhaps some future finds will enable us more fully to reconstruct the fundamental evaluation of the Aggadah by this intellectually most independent of the Babylonian geonim.[30]

Even more complicated was Maimonides' attitude. On the one hand, the jurist-philosopher felt obliged to reject all aggadic concepts running counter to his religious beliefs. In a sharply worded responsum he rejected the well-known mystical work *She'ur qomah* (Measure of the Divine Stature) and altogether denied that it had been written by an ancient sage. "It doubtless is but the composition of one of the Greek preachers," which ought to be totally suppressed as a book propagating the worship of "other" gods, "since a being endowed with a stature certainly is another god." Maimonides could less easily evade the problem of the talmudic *aggadot*. Wherever possible, he glossed over the anthropomorphic passages or those relating to demons or magic, or else tried to give them a rational interpretation. In his juridical works, in particular, he felt free to accept or reject aggadic interpretations in accordance with his own juridical or theological preconceptions. Rarely polemical, he simply ignored those of which he disapproved, or else gave them a new twist which deprived them of their obnoxious features. While restating, for example, the talmudic permission to carry certain objects on a Sabbath because of their alleged utility for magic healing, he generalized that such permission applies to "everything presumed to be useful for healing, provided that its utility is attested by physicians." At times he accepted only a part of a talmudic statement which he considered rationally sustainable, but omitted the rest, as when he upheld the prohibition of gazing at the priests' outstretched hands during the pronunciation of the priestly blessing. Rather than referring to a statement by R. Judah bar Naḥmani that such curiosity, like that prompting people to stare at rainbows or patriarchs, would cause the eyesight to be dimmed, Maimonides gave the reason advanced in the Palestinian Talmud that it might lead to distraction from the main import of the priestly blessing. He passed over in silence R. Judah's two other objects of forbidden contemplation.[31]

On the other hand, the Aggadah could readily be invoked in support of legal doctrines which the codifier welcomed. With his great emphasis on ethics, as well as on law, Maimonides was often at a loss to find support for his ethical postulates in the formal halakhic sources, and had to fall back on the ethical dicta included in the vast mass of rabbinic homilies. The entire first section of his Code, beginning with the "Principles of the Torah," could be restated by him as a part of the Oral *Law* only under the assumption that the Aggadah had been an integral part of it. Certainly the first precepts, enumerated in his *Book of Commandments* and relating to the existence and uniqueness of God, though based on clear and unequivocal statements in Scripture had been more fully elaborated only in the aggadic literature. Similarly, in matters of worldly wisdom and behavior as part of the Jewish way of life, he had to fall back on moralists rather than jurists in the narrower sense of that term. He wanted, for example, to impress upon his readers that "it is the way of men of wisdom that one first acquires an occupation giving him a livelihood and secures living quarters and only then marries a wife . . . but a fool begins by marrying a wife, and then if he is able he acquires a house and only in his later years he looks for an occupation, or else lives on charity." In support he could only cite some Deuteronomic passages and, more indirectly, a talmudic homily. On occasion, the codifier himself turned preacher even in most unexpected places. He concluded, for instance, his detailed restatement of the laws governing lepers and their segregated mode of living with the talmudic explanation that leprosy usually is but a divine infliction for one's "evil tongue." This penalty had been imposed even on Miriam for her false accusation of Moses. How much more severely would it befall ordinary gossipers whose company righteous persons should consistently shun! Maimonides realized, of course, this ambiguity in the use of aggadic materials for juristic purposes. We must doubly regret, therefore, that he never wrote his projected extensive commentary on "all the *derashot* [homilies; this Hebrew term is used in the Arabic text] of the Talmud and other sources." Cognizant of its staggering difficulties, dogmatic as well as scholarly, he lost heart, or, as his son phrased it, was "afraid to come nigh" to it.[32]

From the outset the sage of Fusṭaṭ realized his own minority position. In the programmatic statement preceding the announcement of his projected commentary, he admitted that most Jews were prepared to subscribe to every statement of the Aggadah and to consider impious any doubter of its veracity. There also existed, on the other hand, many skeptics who likewise took the Aggadah literally, but only in order to ridicule it as contrary to reason. Only a small minority had too high an appreciation for the ancient sages to attribute to them evident absurdities, and hence tried to look behind the apparent to the true meaning of each statement. Subsequently, Maimonides gave up his hope of ever persuading the uneducated majority that metaphorical interpretation, too, is legitimate, in fact often necessary. This feeling of frustration must have been deepened by his realization that many of Abraham ben David's strictures on his Code and numerous queries addressed to him by the sages of Lunel and others stressed his departures from the ordinary meaning of homiletical statements, although these inquirers themselves were anything but extreme aggadic literalists. Ultimately, Maimonides' deviations became the opposition's main targets during the anti-Maimonidean controversy of the thirteenth century.[33]

In Maimonides' lifetime, however, the Aggadah, without forfeiting its mass appeal, had already lost its exclusive hold on the extralegal thinking of the Jewish people. Its all-embracing content, which had lent it its unique significance in the ancient nonhalakhic lore, had now become the subject matter of several specialized disciplines and literary genres. It had lost, as we shall see in the next chapter, much of its importance in the very field of Bible exegesis. Even Hai and many like him, who bowed to the authority of the written word, had their misgivings about blindly following the traditional methods of biblical interpretation, the uncritical acceptance of which caused widespread opposition among the new, sophisticated intelligentsia. Historic continuity, to be sure, long reasserted itself. The most popular exegetical work for centuries to come remained Rashi's *Commentary* on the Pentateuch, because of its remarkable blend of philological exegesis with tactfully selected elements of the ancient Aggadah. Yet even Rashi was no longer able freely to produce new hermeneutic interpretations of his own and to read into the biblical text his private moralistic or historical preconceptions. Many new homilies continued to be delivered by preachers, new hermeneutic derivations were suggested to buttress personal views; but they now appeared, as a rule, in separate works of a homiletical or ethical content, not as running commentaries on Scripture.

Similarly the story, another essential ingredient of the Aggadah, now emerged as a separate branch of literature. In his aforementioned apologia for his father's approach to traditional homiletics, Abraham Maimuni suggested a division of midrashic lore into five categories of *derashot* (hermeneutic homilies) and four types of *ma'asiyot* (stories). The first of the latter types, itself broken up into four subdivisions, was the true report of an event mentioned by the sages only in order to impart a moral. A second type consisted of the narration of extraordinary and puzzling occurrences or dreams, such as encounters with demons, which were never intended to be taken literally by listeners or readers. These were expected to use their discretion also with respect to crediting stories of the third type, containing obvious exaggerations and impossibilities. A fourth type consisted of imaginary elaborations of actual events in the form of parables and riddles likewise intended merely to convey some theological or ethical lesson. From the outset many such stories were told without direct reference to biblical passages and hence were devoid of traditional hermeneutics. Now, however, there sprang up a specialized literature devoted to the retelling of old stories circulating in the Mediterranean world from time immemorial, and to the spinning of new yarns, some amusing or edifying, some neither amusing nor edifying.

STORIES AND ROMANCES

From novelistic midrashim to secular stories was but a small step. In Yemen, especially, uncritical collectors included many a secular romance in their sacred literature. Because of the shortage of books, which later caused Yemenite scribes to copy by hand lengthy works printed in Italy or Holland, local students labored to reproduce almost any text that came to their notice. "Who is a scholar?" reads a Yemenite variant from the Sayings of the Fathers; "He who collects from all places" (Abu Manṣur adh-Dhamari). Rather indiscriminately, they included in their libraries many worldly tales, even some with a heterodox tinge. They evinced special curiosity in anything referring to ancient sages, with total disregard of chronology. Nor were Western scholars free from such uncritical acceptance of historical incongruities. An Eastern booklet, bearing the ambitious title *Baraita de-Niddah* (Tannaitic Work on the Menstruating Woman) and circulating in twelfth-century Germany, unabashedly repeated stories involving the Tanna Eleazar ben 'Arakh together with the Amoraim Simon ben Laqish and Abbahu, or Shammai, Eliezer ben Hyrcanus, 'Aqiba and Judah the Patriarch, although in each of these cases nearly two centuries separated the eldest from the youngest of the group. This particular aggadic concoction also contained obvious folkloristic exaggerations, such as that any priest learning of a case of menstruation in his family would automatically be disqualified from the recitation of the priestly blessing. Nonetheless it found sufficient credence among the German rabbis to influence their legal decisions.[34]

Because of these obvious incongruities, Aptowitzer suggested that that *Baraita* was a conscious Karaite fabrication. But this argument is merely an outgrowth of the general pan-Karaite tendencies in recent scholarship. Certainly, popular folklore was never particularly concerned with historical and chronological accuracy, and there has always been freedom within it to attribute to well-known ancient sages any number of expressions of more than average piety. Even the Western talmudist Eliezer bar Joel ha-Levi felt little irritation about these chronological incompatibilities or the attribution to distinguished talmudic sages of acts of supererogation appearing strange or even ridiculous to us. Unconcernedly, he referred to this source in a discussion with his pupil, Isaac bar Moses. Undoubtedly the compiler himself was but a Rabbanite student of the school of Aḥai of Shabḥa and the *Yelamdenu* midrashim, in which Halakhah and Aggadah indistinguishably blended, who wished to impress upon his readers extreme caution with respect to menstrual impurity and privacy in sexual intercourse. He therefore invested such popular "superstitions" with the validity of legal injunctions.[35]

Not surprisingly, erotic interests found here a ready outlet. The ancient and medieval rabbis were not prudes; they freely discussed all marital and sexual relations relevant to their legal or ethical teachings. The compilers of folk tales and popular sayings could, therefore, discuss bedroom behavior without risking widespread disapproval. That same *Baraita de-Niddah* advised any woman who after her ritualistic ablution had met a dog, a donkey, or an illiterate person to undergo in each case a new ablution before cohabiting with her husband, lest she bear him ugly, stupid, or illiterate children. Encounter with a horse, on the other hand, was supposed to be an augury for good-looking and studious offspring. More detailed and intimate were the counsels and injunctions assembled in the erotically overcharged compilation known as *Mishnat Massekhet Kallah*. Allegedly supplying the missing Mishnah to the "minor tractate" *Kallah* (Bride), itself much concerned with sexual problems, this later compilation not only advised against hidden flirtations with other women, but discussed in considerable detail the proper behavior during the sexual act. It, too, regularly threatened the disobedient with physically or mentally malformed progeny. Here and elsewhere such advice was often illustrated by anecdotes, allegedly reporting the conduct or pertinent sayings of some renowned ancient sage. Of course, such popular beliefs had been diffused through many civilizations and, in the Near East, reached back to remote antiquity; some had already penetrated the talmudic letters. But with the greater articulateness and progressive decline of academic controls during the medieval period, writers could the more readily indulge in fanciful descriptions, as their cloak of piety effectively covered up their discussion of intimate improprieties.[36]

Sometimes apothegms were elaborated into regular storiettes with one or more moral lessons. For example, the fairly popular "Story of R. Kahana and His Son Saliq" told at some length of R. Kahana's difficulty with his wife concerning the education of their five-year-old son. Only under the threat of divorce and with the promise not to send the child away from home did he obtain her consent to hiring a teacher. Ultimately he succeeded, at the high cost of a thousand gold pieces, in employing an instructor for twenty-five years, during which time neither master nor pupil were to leave the house. At the age of thirty, finally, Saliq started out into the world, but was keenly disappointed by the lack of appreciation for his learning among his ordinary fellow citizens. One of his relatives, publicly selling flasks of scented water, refused to give him one free of charge. "If you have intensively studied the Torah," the latter declared, "you need not boast about it, for you have been born for it. The Lord has created you to study day and night. Me He has created to draw water, carry it on my shoulders, sell it for a *qasqas,* and thus to support my family." Saliq was appeased, however, when at his father's advice he proceeded to the druggists' quarter. There he found a large assembly of scholars, which anachronistically included Rabbah bar R. Huna and the brothers Shemariah and Samuel, sons of Ḥofni. Here he showed his scholarly prowess by insisting that an animal which was half cow and half dog could be ritualistically slaughtered. This decision, followed by a full-fledged demonstration, secured for Saliq universal acclaim. In most of these tales the rabbis' halakhic and moralistic teachings played a great role, but no effort was made now to attach them to particular biblical verses, which alone had originally justified their inclusion in the "midrashic" literature.[37]

Most tales catered to naive tastes and were told in simple prose without any artistic adornments. True, what we now possess are but literary summaries of lengthy stories told and retold orally with innumerable variants. Papyrus and parchment may have been patient, but they also were quite expensive. Only the introduction of paper and other cheaper writing materials, from the late ninth century on, and the simultaneous growth of the Jewish reading public made possible the rise of a new folkloristic literature, the authors of which have also become individually more identifiable.

One of the earliest and best known works of this type was written by no less an authority than Nissim bar Jacob ibn Shahin of Kairuwan. Nissim was a voracious reader and collector of all sorts of rabbinic materials. In his *Megillat setarim* (Secret Scroll), in particular, he accumulated over many years excerpts from earlier writings or oral reports, which he then used as source material for his commentaries and his encyclopedic *Mafteaḥ* (Key). He copied or paraphrased these data, of which unfortunately only a small fraction has reached us, more or less indiscriminately in either Hebrew or Arabic.

Undoubtedly from that storehouse of information Nissim also selected a number of instructive and edifying tales to which he gave a title, known to us only from its Hebrew translation as *Ḥibbur Yafeh me-ha-yeshu'ah* (The Worthy Book of Comfort). He was stimulated to its composition, he tells us in the introduction, by the death of a friend's son and his desire to place in the mourner's hand some cheerful reading. He also wished to replace a similar storybook stemming from an heretical source.

I shall record in this book [he explained] what I have learned and understood of the words of the sages, stories of happenings and events. Some of the sages were afflicted with miseries, but were relieved of them. Although these are stories affecting individuals, I shall not ignore events which happened to an entire community faced by a crisis and saved from it, except for what has already been assembled in such books as the Scroll of Esther, the Scroll of the Hasmonean children, and other events recorded in the twenty-four books [of the Bible]. . . . I shall record here only what has not become known and familiar except to a few persons.

As a scholar of note, Nissim ibn Shahin doubtless had access to many sources which had escaped the attention of less learned contemporaries; some are no longer extant. He seems also to have borrowed freely from tales current in oral form among his coreligionists in Kairuwan, or which he had heard from travelers, itinerant preachers, or storytellers. Whether stemming from Arabic, Persian, Indian, or Western folklore, these tales quickly lost their original ethnic or denominational character. During their passage from one country to another and from one cultural group to another, they often were retold with numerous modifications to suit the tastes of each new group of listeners. They also were buttressed by references to personalities or events from one's national history and at times provided with homiletical references to the Holy Scriptures of the particular narrator or audience. Such "Judaization" of oriental folk tales, like "Islamization" or "Christianization" of Jewish folk stories, had been going on through the preceding centuries. Certainly few of Nissim's contemporaries were cognizant of their foreign provenance.[38]

Nissim and his readers evinced little concern for these historic connections so vital to modern scholars. Their main criterion was the story's intrinsic plausibility, its usual happy ending, and the moral lesson it imparted. Nissim included, for example, the aforementioned seduction story of "R. Meir," but with one difference. While in the midrashic tale Meir had submitted to his flirtatious hostess in a state of inebriation and had escaped serious injury from the lions to which he had been exposed only because he had been unconscious of his transgression, in Nissim's version he was completely vindicated because the hostess, it turned out, had lied about their affair. Either both versions were current among the populace or Nissim was reluctant to admit even unconscious guilt on the part of so pious a man. He depicted many other love scenes, including several unconsummated seductions. One lengthy narrative, for example, concerned a dissolute rich man, Nathan of Ṣoṣita, who fell in love with the virtuous wife of a poor neighbor. His desire became so overwhelming that he fell seriously ill and was told by doctors that only the possession of that woman would cure him. The communal elders decided, however, that he should perish rather than be allowed to commit adultery. After a while the lady's husband was imprisoned as an insolvent debtor. In desperation he persuaded his wife, after many entreaties, to secure from Nathan the funds necessary for his release at the price of her chastity. At the last moment, however, the lady's speech on the severity of their contemplated sin made Nathan desist. He not only recovered but thenceforth led a saintly life. Many other stories described with much relish various acts of charity, cases of extraordinary compliance with the Jewish commandments, or of the successful pursuit of learning in the face of tremendous difficulties. Nissim also elaborated with much picturesque detail many old rabbinic tales, such as those relating to Nahum of Gimzo, whose name had long been explained by a popular etymology as derived from his valiantly accepting all adversity and constantly reiterating *gam zo le-tobah* (this, too, is for the good).[39]

All these personalities were far overshadowed in the international folklore of the Mediterranean world by the prophet Elijah, whose reputed assistance to a poor man is told by Nissim with particular zest. Here the prophet persuaded the needy man to sell him, a perfect stranger, into slavery in order to sustain the seller's starving family. As a slave Elijah acquitted himself of his obligation by miraculously erecting a beautiful palace for his master, and then vanished. Parts of the ancient apocryphal literature, such as the book of Judith or the books of Maccabees, or rather their contents as reshaped by folk fantasies in centuries of oral transmission, likewise furnished colorful ingredients for many stories. In the case of Judith, Nissim does not even know the heroine's name nor that of her victim. Characteristically, he opens his report by saying: "Know that the correct story has reached us by tradition about one of the infidel kings, powerful and stubborn, who had besieged Jerusalem at the head of a hundred thousand fighters." In this respect as well as in many other details Nissim's formulation differs greatly even from other Hebrew versions current in the

Middle Ages, in one of which the slain enemy is named Seleucus, rather than Holophernes. Evidently the ancient apocryphal books were little known in Nissim's circle. If in some cases Nissim's stories are indebted to Arabic, including Qur'anic, prototypes, and if at times he betrays even linguistic borrowings from the Qur'an, we need not assume his conscious indebtedness to Muslim sources. Many of these Arabic formulations had originated from folk tales and phrases long current in the Near East's cosmopolitan population, or else had subsequently influenced the thinking and speech of all those peoples, including Jews. The latter were for the most part completely unaware of the pagan or Muslim origin of either the tale or its peculiar Arabic garb.[40]

Nor was this head of a Kairuwanese academy at all conscious that some of his ethical postulates would bear such resemblance to certain Mu'tazilite teachings as to enable a modern scholar to designate his work as one of "Aggadic-Islamic syncretism." Not only was he personally not a really informed student of Mu'tazilite philosophy, but there was in his book little reflection of religious "syncretism" in its ordinary sense of a fusion of dogmas and rituals. His *Book of Comfort* rather mirrored the widespread acceptance of moral teachings basically common to Judaism and Islam and only somewhat more sharply formulated by Mu'tazila thinkers. This sharper formulation is, of course, lacking in Nissim's work which neither philosophizes nor defines, but narrates. Precisely because of their more indirect, even imperceptible influence on such unconscious popular exchanges, the migratory tales had long become a most effective vehicle of that cultural diffusion which was so characteristic of the entire Renaissance of Islam.[41]

All these stories, even when written by famous authors like Nissim, never lost the character of folk tales. They were retold with the utter simplicity of the early street-corner narrators who sought to make them immediately intelligible to average listeners. They resembled in this respect the Jewish folk literature which was soon to arise in Germany and later in the Balkans, and which was to form such an essential ingredient of the early Yiddish and Ladino literatures. From there it was but a step to the creation of the truly artistic novel and short story. This branch of literature, understandably enough, developed particularly in the Golden Age of Spain and shared there the fine esthetic qualities of the Spanish Hebrew poetry of the period. Whether consisting of the novel literary form of *maqamas,* of artistic renditions of ancient tales from the East, or of original imaginative contributions by the Spanish and Provençal poets, this literature was often composed in poetic prose and was interspersed with poems of varying length. Its fuller analysis must be relegated, therefore, to the chapter devoted to medieval Hebrew poetry and *ars poetica.*[42]

YOSEPHON AND HISTORICAL FOLKLORE

In the older homiletical and folk narratives the descriptions of events or personalities of the past merely served as ingredients of some moralistic stories. Most homilists themselves did not mean to convey the impression that they were reporting actual historical happenings. At times a great name was mentioned only in the introduction in order to attract greater attention. For example, the so-called *Midrash Va-Yosha'* (Thus the Lord Saved Israel; on Exod. 14:30 ff.), a collection of stories and dialogues in the sequence of the Song of Moses, is prefaced by an elaborate description of the preparations for the sacrifice of Isaac and includes a number of dramatic conversations between Abraham, his son, Satan, and God. Its main connection with the story of the Exodus was merely the example it had set for religious faith and obedience. The story of Esther, told in the Bible with much novelistic flavor, lent itself to many such fictional amplifications. In fact, the so-called *Targum sheni* (the Second Aramaic Version) of the book of Esther is less a translation, or even paraphrase, than a piece of fiction based upon the biblical account. Of a similar kind are several other midrashim, including one entitled *Abba Gorion* simply because that name appears in the opening paragraph. It seems to have been placed there by a relatively late compiler who had lifted it from the proem by R. Berakhiah which followed it.[43]

More popular was the historical midrash called *Sefer Bene Ḥashmonai* or *Megillat Antiochus* (Book of the Hasmonean Children or the Scroll of Antiochus). This story combined elements from the apocryphal books of Maccabees with talmudic legends, particularly the miracle of a small flacon of oil which lasted through the eight days of the rededication of the Temple. Originally composed in Aramaic, it was translated into Hebrew, and was often recited in the Eastern synagogues in either language during the Ḥanukkah festival. The story begins with a brief description of the power of the Syrian King Antiochus residing in the capital built by him "on the shore of the sea" and called Antiocheia, a derivative of his own name. It then tells how in the twenty-third year of the king's reign and the 203d year since the building of the Temple in Jerusalem the Syrians tried to force the Jews to worship Syrian idols, thus provoking the Maccabean uprising. Here Mattathiah and his son Johanan, not Judah, play the roles of chief heroes. Although this scroll may not have been composed before the Muslim regime, Saadiah considered it an authentic record dating from the Maccabean age itself. He either did not find in his copy the concluding passage about the Jewish people having "accepted the reign of the children of the Hasmoneans and their descendants from that day until the destruction of God's Temple," or else he believed that it had been added by a copyist. But among the gaon's rationalist contemporaries there were historically more critical persons who cast doubt on the whole tradition. Saadiah decided, therefore, to append to his Arabic translation of the Scroll of Esther a similar rendition of the story of the Children of the Hasmoneans as a background for the celebration of Ḥanukkah. "The reason," he explained in his introduction, "I took pains to establish it [this story] is that I saw that most of the nation acknowledge it, though they do not fully understand it; how it came to pass and what caused it. Some Jews even reject it." To reinforce its authenticity he searched for hints in the Bible which, in his opinion, must contain some veiled allusions to such a future victory of a levitical family over the Greeks. He thought he had really found them in a combination of verses in Deuteronomy and Daniel, as well as in the prophetic books of Joel and Zechariah. Buttressed by the gaon's prestige, the Scroll, now available also in the familiar Arabic language, became part of the synagogue liturgy for Ḥanukkah, particularly in Yemen.[44]

Of an entirely different order, though closely related in its general outlook on history, is the famous work long attributed to Joseph ben Gurion or Yosephon. This work, often considered by

Jews and non-Jews as the work of Josephus Flavius written for the Hebrews, in contradistinction to his other works addressed to the [Greeks and] Romans, offers a remarkable combination of fact and legend which places it squarely in the twilight zone between the midrashic and historical literatures. The distinction between these two branches of learning was never too sharply drawn; by trying to draw a clear line of demarcation modern scholarship has often come to grief. What Anouar Hatem observed about the *chansons de geste* applies with equal force to much of medieval historiography, Christian, Muslim, and Jewish: they all consisted of (1) entirely imaginary sections, (2) rigorously historical sections, and (3) semihistorical sections in which imagination was given free rein to expand given historical data. Most historical writings, particularly if dealing with events long past and connected with the sacred history of the ancient Hebrews, belong to a greater or lesser extent to the third category.[45]

From the extant older manuscripts it appears that the author of Yosephon utilized Josephus' *Antiquities* (only the first sixteen books), *War,* and to a minor extent *Against Apion,* but not the ancient historian's *Life.* Josephus' authorship of the Hebrew paraphrase seemed be to borne out by the introduction to his *War,* in which he had referred to an earlier version of the book written in the Aramaic speech of his Babylonian coreligionists to whom he had tried to explain his conduct during the great war with the Romans. The historically uncritical medieval mind, accepting that attribution, which indeed had more intrinsic merits than that of many another pseudepigraphon, took it for granted that the ancient writer had fully shared its own biases and historical approaches. Precisely because the book quickly became very popular, it was frequently copied and thus became subject to the usual errors of manual reproduction. Furthermore, the copyists did not consider it a semicanonical book, and knew that its narratives had no bearing on ritualistic or ethical practice. Hence they felt doubly free to "enhance" its value by numerous additions from other sources and the elaboration of many details from their own fertile imagination.

We possess substantially three different versions of Yosephon. The most authentic recension doubtless exists in some of the older, as yet unpublished manuscripts. None of these represents a close approximation of the original text, but at least some have undergone less direct alterations than did the printed versions. A second recension has long been known through the first edition published by Abraham Conat in Mantua about 1480, one of the first Hebrew incunabula. Conat went to considerable pains to secure good manuscripts, but apparently on his own judgment he reduced some of the "legendary" portions as no longer squaring with the scholarly tastes of his generation. Conat's text was inadequately reprinted and provided with a Latin translation by the distinguished Christian Hebraist, Sebastian Münster in 1541. Independently, one Tam ben David ibn Yaḥya published another recension, about a third longer, in Constantinople in 1510. That text was frequently reprinted and, until the awakening of modern historical criticism in the nineteenth century, enjoyed undisputed acceptance. By the usual swings of the critical pendulum it was greatly disparaged for several decades, but it has found some defenders in more recent years. In any case, by the eleventh century Yosephon had already become known and highly revered in western Europe. No less a figure than Gershom bar Yehudah copied the work in his own hand, his copy serving as a major source of information on the history of the Second Commonwealth for Rashi and the latter's disciples. In Spain Samuel ibn Nagrela composed an epitome of it in Hebrew or Arabic. Some such Arabic version was already known to Samuel's Muslim opponent Ibn Ḥazm, who, however, may have relied here as often elsewhere on a second-hand summary. The same or another Arabic translation soon circulated also in the eastern Mediterranean, to be speedily followed by an Ethiopic version, probably from the Arabic, under the title *Zena Aihud* (History of the Jews).[46]

Like the works of Josephus, this medieval compound of history and fiction owed its popularity in the Christian world, where it later appeared in numerous Western translations, to the public's interest in the Second Commonwealth as a background for the rise of Christianity. Modern scholars, too, have often discussed it, particularly in connection with the newly published Slavonic version of Josephus, which reveals some interesting similarities, but also striking dissimilarities, with the Hebrew Yosephon. Without that

Christological bias, however, such Arab historians as Ihn Khaldun leaned heavily on this medieval Hebrew historian and folklorist in their reconstruction of ancient history. Such influence was facilitated by the basic acceptance, on the part of almost all medieval Arab historians, of the biblical reconstruction of the early history of mankind. The division, in particular, of all human races into descendants of Shem, Ham, and Japheth had long dominated the historical outlook of all leading Arab writers, including Mas'udi and Muqaddasi.[47]

A man of considerable vision and wide interests, Yosephon started his narration with a geographic review of the spread of the human race, particularly the children of Japheth. He devoted another section to a Hebraic paraphrase of the Alexander Romance, but either he or one of his predecessors juxtaposed here two distinct layers representing divergent traditions and dating from different periods. From the outset he also tried to synchronize Roman with Jewish history, clearly responding to the influence of the Christians, in whose memory these two lines of historical evolution constantly intertwined. Without fully spelling it out, he clearly intimated that the Roman Empire which had lasted to his day was the fourth most powerful and final empire predicted by Daniel. Therefore, in his speech before the fall of Jerusalem, Josephus the general could assure his coreligionists that they need not be ashamed of submitting to the Romans, whose overlordship had been willed by God. In answering the "rebels" who wished to fight to the last drop of blood, he exclaimed "Inquire about the days of your forefathers! When were you free, without masters, or when was there no Gentile yoke resting upon you?" Even Jacob, Joseph, and their descendants had voluntarily surrendered to Egyptian rule. Later the Jews had served Assyrians, Persians, and Greeks, and they must serve again in the case of Rome. But Rome, too, Yosephon clearly averred, would vanish and give way to the messianic era.[48]

At times Yosephon consciously departed from his main sources. He must have read in both Josephus and Hegesippus that the Herodian dynasty had been of Idumean descent. On one occasion he actually called the founder of that dynasty, Antipater, the "Ascalonite," echoing the Christian tradition that the Idumean statesman had started his career as a temple slave in Ascalon. In a later passage, however, Yosephon accepted the Herodian claim, propagated by Nicolaus of Damascus, that Antipater had descended from one of the noble resettlers from the Babylonian Exile under Ezra and Nehemiah. Very likely our author thus wished to counteract the Christian propaganda that the "scepter" had departed from Judah shortly before the birth of Jesus.[49]

Speeches of the type allegedly delivered by Josephus had been used by historians ever since Thucydides to explain the motivations of leading personalities. Yosephon extensively employed this device, especially in the last section of his book, which is replete with hortatory addresses written in a fine Hebrew prose. For example, to dissuade his forty fellow combatants hiding in the cave after the fall of Jotapata from entering the proposed suicide pact so as not to fall into the hands of Romans, Josephus supposedly delivered a lengthy oration against suicide as such.

> I know [he declared to his comrades] that you are right and that no one would wish to live on such a day. May God say the word, recall my soul and take it back to Him, for death is sweeter than life after all these tribulations. But He knows that it is He who has given me my soul. Who would dare to open what He has locked; He is the one who locks and opens. . . . For you know that this soul is but a trust with us from Him . . . if we throw it away before the stated time He will surely be angry with us and reject us, so that we shall not find our repose with Abraham our father, and with the righteous and the pious.

He cited the examples of Moses, Aaron, David, and Job, who may have prayed for death, but who refused to achieve it by their own hands. The length and repetitiousness of this imaginary harangue may perhaps be explained by its relevance to contemporary discussions. With the growing glorification of religious martyrdom, many Jews even before 1096 must have pointed to the example set by the last heroic fighters of Masada and preached that individual or communal self-extermination was preferable to conversion. In Yosephon's day cases of self-immolation certainly were quite exceptional, but at the first major opportunity the community of Mayence offered those "eleven hundred *'aqedot*," of which its chronicler, Solomon bar Simon, was to speak with that remarkable mixture of bitterness and pride.[50]

Our author's warning against suicide pacts met a genuine need. From a Genizah document, containing a letter from a southern Italian community (probably Bari) to a leader named Ḥisdai, we also learn that during the Saracen raid a distinguished scholar named Isaiah "with his own hands thrust a knife into his throat and he was slaughtered like a sheep in the Temple." The writer believed that the Jewish sufferings had ceased after two days because God had been "pleased by the sacrifice of His pious followers as if by a continual burnt-offering" in the Temple. Even among the Christians the growing glorification by Crusaders of death for one's faith, though partially a reaction to similar Muslim doctrines, was an offshoot of the ancient Judeo-Christian idea of religious martyrdom. This idea, fully developed already in the Maccabean age, colored all the regnant views of the fate and destiny of the Jewish people, which, for lack of a less "weighted" expression, we have called the "lachrymose conception of Jewish history." This conception and, accompanying it, the ever present readiness for martyrdom, remained one of the keynotes of all Jewish life in the dispersion, both in the East and in the West. Probably to counteract some such self-sacrificing proclivities, the rationalist Qirqisani inserted a lengthy "Disquisition on Suicide" into his chief theological treatise. As a Karaite, he could not cite the numerous talmudic utterances reflecting the sages' deep appreciation of human life, and he relied exclusively upon proofs from Scripture. On his part, Yosephon expatiated on these ideas under the guise of a dramatic oration allegedly delivered by Josephus.[51]

Like Nissim and other writers of the period, Yosephon was greatly indebted to oral traditions circulating among the people, although he also borrowed much from literary works by Josephus, Hegesippus, and later Latin writers. To judge from his cultivated Hebrew style, he must have been an informed student of Jewish literature, and echoes of talmudic concepts and legends are often enough distinctly audible in his narratives and speeches. At times he reflects still older Jewish folklore, recorded only in the ancient apocryphal literature. But many ancient theologumena or mythological concepts had unquestionably survived in the oral exchanges of preachers and storytellers. Yosephon may also have used his own hermeneutics in combining certain aggadic statements, and thus derived Hannah as the name of the mother of the seven Maccabean martyrs; in most rabbinic sources either the name Miriam or no name is given. But this identification may either have preceded him or been inserted into some Yosephon texts at a later date.[52]

There is no valid internal evidence, therefore, to deny the date appearing in one manuscript, according to which the book was written in 953. If, as we shall see, the introductory geographic review of contemporary nations may be considered an integral part of the work and likewise best fits the period between 900 and 965, that date remains intrinsically the most plausible of all those hitherto suggested. Nor is there any reason to doubt the long-accepted view, borne out by linguistic as well as historical and geographic data, that the book originated in southern Italy in the sphere of Byzantine influence.[53]

Many of the sources of Yosephon, however, whether written or oral, must have been independently known in many lands. Hence the much-debated passage in Saadiah's *Beliefs and Opinions,* allegedly reflecting Yosephon's influence, was probably indebted to some such earlier source. Perhaps because contemporaries considered the new work but a compilation of familiar narratives, it proved to be an instantaneous success. It is at least possible that a representative of Ḥisdai ibn Shapruṭ (if the Cordovan statesman was the prospective recipient of the obscure letter recovered from the Genizah), traveling in southern Italy after one of the recurrent Saracen raids (some time after 952), learned about its existence and tried to secure a copy for his employer, an ever interested patron of Jewish letters.[54]

Yosephon's extraordinary popularity invited emulation. Utilizing some of his data, but also studying many other historical and homiletical sources, one Yeraḥmeel ben Solomon, poet and scientist as well as historian probably living in the early twelfth century, composed a remarkable world chronicle from Adam to Judah Maccabee. Extant only in a single manuscript compilation of various chronicles, its compass and objectives can only be conjectured. Professing to wish to extol the works of the Lord, the author writes: "It is only possible to recount [but] part of His mighty deeds, to explain what He has done and what He in future will do, so that His great name may be exalted among the creatures whom He has created from one end of the world to the other." Apart from Yosephon, Yeraḥmeel used extensively many Western homiletical compositions otherwise known to us mainly through Moses the Preacher of Narbonne and Raymond Martini. Following his main sources, he concentrated his account on the creation of the world, the story of Adam and his early progeny, inserting an interesting semiscientific chapter on the seven planets; the Hebrew patriarchs; Moses and the settlement of Canaan, curiously preceded by a chapter on the history of Rome and interrupted by a similar brief account of Greek history; that of the Babylonian Exile with the related Daniel and Zerubbabel legends; and finally a lengthy paraphrase of the story of Judah Maccabee as found in Yosephon. Yeraḥmeel reverted to some themes of his book in several didactic poems, including one devoted to the chronological computation of the dates and lifespans of the twelve sons of Jacob. Another poem summarized the chronological sequences in world history, largely based on the rabbinic theory of three world eras of two thousand years each allotted to the duration of the universe.[55]

Far less persuasive is the general assumption of Yeraḥmeel's southern Italian residence. Yeraḥmeel's knowledge of Latin (not of Greek, as suggested by Neubauer) would prove nothing more than that he lived in a Western country. Perhaps we may derive a clue from his great indebtedness to a pseudo-Philonian apocryphon. For lack of a better designation called by its first editor, John Sichardus in 1527, the *Antiquitatum biblicarum liber,* this apocryphon is by itself a remarkable specimen of early Jewish homiletical historiography which, like most ancient apocrypha, owed its preservation mainly to Christian circles. It is generally assumed, on the basis of admittedly inconclusive arguments, that it originated soon after the fall of Jerusalem. Although nothing has remained from either its alleged original Hebrew text or its Greek translation, its stories were familiar to Eastern churchmen as well, and it unquestionably was available to medieval Western Jews in its Latin garb. Several manuscripts written in the eleventh century or soon after are still extant. Their provenance would seem to confirm the general impression that Yeraḥmeel lived in an area under the direct control of the Holy Roman Empire, most probably in northern Italy.[56]

Yeraḥmeel's poems and chronicle alike are available to us only in the compilation by a Rhenish Jew, Eleazar ben Asher ha-Levi, written in 1325. From a life-long hobby of collecting aphorisms and chronicles, Eleazar presented here "records of all events and incidents which had happened from the creation of the world until the present day . . . and as I found, so I copied, and I have deftly woven the materials to form one book." This is a decided overstatement. The individual tracts, loosely connected with one another, include also a much briefer but interesting Hebrew world chronicle from Adam to the destruction of the Second Temple, possibly likewise a part of Yeraḥmeel's original Chronicle. Despite its apparently factual approach, its author's preeminently apologetic purpose is manifest in his enumeration of "the prophets and sages who prophesied and received the Torah and handed it over to one another." While this enumeration includes Balaam, Job, and his friends, he hastens to restate the traditional Jewish view that "from the time of the revelation of the Torah to Israel the Holy Spirit ceased to inspire the nations." With this conviction Jews could readily dispute the authenticity of Mohammed's, if not of Jesus', prophetic messages. Uncritically, but wholly in the temper of his age, the author also quotes an Aggadah stating that "in the days of our teacher Moses many books had been written" describing the earlier history of mankind. Among them was the "Book of Adam" which had depicted the works of Creation and the Divine Chariot.[57]

Another interesting and even more popular work of belletristic historiography circulated under the alternate titles of *Sefer ha-Yashar* (Book of the Just) or *Toledot Adam* (The Generations of Man). Of unknown date, but most probably stemming from late eleventh-century Spain, this book retold the biblical story from the Creation to the death of Joshua. With complete insouciance for historical fact, the author filled in the gaps from legends found in Yosephon, the midrashim, and current folk tales, Jewish and non-Jewish, and apparently also from his own fertile imagination. At the same time he evinced genuine interest in chronology and endeavored to synchronize especially the recorded, or imaginary, events in the history of ancient Israel with those among its neighbors. This attention to chronological detail, and the author's ability to supply many names of heroes and heroines not mentioned in Scripture, doubtless impressed uncritical readers as signs of his intimate familiarity with the ancient history of man. Since they found in the Bible itself several references to a *Sefer ha-Yashar,* many unhesitatingly identified this medieval blend of history and romance with that long-lost ancient work. This identification, at times shared by historically unsophisticated jurists and exegetes, was reinforced by the author's elegant, biblical style and his flowing, connected narration which easily resolved many puzzling passages in the Pentateuch. Its entertainment value, too, was very high. It must have appealed particularly to tired, easy-going, or romantically inclined readers seeking an escape from the exacting studies of Halakhah or philosophy. Its first editor, Joseph ben Samuel of Fez, recommended it especially to preachers and travelers. "Any public speaker who will insert in his address matters taken from it which had not previously been explained by the commentators, will thereby attract the listeners to his speech. . . . All the merchants and travelers who have no time to study the Torah will read it and be rewarded." [58]

JEWISH AND WORLD HISTORIES

In all these writings the homiletical-hermeneutic element predominated. Whether they pursued a primarily apologetic purpose, aimed at the edification and moral exhortation of coreligionists, or were intended merely to amuse their readers, the historical narratives were communicated mainly as object lessons, rather than as records of historical events. In this branch of literature, as in its underlying oral deliveries, the narrators allowed free rein to their vivid imagination.

On the other hand, the growing intelligentsia in Muslim lands soon began demanding more reliable data on the Jewish past. Those attending the cultural conventicles in Baghdad must have been affected by the curiosity in historical facts evinced by many members. In his description of the ninth-century assemblies, Ibn Qutaiba observed that these conversations often brought up names of prophets, kings, and scholars, or referred to historic battles and other events. "Those present usually wish to know precisely which specific event the speaker had in mind, where the area inhabited by the particular tribe was located, when that king lived, and to be informed about the general biographical data of the persons mentioned." At such meetings many Muslims must have learned from their Jewish and Christian interlocutors the main historical facts recorded in the Bible, and stimulated the Jews themselves to inquire more fully about the events of their past. Yet neither the rise of an Arab historiography, culminating in the works of Al-Mas'udi and Al-Biruni, nor the revival of the Greek historical literature in Byzantium during the ninth and tenth centuries, found any responsive echo among the Jewish leaders. Maimonides voiced the regnant opinion of his rabbinic confreres when he advised his readers against studying such historical tracts "as are found among the Arabs describing past events, the governments of kings and Arab genealogy, or books of song and similar works, which neither possess wisdom nor yield profit for the body, but are a sheer waste of time." Apart from objecting to the plethora of anecdotes, Maimonides and other Jewish thinkers must have felt that these books could not serve as models for Jewish historical works. Principally concerned with "political" history, with wars, conquests, dynastic rivalries, and changes in public administration, they appeared of slight relevance to a people with no ordinary political life of its own, and whose past seemed significant only in terms of its religious and intellectual history.[59]

Only one fairly important Jewish historical work of the early Muslim period may have been directly connected with the political struggles of the day. We recall how frequently the authority of the Babylonian princes of captivity was challenged by opponents, both orthodox and sectarian. We are less well informed about the vicissitudes of that branch of the exilarchic family which, in the days of Mar Zuṭra III, had transplanted itself to Palestine and had held sway in Tiberias for several generations. Probably that branch, too, encountered some opposition from local families, even before the arrival of 'Anan's descendants who claimed for themselves the supreme authority as "princes" of Palestinian and world Jewry. Although nowhere recorded, skeptics may have doubted the Davidic descent of all these contestants. In a period when spurious genealogies were often fabricated for political reasons—even Saadiah's claim to purer descent from Judah than King David's progeny could hardly meet the tests of exacting historical criticism—such doubts could not be dismissed lightly. An historical underpinning of the authority of the exilarchic family thus became an urgent public concern. Apart from the great gap in its genealogy during the long period of the Second Commonwealth, there were many obscurities about the decline in the family fortunes at the end of the Sassanian regime and its restoration to power under the early caliphs. The exilarchic family itself doubtless had genealogical records, more or less reliable at least for the first millennium C.E. Curiously, however, except for the various versions of the Bustanai story, some of which were undoubtedly inspired by the exilarchic party, we possess no full-fledged enumeration of the princely line in Babylonia during the Muslim era.[60]

Here the ninth-century compilation called *Seder 'olam zuṭa* (Smaller World Order) partially filled the lacunae by first supplying data on the earlier periods to the days of Mar Zuṭra III. From there on it furnished a list of eleven Palestinian generations, but passed over the Babylonian branch in silence. Doubtless written in Palestine in order to buttress the claims of the Palestinian branch, it has given us important information about the Tiberian leaders during the obscure centuries of late Byzantine and early Muslim rules. Like its famous predecessor, the *Seder 'olam rabbah* (Large World Order) by R. Jose ben Ḥalafta, which in part it copied, it is limited for the most part to a simple enumeration of names and dates. One major exception is its lengthy description of a conflict between the representative of Exilarch Huna and the latter's father-in-law, R. Ḥanina, head of the academy. This controversy ended when the whole exilarchic family died out except for Huna's posthumous son and Ḥanina's grandson, Mar Zuṭra II. After the latter's execution by the Persians, his son Mar Zuṭra III settled in Palestine. Not surprisingly, the Karaite leaders, who generally rejected Rabbanite claims, fully adopted the scheme propounded by our author which helped sustain their own founder 'Anan's Davidic ancestry. Several lists of Karaite princes of Jerusalem are still extant, enumerating the latter's ancestors in accordance with that reconstruction.[61]

Even more fateful for the evolution of the Jewish people was the sectarian strife over the historic transmission of Oral Law. All heterodox currents ultimately had to appeal to history, especially to the biblical record of the past and the messianic goal of the future. Pre-Karaite and Karaite sectarians alike must have been particularly irked by the semisecret nature of the legal traditions within the precincts of the two academies. With the growth of a literary-minded intelligentsia, objections were raised not only against the exclusive controls thus exercised by the academies' "memorizers," but also against the reliability of oral transmission as such. Shortages of talmudic texts could still be explained by their bulk and huge expense of reproduction, but copies of the Mishnah had already been available to outside readers for several centuries. Because of its inclusion of many points debated by the ancient rabbis, the Mishnah served as a ready target for all antirabbinic objectors to its being the main repository of ancient traditions. Some opponents asked, on the other hand, why, despite the ancient prohibition of committing the Oral Law to writing, Judah the Patriarch and his associates had suddenly decided to compile a written Mishnah.

Apart from the various partisan biases, the growing difficulties faced by Muslim students of the law must have stimulated such inner searching among Jews, too. The circulation in all Near Eastern countries of sayings attributed to Mohammed, many of them obviously spurious, had forced the Muslim traditionalists to buttress their authenticity with full-fledged chains of tradition. Intelligent Jews, particularly outside the range of the two academies, could not help being affected by the ensuing skepticism. Even in antiquity, moreover, the chronological setting of each statement had a direct bearing on practical legal decisions because of the primacy of the Tannaim over Amoraim, and of the latter over their saboraic and geonic successors, contrasting, as we recollect, with the opposite principle that the latest authority be allowed to prevail.

For this reason books devoted to talmudic methodology, beginning with the *Seder tannaim va-amoraim* (Order of Tannaitic and Amoraic Sages), had to take cognizance of that chronological factor. Written in 884–86, the *Seder*'s first three chapters were wholly devoted to the chronology of the successive generations of prophets and sages down to the beginning of the geonic age. The author evidently had at his disposal not only the stray data recorded in the Talmud, which he assiduously collected, but also many oral traditions circulating in the Babylonian academies. True, the existing versions reveal many inconsistencies, even obvious errors. Certainly, the computation that from Hillel to Judah the Patriarch 311 years had passed does not square with the facts. Even worse is the statement that "from Rabbah to R. Ashi 204 years elapsed." In the chapter immediately preceding, the three contemporary Amoraim by the name of Rabbah are said to have died in 633, 645, 647, or 663 Sel. era, respectively, while R. Ashi's demise is dated in 738. Much ingenuity has been expended by scholars in harmonizing these figures, but the only satisfactory answer lies in the twin assumptions that the author was quite lax in incorporating mutually exclusive records, and that there was far-reaching despoliation of his text by subsequent copyists. Nevertheless his computations, backed by strong academic traditions, soon enjoyed fairly universal acceptance, although none of the later geonim directly quoted this work. Writing a century later on the same subject, Sherira altogether failed to refer to this important forerunner. If, as a Pumbedita patriot Sherira disliked a tract inspired by the rivaling academy of Sura, this fact should not have discouraged the later heads of that academy, including Saadiah and Samuel ben Ḥofni. Possibly they were all deterred by mistakes which may already then have disfigured the existing texts. They also generally refused to give the stamp of official approval to a work produced by a private scholar. Had not this *esprit de corps* militated even against their adequate use of the far more distinguished juridico-homiletical work by Aḥai of Shabḥa? European Jewry had no such restraints. Introduced into the West by Joseph Tob 'Elem (Bonfils), who personally prepared a careful recension, and recopied by Simḥah of Vitry for inclusion in his *Maḥzor,* the data summarized in the *Seder* underlay all subsequent chronological considerations in the schools of Rashi and the Tosafists. They also served as a basis for the Maimonidean computation of the forty generations of teachers from Moses to R. Ashi.[62]

By Saadiah's time the main outlines of the Rabbanite answer to these challenging questions had already been formulated. But there remained much room for differences of opinion among the Rabbanite leaders themselves with respect to certain significant details. Saadiah's protracted controversy with Ben Meir clearly demonstrated such internal cleavages even in regard to a vital issue like the calendar and the ensuing calculation of the proper dates for the observance of Jewish holidays. Saadiah felt prompted, therefore, to take up the cudgels also in defense of the rabbinic reconstruction of the history of Jewish tradition. As reported by a Karaite controversialist, the gaon had included in his polemical pamphlet, the *Sefer ha-Galui,* the following brief summary of the Rabbanite position:

Our fathers began to compile the Mishnah after the passage of forty years since the construction of the Second Temple, and continued until one hundred and fifty years after its destruction, five hundred and ten [thirty] years in all. The compilers included eleven generations [not counting the first or the last]: the generation of the Men of the Great Synagogue, those of Simon the Pious; Antigonus; Jose ben Yo'ezer and Joseph [Jose] ben Joḥanan; Joshua ben Peraḥiah and Nittai of Arbela; Judah ben Ṭabbai and Simon ben Shetaḥ; Shemayah and Abṭalion; Hillel and Shammai; R. Joḥanan ben Zakkai; R. Eliezer, R. Joshua, R. Gamaliel, R. Ṭarfon and R. 'Aqiba; R. Simon ben Gamaliel; and the Holy Rabbi [Judah]. His [Saadiah's] opinion is that the incentive to this compilation was that, when prophets ceased to preach and the Jews found themselves dispersed, they feared that their tradition might be forgotten. They now placed their reliance on writing. Hence they assembled all the opinions theretofore preserved, wrote them down, and gave the work the title of Mishnah.

Although echoing the chain of tradition already recorded in the Sayings of the Fathers, under whose impact the Tannaim are called here "fathers," the gaon emphasized the successive stages in the *writing* of the Mishnah. He also traced its beginning back to the Men of the Great Synagogue who, according to rabbinic tradition, included the last prophets, Haggai, Zechariah, and Malachi. Perhaps he merely repeated here a contention he had formulated in his biography of Judah the Patriarch which he had written on request while still in Mosul. Despite the great popularity of contemporary Arab biographies, it appears that neither the initiator of that request nor Saadiah was interested in a purely historical exposition, but rather wished to come to grips with the basic problems of the redaction of the Mishnah. Not surprisingly, Sherira refused to follow Saadiah's lead.[63]

SHERIRA AND IBN DAUD

In the meantime, the growth of provincial centers and the spread of literacy had intensified scholarly curiosity in the history of Judaism, if not in that of Jews. The leadership of the Kairuwan community, in particular, raised numerous pertinent questions and thus elicited from informed geonim answers backed by long-range traditions and frequent consultation of the academies' archives.

One such inquiry addressed by Jacob bar Nissim to Sherira caused the gaon to issue in 987 his famous "Epistle," which unwittingly became an historiographic classic. Jacob sought information about when and how the Mishnah, Tosefta, the *baraitot,* and the Talmud had been compiled and what work the Saboraim had done in revising these collections. Jacob wanted to know, especially, "whether the Men of the Great Synagogue had really begun the writing of the Mishnah and the sages of each generation had written [additional] parts of it until Rabbi [Judah] came and completed it." If so, what was the meaning of the general rule that any unnamed mishnah stemmed from R. Meir, most mishnahs falling within that category. Moreover, most Tannaim recorded by name lived at the end of the Second Commonwealth or were the disciples of R. 'Aqiba. Why did the sages of the preceding generations thus leave the definitive formulation of the laws to their late successors? Nor was Jacob entirely satisfied with the sequence of the Mishnaic tractates. Those dealing with the holidays, for example, clearly failed to follow the order of the calendar. Furthermore, why had the important additional tannaitic traditions and explanations in the Tosefta been excluded from the Mishnah itself? Jacob finally wanted to know more about the latest period following that of the Saboraim: "who reigned after them, and how many [scholars] reigned from then to the present?"[64]

Some of these questions could readily be answered on the basis of the existing literature. Sherira clearly disavowed, however, Saadiah's contention that the Mishnah had been compiled in writing over a period of generations. Laying stress upon the predominance of oral transmission, still practiced in his own academy, he insisted that throughout the Second Commonwealth traditions had been handed down reliably from teacher to disciple without arousing any serious controversy. Only after the fall of Jerusalem and Bethar did the confusion among the rabbis themselves lead to differences of opinion which required an authoritative reformulation of the old dicta. Judah the Patriarch arranged them in proper order within each tractate, but he paid less attention to the sequence of the tractates, each of which constituted an independent unit. Without saying it, Sherira also intimated that even after Judah's redaction the Mishnah remained a purely oral document —a view shared by the Franco-German schools which thus interpreted their version of the gaon's "Epistle." [65]

In all this Sherira essentially followed the talmudic record. But in reconstructing the chain of tradition in the posttalmudic period he had to rely principally on the academies' own records, both written and oral. Since this was a rabbinic responsum, he employed in this section, too, the usual care and precision which he accorded to other legal replies. Most of his sources have since disappeared, and it is not always possible to check on the accuracy of his statements. However, whatever external evidence exists, it usually bears him out. Of course, he left many questions unanswered, Jacob and other contemporaries soon soliciting further explanations of particular items. Modern scholarship, too, has for more than a century been busy clarifying many details, especially since Rapoport's famed biographies of Saadiah, Hai, and Nathan ben Yeḥiel. But these critical endeavors have merely underscored our utter dependence on Sherira's "Epistle" for the knowledge of the geonic period, and shown how much confusion still reigns in those areas, for example in the history of the Palestinian gaonate, where Sherira leaves us in the dark. It is small wonder, then, that, written in a lucid talmudic idiom, his "Epistle," which was intended mainly for the private information of a few leaders in Kairuwan, became an important literary source for future generations, indeed, the outstanding historiographic contribution of the geonic era.[66]

For some unknown reason Hai Gaon, who may have collaborated

with his father in the preparation of that reply, felt impelled to include another history of Jewish tradition in a methodological work on the Talmud. The recipient's son, Nissim ibn Shahin, likewise contemplated producing a similar summary. Perhaps both men merely sought to popularize in Arabic Sherira's findings written in a rather technical Aramaic, but nothing further is known about either work.[67]

The task was accomplished on a much broader canvas by Abraham ibn Daud of Toledo (1110–80). Although living at the western end of the Mediterranean, where Jewish heresies had made but slight headway, this outstanding Aristotelian philosopher felt more keenly than any of his compatriots the intellectual challenge of Karaite thinkers and exegetes. Curiously, with complete abandon he asserted that "these heretics never did any good to Israel; they have never written a book lending support to the Torah or containing a matter of wisdom, not even a single poem or liturgical composition, nor a verse of comfort, for they are mute dogs who cannot bark." Almost in the same breath, however, he mentioned the commentaries of Abu'l Faraj (Harun, or Furqan ibn Asad), which he had found theologically and legally so obnoxious that he had written a special pamphlet in reply. At the same time he minimized the effectiveness of Karaite propaganda which had been imported into Spain by Abu'l Faraj's pupil, Sa'id ibn al-Taras, but was sharply repressed by the Rabbanite leaders with governmental assistance.[68]

Nonetheless Ibn Daud considered it his sacred duty to compose, in 1160–61, a special tract, the *Sefer* (or *Seder*) *ha-Qabbalah* (Book or Order of Tradition; a combination of both titles is likewise possible) to answer the Karaite strictures against the veracity and dependability of the traditional law. In its opening paragraph he stated bluntly:

We have written it in order to let the students know that the words of our masters the sages of Mishnah and Talmud are all handed down through tradition by one great and pious scholar who had heard it from the lips of another great and pious scholar, one head of academy and his associates from the lips of another head of academy and his associates—all the way back to the Men of the Great Synagogue who had heard it from the prophets, blessed be the memory of them all. None of the talmudic sages, and still less those of the Mishnah, have ever stated anything from their own heart except when they enacted new ordinances with universal consent, in order to build a fence around the Torah.

The occasional disagreements among them related to details of the implementation of certain commandments, not to the commandments themselves. Abraham assailed Karaites also in many asides, as when he discussed the "great miracle" of the encounter between Simon the Pious and Alexander the Great, which had spared the Jews much suffering. "Nothing like that," he exclaimed, "ever happened to 'Anan or Qirqisani, the heresiarchs!" By naming Qirqisani, next to 'Anan, as the chief spokesman of Karaism, Ibn Daud again betrayed his anger over that heresy's intellectual challenge. Perhaps it was Qirqisani's reconstruction of world and Jewish history which had forced him to take a stand. His complete silence concerning the kings of northern Israel, contrasting with the full list of the Judean rulers, may have been but an emphatic rejection of Qirqisani's theory that the Rabbanite deviation from true, that is Karaite, Judaism, had begun with the schism of Jeroboam I. Ibn Daud tried to show that the Rabbanite view had been championed in each generation by the physical descendants of David and Solomon down to the days of Hillel, the founder of the patriarchal dynasty of Palestine, forgetting that the patriarchs themselves had claimed descent from the Davidic house only through the distaff side.[69]

Abraham employed such asides to grind some other apologetic axes. While mentioning the generation of Joshua ben Peraḥiah and Simon ben Shetaḥ, he emphasized that Jesus had been born in the days of Alexander Jannaeus, or more than 110 years before the Christian era. At the conclusion of his book and in the appendix devoted to the history of Roman rulers he emphasized again that, since the Gospels had thus been written long after Jesus' death, they possessed but slight documentary value. Rather inconsistently with his general theory he implied that one could not rely on the Christians' oral transmission of the life history and words of Jesus. Elsewhere, however, he approximated the Christian dating by placing Jesus' death in the thirty-eighth year of Augustus' reign. With less bias he mentioned the appearance of Mohammed and the Arab conquest of western Asia, but he sharply rebuked Mani, who had allegedly "invented for the Magians a Torah from his own heart" and taught them the dualist doctrine, but ultimately met his death at the hands of "Shabur in his wisdom." [70]

Despite many inaccuracies in detail, particularly with respect to world history, Ibn Daud's chronicle was a major historiographic achievement in medieval Jewish letters. He devotes only about three fifths of his chronicle to the long history of tradition to the end of the Babylonian gaonate which, following him, modern scholars have long dated with the death of Hai in 1038. In this section Abraham is wholly dependent on older sources, though perhaps not on Sherira's "Epistle"; most of these are accessible to us, too. Yet, looking at that geonic period from the vantage point of the critical review of pertinent sources by Samuel ibn Nagrela and Yehudah bar Barzillai, he is able to supplement and clarify many statements in the earlier historical literature. More informative are the remaining two fifths of his treatise, where he records in far greater detail and with much more zest and personal participation the story of the postgeonic century, principally in his native Spain. Here he speaks with authority on the basis of first-hand reports, both written and oral. On occasion, he mentions oral communications by participants or readers of such interesting documents as the aforementioned circular letter addressed by Saadiah to several Spanish communities (pp. 74, 77). Perhaps because he deals here with matters partly within the living memory of prospective readers, he also exercises unusual caution. This part of his Chronicle has, therefore, proved invaluable to all subsequent historical research.

By writing in a vivid Hebrew, with few rhetorical adornments but with much pathos and dramatic illustration, Ibn Daud was able to produce a connected narrative which appealed to many generations of Hebrew readers. True, the organization of his materials leaves much to be desired. Because of his juxtaposition of a primarily chronological with an occasional topical treatment, he is often forced to backtrack. For example, at the end of the amoraic age he reverts to the story of the rise of Sassanian Persia two centuries earlier. He believes that Ardashir successfully overthrew the Roman domination over Iran, just as he assumes that

Nebukadrezzar had previously exercised dominion over Rome. His only evidence is the biblical verse "And all the nations shall serve him." In fact, he asserts with considerable pride that during the entire period from Nebukadrezzar to the Maccabean revolt "the Romans were first under Chaldean, then under Persian, and finally under Hellenistic domination. But when the Hasmoneans prevailed over Antiochus and his kingdom, the Romans, too, rose up in arms, freed themselves from the Greek yoke, and turned the Greeks into their own tributaries." This theory, magnifying the world impact of the Maccabean revolt, may not have been original with our historian-philosopher, since both Christians and Jews had long viewed world history from the standpoint of Scripture, including the Apocrypha, and hence had vastly exaggerated the historical importance to the world of all events in ancient Jewish history. But, as in the case of most medieval authors, we may readily bear with Abraham's inaccuracies, however numerous, when in return we obtain a wealth of dependable information on facts, otherwise incompletely, less accurately, or not at all recorded.[71]

Ibn Daud's great popularity among both Jews and Christians is evident from the numerous editions of his work, beginning with that of Mantua, 1513, and from its translation into Latin, English, German, and other languages. The chronicle served, moreover, not only as an object of emulation by later historians, but also as a gadfly for both epitomes and supplements. Among the former that by the distinguished philosopher Joseph ibn Ṣaddiq is particularly noteworthy. It was included as a chapter of Joseph's *Qiṣṣur Zekher Ṣaddiq* (Epitome of the Memoir of a Righteous Man). The main continuation was produced by Abraham ben Solomon of Torrutiel, who, in a booklet likewise entitled *Sefer ha-Qabbalah* (Book of Tradition), covered the period from Ibn Daud's death in 1180 to 1510.[72]

Compared with the great interest in the history of rabbinic tradition, that in other aspects of Jewish and general history was quite lukewarm. As a philosopher and scientist, Ibn Daud incidentally referred to Aristotle, Hippocrates, Galen, and Ptolemy or his *Almagest* in order to synchronize their dates with the Jewish chronology, just as he tried to integrate Jewish political history with that of the Roman and Persian emperors. He also added two large appendixes devoted to the "History of the Jewish Kings during the Second Temple," and to the "History of Rome." While the general historical information here offered may strike us as quite primitive, it must have come as a revelation to most of Ibn Daud's coreligionists, particularly because of his use of Spanish Christian sources and his explanation of the historic background of certain common geographic designations. He informed them, for example, that during the reign of Emperor Honorius Teuton tribes had invaded their Spanish homeland. As a result the country, formerly called Hispania, received the additional designation of Andalusia, derived from the Vandal conquerors. The mention of Mohammed, on the other hand, gave him the opportunity to refer to the latter's contemporaries, the "great philosopher" Pope Gregory I, and the leading Spanish churchmen, the brothers Isidore and Leander.

Regrettably, both these appendixes, no less biased than the main chronicle, are preserved only in manuscripts and editions even more faulty than those of the "Book of Tradition." Professedly, Ibn Daud's story of the Second Commonwealth was intended "to controvert the heretics who claim that all the works of comfort enunciated by the Israelitic prophets had already been fulfilled under the Second Temple" and that, hence, Jews need not look forward to the coming of the Messiah. Similarly, the Roman history was to prove that "their Gospels were written many years after" Jesus. True, such expostulations need not always be taken at their face value. Many a genuine student of history, even Azariah de' Rossi writing four centuries later, felt the need of justifying before the public his pursuit of such practically "irrelevant" researches. Yet in this case the anti-Christian apologetic purpose is quite transparent. It reflects Abraham's deep concern over the impact on his coreligionists of the gradual Christian reconquest of his beloved Spanish fatherland. His apparent familiarity with the fruits of Spanish Christian historiography could only increase his apprehensions.[73]

Interest in general history, or at least in those general developments which were related to Jewish history, long antedated Ibn Daud, quite apart from some pertinent paragraphs in the folkloristic historiography of Yosephon and Yeraḥmeel. Saadiah, endowed with greater historical vision than any of his geonic predecessors or successors, had produced a *Kitab at-Ta'rikh* (Book of Chronology), a typical blend of world and Jewish historical facts. These data could serve him and his readers as a background, however skeletal, for his other historical writings. Of course, even this general chronology is dominated by the biblical outlook and the centrality of the Jewish people, the main emphasis being placed on the great intellectual trends reflected in the Jewish tradition. The very allotment of space is characteristic. Of the seven chapters into which the treatise, as now extant, is divided, the first two dispose very briefly of the early history of mankind down to Abraham, adding little to the biblical record. The third and fourth chapters, almost four times the size of their predecessors, discuss the ages from Abraham to Moses, and from Moses to the Israelitic monarchy. The largest chapter (the fifth), almost half of the entire treatise, deals with the period of the Israelitic kings and prophets. It is followed by a brief chapter on the Second Commonwealth and the talmudic age, and a still shorter final chapter giving but a few names and dates since the rise of Islam. This chapter is so superficial and has so many obviously later additions that one may question Saadiah's authorship. The public seems to have evinced so little interest in this work of the great gaon that it allowed it to sink into almost total oblivion. Later scholars, too, but rarely copied it or cited it in their own writings.[74]

Among the scholars familiar with Saadiah's work may have been the assiduous collector of geonic materials, Yehudah bar Barzilllai of Barcelona. In his fleeting mention of a "Book of Memoirs on History," Yehudah may have had Saadiah's tract in mind. Qirqisani, the chief Karaite spokesman of the day, may also have been stimulated by the great gaon. Certainly, his historical interests were quite exceptional among his fellow-Karaites, involved as these were in their exegetical, linguistic, and legal studies. Apart from his memorable reconstruction of the history of Jewish sects, Qirqisani evinced as keen an interest as Saadiah in the identification of biblical place names. A quarter-century after the gaon's death a Byzantine writer produced his aforementioned apparently independent compilation, listing the names and dates of several

Hellenistic and of all Roman-Byzantine rulers down to the fourth year of Nicephorus (967). This list, however brief, shows greater familiarity with the imperial succession than is encountered in other medieval Jewish works. For example, the author enumerates three short-lived emperors between Nero and Vespasian. From Justinian on he also includes occasional notes on major events such as Justinian's building of the Church of Saint Sophia, the entry of the Langobards into Italy during the reign of Justinus, the iconoclastic controversy, the rise of the German Empire, and the conquest of Crete and Sicily by the Muslims. While in comparison with the contemporary Christian-Byzantine historians he offers but a few elementary data, he compares favorably even with Ibn Daud's later history of Rome. Finally, we need but mention in passing the fairly independent Samaritan historical literature from the Book of *Asatir* to the chronicle of Abu'l Fatḥ, frequently referred to in our earlier chapters.[75]

None of these chronological compilations, however factual and apparently objective, necessarily reflected detached scholarly curiosity. Even the Byzantine list may have been animated by messianic motivations. But objectivity was never the ideal of medieval historians. Did not even the reputable Byzantine historian of the early thirteenth century, Nicetas Choniates, conclude his history with the Latin Crusaders' conquest of Constantinople in 1204? He simply explained that historical literature, that beautiful invention of the Hellenic spirit, ought not to be abused for the glorification of the deeds performed by barbarians.

CONTEMPORARY CHRONICLES

With a few exceptions such as Yosephon, the "Book of the Just" and Abraham ibn Daud's "Book of Tradition," these general histories could hardly be classified as major contributions to historical literature. Even the most significant historical work of that period, Sherira's "Epistle," is more important as an historical source of information than as a piece of historical writing. Yosephon and the "Book of the Just," on the other hand, belong mainly to belles-lettres and shed more light on the historical outlook and the folklore of Jewry during the High Middle Ages than on either the historical methods of their authors or the dependable factual knowledge of the past among the geonic and early postgeonic intellectuals.

Of even greater significance as historical sources are the chronicles dealing with contemporary events. The craftsmanship of their authors and their accuracy in recording facts vary greatly, as does the sweep and charm of their presentations. Some of them are not even chronicles in the ordinary sense, inasmuch as they merely list certain names and events primarily for liturgical purposes. This is especially true of the German *memor* books intended for use at the recitation of memorial prayers for glorified martyrs. Others are poetic elegies and litanies, in part likewise designed for liturgical use. Most of them, however, whether written in prose, rhymed prose, or verse, reveal a certain freshness of approach and immediacy of their authors' experience which is usually lacking in the more comprehensive historical works. If their bias is completely undisguised, they make up for it by the direct, sometime eye-witness, character of their record and their unique contributions to our historical knowledge of certain events and the motivations behind them.

An early work of this kind was Nathan ben Isaac the Babylonian's "Report," frequently mentioned in these pages particularly in connection with the self-governmental operations of Eastern Jewry. Little is known about the author or the purpose and compass of his remarkable Memoir, of which we possess but a few excerpts in Arabic and Hebrew. He had probably settled in Kairuwan and occupied some position at Ḥushiel's academy in the 960's when he was requested to present to his new compatriots a picture of the activities, mutual competences, and controversies which had affected the highest echelons of communal leadership in his native Babylonia. Obviously, such a request would not have been considered idle curiosity in any country of Jewish settlement feeling the profound effects of the Babylonian world leadership. But in mid-tenth-century Kairuwan this inquisitiveness had direct practical bearing. As we recall, ever since the deposed Exilarch 'Uqba had settled in its midst (about 912), Kairuwanese Jewry, supported by the government, had been building an independent provincial leadership. The constitutional and administrative aspects of Babylonia's Jewish autonomy could serve as both effective models and possible weapons in this struggle for independence from the Eastern leadership then reemerging from its state of eclipse since the turbulent 940's. Nathan satisfied that curiosity by furnishing an elaborate, if nostalgic and romanticizing, description of the high standing of the princes of captivity before the caliph and within the Jewish community. He graphically depicted the ceremonies at the installation of each new exilarch, and the relationships between the exilarchs and the two academies, as well as between the academies themselves. Honestly, he described his "Report" as based "in part on what he had seen in Babylonia, and in part on what he had been told" by others.[76]

Nathan's description of the installation festivities has the earmarks of an eye-witness account. He may indeed have attended such festivities after the election of Yehudah, son of David ben Zakkai, in 940, although the latter was to die within seven months —as it appears, without having secured the necessary caliphal confirmation, perhaps because of the death of Caliph ar-Radi in December of that year and the then generally unsettled state of affairs in Baghdad. Nathan probably refers to this failure when he speaks of the communal leaders having "wished" to place the son in David's seat. He also goes to great lengths in describing the preceding conflict between David ben Zakkai and Saadiah Gaon which, because of the high standing of both contestants, had doubtless made a deep impression in Kairuwan. Possibly to round out the picture, Nathan also described the achievements of "Neṭira and His Sons," that powerful banking house in Baghdad which, during that conflict and for several decades prior to it, had exercised an unofficial ancillary authority over the Jewish community in the capital. Certainly the glorification of these bankers and their allegedly beneficial influence on the Jewish status in the Caliphate must have greatly flattered the newly arisen Jewish plutocracy in the North African community as well.[77]

Of more local interest were the "scrolls" produced by participants in controversies over the regional leadership in Palestine and Egypt. These were in reality political pamphlets using historical arguments to buttress certain partisan views; for instance, with respect to the legitimacy of Bustanai's offspring from the

Persian princess. More comprehensively historical was the so-called *Megillat Abiathar* (Scroll of Abiathar), written in 1094 by Abiathar ben Elijah ha-Kohen. This scion of a long line of priestly geonim tried to prove that his ancestors had presided over the "Tiberian" academy of Jerusalem for many generations with but a brief interruption during the regime of Daniel ben Azariah, the "intruder" from Babylonia's exilarchic family. That "Scroll," or rather "Letter" as it is called by the author himself, was doubtless intended for wide circulation among communal leaders in Palestine and neighboring countries. To it we owe most of our information about the internal evolution of the Palestinian academy in the latter part of the tenth century. Even more limited in scope is the so-called *Megillat Zuṭṭa* (Scroll of Zuṭṭa), describing in much picturesque detail the mismanagement of Jewish communal affairs by the dictatorial Egyptian *nagid* Zuṭṭa (or Sar Shalom) and the latter's final deposition, probably by Saladin. Writing in 1196, the author, Abraham ben Hillel, contrasted the bleak character of this "usurper" with the glorified personalities of the "legitimate" *nagid*, Samuel, "the Mordecai of his time," and Maimonides, "the light of east and west and unique master and marvel of the generation." This pamphlet, written in rhymed prose, was likewise designed as a circular letter to "serve as a permanent memorial for Zuṭṭa." [78]

Since these chronicles were written with the avowed purpose of influencing the readers in current controversies, they concentrate on the more recent past. Even the "Scroll of Abiathar," though furnishing significant facts about the author's ancestors and the Palestinian academy, discusses but briefly Daniel ben Azariah's "usurpation" and aims its main shafts at the spurious claims of his son David to supremacy over Palestinian Jewry through the establishment of an exilarchic office in Egypt. Going back to biblical times, Abiathar argues that the Israelitic priesthood had from the outset been superior in sanctity and permanence to the royal house of David. The latter's selection and the divine grace bestowed on it had been conditioned on the righteous behavior of its members, whereas in fact it included such unregenerate sinners as Ahaz, Menasseh, Ammon, and Jehoiachin. Unhesitatingly, Abiathar asserted that by his behavior David ben Daniel had demonstrated his direct physical descent from these evil kings. David's specific claim to the office of a "prince of captivity" in Egypt was altogether fallacious, because Egypt is not called "captivity" in the Bible. Even the Babylonian exilarchs, moreover, had no authority over Palestinian Jewry, which had, in fact, retained its world control over the calendar. For this purpose, Abiathar inserted a lengthy juristic excursus on the exclusive right of the Palestinian authorities to proclaim the new moon, a right still recognized, according to him, by the Babylonian exilarchs themselves in 835.[79]

No such bias dictated the composition of the Chronicle of Aḥimaaz, the most celebrated Jewish family chronicle of the period. In fact, except for the perfectly simple pride in his ancestry, the author reveals no other motive in compiling this record, which he completed in Sivan 4814 (May–June, 1054). Apart from gathering various family records, probably more oral than written, he left his Capuan residence and spent some time in Oria, the main scene of his ancestors' activities.

And I, Aḥimaaz, son of R. Palṭiel, son of R. Samuel, son of R. Ḥananel, son of R. Palṭiel, son of R. Ḥasadiah, son of R. Ḥananel, son of R. Amittai, the servant of the Lord, . . . asked a boon of Him . . . that He might hearken to my prayer, to let me succeed in finding the genealogy of my fathers. . . . He has granted the wish I have so ardently asked of Him. . . . With God's help I have arranged and written it [that genealogy] in poetic form. I have begun at the beginning; from the captivity of Jerusalem and the destruction of the house of our (my) glory, through the captivity of the city of Oria, in which I have settled, I have come down to the arrival of my fathers in Capua; and have ended with my own time and that of my children. I have collected and compiled it in a book, and narrated it for the generations to come.

This summary is misleading in so far as Aḥimaaz' knowledge of the early generations was limited to the family tradition that its ancestors had arrived in Italy among the captives of Titus. This claim, advanced by many other Italian Jewish families as well, found few objectors among contemporaries and, in view of the uninterrupted Jewish settlement in Rome from the first century B.C.E., cannot be positively refuted even by modern historians. Aḥimaaz' real story begins with Amittai and his three sons, Shephaṭiah, Ḥananel, and Eleazar, living during the second half of the ninth century, and continues through the following two centuries. Only at the very end, perhaps as an afterthought, the author appends a sort of chronological table of the leaders of intervening generations.[80]

The main historical and literary merits of this chronicle consist less in the story of the family fortunes than in its numerous semihistorical and semilegendary anecdotes. Told with much gusto, this blend of history and folklore, so characteristic also of the contemporary Byzantine and Western historical literatures, has shed much new light on the life and thought of the Jewish communities in southern Italy, the place of confluence of the great cultural currents from the Muslim, Byzantine, and Western worlds. True, Aḥimaaz' factual records are so overlaid with these picturesque descriptions that modern historians had to expend much energy in salvaging at least a few dependable facts. Yet these few items have helped to clarify many important aspects in the political, communal, and cultural history of European Jewry during that dark period of its history. While in many respects akin to the folkloristic historiography of a Yosephon or Yeraḥmeel, Aḥimaaz' likely Italian compatriots, our chronicle concentrates on the destinies of but a single family, and hence is able to contribute more detailed insights. At the same time it clearly mirrors the main outlook and aspirations of the Jewish intelligentsia in the Italo-Byzantine sphere of influence.[81]

More limited in scope, but for that very reason even more useful for the reconstruction of historical events, are the Hebrew chronicles relating to the great tragedy of European Jewry during the First and Second Crusades. Although not completely devoid of legendary, even "superstitious" ingredients, these chronicles, supplemented in many significant details by the brief entries in *memor* books and by numerous poems and prayers, have furnished solid information unrivaled by any earlier medieval Jewish records. Because of their great importance for the understanding of a major turning point in Jewish and world history, they have been subjected to close scrutiny for three quarters of a century. Without repeating the conflicting views on the respective dates and merits of the narratives by Solomon bar Simson, Eliezer bar Nathan, and the Mayence Anonymus relating to the First Crusade, or that by Ephraim of Bonn concerning the events during 1146, we need but add here their brief evaluation as parts of the Hebrew historical literature.

Solomon's chronicle was apparently based upon an older account compiled from Jewish and non-Jewish sources, particularly letters and oral traditions, by a more immediate contemporary. This original record was probably intended only for limited circulation within the affected communities themselves. After several decades, however, Solomon and other twelfth-century historians utilized that material to compose narratives for distribution over a wider area as a means of strengthening the faith of many perplexed Jews. By rehearsing the story of the great martyrs, by glorifying their unwavering adherence to their ancestral creed, and by stressing the heart-rending example of eleven hundred *'aqedot* (immolations) performed in Mayence alone in one day, Solomon and his compeers hoped to weaken the impact of anti-Jewish hostility and the Church's missionary efforts. More than their predecessors, they thus sounded the keynote of the "lachrymose conception of Jewish history." Not surprisingly, they are written with the same elegiac overtones as were the numerous contemporary dirges. Possibly from the outset intended for synagogue recitation on a par with their poetic counterparts, these prose narratives performed the same function of helping to inspire the multitude with the idea of unquestioning submission to the inscrutable will of God. Yet because of their length and emphasis on factual detail rather than malediction, they were immediately overshadowed by the poets' lyrical outpourings, whose growing use in congregational services assured them widespread popularity and literary survival. Even Solomon's outstanding narrative was rarely reproduced by copyists. Although translated into Judeo-German before the fifteenth century, its only extant Hebrew manuscript was allowed to lie dormant in the archives until its discovery and publication in the late nineteenth century.[82]

Far briefer, less informative, and historiographically of but secondary interest are the minor records of local or individual persecutions. Mention has already been made of the short fragments, each arbitrarily entitled by their editor "A Horrible Story," which described the sufferings of the Jewish community of Limoges in 992 and the dangers threatening many Western communities less than two decades later. These dangers were averted only through Jacob bar Yequtiel's successful intervention with the pope. Since the former bears the manuscript superscription of "Letter to [!] the Community of Limoges [?]," both documents seem to have been parts of circular letters sent out for the information, and perhaps warning, of neighboring communities. Another such epistle recited the sanguinary experiences of the community of Blois in 1171, which had so profoundly moved Jacob Tam and other contemporaries. On the other hand, a circular letter sent out to the Byzantine communities by an Egyptian Jewish official complaining of the loss of his high position at the court of the powerful vizier Al-Afdhal (1096–1121), belongs to the category of autobiographical records, which abounded in the Muslim literature but were very rare among Jews. All of these epistles clearly merit our consideration as historical sources rather than as contributions to Jewish historiography.[83]

TRAVELOGUES

Much historically relevant material was also contained in the contemporary travel literature. Here eye-witness accounts of the travelers themselves were intermingled with factual reports of local informants and a great many stories and legends. With the broadening of geographic horizons, concomitant with the spread of international trade and the growth of scientific curiosity in other lands and peoples, travelogues, Jewish and non-Jewish, became very popular.

Not surprisingly, Jews were particularly fascinated by reports about distant coreligionists. Their perennial controversies with Muslims and Christians, in particular, made them rejoice whenever they heard that in some remote regions there still existed Jewish tribes not subject to foreign domination. Even such a level-headed diplomat and scientist as Ḥisdai ibn Shapruṭ, as we recollect, instantaneously tried to communicate with the Khazar king, explaining that it was not idle curiosity which had dictated his letter.

He who tests hearts [he assured the king] and searches the reins knows that I have not done all this in order to enhance my honor, but only to ascertain the truth as to whether there indeed exists a place where the dispersed of Israel have retained a remnant of royal power, and where the Gentiles do not govern and oppress them. If I knew that this report is true, I should gladly relinquish my dignity and abandon my family, to render myself speedily through hills and mountains, through seas and lands, until I reached the place where my lord, the king, resides, so that I might view his greatness and majesty . . . and the peace of Israel's remnant.

There is little doubt, indeed, that messengers able to transmit letters from Spain to Khazaria and back found eager listeners among the broad masses. Isaac, Charlemagne's envoy to Harun ar-Rashid, must also have been extremely busy satisfying the curiosity of a host of inquirers during and after his return from his memorable journey.[84]

On a lesser scale other Jewish travelers, commercial as well as scholarly, brought the knowledge of conditions in their home countries to the communities they visited, and brought back similar information about the situation in foreign lands. We do not hear among Jews of such persistent travelers as Ibn Ḥawqal who spent fully thirty years on his journeys, in part it seems in the employ of the Faṭimid intelligence service. But, for instance, Dunash ben Labraṭ undoubtedly brought with him to Spain not only the new approaches of Babylonian Jewish philology and poetry, but also information concerning the general and Jewish ways of life in that great Eastern center. On the other hand, an exiled Spanish scholar like Joseph ibn Abitur, on his arrival in Babylonia, doubtless found interested listeners for his descriptions of the newly arising Western center of Jewish and Arab culture.

Because of the deep-seated blend of popular curiosity and disaffection with existing conditions, even Eldad ha-Dani's venturesome tales enjoyed considerable vogue. Once he reached the more populous Jewish settlements, Eldad doubtless found little difficulty in earning a living as an itinerant storyteller. Judging from the extant fragments of his letters, he was a very gifted narrator. Unfortunately, his limited personal authority and his frequent legal deviations from the established Palestino-Babylonian norms removed the few restraints which medieval copyists were wont to impose upon themselves. In his case, they felt perfectly free to alter his original stories in accordance with their own tastes or those of their prospective readers. Only his reports about the laws observed in his homeland underwent less radical changes. Here the ingrained habit of faithfully transmitting legal traditions helped to preserve the original texts with relative fidelity.[85]

Eldad had a mixed reception in the Western communities. Some Jews felt flattered by his stories about distant Jewish tribes enjoying political independence. Even those who disbelieved his fairy tales raised no serious objections to their diffusion along with purely fictional romances. Leaders and public were disconcerted, however, by the significant legal discrepancies between the usages allegedly prevailing in Eldad's home country and the existing laws. Noticing only a few chance resemblances to familiar schismatic juridical systems, especially that of the Karaites, bewildered scholars of North Africa appealed for guidance to the Babylonian academies (about 880). They were reassured by R. Ṣemaḥ bar Ḥayyim (?) Gaon of Sura and enjoined not to accuse the strange visitor of willful distortion. Some of his variations might be explained, the gaon wrote, by simple forgetfulness during his long and perilous journey. Others were undoubtedly the result of varying local traditions, such as had also caused numerous divergences between Palestinian and Babylonian observances. Later generations, for the most part, gratefully accepted Eldad's reports and attached to them considerable authority. No less a scholar than R. Ḥananel personally copied Eldad's *Halakhot*, later often quoted as "Palestinian Halakhot," or some other designation indicating their great prestige.[86]

Curiously, Eldad found few imitators, except among outright romancers. We know, in fact, of no subsequent Jewish travelogues until their sudden efflorescence in the latter part of the twelfth century. The only significant exception was Ibrahim ibn Ya'qub's Arabic report on his journey to central Europe, preserved merely in fragmentary excerpts cited in a geographic treatise by Al-Bakri (d. 1094) and other Arab writers. Despite protracted efforts by students, especially of early German and Slavonic history, we can merely surmise that he arrived as an envoy of a Spanish-Muslim ruler to Otto the Great in 965, shortly before the emperor's death. He traveled through France and western Germany before reaching Magdeburg, from where he visited both the Baltic areas and Prague. He had the opportunity of conversing with the emperor himself and with other informed leaders, and his general observations in those regions are of vital historic interest. His data concerning Jews, however, are limited to casual references to Jewish traders coming to Prague "from the lands of the Turks," and to a "salt mine of Jews" (or possibly a "Jewish district") in the vicinity of the Saale river. It is small wonder, therefore, that medieval Jews evinced little interest in his report, which left no traces in Hebrew literature. Were it not for its chance preservation by Arab geographers, who found in it rare bits of information on the central European countries, the very fact of that journey would have been completely forgotten. As it is, Al-Bakri was not interested in copying the rest of Ibrahim's report, and but briefly summarized the sections of special interest to him.[87]

Evidently unconnected with these earlier attempts, medieval Jewish travel literature suddenly reached its all-time high point in the reports submitted by Benjamin ben Jonah of Tudela and Petaḥiah bar Jacob of Ratisbon. Though starting from Tudela in northern Spain and from Prague, respectively, some ten or fifteen years apart (about 1165 and 1180), both travelers covered much of the same territory and thus helped confirm each other's observations. Despite their frequent acceptance of hearsay testimony, even of obvious folk tales and legends, Benjamin and, to a lesser extent, Petaḥiah have proved to be extremely valuable guides for the history, population figures, economic occupations, and communal structure of the eastern Jews, particularly those residing outside the major centers of Jewish life. True, their reports cannot always be checked through outside sources. But since many statements are confirmed by the available external evidence, we ought also to give the benefit of the doubt to those lacking outside attestation. In the preceding chapters we have indeed made frequent use of their testimony, as well as of the comments thereon by numerous specialists who, in the course of the last centuries, have translated their works into several western languages and subjected them repeatedly to minute scrutiny. If many problems still await elucidation and the very textual readings often appear dubious or baffling, these shortcomings are largely the result of a highly confused manuscript tradition. The Hebrew transliteration of oriental place names alone created many a pitfall for the often unwary and ill-informed medieval copyists.[88]

Benjamin's general reliability was emphasized already in the earliest known manuscript, that of the British Museum, probably dating from the thirteenth century. In the introduction, which doubtless stemmed from the earliest editor of Benjamin's memoir, the scribe noted that "in every place which he [Benjamin] entered, he made a record of all that he saw, or was told of by trustworthy persons—matters not previously heard of in the land of Sefarad [Spain]." As if speaking of a person still alive, the introduction concluded that Benjamin "*is* a wise and understanding man, learned in the Torah and the *halakhah,* and wherever we have tested his statements we have found them accurate, true to fact and consistent, for he is a trustworthy man." This judgment bears the earmark of official action. While Benjamin's account could not arouse the same suspicions of heterodoxy as had Eldad's legal deviations, it contained enough questionable data to require some sort of public reassurance. Those who had "tested his statements" and "found them accurate" must have been persons of some authority, whose attestation of Benjamin's rabbinic learning, perhaps doubted by his punctilious Spanish contemporaries because of certain weaknesses of his Hebrew style, was evidently aimed at allaying apprehensions.[89]

Benjamin clearly had little opportunity for displaying his halakhic knowledge, but he revealed a keen, almost modern awareness of sociological factors. Wherever he came he tried to ascertain the number of Jews and their economic stratification. He was also greatly interested in their communal organization, their educational facilities, and the level of their intellectual achievements. In many cities he mentioned the local leaders and teachers by name, often serving thus to preserve their memory, and in turn receiving further confirmation and more exact dating for his own record. Although probably not a physician, he evinced keen interest in the medical practices and folkways he had observed. If he himself omitted the dates of his arrivals and departures—a grievous omission for modern investigators forced laboriously to piece together the scraps of available evidence in order to reconstruct a bare chronological outline of his journey—this was doubtless owing to his preparation of the memoir for the exclusive use of contemporaries. He certainly did not perceive how important his data would prove to later generations.

Wherever he failed to supply exact details, Benjamin's narrative has become suspect of having been derived from some second-hand account. Modern scholars have gone too far, however, in denying that he reached the countries east of the Persian Gulf, especially India, merely because of the obvious vagueness of his data in this part of his travelogue. Evidently the further away from the main centers of Jewish learning he moved, the less precise was the information supplied to him by local leaders, who themselves neither possessed nor evinced great curiosity in such exact data. Does not Jewish scholarship in our own "scientific" and highly articulate age suffer from a similar dearth of information concerning the more peripheral Jewish settlements? Hence came also that obvious discrepancy between the moderate population figures reported by Benjamin for the Western and even West Asiatic communities, and the ever larger numbers quoted for the cities further East. Needless to say that, except in the smaller communities where everybody knew everybody else, his best figures are based merely upon rough "guestimates." [90]

Petaḥiah was far less concerned with such factual details. He threw caution to the winds when he quoted the biblical figure of six hundred thousand Jewish inhabitants each for Babylonia, Persia, and Cush (the region of Ethiopia and southern Arabia). Nor is the figure of two thousand disciples who allegedly attended the academy of Baghdad under Samuel ben 'Ali to be taken literally. These and many other exaggerations merely reflected the tremendous impression made by the Near Eastern civilization on this visitor from a backward country. For this reason Samuel, Maimonides' well-known rival, appeared to him as a man "full of wisdom both in the written and the oral law, and in all the wisdom of Egypt. Nothing is hidden from him." Petaḥiah was also amazed by the generally high level of education among Babylonian Jews. "There is no one so ignorant," he exclaimed with his usual abandon, "in the whole of Babylon, Assyria, Media, and Persia, but knows the twenty-four books [the Hebrew Bible] with their punctuation, grammar, the superfluous and omitted letters." Coming from central Europe with its exclusive stress on talmudic learning, such expertness in biblical lore seemed to him truly impressive. From most other countries, however, Petaḥiah regrettably recorded only a few "human interest" stories. For example, starting his journey through Poland, the Ukraine, and the lands under Tartar domination—all countries omitted from Benjamin's itinerary and little known from other contemporary sources—he had an eye only for some exotic customs such as a local blood ritual sealing a compact of perpetual friendship. Even in Khazaria, which must have given him pause because of its Jewish memories (on which, incidentally, he remained conspicuously silent), the only thing he found worth recording from his eight days' journey was the excessive amount of mourning for deceased parents indulged in by the local women. Whatever the motives which induced this apparently wealthy traveler to undertake such an arduous "world tour" (*sibbub ha-'olam*), he evidently learned less from, and communicated less to his readers about, his voyage than his older Spanish contemporary.[91]

Even Petaḥiah, however, remained an isolated phenomenon in the medieval Jewish community. His near-contemporary Jacob ben Nathaniel ha-Kohen left behind merely a brief record of his pilgrimage through the Holy Land, with but a few casual remarks about neighboring Egypt. This genre, richly represented among medieval Christians, was to be cultivated more fruitfully by later Jewish pilgrims, too. But it contributed little to the general geographic information available to educated Western Jews.

More significantly, even Benjamin's and Petaḥiah's travel books, though enjoying a fair degree of popularity, were largely read as belles-lettres for intellectual amusement. They doubtless helped to kindle the imagination of Western Jews, maintain their morale in the midst of successive calamities, and keep alive their perennial yearning toward the Holy Land, which, a generation after Petaḥiah, was to erupt in the dramatic journey of three hundred

Western rabbis to Palestine. Here and there a medieval exegete made use of their data to explain a particularly obscure passage in Bible and Talmud. But from the standpoint of geographic science their works served only as raw material awaiting further exploration, analysis, and integration with other sources. No Idrisis, Yaquts or Qazwinis arose among medieval Jews in either East or West to perform this task. Neither human nor physical geography, except for the latter's philosophically and theologically significant astronomic features, attracted the sustained attention even of the otherwise curious and well-trained Jewish scientists of the period.

Many geographically significant data, to be sure, were discussed by Jewish astronomers and mathematicians in connection with the movements of celestial bodies. Some of them even devoted special treatises to the analysis of the "Shape of the Earth." Many other relevant items are scattered through the entire rabbinic literature, especially the numerous midrashim. Historical works, too, occasionally furnish interesting geographic information on certain regions, localities, and peoples. But only Yosephon made an effort to ascertain the ethnology of a large part of the then known world. In his opening chapter, he discusses the various nations recorded in the tenth chapter of Genesis as descendants of Japheth, son of Noah. In this family of nations, usually identified with the Indo-European group of peoples, Yosephon includes the various Turkic tribes. In fact, because he mentions the Magyars, Bulgars, and Petchenegs as residing on the shore of the Danube and Anatolian Tarsus as still in Muslim possession, modern historians have deduced that this description reflects the ethnographic situation existing between 900 and 965. Since, as we recall, other indications tally with this chronology, there is no reason to attribute this chapter to another author. Yosephon was evidently indebted to non-Jewish predecessors in his identification of contemporary peoples with those recorded in the biblical list, which is the less surprising as the strong impact of biblical ethnology on Jewish and Christian scholarship is illustrated even in our own age by the accepted division between Semitic, Hamitic, and Indo-European races and languages.[92]

HISTORICAL OUTLOOK

Behind all these historical and geographic reconstructions, behind even the biographical legends woven by the people's fertile imagination, loomed a comprehensive, if largely unformulated, outlook on the universe and the historic process. That philosophy of history, if indeed it merits such designation, permeated the thinking of the intellectual leaders and masses alike and was largely shared also by Israel's neighbors, both Christian and Muslim. In its fundamentals laid down by the biblical historians and prophets it had dominated talmudic and patristic thought, and now it set the tone also for the leading Islamic students of history. While ample room was left for differences of opinion in regard to details, particularly those affecting specific religious beliefs, there was basic unanimity in regard to the story of Creation, the divine guidance of history through the instrumentality of man, and the main historic sequences of earlier peoples and faiths.

We shall see that all the resources of secular science and philosophy were used to harmonize the biblical teachings concerning the physical world with those of Greek philosophy stemming from entirely different premises. It was much easier to reconcile the traditional outlook on history with Greek scholarly opinion. Not only were the fundamentals of the geo- and anthropocentric view generally accepted, but in essence the non-Jewish world also conceded to Israel a certain focal position in world history, although the Christians insisted that the Jews had lost it after the appearance of Jesus and the Muslims seriously debated the priority of Ishmael over Isaac. But even they did not gainsay the essential authenticity of the biblical record and its philosophical underpinnings.

No medieval Jews voiced doubts concerning the correctness of their era of Creation, despite minor differences of opinion about the inception of the Jewish calendar. Viewing the past from the standpoint of the late twelfth century, as did Maimonides, the history of the universe divided itself conveniently into two almost equal halves of approximately twenty-five hundred years each, before and after the Sinaitic revelation, which was usually set at 2449 A.M. (1311 B.C.E.). Since Jewish thinkers agreed on viewing all history in terms of the spiritual evolution of man and on treating even the greatest political and military transformations as but subsidiary manifestations of the divine will, the Sinaitic revelation could, indeed, appear as the inception of a new cosmic eon. At the same time, the rabbis subscribed to the aggadic tenet of the Torah's preexistence and the view that, long before Moses, early leaders such as Adam, Enoch, Noah, and the Hebrew patriarchs had been endowed with prophetic gifts and had observed at least part of what was to become the Mosaic law.

In fact, this long pre-Mosaic period often stood in the very focus of discussion by homilists and philosophers, because of the intriguing cosmogony of the book of Genesis, and its story of the emergence of Israel as a religion and a people. With the popular predilection, moreover, for etiological legends, many a sacred locality was associated with ancient heroes. Even Maimonides did not hesitate to explain the superior sanctity of the Temple site in Jerusalem by

> a tradition accepted by everyone that the place where David and Solomon built the altar in the threshing floor of Arauna is the place where Abraham had erected his altar and offered Isaac, and where Noah had built after he left the ark. This is the very altar on which Cain and Abel had offered and on which Adam, too, had brought a sacrifice when he was created; and this was precisely the spot from which he was created. As the sages said, Adam was created from the place of his atonement.

Likewise echoing old legends, Halevi lyrically described Adam as "perfection itself, because no flaw could be found in the work of a wise and almighty Creator." Being born as an adolescent in full possession of his physical and mental faculties, the first man had been spared the difficulties of growing up and of adjusting to the climate, water, and soil. Nor was he burdened by any adverse hereditary traits. "His intellect was the loftiest which it is possible for a human being to possess." Endowed with the prophetic soul in the highest degree, he could commune with celestial beings and "comprehend the great truths without instruction." [93]

Superficially, this picture suggested that the Golden Age had existed at the very dawn of history—a Greek rather than a Jewish idea. In fact, however, medieval Jewish thinkers agreed that, though himself nurtured on the traditions of his grandfather Eber (following the Aggadah, Halevi contended that at his birth Noah had still been alive), Abraham went further than any of his predecessors in formulating the ideas of Jewish monotheism. He, Isaac, and Jacob, as well as the latter's sons, for the first time collectively endowed with the gift of prophecy which had previously been granted to only one outstanding leader of each generation, were further surpassed by Moses, the acme of human personality. Moses was not only a "king" and the greatest lawgiver of all times, but also the greatest of prophets. His prophetic endowment had towered so high above that of any other prophet that, in Maimonides' opinion, only the poverty of human language forces us to use for him the same homonym of "prophet." Moses had also been the only man to receive the divine revelation publicly in the presence of the whole people—a distinction not even claimed by Jesus or Mohammed. This attestation of Moses' mission by 600,000 adult males was indeed to play a great role in the religious controversies of the period. At the same time Maimonides conceded that some Gentiles could share in the prophetic gifts of the lowest order. Only Halevi's nationalist fervor made him deny even proselytes the ability to acquire that native endowment, although he must have realized that this doctrine was running counter to the scriptural record concerning Balaam, Job, and other Gentile seers, and the Aggadah's classification of Prophet Obadiah as an Edomite proselyte. At the other extreme, the author of *Seder Eliyahu rabbah* taught, "I invoke the testimony of heaven and earth that whether Israelite or Gentile, man or woman, male or female slave, in accordance with his deeds the Holy Spirit rests upon him." [94]

After reaching the unexcelled heights of the Sinaitic revelation, Israel and mankind began declining. In this respect Jewish opinion shared the "devolutionary" view of history prevailing among its neighbors. However, Israel still boasted of the great intellectual and spiritual achievements of the Israelitic prophets, including David and Solomon, in the 440 years which supposedly elapsed from its entry into Canaan to the erection of the First Temple, and the 410 years of the latter's existence. Even when prophecy was terminated some forty years after the return from the Babylonian Exile, the bearers of Jewish tradition continued to evolve ever new applications of the old principles.

Going further than most of his contemporaries, Maimonides decided that "there never was a time in which speculation and the discovery of new matters were amiss; the sages of every generation placed great stock in the words of their predecessors and learned from them, and then discovered new things. Only with respect to basic principles of tradition were opinions never divided." In the Maimonidean enumeration of "forty" generations of the chief bearers of tradition, fully twenty belonged to the prophets of the preexilic period. Several postexilic prophets were counted among the Men of the Great Synagogue, who were succeeded by sages without the call to prophesy. Through much of that time Jews suffered from Gentile hostility and, after the Exile, from constant oppression. The tragedy of Exile, which loomed large in all considerations of Jewish fate, also helped to explain the loss by the Jews of their intellectual world leadership. According to a belief widely shared also by non-Jews, the Greeks had learned the main elements of their science and philosophy from Jewish sources (according to legend, Aristotle himself ultimately adopted Judaism) which the Jews subsequently lost on their perennial migrations. In general, the period following the second fall of Jerusalem, and particularly since the conclusion of the Babylonian Talmud, marked the nadir of Jewish history. Full recovery could be expected only from the miraculous liberation of the people and the restoration of its prophetic gifts after the advent of the Messiah, who would usher in the real Golden Age of man on earth and of the universe as a whole.[95]

Spiritual and intellectual achievements so overshadowed all other aspects of history that even the Maccabean uprising and the Roman Jewish wars appeared as but minor episodes, significant only in so far as they helped explain the Maccabean renovation of the Temple and its destruction by the Romans. The Exile also had deep spiritual implications, because residence in the Holy Land, especially endowed by its position in the heart of the fourth climate and other extraordinary features, carried distinction also in the spiritual realm. Such an interpretation of history could only arise from the dominant belief, expressed by Saadiah, that "Israel is a nation only by virtue of its laws." Since, on the other hand, Israel's historic evolution appeared as the core of all human evolution, Jewish thinkers found no difficulty in subsuming the main developments in the outside world under the successive phases of their own "sacred" history.[96]

On the whole, the medieval Jews thus merely adhered to their ancient historic heritage, already greatly refined in talmudic and patristic letters. Even the basic chronology had been fully laid down by Jose ben Ḥalafta and his early successors. Only occasionally could a distinguished poet and thinker like Yehudah Halevi contribute noteworthy variations on these old themes out of his fertile imagination and pent-up nationalist emotions. Apocalyptic visionaries and messianic dreamers likewise added ever new hues to the multicolored pattern of Jewish historical monotheism. But in essence they all merely perpetuated the historical outlook of the ancient Aggadah.

Abraham bar Ḥiyya, the distinguished scientist, was able to add still another dimension to the traditional outlook by opening up new chronological and astrological vistas. His chronological elaboration of scriptural and aggadic data, ingeniously reinterpreted, evoked considerably less opposition than his attempt to apply astrological methods to the interpretation of history, especially since he trod on dangerous ground in thus trying to ascertain the date of the Messiah's arrival. Abraham's daring was but slightly mitigated by his offering several alternate and distant dates. The astrological method in its application to Jewish history also ran counter to the age-old talmudic conviction that, unlike other nations which were governed by particular stars, "Israel has no lucky star" of its own. Yet Abraham believed that the course of stars could explain both past and future events, although future destinies still largely depended on the will of God, who might at any time alter what appeared to be decreed by the stellar constellations.[97]

Bar Ḥiyya did not hesitate to borrow extensively both from the vast astrological literature and from Augustinian and Isidorian concepts, probably familiar to him through works of later disciples and imitators. His main contention was that, since the "week" assigned to the duration of the universe totaled six thousand years, each cosmic "day" amounted to slightly more than 857 years. Accordingly, the Sinaitic revelation in 2449 A.M. and the Israelite settlement in Canaan forty-seven years later occurred toward the end of third "day." One could, therefore, expect the arrival of the Messiah toward the end of the sixth "day," or some time before 5142 A.M. (1382 C.E.). Elaborating this theory in minute detail, Bar Ḥiyya interpreted in its light certain crucial passages in the Bible and the recorded evolution of world history. Here he committed a number of factual blunders; for instance, with respect to the successors of Alexander the Great, the position of Cleopatra, or the struggle between Rome and king "Shabur" in the days of the Maccabean and Herodian dynasties. But he betrayed keen awareness of the necessary integration of world and Jewish historical developments to an extent rarely encountered among his coreligionists, including even his early successor, Ibn Daud.[98]

HISTORY AND FOLKLORE

Abraham's blend of hermeneutics and science with historical reinterpretation, all placed in the service of theological preconceptions and messianic yearnings, was unusual only in his application of mathematical and astrological methods. Otherwise his reasonings and objectives represented the well-nigh universal approach of his Jewish contemporaries. None of them was really interested in history per se. Whatever they thought of the didactic value and purposes of all historical investigations, they certainly saw in them mainly an instrument for proving their theological and ethical teachings.

Few Jewish, and for that matter non-Jewish, thinkers were genuinely interested in objectively ascertaining specific historical facts. Many undoubtedly felt, as did Goethe at the ushering in of the great era of historical criticism, that detached critical analyses would, "through some pedantic truth, displace something great which is of superior value for us." Conceding that the ancient Roman stories about Mucius Scaevola and Lucretia had been relegated by historians to the limbo of myth, the poet exclaimed, "If the Romans were great enough to invent such stories, we should at least be sufficiently great to believe them." Medieval thinkers and public alike resented the "useless" quest of mere facts from the dim and distant past. That is why the transition from history to legend was so facile. Legend was there to elaborate the meager material left behind in the older records, in themselves partly legendary, so as to arouse the wish to emulate the desirable traits and to avoid the pitfalls of the heroes of past ages. It was also to serve to harmonize contradictions in the authoritative older writings, to interpret away certain unsavory aspects or interpret into the texts certain laudable features, or even merely to fill in obvious gaps in the sources to satisfy their devoted students.[99]

In that twilight zone between truth and fiction, or what some may call artistic "higher truth," such semihomiletical interpretations did not necessarily claim to offer historically authentic explanations. Rather like other hermeneutic or exegetical devices, they often intended to offer merely alternative insights into the meaning of certain texts and their hidden implications. In time, however, many such putative suggestions, buttressed by the authority of their initiators, came to be considered final truths. For this reason the transition from Midrash to historical literature was often so tenuous. All midrashim contained semihistorical elaborations of historical facts; many were primarily historical in content. On the other hand, purported historical works often consisted mainly of collections of semilegendary narratives. Certainly, there was but a shadowy line of demarcation between the midrashic legends concerning ancient sages and books like Yosephon or the "Book of the Just." Even purely chronological lists, like those included in the two "World Orders," indiscriminately organized historical and legendary materials as handed down by tradition. Only where it really mattered from the standpoint of Jewish law and ritual, as in the historical sequence of the talmudic and post-talmudic sages, did works like Sherira's "Epistle" or Ibn Daud's "Book of Tradition" approximate the quest for genuine historical facts.

Indifference toward such facts grew ever deeper as exilic life appeared less and less satisfactory to the majority of Jews. Accepting it as the justified divine retribution for their forefathers' sins, they nevertheless believed in the indestructibility of their people and viewed the Exile, whatever its duration, as but a transitory state. Hence their eyes turned back yearningly to the glorious past reflected in the Bible and to a lesser extent in their talmudic sources. On the other hand, they looked forward toward the messianic future which would redeem them from that "valley of tears." They viewed their long deprivation of the Holy Land and Temple as but a protracted nightmare, a period of trial and suffering, designed so that they might the better bear witness to the truth of Judaism. Details of that experience mattered only in so far as they bore out that "lachrymose conception of Jewish history." That is why next to the facts concerning the transmission of ancient traditions and its exponents, those relating to martyrs and anti-Jewish persecutions alone were recorded with relative precision, although neither set of descriptions was devoid of didactic and hortatory trimmings. This exclusive concentration on the *Leidens- and Gelehrtengeschichte,* to cite Heinrich Graetz's oft-quoted dictum, had thus, indeed, dominated the historical outlook of all thoughtful medieval Jews.

Nonetheless, even medieval Jewry never wavered in its acceptance of the fundamentals of historic monotheism and the current notions of the divine guidance of all history. It viewed all happenings under the aspect of long-range historic implications, in which a generation, even a century, mattered little because the basic lines of evolution had long been predicted by the ancient prophets. If asked, most medieval Jews would unhesitatingly have asserted that they were more apt to detect the true meaning of contemporary events by restudying the ancient prophetic messages than by pondering over minute details of these events themselves. For this reason the constant immersion in the words of Scripture, the "turning over and over" (*hafokh bah*) of its all-embracing contents, appeared to the majority as far more useful a pursuit for the understanding of their own time than the ascertainment of specific facts of their contemporary experience. Bible and tradition thus became the main guideposts for historical understanding, as they were important vehicles of the historical evolution itself.

XXIX

RESTUDY OF THE BIBLE

Few medieval Jews ventured to deny the authority of Scripture. Even the rationalists bent every effort upon squaring the biblical tradition with the dictates of "reason." The minority, apparently very small, of those who in their hearts may have rejected the idea of a supernatural revelation as such, as a rule kept their thoughts to themselves. We have no record of such skeptics among Jews, though there were some among the Arabs. In any case, they were not propagandists for the cause of free thought, and seldom did they care to appear in a public debate. Such disputations were fraught with dangers even for Muslim heretics (*zindiqs*) or orthodox "protected subjects." They must have been doubly dangerous for Jewish agnostics deprived of the protective arm of their own community.

One of the main issues was whether the existing biblical texts were genuine testimonies of God's revealed word, or whether they had undergone alterations at the hand of man. Such alterations might have been willful falsifications, as the Muslims charged, or they might have resulted from mistakes in transmission or interpretation. It was of extreme interest, therefore, even to the heterodox Jew to prove that he possessed an authentic record from which he might derive valid lessons for his faith. No sectarian leader had any chance of convincing his followers, or perhaps even himself, of the legitimacy of his brand of Judaism unless he could invoke in its behalf relevant scriptural passages through some novel, if often twisted, exegesis.

Nevertheless, Rabbanite Jewry and its geonic leadership were so deeply engrossed in the tremendous undertaking of consolidating and unifying all Jewry under the aegis of talmudic law that they paid less concentrated attention to biblical studies. We have the aforementioned testimony of Naṭronai Gaon that at least adult education had departed from the talmudic scheme of assigning an equal amount of time to the study of Bible, Mishnah, and

Talmud in favor of the latter. The gaon blamed this lack of balance upon the general impoverishment of the people and the necessity for students to devote a disproportionate amount of time to earning a living. "Hence, they have concentrated on the Talmud alone and neglected Bible and Mishnah, relying on the saying [of the Midrash]: 'All rivers run into the sea,' that is Scripture, Mishnah and Midrash," selections of all of which were to be found in the Talmud. This rationalization, based upon an innocuous homily, was to play havoc with the biblical studies of later medieval Jews. Jewry of the Great Caliphate, however, was spared this lapse into one-sided talmudism by the new intellectual ferment which seized the intelligentsia of all faiths; by the example of endless debates among the Muslims themselves about text and interpretation of the Qur'an; and by the need of defending the Jewish tradition against the onslaughts of powerful enemies. Above all the internal sectarian controversies enforced constant appeals to the text and meaning of Scripture.[1]

DEFINITIVE TEXT

Paramount, of course, was the question of the reliability of the accepted texts. Rabbanite Jewry may at first have thought that this problem had been settled in ancient times. The sectarian controversies raging during the Second Commonwealth must already have helped to clarify and consolidate the textual tradition of the Pentateuch. Certainly the thousands of variants even now extant in the Samaritan Bible must have offered many an opportunity for the buttressing of sectarian views through the word of God and, hence, must have forced the Jewish leaders to establish authoritative texts. Such were undoubtedly kept in the custody of the Jerusalem priesthood before the fall of Jerusalem, especially as the latter, with its predominantly Sadducean orientation, placed its supreme reliance on the written words of the Torah. According to a talmudic tradition, there also were special correctors of biblical books who were salaried by the Temple treasury. The basic identity of existing texts was, indeed, taken for granted by both Philo and Josephus. Emphasizing the deep-rooted and, if need be, self-sacrificial Jewish reverence for the Bible, the ancient Jewish historian boasted before his Graeco-Roman readers that "although such long ages have now passed, no one has ventured either to add, or to remove, or to alter a syllable." Less uniformity prevailed in the textual transmission of the Prophets and Hagiographa, but it stands to reason that, as soon as a particular book achieved canonical standing by inclusion in Scripture, an effort was made to ascertain, and subsequently to adhere to, the correct text.[2]

After the fall of Jerusalem, the anxiety of the rabbinic leaders that uncontrolled copying by uninformed and unreliable scribes throughout the far-flung Diaspora might undermine the foundations of their faith induced them to review in minutest detail the existing tradition, and to record it with the aid of mnemotechnic rules. Professional scribes, whose occupation was usually hereditary, applied these rules in practice and helped preserve them for posterity. One such libellarius had already been warned by R. Ishmael to be extremely careful in plying his trade: "Your work is sacred because by leaving out a single letter or adding a single letter you might destroy the whole world." The professional "readers" in the synagogues, whose services became increasingly indispensable, welcomed such guidance in the correct recitation of scriptural lessons, without which they might have become involved in endless controversies with their own congregants. They also found their work facilitated by uniform rules governing both the cadences of scriptural readings (the Talmud speaks of *ṭeʿamim*) and liturgical cantillation, which led to the development of a comprehensive system of Hebrew accents.[3]

As in all other legally significant problems, the talmudic sages placed their reliance on oral transmission. That here, too, they were essentially right in trusting the memory of faithful recorders may be seen from the early medieval literature on Masorah. Although all masoretic work still was concentrated in but a few schools and even families, the scriptural fragments from that period show greater divergences in detail than was possible under the more or less esoteric oral tradition.

The intensive efforts of these academicians to stabilize the textual tradition may be illustrated from the few passages recorded on a single page of the Babylonian Talmud. A tannaitic source had already stated that the Pentateuch contained 5,888 verses; the book of Psalms exceeded it by eight verses, and the book of Chronicles had eight less. Another tradition, attributed to the "scribes" of the early Second Commonwealth, had it that "the *vav* of the word *gaḥon* [belly; Lev. 11:42] stands in the middle of all the letters of the Torah, the words *darosh darash* [diligently inquired; Lev. 10:16] in the middle of all its words, the verse beginning *ve-hitgalaḥ* [then he shall be shaven; Lev. 13:33] in the middle of all its verses. The letter *'ayin* of *mi-ya'ar* [out of the wood; Ps. 80:14] stands in the middle of the letters of the book of Psalms, the verse beginning *ve-hu raḥum* [but He, being full of compassion; Ps. 78:38] in the middle of all its verses." In the ensuing discussion R. Joseph raised the question as to whether the letter *vav* and the word *ve-hitgalaḥ* were themselves to be counted in the first or the second half (he was apparently prepared to split *darosh darash,* as did the later tradition). He rejected the suggestion of pupils that he check existing copies by disclaiming any competence in the intricate problems of the full or deficient spelling of the words (with or without the *matres lectionis*) and of the division of the scriptural text into verses. These matters were in the hands of specialists. Moreover, as the Talmud here admits, there had arisen differences between the Palestinians and the Babylonians. For example, upon his arrival in the Euphrates Valley, R. Aḥa bar Adda reported that the verse in Exodus 19:9 was divided in Palestine into three verses.[4]

Countless individuals toiling over many generations thus produced for Palestine and Babylonia, and through them for the other countries of Jewish settlement, fairly uniform recensions. The old differences, such as had existed between the copies which underlay the Septuagint translation and the equally Egyptian Nash papyrus, or between the Isaiah Scroll of the Qumran sectarians and the masoretic text, now were gradually reduced to a few minutiae of spelling or, somewhat more frequently, of reading. The posttalmudic author of the tractate *Soferim* could, therefore, compile for the benefit of scribes a considerable number of accepted rules which reflected widely adopted practice among all Jewry.

However, some minor differences in spelling, pronunciation,

and verse division remained between Palestine and Babylonia, as well as among the Palestinians themselves, and between such Babylonian centers as Nehardea-Pumbedita and Sura. As in most other matters, Nehardea had retained many ancient Babylonian conventions, modified but not suppressed by the importation of Palestinian teachings. If we may accept a medieval report, couched in terms of a typically Muslim chain of tradition and perhaps therefore equally artificial, it was a Palestinian refugee, Naqqai, in the days of Bar Kocheba, who brought with him to Nehardea the Palestinian method of pronunciation. If transmitted orally, such vocalization did not necessarily indicate any formal punctuation, although written aids in memorizing some disputed or ambiguous readings could have been developed by that time. The new system also included some rudimentary interpunction. A good case has been made for the early adoption of certain Hebrew letters as symbols for major sentence divisions (the Talmud speaks of *pissuq ṭe'amim*) in imitation of the extensive use of Greek letters for that purpose throughout the Hellenistic world. The later "Babylonian" accents retained this utilization of the Hebrew alphabet. A single exception is even more revealing. The sign for *atnaḥ* (roughly the equivalent of our semicolon, mentioned as early as the tractate *Soferim*) seems to be a direct vestige of the Greek *lambda*. On the other hand, when Rab established his academy in Sura he could make a fresh start in the light of the Palestinian teachings and practices with which he had become imbued at the school of Judah the Patriarch. Conversely, Babylonian views influenced Palestine, particularly when Mar Zuṭra III became the head of the academy of Tiberias, which soon grew into a chief center of masoretic research.[5]

Even more important in some respects was the securing of a uniform Aramaic translation of the Bible. From time immemorial there circulated among the Palestinian Jews vernacular versions of Scripture, out of which there gradually emerged the dominant translation known as the Targum Onkelos. The story of these translations has been discussed by us briefly in their ancient context and will be further analyzed later on in this chapter. But it is important to understand the reciprocal influences of the preservation of a correct Hebrew text and the efforts made at securing uniformity in the translation of that text. Precisely because Aramaic was at that time, in contrast to Hebrew, a widely spoken language, it showed not only greater dialectal variations, but also far greater changes in spelling and pronunciation from generation to generation. The tendency to slur over vowels and weaker consonants must have created a great many like-sounding words which, if substituted for one another, totally altered the meaning of entire sentences. This slovenliness in speech, doubtless aggravated by the influence of the Greek *koinė* (itself the result of such negligent mixtures) particularly on the mispronunciation of Semitic gutturals, had begun to affect even the sounds of Hebrew words. The Talmud had therefore to warn congregations not to invite synagogue readers from certain Palestinian regions where the popular dialects failed to distinguish clearly between an *alef* and an *'ayin*. That this was not only aesthetically significant is illustrated by Judah the Patriarch's censure of the speech habits of his eminent Babylonian disciple, R. Ḥiyya. Failing to distinguish clearly between *he* and *ḥet,* would not R. Ḥiyya, the Patriarch inquired, be guilty of blasphemy when mispronouncing, for example, *ve-ḥikkiti la-Adonai* (and I will wait for the Lord; Isa. 8:17) by *ve-hikkiti* (and I will beat the Lord)? In another connection the rabbis pointed out that five different words had exactly the same sound in the mouth of a "foolish Galilean." How much more anarchical could the reading of the Aramaic version become, if the speech of the street were allowed untrammeled control! [6]

It became, therefore, doubly important for the rabbinic leaders to establish not only the definitive text but also the pronunciation of both their Hebrew Scripture and its authoritative translation. This seems to have been indeed one of the major contributions of those obscure generations of "epigoni" from the fifth to the seventh centuries. Just as the Saboraim, replacing the more dynamic Amoraim, concentrated on revising and establishing a definitive recension of the Babylonian Talmud, other students focused their work on biblical texts in both Hebrew and Aramaic. Not surprisingly, a major center of these studies arose in the ancient city of Nisibis, where Jews lived side by side with an intellectually alert and Bible-minded Christian population. Exposed to the combined influence of East and West, to the Persian as well as the Greek language, the leaders of both denominations had to take the necessary precautions to safeguard the correctness of their respective Aramaic and Syriac versions. We learn from Cassiodorus that in the middle of the sixth century a Jewish and a Christian school in Nisibis were engaged in intensive biblical studies, which this churchman wished to emulate in his projected biblical academy in Rome. The same needs which caused James of Edessa and other Syriac scholars to develop during the last pre-Islamic generations a system of punctuation and vocalization for their sacred Syriac texts doubtless determined their Jewish colleagues to devise some such symbols for their own texts, perhaps first Aramaic and later also Hebrew. In view of their close social interrelations, already censured by Aphraates, it is more than likely that Christians and Jews mutually influenced one another.[7]

While our knowledge of that evolution is extremely limited, it would seem that the Jews could claim both historic priority and greater influence on their neighbors. The fact that their "Babylonian" system of punctuation goes back to a more primitive "Palestinian" system lends considerable weight to the aforementioned tradition that some such rudimentary forms had been imported to the Euphrates and Tigris valleys in the critical days of the Bar Kocheba revolt, when Hadrian had outlawed all organized instruction in Jewish studies in the homeland. Moreover, through the ages, Christian students of the Old Testament, like Jerome, had more reason to consult Jewish experts in the Hebrew original, than Jews had to make use of Christian interpretations, even when they did not altogether reject these on dogmatic grounds. Unconsciously, however, Jews, too, were greatly affected by the deepened concern of their Christian neighbors for the textual exactitude of the Peshiṭṭa and the newer techniques developed by the Christian commentators in meeting exigencies similar to their own.[8]

Understandably, these new inventions did not find immediate acceptance even throughout Babylonia. There were local and probably even individual variations among copyists. Palestine continued to pursue its own independent course, as was noted, for example, by Ṣemaḥ Gaon in his reply to Kairuwan concerning Eldad. Here it was the great mystical *Sefer Yeṣirah* (Book of Creation) which, because of its deep interest in numbers and hence also in the numerical value of letters, made significant contributions to Hebrew phonetics and, indirectly, to the stabilization of the biblical text. As we shall see, the date of this composition is uncertain. Saadiah, whose commentary on the longer version of this work, written in 931, marked another advance in Hebrew linguistic studies, considered it of hoary antiquity. The very keynote of its treatment, expressed in its initial paragraph, *sefer, sefar,* and *sippur* (book, number, and word), showed how much depended on the proper vocalization of the same three Hebrew consonants. It clearly reflected, and contributed to, the growing interest of the Palestinian intelligentsia, if not in philological problems as such, at least in their hermeneutic and mystical derivatives.[9]

All these minute differences between countries and schools, however, seem to have disturbed the Jewish leaders of the pre-Islamic age even less than did the numerous ritualistic divergences between Palestine and Babylonia. Confident of its essential unity, talmudic and early posttalmudic Jewry took these regional variations in its stride.

PARTISAN ISSUES

Under the rule of Islam this relative equanimity gradually gave way to increasing concern. All the factors which accounted for the geonic drive to secure the over-all supremacy of the Babylonian Talmud, while tolerating minor regional diversities, operated with redoubled strength in this area. Under the unceasing Muslim denunciations of Jewish forgeries of Scripture, apparently reinforced by the lack of complete uniformity of the texts venerated by the Jews themselves, Jewish leaders began looking askance at these "minor" disparities. Moreover, the Muslims set the pace for literal intransigence, probably not without reciprocal Jewish influence. Although, unlike most biblical writings, the Qur'an had been composed in the full light of history, the basic difficulties of the Semitic consonants, often distinguished only by diacritical marks and hence readily mistaken for one another and a vocalization which had been added as a mere afterthought, made themselves felt here, too, almost immediately after the days of Mohammed.

The Herculean efforts of Caliph 'Uthman (644–56) and his associates produced a certain standard text, against which all future generations were to measure the conformity of their own copies. But much latitude still remained for divergences in readings and ensuing casuistic controversies on law and dogma. Not by sheer coincidence it was a converted Jew, Harun ibn Musa (died *ca.* 796), who wrote the first critical book on the Qur'anic text. This work was followed by many other detailed investigations. As late as the tenth century, the theologian Abu Bakr al-'Attar (died in 965) still vigorously defended some readings differing from the official redaction. Despite the burning of his books and his own enforced public repudiation of such "heretical" arguments, he insisted that the text be reproduced without vowel-points, since in classical Arabic any punctuation which yielded good sense was permissible. Jews could not long remain insensitive to these raging disputes, nor to the spectacle of another theologian of that period being flogged on orders of the vizier and made publicly to recant some six harmless variants in the Qur'anic text. The generally awakened passionate and all-embracing intellectual curiosity likewise added zest to the search for reliable texts and for readings hallowed by chains of tradition.[10]

Sectarian controversies, too, soon began affecting not only the accepted consonantal text of Scripture, but also its vowels and accents. 'Anan himself often drew conclusions in good rabbinic fashion from the difference between the reading and spelling of biblical words (for instance, from the plural reading of the word *azenekha* [thy weapons], contrasted with its singular spelling in Deut. 23:14). But some of his successors, realizing that by implication they would thus recognize the validity of the Rabbanite claim that Scripture could not be properly read without the aid of oral traditions, rejected the distinction between *qeri* (reading) and *ketib* (spelling), and insisted upon the exclusive validity of the written forms. For this reason they ascribed Mosaic origin to the vocalization of the Bible. A later legend, doubtless communicated to Maqrizi by his Karaite informants, even claimed that 'Anan had in his possession a copy of Deuteronomy written in Moses' own hand. That is also why they did not distinguish between copies of the Torah used for study and those employed in the liturgical recitation. This question, heatedly debated among the Muslims ever since Malik ibn Anas (died in 795) had forbidden the liturgical use of vocalized Qur'an texts, was aired also among Jews. An inquiry addressed to Naṭronai Gaon elicited a clear prohibition to use vocalized Torah scrolls for the recitation of scriptural lessons in the synagogue. The Karaites, on the contrary, despite Qirqisani's objections, encouraged such recitation from vocalized scrolls or even codices.[11]

On the other hand, Karaite use of Prophets and Hagiographa on a par with the Five Books of Moses as sources of Jewish law and dogma necessarily broadened the scope of biblical interests. If we may generalize the impression created by the midrashic collections, the Jewish public had previously focused its attention on the Pentateuch, the prophetic *hafṭarot* for Sabbaths and holidays, the book of Psalms and the five "scrolls" (Canticles, Ruth, Lamentations, Ecclesiastes, and Esther). All of these had long been popularized by the synagogue liturgy. Karaites, however, forced to exploit the full resources of biblical research for the reconstruction of a ramified legal system for their own time, evinced equal interest in the rest of Scripture and thereby stimulated basic studies affecting the entire text of the Old Testament.

Not that such concentration was necessarily conducive to greater original contributions. Certainly, none of the distinguished Karaite translators and commentators ranked as high as Saadiah Gaon. Saadiah's contemporary, Qirqisani, bitterly complained of the Rabbanite assertion that "they are the (highest) authority in the Hebrew language, the learned ones [*al-maskilim*] and the teachers." At the same time the rank and file of the Karaite intelligentsia seems to have had a greater understanding for the problems of biblical scholarship than did the average Rabbanite intellectuals. One Rabbanite author derisively quoted the Karaites as boasting that the Bible was their peculiar heritage and that "we know Scripture with all its verbs; nothing in it from beginning to end remains [alien] to us." But even he had to admit that most Rabbanites relied mainly on their secondary knowledge of the Bible incidental to talmudic learning. He also unwittingly confirmed, in part, the Karaite claim by censuring the sectarian scholars for their excessive preoccupation with externals like vowels and accents, rather than with the real spirit of the biblical texts.[12]

Large numbers of Karaite students seem to have joined the Palestinian schools which had assumed leadership in masoretic research. We know very little about Babylonian personalities engaged in this work; their individual contributions were imbedded in the mainstream of the dominant, largely anonymous, oral transmission, and few if any Karaites were in a position to enter the academic ranks there. But in the ninth century the center was moving westward. The famous Leningrad manuscript of Prophets, written in 916 in Babylonia, shows that the "Tiberian" rules of punctuation had already begun replacing there the "Babylonian" system. Saadiah was the last expert really familiar with the underlying principles of the eastern schools. Symbolically, even wealthy donors from Baṣra and Nisibis are recorded as the purchasers of tenth-century western Bibles.[13]

In Palestine a fresh start was made during the crucial century and a half between 775 and 930. Two rather obscure lists cite a number of names, among "many others whose names are not mentioned," of Masorites active especially before and after 800 C.E. (Riqat, his son Abraham, and others). Some of these scholars may have been Karaites or Karaite sympathizers, although at least one of them, Phineas "head of the academy," seems to have presided over the Rabbanite academy of Jerusalem which, originally founded in Tiberias by his ancestor, Mar Zuṭra III, had in the interim been transferred to the Holy City.[14]

A strong case has been made for the Karaite orientation of Aaron Ben Asher, the "last of the chain" of five or six generations of leading Tiberian Masorites going back to Asher, "the great Sheikh," of the eighth century. Although Graetz's original arguments to this effect had largely been vitiated by his excessive reliance on texts doctored by the modern Karaite apologist, Abraham Firkovitch, fresh and better evidence examined by Benjamin Klar has demonstrated the great Masorite's Karaite leanings. This does not necessarily mean that he had formally joined a Karaite congregation or school. Possibly a typical "cloistered" scholar, he seems to have stayed out of the public controversies of the day. In this respect he may have resembled scholars of similar temperament today who steer clear of political disputes. Yet, wholly engrossed in biblical research, he may have been deeply impressed by the Karaite viewpoint and methods. It probably was against him that Saadiah wrote one of his polemical poems, named by its initial words, *Essa meshali*. Careful reading of the famous colophon written in 895 by Aaron's father, Moses Ben Asher, at the end of the biblical manuscript revised by him, likewise betrays in spirit and phraseology Karaite predilections. On the other hand, we have no record of any organized Karaite community in Tiberias. While there undoubtedly were some Karaite individuals in this ancient seat of Jewish learning, we know nothing about a Karaite academy or even synagogue in any Palestinian community outside Jerusalem and Ramleh.[15]

Modern scholarship seems to have taken too rigidly an "either-or" attitude in this matter. We recall that the Karaites themselves admitted the existence of many half-Karaites and other more or less convinced sympathizers with their faith. Nor was the separation between the two communities, occasional Rabbanite bans notwithstanding, nearly as sharp as it became in later generations. There is little doubt that in isolated settlements Karaites frequented Rabbanite synagogues (we remember Sahl ben Maṣliaḥ's wondrous accusation that the Rabbanites illumined their synagogues on Sabbath evenings only for the purpose of keeping Karaites away) and lived an ordinary Jewish life. Certainly, neither group hesitated to make use of authoritative manuscripts produced by Aaron Ben Asher and his school. The most famous of all biblical manuscripts, prepared by him in the early tenth century, was donated by Israel ben Simḥah of Baṣra to the Karaite synagogue in Jerusalem for use during the three holidays.

If any man from all the offspring of Israel [the donor further provided], among Karaites or Rabbanites, should wish to consult it on other days of the year, in order to find what is written fully or defectively, irregularly or according to a certain order, with closed or open lines [at the end of certain sections as prescribed by law] or to verify any accent from among the biblical accents, they [the synagogue authorities] shall produce it for him for examination and study, but not for recitation or exegesis.

When this manuscript, after being redeemed in 1105 from King Baldwin of the crusading conquerors of Jerusalem, was transferred to the Rabbanite synagogue in Cairo, local Rabbanites did not hesitate to consult it. In fact, Maimonides himself considered this copy a model biblical text and codified his laws in accordance with it. Some time before the end of the fifteenth century this manuscript was transferred to the Rabbanite community of Aleppo, where it made history in modern masoretic research.[16]

Masorah required extreme concentration on details. In later generations some speculative individuals were inclined to disparage this "mechanical" recension of textual minutiae. Others, however, realized how much philological and biblical learning went into each decision of vocalizing or accenting a particular word. Some, like Yehudah Halevi, saw in it a "profound study" and a sort of inspired wisdom incomparably superior to the ordinary exploits of the human mind (*Kitab al-Khazari,* II.80 end; III.31).

These evidently cloistered scholars may well have turned their backs on the raging controversies of the age and discarded sectarian arguments even where they sharply differed among themselves on masoretic problems. Certainly, there is nothing in our sources to indicate that Moses (ben David) Ben Naphtali, Aaron Ben Asher's main rival and spokesman for an important independent tradition, was likewise a Karaite sympathizer. And yet we never hear of their reaching divergent decisions on the basis of sectarian preconceptions, or of their attacking each other's orthodoxy on this score. It would have been very difficult, indeed, to persuade readers that heretical motives inspired Ben Naphtali to object to the frequent use of the hyphen (*maqqef*), his special accentuation through the different use of the *meteg* symbol, and his different vocalization of the name *Yissakhar* or the term *qanno,* instead of *qanna* ("a jealous God"; Josh. 24:19). Nor were subsequent Masorites guided by religious considerations when they preferred in the latter case Ben Naphtali's reading, while they followed Ben Asher's punctuation (though not pronunciation) of *Yissaskhar*—both perchance the less "regular" forms. Very soon there began circulating among interested readers long lists of *ḥillufim* (differences) between the two schools, without their compilers betraying in any way their private sectarian biases. While the prominent Karaite author, Levi ben Jephet compiled such a list, one of the earliest and most authoritative studies was made, probably likewise in the eleventh century, by Mishael ben 'Uzziah, apparently a Rabbanite.[17]

The Masorites' chief concerns seem to have been clarity and consistency of spelling, pronunciation, and accentuation, in so far as these were reconcilable with tradition. From time immemorial, we recall, the rabbis had waged a fight against the popular tendency of slurring over vowels and even weak consonants (*alef, he, vav, ḥet, yod,* and *'ayin*). Much has been made by Joseph Halévy, Franz Wutz, Paul Kahle, Alexander Sperber and Einar Brønno of the pronunciation of Hebrew as reflected in the transliterations of the second column of Origen's *Hexapla* and those scattered through the writings of Jerome. These negligent forms, though less serious than in Aramaic where an original five-letter word like *tehevi* (תיהוי) was gradually sliced down to two letters *te* (תי), are in part confirmed by the Palestinian Talmud and by rhymes used by the seventh-century liturgical poets Yannai, Ḥaduta, and others. Similarly, the distinction between the letters *B, G, D, K, P* and *T* with and without a *dagesh* was often blurred. Jerome, for example, consistently renders the letter *pe* by *f*.[18]

All the evidence hitherto adduced, to be sure, reflects only popular usage, and not necessarily the traditional reading of the Bible in the academies of Palestine and Babylonia. Neither Origen nor Jerome were trained phoneticists. Origen undoubtedly incorporated in his work whatever he may have heard from a more or less learned Jew in Caesarea before the foundation there of R. Abbahu's academy. Jerome, as has long been conceded, quoted his various sources indiscriminately and without any regard for consistency. On the other hand, the rabbis had always insisted that "the language of the Torah is apart from that of the scholars." While this rule was chiefly applied to vocabulary and plural forms, it doubtless referred also to the existing differences in pronunciation. To safeguard continuity, the sages taught that "one must repeat precisely the speech of one's master." They illustrated this statement by mentioning Hillel's pronunciation of the biblical measure, *hin*. The old tradition, communicated by Maimonides, that on Hillel's lips this word sounded like *in* is undoubtedly correct, except that the source of this mispronunciation probably was Hillel's early Babylonian teacher, rather than either of his Palestinian masters, Shemaya or Abtalion. Subject to such regional differences, however, which exist today, too, among various segments of the Jewish people, the academies must have maintained a fairly uniform way of reading Scripture. They bent every effort to safeguard it against the encroachments of popular dialects. Explaining the statement of R. Isaac that the correct reading of the pausal forms *areṣ* or *shamayim* (with a *qameṣ*) was an ancient Mosaic tradition, a gaon (Hai?) commented, "Know ye that in those years many of the uneducated read [such words] erroneously, and that there also were books which lacked precision in their readings. Only the scribes and a minority of readers" had preserved the correct phonetic sounds. A gaon also impressed upon his audience the great need of correctly pronouncing the weaker consonants by pointing out that the divine name YHWH was wholly composed of such consonants.[19]

MASORETIC REFINEMENTS

Upon these solid foundations the Masorites built their imperishable structure. By approaching the biblical text not only empirically, but on the basis of newly developed grammatical and phonetic principles, they introduced far-reaching reforms. Discarding the old "Palestinian" punctuation as entirely inadequate and, for some other reason doubtless rooted in tradition, disliking also the more complicated "Babylonian" system, they devised a new comprehensive range of symbols designating the various sounds and accents. They made more extensive use of the *sheva,* both quiescent and mobile, and added to it the related *ḥatef* and *pattaḥ furtivum*. Wherever this punctuation proved insufficient, they inserted an accent (*meteg*) into dubious syllables. Through these measures they succeeded especially in securing the full pronunciation of the weaker consonants. They also hyphenated many words by inserting the newly introduced *maqqef* and, conversely, separated words by the equally new symbol, the *paseq*. They differentiated sharply, perhaps even more sharply than was warranted by the accepted official reading, the double pronunciation of the aforementioned six letters (*B-V, G-J, D-Th, K-Kh, P-F, T-S*).[20]

In all this reformatory work, the Arabic environment, especially the use by cultured persons of phonetic sounds akin to those of Hebrew and the new stress on clear and distinctive enunciation, doubtless created a climate of opinion favorable to related Hebrew studies. It also influenced the Hebrew speech of Jews long inured to the daily use of Arabic. But all more direct influences on the work of the Masorites with respect to the reading of Scripture (such as are postulated by Kahle) are far more problematical. It is very doubtful, for example, whether the inconspicuous *hamza* sign of the Qur'an writers was in any way responsible for the development, by the Tiberian Masorites, of their vast and complicated phonetic symbolism, which was mainly but an elaboration of the relatively primitive "Palestinian" punctuation of pre-Islamic days. One should rather assume that, like the Syrians, the Arab students of the Qur'an in the crucial first two centuries after Mohammed were themselves more deeply indebted to the older "people of the book," which had long cherished and cultivated every iota of its scriptural heritage.[21]

On the whole, the Masorites were reformers, not revolutionaries. They accepted, where they found it, any particular pronunciation deeply rooted among the people, as in the Song of Moses, which at that time was recited daily in many synagogues. For example, they incorporated in that Song, contrary to their own rules, the *d*'s in the words *ne'ddar* (not *ne'edar*) and *ne'ddari* with a *dagesh* and in the word *miq-dash* without a *dagesh*. But they made it clear that this was an exception.[22]

Similarly, knowing that the Palestinians of their day had insisted on pronouncing the ancient ā sound (still maintained by the Babylonians) å, they used the *qameṣ* to render both the former long ā and the short derivative of their *ḥolam,* pronounced ŏ. This distinction still underlies the differences in Jewish dialects today. As in law and ritual, Spain largely followed the Babylonian practice. Hence the Sephardic pronunciation of the *qameṣ* varies between ā and ŏ. But the Ashkenazim, generally more influenced by Palestinian models, still read it invariably ō and ŏ. Ironically, modern Palestinian Hebrew has reverted to the Babylonian-

Sephardic, rather than to its own medieval tradition, which almost certainly had been a departure from the ancient usage. On the other hand, it has maintained only the double pronunciation of *B, K,* and *P,* discarding not only the double *G,* now current only in a few Arabic-speaking countries, but also the double *D* cultivated in Babylonia, Yemen and medieval France and abandoned in Germany only at the beginning of the modern era. It has also neglected the double *T,* still emphasized by Ashkenazic Jewry today.[23]

To systemize their readings and, even more, to secure them against future mistakes by copyists, the Masorites summarized their findings in the *Masorah* (Tradition). Even in its final formulation, this work betrayed its origin from a long oral tradition and its reliance upon the faithful memory of oral recorders. That is why it retained a great many mnemotechnic aids, sometimes quite witty and easily remembered, but essentially superfluous in written lists. For example, to indicate that the term "at midnight" (*ba-ḥaṣi ha-lailah*), when "the Lord *smote* all the first-born in the land of Egypt" (Exod. 12:29), occurred but twice more in Scripture, namely in connection with *Samson* (Judg. 16:3) and *"the man"* (Boaz) who "was startled, and turned himself" (Ruth 3:8), the Masorah impressed this fact on the minds of readers by means of an epigram, "Samson smote the man." To remind the reader that Ezekiel's prophecy concerning the man who "hath *not eaten* [*akhāl*] upon the mountains" (18:6) is written with a long ā (*qameṣ*) whereas that concerning the man who "hath even *eaten* upon the mountains" (18:11) is spelled with a short ă (*pataḥ*), the Masorites punned: "He who had eaten opened [*pataḥ*] his mouth, he who had not eaten pursed [*qamaṣ*] his mouth."

Quite early the Masorah was divided into a longer and a shorter section, the so-called *Masorah magna* and *Masorah parva.* The shorter section, usually appearing in later manuscripts and editions on the margin, registered principally the correct readings of particular words, stated whether a full or a defective spelling was indicated, and occasionally gave statistics concerning the proper use of certain words. The longer section, mostly copied or printed at the top or the bottom of the page but often relegated to the end of the book, was concerned with broader rules and, despite its extreme brevity, contained many grammatical and phonetic excursuses. We need but cite one example of the effective use to which it was put already at the end of the tenth century. In combating certain "erroneous" interpretations, David ben Abraham al-Fasi rejected the equation of the words, *shamerah nafshi* spelled exactly alike in two Psalms (86:2 and 119:167). He decided that one is to be translated as an imperative ("keep my soul"), whereas the other was to be treated as a perfect ("my soul hath observed"). This is, indeed, the accepted rendering in the King James and many other versions. In support of his explanation David quoted the Masorah. "For in the *Masorah magna,*" he stated, "it is written: '*shamerah* of I Chron. 29:18 has none like it [as an imperative] elsewhere in Scripture. But in Psalms every *shamerah* is like it, except one: Psalm 119:167.' " [24]

In addition, some other Masorites wrote detailed monographs, somewhat resembling the halakhic treatises on special subjects composed by their geonic contemporaries. In these tracts they were able to elaborate the newly discovered principles and to illustrate them by a wealth of details. Aaron Ben Asher's *Diqduqe ha-ṭe'amim* has long been a classic in this field. So was the alphabetical listing of all words occurring in the Bible both with and without a *vav,* known by its opening two words as *Okhlah ve-okhlah.* This book seems to have been known to David al-Fasi, and it is expressly quoted by the great eleventh-century Spanish grammarian, Jonah (Abu'l Walid Merwan) ibn Janaḥ. Of importance were also the aforementioned treatises on the differences between the schools of Ben Asher and Ben Naphtali. All these works bear out the high praise showered upon the Masorites by Ibn Janaḥ when he urged readers neglectful of their grammar to follow the shining example set by the former's

> painstaking care, deep insight, extraordinary industry and toil in ascertaining the full and defective spellings, distinguishing between the penultimate and ultimate accents, diligently counting the verses containing the letters of the alphabet, and in all those other matters which they carefully examined out of their solicitude for the sacred writings so that they may be preserved in proper form.

It is, indeed, difficult to overestimate the devotion and learning which went into these final products of a long chain of tradition, cultivated and elaborated by generations of selfless, and hence largely anonymous, students of the revealed words of Scripture.[25]

Work of so high a degree of excellence secured for the Tiberian Masorites speedy and universal acceptance. Not only did Rabbanites and Karaites bury their hatchets with respect to this potentially most explosive area of disagreement, but the Jews of various lands quickly bowed to the superior mettle of the Tiberian experts. What self-abnegation this must have required on the part of the proud Babylonians can readily be imagined in view of Pirqoi ben Baboi's earlier attempt to impose Babylonian rituals and observances upon Palestinian Jewry. In Aaron Ben Asher's and Ben Naphtali's lifetime the Babylonian academies tried to wrest from Palestinian leadership even its time-honored prerogative of proclaiming the new moon. And yet several years before Saadiah's controversy with Ben Meir, the Babylonian copyist of the Leningrad manuscript of Prophets largely abandoned the traditional eastern punctuation in favor of the Tiberian system. The Tiberian principles penetrated the very work of "punctuators" who externally still used the older symbols. Far-off Yemen, which for centuries thereafter remained faithful to the Babylonian supralinear punctuation, kept on revising it in accordance with the principles laid down by the Tiberians.[26]

Directly and indirectly, the Masorites thus contributed to the intellectual upheaval which marked all facets of Jewish life under early Islam. Theirs was a constructive force. By placing in the hands of students reliable and uniform biblical texts, they prevented further splits in the ranks of Jewry which would doubtless have resulted from the availability of many different, equally authoritative recensions. As a result of their efforts, the biblical manuscripts of the tenth to the twelfth centuries show fewer and fewer variants. Qualitatively, too, these variants are for the most part of minor consequence.

To be sure, in his discussion of the laws requiring certain sections in the Torah scroll to be concluded with open or closed lines, Maimonides noted "great confusion" in the existing scrolls, as well as in the writings of Masorites on this subject. He decided, therefore, to follow the aforementioned Ben Asher codex. But this was a legal rather than purely masoretic problem, and hence was subject to the usual juristic interpretations and disputes. In fact, Maimonides' decisions were controverted by the French Tosafists, and for generations thereafter the Jewish communities followed at least two schools of thought on this scribal detail.

Far more reflective of reality was Abraham ibn Daud's eloquent defense against the Muslim accusations of Jewish tampering with the scriptural text. He argued that Ezra could not possibly have brought with him from Babylonia an altered Torah without provoking sharp opposition. And yet Ezra's recension had found unquestioned acceptance throughout the far-flung Jewish dispersion.

> We indeed find today [Ibn Daud added] the Torah, written in exactly the same text without the slightest change, publicly displayed in all Jewish communities from India to the ends of Spain and Morocco in the civilized world, and from the borders of Ifriqiya, Ethiopia, and Yemen in the south to the last cities of Almagos in the Arctic Ocean to the north. Not one segment of the people differs [in this respect] from another, down to the three small letters *nun* which, occurring in the earliest texts, are still found in all recensions known throughout the world.

Maimonides himself, moreover, assumed complete unanimity in all legally noncontroversial matters. He insisted, therefore, that Torah scribes be particularly careful in reproducing oversized, undersized, and other unusual letters which they must copy precisely "as the scribes had copied them one after another" through the generations. He also enjoined them to "be careful in regard to the number of [ornamental] strokes, since some letters have but one stroke, while others have [as many as] seven strokes." Maimonides and Ibn Daud might have reinforced their arguments by pointing out that even the Jewish sectarians never claimed possession of differing texts. Although Mesvi al-'Ukbari and others felt free to suggest emendations and additions to solve exegetical difficulties, they supported their heterodox teachings more by interpretation than by citing readings at variance with the masoretic version. This fair degree of unanimity contrasted sharply with the endless debates among the Muslim parties, both political and religious, concerning the authenticity of traditional readings in the Qur'an, their alleged omissions and willful misspellings. After 1200, even the minor regional variations largely disappeared from Mediterranean communities, so that the numerous manuscripts used by Jacob ben Ḥayyim in preparation of the famous *Biblia Rabbinica* (published by the Bomberg press in Venice in 1524–25), and the still larger number of texts at the disposal of Benjamin Kennicott and Giovanni Bernardo de Rossi two and a half centuries later, showed but microscopic variations.[27]

Indirectly, too, the Masorites helped lay the foundations for the development of the new linguistic studies which culminated in the immortal work of the western grammarians of the eleventh century. Nor could the flowering of Spanish-Hebrew poetry have come about at the time and in the way it did without the ground having been carefully tilled by these textual "pedants." In short, theirs is no mean share in that remarkable renaissance of the Hebrew language and literature which accompanied the Renaissance of Islam.

ARAMAIC VERSIONS

Almost as important as the task of securing a correct scriptural text was the authoritative review of existing translations and the preparation of new ones for the benefit of the masses. Despite the constant growth of literacy in the urban centers of the Caliphate, many Jews were unable to comprehend the traditional juristic lingo and perhaps did not even know how to read or write in any language. A gaon, discussing the illiteracy of witnesses, did not controvert an inquirer's contention that "today the majority, and sometimes all, of those who sign a deed cannot read it, or do not understand its content." He merely advised his correspondent not to disturb the existing credit facilities and to examine such witnesses only if there is *prima facie* evidence of their ignorance (*Teshubot ha-geonim,* ed. by Harkavy, Nos. 231, 238). As the Aramaic language, so closely related to Hebrew, was gradually displaced by Arabic, even the more intelligent Jew had to work much harder in learning biblical or mishnaic Hebrew.

Of course, this process of acculturation did not develop with equal speed throughout the empire. Perhaps abetted by neighboring Persia's effective resistance to the overwhelming assimilatory influences of Arab culture, Babylonia retained its Aramaic speech much longer than Syria or Palestine. In a late tenth-century responsum, signed jointly by Hai and Sherira, we are told that "Babylonia has been from time immemorial the locale for the Aramaic and Syriac languages. Until today all inhabitants, Jews as well as Gentiles, in all hamlets speak Aramaic or Syriac." In another context, Hai referred to the Talmud's Aramaic proverbs as still current among Babylonian Jews. In Palestine, on the other hand, the rapid spread of Arabic rendered less and less intelligible the eastern Aramaic dialect of the Babylonian Talmud which, from the outset, had had an unfamiliar ring to western ears. That is why Palestinian scholars (for instance, Abraham ben Shabbetai in 1089–90) translated some of the Babylonian homilies into Hebrew.[28]

In their endeavor to make the Torah the common possession of the whole people the talmudic rabbis had introduced the obligatory reading of the weekly lessons in both the Hebrew original and the Aramaic version. They also believed in that version's intrinsic antiquity, finding an allusion thereto in the story of Ezra making the people "read in the book, in the law of God, distinctly" (*meforash,* that is with distinct explanation). But in the earlier period they evinced little concern for the absolute uniformity of the Aramaic texts. They apparently allowed not only for considerable dialectal divergences, especially between Palestine and Babylonia, but also for fairly free homiletical accretions. In fact, some rabbis insisted that "he who translates a biblical verse literally is a liar, and he who adds to it is a blasphemer." This latitude was reversed, however, after the rise of Christianity, when the Palestinian rabbis collaborated in the pedantically literal Greek translation by Aquila, intended to counteract the hermeneutically lax Septuagint. In Babylonia an effort was made to purge these aggadic accretions also from the Targum and to secure a fairly precise version. It was, therefore, not completely devoid of historic justice that in its final Babylonian formulation, the Aramaic translation came to be known under the name of "Onkelos"—evidently but an Aramaic variant of the name Aquila ('Aqilas), continually used in Palestine for both the Greek and Aramaic translators.[29]

Perhaps here, too, the school of Nisibis and its contacts with

Christian scholars contributed greatly to the ultimate revision of the accepted text. A good case has been made for the origin of the Christian-Syriac *Peshiṭṭa* (this name is first mentioned in the ninth century) from among Jewish and Christian missionaries in the eastern lands. The merchant Ananias, who in the first century had converted the royal house of Adiabene, must have placed in the hands of the new devotees a text of the Pentateuch, perhaps of the entire Old Testament canon of that time, in a language understandable to them. He probably adjusted one of the existing Palestinian versions to the eastern dialect of his royal disciples. The example, set by him and other like-minded Jews, was doubtless emulated by Christian missionaries who, here as elsewhere, appealed to their Gentile neighbors principally through the Old Testament. Tatian, the "Assyrian" or native of Adiabene, certainly was not alone in being converted to Christianity after an intensive study of the Old Testament canon.

Out of these early Jewish versions gradually grew the Peshiṭṭa, largely by the revision of the text in the light of Septuagintal interpretations in their elaboration by the Greek and Syriac Fathers. Greek prototypes were often followed even in matters of slight theological significance. For example, the musical symbol *selah* in Psalms, which the Syriac translators no longer understood, is rendered by the Septuagintal loan word, *diapsalma*. But whatever one thinks of these beginnings of the Peshiṭṭa (they were already obscure to Theodore of Mopsuestia early in the fifth century) and its hypothetical relation to some ancient Jewish version in eastern Aramaic, the mere presence of a related Christian translation must have forced the Babylonian Jews to pay greater attention to their own Aramaic version.[30]

For a time, to be sure, these rivalries may have contributed to the rabbis' aversion to the circulation of written Aramaic translations. Even later they enjoined at least the public interpreter in the synagogue to recite the weekly lesson in Aramaic without consulting a written Targum. This prohibition was epigrammatically restated, "The interpreter must not consult any manuscript, while the reader [of the Hebrew Scripture] must not take his eyes off the Torah." In explanation R. Judah son of R. Shalom stated:

Moses wanted to have the Mishnah [or Oral Law] in writing. But the Holy One, blessed be He, foresaw that the nations were going to translate the Torah, read it in Greek and contend that "They [the Jews] are not [no longer] Israel. . . . Now the scale would be balanced [and one could not decide who was right]. But the Holy One, blessed be He, told the nations: "You claim that you are My children; I know that only he who possesses My mysteries is My child." They asked: "What are Thy mysteries?" He replied: "They are the Mishnah."

Sooner or later, however, opposition to written Aramaic versions, as to written compilations of the Oral Law, had to yield to the real needs of a far-flung dispersion, less and less effectively controlled from the Palestinian center.[31]

The outcome of these labors was a carefully revised text of "Onkelos" to the Pentateuch. Intended for use in the whole Aramaic-speaking world, it steered clear of pronounced dialectal connections with Babylonia, and used an apparently artificial literary language which had enough in common with all Aramaic dialects to be understandable to most Aramaic-speaking persons.

Needless to say, even a faithful translation necessarily reflected certain basic theological attitudes. Its exegetical functions were, indeed, taken for granted by the rabbis when they discovered an allusion to it in Nehemiah's aforementioned reference to the reading of the law "distinctly." The underlying objectives of "Onkelos" are well stated by Alexander Sperber: (1) elimination of all anthropomorphisms, (2) unquestioned acceptance of the rabbinic exegesis, and (3) use of the translators' own exegetical methods. Anthropomorphisms had become obnoxious already to readers of the Septuagint. They appeared even more objectionable after the religious controversies which accompanied the rise of Christianity and of the Neoplatonic schools of philosophy. That is why "Onkelos" inserted such qualifying terms as the "word" of God, to remove any shadow of corporeal action or human affect from the Deity. Equally important was that the translation bear out, or at least not controvert, accepted rabbinic teachings hermeneutically derived from the biblical texts. For example, the reiterated biblical injunction, "Thou shalt not seethe a kid in its mother's milk" (Exod. 23:19), is translated blandly: "Ye shalt not eat meat in milk." (In its customary way Targum "Jonathan" expands this translation to include both cooking and consumption under the threat of the divine wrath.) The biblical provision, "And he that stealeth a man . . . he shall surely be put to death" (Exod. 21:16) is qualified by Onkelos through the translation "a man of the children of Israel." Nor does he refrain from utilizing aggadic explanations in reproducing puzzling, particularly poetic passages. The rather difficult phrase in Jacob's blessing of Reuben (Gen. 49:3), "The excellency of dignity, and the excellency of power," is interpreted with the Aggadah to mean that Reuben had originally been predestined to hold all three dignities of first birth, priesthood, and kingdom. At the same time much leeway remained for the translators' personal interpretations wherever they did not infringe on authoritative rabbinic doctrines.[32]

To make sure that the artificial language of their text would not undergo too many arbitrary adjustments to the dialects spoken in various countries, the rabbis provided their growingly authoritative version with vowel points and accents akin to those used for the Hebrew original. In fact, the Aramaic version was perhaps vocalized and accented first precisely because it required many more safeguards to maintain its textual and phonetic integrity. Possibly it is for this reason that we possess many early manuscripts of vocalized Targumim, some antedating comparable biblical texts. To reinforce their vocalization and accentuation, experts developed also a special Masorah for the Targum. Couched in the same language as that relating to the Hebrew text, this systematic summary was frequently appended to biblical manuscripts; it finally appeared in the famous Sabionetta (1557) edition of the Targum. Unfortunately, here too the Babylonian system was replaced in manuscripts now extant by Tiberian symbols and methods, so that the accompanying Babylonian Masorah no longer fully corresponded to the text. The ensuing attempts at harmonization so thoroughly confused many issues that the original texts can now be recovered only with extreme difficulty.[33]

Confusion was further increased by the use made in some countries of the newly developed technique of vocalization and accentuation for writings other than the Bible and its Aramaic versions. In the hands of less well trained and disciplined scribes this delicate instrument, then still in the process of being shaped, threatened to become a weapon of controversy rather than a means of unified control. Some students of Mishnah and Talmud tried to prevent misunderstandings by inserting vowel points and accents in equivocal passages. Numerous folios, using either the Babylonian, or the Tiberian system, are still found in Cambridge, Oxford, and elsewhere. Once, in 1553, an enterprising publisher printed the entire Mishnah with vowels and accents. Medieval poets from the days of Yannai seem to have vocalized, though not accented, their poems. Other ancient and more recent texts like Ben Sira, the Pesiqta de-R. Kahana, the "Scroll of Antiochus," and a work written in Kairuwan in the days of Saadiah Gaon—all used the biblical system of punctuation. Nevertheless, when Saadiah, with his penchant for antiquarian flourish, provided some of his works with these symbols, he was accused of donning the mantle of prophecy.[34]

Understandably, far less effort was expended on securing an authorized and uniform translation of biblical books other than the Pentateuch. These versions, like the other nonsacred Targumim of the five books of Moses, were sharply differentiated from "Onkelos," Sar Shalom Gaon adding, "We have heard from ancient sages that the Holy One, blessed be He, had conferred a great favor on Onkelos the Proselyte by making him compose that Targum." In these versions literalness was completely superseded by dogmatic preconceptions. For example, by interpreting the two letters *he* in the verbs of Ecclesiastes 3:21 as definite articles (this is indeed indicated by the masoretic vocalization), the query "whether" of the skeptical author was converted into an affirmation of man's immortality. Some of the existing Aramaic versions of Prophets and, to a lesser extent, of the Hagiographa were early ascribed to Jonathan ben 'Uzziel, one of Hillel's brightest pupils. Perhaps to counteract the menacing implications of Sar Shalom's decision, Hai Gaon taught that the only difference between Onkelos and Jonathan consisted in the qualitative difference of the Pentateuch and the other biblical books. According to talmudic tradition, both translators were advised by such authoritative masters as R. Eliezer and R. Joshua, or by the prophets Haggai, Zechariah, and Malachi. But modern scholarship is fairly unanimous in denying Jonathan's authorship. S. D. Luzzatto has plausibly suggested that "Jonathan" was as much the

Hebrew-Aramaic equivalent for the Greek translator, Theodotion, as the name Onkelos was a derivation from 'Aqilas-Aquila. Targum Jonathan occasionally betrays its final formulation in the Muslim age by curious anachronisms, as when it expatiates on the biblical reference to Ishmael's marriage by supplying the wives' names, Ayesha and Faṭima—an obvious borrowing from Mohammed's biography. But this passage may be a later insertion.[35]

In any case, this Targum, too, is undoubtedly based on previous Aramaic translations current in ancient Palestine, orally if not in writing. In its present form, however, it is also principally the product of intensive revision in the Babylonian academies, which did not consider it sufficiently weighty to safeguard its textual integrity by a special Masorah. It, too, rather faithfully follows the Hebrew original, except where it wishes to convey some special religious meaning. For example, it allegorizes the Song of Deborah, but it offers no variants of such factual data as numbers, which otherwise are most likely to suffer from errors in transmission.[36]

Palestine, on its part, continued to cultivate its own preferred versions together with their hermeneutic and homiletic elaborations. The extant residua of what is still called the "Palestinian Targum" were, even less than the Palestinian Talmud, the product of conscious editorial efforts extending over several generations. This translation undoubtedly circulated in a variety of related formulations, of which some enjoyed great popularity, and possibly also official recognition. Such anarchical diffusion would ordinarily have called forth an effort at consolidation on the part of the leading academies. But Justinian's outlawry of all instruction in Oral Law doubtless stimulated the Palestinian sages themselves to insert more and more of their aggadic teachings into their accepted and, hence, legally permissible Aramaic translations.

For all these reasons the "Palestinian Targum" was allowed to drift for itself without strict supervision by authoritative transmitters of its textual tradition. Hai Gaon on one occasion decided that that translation, consulted by several outstanding talmudic sages, ought to enjoy the same standing as "our Targum." But in another reply he admitted that "we do not know that version itself and have heard only little about it." Somewhat later Rashi was rather convinced that "there exists no Targum of Hagiographa," although soon thereafter his younger compatriot, Joseph Qara, occasionally quoted it in his commentaries. After the Arab conquest, moreover, the general intellectual supremacy of Babylonia paved the way for the undisputed sway of "Onkelos" in Palestine as well. Before long Arabic displaced Aramaic in popular use and the great Tiberian Masorites now concentrated entirely on the Hebrew text, utilizing the Targumim merely as welcome sources of linguistic and exegetical information.[37]

Because the talmudic sages had wished that the whole congregation understand the meaning of the scriptural lessons, they insisted upon the regular weekly recitation of the Aramaic version together with that of the Hebrew text. This regulation, sanctified by custom, persisted long after the majority of Jews ceased speaking Aramaic—in fact, found the Aramaic translation far less intelligible than the Hebrew original. Hai Gaon expressed serious doubts about rumors that Spanish Jews, for whom Aramaic never had been a native tongue, had discontinued the public recitation of the Aramaic version. In Spain proper Samuel ibn Nagrela tried to explain in a long-winded and rather implausible dissertation that such neglect consisted in occasional lapses caused by considerations for foreign visitors and numerous other demands on the time allotted to services by local leaders. But he insisted that, as a rule, the Spanish congregations, proud of their ancient traditions, still staunchly cultivated the old custom. Yehudah bar Barzillai, on the contrary, to whom we owe the lengthy quotation from the *nagid*'s statement, declared bluntly, "It appears to us that in most places the people sin outright and do not publicly recite the Targum at all, so that the majority of men, and especially the unlearned among them, have completely forgotten the commandment relating to the targumic readings." He exhorted his coreligionists to reintroduce the Aramaic recitation, even if it meant eliminating, or curtailing, some other part of their services, including lengthy sermons. But he himself was keenly aware of the difference in this respect between Onkelos and the Palestinian Targum. The latter, he declared, "contains many aggadic accretions, inserted by synagogue readers on their own. The rabbis taught that one may recite in the synagogue [that Targum, too,] because it may be classified as a commentary." Beyond their role in the scriptural recitations the various Aramaic versions greatly stimulated the output of liturgical poetry in that language. They thus paid back the debt they had undoubtedly owed to some ancient Aramaic prayers. Liturgical passages, moreover, not only found their way into the targumic texts themselves, but also became part of special Aramaic prayers introducing the public recitation of the Aramaic version.[38]

ARABIC TRANSLATIONS

Without such liturgical supports, the progressive adoption of Arabic, especially by the western provinces of the Great Caliphate, made ever more urgent the task of replacing the traditional Aramaic by a good Arabic version of Scripture. Even in pre-Islamic days Jews and Christians of the Arabian Peninsula and the Arabic-speaking buffer states must have had access to some Arabic translations, or paraphrases, of their sacred writings. But these versions may have been known only through oral transmission. As soon, however, as Arabic developed into the main medium of intellectual communication between the ancient cultural centers of Egypt, Palestine, Syria, and Babylonia, the scriptural traditions of the "people of the book" became of immediate concern to the Muslim intelligentsia, as well as to the Arabic-speaking *dhimmis* themselves. According to Michael the Syrian, a very careful Arabic translation of the Gospel had been prepared in 639 as a result of the important debate between the Monophysite patriarch John I and Arab generals. A mid-eighth-century Vatican MS attests the existence of such an Arabic version in that period, although a century later 'Ali aṭ-Ṭabari still preferred to quote the official Syriac version and occasionally even to compare it with both the Septuagint and the Hebrew text. At the same time 'Ali betrayed, at least in one passage, that his Hebrew text had already been doctored, possibly by some Jewish converts to Islam, to provide better ammunition for Muslim controversialists.[39]

A new impetus to biblical versions in Arabic was given by the large-scale endeavors, partly subsidized from the governmental treasury, to secure Arabic translations of all available ancient classics. Ultimately, we are told by Ibn Daud, the Spanish 'Umayyad Al-Ḥakam (961–75) induced the Cordovan Jewish scholar, Joseph ben Isaac ibn Abitur (or Ibn Satanas), to translate for him the Babylonian Talmud into Arabic. We do not know whether this order really concerned "the entire Talmud" or merely the Mishnah or some other parts thereof, and whether by referring to an "exposition" (*perush*) Ibn Daud meant an epitome of that voluminous compendium, or a regular translation. Nevertheless the royal interest in that Jewish classic, though perhaps stimulated by the king's curiosity about the legal practices of his Jewish subjects, is characteristic of the breadth of contemporary intellectual interests. The Bible, naturally enough, carried a far greater appeal to Muslims, as well as "infidels." The same Syriac Christian, Ḥunayn ibn Isḥaq al-'Ibadi (809–73), who together with his son Isḥaq and his nephew Ḥubaysh was responsible for the translation of most extant Greek writings in science and philosophy, also produced a translation of the Old Testament from the Septuagint. His procedure of trying to secure at least three reliable manuscripts of each work may well have served as a model also to Jewish translators, although these doubtless placed greater reliance on the work of their Masorites. By the middle of the ninth century Naṭronai bar Hilai Gaon insisted on regular congregational recitation of the Aramaic Targum, but allowed the community to appoint an additional person to "interpret [Scripture] for them in their language." This decision was soon thereafter quoted as authoritative in Amram's prayer book. Obviously, the two geonim yielded only to existing real needs. From the tenth-century grammarian Yehudah ibn Quraish of Tahort, Algeria, we learn that the North African communities had long before those of Spain abandoned the reading of the Aramaic Targum. Ibn Quraish was prompted, therefore, to send a special missive (*risala*) to Fez pointing out the Targum's universal use in Babylonia, Egypt, Ifriqiya, and Spain, and its great usefulness for the understanding of Scripture. He hoped thereby to "awaken in them the desire to study the Aramaic version, to make them love it and appreciate its usefulness, as well as to deprecate its neglect." Several generations later Hai Gaon was fully reconciled to the use of an Arabic translation. Reiterating the decision of his geonic predecessors, he merely warned of the difficulties of finding the middle ground between excessive literalness and a free translation. He twice reminded correspondents of the aforementioned talmudic condemnation of the pedant clinging to the literal sense of each biblical verse.[40]

Regrettably, we know practically nothing about the early Arabic Jewish translations. The translators' names alone have been, in part, preserved by Qirqisani and Mas'udi. The former mentions versions by "Al-Ashkenazi, Ar-Ramli, Ibrahim ben Nuḥ, and their confreres," whereas the Arab historian apparently refers to a similar work by Saadiah's teacher, Abu Kathir of Tiberias, with whom he had discussed religious problems of mutual interest. Although Qirqisani explains in this context phrases from Nahum and Joel, we cannot be sure whether these authors reproduced only the Pentateuch, or other biblical writings as well. Other translations of Jewish origin may likewise be hidden behind the various Arabic versions of the Old, as well as the New Testament, listed in 988 by Ibn an-Nadim in his *Fihrist*. This list includes an early version prepared by one Aḥmad ibn 'Abd Allah ibn Salam in the days of Harun ar-Rashid.[41]

We do not have to search too far for the reasons for this nearly total oblivion. Saadiah's translation of the Hebrew Bible, on which the great gaon had spent much of his extraordinary ability and industry over a period of many years, proved so much superior to those of all his predecessors that it immediately became the standard Arabic version for Jews of all lands. Only where no translation by Saadiah was available did some later work, largely based on it, take its place. According to a persistent Yemenite tradition Saadiah himself never translated the First Prophets, Ezra, Nehemiah and Chronicles; the few fragments of his alleged translation of *Hafṭarot* taken from the First Prophets are, in fact, the products of some disciples. Unfortunately, considerable parts of the gaon's authentic versions, too, were allowed to disappear, while those preserved have often undergone substantial alterations, precisely because they were so constantly used. At times some of its best readings must be recovered from later quotations and other outside sources.[42]

From the outset Saadiah seems to have prepared his version, which he called *tafsir,* connoting both explanation and translation, not only for the benefit of his coreligionists, but also for the information of interested Gentiles. This intention colored in many ways both form and substance of his work. He refrained from using language appealing only to the intelligentsia, and occasionally even lapsed into colloquial terms, for which he was attacked by some Samaritans. Unlike most other medieval Jewish authors, he wrote his text in the Arabic, rather than the Hebrew, script. Not to lend support to the frequent accusation of Muslim polemists that the Jews themselves often no longer understood many biblical phrases and hence were no longer in possession of an unbroken chain of tradition, he forced himself to reproduce the most obscure and, in the opinion of modern critics, textually corrupt passages. When the text lent itself to a variety of interpretations, he mentioned this fact in his commentary, but in the translation he followed consistently but one alternative. Even in his rendition of Job he did not admit to being stumped by any of the *cruces interpretum* characteristic of this immortal symposium. This effortless gliding over numerous rough spots in the scriptural text aroused the ire of Ibn Ezra and other commentators who were not wholly aware of Saadiah's defense motivations.

Primarily for apologetic reasons Saadiah also refused to admit ignorance, as did later Jewish exegetes, of the identity of places, persons, animals, plants, or minerals mentioned however casually in Scripture, but courageously supplied their Arabic equivalents. For example, he identified the river Pishon (Gen. 2:11) with the Egyptian Nile, although the Targumim left the word untranslated. This identification was accepted by Rashi and, despite Ibn Ezra's strictures, also by Naḥmanides. So highly did Saadiah value these contemporary identifications that he even sacrificed to them elementary consistency. In the same chapter of Daniel he translated the words *negeb* (south) and *ṣafon* (north) once by (sovereigns of) "Syria" and (king of) "Iraq" (11:15), and the second time by (kings of) "Rome" and "Persia" (11:40). He also wrote a special treatise explaining, with the aid of somewhat crude comparative linguistics, seventy (or ninety) *hapax legomena* in Scripture, doubtless intended in part to justify his own translation of these terms as well as to point out to Karaites how dependent on rabbinic tradition was even the simple textual meaning of Scripture. Saadiah's avowed anti-Karaite purpose, however, allegedly noticeable also in his selection of *hapax legomena* best explainable by talmudic nomenclature, would hardly have justified the effort. Dependence on linguistic tradition could not possibly be denied by any reasonable Karaite who used all Hebrew and Aramaic words in their "accepted," that is "traditional," meaning. Certainly 'Anan, Benjamin, and others did not hesitate to use freely the talmudic idiom. Saadiah's Karaite successors, especially Jephet ben 'Ali, were rightly irked by his rather irrelevant demonstration of "men's need to study the Mishnah for linguistic purposes." Of a different order were, of course, Saadiah's reiterated arguments that, without the explanations given by the rabbis, one could not gauge the *substantive* import of the biblical commandments.[43]

More important was the basic polarity in Saadiah's general approach. On the one hand, he believed that Scripture could not possibly contradict reason and that, hence, all passages running counter to accepted rational truths must be understood metaphorically. On the other hand, he insisted that the Bible itself was but one of the sources of Jewish tradition, and hence could be properly understood only in the light of the other authoritative Jewish writings. Like the author of Targum before him, he had to make sure that his version should at least not controvert any basic hermeneutic deductions by talmudic sages. The crucial word *shabbat,* for example, in Leviticus 23:11, 15, and 16, that stormy petrel of raging sectarian controversies concerning the observance of the Festival of Weeks, he rendered inconsistently twice by "the morrow after the *day of rest,*" that is after the first day of Passover, and the third time by "the morrow after the *seventh week,*" thus justifying the observance of the Pentecostal holiday on any day other than Sunday. Above all, Saadiah was even more deeply concerned about the frequent anthropomorphisms in Scripture than had been "Onkelos." The attribution of corporeality and human passions to God not only offended now the sensitivities of sophisticated Jews, but had also become the choice target for Muslim controversialists. Even Karaites, although finding themselves in the same quandary with respect to the Bible, had aimed their shafts at the numerous anthropomorphic passages in the Aggadah. It was of vital importance for Saadiah, therefore, to reproduce such obnoxious phrases with some circumlocution. For instance, the formulation that God "rested on the seventh day from all His work which He had made" (Gen. 2:2), reads in his version: "He stopped on that day from creating further anything of the type of creation which He had made." He intimated thereby that the biblical view was neither inconsistent with the philosophic ideas of continued creation (though no longer *ex nihilo*) and uninterrupted divine Providence on all days including the Sabbath, nor with the juristic derivatives from that text as to which types of work were prohibited on the Sabbath.[44]

Apart from these dogmatic and apologetic considerations Saadiah's translation clearly reflected the new philological and exegetical approaches. He believed that the scriptural sequences had an inner logic of their own, to the unraveling of which he devoted much space in his introductions to the individual biblical books. The very succession of aphorisms in the book of Proverbs appeared to him far from accidental. On one occasion he even dared to transpose three verses (Prov. 9:10–12) from their traditional place in the middle to the end of the chapter, in order to achieve a sharper contrast between the first nine verses dealing with the praise of wisdom and verses 13–18 devoted to the censure of folly. Similarly, he added or subtracted a word or two for the sake of clarity. His effort to write a smooth and idiomatic Arabic, however, occasionally had untoward consequences with respect to meaning. Nor was his type of Arabic purism always appreciated by his Arab contemporaries, as when he freely used the contemporary term "caliphs" for ancient Israelitic kings, called Moses the "Messenger," a title usually reserved for Mohammed, and even applied the term, "Qur'an" to the Hebrew Scriptures. But in this way his translation made up in vividness for what it lost in historic accuracy. On the other hand, wherever possible, he preferred to use like-sounding Arabic words despite their different connotation, and at times even created for this purpose a new Arabic vocabulary (for example, in rendering the *na' ve-nad* [a fugitive and a wanderer] of Gen. 4:12, 14). On one occasion, perhaps inadvertently, he rendered the biblical pun on the origin of *ishshah* (woman) from *ish* (man; Gen. 2:23) by a corresponding Arabic phrase which removed the ground from under the midrashic demonstration that Adam must have spoken Hebrew.[45]

Saadiah's translation, and the underlying exegesis, had one major shortcoming, namely the utter lack of historical criticism. In this respect the gaon was merely the child of his age. Like most of his contemporaries he blandly assumed that all the prophetic books were written by the prophets after whom they were named, that all the Psalms had been composed by David, and all the Proverbs by Solomon. Even where the Bible itself gives other names in Psalm headings or in the last chapters of Proverbs, he explained them away as names of persons for, or about whom, they were written. Using the presence of 600,000 adult males together with their wives and children at the Sinaitic theophany as a major historical proof for the veracity of the revelation to Moses, he also was a firm believer in the miracle of the manna, "the most amazing of all miracles." Occasionally Saadiah allowed his dogmatic and exegetical predilections to run away completely with his historical judgment. He "detected" biblical proofs for the correctness of the rabbinic calendar, and from the story of the children of Issachar (I Chron. 7:1–5), he even deduced the Mosaic origin of its underlying astronomic computation. This defiance of a long-accepted historical fact must have shocked even his confirmed Rabbanite contemporaries and was unanimously repudiated by his successors, including Hai Gaon, Abraham bar Ḥiyya, and Maimonides. Nor did he hesitate, as we recall, to ascribe the obviously apocryphal *Megillat bene Ḥashmona'i* to the five Maccabean brothers themselves, although Judah's death is mentioned in it. Neither the gaon nor most readers were primarily interested in the story narrated in that apocryphon, but rather in its edificational and apologetic implications. To Saadiah it decidedly seemed to offer documentary proof for the festival of Ḥanukkah repudiated by the Karaites.[46]

Rabbanite Jewry in eastern lands was, on the whole, satisfied with Saadiah's concise translation of the Pentateuch and several other biblical books. Whatever criticisms transpired were aimed at individual interpretations, for the most part given in the gaon's commentaries, rather than at the translation as such. Only Mubashshir ha-Levi, as we recall, wrote a special critique of Saadiah's works, in which he concentrated his shafts on the gaon's biblical writings, but also tried to underscore the weaknesses in all other publications as well. More extensive were the criticisms sounded in the West. Soon after the gaon's death Dunash ben Labraṭ also composed a special treatise attacking his interpretations, even where they were based merely on different vocalization. Referring, for instance, to Saadiah's version of Job 31:18, which assumed the reading *ke'eb* (pain) instead of *ke'ab* (as with a father), Dunash exclaimed: "This is the ruin of language. We must beware of explaining [Scripture] in a way leading to the removal of but a single vowel [or dot, *nequdah*] from the Hebrew tongue in which angels sing in Heaven and Israel on earth." However, even there Dunash's successors, and particularly Abraham ibn Ezra, for the most part sided with Saadiah against his critics. At any rate, neither in the East nor in the West did Jewry encourage further efforts at translating Scripture into Arabic. All previous and many subsequent such attempts, still known to Ibn Janaḥ, were confined to the library shelves of erudites. Only where no version by Saadiah was available could another's secure a toehold in communal usage, as in the case of Yehudah ibn Gayyat's work on Ecclesiastes. In Yemen Saadiah's translation was hallowed by the traditional name Targum. Soon legends grew about Saadiah's alleged origin from and long sojourn in that southern land. Elsewhere, too, Saadiah's version took the place of the Targum, and Yehudah ibn Tibbon specifically enjoined his son on every Sabbath to recite the weekly lesson in that Arabic translation.[47]

Karaites, naturally enough, were far less pleased. Joseph ben Nuḥ and Jephet ben 'Ali supposedly prepared new translations of the entire Old Testament. Joseph's work is completely lost. But we possess substantial sections of Jephet's version, including some which were adopted, however reluctantly, by Rabbanite Jewry to fill in gaps left by the unavailability, for whatever reason, of portions of Saadiah's text. Though deeply indebted to his great geonic predecessor, Jephet made a valiant effort to render the biblical text with even greater precision. Perhaps seeking to undermine the foundations of the rabbinic midrash, his version approaches in some respects the extreme literalness of Aquila, readily sacrificing for it the elegance of the Arabic diction.[48]

Most remarkably, the Samaritans first adopted Saadiah's version as their own. For nearly three centuries, in fact, they had no other Arabic translation than that borrowed from their Jewish "enemy," although many alterations gradually crept into their texts. Only in the thirteenth century did one Abu Sa'id ibn Abu'l Ḥusain produce a revised translation, often sharply criticizing in his marginal notes Saadiah's renditions. In fact, according to Kahle, some of the most authentic readings of Saadiah's original version are those preserved in older Samaritan manuscripts, despite their transliteration into the Samaritan script. The twelfth-century Samaritan Triglot (Hebrew, Samaritan, and Arabic) of the Pentateuch especially, now in the British Museum, offers one of the most authentic recensions of Saadiah's original text. Saadiah's influence on Christian translations is likewise marked. But these, often based on Ḥunayn's work and otherwise starting with the Septuagintal or Peshiṭṭa version rather than the Hebrew canon, naturally included substantially different readings.[49]

Compared with the Aramaic, Syriac, and Arabic translations, those into other Near Eastern languages have remained practically unknown. To be sure, the fifth-century bishop Theodoret of Cyrrhus alludes to an existing old Persian translation of the Bible. But we know neither whether it really covered the entire Bible, nor whether it had been prepared by Jews or Christians, although at that early date, before the mass immigration of Nestorians into the Sassanian Empire, a Jewish translation appears more likely. Maimonides perhaps referred to that very version when he spoke of a Persian rendition in existence before the rise of Islam. Since no fragment thereof is extant even in direct citation, we cannot ascertain its nature or accuracy. We cannot even tell whether Mardan Farukh, who made extensive use of the Bible in his attacks on both Judaism and Christianity, had consulted such an Iranian version, or merely had access to some Syriac or Arabic translation. The same may be true of Firdausi, whose considerable indebtedness to the biblical legends may likewise have been derived from an Arabic version, or even from some second-hand source. In any case, the numerous Jewish sectarians of the seventh to the tenth centuries, who hailed from the Iranian Plateau, always invoked the testimony of the Hebrew, not the Persian, text in support of their teachings. Not only the great Karaite scholars, moreover, but also the skeptic Ḥivi ha-Balkhi constantly interpreted Hebrew passages with no reference to textual interpretations of a Persian version. It stands to reason, therefore, that the majority of educated Persian Jews understood the Hebrew original without requiring the aid of a Persian translation.[50]

WESTERN TRANSLATIONS

Little more is known about the Jewish share in the Western translations. Reference has already been made to the probable existence in ancient times of Jewish paraphrases into Latin of certain parts of the Bible, as well as to St. Jerome's Jewish assistant or assistants. But it appears that most Jews living in Latin-speaking countries were satisfied with a basic version carried down the ages from teacher to pupil by word of mouth, very much like the Yiddish renditions which had been current in the East European schools for the past several centuries. Although subject to individual variations in unnumerable details, these translations were basically uniform and fairly independent of the coexisting literary reproductions. Umberto Cassuto was, therefore, perfectly justified in utilizing many peculiar phrases used by Italian Jewish elementary teachers in modern times for the reconstruction of underlying textual traditions reaching back to antiquity. Individual Jewish scholars may also have proved helpful to such Christian students of the Bible as Alcuin, Odo, Andrew of St. Victor, or Peter Comestor. Of course, most Christian scholars simply followed the existing Latin translations, especially the Vulgate. Some had at their disposal earlier Latin versions or their derivatives, but quite a few also realized the superiority of the Hebrew text and took St. Jerome as their model. Abelard, who as we recall was able to present a fairly dispassionate dialogue between a Christian, a philosopher, and a Jew, once told Heloise of having listened to the discourse by a Jew on the text of the book of Kings. From

Abelard's school also emanated a short theological treatise, *Ysagoge in theologiam* (written in 1148–52), which quoted the Ten Commandments and certain prophecies in Hebrew as well as in Latin. In the same period, a Cistercian monk, Nicholas Manjocaria, not only declared his preference for Jerome's *Hebraica* over all other existing translations of the Psalter, but also acknowledged the superiority of the Hebrew original, or what he called the *Hebraica veritas* over them all. Toward the end of the century, Herbert of Bosham, a pupil of Andrew of St. Victor and Peter the Lombard, criticized the *Hebraica* in the light of the original which, as probably the most learned native Christian Hebraist of his day, he had studied with concentrated attention. On the other hand, an unnamed apologist of the twelfth or thirteenth century took up the cudgels in favor of the Christian allegorical interpretation by addressing a number of direct questions to contemporary Jews.[51]

Even those unable to consult the original Hebrew Bible hardly ever dared to declare publicly that they considered any translation superior to the original. Such an attitude, almost ridiculous to modern linguists, had indeed been expressed with respect to the Septuagint by the Byzantine Georgius Syncellus. In the West, the Septuagint itself had lost almost all authority, particularly after the separation of the Eastern Churches. John Scotus Erigena, who knew enough Greek to express preference for the Greek original of the Fourth Gospel over its Latin version, admitted on another occasion that he had no Septuagint at hand. Hebrew texts were more readily accessible at least through the mediation of Jews. It is even possible that such ecclesiastics as Odo had at their disposal premasoretic Hebrew texts still current among European Jews. Certainly the seventy-eight Hebrew passages recovered from one of Odo's manuscripts represent too many variants from the masoretic text to be explained away as mere corruptions by an uninformed scribe. Just as in the area of Jewish law, or its neglect, the Western Jews must have carried with them certain textual traditions from Roman days which were subsequently submerged by the hegemony of talmudic-masoretic teachings instituted by the schools of Gershom and Rashi.[52]

If the presence of numerous learned Jews proved helpful to Western students of the biblical text, Jewish assistance had even greater bearing on other aspects of the medieval Christian interpretations of the Bible. Briefly mentioned later on in this chapter, these interrelations between Jewish and Christian Bible exegesis will be treated more fully in their far better known later medieval connections. The Jewish translations of Scripture into western vernacular languages, for the most part likewise dating from that later period, will also shed additional light on both the earlier Jewish oral traditions and the Jewish contributions to the literary work by Christian authors during the High Middle Ages.

RATIONAL EXEGESIS

Saadiah's translation differed from its Aramaic predecessors not only in its linguistic medium. Less slavish in its literal adherence to the Hebrew text than Onkelos, it allowed occasional theologically inspired readjustments of the meaning of scriptural passages, but kept aloof from the ancient hermeneutic elaborations characteristic of the other Aramaic versions. Not that the gaon, or any other Jewish translator, totally ignored the vast linguistic resources and the intellectual penetration of the Bible's inner meaning accumulated in the course of ages in the homiletical literature. On the lowest level they all derived from it lexicographical aids for the identification of words and terms, and found in it helpful insights into the ordinary meaning of many puzzling phrases. But they felt free to disregard its purely aggadic elements. This freedom of choice was reflected also in their biblical commentaries, which now began to proliferate in both East and West.

External and internal pressures combined to force Jewish intellectual leaders to develop new approaches to biblical studies. In its three-cornered struggle with Islam and Christianity, the Jewish intelligentsia became ever more aware of the difference between its own adherence to the ordinary meaning of Scripture and the more typological Christian exegesis. The Bible had now come under the attack of Muslim propagandists because of its alleged "forgeries," not so much with respect to its text, which was largely accepted and freely quoted by the Muslim theologians as well, but rather in its allegedly misleading traditional interpretations. Unavoidably, the Jewish apologists, too, became ever more conscious of the difference between the simple meaning of the scriptural text and its hermeneutic amplification. They now increasingly turned to that simple meaning, the *peshaṭ,* or to what the Arabs styled the *zahir.* In this straightforward interpretation they now detected a new source of strength against Muslim imputations, as well as a vehicle of counterpropaganda among Christian neighbors. A traveler from Muslim to Christian lands like Abraham ibn Ezra became doubly aware of the difference between the Jewish and Christian exegetes, the latter finding "the whole Torah to consist of riddles and parables." That is perhaps why Maimonides taught that the old prohibition of teaching Torah to Gentiles applied only to Muslims and pagans who denied the authenticity of the biblical tradition, but not to Christians who, conceding the canonical value of the Old Testament, were misled only by their faulty interpretations. To rectify these by proper instruction might actually be considered a good deed.[53]

No less powerful was the impact of the large and ever more heatedly debated exegetical literature on the Qur'an. In many ways fathered by Jewish converts to Islam, especially K'ab al-Aḥbar and 'Abdallah ibn Salam, influential advisers of 'Abdallah ibn 'Abbas, Qur'anic studies soon became a major preoccupation of Muslim scholarship; reciprocally they influenced Jewish students of Scripture. This new attitude affected not only specialists. Since support by scriptural testimony affected all sectarian and most political controversies, the "correct" interpretation of relevant passages decisively concerned leaders in all walks of life. General intellectual curiosity, the growing demand for more scientific evidence and precision, and the prevailing combination of worship of authority with independent rational investigation likewise stimulated the new type of biblical research. We shall see how deeply optimistic the savants of the Great Caliphate, "unbelievers" as well as Muslims, had become in regard to the ultimate solutions offered by human reason for all riddles of existence. Such conviction necessarily challenged the naive acceptance of the traditional lore and enforced a considerable amount of rethinking on the part of theologians of all faiths.

Equally important was the internal struggle with Karaites and other sectarians. By repudiating the authority of Oral Law, these heterodox groups rejected the entire body of talmudic and midrashic interpretation of Scripture and had a field day in attacking particularly midrashic expositions of the anthropomorphic and "superstitious" kind. Certainly fighting words, like those coined by 'Anan, "Search well in the Torah," placed the responsibility squarely on the shoulders of every student of the Bible.

Before long the Karaites began practicing what they preached and thus helped develop the new discipline of rational Bible exegesis. Theirs was the initiative in time, if not in quality and enduring influence. None of their writers attained the eminence of Saadiah the interpreter, any more than he rivaled Saadiah the translator. But long before Saadiah, some Karaite scholars tried to review the entire Canon in the new vein. Benjamin al-Nahawendi, as we recall, had already written exegetical works on a number of biblical books. The brief extant fragments of, or quotations from, his commentaries (on Exodus, Isaiah, Canticles, and Ecclesiastes) betray, despite their allegorical overtones, the same directness and brevity which characterized his legal treatise. More comprehensive and also better preserved are the exegetical contributions by Daniel al-Qumisi and his immediate disciples. Directly or indirectly, this Karaite preoccupation also influenced Saadiah, particularly during his stay in Palestine, where Daniel's pupils had continued the work of their master and where the efforts of Masorites were just reaching their fullest fruition. The gaon did not hesitate to accept specific explanations from his Karaite predecessors in so far as these did not entail any substantive deviation from orthodox Judaism.[54]

Saadiah's towering personality impressed itself on the minds of all his successors, Karaite as well as Rabbanite, in the exegetical domain, too. His general approach and a great many detailed interpretations eclipsed all earlier works, which were allowed to sink into oblivion even among the Karaite admirers of Benjamin and Daniel. Solomon ibn Parḥon voiced a widely accepted notion when he described Saadiah as "the chief spokesman and pioneer commentator who explained Scripture properly and placed it in its right framework. All [later] commentators learned from his wisdom" (*Maḥberet he-'Arukh,* ed. by Stern, fol. 54c). While often attacking individual statements by the gaon and sharply disagreeing with some of his generalizations, the distinguished Karaite exegetes of the following two centuries, Jephet ben 'Ali, Abu'l Faraj Harun, Yeshu'a ben Yehudah, and 'Ali ben Suleiman, expressly or tacitly related their expositions to Saadiah's translation and commentaries.

The same may be said, with even fewer reservations, concerning the more prominent Rabbanite commentators. Apart from the outspokenly antagonistic Mubashshir ha-Levi, it was only Dunash ben Labraṭ, a near contemporary, who ventured to publish a refutation of Saadiah's special monograph on the *hapax legomena* in the Bible. Others, like Tobiah ben Eliezer of Byzantine Castoria, or the Spaniards Moses ben Samuel ibn Chiquitilla and Yehudah ben Samuel (Abu Zakariya Yaḥya) ibn Bal'am (all of the late eleventh and early twelfth centuries), whether in agreement or disagreement, were deeply indebted to their geonic predecessor. Ibn Bal'am, in one of his frequent fits of ill temper, may have attacked Saadiah's translation of a phrase in Isaiah as "the invention of a man ignorant of the meaning of a word," and yet he could not avoid constantly learning from that version and the gaon's comments, which had become common property by that time. In rarely mentioning him by name, these commentators merely followed the accepted fashion of the age when the truth or falsity of views and doctrines were considered far more significant than their authorship. Even Abraham ibn Ezra (*ca.* 1092–1167), Saadiah's ardent admirer, only occasionally mentioned the gaon while quoting his views. It has been shown that, for example, in his *Commentary* on Job (written about 1140), Ibn Ezra referred to Saadiah expressly only six times, while forty other statements cited anonymously, and sixty more containing no reference to any predecessor, can be traced back to similar views expounded by him.[55]

Ibn Ezra's own work was in many ways, as we shall presently see, the final link and the crowning achievement of that classical period of Jewish Bible exegesis. Facing a large and economically highly differentiated public, the eastern and Spanish commentators developed a new kind of sophistication, even intellectual snobbery. Because they addressed themselves principally to the intellectual élite, Saadiah and his Karaite and Rabbanite successors in the Near East and Spain could use an increasingly refined technical language, develop a precise terminology and relate their biblical to the general philosophic and scientific studies then in vogue among their fellow intellectuals. This approach made their cumulative work of superior scientific quality, and modern, scientifically oriented biblical scholarship could learn from it a great deal. But it was largely a closed book to the masses. On the other hand, pursuing a somewhat independent course, German Jewry contributed a masterly and superlatively popular exposition of Scripture by Rashi (R. Solomon Yiṣḥaqi, 1040–1105). Basing his interpretations primarily upon the Eastern traditions, which via Italy had gradually been accumulating in the Rhenish academies, but also familiar with the works of Menaḥem ben Saruq and Dunash ben Labraṭ written under western Islam, Rashi presented concise and luminous commentaries on both the Bible and the Babylonian Talmud, in which subsequent generations of students were to be trained from their childhood on. Among many adults the words of Rashi and those of the Bible became so indistinguishably blended that, when citing from memory, they often were uncertain as to which they were quoting. Although apparently originating in part from the author's notes prepared for his private benefit and in part from expositions in his small academy, these comments were always geared to a talmudically well-trained, but scientifically rather naive, audience such as lived in the small and socially homogeneous northern communities. Because of his warm-hearted, popular approach, Rashi reflected more clearly the spirit of talmudic sages and also of Scripture as seen through the eyes of these sages.[56]

Rashi's works were immediately accepted as authoritative in the north. All his successors, including such independently distinguished authors as his associate Joseph Qara, his grandson Samuel bar Meir, Joseph Bekhor Shor, and Eliezer of Beaugency (all 12th cent.), leaned heavily upon his shoulders and, even in disagreement, bent in appreciation before the master. Others wrote merely *tosafot* (additional notes) on his commentaries. Within a century after his death his fame spread to other countries. Abraham Zuṭra of Thebes (about 1200) initiated what was to become a long series of supercommentaries on Rashi, since, despite their utter simplicity and lucidity, Rashi's comments often opened up new vistas which required further elucidation. Not long thereafter Daniel the Babylonian, a resident of Damascus, spoke reverently of the sage of Troyes as "the greatest exegete who illumined the eyes of the people in the dispersion." Nor was it purely accidental that, when Hebrew printing presses were established in 1475–76, the first book to be published in both Italy and Spain was Rashi's *Commentary* on the Pentateuch. Since that time a great many Bibles, just as almost all editions of the Babylonian Talmud, include Rashi's commentaries.[57]

We shall see that, like most Jewish commentators in Christian lands, Rashi continued in part the long-accepted patterns of midrashic exegesis, intermingling it with the newly awakened appreciation of the simple meaning of the scriptural text and its philological underpinnings. Compared with his Christian contemporaries, even Rashi could be considered a rationalist interpreter. He certainly steered clear of the purely allegorical or typological exegesis of Gregory the Great, the Venerable Bede or most of their immediate successors. Bede may have exaggerated the difference between the two denominational approaches when he asked: "If we follow the letter of Scripture only, in the Jewish way, what shall we find to correct our sins, to console or instruct us . . . when we open the book of the blessed Samuel and find that Elcana had two wives; we especially, who are celibate ecclesiastics?" Certainly, Jewish interpreters, too, found in the Bible many passages which did not square with their consciences and which they explained metaphorically. Yet even the homilists as a rule admitted that "Scripture never departs from its ordinary meaning." In Rashi's time, moreover, even Latin Christianity was gradually veering away from the purely allegorical toward a more rational exegesis—a transition undoubtedly promoted by the growing intellectual contacts between Jewish and Christian scholars.[58]

For Ibn Ezra the midrash, though not tradition in general, played but a secondary role. His epigram on Saadiah well describes his own work: "Although in some places he [the gaon] sauntered after the *midrashim,* we know that he was far better acquainted with the *shorashim* [grammatical roots]." Ibn Ezra integrated the great philological and exegetical attainments of Jewish scholarship in Muslim countries into a new comprehensive reinterpretation. Modern scholarship has often been inclined to minimize the "originality" of Ibn Ezra's exegetical work and to echo Profiat Duran's snide remark concerning Ibn Ezra the grammarian. "After him [Ibn Janaḥ]," wrote this fifteenth-century apologist, "Abraham ibn Ezra wrote nice works in this field, but he contributed in them little that was new." Perhaps this was a historic retribution for the rather rough handling Ibn Ezra's sharp satirical pen had meted out to many of his predecessors. In fact, however, this globe-trotting polyhistor not only summarized for the benefit of Western readers the monumental findings of Arabic-writing scholars, but very frequently he subjected the pertinent problems to independent scrutiny and presented the results in a concise manner. At times he was so concise as to become intentionally obscure and to call forth a host of supercommentaries. He also sprinkled his exposition with felicitous epigrams and witty allusions which made its study a sheer delight to generations of students. Popular fancy later wove around his intriguing personality an endless array of legends which, while often distorting essential features of his character, brought him closer to the folk psyche of Jews of various lands and varying cultural levels.[59]

An intermediary position between Ibn Ezra and Rashi was taken by David ben Joseph Qimḥi (Qamḥi, *ca.* 1160–1235), whose biblical commentaries were to enjoy great vogue also among "enlightened" Christian readers during the Renaissance age. Living in the Provence, that crossroad between the Spanish and Franco-German schools, David took over many philological and philosophic interpretations of his Spanish predecessors, but he combined with them the popular touch of Rashi's adherence to the living springs of Hebraic tradition. In many asides, of which he may not have been fully aware, he showed himself deeply steeped in the local aggadic heritage transmitted by the hermeneutic school of Moses the Preacher. In his interpretation of crucial passages Qimḥi was also ever mindful of their theologically controversial aspects. Less concerned about Karaite views, he was a sufficiently outspoken anti-Christian apologist to take full cognizance of the divergent scriptural interpretations of the two faiths. He explained, for instance, the reason for the inclusion in the Bible of prophecies addressed to Gentile nations as intended "to announce their forthcoming punishment for their persecution of Israel." But his interpretations never transcended the bounds of moderation and good taste. Once they realized that, as a Jew, Qimḥi could not possibly subscribe to the Christological interpretation of the biblical "testimonies," later Christian commentators had no difficulty in accepting his general explanations.[60]

CHANGING FASHIONS

Apart from personal temperaments and inclinations, chronological and environmental differences account for the varying approaches of these leading medieval Bible scholars. Ibn Ezra, who spent most of his life as a traveler in Christian countries, seems not always to have been fully cognizant of the peculiar fashions of scriptural exegesis in Eastern lands. That is why he was so deeply puzzled, for example, by Saadiah's attempt at identification of biblical names and anonyms. Objecting to the gaon's aforementioned equation of the river Pishon with the Nile (Gen. 2:11), Ibn Ezra wrote,

He [Saadiah] had no tradition to this effect. He did the same with respect to families, countries, animals, birds, and stones. Perhaps he saw them all in a dream. He erred, indeed, in some of these comparisons, as I shall explain them in their contexts, and we shall not rely on his dreams. Perhaps he did it only for the glory of God, since he translated the Torah into the language and script of Ishmael [Arabic], and feared lest they [the Arabs] assert that there are words [in Scripture] unfamiliar to us.

Consciously or unconsciously, Ibn Ezra merely restated here an old talmudic rationalization. After supplying the names of the mothers of Abraham, Haman, David, and Samson, not mentioned in the Bible, the Talmud explained that this was necessary "as an answer to heretics." R. Gershom, "the Light of the Exile," interpreted this saying to mean "that they may know and recognize that no subject escapes the attention of scholars."[61]

On the other hand, our polyhistor knew quite well the pertinent Arabic Jewish letters. His introductory critical survey of the existing exegetical literature, in itself a remarkable innovation, served despite its brevity and studied ambiguity as the main guide for the history of that literature to many generations until the opening of the world's vast manuscript resources during the last century.[62]

Unfamiliarity with the mainstream of Muslim exegesis, however, explains Ibn Ezra's frequent strictures against the excessive length of earlier works. A commentary in two books by Isaac ben Solomon Israeli, the distinguished North African Jewish scientist, covered only the first chapter in Genesis. It ended with the verse "Thus the heaven and the earth were finished" (*va-yekhullu;* Gen. 2:1), which gave Ibn Ezra the opportunity to pun, "And the plethora of his words still is unfinished [*lo khalu*]." This master of brevity did not realize that such an interminable flow of explanations was a more or less common failing of scriptural commentators of all faiths in Muslim lands. A carryover of ancient hermeneutics, when the scriptural word served as but a peg to which to attach all sorts of dogmatic and moral lessons, this method of detailed elaboration and discursive review of related but decidedly secondary issues was generally accepted. Otherwise the famous commentary (*tafsir*) on the Qur'an by Mohammed ibn Jarir aṭ-Ṭabari (838–923), a model for most subsequent exegetical efforts, could not cover 30 volumes totaling approximately 5,200 quarto pages, as it does in the Cairo edition of 1911. Half a century later, the Egyptian Al-Adfuwi composed a commentary in 120 books. Had not Theodore of Mopsuestia, even before the rise of Islam, written forty-one books, largely of an exegetical character? [63]

Such prolixity was the necessary effect not so much of garrulity as of the profound reverence for the divine word as the acme and synthesis of all wisdom. Even the rationalist exegetes did not seek merely dispassionate understanding of Scripture, but rather looked for broader information about vocabulary, grammar or style, law or ethics, dogma, philosophy, or even science. The more the exegetical literature proliferated, the lengthier became the comments analyzing the views of earlier authorities and passing judgment on controversial points. Before long the Baghdad teacher Ibn Salama (died in 1019) felt constrained to limit his observations to but 201 selected passages in the Qur'an which he explained on the basis of ninety-five earlier commentaries. Somewhat later Ibn Bal'am's commentary on Genesis bore the characteristic title, *Kitab at-*

Tarjiḥ (Book of Selection), namely selection of the most likely opinions as well as passages.[64]

No gargantuan efforts such as Ṭabari's are known to us from the Jewish literature of the period. But here too we may pursue the gradual growth of the exegetical works in both size and complexity. Benjamin al-Nahawendi and Daniel al-Qumisi still wrote rather concisely and more or less to the point, although the former frequently used the biblical word as a vehicle for the allegorical buttressing of his philosophic doctrines, and Daniel utilized it for the legalistic justification of cherished preconceptions, both dogmatic and juridical. Among Qumisi's successors the trend toward fuller and fuller elaboration became distinctly noticeable. One need but compare the fairly simple comments on Genesis which seem to stem from either of these authors with two theological expositions, probably dating from the late ninth century and based on the early verses of that book. Benjamin or Daniel had apparently devoted only two folios to the explanation of the last four verses of the first chapter. God's blessing to Adam and Eve, "Be fruitful, and multiply" (Gen. 1:28), is explained: "If [the Bible] had said only, 'Be fruitful,' without adding 'and multiply,' one might assume that having one child was enough. For this reason Scripture adds 'and multiply,' that is until man replenishes the earth, 'and subdue it,' that is until he conquers all lands." The commentator clearly intimated here that these words had been intended to serve as an injunction for man to proliferate, which corresponded to the long accepted rabbinic interpretation. Although somewhat more wordy and frequently, for stronger emphasis, quite repetitious in his analysis of the theologically very difficult beginning of the second chapter, the author is satisfied with the explanation that God's "ending" the work and resting on the seventh day (2:2–3) does not mean that part of the work had been done on the Sabbath. By making heaven and earth, God had in fact completed the whole work of creation. "Do not think that 'In the beginning' [Gen. 1:1] indicates the time of the beginning of creation, for there was no time before creation, just as the world was not created in space, for there was no space before creation." [65]

In contrast thereto the other two discourses on the early parts of Genesis (simultaneously published by Mann) are so elaborate and detailed that, at first glance, they hardly deserve the designation of commentaries. Their editor styles them, therefore, "Two Theological Works on Biblical Subjects," and does not consider them part and parcel of any original commentary. In the first fragment (F) its author argued against "the fools who contend that *tohu va-bohu* (Gen. 1:2) refers to the time before the creation of the world," for there could be no emptiness before the container. Hence Scripture merely wishes to indicate the condition of the earth *after* its creation. The author of the second fragment (G) merely insists that the *tohu va-bohu* really means "empty" and "waste"—a simple inversion of the Aramaic renditions. He then proceeds to explain the "darkness upon the face of the deep." He considers "darkness" the permanent accompaniment of the universe interrupted only by occasional periods of light. Or, to quote his graphic description: "Darkness is permanently settled upon it [the earth], is its citizen, whereas light is but a stranger on it, entering through one gate and leaving by another." [66]

Conceivably, however, all the fragments from the early Karaite exegetical literature here discussed may stem from the same author or authors. Not only could the same writer use a different phraseology and propose different explanations at different times, but the intermingling of brevity and conciseness in certain expositions with great prolixity in others was a frequent feature of contemporary exegesis, both Muslim and Jewish. Admirer though he was of Al-Muqammiṣ's "fine commentary on Genesis," Qirqisani censured it for being too brief in some parts and too verbose and irrelevant in others. A glance into the extant fragments of Saadiah's exegetical works also shows how frequently entire paragraphs of Scripture were explained briefly or not at all, while individual verses were accorded lengthy treatment. Few early exegetes frankly admitted to having written mere glosses on selected verses. Ibn Bal'am alone, as we recall, candidly called his work a "Book of Selections." The later Spanish commentaries were far better balanced. In accordance with the newly developed tastes of his readers, Ibn Ezra sharply censured the tiresome and frequently irrelevant excursuses by Isaac Israeli, Samuel ben Ḥofni, and even the revered Saadiah. Punning on Samuel's patronymic, he declared that the gaon had only "gathered wind in his fists [*be-ḥofnav*]," and that his "commentary had no merit except length." [67]

Sometimes purely formal considerations determined the choice between alternative interpretations even in matters of great theological import. In his translation of Genesis 2:2, for example, Saadiah rendered this obscure passage by "And the earth was plunged into an abyss and covered by water." We do not possess his commentary on Genesis, where he undoubtedly sought to justify this translation at great length, but it was clearly derived from his identification of *tohu* with *tehom* (abyss, for which he was censured by Jephet ben 'Ali and Ibn Ezra). He evidently resorted to this strained interpretation mainly because he wished to preserve the parallelism with the remainder of the verse, "And darkness was upon the face of the deep [*tehom* = abyss]; and the spirit of God hovered over the face of the waters." [68]

This translation is characteristic of Saadiah's entire exegetical approach. A zealous systematizer by native endowment and training, he had a passion for unity and always sought to integrate elements of thought and letters, however externally disjointed. His attempt to introduce systematic sequences into verses, chapters, and even entire books of the Bible is perhaps the outstanding and, despite its obvious artificiality, most ingenious and alluring feature of his exegetical method. For this reason he prefaced his translation of each biblical book with a lengthy introduction, in which he not only laid down the general principles guiding his interpretation, but also made a valiant effort to show the integral unity of that book and the logical sequence of its successive chapters.

We need but consider his commentary on the book of Proverbs which, superficially, appears as but a loose collection of moralistic apothegms. Not so to Saadiah. Convinced that the entire book was designed by Solomon as an aid to the "Quest for Wisdom" (he gave this title to his translation), the gaon launched into a lengthy tirade on the perennial conflict between man's natural propensities and his reason, which requires his never ending vigilance and disciplined ethical behavior. Only thus could reason overcome nature and secure man's genuine happiness. "That is why," Saadiah concluded, "this book and others like it have been written to teach man what is in accord with reason and to point out to him matters to which he had paid no attention. This is the purpose of [the exhortation] 'O ye thoughtless, understand prudence; and, ye fools, be ye of an understanding heart' [8:5]." The gaon then listed twelve major themes of the book covering the entire range of wisdom except the complex cosmological problems, speculation on which would prove futile (30:2–4) to the ordinary, philosophically untrained reader. In his detailed exposition, finally, he tried to reconstruct each chapter as part of a unified composition and, on one occasion, even transposed three verses from the middle to the end of the ninth chapter in order to achieve a more logical sequence.[69]

At the same time, Saadiah as a rule refrained from doing violence to the simple meaning of the text. With a fair degree of consistency he adhered to the general principles he was to lay down in his major philosophic work. In connection with the old *crux interpretum* of finding scriptural proof for the doctrine of resurrection, he asserted:

> We, the congregation of Israelites, accept in its literal sense and its universally recognized meaning whatever is recorded in the books of God that have been transmitted to us. The only exceptions to this rule are those instances in which the generally recognized and usual rendering would lead to one of the four [following] results: either (a) the contradiction of the observation of the senses . . . ; or (b) the contravention of reason . . . ; or (c) a conflict with some other Scriptural utterance . . . ; or, finally, (d) a conflict with what has been transmitted by rabbinic tradition. . . . Now the method of interpretation to be adopted in these exceptional cases is to look for a rendering of the expressions, which would be permissible in the usage of the Hebrew language and would make it possible for the contradictions to be reconciled.

The latter principle, widely adopted also in the Muslim exegetical literature, naturally opened the gate to a wide variety of interpretations. In this formative period of Hebrew philology, a decision as to the permissibility of a particular explanation often hinged on the acceptance or rejection of grammatical rules and lexicographic identifications which themselves still were in a state of flux.[70]

Methodological statements of this kind became quite customary after Saadiah. His younger contemporary, Qirqisani, not only wrote commentaries on several books of the Bible and a detailed exposition of the non-legal sections of the Pentateuch to supplement his *Kitab al-Anwar,* but he also prefaced that exposition by a lengthy introduction. Here he analyzed thirty-seven exegetical propositions which were to guide him in his work. Only a fragment of this commentary is extant, but its editor was able to reconstruct twenty-four of these propositions, about equally divided between general exegetical-theological principles and philological rules. As elsewhere, Qirqisani was rather moderate. Hardly any of these propositions would have been rejected by Saadiah, had he been able to read them. They included such rabbinical rules as that the Torah often "spoke in the language of the man of the street," and hence many of its formulations must not be taken literally; that there was no exact sequence (the rabbinic *muqdam u-me-'uḥar*) in Scripture, but that matters left open in one context were more fully explained in another; that some difficult passages must be understood in a way which, even if at variance with their ordinary meaning, is reconcilable with human reason; and that, more generally, many statements in the Bible may be subject to different interpretations, all more or less equally legitimate and applicable to different situations. While not quoting here R. Isaac's old dictum concerning the forty-nine *panim* (faces or modes) wherewith the Bible may be explained as favoring a legal point, and forty-nine other modes opposing it, the leading Karaite accepted this basic approach of talmudic hermeneutics.[71]

Apart from the influence of Saadiah's exegetical methods, to which Qirqisani seemed to refer when he spoke of "another fine book similar to that of David [al-Muqammiṣ]" composed by a contemporary, there was the irresistible logic of circumstances. Since Scripture was considered the fountainhead and sum total of all wisdom, it had to contain allusions to an endless variety of subjects which could be read out of, or rather into, it by concurrent explanations. This logic, which imposed itself also upon Muslim and Christian exegetes, led to the increasing vogue of citing various alternatives suggested by predecessors, named or quoted anonymously. Later commentators, like 'Ali ben Suleiman or Ibn Ezra, frequently mentioned such alternate meanings, rejecting some, giving preference to others as "the more likely," or simply leaving the decision to the reader. Far from being a sign of intellectual exhaustion and the work of epigoni, these extensive citations were merely the result of the growing accumulation of scholarly findings in this field which forced every new writer to take cognizance of the work of his predecessors.[72]

For similar reasons one had to explain every word in Scripture with appropriate gravity. Satirical statements against idolatry were readily taken as such. But other humorous passages were interpreted in a way effacing all suspicions of levity. For one example, to explain the proverb "Let a bear robbed of her whelps meet a man, rather than a fool in his folly" (17:12), Saadiah supplied the legalistic reason that a bear may be difficult to keep away, but at least one can kill it with impunity and without being cursed for it (*Oeuvres,* VI, 89).

As bitterness mounted in the latter part of the tenth century, the Karaite commentators often vented their spleen on the Rabbanite exegesis and its chief exponent, Saadiah. Salmon ben Yeruḥim particularly, preeminently a fighter, frequently assailed the gaon also in his commentaries, although he was evidently much in debt to Saadiah's method of translating Hebrew words by like-sounding Arabic terms, and of attempting to integrate into a single whole a book of so diverse a nature as the book of Psalms. On every possible occasion Salmon injected unbridled attacks on the Rabbanite point of view, as well as on Islam and Mohammed. At times his polemical excursuses appeared both dangerous and irrelevant to Karaite copyists themselves. For this reason, it appears, the Leningrad manuscript of Salmon's comprehensive commentary on Psalms omits what must have been a lengthy exposition and rendition of Psalm 74:4–60, because it contained a sharp diatribe on the dominant religion and its forthcoming downfall. No copyist hesitated, however, to reproduce Salmon's frequent excursuses on alleged Rabbanite misinterpretations, however little germane these appeared to the verse under review. Salmon took the occasion, for example, of explaining the verse, "Be surety for Thy servant for good; let not the proud oppress me" (Ps. 119:122) to assail the "proud" Rabbanites for their effrontery in postulating the coexistence of two Torahs (the written and the oral laws) and to show how badly the very Ten Commandments fared at the hand of Rabbanite expositors.[73]

Even the generally more moderate Jephet ben 'Ali, deeply indebted to both Saadiah's translation and commentaries, indulged in occasional sharp observations on the methods employed by the gaon, or the Rabbanite schools in general. Interpreting the prophecies addressed to Hosea as relating not only to the evil ways of ancient Israel, but also as an adumbration of contemporary developments, he stated:

> The meaning of "thou shalt not play the harlot, and thou shalt not be any man's wife" [Hos. 3:3] is that the multitude of the people in Captivity shall worship none but God and proclaim, "the Lord is our God, the Lord is one"; they shall firmly believe that Moses and his law is truth; they shall equally believe in the other prophets and their books, and that none other except Jerusalem is the Ḳibla. Yet, they [the Rabbanites] change many of the divine laws according to methods of interpretation employed by their early sages whom they follow. It is imperative that they turn away from the corrupt doctrines which their predecessors [falsely] deduced [from the biblical text], and according to whose judgment they act. But if they repent not, they shall remain in Captivity, seized as hostages in the hands of the enemies, as it is said, "And they that are left of you shall pine away in their iniquity in your enemies' lands" [Lev. 26:39].

Hosea's exhortation to ancient Israel to "return unto the Lord" (14:2–3) gave Jephet a welcome opportunity to enumerate some of the major legal and ritualistic differences between the Rabbanites and the Karaites, and to insist that only by giving up these deviations could the former return to the Lord.[74]

Curiously, it was in the interpretation of this very prophecy that Jephet's indebtedness not only to Saadiah's translation and commentaries, but also to his main philosophical treatise came clearly to the fore. While Saadiah's commentary on Hosea is not extant, and hence no detailed comparison is possible, it is certainly more than mere coincidence that every one of the fourteen interpretations cited from Saadiah in Qimḥi's *Commentary* is also given by Jephet. We are better able to ascertain both similarities and dissimilarities in their respective commentaries on Proverbs, both of which are available substantially in their original form.

Jephet's introduction was much briefer than Saadiah's and much less bent on the unification and systematization of the book in philosophic-ethical terms. But individual comments revealed striking similarities. Even externally both authors withheld lengthy comments on the individual verses of the first chapter, but concentrated their observations on the crucial verses 7, 19, and 33. Only Saadiah's brief comment on verse 9 was not emulated by his Karaite adversary, probably because Saadiah had stressed the great rewards of consulting "wise men," that is the rabbinic leaders. On the other hand, Jephet drew a sharper line of demarcation between the "external" or ordinary, and the "internal" or allegorical, meaning of scriptural phrases. He also was generally far more concise and, making use of some of the intervening advances in the philological investigations of Hebrew, sometimes offered a linguistically more acceptable solution. This of course did not justify his occasional attacks on the gaon, who, in his opinion, had often "lacked right direction in the way of language." It was only historic justice when Ibn Ezra retaliated in kind. In his survey of the existing exegetical literature the sharp-witted Spanish commentator attacked 'Anan, Benjamin, Ben Mashiaḥ, Yeshu'a, "and every heretic who does not believe in the words of the transmitters of religious tradition. He tends to turn left or right, and arbitrarily to interpret verses, even commandments and laws. These men are devoid of the knowledge of the principles of the Hebrew language and hence go astray even in their grammatical expositions." [75]

Remarkably Jephet and Ibn Ezra were both right. In the tenth century, despite Saadiah's magnificent contributions to Hebrew philology, the Karaites as a group still seemed superior in their linguistic equipment. In the century and a half, however, which elapsed between Jephet and Ibn Ezra, further Karaite advances in the domain of grammar and lexicography were far outranked by the magnificent work of the Spanish Rabbanites. Although Ibn Ezra himself unwittingly paid homage to the "unknown Jerusalem scholar," namely the Karaite Abu'l Faraj Harun, whose eight grammatical works (*sefarim*) were like "precious sapphires" (*sappirim*), these achievements were far outstripped by the superlative contributions of Yehudah (Abu Zakariya Yaḥya) ben

Ḥayyuj and Jonah (Abu'l Walid ibn Merwan) ibn Janaḥ. After them no Bible exegete dared use linguistic criteria without reference to their vital discoveries. Ibn Ezra himself may but rarely quote these predecessors verbatim or by name, but his dependence on them is evident at every turn. In his commentary on Job, for instance, the name of Abu'l Walid is expressly mentioned only once, but Ibn Janaḥ's explanations of biblical phrases and words are followed on more than one hundred occasions. Ibn Ezra's predecessor, Ibn Chiquitilla, too, had made extensive use not only of the methodological innovations, but also of many detailed expositions of Ibn Janaḥ, his fellow townsman of Saragossa. He was followed therein by his archenemy Ibn Bal'am, despite the latter's effort to revert wherever possible to talmudic interpretations. In 'Ali ben Suleiman's clear dependence on Ḥayyuj and other Rabbanites we already witness the eclipse of Karaite Bible exegesis in comparison with that of the Western Rabbanites.[76]

BIBLICAL CRITICISM

The great influence of Ḥayyuj, Ibn Janaḥ, and other grammarians on Bible exegesis was the result of the new "scientific" approaches, combined with the continuing quest for biblical support for sectarian or academic biases. For centuries past the Bible had been quoted by jurists and preachers, both Jewish and Christian, as authority for any doctrine they wished to impart, any law they wanted to have observed. But while previously any connection, however remote, between the biblical text and its hermeneutic derivation satisfied the expounder and his audience, he now had to prove to the satisfaction of far more critical readers that his interpretation was at least reconcilable with the accepted philological evidence.

Unlike the Muslims, Jews did not heatedly argue the "inimitability" of their Scriptures. Since Hebrew was no longer a widely spoken and ever changing language, and since all its basic properties and rules could in the ultimate sense be derived only from a careful scrutiny of the Bible, no one questioned its supreme linguistic excellence. Even those Muslim scholars who accused Jews of theologically inspired scriptural "forgeries," or those Christian critics who, like Rufinus, claimed that the rabbis had despoiled their biblical texts out of envy of Christians, conceded that these texts were the only surviving monuments of ancient Hebrew. Most students felt with Ibn Chiquitilla that "no one is left from whom we may learn the properties of the [Hebrew] language, and none remaining from whom we may acquire all its meanings, but only what we may understand from the materials afforded in the Holy Scriptures, and learn from the prophetical books." Certainly, Jewish life had no room for a counterpart to Ar-Rawandi's contention that the prose of some later writers was more beautiful than that of the Qur'an. In fact, so dependent were even the great Hebrew poets of the Golden Age of Spain on their peculiar understanding of biblical words and phrases, that Klar could pick out of their poems a long series of interpretations demonstrating the unconscious Bible exegesis practiced by these creative molders of the new Hebrew style. This is, of course, even more true of the philologists themselves, and careful reviews of Ibn Janaḥ's grammatical works have revealed his significant, if incidental, exegetical contributions as well. The average educated Jew, too, derived much of his familiarity with Hebrew from his frequent recitations of biblical lessons and the liturgical texts using biblical sentences or paraphrasing them. Had not Augustine already noted that Christians, raised on Latin Bibles, had become so deeply inured to the latter's linguistic peculiarities that they disparaged many equally good or better expressions employed by classical authors? The Hebrew Bible had no such rivals.[77]

Nor did Jews voice any doubts concerning the correctness of the Old Testament text. Although knowing from daily experience that copyists were bound to make mistakes and perfectly ready to suggest corrections in other manuscripts, generation after generation of scientifically trained Bible students, among Rabbanites and Karaites alike, professed unbounded confidence in the masoretic text. Even their Muslim neighbors, though confronted with a less uniform and controlled textual transmission of the Qur'an, generally adhered to the principle that one was free to choose between alternate versions only with the support of a reliable chain of tradition from the Messenger himself. True, Saadiah found few followers in his endeavor to derive independent meanings from the divergent spelling and pronunciation (the *ketib* and the *qeri*) of every word recorded in this double form in the Masorah. He contended that while the indicated pronunciation reproduced the simple sense, the original masoretic spelling, if retained in the official text, necessarily possessed also some hidden significance. Yet the eleventh-century Spanish physician, Isaac (Abu Ibrahim) ibn Yashush, was alone in suggesting occasional emendations, as when he identified the Edomite King Jobab the son of Zerah (Gen. 36:33) with Job. The overwhelming majority was prepared to accept the existing textual oddities with utter resignation and declare, with Abraham Maimonides, "These are matters handed down to us by tradition. Their mysteries escape us and we do not know their real reasons." [78]

Others, like Ibn Janaḥ, developed a series of rationalizations. An entire chapter in Ibn Janaḥ's grammar is devoted to illustrations of what he considered the good biblical usage of "expressing something in one word and intending another." If, for example, in his dire prophecies about Damascus, Isaiah referred to "the cities of Aroer" being forsaken (17:2), he

> did not mean Aroer herself, but rather Damascus. He called her Aroer to indicate that her affairs would take an evil turn so that she would become like Aroer located in the desert apart from civilization, as it is written, "And be like a tamarisk [*ka-'aro'er*] in the wilderness" [Jer. 48:6]. That is to say that these cities and their environs would become waste and deserted so that they would resemble [the city called] Aroer. . . . And proof of this explanation is that Aroer is not counted among the cities of [the district of] Damascus, but among the cities of Moab, as it is said about Moab, "O inhabitant of Aroer, stand by the way, and watch" [Jer.48:19].

Similarly, the biblical historian recording "the five sons of Michal, the daughter of Saul" (II Sam. 21:8) merely replaced, by Michal, the name of her sister Merab, who alone fits the previous biblical narratives (I Sam. 18:19, II Sam. 6:23). Although the reading Merab is supported not only by Targum and Septuagint but also by some Hebrew manuscripts, it did not occur to Ibn Janaḥ and his school thus to emend the verse. They only considered such substitutions a perfectly legitimate technique of the biblical writers, or as Ibn Parḥon graphically expressed it, "They say one thing, and in their heart mean another." Ibn Ezra actually saw in the preservation of the substitute words, rather than of their more correct originals, a clear demonstration of the faithfulness of the transmitted texts.[79]

Emendations were even further from the thought of the midrashic writers who often derived homiletical lessons from suggested different readings. Neither the homilist himself nor his audience ever conceived that he had wished to replace the existing text. Only the Karaites, willfully misinterpreting the aggadists' intentions, frequently ridiculed these *al tiqris* (do not read thus but thus), evoking an eloquent defense of this homiletical expedient by Maimonides. The sage of Fusṭaṭ was convinced that all linguistic techniques may readily be employed in order to secure from the revealed word of God the necessary guidance for the complexities of human existence. After all, he reminded his readers, the Bible "has been the guide of past and present generations," not just a history book or a volume of poems, intended for casual perusal (*Guide,* I.2; III.43; in Friedländer's translation, pp. 15, 354).

Few were, indeed, the medieval men who approached the study of the Bible without some such pragmatic objective. In Christian countries, in particular, the legal, dogmatic, or ethical derivatives from the biblical text by way of hermeneutic interpretation so indistinguishably blended with its ordinary meaning that even the more rational exegetes, such as the French Menaḥem bar Ḥelbo and Rashi, often crossed the invisible boundary between these two domains with perfect insouciance. Joseph Qara on several occasions declined to use aggadic materials and once roundly declared that "in all the twenty-four books [of the Bible] no prophet states his ideas so obscurely as to require explanation through the words of Aggadah." Nonetheless he frequently quoted the simple and the hermeneutic explanations side by side, intimating their equal legitimacy.[80]

The first northern commentator to pursue the rational line with considerable consistency was Samuel bar Meir (Rashbam). In a programmatic passage, inserted as a tacit polemic against an aggadic interpretation by his grandfather Rashi, he wrote:

> Friends of reason shall clearly understand the teaching of our sages [Yebamot 11ab, etc.] that Scripture never loses its ordinary meaning.

To be sure, the main objective of the Torah is to teach us [conduct] and to give us pertinent information through the various methods of ordinary as well as aggadic or halakhic interpretation, even through excessive verbiage, with the aid of the thirty-two modes of R. Eliezer son of R. Jose the Galilean and the thirteen modes of R. Ishmael. For this reason the older sages, in their great piety, immersed themselves completely in the hermeneutic teachings which are essential [for practical conduct] and failed to delve into the profundities of the ordinary meaning [one of Rashbam's pet phrases]. . . . However, our teacher Solomon, my mother's father, has enlightened the eyes of the dispersion by commenting on the Law, Prophets, and Hagiographa and paying attention to the simple meaning of Scripture. And I Samuel, son of his son-in-law Meir, of blessed memory, have often debated the issue with him. He admitted to me that if he had more time he would consider it necessary to rewrite his commentaries in the light of the ordinary meanings being detected every day.

Although Rashi never found the leisure to write new commentaries, he inserted some additions and corrections into the final versions of his exegetical works in the light of his debates with this independent grandson. Samuel did not hesitate to follow the ordinary meaning, even if he thereby removed the ground from under some important legal interpretation. He was prepared, for example, to see in the biblical phrase "And there was *evening* and there was *morning,* one day" (Gen. 1:5) rather than *night* and *day,* a sign that the day ended with the daybreak of the next morning, and that, hence, the night followed the day. Similarly, he understood the saying "And it shall be for a sign unto thee upon thy hand" (Exod. 13:9) as a pure metaphor for permanent remembrance, rather than as a reference to phylacteries.[81]

Certainly Rashbam had no intention of espousing heretical views. In his sheltered French environment he probably was not even aware of anyone wishing to apply such purely theoretical expositions to practical deviations from Jewish orthodoxy. However, there was enough ambiguity in this general approach for Samuel's successors, including his younger brother, Jacob Tam, and the latter's pupil Joseph Bekhor Shor, to moderate it greatly. Later generations of Franco-German scholars increasingly reverted to that intimate blend of literal and homiletical interpretations which had lent Rashi's commentaries their unparalleled charm. While the latter retained their freshness and popularity throughout the ages, those by Samuel were all but forgotten after their author's death, and they were resuscitated only by the antiquarians of the nineteenth century. It is small wonder, then, that half a century later David Qimḥi, searching in Narbonne for materials in preparation of his commentary on Exodus, found there only exegetical works, "the names of whose authors I did not know for they mostly followed the hermeneutic method."[82]

Even in Muslim countries, at the very height of the Hebrew rational exegesis, pragmatic interpretations of Scripture permeated the whole fabric of intellectual life. Characteristically, most of our quotations about Saadiah's exegetical principles and methods were taken from his main philosophic work, rather than from his commentaries or even from his illuminating introductions to individual biblical books, which between them have not unjustly been viewed as an early "Introduction to the Old Testament." With his fine feeling for the biblical language the gaon was, indeed, able to derive many startlingly new meanings from long familiar phrases. Nor was he totally averse to outright homiletical embellishments. He not only made free use of midrashic teachings, old and new, for his liturgical compositions, but he seems to have produced a booklet on the Ten Commandments, which was more homiletical peroration than commentary (*tafsir*), as he called it. To be sure, the texts now extant, which thirty generations of Arabic-speaking Jews unquestioningly attributed to the gaon, seem to be products of later medieval piety. Algerian Jewry still recites them at its synagogue services of the first day of the Festival of Weeks. However, their leading ideas very likely go back to an authentic composition by Saadiah.[83]

Such biblical semantics not only played a great role in all mystical and metaphysical speculations, but were also constantly employed for moral and legal guidance. Baḥya ibn Paquda, for example, built entire phases of his philosophic theory around the differences in the shades of meaning of the ten biblical synonyms of confidence (*biṭṭaḥon*—faith) and of the eleven synonyms of humility. Commenting on the three terms for "sin" employed by the psalmist in a single verse (32:5), Abraham bar Ḥiyya explained that one (*ḥatat*) stands for sins committed through action, one (*'avon*) for sinful thought, and one (*pesha'*) for sinful speech.[84]

Contrary to some medieval reports, Maimonides never wrote a commentary on the Bible; his successors may have confused him in this respect with his father, Maimon. Yet he devoted most of the first book of his philosophical magnum opus to an elucidation of biblical synonyms and homonyms. This semantic exercise appeared to him a requisite preparation for the systematic exposition of his own views, many of which might otherwise seem to run counter to the accepted literal meaning of Scripture. He also emulated Saadiah in constantly citing biblical passages, often with surprisingly new insights, in support of his own teachings, as well as in justification of certain general juridical principles, or particular laws. In all this he revealed himself as a biblical exegete of no mean attainments, and modern scholars were justified in carefully analyzing his exegetical methods. At times he was reluctant to divulge some of his unusual interpretations, lest they offend the sensibilities of orthodox members or Arab neighbors. Conceding that the rabbis had reversed the simple meaning of the biblical laws of direct physical retaliation, Maimonides merely expostulated, "They [the members of the Sanhedrin] have the power temporarily to dispense with some religious acts prescribed in the Law, or to permit what it forbids." He frequently confided such private views only to his young son, Abraham, however, who, fortunately, recorded a few in his own commentaries.[85]

In contrast to Maimonides—in fact, to all other medieval Jewish philosophers—Ibn Gabirol refrained from quoting the Bible in his main philosophic work. But in his other writings he indulged many allegorical interpretations, which made the rounds in the subsequent exegetical literature. His explanation of Jacob's dream (Gen. 28:12), for example, though rejected by Ibn Ezra, was widely quoted. By viewing Jacob's ladder as a symbol for the "higher soul" and the angels as representing the "thoughts of wisdom," Ibn Gabirol was able to integrate this dream into his general ideology. Saadiah's warning against allegorizing Scripture thus was disregarded even by Maimonides, who sometimes referred to the hidden meanings of the Bible in such a vein that, by a curious historical irony, he was claimed by later kabbalists as one of their own. Of course, mystics of all schools, beginning with the author of *Sefer Yeṣirah,* had a field day in reading into the Bible all of their pet convictions and speculations. The scientist Abraham bar Ḥiyya, on his part, subjected a great many scriptural passages to a searching astrological interpretation. In short, the all-pervasive biblical tradition became an eminent vehicle for the defense of almost any point of view which had found a champion within the Jewish community or, for that matter, among Christian ecclesiastics.[86]

RATIONALIST CRITIQUES

There was no lack, however, of men who questioned the very fundamentals of biblical tradition. The constant bickering between the sects in the Empire and their frequent disputations, private or public, accumulated enough material for anyone wishing to point out the weaknesses of all scriptural records. With eyes sharpened by hatred, opponents detected every inconsistency or irrationality which readily escaped the attention of the sworn partisans of each particular sacred text. In the grand debate extending over many centuries between Graeco-Roman polytheism, Judaism, and Christianity, particularly heterodox Christianity of the Marcionite kind, every word in the Old Testament was scrutinized for possible arguments against the mother or daughter religion. The gnostics, who had hated Jews and Judaism with unreasoning hatred; the followers of Mani, who wished to synthesize all existing faiths and thus to displace them all; and the Muslims, who, for purposes of self-justification, had to claim that their Qur'an had dislodged earlier Scriptures which, though originally genuine, had been corrupted by endless "forgeries"—all looked for every possible flaw in the Old Testament to support their own contentions. All this was grist for the mill of skeptics and freethinkers of all faiths, whose number was not inconsiderable during the height of the Islamic Renaissance.

Among Jews we hear little of outright atheists of the kind of the Muslim school of Dahriya. However, Ibn ar-Rawandi, the much-hated persistent questioner of the established order, seems to have been born of an heretical Jewish father and to have frequently associated with Jews. According to Ibn al-Jauzi, some Jew warned the Muslims that Ibn ar-Rawandi would spoil for them the

Qur'an, as his father had spoiled the Torah for the Jews. When the heretical agitator had to escape from threatening arrest, he went into hiding in the house of a Jew, Levi (Abu 'Isa ben Levi), for whom he allegedly composed his *Destroyer of the Brain,* with its virulent attacks on the Qur'an and Mohammed.[87]

No other Jew of the period, certainly none of the Jewish writers, was quite as radical as this son of a Jewish apostate. Nevertheless, even in the Jewish camp, the sectarian Isma'il al-'Ukbari insisted "that some things in the Scripture were not [originally] as they are now written." More, Rabbanite extremists such as Ḥivi ha-Balkhi (of Balkh in what is today Afghanistan) ventured to question the authority of the Bible itself. Living in the second half of the ninth century at the height of the Jewish sectarian conflicts and in a region where Zoroastrianism was fighting its losing battle for survival against the onslaughts of Judaism, Christianity, Manichaeism, and Islam, Ḥivi seems to have formulated two hundred questions aimed at demonstrating the Bible's shortcomings from the point of view of reason and ethics. No fragment of, nor even any full quotation from, Ḥivi's own work has come down to us. We must rely, therefore, on the ever hazardous expedient of trying to reconstruct his ideas from statements by opponents, of which only a small portion has survived. We possess, for instance, none of the replies given, according to Qirqisani, by Ḥivi's near contemporary, the sectarian leader Abu-'Imran al-Tiflisi (Musa al-Za'frani). But it seems that Ḥivi had published his queries in a rhymed Hebrew text, which lent itself to wide circulation, perhaps both in oral and in written form.[88]

Ḥivi's criticism differed radically from the previous questioning of the Jewish interpretation of the Bible by both Christians and Muslims, inasmuch as he applied rational standards, rather than those of opposing dogma. This difference did not hinder him, however, from borrowing Christian or Muslim arguments whenever it served his purpose. That he was also deeply indebted to the Jewish Aggadah (whose inquisitive remarks on some scriptural passages he reproduced without quoting its answers), to Zoroastrian dualism, and to ancient gnosticism, makes him an even more alluring symbol of the awakened intellectual curiosity of his age. His method consisted mainly in pointing out sharply the apparent or real contradictions in Scripture, and in offering rational explanations for miracles such as the crossing of the Red Sea or the gift of manna. According to the Karaites Joseph al-Baṣir and Ibn Ezra, he contended that Moses knew of a spot in the Red Sea which ran dry once in a thousand years. The Hebrew lawgiver led the Israelites there in perfect safety, while the less informed Egyptians drowned upon the return of the waters. The manna was but a fairly common variety of a desert plant, called in Persian *tarnjabin*. Ḥivi also interpreted the biblical narrative concerning the appearance of Moses' face after his descent from Sinai (Exod. 34:29–30) as referring not to a miraculously "shining" face, but to a face become "horny" (an equally admissible translation of the crucial word, *qaran*), or wizened, because of the prophet's forty-day starvation.[89]

Curiously, in these and other strictures Ḥivi never suggested that the biblical text might be corrupt. In fact, he often presupposed a rabbinic interpretation of the biblical stories as if it were part and parcel of the Bible itself. In his question, for example, as to why Isaac so willingly submitted to his intended sacrifice, he evidently assumed, with the rabbis, that Isaac was a grown man (according to some traditions aged thirty-seven) and fully aware of the danger. He also accepted the rabbinic contention that the biblical commandments frequently lacked detailed explanations left to be clarified by Oral Law, but he merely argued that God should not have thus left the reader in the dark about the implications of each commandment and its underlying reasons. Nor did he allow for any lapse of time between God's blessing of Abraham, "I will multiply thy seed as the stars of the heaven" (Gen. 22:17), and the Deuteronomist's exclamation, "For ye were the fewest of all people" (7:7).[90]

Like other contemporary opponents, Ḥivi attacked biblical anthropomorphisms. He queried, in particular, why God should have demanded fat and blood as sacrifices and accepted them as a "sweet savour" (Gen. 8:21). He also denounced God's alleged changes of mind as a serious reflection on God's omniscience. If God considered the criminal's death a just penalty for murder, why did He not destroy Cain? Referring to God's anger at the recalcitrant Israelites during their desert migrations (Num. 14:23),

Ḥivi objected: "Since God had already sworn to the patriarchs to give their children this particular land, how did it become Him to swear to prevent them from entering it, and thus annul His former oath?" [91]

Above all, Ḥivi dared question the very fundamentals of the Jewish faith. How can we believe in God's omnipotence, he asked, if He could not keep Adam from reentering the Garden of Eden without the help of the cherubim and the flaming sword? Why did not God prevent Cain's murder? Why was He afraid of the Tower of Babel? If God is really omniscient, why did He have to try Abraham? Why did God leave the angels, and decide to dwell among the inferior humans? Ḥivi subjected the institutions of circumcision and sacrifices to no less searching scrutiny than the belief in reward and punishment. He also pointed out that, according to the story in Genesis, God appears to have partaken of food ritually forbidden (meat with milk) and, thus bribed, He promised Abraham a son. A distinct echo of Islamic-Jewish controversies is discernible in his query as to why God had allowed Ishmael (the ancestor of the Arabs) to be born, and why He broke His pledge to Abraham to make Israel a great nation. Contrary to Isaac's blessing of Jacob, the descendants of Esau (Romans or Christians) were both more numerous and more prosperous than the children of Jacob. In fact, "Israel is today in servitude during its captivity in Se'ir." [92]

To be sure, Ḥivi is an exceptional phenomenon. In so far as one can judge from answers by opponents, he seems to have been one of those "smart-alecky" eclectics who took his arguments wherever he could find them, without necessarily committing himself to any particular set of beliefs. In the Arabian world at large, Ḥivi's was the generation which first embarked upon a scientific study of comparative religion, often in a positively heretical, even freethinking vein; it was a generation which produced Ibn ar-Rawandi's *Destroyer of the Brain* and *Emerald,* and soon also Ar-Razi's (Rhazes') *Impostures of Prophets.* In fact, as we recall, Louis Massignon traced back the notorious medieval phrase of the "three impostors" (Moses, Jesus, Mohammed) to a tenth-century document emanating from the Muslim sect of Qarmatians. Among the surviving Zoroastrians, Mardan Farukh, author of the

Pehlevi work, *The Decisive Solution of Doubts,* voiced opinions often strikingly similar to Ḥivi's.[93]

Whatever its borrowings from the outside, however, Ḥivi's critique was a novelty in Jewish literature and probably also in Jewish communal life. And yet it seems to have enjoyed a relatively wide acceptance in Jewish circles. In a crucial, though rather obscure, passage, Ibn Daud praises Saadiah highly for having "composed replies to heretics and deniers of the Torah. One of these was Ḥivi al-Balkhi, who had fabricated a Torah of his own. R. Saadiah testified that he had seen elementary teachers giving instruction in it in books and tablets until he [Saadiah] arose and overcame them." Most likely, Ḥivi's new Torah consisted merely of some revised version of the Pentateuch in which "objectionable" passages were deleted or altered. That, whatever its nature, this new concoction should have gained circulation in elementary schools is doubly remarkable, as school teachers generally considered themselves guardians of the traditional lore and were, indeed, accused by another contemporary of excessive conservatism. Their young pupils, too, doubtless evinced far less interest in the fine theological distinctions underlying most of Ḥivi's criticisms than in his "clever," though irresponsible, attacks on the canonical texts.[94]

All efforts to make of Ḥivi a convert to another faith have proved unsuccessful. Some scholars, remembering Pseudo-Baḥya's reference to him as a follower of the Magi, postulated at least Ḥivi's profound indebtedness to the *Decisive Solution of Doubts.* This is unlikely. Apart from the probability that Ḥivi wrote before Mardan Farukh, we must bear in mind that Ḥivi's stricture on Deuteronomy 32:9 had, if anything, a polytheistic rather than a dualistic coloring. His query concerning the *tohu va-bohu,* cited by Pseudo-Baḥya, likewise indicated his objection to, rather than approval of, any dualistic inference. In his few direct points of contact with the Parsee account, as in his critique of the anthropomorphism of God's (or the angels') visit to Abraham, the two stories bear but remote resemblance. Certainly Ḥivi was too well informed to accept the utter nonsense dished out by Mardan Farukh to unsuspecting readers (doubtless from some third-hand aggadic sources) as the official Jewish version of that visit. On the other hand, Mardan Farukh's ethical argument clinching his critique of the biblical story of creation and the sufferings of all later generations for Adam's sin, probably had its counterpart in Ḥivi, who frequently harped on the theme of the injustices attributed to God by the Bible. He complained, for instance, of the prohibition of admitting Moabites and Ammonites to the fold, as well as of God's infliction of the Egyptian bondage "against them that did not sin" because of their forefathers' transgressions.[95]

With more justice, Ḥivi's questions were linked with age-old strictures on the Old Testament, advanced by various Manichaean and other gnostic groups, Menahem Stein calling him the "Jewish Marcion." Harping on the sudden transition from the plural to the singular in the story of the visit of the three angels to Abraham (Gen. 18:2–3), Ḥivi, following many Christian authors, tried, according to Saadiah, "to divide into three the God who lifteth up and bringeth low." Ḥivi's objection to the anthropomorphism of this biblical narrative which makes it appear as if God had been fed by Abraham and, thus bribed, had promised him progeny, was answered by the gaon with an obvious allusion to the Christian Eucharist: "Thou knowest all the wickedness which thy heart is privy to that thy Master hath been eaten and drunk and absorbed and mixed up." We must, however, discount much from assertions of any fervent controversialist. Had Ḥivi been a Christian convert, Saadiah would neither have failed to mention this fact, nor have been likely to find it altogether necessary to write any apologetic treatise against him. Among the Jews, Ḥivi's conversion alone would have disposed of the entire issue.[96]

Other Jews in a similar position doubtless preferred to leave the Jewish faith altogether, and to share the economic and political advantages of the dominant group. Samau'al ibn Yaḥya, for example, joined the ranks of the Muslim literary polemists against Judaism. But there must have been other skeptics who remained Jews outwardly, though no one has cared to preserve their memory. What would have remained of Ḥivi's ideas, were it not for the fulminating replies of Saadiah, Salmon ben Yeruḥim, and Ibn Ezra?

Despite its intemperate tone and frequent emulation of Ḥivi's own irresponsibility, Saadiah's polemic poem seems to have checked the latter's popularity. Ḥivi's "Questions" were still known and cited by Qirqisani, Salmon, Pseudo-Baḥya, the two Ibn Ezras, and several anonymous writers of the eleventh and twelfth centuries. However, these citations increasingly give the impression of second-hand borrowings. Since to some writers Ḥivi had become the symbol of extreme Bible criticism as such (for this reason alone he has been accorded here, too, an inordinately lengthy treatment), it is rather astonishing that he was not quoted with even greater frequency and venom.

Ḥivi's sources seem to have included the numerous "questions and answers" (*eroteseis kai apokriseis*) and "difficulties" (*aporiai*) in the understanding of the Bible raised from ancient times by Jewish and Christian exegetes and assembled, among others, in the works of Theodoret of Cyrrhus, Maximus Confessor, and Anastasios Sinaites (5th–7th cent.). These Christian writers were not iconoclasts. Their principal aim was to point up the difficulties raised by opponents, or otherwise agitating the minds of attentive students, in order to furnish appropriate answers. While in quiescent periods Jewish leaders could limit themselves to more oblique references and indirect resolutions of difficulties, the growth of sectarian controversies in the posttalmudic age demonstrated the importance of these critical problems and the need to furnish definite guidance to conscientious readers. Had not the second-century school of R. Ishmael already included in the "modes" of interpretation of Scripture the category of "two contradictory verses," the meaning of which is determined by a third verse? From here was but a step to the deduction (to quote Abraham ben David's comment on that passage) that "it is our duty to study and harmonize all (two) verses which are difficult to reconcile with one another." This view was shared by Saadiah who, without spelling it out, furnished in his treatise on "The Thirteen Modes of Interpretation" three significant examples (including the contradictory figures relating to King David's census) of how superficially contrasting assertions could be explained with the aid of some apparently unrelated verses. In fact, there existed a medieval midrash entirely devoted to the harmonization of such contradictory statements in the Bible. It tried to explain, for example, why the

Torah, which is rightly called by the Psalmist "the law of the Lord" (19:8), is styled by Malachi "the law of Moses" (3:22). Another midrash of which only a small fragment is now extant seems to have raised many pertinent questions on the Pentateuch, without even bothering to supply the answers.[97]

The most notable example of this type of exegetical-apologetic literature is "The Oldest Collection of Bible Difficulties by a Jew," originally published by Schechter from a Cambridge Genizah manuscript. Unfortunately, even with some additional fragments uncovered by Louis Ginzberg and Alexander Scheiber, we seem to possess in all less than half of this composition. Neither its author nor its date can be ascertained, although there are indications that it was written in the tenth or eleventh century by a Babylonian or Palestinian writer, who at the age of eighteen had left one of the Central Asian provinces. Coming from an area where Ḥivi's type of questioning still was very much in vogue, our poet was evidently antagonized by the excessive self-assurance with which the Palestino-Babylonian Bible exegetes, particularly the Karaites, presented their interpretations. He was especially distressed by their lack of unanimity on any fundamental problem. "They foregather all," he exclaimed, "in search of a solution, they circle and tremble like angels of intoxication, and to the last one states one thing while a second tells the opposite. Their leader 'uttereth his mischievous desire' without any advantage, 'and he restraineth them not.' "[98]

Above all our author was convinced that human reason, unaided by tradition, could neither penetrate the mysteries of the universe nor understand the true meaning of Scripture. "Try to answer my questions from Scripture," he challenged his opponents. Taking up the biblical story of creation, he defied these self-proclaimed biblical experts to explain to him (1) the nature of heaven and how God had created it; (2) the place of darkness in the scheme of the universe and how the Creator had woven light into it and assigned to the latter its place in the daytime; (3) the meaning of *tehom*—"hast thou walked in search of the depth?"; and (4) the nature of man whom God created upright. Undoubtedly stimulated by some Zoroastrian debates on the dualistic principles of light and darkness—Mardan Farukh attacked this part of the biblical cosmogony with greater vehemence than any other —our poet dismissed with disdain the individualistic speculations on this score among such Karaite students of the Bible as Nahawendi or Qumisi. He was equally emphatic that, without the assistance of oral tradition, students would helplessly confront the numerous contradictions in Scripture, particularly those relating to numbers, and understand very little of the implications of terse biblical laws.[99]

In contrast to Ḥivi's negativistic critique, this type of questioning evidently pursued constructive purposes. In many ways our author anticipated the situation which was to arise in the Christian world after the Reformation. If, like the later Protestants, Karaite and other opponents of tradition called for a return to the Bible and its individual interpretation, Rabbanite leaders reacted in the same way as such spokesmen of the Catholic Counter Reformation as Richard Simon in his *Critical History of the Old Testament,* and contended that, without tradition, Scripture itself would remain contradictory and often wholly unintelligible.[100]

HISTORICAL CRITICISM

Lagging far behind the tremendous effort of Jewish exegetes and grammarians to come to grips with the Bible's complicated textual problems was the concern of scholars and public alike in its historical aspects. Such neglect becomes doubly manifest when one compares it with the considerable ingenuity which went into the raising and solving of theological, scientific, and ethical problems arising either from apparent contradictions in Scripture itself, or from the reluctance of later generations to accept certain implications of the biblical record for their own time. This is the less surprising, as the very historical literature of the period had built its reconstruction of world and Jewish history on the foundations of the biblical narratives without applying to them even its usually moderate critical standards.

Not that the Bible's historical sections were neglected. In fact, the author of our "Oldest Collection" devoted as much space to the difficulties arising from a comparison of historical data as to those stemming from alleged legal or ethical ambiguities in the

Bible. Chronological problems, in particular, because of their numerous practical implications, were extensively discussed and rediscussed by students, including Saadiah and Maimonides. The author of *Pirqe de-R. Eliezer* had devoted two or three chapters to chronological problems, in their aggregate constituting "the first Hebrew treatise on the fixed calendar." Later Saadiah composed several monographs on problems of chronology and the calendar. Maimonides went to great lengths to explain the chronological foundations of the continued Jewish observance of the year of fallowness. Moreover, Jews could not help being stimulated by their Arab neighbors' great interest in biblical chronology, which reached a climactic achievement in the work of Al-Biruni. Ḥamza al-Isfahani, a contemporary of Saadiah, even tried to reconstruct the chronology of all unbelievers.[101]

Other historical aspects, however, were treated naively or not at all. Even Muslim controversialists, who harped on the theme of alleged Jewish "forgeries," constantly invoked even indirect allusions or remote reconstructions in the Bible as indisputable evidence for the genuineness of their Messenger and his prophecies. In fact, there was so little dispute about the Bible's revealed origin that the Jewish community showed little interest in the problem of its "createdness"—a problem which, as applied to the Qur'an greatly agitated the minds of contemporary Muslim thinkers. Maimonides merely voiced accepted opinion when he declared it to be an article of faith (the eighth in his enumeration) that "the whole Pentateuch given to us through Moses is in its entirety revealed by God." [102]

Jewish exegetes unquestioningly accepted also the conventional attribution of biblical books to certain authors. Explaining away the numerous difficulties, Saadiah asserted that "a divine voice revealed the entire book [of Psalms] to David, as the whole people agrees in calling them the 'songs of David' and as Scripture itself in many passages attributes them to David." In fact, he considered it his duty to disprove contentions that David had written this book from his own mind, for "all these are the words of God . . . as is attested by truthful Masorites." David Qimḥi, with extreme insouciance, adopted the various legendary attributions of individual psalms to biblical heroes of the pre-Davidic age. So convinced was Abraham Maimuni of Solomon's authorship of both Proverbs and Ecclesiastes that, in a responsum, he invoked the testimony of this much-married king himself as a warning: "Give not thy strength unto women, nor thy ways to that which destroyeth kings" (Prov. 31:3), and he contended that Solomon had his own frailty in mind when he expostulated "For there is not a righteous man upon earth, that doeth good, and sinneth not" (Eccles. 7:20). Ibn Ezra argued even against the talmudic suggestion that Job was not the author of the book named by him, indeed may never have existed. The fact that Job was mentioned by Ezekiel (14:14), along with Noah and Daniel, appeared to him to be sufficient proof of both his historicity and identity. Ibn Ezra further suggested that Job had probably written the work in a foreign language from which it was later translated into Hebrew. That is why, he declared, the text "is so difficult to interpret, as is the case in every translated book." [103]

Perhaps the greatest culprits in neglecting even rudimentary historical approaches were the Karaite exegetes. Having rejected tradition, they had to resort to the Bible for exclusive guidance and hence sought in it also hints for all subsequent history and contemporary situations. Jephet ben 'Ali was fairly representative of his fellow sectarians, when he viewed the prophecies of Hosea as object lessons for his own time. His comment on the "knowledge" with which the three youths brought before Nebukadrezzar were supposed to have been endowed (Dan. 1:4) was likewise typical. It was, he wrote,

> most probably knowledge, like Solomon's, in the different departments of philosophy. The children of Israel were never destitute of its elements, but always taught them to their children. Even in times of their idolatry and wickedness, the votaries of wisdom and knowledge never failed among them.

Nor did Jephet show the slightest hesitation in interpreting Daniel 11:21 ff. as a prophecy foretelling the events which were to shape the destinies of the world and Israel after the conquest of Islam. He even found therein hints of such details as the battle which preceded 'Umar's conquest of Jerusalem. Similarly, by identifying the Arabs with Moab in Isaiah 16:4, David ben Abraham al-Fasi interpreted the Isaianic prophecy to mean that the Jewish "outcasts" would ultimately find shelter under the Arab dominion and even be allowed to settle again in Jerusalem.[104]

Apocalyptic visions like Daniel's lent themselves particularly well to intimate blending of the past, present, and future. As the Messiah was essentially timeless, speculations based upon the Bible's messianic passages could easily transcend the boundaries of time and space. To Jephet it was perfectly clear that Nahum's prophecy about God who "rebuketh the sea" (1:4–5) pointed "to the great kingdoms, Edom (Byzantium) and Ishmael (the Arabs), whose rule extends along the ocean of the world. Their armies toss about as the waves of the sea, but God rebukes them and destroys these kingdoms." Apart from similarly foretelling the downfall of Israel's enemies, in Jephet's opinion Daniel's predictions included also the coming of the time when "the doctrines of the chiefs of Jews shall be exploded," and when it would "become clear to the multitude, who accept their authority, that the truth is with the [Karaite] sect, and that by it the redemption shall come." Jephet disagreed violently with Saadiah's effort to fix the date for the coming of the Redeemer by a peculiar exposition of Daniel's obscure chronology, just as he disagreed also with some messianic interpretations of his own coreligionists, Benjamin and Salmon. But neither he, nor any of the Rabbanite objectors to attempts at computing the end of days, denied that some such hints might, indeed, be found in Scripture.[105]

In the invigorating intellectual climate of Spanish Jewry, however, even such long accepted historical truisms were not allowed to stand unchallenged. Isaac ibn Yashush, the intrepid textual critic, ventured also to defy the accepted literary assumptions and to subject the very Pentateuch to searching historical scrutiny. His rationalist bent rebelled against the then regnant opinion that the list of Edomite kings (Gen. 36:31 ff.) had been inserted, long "before there reigned any king over the children of Israel," by Moses writing under divine inspiration. By comparing some names in this list (36:39) with those recorded by the biblical historians in other connections (I Chron. 1:50 and I Kings 11:19), he came to the conclusion that the list originated in the days of Jehoshaphat. This was outright heresy even for a rationalist like Ibn Ezra who not only punned on Ibn Yashush's first name, Isaac-Yiṣḥaq ("every listener shall laugh at him"), but also irately called for the burning of Ibn Yashush's book.[106]

Ibn Yashush's work was never formally banished, but the tacit opposition among Jewish literati sufficed to suppress his views. Scribes and booksellers refused to reproduce them in quantities which might have assured their survival in modern libraries. The more moderate Moses ibn Chiquitilla was somewhat more fortunate. He seems to have abstained from any historical criticism of the sacrosanct books of Moses. Only some twenty-four of his comments on the Pentateuch have been reconstructed; almost all of them are purely philological in content. Even where (as in Exod. 16:15 ff.) he was disturbed by the historic sequence of events, he evaded the issue by the time-honored expedient of assuming that one need not expect regular sequences (*muqdam u-me'uḥar*) in Scripture. On the other hand, he publicly denied the unity of the book of Psalms and its Davidic authorship; in the case of several psalms (42, 47, 102) he stated bluntly, "This poem was composed in Babylonia," or "This poet lived in Babylonia." He is also the first man on record to have pointed out the disparity between the first thirty-nine chapters of the book of Isaiah and the section beginning with Chapter 40. Although not necessarily denying Isaiah's authorship of that section, and in one passage (52:13) actually relating God's "servant" to Hezekiah, he nevertheless noted on the prophecy "Comfort ye" (40:1) that "these are the first comforting prophecies from the middle of the book which pertain to the Second Temple." [107]

Ibn Chiquitilla had a special predilection for relating messianic statements, even if made by such indubitably preexilic prophets as Micah or Zephaniah, to the Second Commonwealth, although he thereby removed the props from under certain messianic expectations for the ultimate end of days. At the same time he tried to ascertain, in the vein of modern biblical students, the date of the prophet Joel. Not only from the mention of the valley of Jehoshaphat, but also from other allusions in the book, he deduced that "this prophet perhaps lived in the days of King Jehoshaphat." He was equally critical in assessing some of the biblical miracles. Without altogether denying the possibility of God's supernatural intervention and its occasional alteration of the course of nature, he refused to subscribe to the accepted notion that, at Joshua's command (10:12), the celestial bodies had come to a standstill. Since, in his opinion, the universe could not cease moving, the miracle at Gibeon consisted only in the sunlight continuing to permeate the atmosphere after the sun had set. For similar reasons Ibn Chiquitilla repudiated the literal interpretation of the very biblical sayings that the heavens and earth would "perish" or "vanish away like smoke" (Ps. 102:27, Isa. 51:6). He explained them as referring merely to the disappearance of creatures living in the respective heavenly spheres and their earthly center. This view, too, was sharply repudiated by Ibn Bal'am as smacking of the atheistic doctrines of the Dahriya. Although based on scientific rather than historical criticisms, these radical interpretations of the Saragossan critic seem to have found few followers even among the Spanish students of philosophy.[108]

These were daring views, however cautiously expounded. Ibn Bal'am, to whose report of a private conversation we owe our knowledge of Ibn Chiquitilla's interpretation of the miracle at Gibeon, sharply attacked it along with Ibn Chiquitilla's other views which he found "perplexing and corrupt." This altercation may actually have stimulated Ibn Bal'am to compose a special treatise analyzing all miracles mentioned in the Pentateuch or Prophets. By no means a rigid conservative (he did not hesitate to quote the Qur'an or ancient Arabic poetry), Ibn Bal'am bitterly resented also Ibn Chiquitilla's application of many prophecies to more or less contemporary events, in which he saw a conscious stratagem to undermine the readers' faith in ultimate redemption. These irate remarks seem to have strongly influenced the later exegetes. Even Ibn Ezra, though greatly indebted to Ibn Chiquitilla's philological exegesis, steered clear of most of the latter's historical criticisms. Only by popularizing his suggestion of a break in the continuity of the book of Isaiah (of course, without naming his predecessor) this widely read commentator salvaged some vestiges of Ibn Chiquitilla's (and Ibn Yashush's) revolutionary historical approaches for later, more sympathetic generations of biblical critics.[109]

PRECIOUS POSSESSION

In the first three and a half dark and inarticulate centuries after the conclusion of the Talmud (500–850), Jewish intellectual leadership laid the foundations upon which the vocal and creative generations of the following three and a half centuries (850–1200) erected the magnificent structure of medieval Jewish biblical learning. Their joint efforts resulted in a permanent achievement unsurpassed in all essentials. With hard toil and self-discipline they reviewed the existing texts and established a uniform, canonical recension of Scripture, which they fortified and made secure by a multitude of masoretic rules, exceptions therefrom, and exceptions from exceptions. Both text and rules were agreed upon by the most authoritative expounders of the scriptural tradition and ultimately recognized by Rabbanites and Karaites alike, as well as by interested Christians and Muslims. These groups of devoted disciples also reviewed the existing Aramaic translations, in part going back to immemorial antiquity, and finally secured agreement on a masoretic recension of their "Onkelos" which ranked second only to the Hebrew Bible itself in canonical authority. Soon thereafter, to meet growing needs of the Arabic-speaking majority of world Jewry, the superlatively gifted Saadiah Gaon produced an Arabic translation of the Bible, which ranked high in the history of translation literature.

Equipped with such reliable texts, Jewish scholarship began exploring with renewed zest every nook and corner in the Bible. It brought to bear on this task both its accustomed hermeneutical methods and the newly discovered scientific approaches that were philological-critical and, to a lesser extent, historical. It had greatly refined these tools in continually defending its ancestral faith against the onslaughts of Muslim and Christian controversialists who spoke the same lingo and largely shared the same set of beliefs, disbeliefs, and prejudices. Following the example set by such Karaite scholars as Benjamin and Daniel, Saadiah again made literary history through his superb commentaries. Only their overambitious compass and sophistication in both form and substance militated against their popularity and prevented their becoming a household possession of Arabic-speaking Jewry on a par with the gaon's translation. Although greatly admiring his qualities as an exegete—an enthusiastic modern literary historian (B. Z. Halper in *Hatekufah,* XXIII, 273) called Saadiah "the greatest Bible commentator of all time"—the following generations turned to such more popular expositions as those of Rashi and Ibn Ezra, who had made good use of the further philological advances of the intervening century or two.

Far beyond the progress of biblical research, the Bible as such became, perhaps more than in any other historical period, the common possession of the people at large. As a combined result of the general spread of popular education in Muslim lands and the growing interest of all faiths in their scriptural traditions, a substantial Jewish intelligentsia now shared in the process of rediscovery of its ancient treasures, linguistic, historical, and religious. Gone was the time when Naṭronai Gaon had to expostulate for the public's relative neglect of biblical studies in favor of exclusive concentration on rabbinics. Now the geonim themselves, doubtless stimulated by Karaite competition, urged their correspondents to address to them questions on exegetical problems in the Bible as much as on fine points of the law. In fact, as late as the days of Abraham Maimuni, such exegetical inquiries were commonplace; they occupy about a third of the collection of his "rabbinic" responsa (Nos. 9–45).

Through both intensity of effort and popular participation, the Jewish people now recaptured its most treasured possession, which one of its psalmists had already called "more precious than gold." More than ever it now justified its designation as the "people of the book." Jewish law now extended to the exegetical literature some of the safeguards long given to the Bible itself. According to Maimonides, it was "forbidden to burn or to destroy by hand the holy Scriptures as well as their translations and commentaries," except if they were written by heretics (*M.T.* Yesode ha-torah, vi.8). Confident of the ultimate truths contained in their revealed documents, and believing that their careful exploration would shed light on every phase of human knowledge, medieval Jewry was prepared to weather all storms in its intellectual encounters with the outside world.

NOTES

ABBREVIATIONS

AHDO	Archives d'histoire du droit oriental
AJSL	American Journal of Semitic Languages and Literatures
'A.Z.	'Abodah Zarah (talmudic tractate)
b.	Babylonian Talmud
Baron Jub. Vol.	Essays on Jewish Life and Thought. Presented in honor of Salo Wittmayer Baron. New York, 1958
BASOR	Bulletin of the American Schools of Oriental Research
B.B.	Baba Batra (talmudic tractate)
BJRL	Bulletin of the John Rylands Library, Manchester
Blau Mem. Vol.	Zikhron Yehudah. Tanulmanyok Blau Lajos. Budapest, 1938
B.Q.	Baba Qamma (talmudic tractate)
BZ	Byzantinische Zeitschrift
CHE	Cuadernos de historia de España
EJ	Encyclopaedia Judaica
Festschrift Berliner	Festschrift zum siebzigsten Geburtstage A. Berliner's. Frankfort, 1903
Festschrift Harkavy	Festschrift zu Ehren des Dr. A. Harkavy. St. Petersburg, 1908
Gedenkbuch Kaufmann	Gedenkbuch zur Erinnerung an David Kaufmann. Breslau, 1900
Ginzberg Jub. Vol.	Louis Ginzberg Jubilee Volume. 2 vols. New York, 1945. A volume each of English and Hebrew essays
GK	Ginze Kedem
Goldziher Mem. Vol.	Ignace Goldziher Memorial Volume. Budapest, 1946
GSAI	Giornale della Società asiatica italiana
Gulak-Klein Mem. Vol.	Sefer Zikkaron (Studies in Memory of Asher Gulak and Samuel Klein). Jerusalem, 1942
Hildesheimer Jub. Vol.	Jubelschrift zum siebzigsten Geburtstag Israel Hildesheimers. Berlin, 1890
HJ	Historia Judaica
HTR	Harvard Theological Review
HUCA	Hebrew Union College Annual
IC	Islamic Culture

j.	Palestinian Talmud
JA	Journal asiatique
JBL	Journal of Biblical Literature and Exegesis
JJLG	Jahrbuch für jüdische Geschichte und Literatur
JJS	Journal of Jewish Studies
JNES	Journal of Near Eastern Studies (continuation of *AJSL*)
JQR	Jewish Quarterly Review (new series, unless otherwise stated)
JRAS	Journal of the Royal Asiatic Society
JSS	Jewish Social Studies
Kahle Jub. Vol.	Studien zur Geschichte und Kultur des Nahen und Fernen Ostens; Paul Kahle . . . überreicht. Leiden, 1935
Kohut Mem. Vol.	Jewish Studies in Memory of George A. Kohut. New York, 1935
Krauss Jub. Vol.	Sefer ha-Yobel la-Professor Shemuel (Samuel) Krauss. Jerusalem, 1937
KS	Kirjath Sepher, Quarterly Bibliographical Review
Lewin Jub. Vol.	Sefer ha-Yobel la-Doctor Binyamin (Benjamin) Menasheh Lewin. Jerusalem, 1940
MGWJ	Monatsschrift für Geschichte und Wissenschaft des Judentums
MJC	Mediaeval Jewish Chronicles, ed. by R. Neubauer
M.T.	Moses ben Maimon's Mishneh torah (Code)
MW	Moslem World
MWJ	Magazin für die Wissenschaft des Judentums
O.H.	Oraḥ Ḥayyim (sections of Jacob Ben Asher's *Turim* and Joseph Karo's *Shulham 'Arukh*)
PAAJR	Proceedings of the American Academy for Jewish Research
Poznanski Mem. Vol.	Livre d'hommage à la mémoire du Samuel Poznanski. Warsaw, 1927
Rashi Anniv. Vol.	American Academy for Jewish Research. Texts and Studies, Vol. I. Rashi Anniversary Volume. New York, 1941
RB	Revue biblique (includes wartime *Vivre et Penser*)
REJ	Revue des études juives
Resp.	Responsa
R.H.	Rosh ha-Shanah (talmudic tractate)
RHR	Revue d'histoire des religions
RMAL	Revue du moyen âge latin
Saadia Anniv. Vol.	American Academy for Jewish Research. Texts and Studies, Vol. II. Saadia Anniversary Volume. New York, 1943

SB	Sitzungsberichte der Akademie der Wissenschaften (identified by city: e.g., *SB* Berlin, Heidelberg, Vienna)
Schwarz Festschrift	Festschrift Adolf Schwarz. Berlin, 1917
Shorter EI	Shorter Encyclopaedia of Islam, ed. by H. A. R. Gibb and J. H. Kramers. Leiden, 1953
Sokolow Jub. Vol.	Sefer ha-Yobel li-khebod Nahum Sokolow. Warsaw, 1904
T.	Tosefta, ed. by M. S. Zuckermandel
VT	Vetus Testamentum
WZKM	Wiener Zeitschrift für die Kunde des Morgenlandes
Yearbook CCAR	Yearbook of the Central Conference of American Rabbis
ZAW	Zeitschrift für die alttestamentliche Wissenschaft und die Kunde des nachbiblischen Judentums
ZDMG	Zeitschrift der Deutschen Morgenländischen Gesellschaft
ZHB	Zeitschrift für hebräische Bibliographie
Zlotnik Jub. Vol.	Minḥah li-Yehudah. Jubilee Volume in Honor of Judah Leb Zlotnik. Jerusalem, 1950
ZNW	Zeitschrift für die neutestamentliche Wissenschaft und die Kunde der älteren Kirche

NOTES

CHAPTER XXVII: REIGN OF LAW

1. See esp. the three volumes of the *Syrische Rechtsbücher,* ed. in Syriac with a German trans. by E. Sachau, and V. Aptowitzer's detailed analyses: *Beiträge zur mosaischen Rezeption im armenischen Recht; Die syrischen Rechtsbücher und das mosaisch-talmudische Recht;* "Die Rechtsbücher der syrischen Patriarchen und ihre Quellen," *WZKM,* XXIV, 180–224; "The Controversy over the Syro-Roman Code," *JQR,* II, 55–74; and his briefer summaries cited *supra,* Vol. II, p. 432 n. 14. On the influence of ancient Babylonian institutions, see D. H. Müller's observations in "Das syrisch-römische Rechtsbuch und Hammurabi," *WZKM,* XIX, 139–95 (affirming, against L. Mitteis, the impact of the ancient Babylonian institutions). Now with vastly richer materials available, a careful search for the surviving vestiges of the ancient Babylonian legal evolution in both the talmudic-geonic and the Syriac Christian jurisprudence ought to prove doubly rewarding. On the Western origins of the Syro-Roman Code, see "Un' Ipotesi intorno all' originale greco del libro siro-romano di diritto," advanced by E. Volterra in the *Rendiconti* of the Accademia nazionale dei Lincei, 8th ser. VIII, 21–37. But even in its Greek original this code represented mainly provincial practice as distinguished from the imperial law codified by Theodosius and Justinian. As such it showed somewhat greater affinities with Jewish observances than did the imperial legislation. See the interesting papyrological documentation adduced by R. Taubenschlag in "Il Diritto provinciale romano nel libro siro-romano," *Journal of Juristic Papyrology,* VI, 103–19. See also several earlier studies by C. A. Nallino, reprinted in his *Raccolta,* Vol. IV, devoted entirely to studies of Muslim and Eastern Christian law; it includes a previously unpublished address of 1933, "Considerazioni sui rapporti fra diritto romano e diritto musulmano" (pp. 85–94).

Nor need we be astonished at the extent of Jewish juridical influences on the Syriac Christians despite the deep animosities between the two groups. We need but recall E. Robertson's observation that "the Samaritan acceptance of the Jewish lead in spite of their mutual hostility is a supreme tribute to the value of the Jewish solutions of their eternal problem, how to get God to pronounce on every problem of human life and conduct through His Scriptures." See Robertson's "Law and Religion amongst the Samaritans," in *Judaism and Christianity.* Vol. III, ed. by E. I. J. Rosenthal, p. 87. The domain of family laws lent itself particularly well to such parallel Judeo-Christian interpretations of the biblical legislation. An interesting example of talmudic influence on Christian family laws in early Muslim Palestine is furnished by Papyrus Nessana (formerly Colt), No. 14, dated in 689 and published by C. J. Kraemer and N. Lewis in "A Divorce Agreement from Southern Palestine," *Transactions* of the American Philological Association, LXIX, 117–33. This indebtedness is the more remarkable as C. C. Torrey could not detect in that document any linguistic borrowings from Semitic languages (*ibid.,* pp. 132 f.). Cf., however, A.

Steinwenter's reservations in "Eine Ehescheidung aus dem Jahre 689," *Zeitschrift der Savigny Stiftung,* Rom. Abteilung, LXIII, 415–30.

2. See *infra,* n. 10. To be sure, the specifically Christian reinterpretation of the Graeco-Roman doctrine of the *jus naturale* was essentially derived from biblical and even some postbiblical Jewish concepts. Yet here even less than in other aspects of its world outlook was the Jewish people able or willing completely to transcend the "particularist" aspects of its faith. We shall see (*infra,* n. 167), however, that considerable room was left in Jewish law for certain approximations of both the *jus gentium* and the *jus naturale.* On the latter, as well as on the indebtedness of the Code of Justinian to Eastern, including Jewish, models, see the examples cited *supra,* Vol. II, pp. 431 f.; E. Volterra's "Introduction à l'histoire du droit romain dans ses rapports avec l'Orient," *AHDO,* IV, 117–59 (furnishing also an historical sketch of the research in this field); H. J. Scheltema's search for "Les Sources du droit de Justinien dans l'empire d'Orient," *Revue historique du droit français et étranger,* 4th ser. XXX, 1–17; and particularly L. Wenger's observations in *Die Quellen des römischen Rechts,* pp. 298 ff., 869 ff.; and B. Biondo's three-volume work, *Il Diritto romano cristiano,* of which Vol. I is devoted to a detailed analysis of the *Orientamento religioso della legislazione.*

3. Obviously, the interrelations of Jewish and Christian laws in the Near East were not limited to those written in the Syro-Aramaic or Armenian language. Much of the juridical literature composed in Greek, especially by canon jurists, betrayed by its very origin from biblical hermeneutics strong affinities, if not direct indebtedness, to Jewish law. Even more than in the theological domain the Old Testament, with its pronounced legal emphases, served as the main foundation for the juridical thinking of experts of both faiths. That is why a legal investigation into the Jewish ingredients in the thought and observances of the Church Fathers and the later canonists is likely to prove even more informative than have the manifold researches by L. Ginzberg and others about the relationships between the Aggadah and the patristic letters. Funk's and Gavin's aforementioned analyses of the anti-Jewish polemics of Aphraates, with their main accents on Jewish law to which the fourth-century Syriac Father himself was more deeply indebted than he was willing to acknowledge, have merely served to whet the appetite for broader investigations of the Byzantine and even Western letters from this angle. Old Testament concepts were to color deeply, for instance, the monarchical theory, as well as the oaths in vogue even among the ruling Teuton circles of the Carolingian Empire, according to the studies by E. Rieber and M. David, cited *supra,* Chap. XX, n. 67. It appears that postbiblical Jewish views and interpretations, too, influenced some of these concepts even more strongly than they had the earlier Teuton laws, as shown by J. J. Rabbinowitz's investigations.

For this reason the impact of Jewish law on Muslim law, presently to be discussed, may have been not only direct but also indirect, that is, via the legal institutions found by the conquering Arabs among their Christian subjects. That there had existed a Christian literature in Arabic even before the rise of Islam has been convincingly shown by A. Baumstark in "Das Problem eines vorislamischen christlich-kirchlichen Schrifttums in arabischer Sprache," *Islamica,* IV, 562–75; and by G. Graf in his *Geschichte der christlichen arabischen Literatur,* I, 27 ff. See also the debate between R. S. Lopez and B. Sinogowitz, discussed *supra,*

Chap. XIX, n. 16; the complementary studies by S. V. Fitzgerald, "The Alleged Debt of Islamic to Roman Law," *Law Quarterly Review,* LXVIII, 81–102; and by Abdel-Rahman Hassam, "Le Droit musulman et le droit romain," *AHDO,* IV, 301–21 (includes "Observations" by J. Wigmore, both denying far-reaching influences of the latter on the former); and, more generally, C. de Clercq's "Introduction à l'histoire du droit canonique oriental," *ibid.,* III, 309–48.

4. Regrettably, these observations are still as true today as they were twenty years ago when they were first written for the earlier edition of this book. In the meantime, the investigation of the interrelations between Jewish theology and the early Muslim traditions has made some further progress. See esp. G. Vajda's "Juifs et Musulmans selon le Ḥadiṭ," *JA,* CCXXIX, 57–127; supplemented by his "Jeûne musulman et jeûne juif," *HUCA,* XII–XIII, 367–85; and the literature mentioned *supra,* Chap. XVII, nn. 12, 15. But a more comprehensive and thorough investigation into the parallels, as well as the differences, between Muslim and Jewish law is still a desideratum. Research into the enormous mass of available Muslim sources, both in printed and manuscript form, has been facilitated by the progressive publication of A. J. Wensinck's voluminous *Concordance et indices de la tradition musulmane* and his briefer *Handbook of Early Mohammedan Tradition, Alphabetically Arranged.* See also G. Bergsträsser's *Grundzüge des islamischen Rechts;* D. Santillana's *Istituzioni di diritto musulmano malichita* (with constant reference also to the Shafi'ite school); J. Schacht's searching inquiry into *The Origins of Muhammadan Jurisprudence;* his briefer *Esquisse d'une histoire du droit musulman;* L. Milliot's *Introduction à l'étude du droit musulman;* and M. Khadduri and H. J. Liebesny's *Law in the Middle East,* Vol. I. At present, there are but a few monographs on the Judeo-Muslim interrelations in special branches of law, such as those by S. Bialoblocki, *Materialien zum islamischen und jüdischen Eherecht;* Y. (I.) Epstein, "The Jewish Deed of Gift to a Wife and the Muslim Law of Sadaq" (Hebrew), *Ha-Mishpaṭ ha-'ibri,* IV, 125–34; and S. Rosenblatt, "The Relations between Jewish and Muslim Laws Concernings Oaths and Vows," *PAAJR,* VII, 229–43.

In *Zur Entstehungsgeschichte des islamischen Gebets und Kultus,* p. 42, E. Mittwoch sweepingly asserted that an examination of this and other phases of Islamic law will show that "they all reveal distinct influences of Jewish law in their general structure, as well as in a great many details." Unfortunately, the comprehensive work on Jewish and Muslim legal interrelations, which Mittwoch had been preparing in the last years of his life (see E. Rosenthal's "Islam" in *Judaism and Christianity,* ed. by H. Loewe *et al.,* II, 167), was never completed. It is to be hoped that the establishment of Israel in the midst of nations governed by Muslim law, the need of synthesizing there traditional Jewish legal teachings with the existing Turkish heritage in the country, and the further development of advanced legal thinking will stimulate researches into this significant domain of comparative jurisprudence.

5. See A. J. Wensinck's analysis of *The Muslim Creed, Its Genesis and Historical Development;* J. J. Rivlin's aforementioned Hebrew essay on "Mohammed as a Legislator" in *Keneset,* VII, 294–310; his *Das Gesetz im Koran* (mainly discussing cult and ritual); and more generally J. Schacht's "Foreign Elements in Ancient Islamic Law," *Journal of Comparative Legislation,* 3d ser. XXXII, Parts 3–4, pp.

9–17; and *supra,* Chap. XVII, n. 13. Some of the "foreign elements" attributed by Schacht to the impact of Christian laws were, in fact, of Jewish origin. For example, the doctrine of adultery as an impediment to marriage, adopted by some Muslim sectarians, had its origin in an ancient Jewish law for which R. Joshua ben Ḥananiah and R. 'Aqiba had already sought support in the Bible. See M. Soṭah v.1; b. 28a; and Schacht, pp. 16 f. On the question of the reciprocal indebtedness of Maimonides' "thirteen principles" to Muslim prototypes see *infra,* Chap. XXXIV.

6. Menaḥot 29b, elaborated in the mystical midrash *Alpha-Beta de-R. 'Aqiba,* letter *Ṣadi,* ed. by Jellinek in *Bet ha-Midrasch,* III, 44 (in J. D. Eisenstein, *Ozar Midrashim,* p. 422a); C. Snouck Hurgronje, *Mohammedanism,* p. 113; M. Gaudefroy-Demombynes, "Sur les origines de la justice musulmane," *Mélanges syriennes . . . René Dussaud,* II, 828; J. Müller, *Mafteaḥ li-teshubot ha-geonim* (Einleitung in die Responsen der Babylonischen Geonen), pp. 67, 183. True, the ancient Christian-Persian heritage did not entirely disappear. In the early centuries of Islam, some pietistic Muslims objected to serving as *qadhi*s, not only because of the creeping corruption which growingly undermined the judiciary's religious prestige, but also because they felt sharply the chasm between the theoretical postulates of Islamic law (*shari'ah*) and the necessary compromises imposed on the practical administrators of justice. See N. J. Coulson, "Doctrine and Practice in Islamic Law: One Aspect of the Problem," *BSOAS,* XVIII, 211–26. Nevertheless the growth of law consciousness among the intelligentsia and the exigencies of the far-flung empire assured the legal expert a preponderant role in Muslim society. So large, indeed, loomed the *qadhi*'s importance in Islamic constitutional law that, for instance, the celebrated jurist Al-Mawardi devoted to that office an entire chapter (vi) in his *K. al-Aḥkam as-Sultaniyah* (Constitutiones politicae), ed. by M. Enger, pp. 107 ff.; and in E. Fagnan's French trans., entitled *Les Statuts gouvernementaux ou règles de droit politique et administratif,* pp. 131 ff. At first the Arabs naturally had to recruit most of their personnel for that office from among the native populations but recently converted to Islam. According to a story told about Caliph Hisham, he had found that all the important jurists of Mecca, Medina, Yemen, Syria, Mesopotamia, Baṣra, and Khorasan were "clients," and that only Kufa had an Arab *faqih.* Cf. C. C. Adams's remarks in *MW,* XXXVI, 219. Understandably, many of these clients, including some fairly recent converts from Judaism, often synthesized the new teachings with their own juristic traditions and practices, thus injecting ever new foreign ingredients into the entire fabric of Islamic law.

7. *Teshubot ha-geonim,* ed. by Harkavy, pp. 80 f. No. 180; Sanhedrin 14a; Maimonides' *Commentary* on M. Sanhedrin 1.3, ed. by M. Weisz, pp. 3 f.; and Samuel's responsum, ed. by S. Assaf in *Tarbiz,* I, Part 2, p. 82. See also *supra,* Chap. XXIII, nn. 1, 19. In view of this newly acquired status, the judge's probity became a matter of extraordinary social importance. The opportunities for abuse were greater and the restraints smaller for the Muslim than for the Jewish judge. Hence the corruption of Muslim courts was far more rampant, and Jews were not alone in distrusting their honesty. See E. Tyan's *Histoire de l'organisation judiciaire en pays d'Islam,* I, 428 ff., and the geonic sources cited in my *Jewish Community,* III, 38 n. 10. However, miscarriage of justice by prejudiced, if not altogether corrupt, Jewish judges was frequent enough for Hai to write a special

K. Adab al-qadha (Book of Conduct of Judges). See the few excerpts collected by S. Assaf in *Tarbiz,* VII, 217–18. Somewhat later the Barcelonian scholar Yehudah bar Barzillai suggested a characteristic formula of appointment for a local leader, who was expected to be "wise, understanding, pious, wealthy, and incorruptible." See his *Sefer ha-Sheṭarot* (Book of Deeds), pp. 7 f.

8. See the brief survey of the various Muslim ecclesiastical officials in S. M. Zwemer's "Clergy and Priesthood of Islam," *MW,* XXXIV, 17–39, going to great length to prove their importance. See also the older semipopular review of *The Religious Orders of Islam* by E. Sell; F. Taeschner, "Das Futuwwa-Rittertum des islamischen Mittelalters" in Hartmann's *Beiträge zur Arabistik,* pp. 340–85; and G. Salinger, "Was the *futūwa* an Oriental Form of Chivalry?" *Proceedings* of the American Philosophical Society, XCIV, 481–93 (includes a fairly extensive bibliography). On the position of the contemporary "priests" in the Eastern communities, see the interesting document published by Mann in *Jews in Egypt,* II, 205 f., and the caustic letter purportedly addressed by Hai Gaon to the priests of Ifriqiya in B. Lewin's ed. in *GK,* IV, 51–56, 111.

9. *Sha'are Ṣedeq,* I.17, fol. 2b f.; Maimonides, *Qobeṣ,* II, 28c. On Hulagu's inquiry, see Reuben Levy, *Sociology,* I, 313. See also J. H. Kramer's analysis of the contrast between "Droit de l'Islam et droit islamique," *AHDO,* I, 401–14; and *supra,* Chap. XXIII, n. 48. So important in both faiths was the role of the juristic expert that not only "clients" but also foreigners endowed with superior juridical learning quickly achieved eminence in their new places of residence. The startling careers of the Egyptian Saadiah and the Moroccan Solomon ben Yehudah in Babylonia and Palestine had many counterparts in other lands, such as Spain. The same holds true for the Muslim communities. In his careful list of all the recorded Spanish-Muslim jurists of the first three centuries after the Arab conquest, R. Castejón Calderón has shown that among the early leaders the majority had come from the East, and only gradually did the locally trained scholars attain equal eminence. See *Los Juristas hispano-musulmanes (años 711 a 1031 de C.).* Did not Spanish Jewry, too, acknowledge the origin of its higher rabbinic learning from one of the four Eastern captives? We shall see that this phenomenon repeated itself also in other domains of learning. See esp. *infra,* Chap. XXX, n. 19.

10. Bukhari, *Traditions,* II, 162 f.; Sanhedrin 59a; Maimonides, *Resp.,* pp. 331 f. No. 364, with the editor's comments thereon; *Sha'are Ṣedeq,* III.6, 29 and 36 (fol. 26ab); Ginzberg, *Geonica,* II, 83 f., with reference to R. Joshua ben Levi's statement in Ketubot 28a. Remarkably, this intellectual aloofness from members of other faiths in the domain of law and ritual was cultivated also by heterodox leaders, although their sharp dissent from majority opinion necessarily led them to frequent adoption of concepts and observances current among their non-Muslim neighbors. That is why Abu Ḥanifa an-Nu'man (d. 974), chief *qadhi* of the Faṭimid Caliph Al-Mu'izz, so urgently enjoined his Isma'ili followers not to imitate Jews, Magians, and Christians in their dress or physical appearance, nor to say Amen after the recitation of the first Sura, nor to transport bodies to another locality, as the Jews do in conveying some of their dead to Jerusalem, and the like. See his recently published *K. Da'ā'imul-Islām* (Foundation Stones of Islam), Vol. I, analyzed by R. Strothmann in his "Recht der Ismailiten," *Der Islam,* XXXI,

131–46, especially pp. 141 f. And An-Nu'man himself had been a sufficiently rugged individualist to start his career as a devout Malikite, then turn to the Shi'ah, and, finally, embrace the Isma'ili viewpoint! The study of law was certainly not intended for people who denied its very foundations, which always were denominational in character.

11. See I. Friedlaender, "'Abdallāh b. Sabā, der Begründer der Ši'a und sein jüdischer Ursprung," *Zeitschrift für Assyriologie,* XXIII, 296–327; XXIV, 1–46 (also reprint). True, subsequent research has modified some of Friedlaender's contentions. Yet there has remained a solid kernel of truth in his view that 'Abdallah, and undoubtedly also other Jewish converts in a similar position, exerted great influence on Muslim teaching, both orthodox and sectarian. See also *supra,* Chap. XXV, n. 30.

12. See Manhana Muḥammad Ali's *Religion of Islam,* pp. 315 ff.; J. J. Rivlin's brief analysis of the ritualistic ingredients of *Das Gesetz im Koran,* Vol. I; Abu Huraira, quoted by W. R. Taylor in his "Al-Bukhari and the Aggada," *MW,* XXXIII, 200; J. Horovitz's "Bemerkungen zur Geschichte und Terminologie des islamischen Kultus," *Der Islam,* XVI, 249–63; other data and literature quoted by G. Vajda in *JA,* CCXXIX, 78, 84, 121; and *HUCA,* XII–XIII, 367 ff.; and particularly E. Mittwoch's *Zur Entstehungsgeschichte des islamischen Gebets und Kultus.* A. Baumstark's opposite conclusion ("Jüdischer und christlicher Gebetstypus im Koran," *Der Islam,* XVI, 229–48) seems to follow too closely T. Andrae's general "either-or" attitude. Cf. *supra,* Chap. XVII, n. 15. Cf. also A. J. Wensinck's "Entstehung der muslimischen Reinheitsgesetzgebung," *Der Islam,* V, 62–80 (showing its decided indebtedness to Jewish prototypes); G. H. Bousquet's more sociological study of "La Pureté rituelle en Islam," *RHR,* CXXXVIII, 53–71; Becker, *Islamstudien,* I, 472 ff.; and *infra,* nn. 15, 24.

13. Maimonides, *M.T.* Tefillah IV.3, 6; *Qobeṣ,* I, fols. 25b No. 140, 51cd (reported by Abraham Maimuni); *Resp.,* pp. 32 ff. Nos. 35–39, 79 f. No. 81; *Guide,* III.48; and other sources cited in N. Wieder's comprehensive analysis of *Hashpa'ot islamiyot 'al ha-pulḥan ha-yehudi* (Islamic Influences on the Hebrew Ritual). No wonder that Abraham ben David (in his stricture on *M.T.* Tefillah IV.3; see Joseph Karo's *Commentary, ad loc.*) expressed amazement at the requirement of washing one's feet, wholly unknown in Christian lands. Nor were Maimonides' older or newer commentators (for instance, A. I. Bromberg, *infra,* n. 120), able to supply any talmudic source. David ibn abi Zimra's abrogation of the Maimonidean reform is recorded in the former's *Resp.,* Sudzilkov ed., Vol. IV, fols. 3c No. 5, 21 No. 94. In reaction to Muslim taunts, however, some Jewish apologists, particularly among the Karaites, placed the Muslims among those that "purify themselves," upon whom Deutero-Isaiah had heaped his scorn (66:17). Cf. the passage quoted by M. Steinschneider in his *Polemische und apologetische Literatur,* pp. 329 f.

14. Naṭronai bar Hilai Gaon's responsum in Ginzberg, *Geonica,* I, 114 ff.; Amram Gaon's *Seder* (Prayer Book), ed. by A. L. Frumkin (Part I also ed. by D. Hedegard); Saadiah's *Siddur, passim;* Hai Gaon in *Teshubot,* ed. by Harkavy, No. 208 (referring to "all the copies of the gaon's prayer book which we have seen"). On Saadiah's compilation see also the "Fourteen New Genizah Fragments of Saadya's *Siddur*

Together with a Reproduction of a Missing Part," collected and interpreted by N. Wieder in *Saadya Studies,* ed. by E. I. J. Rosenthal, pp. 245–83; B. Klar's and D. Goldschmidt's reviews of the ed. by Davidson *et al.* in *KS,* XVIII, 336–48; and I. Elbogen's "Saadia's Siddur" in *Saadia Anniv. Vol.,* pp. 247–61. Curiously, it was perhaps that prayer book's initial popularity, followed by its relatively speedy eclipse outside of Yemen, which accounts for the early copies having been used up so thoroughly that not a single complete version and, apart from the main Bodleian manuscript, only a few stray fragments have reached us. All these works and other aspects of Jewish worship will be more fully discussed *infra,* Chap. XXXI.

15. Saadiah's *Siddur,* p. 117; Aaron ibn Sarjado's accusation in Harkavy, *Zikhron,* V, 227; B. Klar's attempt at reconstruction of Saadiah's *Ma'amar Ner Shabbat* (Treatise on the Sabbath Light, mentioned by Abraham Ibn Ezra in his long commentary on Exod. 35:3) in his *Meḥqarim ve-'Iyyunim* (Studies and Researches in the Hebrew Language, Poetry and Literature), pp. 242–58; Ginzberg, *Ginze Schechter,* II, 541; Maimonides, *Resp.,* pp. 39 f. No. 41 (with special reference to Saadiah's *Siddur*); Halevi's *K. al-Khazari,* II.50; III.20, pp. 110 f., 172 f. (Hebrew and Arabic), 113 ff., 158 f. (English). The *ḥadith* relating to Jewish postures were quoted by Goldziher and summarized by G. Vajda in *JA,* CCXXIX, 84. Cf. also J. Zimmels's "Zur äusseren Haltung im Gottesdienst," *Nathan Stein-Schrift,* pp. 140–54 (I owe it to the courtesy of Professor Stein that I was able to consult one of the few surviving copies of this jubilee volume not destroyed by the Nazis); and S. Muntner's related Hebrew study of "The Swaying Posture of Jews during Prayer and Study," *Molad,* XI, 285–89. There obviously was considerable justification for the inclusion in the well-known prayer, *Yismaḥ Mosheh* in the Sabbath *'Amidah,* of the formula "Of its rest no Yishmaelites [Arabs] shall partake." This was hardly an invention of later generations of Jews who, living in Christian countries, sought to avoid difficulties with censors, as suggested by M. Steinschneider in his *Polemische und apologetische Literatur,* pp. 274 f. If Maimonides, in his formulation, substitutes *'arelim* (uncircumcised) for "Ishmaelites" (cf. *M.T. Seder Tefillot* at the end of the second book; here switched to the *Musaf* prayer), this was merely in line with his general preference for Islam as against Christianity. See also I. Elbogen, *Der jüdische Gottesdienst,* pp. 114 f.; and I. Davidson, *Oṣar ha-shirah,* II, 447 No. 4101, neither of whom, however, mentions these significant variants; and *supra,* Chap. XXIV, n. 5. On the controversies between Rabbanites and Karaites concerning the Sabbath and its prayers, see *supra,* Chap. XXVI, n. 43.

16. Samuel ben 'Ali's letter, cited *supra,* Chap. XXIII, n. 64; Hai's responsum in *Teshubot ha-geonim,* Lyck ed., No. 46. In another, sharper formulation Hai explained that "in matters decided in our Talmud we do not rely on the Palestinian Talmud, because learning had been interrupted there on account of persecutions for so many years that the conclusion had to be clarified in this country." Cf. the text in Assaf's *Teshubot,* 1928, pp. 125 f.; the editor's comments there, pp. 124 f.; and B. M. Lewin's introduction to his edition of *Metibot,* pp. v ff. This propaganda line of the Babylonian geonim since Yehudai was doubtless repudiated by the Palestinians and their partisans abroad, but with little success. See *infra,* n. 22. On the "Babylonian-Palestinian Variations in the Mishna" see M. Shackter's essay in *JQR,* XLII, 1–35; and the literature cited *supra,* Vol. II, pp. 425 n. 1, 427 ff. n. 6. Characteristically, medieval French rabbis did not hesitate to attribute the varia-

tions between the two Talmudim to differences in the existing legal institutions and opinions in the two countries. See *Tosafot* on Bekhorot 22b *s.v. Terom.*

17. Sherira's *Iggeret,* ed. by B. M. Lewin, pp. 59, 69 ff.; the geonic responsum reproduced by Lewin, *ibid.,* p. ix, Appendix No. 12. The unnamed author of the latter resp., possibly Sherira himself, admits that he had never seen the Book of Adam and that it was no longer to be found anywhere. Yet he fully believed in the authenticity of that statement attributed to Mar Samuel, as found already in B.M. 85b f.; and Gen. r. XXIV.2, ed. by Theodor and Albeck, pp. 230 f. See L. Ginzberg's attempted reconstruction of an ancient Jewish apocryphon by that name in his "Book of Adam," *Jewish Encyclopedia,* I, 179–80. This apocryphal work may have antedated the fall of Jerusalem, however, and hence was not necessarily identical with the book alluded to in the above passages of Talmud and Midrash. In any case, the second part of the statement attributed to Samuel in his imaginary conversation with Judah the Patriarch, together with the curious phonetic derivation of the names Ashi and Abina from Ps. 73:17, is a good example of a saboraic or early geonic gloss which had penetrated the very text of the Talmud.

18. Abraham ibn Daud's enumeration of the five generations of Saboraim (in his Chronicle, *MJC,* I, 61 f.) from R. Yose to the death of R. Sheshna in 689, or a total of 187 years, erred only in including the generation which had followed the greetings extended to 'Ali by the academy of Firuz Shabur. True, Ibn Daud seems to have had no independent sources at his disposal. His is but a reconstruction from Sherira's *Epistle* and other geonic sources, largely accessible also to modern scholars. See esp. the literature listed in the next two notes. But in their almost exclusive concentration on literary documents and the inner workings of the halakhic processes, most of these scholars were prone to forget the great transformation in the entire fabric of Jewish life which had begun in the middle of the seventh century.

19. *Seder tanna'im va-amora'im* (Chronology of Tannaitic and Amoraic Sages), ed. by M. Grossberg, II, III, VI, pp. 65 f., 68, 105 ff.; ed. by K. Kahan, §§ 4b, 6c, pp. 6, 9 (Hebrew), 3 f. (German), and his notes thereon, pp. 28 ff. (on this work which is extant in various recensions, see *infra,* n. 32); N. Brüll in "Die Enstehungsgeschichte des babylonischen Talmuds als Schriftwerkes" *Jahrbücher für jüdische Geschichte und Literatur,* II, 1–123, following Sherira's brief hints in his *Iggeret,* pp. 71 ff.; H. Klein, "Gemara Quotations in Sabara," *JQR,* XLIII, 361; and B. Lewin's *Rabbanan Sabora'i ve-talmudam* (Our Teachers the Saboraim and Their Talmud). Lewin's brief study is particularly valuable because of its extensive illustrations, from both printed and manuscripts sources, of the manifold activities, credited to the Saboraim by Sherira and other early authors. See also H. Klein's earlier study of "Gemara and Sabara," *JQR,* XXVIII, 67–91; and particularly the significant researches by A. Weiss mentioned in note 20. No effort has as yet been made by any scholar to compare these saboraic methods to those used at the same time in the Syriac schools of jurisprudence, and soon also among the Muslim traditionalists. On Nyberg's theories concerning the Zoroastrian Scriptures and their relevance for Jewish oral transmission as well, see *infra,* Chap. XXVIII, n. 95.

20. See Weiss's stimulating lecture, *Ha-Yeṣirah shel ha-Sabora'im* (The Creativity of the Saboraim: their Share in the Creation of the Talmud), p. 18. Here Weiss suc-

cinctly summarizes his extensive investigations of the processes of evolution which had led to the formation of the Babylonian Talmud. Cf. *supra,* Vol. II, pp. 425 f. n. 2. Largely following the ingenious and well-informed, though somewhat overconfident, theories of I. Halevy in his *Dorot ha-rishonim,* III, 1 ff., 23 ff., Z. Jawitz tried to reconstruct the lives and accomplishments of the leading Saboraim, mainly from Sherira's all-too-succinct résumé. See his *Toledot Yisrael,* IX, 5 ff., 213 ff. Apart from some such chronological misconceptions as that Rabina II had died in 474, and that hence the saboraic age had begun in 474 and ended in 589, Jawitz's reconstruction still offers the most lucid summary of the available biographical and chronological data. However, his neat division of the saboraic work into three stages is too schematic to seem acceptable. According to him, the first generation alone dared to enter into the Talmud itself halakhic decisions in cases left unfinished by Rabina and his associates. Later Saboraim introduced only additional discussions and explanations of existing texts, while the latest members of the group merely inserted certain technical guideposts of one or two words each to facilitate the study of these texts. As a matter of fact, however, these youngest members and even their early geonic successors did not hesitate to decide many a legal issue inconclusively debated in the Talmud.

21. Maimonides, *M.T.* Malveh xv.2; Yehudah bar Barzillai, *Sefer ha-'Ittim,* p. 267 (*supra,* Chap. XXIII, n. 56); Ibn Daud's Chronicle in *MJC,* I, 72 f. Yehudah's explanation that Naṭronai "wrote" (?) the Talmud from memory "lest they begin quarreling" merely restates the traditional suspicions. In his reply to Jacob bar Nissim's query as to how the Mishnah and Talmud were written down, Sherira emphasized that "the sages had been careful in recording them orally," because of the old talmudic injunction against committing to writing what God gave to Israel in oral form (Temurah 14b). See his *Iggeret,* pp. 71 f.; and, on the differences of opinion on this score among the geonim themselves, *infra,* Chap. XXVIII, nn. 62, 65. But Sherira failed to mention when, and under what circumstances, this rule was ultimately broken and written copies of both Talmudim became available to interested readers, particularly outside the central academies. We may assume that the growing literacy of the public and the rise in Baghdad and elsewhere of a powerful intelligentsia unaffiliated with any major academy forced the hands of the leaders to relinquish their monopoly. Islam, too, faced similar problems. After a centuries-long debate on the permissibility of writing down traditions stemming from the Messenger and his companions, the jurists yielded and adopted an affirmative position. See the summary of the divergent opinions assembled by Al-Khatib al-Baghdadi in *La Transmission écrite du Hadith,* ed. with an "étude critique" by Youssef Eche (Yusuf al-Ash).

22. See the illuminating survey of the earlier researches into the relations between "The Geonim and the Palestinian Talmud" in S. Poznanski's *'Inyanim shonim* (Studien zur gaonäischen Epoche), pp. 1–10. In his *Tequfat ha-geonim,* pp. 135 f., S. Assaf lists a number of passages which had crept into the Babylonian Talmud from the early geonic literature. He assumes that these were originally marginal notes which, in some way, found their way into the main text. But it is more likely that, as long as the entire Talmud was transmitted by word of mouth alone, many a novel interpretation by an early gaon was incorporated by a memorizer in his talmudic text, either unconsciously or by design. At times even a great jurist re-

peated from memory some tradition he had heard, unaware that that particular saying had already become part and parcel of the official talmudic text. Many such readings must have remained in flux, particularly in the recensions current at the two academies, to the end of the eighth century and beyond.

23. Hai's responsa cited in Yehudah bar Barzillai's *Sefer ha-Sheṭarot,* p. 126; and in *Teshubot ha-geonim,* ed. by Harkavy, p. 107 No. 228; Lewin's *Otzar ha-gaonim,* VIII, 48 No. 151; Sherira's *Iggeret,* p. 105; and his resp. in *Teshubot geone mizraḥ u-ma'arab,* ed. by J. Müller, fols. 33b f. No. 140. See Assaf's *Tequfat ha-geonim,* pp. 131 ff.; and *infra,* n. 129, and Chap. XXVIII, n. 66. Of course, none of these traditions were supposed to controvert any talmudic law. Similarly, with respect to the Muslim traditions, Shafi'i adapted what had long been accepted lore among the rabbinic sages: "The *sunna* of the Messenger is never contradictory to the Qur'an but explanatory; no tradition from the Messenger can possibly be regarded as contradicting the obvious meaning of the Qur'an." Cf. his *Risala,* p. 33; and Schacht's *Origins,* pp. 15 f.

24. Lewin's introduction to his edition of *Metibot,* pp. i ff., and other sources listed *supra,* Vol. II, pp. 207, 405 n. 39; and Chap. XXIII, n. 27. Lewin has gone too far, however, in postulating a Palestinian background for some of Sura's practices, where local origins are more likely. Certainly, the divergences between the two academies concerning public fasts are decidedly inconclusive. Asked by an unnamed community (Fez?) about liturgical recitations during a locally proclaimed fast, Sherira and Hai pointed out that, in the absence of a patriarch solely entitled to issue the required proclamation, no new fast could be regarded as an official public fast requiring such recitations. Nevertheless, the two geonim admitted, fasts of that kind had spread to Babylonia as well: "Members of the academy of Meḥasiah while located in Sura [before it moved to Baghdad] took a very lenient view in this matter and proclaimed an annual fast in the academy's precincts. But members of our academy [of Pumbedita] were more stringent and allowed it only during a major emergency and in a locality having numerous scholars or one outstanding scholar. . . . We ourselves have already instituted several such fasts." See their resp. in *Teshubot,* ed. by Harkavy, pp. 133 No. 259, 364; Lewin's *Otzar ha-gaonim,* V, Part 2, pp. 26 f. These statements prove nothing with respect to Sura's indebtedness to Palestinian patterns. The two geonim, quoting j. Ta'aniyot II.1, 65b, specifically emphasized that the Palestinians, too, had refrained from calling official public fasts "when they had no patriarch," although the latter phrase is missing in our Palestinian text. Even in the controversy between Saadiah and David ben Zakkai, the Pumbedita faction accused the gaon not of instituting a public fast in order to stem the spread of a pestilence, but rather of unjustly boasting that his proclamation had saved many lives. See Ibn Sarjado's pamphlet, ed. by Harkavy in his *Zikhron,* V, 229.

Similarly questionable is Lewin's assumption that Sura had followed Palestine's lead in permitting pious men to fast on the New Year's day and on the following Sabbath, whereas the Pumbeditans considered fasting a desecration of these holidays. We may perhaps concede that one responsum allowing, and even encouraging, that practice had, in fact, originated in Palestine. But certainly the other responsa referring to such a "custom in the two academies" could only have been written in Babylonia. See his *Otzar ha-gaonim,* I, 125; IV, Part 1, pp. 24 f. Nos. 48–49.

More, rabbinic opinion in Sura itself seems to have been divided. While some of its heads were in favor of such expiatory fasts, others opposed them sharply. Cf. the statements by Yehudai Gaon, Pirqoi ben Baboi and Saadiah, cited by Lewin himself *ibid.*, V, 188 ff. Nos. 39–41. A similar dichotomy concerning the fasting on the Muslim Sabbath (Friday) existed also under Islam, but some *ḥadith* forbade also fasting on Saturday; according to one of the Muslim savants, because one ought not thus to lend distinction to the Jewish day of rest. See the data cited by G. Vajda in his "Jeûne musulman et jeûne juif," *HUCA*, XII–XIII, 379 f.

Evidently, the difference in the attitude toward "public" and holiday fasts lay not so much between the two countries, and still less between the two academies, as between periods and individuals of more or less pronounced ascetic leanings. Nor may we neglect altogether the environmental pressures. While in their inception Muslim fasts indubitably owed much to Jewish prototypes, in later years the Muslim teachers' great stress upon fasting and numerous local observances evolving in various parts of the Muslim world must have affected Jews, too. The reaction of Jewish leaders varied in different periods and with different individuals. In his aforementioned essay, G. Vajda has supplied some interesting general parallels, but could pay no attention to the differences in time and locality. Not surprisingly, self-mortification through fasting so greatly appealed to the pietistic circles in medieval Germany that their very jurists took no umbrage to it, although they generally followed the lead of the last Pumbedita geonim. See Eliezer bar Joel ha-Levi's *Sefer Rabiah*, ed. by V. Aptowitzer, II, 206 f., 246 f., with the editor's notes thereon. Even discounting Lewin's exaggerations, however, there seems to remain a solid kernel of truth in his assumption of greater pro-Palestinian leanings of the Sura geonim. See also S. Assaf's analysis of "The Differences of Customs and Teachings of the Academies of Sura and Pumbedita" in his *Tequfat*, pp. 261 ff., 268; and *infra*, n. 142.

25. Alfasi's *Halakhot* on 'Erubin, end. On the long-debated relationship of the geonim to, and their use of the Palestinian Talmud, see esp. S. Poznanski's *'Inyanim shonim*, Part 1; and L. Ginzberg's *Perushim* (Commentary on the Palestinian Talmud), I, 83 ff. See also C. Tchernowitz's *Toledoth ha-Poskim* (History of the Jewish Codes), I, 29 ff.; *supra*, n. 16; and Vol. II, p. 425 n. 2. Incidentally, the Palestinian Talmud, still thus designated in most geonic writings (it also appears there under the synonyms of "western" or "of the westerners"), was soon increasingly named the *Yerushalmi*, the Talmud of Jerusalem. This title would have made no sense under Roman-Byzantine domination when Jews were officially barred from residence in the Holy City, but was quite appropriate after the Muslim conquest and the reestablishment of the Jewish academy in the Holy City.

26. S. Assaf's *Teshubot ha-geonim*, 1942, pp. 20, 29 f.; Ḥananel's *Commentary* on 'Erubin 26a, 83b, and so forth; the analyses by A. Schwarz, "Das Verhältnis Maimuni's zu den Gaonen" in Jakob Guttmann *et al.*, *Moses ben Maimon*, I, 409; F. Rosenthal, "Die Kritik des maimonidischen 'Buches der Gesetze' durch Nachmanides," *ibid.*, pp. 475–95; and I. Unna, "Naḥmanides as Defender of his Predecessors" (Hebrew), *Sinai*, II, Nos. 16–17, pp. 212–17. Schwarz's data are limited to the quotations in the Maimonidean code. Fully twenty-seven of these references to geonim, moreover, are to be found in Books XII–XIII, dealing with civil law. They clearly reflect legal adjustments of talmudic law necessitated by the more advanced economy of the

Caliphate. Many other references to geonic teachings are scattered in Maimonides' other works. See also my remarks in *PAAJR*, VI, 85 f.; and *infra*, n. 115. On the other hand, the Frenchman, Jacob Tam, was fully convinced that the geonim had unflinchingly adhered to ancient traditions, to which they had far closer and more intimate access. He could not envisage, therefore, their deviating in the slightest from the talmudic law. He even tried to explain their clear innovation for creditors and wives to collect claims from debtors' movables as the mere application of an enabling provision in the Talmud. See his *Sefer ha-Yashar* (Juridical Treatise), Vienna ed., fols. 47d f. No. 502; and his *Resp.* under the same title, ed. by F. Rosenthal, p. 131 No. 57, 3. Needless to say, many geonim and their rabbinic contemporaries in other lands (Ḥananel, Alfasi, Nathan of Rome, and the like) were not only familiar with the two Talmudim, but also with the halakhic midrashim and the Tosefta. See the data assembled by M. Higger in his "Tannaitic Writings during the Geonic Period" (Hebrew), *Ozar Hachaim*, XIV, 95–120, 143–64, 167–75.

27. See H. Lammens's *Islam*, pp. 76 f.; Shafi'i's *K. al-Umm*, in Schacht's English rendition in *The Origins*, p. 12 ("Shafi'i repeats and elaborates this statement . . . with tedious monotony"); Naḥmanides' letter to the rabbis of France in Maimonides' *Qobeṣ*, III, fols. 8d f. On the Muslim *isnad* (chain of tradition) and its likely Jewish antecedents, see J. Horovitz's "Alter und Ursprung des Isnad," *Der Islam*, VIII, 39–47. See also, from another angle, the detailed list in L. Massignon's "Etude sur les 'isnad' ou chaînes de témoignages fondamentales dans la tradition musulmane hallagienne," *Mélanges . . . à la mémoire de Félix Grat*, I, 385–420. Numerous examples of the free, apparently uncontrolled, but intrinsically highly disciplined, evolution of the postgeonic *halakhah* will be given in the following sections of this chapter.

28. Hezekiah's letter, published by A. Cowley in *JQR*, [o.s.] XVIII, 401, and reprinted in Lewin's ed. of Sherira's *Iggeret*, Appendix, p. xxiii. On Hezekiah ben Samuel who, as *rosh ha-seder* of Pumbedita, sent a responsum in his own name, see Ginzberg, *Geonica*, II, 54 ff.; Mann, *Texts and Studies*, I, 559. As mentioned above, the Spaniards, who later claimed to have cultivated Jewish lore from ancient times, received their first inkling of the official talmudic text in oral form some eighty years before. That they now wished to have a complete written copy with whatever interpretation the gaon would volunteer to give them, is not surprising. The absence of complete and authentic texts must have hampered even leading scholars in their pursuit of learning. According to the well-known story of the four captives, Moses ben Ḥanokh owed his sudden rise to eminence in Cordova to his correction of a simple misinterpretation by the local judge, Nathan, of a passage in the Tosefta. Cf. T. Yoma IV.2, ed. by Zuckermandel, p. 187; Ibn Daud's Chronicle in *MJC*, I, 68; Assaf's *Tequfat ha-geonim*, pp. 137 f.; *supra*, n. 21; Chap. XXIII, n. 56; *infra*, n. 30; and Chap. XXX, n. 12.

29. See J. N. Epstein's ed. of *Perush ha-geonim le-seder Ṭeharot* (Der gaonäische Kommentar zur Mischnaordnung Teharoth zugeschrieben R. Hai Gaon); his illuminating analysis thereof in his dissertation, *Der gaonäische Kommentar zur Ordnung Tohoroth, passim;* and his more recent "Supplement to the Gaonic Commentary on Teharot" (Hebrew), *Tarbiz*, XVI, 71–134. This commentary is for the

most part quoted under its Hebrew title, *Perush;* occasionally under that of *Teshubah,* for it had probably originated from an inquiry addressed to the academy of Sura, see *Der gaonäische Kommentar,* pp. 20, 152 f. The author quotes earlier commentaries, at least some of which must have been available to him in written form. He or one of his predecessors may also have used some such lexicographic handbooks as the Mishnaic-Greek vocabulary, a fragment of which was published by A. Papadopoulos-Kerameus in his "Glossarion hebraikoellenikon" (Greek), *Festschrift Harkavy,* pp. 68–90, 177, and in J. Starr's revised text in "A Fragment of a Greek Mishnaic Glossary," *PAAJR,* VI, 353–67. While the first editor dated this fragment in the seventh century, Starr attributes it, largely on palaeographic grounds, to the period after 900. There is, of course, the possibility of its being but a copy or paraphrase of an older glossary. Saadiah's essential authorship of the *Perush* has been later questioned by Epstein himself, who has more recently suggested that it may have been written a century before the gaon by Simon Qayyara, author of *Halakhot gedolot.* See his rather inconclusive observations in *Tarbiz,* XVI, 76 ff. Similarly, the copyist of its present extant version (or possibly paraphrase) is unknown, M. Margulies suggesting some writer in tenth-century southern Italy as the most likely choice. See the introduction to his edition of *Halakhot qeṣubot,* pp. 7 ff. Be this as it may, the *Commentary* certainly antedates Hai Gaon, to whom it is generally attributed in the later Franco-German halakhic literature.

30. Ṣemaḥ Gaon's *'Arukh* is known to us principally from quotations by the sixteenth-century historian Abraham Zacuto. See his *Sefer Yuḥasin ha-shalem* (Lexicon biographicum et historicum), ed. by H. Filipowski, pp. 100b, etc. More questionable is its use by Nathan ben Yeḥiel, postulated (against Rapoport's view) by A. Kohut in the introduction to his edition of the latter's *'Arukh ha-shalem,* I, xvi ff. See also H. Z. Taubes, "The *'Arukh* [Dictionary] by Nathan of Rome and the Ancient *'Arukh* by Ṣemaḥ bar Palṭoi Gaon," in *Scritti in Memoria di Sally Mayer (1875–1953),* Hebrew section, pp. 126–41. On the doubts expressed by L. Ginzberg concerning Ṣemaḥ's identity and the probable character of his compilation, see *infra,* Chap. XXX, n. 12.

31. See Assaf's *Tequfat ha-geonim,* pp. 223 ff. Assaf culled from various geonic sources an impressive array of seventy-four rules advanced by one or another of the geonim. Only a small fragment of Samuel's letter, written in the vein of Sherira's more famous *Iggeret* and his own "Introduction," has thus far been published from a Cambridge MS, *ibid.,* pp. 281–85. This is doubly regrettable, as its composition may have antedated by two years the dispatch of Sherira's *magnum opus* (985 and 987, respectively). However, the date of Samuel's epistle happens to be quoted in a perforated passage of the MS and is admittedly uncertain. On the related, equally independent approach of Samuel ben Ḥofni to the modes of interpretation of the biblical text, see *infra,* Chap. XXVIII, nn. 8, 15, and 30.

32. *Seder tanna'im,* IV–VI, in M. Grossberg's ed. of *Seder 'olam zuṭa,* esp. pp. 76 ff., 91 ff.; in K. Kahan's ed., esp. pp. 12 ff. (Hebrew), 5 ff., 11 (German), with his significant comments thereon, pp. 37 ff. The passage concerning the qualifying clauses allegedly indicating a Mosaic tradition, although appearing in exactly the same form in Simon Qayyara's *Halakhot gedolot* (ed. by Hildesheimer, p. 469, with the editor's note 96 thereon) before, and Samuel ibn Nagrela's *Introduction to the Talmud*

(end) after our author, caused much difficulty to later commentators from the days of Rashi. Cf. Kahan's note, pp. 37 f. Even if we eliminate the word, *bi-zeman* (at the time), which occurs most frequently, although it is present in almost all versions of our tract, there still remain in the Mishnah alone far too many passages containing these clauses for all of them to have been acclaimed as "Mosaic" traditions. In his *Ha-Massoret be-sifre ha-Rambam* (Maimonides' Conception of Tradition), pp. 25 f., E. Z. (H. E.) Revel reviewed previous explanations, all of them forced, and came to the conclusion that our text must be corrupted. He suggested that an original brief statement, referring to passages of this kind as representing each a *halakhah* (binding law), was expanded by some copyists into *halakhah le-Mosheh mi-Sinai* (tradition from Moses on Sinai). This desperate emendation does not meet, however, the problem of how that faulty conception could have appeared justified to Qayyara and Ibn Nagrela. It was clearly disregarded by Maimonides. A useful compilation of the mnemotechnic aids in rabbinic literature was published by P. J. Kohn in his *Sefer ha-Simanim ha-shalem* (A Complete Collection of All the Mnemonics . . . in the Talmud, Old Manuscripts, and Later Literature).

Because of its great brevity and utility the *Seder tanna'im* was extensively used throughout the later Middle Ages, and hence has come down to us in at least six different versions. Much ingenuity has been expended by modern scholars, including I. H. Weiss, A. Epstein, and A. Jellinek, in analyzing their origin, selecting the preferred readings, or in harmonizing them in accordance with the subsequent methodological researches. Cf. the older editions and other bibliographical data listed by M. Steinschneider in *Die Geschichtsliteratur der Juden,* pp. 12 ff.; and A. Marx in "Neue Texte des Seder Tannaim we-Amoraim," *Festschrift Israel Lewy,* pp. 392–99, Hebrew section, pp. 155–72. The latter essay includes a number of additional fragments, some of rather dubious authenticity. More recently K. Kahan published a more critical edition of the text with a German translation, using more than a score of extant recensions, both handwritten and printed. The tract's historical sections will be more fully analyzed in the next chapter (XXVIII, n. 62). Here we need but concern ourselves with its contributions to talmudic methodology in the narrower sense, in which, too, it performed a striking pioneering service.

33. Ginzberg, *Geonica,* II, 32, 85 f.; Ḥananel's *Commentary* on Shabbat 19a; and the other sources cited in Assaf, *Tequfat,* p. 226. Of course, in the hierarchy of scholars even the posttalmudic sages soon enjoyed varying ranks. Discounting the Saboraim, whose work was entirely immersed in either the talmudic text or in some traditions anonymously carried down into the geonic age, there was a decided difference between the geonim and the so-called *rishonim* ("first" among the post-geonic teachers). We recall with what hesitation even contemporaries like Ḥananel controverted accepted geonic decisions. While an independent mind like Maimonides' occasionally ventured to defy these revered predecessors, there gradually emerged the conviction that, just as in the conflict between an Amora and a gaon, the gaon's opinion had to lose out, unless it could somehow be harmonized with that of his predecessor, so did geonic doctrine have decided precedence over that of later teachers.

34. Petaḥiah of Ratisbon's *Sibbub,* XII, ed. by Grünhut, pp. 12 (Hebrew), 16 (German); in Benisch's English trans., p. 23; Bezalel Ashkenazi's *Kelale ha-talmud* (Talmudic Rules), ed. from a Jewish Theological Seminary MS by A. Marx in

Festschrift David Hoffmann, pp. 369–82, Hebrew section, pp. 179–217, especially Nos. 228, 229, 319, 369, 372; Saadiah's *Perush yod-gimmel middot* (Commentary on the Thirteen Modes), now readily available in the Hebrew translation by Nahum ha-Ma'arabi, first edited by S. Schechter and then republished by J. Müller in Saadiah's *Oeuvres,* IX, 73–83 (and again from the Oxford MS by H. J. Ehrenreich). In his introduction, pp. xxiii ff., xlii (Hebrew), xviii ff. (French), Müller cited several quotations from Saadiah's work by later Karaites, and also reported in behalf of Joseph Derenbourg that the Arabic original of that *Commentary* was still extant in the Baron Günzburg Library, now in Moscow. See also H. Malter, *Saadia Gaon,* pp. 159 f., 341 f., 400 f., 427. The publication of the Arabic text ought to prove doubly worth while, in as much as the gaon seems to have had at his disposal somewhat different readings in R. Ishmael's famous *Baraita.* These variants were subsequently replaced by the standardized version, either by the Hebrew translator of the thirteenth century, later copyists, or both. See also *infra,* Chap. XXVIII, n. 63.

35. See A. Cowley's edition of a fragment of "Samuel ben Ḥofni's Introduction to the Talmud" in his Hebrew essay under this title, *Festschrift Harkavy,* Hebrew section, pp. 160–63; and the latter's methodological Epistle mentioned *supra,* n. 31; and *infra,* Chap. XXVIII, nn. 8, 15, 30. Since Samuel ibn Nagrela's Introduction is preserved only in fragments which do not coincide with the few published excerpts from Samuel ben Ḥofni's similar work, one cannot judge definitely the extent of the former's indebtedness to the geonic work. That the Spaniard merely paraphrased the Arabic work of his predecessor, here and there adding a few observations of his own (like the story of the four captives which may have served as a source for Ibn Daud), has been suggested long ago by scholars cited in M. Steinschneider's *Catalogus librorum hebraeorum in Bibliotheca Bodleiana,* II, 2471 f. No. 2. In the present state of our knowledge this suggestion can be neither proved nor rejected. One may expect, however, fuller light on this subject from M. Margulies's forthcoming edition of Samuel's major juridical work. See *infra,* n. 80. See also "A Geonic Fragment concerning the Oral Chain of Tradition" recently ed. in a Hebrew essay by A. N. Z. (E.) Roth in *Tarbiz,* XXVI, 410–20; and immediately identified by S. Abramson as part of "R. Samuel ben Ḥofni's Introduction to the Talmud" (Hebrew), *ibid.,* pp. 421–23.

36. Nissim bar Jacob's introduction to his *Mafteaḥ le-man'ole ha-talmud* (*Clavis talmudica;* Key to the Locks of the Talmud) was first published, from a Vienna MS of the Hebrew version, by J. Goldenthal, and then made widely popular by its republication, together with the author's commentary, in the first three talmudic tractates of the Vilna edition of the Talmud (the intro. opens here the tractate Berakhot). The work was originally written in Arabic, but only small fragments of the original are extant today. See esp. the texts published in Ginzberg's *Ginze Schechter,* II, 332 ff.; and S. Abramson's "From the Works of Rab Nissim Gaon: I. Sefer Ham-Mafteaḥ" (Hebrew), *Tarbiz,* XXVI, 49–70 (listing also other fragments published so far). On the example of Nissim's original comments on Shabbat, Ginzberg has also shown (II, 282, 287 f.) that the Hebrew version is frequently quite inaccurate.

We are somewhat more fortunate with respect to the *Megillat setarim* (Secret Scroll) which consisted of both Arabic and Hebrew notations. Responsa were usually entered in Arabic, the language in which Ibn Shahin corresponded with his inquirers, whereas his exegetical and folkloristic notes he wrote in the usual rabbinic mixture of Hebrew-Aramaic. A section of the text was published from a Cambridge MS by S. Assaf, together with a fairly complete summary of the whole work prepared by an almost contemporary admirer. See Assaf, "The Book *Megillat Setarim* by R. Nissim bar Jacob of Kairuwan" (Hebrew), *Tarbiz,* XI, 229–59; XII, 28–50, where the older literature is also listed. Nissim seems to have started his notebook fairly early in life, and used the materials here accumulated in his later major works. That is why there was considerable repetition, and later scholars could quote similar statements either from the notebook, or from the *Mafteaḥ*. For example, an explanation of R. Johanan's reputed strange behavior after the tragic demise of his tenth son (Berakhot 5b) is quoted by some later students from the "Key" as the view held by Sherira and Hai, while others mention as their source but the "Secret Scroll" without any reference to geonic predecessors. Before long the Scroll attained such a reputation that it was often quoted without its author's name; for instance, in the *Commentary* on *Massekhet Sheqalim* (Tractate Sheqalim) by an unnamed pupil of Samuel ben Shne'ur, ed. by A. Schreiber (Sofer), p. 44. On Nissim's biographical data and his important folkloristic work, see *infra,* Chap. XXVIII, nn. 38 ff. It was probably more than mere coincidence that tenth-century Kairuwan became also the center of intensive Muslim juridical studies. See, e.g., H. R. Idris, "Deux jurists kairouanais de l'époque Ziride: Ibn abi Zaid et Al-Qâbisî (X^{e} et XIe siècle)," *Annales* of the Institut d'Etudes Orientales of the University of Algiers, XII, 122–98.

37. Naṭronai Gaon's resp. in *Teshubot ha-geonim,* Lyck ed., fol. 28b No. 90; Jacob Tam's comment in *Tosafot* on Qiddushin 30a, *s.v. Lo;* and, more generally, S. Assaf's *Meqorot le-toledot ha-ḥinnukh* (Sources to the History of Jewish Education), *passim;* and my *Jewish Community,* II, 192 f.; III, 167 n. 20. See also *infra,* Chap. XXIX, n. 1. This exclusive concentration on talmudic studies was characteristic more of the Franco-German schools than of the geonic age in the East or of the Sephardic areas at any time. Yet the incipient signs of such limitations of educational horizons were already noticeable in some academic circles before Saadiah. To these men such a rationale as offered by Naṭronai, and later Jacob Tam, came as a welcome relief against the overt injunction in the Talmud.

38. Nathan the Babylonian's Report in *MJC,* II, 84; *supra,* Vol. II, pp. 280 ff., 422 f. See also the formula introducing the discourse by an exilarch or another grandee in S. Assaf's comments on his ed. of an excerpt from "A Benediction in Honor of Exilarch Ḥisdai ben David" (Hebrew), *GK,* IV, 63–64. This benediction was undoubtedly recited in behalf of the powerful exilarch Hezekiah (before 1021–58) when he took the floor to deliver his oration. The quadripartite division here indicated can only be reconstructed with some difficulty from Aḥai of Shabḥa's *She'eltot,* although an intimation of similar public discourses combining legal with homiletical elements is found in various talmudic passages, especially Shabbat 30ab. As we shall presently see, however, R. Aḥai's work is but incompletely preserved and has been disfigured by later interpolations and, more importantly, many omissions by copyists. Hence no homily is completely preserved in its original form. For this reason it was possible for L. Ginzberg to suggest that these four parts were followed by still another devoted to a "homily." See his *Geonica,* I, 90 f. However,

the solitary word *derashah,* which appears in various editions and MSS at the end of some pericopes, is not sufficient evidence for such duplication of homiletical efforts in the third and fifth stages of the proceedings. More likely the word was either transposed from the third section by some early copyists, or else this fifth section consisted entirely of talmudic quotations, resembling somewhat a documentary appendix. In the eighth century, we must remember, copies of the Talmud still were very scarce and such quotations must have proved very helpful to students. When the talmudic texts became freely available, such excerpts seemed redundant and were legitimately omitted by copyists.

39. Menaḥem Me'iri's Introduction to his *Bet ha-beḥirah* (Habchira; a commentary) on Abot, ed. by S. Waxman, pp. 63, 64 (also in the excerpt in *MJC,* II, 224). Me'iri's obvious chronological errors need not make us too skeptical about Aḥai's death in 752. Nor need we doubt his report, based on a "trustworthy tradition," of the personal stimulus to the composition of *She'eltot* merely because we are reluctant to "believe that the first work of importance after the close of the Talmud owed its existence to the laziness of an unruly boy" (Ginzberg). We must not forget that, for instance, Moses Mendelssohn's German Bible translation, which marked a similar turning point a millennium later, likewise originated from such parental solicitude. Be this as it may, the century-old discussion about the place where Aḥai wrote his tract has not been brought any nearer to a solution by the fragments discovered in recent years. The few quotations from the Palestinian Talmud (Reifmann, Halevy, Ginzberg, and Poznanski have established a maximum of fourteen such references) could certainly have been added by Aḥai after his arrival in the Holy Land. Parts of that Talmud, moreover, had doubtless been known for some time in Babylonia's academic circles. See *supra,* n. 22. Certainly, the language of the whole tract is predominantly of the Babylonian variety. See esp. J. N. Epstein's "Notes on Post-Talmudic Aramaic Lexicography, II," *JQR,* XII, 299–390.

Literary and juridical problems of Aḥai's *She'eltot* have likewise been under constant debate. Its age as the reputedly oldest extant posttalmudic codification of Jewish law; its great influence on subsequent codifiers, whether or not it is quoted by name; its unorthodox approach to the presentation of legal findings in a series of halakhic as well as aggadic discourses arranged in the form of questions and answers on the weekly lessons in the Pentateuch; the numerous variants in talmudic texts quoted therein; the personality of its author; and its whole extraordinary background and aims—all have long intrigued modern scholars. See esp. Ginzberg's *Geonica,* I, 75 ff.; B. M. Lewin's "On the Study of R. Aḥai Gaon's *She'eltot,*" *Jüdische Studien Wohlgemuth,* Hebrew section, pp. 32–39; and V. Aptowitzer's "Untersuchungen" in *HUCA,* VIII–IX, 373 ff. Much of that discussion may be obviated, however, if we assume that Aḥai did not necessarily originate most of the "Propositions" contained in his book but that he merely incorporated in it some of the extended debates at the academies. See A. Kaminka's observations on "Die Komposition der Scheëltot des R. Achai und die Rhetorik in den babylonischen Hochschulen," *Schwarz Festschrift,* pp. 437–53; and his "Order and Purpose of R. Aḥai Gaon's *She'eltot*" (Hebrew), *Sinai,* III, No. 34, pp. 179–92. Assuming such a composite origin, many ingredients may indeed be of Palestinian vintage, previously imported into the Euphrates Valley by immigrants from the Holy Land or through other intellectual exchanges. On the meaning of the term *She'eltot* as "propositions" rather than "queries," see S. Mendelsohn's *"Sha'al, She'elta* et *She'eltot," REJ,* XXXII, 56–62; and H. Leshitz's more recent analysis of "Sha'al, She'ilta, She'eltot" (Hebrew), *Sinai,* XVII, No. 205, pp. 338–42 (the term embraces both question and affirmation).

Despite these extended debates, we do not yet have the desired critical edition of Aḥai's text. Published first in 1546, it has been frequently republished, with several important commentaries by modern rabbis. The fullest edition now available is that published by the Kuk Foundation in Jerusalem, 1953; it is based on the Vilna edition of 1861 with commentaries by Isaiah Berlin and Naphtali Zvi Yehudah bar Jacob, with some additions and corrections from a manuscript. Cf. also the other recent edition with a new commentary *Reqaḥ Mordecai* (Mordecai's Concoction) by E. M. König; J. N. Epstein's edition of "She'eltot Fragments" (Hebrew), *Tarbiz,* VI, 460–97, 542; VII, 1–30; VIII, 5–54; X, 283–308; XIII, 25–36 (from Oxford and Leningrad MSS, as well as from quotations in *Halakhot gedolot* and *pesuqot*); and further fragments described by A. N. Z. Roth in his "Geonic Writings in the Kaufmann Collection" (Hebrew), *Sura,* II, 283 f. Cf. also the textual notes, together with a MS fragment, in B. M. Lewin's essay in *Jüdische Studien Wohlgemuth.* The more critical edition, however, begun half a century ago (1908) by A. Kaminka has not progressed beyond a small "sample issue." All these efforts may soon be largely superseded by S. K. Mirsky's projected definitive edition on the basis of ten manuscripts and all early prints. See for the time being his "New She'eltot Hidden in Unpublished Manuscripts" (Hebrew), *Talpioth,* V, 411–46 (publishing two "propositions" from a Paris and two Bodleian manuscripts); and, more generally, his *Sheeltot de-R. Aha: a Critical and Annotated Edition of the Book of Genesis Based on MSS with an Introductory Study on the Nature and Form of the Sheeltot* (Columbia University dissertation, microfilm; includes ed. and trans. of 37 *she'eltot*).

40. Aḥai's *She'eltot,* Vilna ed., Nos. 4, 7. As pointed out by S. Assaf, the speculation over Genesis 12:5 and its application to the educational duties of every Jew, seemed doubly appropriate in the context of that scriptural lesson (*Lekh lekha*). The Sabbath when it was recited had long been used by the exilarchic court for public assemblies at which scholars delivered discourses of the kind represented by the *She'eltot.* See Assaf, *Tequfat,* pp. 155 f.

41. Aḥai's *She'eltot,* Nos. 88 (on plagues, with reference to Lev. 14:33 ff., 'Arakhin 16a); 7, 142 (education); 10, 34–37, 93 (circumcision); 23, 29, 30, 53, 121, 136 (vows and oaths). With the pan-Karaite tendency of recent scholarship it is not at all surprising to find that C. Tchernowitz attributes these repetitions to the author's alleged relentless opposition to Karaism, as well as his insistence upon the primacy of such rabbinic laws as those allowing scholars to dissolve vows, or demanding the universal kindling of lights on a Sabbath eve (Nos. 63 and 162). See Tchernowitz's *Toledoth ha-Poskim,* pp. 64 ff. The obvious objection that Aḥai had died some fifteen years before 'Anan's heresy could still be answered by assuming that these discourses aimed at combating certain antitalmudic manifestations antedating 'Anan. But Aḥai's equal emphasis on such noncontroversial subjects as educational obligations and charities, especially toward the dead and neighbors in need of loans (Nos. 14, 31, 34, 62, 114), and on unfair business practices (Nos. 4, 32, 102), could not possibly have pursued any but general ethical aims.

42. The relationship between R. Aḥai's work and the midrashim with juridical overtones have often been discussed. See, e.g., L. Zunz and H. Albeck's *Ha-Derashot be-Yisrael,* pp. 110 f., 372 n. 69; V. Aptowitzer's "Scheeltoth und Jelamdenu," *MGWJ,* LXXVI, 558–75; and *infra,* Chap. XXVIII, n. 21. Similarly, the astonishing contrast between the high appreciation of Aḥai's work by such Western scholars as Rashi, Nathan ben Yeḥiel, and their successors, and the almost complete absence of direct quotations therefrom in geonic responsa, except for two written by Sherira and Hai only one of which mentioned Aḥai's name, has long been noted. Cf. *Teshubot ha-geonim,* ed. by Harkavy, pp. 191 f. No. 376 (with reference to *She'eltot,* No. 124); ed. by Assaf, in *Madda'e ha-yahadut* (Scripta Univ. Hierosolymitanae), II, 79 f. No. 61 (quoted by Yehudah bar Barzillai). Ibn Daud voiced a widely held Western opinion when, in his chronicle, he wrote admiringly of Aḥai's *She'eltot* as "relating to all the commandments stated in the Torah. This book is available to us today, and all of his [Aḥai's] successors have carefully examined it. We understand that until today no mistake whatsoever has been detected in it" (*MJC,* I, 63). We must bear in mind, however, that in their responsa the geonim rarely quoted any but talmudic authorities, and still less frequently referred to those who did not occupy a geonic seat. In their halakhic compilations they were somewhat more generous, and, as pointed out by A. Epstein and V. Aptowitzer, there are many (about one hundred) quotations from Aḥai's book, four or five of them under his name, in Simon Qayyara's *Halakhot gedolot.* In fact, in the responsum dated in 992, Sherira had already noted that a passage in that famous code was but a citation from Aḥai's work. See *Teshubot,* ed. by Harkavy, *loc. cit.;* and, more generally, V. Aptowitzer's persuasive arguments in his "Untersuchungen zur gaonäischen Literatur," *HUCA,* VIII–IX, 373 ff. On divergent readings in *She'eltot* as a possible reason for the conflicting opinions of Alfasi and R. Zeraḥiah ha-Levi, see Ginzberg's *Ginze Schechter,* II, 72. However, even in cases of close verbal resemblance one cannot entirely rule out the possibility of independent citation from the vast mass of oral traditions faithfully recorded by the academic memorizers. Certainly, Yehudai Gaon, Aḥai's contemporary who, as we shall see, was highly praised for his unwavering adherence to older traditions, would have been more inclined to quote older sayings known in Pumbedita than those but recently formulated by a former colleague. See also Aptowitzer, pp. 377 f.

43. Raba's *Halakhot pesuqot* in the fragments published by S. Schechter in his "Halakhot in the Order of Weekly Lessons" *Festschrift Hoffmann,* Hebrew section, pp. 261–66; and esp. from a Bodleian MS by J. N. Epstein in "R. Abba's Halakhot" (Hebrew), *Madda'e ha-yahadut,* II, 149–61; *Sefer Ve-hizhir* (And [God] Warned), ed. from a Munich MS with a commentary *'Anfe Yehudah* (Ramifications of Judah) by J. M. Freimann; and H. G. Enelow's "*Midrash Hashkem* Quotations in Alnaqua's *Menorat ha-Maor,*" *HUCA,* IV, 311–43. The early date of that midrash is evidenced by a reference to it and the *She'eltot* in that order in Nissim's *Mafteaḥ.* See the fragment published in Assaf's edition of *Teshubot,* 1942, p. 197. The mutual relationship of the latter two works has been under debate ever since L. Zunz had suggested that they represented the same book under different names. See his and Albeck's *Ha-Derashot be-Yisrael,* pp. 141, 428 n. 25. Once again many of these discussions are vitiated by their exclusively literary approach. Because certain passages in *Ve-hizhir* appear identical, or nearly identical, with some medieval

quotations from *Hashkem,* the indebtedness of the one to the other is usually taken for granted. However, with our fuller recognition of the importance of long-range oral traditions underlying all these early geonic works, we must be doubly wary of drawing hasty conclusions concerning their direct interdependence.

44. See Naṭronai's responsa published by Ginzberg in his *Geonica,* II, 293 ff., 319 ff. Nos. VIII, XXVI; and by Assaf in his edition of *Teshubot,* 1928, pp. 147 ff., esp. p. 157 No. 19, and the numerous sources relating to the problem of flagellation cited by Assaf, p. 150; and by A. Aptowitzer in *Ha-Mishpaṭ ha-'ibri,* V, 33–104. The gaon also explained to his distant inquirers unusual geographic terms. For example, he informed them that Ḥarta de-Argiz (Shabbat 19b) is "the name of a town one parasang distant from our town [Baghdad?]. Its name is derived from [its founder] Argiz who was a Magian. This was [the residence of] R. Hammuna, whose burial place is still there." Assaf ed., p. 155 No. 7; and Rashi's comment *ad loc.* As pointed out by Assaf, Nathan ben Yeḥiel replaced the vague phrase, "our town," by Baghdad. This description of the capital by Naṭronai of Sura is rather unusual, however. On the smaller city's location, its identity with the famous pre-Islamic town of Ḥira, and the possible identification of Argis with a Christian martyr Warjiz (Ghorgios), see J. Obermeyer's comments in *Die Landschaft Babylonien,* pp. 143 f., 233 f., 318 f. It may be noted that Naṭronai's explanations were extensively used in the later exegetical and lexicographic literature, especially the aforementioned geonic commentary on Ṭeharot from the school of Saadiah and Nathan ben Yeḥiel's dictionary. Nathan alone quoted no less than seventy-five comments from the fragments now extant, without mentioning Naṭronai's name, perhaps because he was no longer familiar with that gaon's authorship. See Assaf ed., p. 148.

Naṭronai's early correspondence with Spain has long been known from Amram Gaon's *Seder,* ed. by Frumkin, I, fol. 25ab; ed. by Hedegard, pp. 3 (Hebrew), 5 f. (English), with Hedegard's note thereon. Cf. Assaf's remarks in *Ha-Shiloaḥ,* XXXV, 405. If these inquiries had indeed come from Spain, they would indicate a fairly high level of learning on the Iberian Peninsula in the middle of the ninth century. The afternoon prophetic readings were to appear puzzling even to Rashi, who quoted the interpretation here given as one offered by the "geonim." Cf. his *Commentary* on Shabbat 24a *s.v. Ha-Mafṭir;* and Lewin's *Otzar ha-gaonim,* II, Part 1, pp. 26 f. Nos. 79–81. Of course, such explanations of selected passages, even if presented in the sequence of the talmudic discussions, may be considered but rudimentary forms of exegetical writings. They did not greatly differ from similar comments strewn through the entire responsa literature.

45. See Naḥshon's commentaries in *Teshubot geonim qadmonim,* ed. by Cassel, fols. 39b–42b; ed. by Assaf, 1942, pp. 146–56; Saadiah's *Commentary* on Berakhot intermingled with other geonic comments, readily available in Lewin's *Otzar ha-gaonim,* I, Part 2, pp. 103–14; his *Commentary* on the Mishnah mentioned *supra,* n. 34; Samuel ben Ḥofni's letter of 985, published from a Cambridge Genizah fragment in Assaf's *Tequfat,* pp. 299 ff., with the editor's notes thereon. Cf. *infra,* n. 78; and *supra,* n. 31; and Chap. XXIII, n. 24.

46. Sherira's commentaries in *Teshubot,* ed. by Assaf, 1942, pp. 93 f., 101, 172–79; Mann, *Texts and Studies,* I, 568 ff.; B. M. Lewin in "A Commentary by Sherira and Hai on Baba Batra 36b–37a" (Hebrew), *GK,* V, 17–23 (also listing other texts);

Hai's more fully preserved commentaries on seven tractates listed and analyzed by Assaf in *Tequfat,* pp. 139 ff. (with additional bibliographical data); and S. Löwinger's more recent excerpts from "Gaonic Interpretations of the Tractates Gittin and Qiddushin," *HUCA,* XXIII, Part 1, pp. 475–98 (with facsimiles). In his review of this essay in *KS,* XXIX, 64–65, however, S. Assaf considers these excerpts as parts of *responsa* probably written by Hai. Some of these commentaries enjoyed almost instantaneous popularity; one was copied within thirty years of the gaon's death (1067) by a leading official of the Palestinian academy "for his own use." See S. D. Goitein's text and facsimile of "A Colophon to R. Hai Gaon's Commentary to Ḥagigah and to the Book of Laws by R. Ḥananel" (Hebrew), *KS,* XXXI, 368–70. See also the fragments of unnamed geonic commentaries, largely in response to inquiries and limited to selected talmudic passages, in Ginzberg's *Ginze Schechter,* II, 379 ff. (on Ketubot), 395 ff. (on Sanhedrin-Makkot); J. N. Epstein's analysis of "Le Commentaire de Scherira sur 'Baba Batra,'" *REJ,* LXIV, 210–14; and his observations "On Sherira and Hai's Commentary on Baba Batra" (Hebrew), *Tarbiz,* V, 45–49.

Most of these works, together with fragments from the slightly younger commentaries by Nissim bar Jacob and Ḥananel bar Ḥushiel, are now conveniently assembled and arranged according to the sequence of the talmudic tractates in Lewin's *Otzar ha-gaonim,* which includes sections devoted to "Commentaries." This standard work, even more useful with respect to the widely scattered geonic and early postgeonic responsa, has, owing to the compiler's demise, remained incomplete; only 13 of the projected 20 volumes have seen the light of day. But it is to be hoped that various plans, now under review, to bring this work to completion, will prove successful. On the merits of the parts hitherto published, see, e.g., S. Abramson's critical evaluations in his Hebrew reviews of Vols. X–XII: *KS,* XIX, 89–91; XXI, 238–42.

47. See the geonic comments on Berakhot 21a and Ketubot 45a, reproduced in Lewin's *Otzar ha-gaonim,* I, Part 2, p. 26 Nos. 82–84; VIII, Part 2, p. 28 Nos. 27–28; and *infra,* Chap. XXXI, n. 53. Such clear-cut rejection of geonic interpretations could be indulged only by such early Spanish authorities as Ibn Nagrela or Alfasi rather than by their successors (see *supra,* n. 26). But from time immemorial there existed a fairly sharp line of demarcation between purely theoretical interpretations of scriptural or talmudic passages and such as had direct bearing on legal practice. The far greater freedom of more abstract inquiries alone made possible the growth of the new Bible exegesis, and also encouraged a freer explanation of talmudic texts.

48. See B. M. Lewin's "Rabbenu Nissim's Commentary on 'Erubin," *Festschrift Jakob Freimann,* Hebrew section, pp. 72–80, publishing a fragment from an Adler MS and excerpts from Nathan ben Yeḥiel's *'Arukh.* See also the very useful revised "List of the Early Commentaries on the Talmud" by Aron Freimann in *Ginzberg Jub. Vol.,* Hebrew section, pp. 323–54, where many texts extant in both manuscripts and printed volumes are enumerated; and P. J. Kohn's more comprehensive *Oṣar ha-bĕurim wĕ-ha-perushim* (Thesaurus of Hebrew Halachic Literature).

49. Ḥananel's *Commentary* on Berakhot 59a and Pesaḥim 64a. The former was first published from an Oxford MS by B. M. Lewin in his "R. Ḥananel's Commentary on Berakhot 59a" (Hebrew), *GK,* I, 26–45; and then reproduced in his *Otzar ha-*

gaonim, I, Part 3, pp. 62 ff. In the continuation of this lengthy comment, Ḥananel also took issue with the starkly anthropomorphic talmudic characterization of demons as sharing three characteristics with human beings and three with angels. "All talmudic scholars," he exclaimed, "familiar with the teachings of the talmudic sages unanimously explain these words as mere allegory." In a greatly abbreviated and emasculated form this interpretation has long been known from Nathan ben Yeḥiel's *'Arukh, s.v. Uba,* ed. by Kohut, I, 3b. On Ḥananel's decisions in cases left open by the Talmud, see the interesting analysis offered by V. Aptowitzer in his "On the Study of the Halakhah," *Festschrift Jakob Freimann,* Hebrew section, pp. 14 ff. The medieval Jewish attitudes to such scientific problems as the measurement of the earth's surface will be more fully discussed *infra,* Chap. XXXV.

50. Ḥananel's *Commentary* on Shabbat 131a, 145a (in the Vilna ed.); on Ta'anit 14a; and on Berakhot 2b, 19a, in Lewin's *Otzar ha-gaonim,* V, Part 2, p. 59 No. 141; I, Part 3, pp. 1 No. 2, 18 No. 68. In his succinct analysis of Ḥananel's *Commentary,* I. H. Weiss figured out that the Kairuwan scholar had quoted the Palestinian Talmud on more than two hundred occasions. See his *Dor dor ve-doreshav,* IV, 239. This number has greatly increased by the additional fragments which have come to light since. Another decision in favor of the Palestinian Talmud was quoted from Ḥananel by the well-informed twelfth-century French author Simḥah of Vitry in his *Maḥzor Vitry,* ed. by S. Hurwitz, p. 244. In this case, however, the Kairuwan exegete could invoke the support of Naṭronai Gaon of Sura. See Aptowitzer's ingenious reconstruction in *HUCA,* VIII–IX, 428 n. 22; and *supra,* n. 26.

Aptowitzer advanced here also the somewhat venturesome theory that, unlike their confreres Jacob bar Nissim and his son Nissim, Ḥushiel and Ḥananel maintained no direct contacts with the Babylonian academies; in fact, they were regularly bypassed by the latter because of their excessive independence and their reliance on their own Italo-Palestinian heritage. But this theory hinges around the identification of the term *talmidim* (disciples) in several geonic responsa with Ḥushiel and his school. Apart from the intrinsic improbability of that identification, the geonic censure of these "disciples" for permitting the appropriation of money owned by illiterate persons (see *supra,* Chap. XXV, n. 40) corresponds more fully to the unsavory conditions in Babylonia during the dissolution of the Caliphate than to what we know about the situation in North Africa. Certainly, the Italo-Palestinian traditions, including the record of the Palestinian Talmud, revealed no greater hostility toward the illiterate *'am ha-areṣ* than did the Babylonian Talmud. But Aptowitzer is undoubtedly right in rejecting J. Mann's theory of the existence of two Ḥushiels. Through this desperate expedient Mann had undertaken to reconcile S. Schechter's publication of a Genizah fragment showing that Ḥushiel had been detained in Kairuwan on a peaceful journey from Italy to Egypt, with the well-known legend concerning the four captives including Ḥushiel. See Schechter's "Geniza Specimen: a Letter of Chushiel," *JQR,* [o.s.] XI, 643–50 (with facsimile); Mann's aforementioned observations on Elḥanan ben Ḥushiel in *JQR,* IX, 160 ff.; his *Texts and Studies,* I, 110 ff.; his essay in *Tarbiz,* V, 286 ff.; *supra,* Chap. XXIII, n. 56; and Aptowitzer's *R. Chuschiel und R. Chananel.*

51. Ḥananel's *Commentary* on B.Q. 73a, and 'A.Z. 9a (Vilna ed.). While some portions of that *Commentary* have long been known, others have been pieced together laboriously and incompletely in recent years. A description of the MSS

(Vatican, Munich, London, and others) used in the Vilna edition of the Talmud is furnished in the "Postscript" by the publisher (the Widow and Brothers Rom) in the last volume of that monumental work, p. 5. Other fragments (on B.B.) have been assembled by Ginzberg in *Ginze Schechter,* II, 348 ff.; Lewin in *GK,* II, 13–15; V, 17–23; Assaf in his edition of *Teshubot,* 1942, pp. 206 ff.; and others. As shown by J. N. Epstein, some fragments previously attributed to Sherira and Hai really stemmed from Ḥananel's pen. See his essays cited *supra,* n. 46. It seems that, from the outset, the Kairuwan savant restricted himself to commenting on those tractates of the Talmud which contained the *gemara.* He skipped, therefore, all sections of the first order, *Zera'im,* other than Berakhot. He commented also on Zebaḥim, Ḥullin, and Niddah, but perhaps not on the other tractates of the fifth order, although the distinguished eighteenth-century bibliographer Ḥayyim Joseph David Azulai claimed, at least according to one version, that Ḥananel had written a commentary on the entire Talmud. Some comments on such later passages are indeed quoted in subsequent literature. But these may have been taken either from his observations in the earlier sections of his *Commentary,* or from his responsa, but few of which are extant today. See I. M. Ben Menahem's edition of Ḥananel's *Perush la-massekhet Zebaḥim* (Commentary on the Tractate Zebaḥim: the last three Chapters); the literature listed in Ginzberg's *Ginze Schechter,* II, 344, 346 f.; and Azulai's *Shem ha-gedolim* (Renown of Great Men; a biographical dictionary), ed. by I. A. Benjacob, I, fol. 26cd. In using subsequent quotations, moreover, we must bear in mind that different versions of Ḥananel's *Commentary* circulated in the later Middle Ages. See Aptowitzer's observations in his edition of Eliezer bar Joel ha-Levi's *Sefer Rabiah,* II, 396 n. 21, 584 n. 12; and his *Hossafot ve-tiqqunim* (Addenda et emendationes), *ibid.,* p. 135. Nevertheless, continued efforts to cull from the medieval citations as many of the lost statements by Ḥananel as possible, a task but incompletely performed in Lewin's *Otzar ha-gaonim,* would go far in reconstructing the text of that first comprehensive commentary on nearly the entire Talmud.

Ḥananel's great influence on the subsequent juridical, as well as exegetical, literature is evidenced, for example, by some two hundred quotations therefrom in Eliezer bar Joel's work, ed. by Aptowitzer. See the latter's *Mabo le-Sefer Rabiah,* p. 251. See also A. I. Bromberg's "R. Ḥananel and Maimonides" (Hebrew), *Sinai,* XI, Nos. 128–30, pp. 4–13, showing the former's influence on the sage of Fusṭaṭ, both directly and through Alfasi.

If neither Alfasi nor Nathan ben Yeḥiel cited the comments by Ḥananel or Nissim in their names, the latter would have had the less reason to complain, as this was also their own usual procedure. For one example, Ḥananel unperturbedly borrowed Hai's naturalistic explanation of the talmudic legend concerning a harp, suspended over King David's bed, which on every midnight was struck by the North Wind and of itself began playing a tune to awaken the king for the study of Torah (Berakhot 3b). Both the gaon and the Kairuwan scholar explained that this harp had been provided with a clock-like contrivance which sounded off at midnight. See Hai's comment in Lewin's *Otzar ha-gaonim,* I, Part 2, p. 4 No. 9; and that by Ḥananel published from a Cambridge fragment in Ginzberg's *Ginze,* II, 358 (on the general relations between the two men, see n. 52). This idea readily occurred to inhabitants of the world of Islam during the tenth and eleventh centuries, a period in which advanced technology combined with the availability of a mass market to stimulate the invention of all sorts of gadgets, whether useful or merely entertaining. See especially the studies by E. Wiedemann and others listed by A. Mieli in *La Science arabe,* p. 155; and *infra,* Chap. XXXV.

52. See M. C. Welborn's "Lotharingia as a Center of Arabic Scientific Influence in the Eleventh Century," *Isis,* XVI, 188–99; the older but still fundamental analysis of "Der Gershom Meor ha-Golah zugeschriebene Talmud-Commentar," by A. Epstein in the *Festschrift . . . Moritz Steinschneider,* pp. 115–43; Aptowitzer's *Mabo,* pp. 249, 330 ff.; and S. Eidelberg's more recent summary in the introduction to his edition of Gershom's *Teshubot,* pp. 26 ff. Curiously, although living in Mayence, Gershom used French rather than German equivalents in explaining some difficult talmudic terms. See the mutually complementary studies by L. Brandin, *Les Gloses françaises (loazim) de Gershom de Metz;* and B. Königsberger, *Fremdsprachliche Glossen bei jüdischen Commentatoren des Mittelalters,* Vol. I (that volume, devoted to Gershom, was to be followed by one reviewing the works by R. Isaac of Siponte). R. Gershom's alleged "ordinance" against careless copying of the talmudic texts is largely based on a misunderstood report in the introduction to Jacob Tam's *Sefer ha-Yashar.* Probably Gershom once irately uttered a curse against malefactors who, through their carelessness, imperiled the orderly processess of both study and judicial administration. But this was not one of the famed communal ordinances adopted under Gershom's leadership by the Franco-German rabbinate. Cf. L. Finkelstein's observations in his *Jewish Self-Government in the Middle Ages,* p. 32; and *infra,* nn. 156 ff.

The fullest as well as most readily available texts of Gershom's commentaries are included in the Vilna edition of the Talmud. Based upon several MSS and earlier prints (see their description in the aforementioned "Postscript" by the publisher), this is a good, though not "critical," edition according to modern standards. Even without unraveling Gershom's personal contributions from those of the "Mayence school," a critical edition might help recapture at least some of the basic texts of that Mayence commentary which so vitally determined the subsequent course of talmudic exegesis throughout Ashkenazic Jewry. We possess only a small fragment of "Gershom's" *Commentary* on Berakhot, quoted by the southern Italian rabbi Barukh ha-Sefardi (see S. Assaf's remarks in "A Portion of an Old Commentary on Berakhot by One of Maimonides' Contemporaries," *Abhandlungen Chajes,* Hebrew section, pp. 30, 46, 48). We cannot tell, therefore, to what extent the brief comments on that tractate, apparently written by an early Franco-German scholar, were indebted to it. See the small excerpt published in Ginzberg, *Ginze Schechter,* II, 371 ff. But such indebtedness is more probable than that author's borrowing from Rashi. The single passage therein verbatim similar to Rashi's interpretation and relating to the ancient Persian outhouses, whose construction certainly was not known in France, was doubtless taken by both authors, too, from some older Eastern tradition cited in the "Mayence commentary." We shall see that even Maimonides, unfamiliar though he was with Rashi's work, nevertheless included many strikingly similar statements in his *Commentary*—evidently because he derived them from the same source. In any case, we should find it truly surprising if, after Rashi, someone in his immediate environment had undertaken to write an independent brief commentary on the Talmud. See *infra,* n. 99.

53. See W. Bacher, *Die Agada der Tannaiten,* II, 454 ff., quoting the talmudic sources concerning the various teachers under whom Judah the Patriarch had

studied. The date of Rashi's birth still is somewhat uncertain, although the prevailing assumption that he was born in 1040, rather than in 1028, the year of Gershom's demise, has not been controverted by V. Aptowitzer's arguments in his *Mabo,* pp. 395 ff. Even if separated by a dozen years, Gershom's death and Rashi's birth were close enough to create in the minds of later chroniclers the image of a new sun rising after the older sun had set. See the chronology of scholars included in the *Resp.* by the great sixteenth-century scholar Solomon Luria, Lublin ed., 1599, fol. 23cd No. 29. Aptowitzer is right, however, in reversing the accepted order of Rashi's studies and postulating that the young student of Troyes first spent some time in Mayence and then proceeded to Worms. On the other hand, the frequent assumption that Rashi also studied in Spires (see, e.g., I. H. Weiss's biography, in his *Toledot gedole Yisrael* [Biographies of Leading Scholars], II, 5 n. 7; and his *Dor dor,* IV, 285) is based on the erroneous identification of the speaker, "I have seen in Spires," in Rashi's *Sefer ha-Pardes* (ed. by Ehrenreich, p. 216); it indubitably stemmed from one of Rashi's pupils. Also the reference there to a teacher, Eliakim, who had protested against a Spires custom, and the remark "I do not know the reason for it, except that I have seen the action" (*ibid.,* p. 262), were not written by Rashi himself. In another context, Eliakim testified to having observed an event in Mayence (*ibid.,* p. 78). Since the very foundation of the Jewish community of Spires does not antedate 1084, even a brief visit by Rashi there in his later years appears unlikely, notwithstanding the scholarly distinction of the three recipients of Henry IV's privilege in favor of the Spires community in 1090. See *supra,* Chap. XX, nn. 86–87; and M. Frank's *Qehillot Ashkenaz,* p. 2.

Similarly, the so-called Rashi script was obviously not invented by Rashi. It is a cursive script developed in the Middle Ages and early used for the speedy writing of commentaries on ancient classics, which were copied in square characters. Undoubtedly Rashi's popular commentaries belonged to the earliest and most widespread specimens of such writings, and were thus distinguished from the main texts also in the early prints. See M. Steinschneider, *Vorlesungen über die Kunde hebräischer Handschriften,* p. 30; and S. Birnbaum, *The Hebrew Scripts.*

54. Isaac bar Moses' *Sefer Or Zaru'a,* I, No. 61. The modern literature on Rashi is truly enormous. Scholarly investigation of his work began in 1823 when L. Zunz wrote his "Salomon ben Isaac, genannt Raschi," *Zeitschrift für die Wissenschaft des Judentums,* I, 277–384. Translated into Hebrew with additional notes by S. Bloch, this biography has served as the basis for many subsequent biographical studies, including those by Weiss and Aptowitzer mentioned above, and the books by M. Liber, *Rashi,* an English trans. from the French; E. M. Lipschütz, *R. Shelomoh Yiṣḥaqi* (Raschi, sein Leben und sein Werk), and, on a more popular level, but with a few more recent bibliographical references, by I. Spivak, *R. Shelomoh Yiṣḥaqi* (Rashi: His Period, Life and Work), both in Hebrew. A host of monographs was produced especially in connection with the eight-hundredth anniversary of Rashi's death in 1905, and again on the nine-hundredth anniversary of his birth in 1940. The latter celebration, though hampered by war-time conditions, produced numerous essays of fairly lasting value. Somewhat less of a flurry took place in 1955–56. Some of the more important studies will be cited in the following notes here; in Chap. XXIX, nn. 56–57; and other contexts. Cf. also I. Rivkind's description of the *Ta'arukhat Rashi* (Rashi Exhibition at the Library of the Jewish

Theological Seminary of America). A critical and up-to-date bibliography of the writings by and on Rashi should prove very useful, indeed.

55. Menaḥem ibn Zeraḥ's *Ṣedah la-derekh,* Intro., in *MJC,* II, 242; and *infra,* n. 58. Eliezer bar Nathan had already objected to certain individuals who, under false pretenses, had attacked a decision by Rashi, "whose waters we drink and from whose lips we live." See his *'Eben ha-'ezer,* No. 107 beg., ed. by Albeck, p. 78b. On the early prints of Rashi's commentary, see R. N. Rabbinovicz's *Ma'mar 'al hadpasat ha-talmud* (Essay on the Printing of the Talmud), pp. 7, 22 f. (also in the recent edition revised by A. M. Habermann); A. Freimann's *Thesaurus typographiae hebraicae,* Index, p. 7 (listing 5 incunabula of Rashi's commentaries on Bible and Talmud, with facsimiles); and E. N. Adler's brief observations on "Talmud Incunables of Spain and Portugal," *Kohut Mem. Vol.,* pp. 1–4 (with and without Rashi).

56. Mordecai Jaffe's *Sefer Lebush ha-Orah* (Vestment of Light; supercommentary on Rashi's Bible Commentary), on Gen., Prague ed., 1604; H. J. D. Azulai's *Shem ha-gedolim,* ed. by Benjacob, fol. 74b, quoting an autograph scroll by the famous kabbalist Ḥayyim Vital Calabrese; and other interesting illustrations furnished by I. Maarsen in his "Rashi's Image in the Course of Ages" (Hebrew), *Bitzaron,* II, 333–45. On Rashi's unconcern over anthropomorphic teachings and his explanation of R. Ishmael's ascension, see his *Commentary* on Berakhot 51a *s.v. Ematai;* Ḥagigah 14b *s.v. Nikhnesu.* In the former case, he simply quoted as a tannaitic source (*baraita*) the *Merkabah* literature attributed to R. Ishmael. See *infra,* Chap. XXXIII.

57. Rashi's *Commentary* on Gen. 1:1; his *Teshubot* (Responsa), ed. by Elfenbein, pp. 56 f. No. 59; his *Commentary* on Sukkah 40a *s.v. Eṣim.* At times he used the text of the Palestinian Talmud to correct, or at least to interpret accordingly, certain parallel passages in the Babylonian text. That he used this obvious method rather sparingly was doubtless owing to the scarcity of the Palestinian version in western Europe. Sometimes he quoted Palestinian statements from a tractate other than the one he was explaining, or relied on some secondary work, simply because the full text of that Talmud was not at his disposal. See the illustrations assembled by M. Higger in "The Yerushalmi Quotations in Rashi," *Rashi Anniv. Vol.,* pp. 191–217; and by A. I. Bromberg in his "Rashi and the Yerushalmi" (Hebrew), *Sinai,* VIII, Nos. 94–99, pp. 62–72, 193–99, 277–90; XVII, No. 210, pp. 165–69, 240–44. The startling unevenness of these quotations may perhaps best be explained by Rashi's consultation, during his sojourn in Mayence or Worms, of some texts which were no longer avilable to him in Troyes. The dearth of well-trained scribes, combined with the high price of writing materials, must have made such large compendia extremely rare—a condition which had only begun to become alleviated toward the end of Rashi's life through the general increase of the Jewish population and the establishment of tanneries in Troyes and elsewhere. See my remarks in *Rashi Anniv. Vol.,* pp. 50 f. Simple availability of complete copies, rather than personal preferences or acquaintance with Ḥananel's *Commentary,* explains the fuller use of the Palestinian source by such later scholars as the brothers Isaac and Simson, sons of Abraham, Eliezer bar Nathan, and the latter's family. Cf. E. Urbach's *Ba'ale ha-tosafot,* pp. 543 ff., with the views previously held by Aptowitzer and Ginzberg. Rashi's use of other ancient, particularly midrashic, sources has long preoccupied the foremost students of his works, such as L. Zunz and A. Berliner. Some new

material has been assembled by J. L. Fishman (Maimon) in his "Israel's Masterly Teacher" (Hebrew) in *Sefer Rashi* (Rashi Volume), ed. by him, pp. 373–488. But much remains to be done. See also, from a broader range, M. A. Amiel's penetrating observations on "Rashi's Halakhic Approach" (Hebrew), *ibid.*, pp. 153–73.

Urbach (pp. 47, 527 ff.) has also pointed out how inconsistent Rashi's and his disciples' attitude was toward emending the talmudic text on the basis of mere reasoning. Rashi may not have heard of Hai Gaon's warning, "We must not correct the Mishnah or Talmud because of any question we may raise against it." See Lewin, *Otzar ha-gaonim,* VIII, Part 1, p. 207. But he certainly was familiar with Gershom's "curse" against precisely such proceedings. Yet he could no more refrain from correcting the existing recensions whenever he felt that they misrepresented the sages' original intent than could Jacob Tam or other exegetes. On one occasion, for example, Alfasi reported Hai as quoting four different versions of a single word in the Talmud, Alfasi himself choosing still another as the "reading of the academy." Yet Rashi had a further variant of his own which, because of his immense popularity, was incorporated in our printed editions. Though also accepted by Zeraḥiah ha-Levi, Rashi's version evoked some serious questioning on the part of Naḥmanides, who claimed that, had Rashi known of Hai's readings, he would not have suggested his own. See Rashi's *Commentary* on Sanhedrin 65b *s.v. Bi-re'iyyah;* Alfasi's *Halakhot* on Sanhedrin VII, with Naḥmanides' comment thereon in his *Milḥamot Adonai* (Wars of the Lord; a commentary on Alfasi), *ad loc.*

58. Rashi's *Commentary* on *Giṭṭin* 90b *s.v. U-perumah;* and numerous other illustrations furnished in A. Berliner's lecture, *Blicke in die Geisteswerkstatt Raschi's;* and P. Klein's aforementioned dissertation on *La Vie privée.* On the foreign vocabulary see A. Darmesteter and D. S. Blondheim's careful analysis of *Les Gloses françaises dans les commentaires talmudiques de Raschi,* backed up by Blondheim's examination of numerous Rashi manuscripts and his comparative study of the Italian words inserted in Nathan ben Yeḥiel's *'Arukh.* See his "Liste des manuscrits des Commentaires bibliques de Raschi," *REJ,* XCI, 71–101, 155–74 (also reprinted with a supplementary Index of Names); and his "Notes on the Italian Words in the 'Aruk Completum" (private preprint). Apart from their linguistic significance, these foreign terms, properly reexamined, are apt to shed much new light on the socio-economic life of the period, including the then employed technological processes. See the interesting examples assembled by J. Wellesz in his Hebrew essay "Rashi" in *Ha-Goren,* VI, 5–25 (reprinted under the title "On the Character of Rashi's Commentaries" in *Sefer Rashi,* ed. by Fishman, pp. 174–93), as well as by M. Narkis in his "Niello" (Hebrew) in the same anniversary volume, pp. 535–42, with four telling illustrations. See also *supra,* n. 52; and *infra,* n. 99. Apart from using such foreign words, Rashi utilized to the full the internal resources of the talmudic and targumic vocabulary, as well as traditions current in the academies, to identify rare objects and terms. See B. Cohen's pioneering examination of "Rashi as a Lexicographer of the Talmud," *Rashi Anniv. Vol.,* pp. 219–48; and other literature cited *infra,* Chaps. XXIX, n. 56; XXX, n. 33. Rashi's primarily exegetical aims, however, colored his identifications, the same word being often reproduced differently in various contexts. See, e.g., the four different renditions of such a simple word as *adamah* (earth), three of them with the aid of French translations (Cohen, p. 229).

Rashi followed the same procedure also with respect to his substantive interpretations. For this reason V. Aptowitzer suggested that the existing commentaries essentially reproduce the initial oral presentations by the master at his school in Troyes. Facing a class, a teacher would normally use a different verbiage each time he explains a similar passage. See Aptowitzer's extensive illustrations in "The Genesis of Rashi's Commentary on the Talmud" (Hebrew), *Sefer Rashi,* ed. by Fishman, pp. 98–139 (also reprint; partially reproduced in English in *Rashi Anniv. Vol.,* pp. 149–89). Since, however, either Rashi or his pupils speedily committed these commentaries to writing, the innumerable variants could not have escaped his attention, especially as he kept on revising his texts. Nor does A. Epstein's earlier suggestion that the three recensions of the *Commentary* originated during the years of Rashi's respective sojourns in Worms, Mayence (or the reverse, see *supra,* n. 53), and Troyes, answer our problem. See Epstein's "Schemaja, der Schüler und Secretär Raschi's," *MGWJ,* XLI, 258 n. 2; together with the additional notes by I. Werfel, appended to the Hebrew trans. of that significant essay in *Sefer Rashi,* ed. by Fishman, pp. 342 ff. (also in Epstein's *Kitbe,* ed. by Habermann, I, 269–300). Apart from its overneatness and lack of supporting documentation, this suggestion would presuppose Rashi's almost uncritical acceptance of divergent explanations by his teachers without any effort to harmonize them in later recensions. Probably most of these variants were quite intentional, Rashi wishing to bring home the meaning of such parallel statements in two or more different ways. Of course, we possess but few of the original formulations, most of our texts being derived from the final recension. But some of the early versions are preserved in quotations by Tosafists and their successors (especially Bezalel Ashkenazi), unless later copyists here, too, freely used their discretion in harmonizing and, hence, leveling down variations. Since, on the other hand, these copyists were also guilty of introducing new elements at variance with the master's teachings, they created numerous fresh inconsistencies. See the examples independently adduced by S. Grünberg in his "Alterations in and Additions to Rashi's Commentary on the Talmud" (Hebrew), and by Z. P. Frank in his "Divergent Interpretations in Rashi's Commentary" (Hebrew), in *Sefer Rashi,* pp. 345–59 and 360–72. These examples could easily be multiplied.

More consistent were Rashi's methodological approaches. Although obviously bent on communicating only those rules of juristic determination and those historical sequences which would facilitate the understanding of each particular text, he fully realized their important legal implications. See J. L. Fishman's observations in *Sefer Rashi,* pp. 120 ff., and "The Material for an Introduction to the Talmud in Rashi's Commentaries" assembled in a pertinent Hebrew essay by M. Zucker in *Bitzaron,* II, 378–89. See also the other essays in this special "Rashi Issue."

59. See the Vilna edition of the Talmud *ad loc.* Only a small portion of the independent talmudic commentaries by either Yehudah bar Nathan or Samuel bar Meir have appeared in print, or are extant in MSS. Most of our knowledge about them is derived from quotations in later literature, especially the works of Eliezer bar Joel and Isaac Or Zaru'a. See J. N. Epstein's edition of Yehudah's *Perushe* (Commentaries) on Ketubot; his apt analysis of "Yehudah bar Nathan's Commentaries and Those of Worms" (Hebrew), *Tarbiz,* IV, 11–34, 153–92, 295–96; Aptowitzer's *Mabo,* pp. 340 f., 409 ff.; E. Urbach's *Ba'ale ha-tosafot,* pp. 36 ff., 42 ff.; and the literature listed *infra,* Chap. XXIX, nn. 81–82. The genuineness of several Rashi commentaries has been under debate ever since Zunz's aforementioned biography of Rashi. Even conservatives like the family Rom, publishers of the Vilna edi-

tion, published side by side two versions, one allegedly authentic and another spurious, of Rashi's commentaries on Bekhorot 57b–61a, Menaḥot 72b–94a, the latter following a MS left behind by Bezalel Ashkenazi. Among the main contributors to the debate were J. Reifmann and A. Berliner. See the convenient summary in Lipschütz's *R. Shelomoh Yiṣḥaqi,* pp. 64 ff. More recently, S. Liebermann has attributed also the existing commentary on Sanhedrin, Chap. x, to Yehudah bar Nathan, rather than his father-in-law, but he has argued for the existence at one time of a genuine commentary by Rashi, of which certain vestiges may still be detected. See his *Shkiin,* pp. 92 ff. On the other hand, fragments of Rashi's genuine commentaries were recovered from a Vienna MS by J. Freimann and published in *Ha-Zofeh,* XII, 241–51 (on Nedarim fols. 1–4). The time seems long overdue for specialists to draw all these researches together, and particularly to attempt a careful critical edition of all talmudic commentaries by Rashi, based upon MSS, early editions, and particularly the innumerable citations by Rashi's successors. This task is complicated, of course, by the absence of a critical edition of the underlying talmudic text. Both interrelated undertakings will benefit greatly from the Talmudic Concordance by C. J. Kasovski now under way. On the relations between the two classical contributions by Rashi, so totally different in approach and often resulting in divergent, even contradictory explanations, see I. Maarsen's "Keren hapukh [Reversed Projection]," in *Blau Mem. Vol.,* Hebrew section, pp. 170–73.

60. The vast older literature dealing with the school of Tosafists or its individual members, has largely been superseded by Urbach's *Ba'ale ha-tosafot.* See J. Katz's review of that volume in *KS,* XXXI, 9–16; and that by I. A. Agus in *JQR,* XLVI, 366–78. Many of their criticisms, however, are merely semantic, or in quest of unnecessary definitions. Despite Urbach's legitimate strictures (p. 31 n. 1), P. Tarshish's bio-bibliographical index to the *Ishshim u-sefarim ba-"tosafot"* (The Personalities and Books Referred to in Tosafot), ed. by S. A. (H. S.) Neuhausen, is useful for ready reference. Of interest also are such outright commentaries on talmudic tractates as that on *Sheqalim* mentioned above (n. 36) by a pupil of Samuel ben Shne'ur, ed. by A. Schreiber together with a *Commentary* thereon by Meshullam, pupil of David bar Kalonymus of Münzberg. These commentaries are perhaps particularly noteworthy because of their more extensive use of the Palestinian Talmud to explain the Babylonian text. Cf. the entries listed in Schreiber's introduction, pp. viii f. Cf. also the newly published text of "The *Tosafot* of R. Isaac ha-Laban [the Blond] on Tractate Yoma" (Hebrew), ed. by D. Genchovsky in *Sinai,* XIX, Nos. 230, 232–35; with the editor's comments "On the Teaching of Isaac ha-Laban" (Hebrew), *ibid.,* No. 237, pp. 345–55; and the older literature listed *ibid.,* p. 309; and in Urbach's *Ba'ale,* pp. 185 ff. This Isaac bar Jacob, Jacob Tam's pupil, helped to transplant Jewish lore to Prague and Ratisbon, from which community his brother Petaḥiah started out on his memorable journey.

61. See W. Windfuhr's *Französische Wörter im Mischnacommentar des R. Simson von Sens;* the broader, though no longer up-to-date "Etude sur Simson ben Abraham de Sens" by H. Gross in *REJ,* VI, 167–86; VII, 40–77. The peculiarities of talmudic dialectics are analyzed in the various methodological and comparative studies listed *supra,* Vol. II, especially pp. 429 ff.; J. Banner's "Essai sur la dialectique rabbinique dans le Midraš et le Talmud," *Annales Universitatis Saraviensis,* Philosophie-Lettres, II, 81–88; R. Bloch's "Note méthodologique pour l'étude de la littérature rab-

binique," *Recherches de science religieuse,* XLIII, 194–227; and in T. Boman's comparative study of *Das hebräische Denken im Vergleich mit dem griechischen.* Cf. also I. Heinemann's Hebrew review of the latter volume in *KS,* XXIX, 225–29. On the approaches of the Tosafists as such, cf. the older but still useful analysis by P. Buchholz, "Die Tosafisten als Methodologen," *MGWJ,* XXXVIII, 342–59, 398–404, 450–62, 549–56. In fact, the sharp dialectics of the Frenchmen appeared unrealistic even to their early German colleagues. See J. N. Epstein, "Aeltere Tosafot aus Deutschland," *MGWJ,* LXXXIII, 346–55. Jacob Tam himself once expressed amazement at the overingenious speculations of Isaac of Dampierre. The parallels between the Tosafists and the glossators are briefly mentioned by Urbach in *Ba'ale,* pp. 27 ff. The contrasts, as well as the similarities with canon jurists may be gleaned from the literature cited *supra,* Chap. XX, n. 19; and especially from such analyses as that of "Die Rechtslehre des Magisters Gratians" by F. Arnold in *Studia Gratiana,* I, 451–82; and other studies in that work. But this important and ramified subject would merit fuller monographic treatment.

62. Isaac bar Sheshet, *Resp.,* No. 394 beg. The authorship of the *Pisqe ha-tosafot* (Legal Decisions of the Tosafot), found in many Talmud editions, still is uncertain. There is even some question as to whether they emerged from a single original collection, or from two collections which were subsequently merged. The compilation has been variously attributed to Asher bėn Yeḥiel, an assiduous copyist of earlier *Tosafot,* his son Jacob, or even to earlier authors. Cf. the list in I. A. Benjacob's *Ozar ha-sepharim* (Bibliographie der gesammten hebräischen Literatur), p. 491 No. 1016; and Urbach's *Ba'ale ha-tosafot,* pp. 460 n. 9, 566 f.

63. Abraham ben David's stricture on the Tosafists is included in his replies to two inquiries from Béziers and reproduced in the collection *Temim de'im* attributed to him (Warsaw ed., 1897, fol. 24d No. 113). Here the irate author also delivered a blast against the inquirers: "All of Provence has followed the practice as taught by us and our colleagues have agreed with us, and have not rejected our decision as you are reported to have done." See Naḥmanides' introduction to his tract, *Dine de-garme* (Laws of Damages by Indirect Action); and Yehudah ben Samuel ibn 'Abbas' *Ya'ir netib* (Illuminating the Path), cited in S. Assaf's *Meqorot le-toledot ha-ḥinnukh be-Yisrael,* II, 30; Urbach, *Ba'ale ha-tosafot,* p. 22. Understandably, the juridical content of these interpretations interested also some early compilers of *Tosafot.* Halakhic interests predominated, for example, in the collection known as the *Tosefot Sens,* emanating from the school of R. Simson, while a similar collection prepared by Eliezer of Touques and circulating under the name of *Tosefot Tukh* pursued more directly exegetical aims. There were also other collections. Much speculation has been attached, for example, to a collection called *Tosefot Gornish,* variously attributed to Simson of Sens and other scholars. It has even been suggested that those were really the product of English scholars and that their original name was *Tosefot Norwich.* See *supra,* Chap. XX, n. 113. All these suggestions are quite venturesome, however, and Urbach (pp. 238, 245 f.) is quite right in warning against any hasty conclusions until the two MSS now preserved in the Günzburg collection in Moscow will be fully examined. Out of all these texts the printers of the first Talmud edition compiled our present *Tosafot* in a somewhat arbitrary manner. See Urbach's illuminating analysis, pp. 447 ff.

64. Nathan ben Abraham's "Commentary on the Six Orders of the Mishnah" was first described on the basis of a modern Yemenite MS by S. Assaf in a pertinent Hebrew essay in *KS,* X, 381–88, 525–45; reprinted in his *Tequfat,* pp. 295 ff. We know very little about that author's life and background, although he probably was the grandson, as well as namesake, of the Gaon Nathan ben Abraham. See Mann's *Jews in Egypt,* I, 151, 193 f.; his *Texts and Studies,* I, 323 ff.; and *supra,* Chap. XXIII, n. 38.

65. Maimonides' *Commentary* on the Mishnah, general introduction (ed. by B. Hamburger, pp. 60 f. [Arabic and Hebrew], and in the Vilna ed. at the end of Berakhot, fol. 110b); on tractate 'Oqṣin end (Vilna ed., last volume fol. 77a: read "thirty-three" instead of "thirty"); and his *Resp.,* ed. by Freimann, pp. 225 f. No. 240. Regrettably, we still have no really critical edition of either the Arabic original or the Hebrew translations of that outstanding commentary. Many portions of the Arabic text, some of them accompanied by German translations, have appeared as dissertations at various German-speaking universities ever since 1879. See the fifty-four entries in A. Yaari's "Maimonides' Commentary on the Mishnah: a Bibliography of the Edited Parts" (Hebrew), *KS,* IX, 101–9, 228–35, and XXIX, 176, with a supplementary list of four items by B. Simches, *ibid.,* XII, 132. Prepared by tyros, though including a Jacob Barth or an Eduard Baneth, who later achieved eminence in the field of Judeo-Arabic studies, some of these editions leave much to be desired. Prospects for a complete critical edition are promising, as we are fortunate in possessing a few leaves from the author's own hand which, although covering but tiny fragments, may nevertheless shed light on the critical value of other medieval copies. Cf. Yaari's brief note on "Maimonides' Commentary on the Mishnah in His Own Handwriting" (Hebrew), *KS,* XVIII, 208; the four manuscripts recently described by S. M. Stern in his "Autographs of Maimonides in the Bodleian Library," *Bodleian Library Record,* V, 180–202; and J. M. Toledano's ed. of "Maimonides' Commentary on the Mishnah Tractate Sheqalim" (Hebrew), *Sinai,* XIV, Nos. 159–60, pp. 52–61; XVI, 133–52. On the other hand, in the introduction to his edition of Maimonides' *Hilkhot ha-Yerushalmi* (see *infra,* n. 100), S. Lieberman marshaled strong evidence to show that most of the texts current today represent neither the first nor the final recension of the *Commentary,* but rather an intermediate stage. Other Maimonidean autographs, as well as some of the enormous secondary literature, will be listed *infra,* n. 102, in connection with the Maimonidean code, the master's supreme contribution to the development of Jewish law. See also *infra,* Chap. XXX, n. 7. These and other sources are used in the photographic ed. of Maimonides' *Commentarius in Mischnam,* edited from one Sassoon and two Bodleian MSS by S. D. Sassoon as part of a general *Corpus codicum hebraicorum medii aevi* under the general editorship of R. Edelmann. Thus far only Volume I, giving the text for Zera'im and Mo'ed, has appeared; it includes forty-two facsimiles of other known autographs.

The biographical data here given are supplied by Maimonides himself in his aforementioned postscript to 'Oqṣin. On the unfortunate deletion in some manuscripts there of the word *shalosh,* which made it appear that Maimonides had completed his *Commentary* at the age of thirty in Morocco, rather than thirty-three in Egypt, see A. Geiger's "Moses ben Maimon" (1850), reprinted in his *Nachgelassene Schriften,* ed. by L. Geiger, III, 86 n. 41. We do not know when and to what extent Maimonides consulted Nathan ben Abraham's commentary, nor whether he had even read any portion of Saadiah's earlier exegetical work on the Mishnah, for he generally refers to but few of his authorities by name. On his family background, see A. H. Freimann's genealogical data in *Alummah,* I, 9–32, 157–58; and J. M. Toledano's "Maimonides' Family, Its Origin and Vestiges" (Hebrew), *Sinai,* XIX, No. 230, pp. 281–87, and other literature listed *infra,* n. 114.

Evidently unfamiliar with Rashi's similar work (see *infra,* n. 118), Maimonides undertook in his younger years to produce also a commentary on the whole Babylonian Talmud. But after writing on the three major orders of Mo'ed, Nashim, and Neziqin, with the exception of four tractates, as well as on the tractate Ḥullin (see the aforementioned general introduction to his Mishnah *Commentary*), he seems to have decided not to circulate this work. In fact, very little of it has come down to us. The commentary on the tractate Rosh ha-Shanah, attributed to him and published in 1865, is of dubious authenticity. On the other hand, "An Old Commentary on the First Chapter of Shabbat," ed. in Hebrew by B. M. Lewin in his *GK,* V, 157–60, and quoting both Ḥananel and Joseph ibn Megas, has been identified as a likely fragment from Maimonides' pen by A. H. Freimann. See his note on Abraham Maimonides' *Resp.,* ed. by him and S. D. Goitein, p. 8 n. 4. "A New Fragment of Maimonides' Commentary on the Talmud Tractate Shabbat" was detected in the texts published by Assaf in his *Mi-Sifrut ha-geonim,* pp. 192–95, by M. J. L. Sachs. Cf. his pertinent Hebrew essay in *Sinai,* XIII, Nos. 153–54, pp. 66–68, 248. On Maimonides' work on the Palestinian Talmud, which is more juridical than exegetical, see *infra,* n. 99.

66. Maimonides' aforementioned general introduction to his *Commentary;* his comment on M. Ketubot 1.6, ed. by S. Frankfurter, pp. 5 f. (Arabic and Hebrew), 27 (German); and the introduction to his *Sefer ha-Miṣvot* (Book of Commandments), in the Arabic ed. by M. Bloch, p. 1; and in Moses ibn Tibbon's Hebrew trans., ed. by C. Heller, p. 1a. His deviations from the meaning given the Mishnah by geonim and even Amoraim have often been noted by such later commentators as Yom Tob Lippmann Heller. See the illustrations cited by Geiger, in his *Nachgelassene Schriften,* III, 84 f. n. 35, which have not been explained away by Jacob Horovitz's arguments in the essay cited *infra,* n. 99. See also I. H. Weiss's biography of Maimonides in his *Toledot gedole Yisrael,* I, 9, n. 13; and, more generally, *supra,* n. 26; and *infra,* n. 115.

67. M. D. Gaon's analysis and text in "The Reading of the Thirteen Principles in Sephardic Congregations" (Hebrew), *Yeda 'Am* (Journal of the Israel Folklore Society), III, 39–41; E. Pococke's ed. of *Bab Musi Porta Mosis* (Arabic text, with Latin translation of parts of Maimonides' *Commentary;* reprinted in Pococke's *Theological Works,* ed. by L. Twells, I, 1–125; cf. C. Roth, "Edward Pococke and the First Hebrew Printing in Oxford," *Bodleian Library Record,* II, 215–19); J. I. Gorfinkle's ed., with an English trans., of the Hebrew version of Maimonides' *Eight Chapters.* These and other lengthy excursuses by Maimonides, dealing with a vast range of subjects of interest for his time and teachings, have been, and will be, quoted here in various connections.

68. See Al-Ḥarizi's preface to his translation of Maimonides' general introduction; Joseph ben Isaac ibn al-Fawwal's preface to his translation of the rest of the first order (Zera'im at the beginning of tractate Terumot); that by Solomon ben

Joseph ibn Ya'qub to his translation of the fourth order (at the beginning of B.Q.); and Joseph Karo's *Bet Yosef* (House of Joseph; a commentary on Jacob ben Asher's *Ṭurim*), O.Ḥ. 128, Warsaw ed., 1861, fol. 112a. Maimonides included the text of the Mishnah itself before adding his own comments. But, since copies of the Mishnah were readily available, these quotations were omitted by many translators and copyists of both the Arabic version, and the Hebrew translations. A laudable exception was Jacob ben Moses ibn Abbasi, translator of the *Commentary* on the third order (Nashim). In the preface to his translation (at the beginning of Yebamot), Jacob censured his predecessors for omitting the text of the Mishnah, which must be held before the reader's eyes if he is to understand the Maimonidean comments. To us today these omissions appear doubly grievous, for, if faithfully copied, some of the Maimonidean readings might have proved useful in ascertaining early variants in the Mishnah text itself.

69. Simon bar Ṣemaḥ Duran's *Magen Abot* (Commentary on Abot), Intro., ed. by J. Schlossberg, fol. 2b; Ibn Daud's Chronicle in *MJC,* I, 69, 76; Abraham ben David's *Ḥiddushe* (Novellae) on Tractate Baba Qamma, ed. by S. H. Atlas (listing also other parts published before, including the spurious commentary on Tamid); A. H. Freimann's review of that edition in *KS,* XX, 25–28; Solomon ben ha-Yatom's (ha-Jatom's-Hitam's?), *Perush 'al massekhet Mashqin* (Kommentar zu Mašqin), ed. by H. P. Chajes; Isaac ben Melchizedek's *Commentary* on the first order of the Mishnah (Zera'im), published from a Bodleian MS in the Vilna edition of the Talmud (cf. the publisher's "Postscript" in the last tractate); Benjamin's *Massa'ot,* ed. by Adler, pp. 10 (Hebrew), 8 (English). Living in a region, where important segments of the population still retained vestiges of both the Greek and the Arabic speech, these Italian scholars made extensive use of Arabic, Greek, and Italian equivalents, in interpreting difficult talmudic terms. In his introduction to Solomon's commentary (pp. xxxi ff.), Chajes assembled no less than twenty-five Italian and thirty Arabic terms (in a dozen cases both languages were used), occurring in the rather brief text on that single talmudic tractate. This fact does not necessarily suggest Solomon's Eastern origin, as proposed by Chajes. If he seems less proficient in Greek—the few Greek terms seem to be derived from second hand—we must not forget that in the Norman period Greek rule had been a matter of a more distant past than that of the Muslims. On Isaac ben Melchizedek, see H. Gross's "Isaak b. Malki-Zedek aus Siponto und seine süditalischen Zeitgenossen," *MWJ,* II, 21–22, 25–26, 29–30, 33–34, 37–38, 42–44; and *supra,* n. 52.

Even the few works of the Spanish school which have come down to us are in a bad state of preservation. Typical of these deficiencies are the complaints voiced by the first editor of Joseph ibn Megas' *Ḥiddushim* (Novellae) on Baba Batra. The copy from which he prepared the publication, he claims, was "erroneous and corrupt, as if a stupid child had written it. . . . It seems that the copyist transcribed from a Sephardic into an Ashkenazic handwriting without properly discerning the letters." The editor himself, however, seems to have gone too far in correcting the text not only on the basis of subsequent quotations in rabbinic literature but also from his own reasoning, "out of necessity." Better, but far from "critical," is the recent edition of that work (also on Shebu'ot), provided with a detailed commentary *Ne'eman Shemu'el* by Samuel Isaac. Two interesting excerpts from Ibn Megas's commentary transcribed from Moses Maimonides' autograph copy in his *Commentary* on Shabbat are included in Abraham Maimonides' *Resp.,* pp. 8 f. No

2, 10 ff. No. 3. See also, more generally, A. L. Grajewsky's very brief biographical sketch of *Rabbenu Joseph ha-Levi ibn Migash* (R. J. i. Megas: Contributions to His Teaching, Life, and Epoch).

Still less fortunate was Isaac ibn Gayyat, a distinguished poet as well as jurist. While, as we shall see, some of his halakhic decisions have been preserved, his commentaries on Mishnah and Talmud have totally vanished, except where his comments had penetrated the juridical literature via subsequent quotations. According to Isaac ben Abba Mari (in his *Sefer ha-'Iṭṭur,* ed. by S. Schönblum, I, 15), Ibn Gayyat had quoted his own commentary on Ketubot, since lost. The latter also left behind a *Sefer ha-Ner* (Book of Light), a Hebrew rendering of a *K. as-Siraj* similar in nature to that of Maimonides. However, the Hebrew translators usually preferred to render that Arabic title by *Sefer ha-Ma'or.* See Maimonides' *Resp.,* p. 131 No. 136 with the editor's comments; and S. Assaf's observations on "The Book of Light by R. Isaac ibn Gayyat" (Hebrew), *Tarbiz,* III, 213–14, 339. Least well-known is the work of Isaac al-Balia. Devoted to the explanation of more difficult talmudic passages, his commentary, bearing the picturesque title of *Quppat ha-rokhlim* (The Peddlers' Basket), seems never to have been completed and is totally lost. See Ibn Daud's Chronicle in *MJC,* I, 74. Perhaps Al-Balia's speedy rise to political leadership through his connection with Al-Mu'tamidh, ruler of Granada, interrupted his literary creativity. All these men's renown was eclipsed by that of Isaac Alfasi, with whom they often violently disagreed.

One of their Provençal successors, Moses ben Joseph of Narbonne, who likewise sharply dissented from Alfasi's views, has shared their fate. His *Novellae* on most talmudic tractates (Berakhot, Ḥullin, and the entire second, third, and fourth orders) have disappeared, except for the few quotations preserved mainly by his eminent disciples, Zeraḥiah ha-Levi and Abraham ben David. Cf. B. Z. Benedikt's "R. Moses ben Joseph of Narbonne" (Hebrew), *Tarbiz,* XIX, 19–34. From Benedikt's data it clearly appears that Moses' work consisted of elaborate comments on selected passages of the kind of Joseph ibn Megas' *Ḥiddushim,* rather than of a consecutive commentary à la Rashi. Hence the term *ḥiddushim* (*novellae*), or *nimmuqim* (reasonings), used by Naḥmanides, has a more technical ring than Zeraḥiah's nondescript *perushim* (commentaries). See *ibid.,* pp. 24 f. Moses' pupil Abraham ben David likewise composed works belonging to the category of *novellae,* rather than commentaries, although few contemporaries drew a sharp line of demarcation between these two genres. More directly exegetical, though always with an eye for both the juridical implications and complex talmudic debates, were Abraham's quite extraordinary commentaries on the otherwise neglected halakhic midrashim. While his expositions of the *Mekhilta* and *Sifre* seem definitely lost, that of *Sifra* was published, from an Oxford MS, with a good critical analysis, in I. H. Weiss's edition of that tannaitic classic. See also the literature listed *infra,* n. 98.

70. Berakhot 22a; M.Q. 26b; *Massekhet Soferim* (Tractate Soferim), XIII.9, ed. by Higger, p. 246; Jacob Tam's *Sefer ha-Yashar,* Vienna ed., fol. 73c No. 619; ed. by Rosenthal, p. 81 No. 45, 3. See also the various other Minor Tractates ed. by Higger (listed *supra,* Vol. II, p. 428 n. 6), and the editor's detailed introductions. The Palestinian origin of these tractates and their composition in the early posttalmudic era have long been recognized. True, with respect to the tractate *Soferim* doubts have arisen because of its frequent citations from the Babylonian Talmud and its reference to the Diaspora's double holidays. See W. Jawitz's observations in his

Toledot, pp. 16 f. However, its indebtedness to the Palestinian Talmud is far more noticeable, which would be more surprising were the compiler a Babylonian scholar than would a Palestinian writer's familiarity with the Babylonian compendium. More decisively, there is a prevalence of Palestinian customs throughout the booklet. On the various theories relating to its origin, see Higger's review in the introduction to his edition of *Massekhet Semaḥot* (Treatise Semaḥot), pp. 9 ff.; and that to *Soferim*, especially pp. 78 ff. At times its compiler refers to traditions and customs unrecorded in either Talmud, as when he gives a rather unusual twist to the required length of the *hafṭarah*. While the Talmudim discuss the minimum length of that prophetic lesson of twenty-one or twenty-four verses, corresponding to the minimum of three verses for each of the seven or eight men summoned to the Torah on Sabbaths (j. Megillah IV.3, 75a; b. 23b–24a), *Soferim* has the unique version of a requisite number of twenty-two verses, namely twenty-one for the seven readers and one for the synagogue precentor (XIII.15, p. 250). Cf. J. Mann's brief observations in *The Bible as Read and Preached in the Old Synagogue*, I, 9.

71. *Sefer ha-Ma'asim*, ed. by Mann in *Tarbiz*, I, Part 3, pp. 11 f.; Hai Gaon's resp. quoted in the *Sefer ha-Makhria'* (Book of Decisions; on selected laws) by the thirteenth-century jurist, Isaiah bar Mali of Trani, fols. 27bc No. 36, 31cd No. 42. On the date of the "Ordinance concerning the Obstreperous Woman" and its limited acceptance in various countries, see the numerous sources analyzed by H. Tykocinski in *Die gaonäischen Verordnungen*, pp. 4–33; and *infra*, n. 153. Ever since the publication of the several fragments of the *Sefer ha-Ma'asim* by Lewin, Epstein, and Mann in *Tarbiz*, Vols. I–II, this curious compilation has intrigued scholars. The fairly general consensus still is that this is largely a collection of legal precedents, probably from the tribunal of Tiberias. See S. Lieberman's observations on "Sefer ha-Ma'asim—the Book of Decisions [Precedents]" (Hebrew), *Tarbiz*, II, 377–79. The extant texts are not quite uniform. Only one fragment published by Lewin bears such earmarks of the original compilation as the absence of the heading *Ma'aseh* and of authors of particular talmudic statements; the general paucity of Babylonian influences; the frequency of Greek terms, some of them quite unusual; and the lack of any connection between the successive entries which apparently followed the order of the Tiberian court ledger. The other published parts, on the other hand, evidently represent works by later compilers using the original *Sefer ha-Ma'asim* as their main source.

Some of these compilers may actually have lived in southern Italy in the tenth century, as suggested by Aptowitzer in his *Meḥqarim be-sifrut ha-geonim* (Studies in Geonic Literature), pp. 78 ff., 150 ff. This hypothesis is not necessarily controverted by Lieberman's demonstration of the close linguistic affinities between this "Book of Precedents" and the Palestinian Talmud. See his "On the Book of Precedents for the Population of Palestine" (Hebrew), *GK*, V, 177–85. Of course, an Italian epitomizer would have had no compelling reasons to change the linguistic forms of the original Palestinian passages quoted by him. More serious is the absence of any Latin loan words, contrasted with the presence of quite a few borrowings from the Greek. Even in Sicily before the Muslim conquest one might legitimately expect the incursion of some Latin elements, whether from literary sources or the "vulgar" speech of the local majority. Cf. also S. Assaf's critical, though inconclusive, observations in his review of Aptowitzer's *Meḥqarim*, in *KS*, XVIII, 323 f., 328. See also Mann's "Varia on the Geonic Period" (Hebrew), *Tarbiz*, V, 300 f., and, particularly,

M. Margulies's succinct analysis of the available fragments in his Hebrew lecture, "Something about Palestine's Halakhic Literature during the Geonic Period," *Ha-Kinnus ha-'olami,* I, 255–58. In any case, Mann's reiterated suggestion (*Tarbiz,* I, Part 3, pp. 5 f.) that the compiler of the Tractate *Soferim* borrowed from the *Sefer ha-Ma'asim* is unlikely. Either the reverse is true, or else both authors independently derived their rules from observation of the contemporary liturgical practices in the Holy Land. On the medieval German law books, see *infra,* nn. 83–84.

72. *Shimmusha Raba* (Raba's Legal Practice), in Asher ben Yeḥiel's *Halakhot qeṭanot* (Small Halakhot), appended to the latter's comprehensive legal code *Halakhot* at the end of the tractate Menaḥot (Vilna ed., fol. 123bc). Asher himself does not indicate where he had found the manuscript. Some texts mention, however, that the critical comment at the end of the tract stems from "the Barcelona rabbi." See Yom Tob Lippmann Heller's *Ma'adane Yom Tob* (Yom Tob's Delights; a commentary on Asher ben Yeḥiel's *Halakhot*), *ad loc.* There is little doubt that this observation refers to Yehudah bar Barzillai, the avid collector and critical reviewer of geonic materials. The title *Shimmusha* has been explained as the equivalent of *halakhot* (laws) by M. Margulies in his edition of *Halakhot qeṣubot* (Adjudicated Laws; see *infra,* n. 91), p. 110 note. See also Assaf's *Tequfat,* p. 209. From subsequent quotations it appears that our tract was not limited to the laws of phylacteries, but probably covered a wider range of ritualistic regulations. For example, Simḥah of Vitry quotes from it the legend concerning God's appearance before Moses in the shape of a synagogue reader to teach him a prayer for fast days, a variation of R. Johanan's statement in R.H. 17b. See Simḥah's *Maḥzor Vitry,* ed. by Hurwitz, p. 234 No. 272. See also *ibid.,* pp. 639 n. 4, 641 n. 4, 644, all relating to phylacteries.

73. A full bibliography of Saadiah's juridical writings is available in Malter's *Saadia Gaon,* pp. 163 ff., 344 ff., with some supplementary data by I. Werfel in *Rav Saadya Gaon,* ed. by Fishman, p. 651; and by S. Assaf in his *Tequfat,* pp. 185 ff. See also the next notes. In view of the bad state of preservation of most extant fragments—not to speak of the monographs totally lost—it is almost impossible to ascertain the time and circumstances of their original composition. Moreover, Saadiah himself kept on revising and reworking his tracts as he gained more knowledge and experience. Ibn Daud was clearly mistaken when he wrote that David ben Zakkai had "sent to Egypt and brought from there" Saadiah to head the academy of Sura, and that after his break with the exilarch Saadiah "went into hiding for about seven years, during which period he wrote all his books." See Ibn Daud's Chronicle in *MJC,* I, 65, and my remarks in *Saadiah Anniv. Vol.,* pp. 69 ff. During his controversy with Ben Meir in 921–22, Saadiah had already revealed expert familiarity with various domains of Jewish law. Moreover, only such expertness enabled him to gain sufficient recognition from the Babylonian academicians who allowed this recent arrival to assume the leadership in their struggle for supremacy with the Palestinian teachers. His appointment as *alluf* of the academy was likewise predicated principally on his juristic, rather than his philosophic or philological, training. It stands to reason that during the busy years of his gaonate, as well as during the melancholy interlude of his unfortunate struggle with David ben Zakkai, he probably could spare but little time and energy for his literary work, other than the composition of his main philosophic treatise and the writing of his numerous responsa. At best he could only pay some attention to the revision of his earlier

books. Apart from satisfying the general historical curiosity, a more exact knowledge of the dates and the nature of these juridical monographs might help to answer many another intriguing problem, such as the extent to which the Babylonian Talmud and its legal institutions had been accepted in Palestine and Egypt during the early tenth century.

74. See the excerpts from Saadiah's introduction to his "Book of Deeds," ed. by H. Hirschfeld in "The Arabic Portion of the Cairo Genizah," *JQR,* [o.s.] XVI, 295 (English), 299 (Arabic); and, more fully, in S. Assaf's "R. Saadiah's Book of Deeds" (Hebrew), in *Rav Saadya Gaon,* ed. by Fishman, pp. 65–99, 674–76, especially pp. 76 f., 82, 93, 97. Only through these excerpts has it become evident that the gaon formulated here a total of fifty-four private and ten public documents, not, as has long been deduced from a statement by Yehudah bar Barzillai, that there were forty and fourteen formulas, respectively. Evidently, in composing his own "Book of Deeds" (*infra,* n. 81) Yehudah no longer had before him a complete copy of the gaon's tract written less than two centuries earlier. See also the "Two Fragments from the Kitâb al-Šahâdât wa-l-Waṭâ'iq of Saadiah," ed. by A. Scheiber in *Acta Orientalia,* V, 231–47 (also with a Hebrew trans. of these fragments which supplement those previously identified in the Bodleian Library in *Tarbiz,* XXV, 323–30).
The punctiliousness with which deeds used to be written even in Jewish antiquity is evident not only from the ramified talmudic discussions on this subject, especially with reference to writs of divorce on whose exactitude depended the divorcée's right to remarry, but also from the numerous extant documents. See *supra,* Vol. I, pp. 111 ff., 347 ff., especially nn. 12–13; and among the latest archaeological finds, "Un Contrat juif de l'an 134 après Jésus-Christ," ed. by J. T. Milik, in *RB,* LXI, 182–90, with a "Note additionelle" thereon, *ibid.,* LXII, 253–54; the interesting comments, both linguistic and substantive, by J. J. Rabinowitz and the corrected text with English trans. by S. Abramson and H. L. Ginsberg, in *BASOR,* 136, pp. 15–19. From the Middle Ages, too, a host of actual deeds have reached us from both East and West. The Eastern documents (like the geonic formularies ed. by Aptowitzer; see *supra,* Chap. XXIII, n. 20) have largely been preserved in the Cairo and other genizahs, while the Western texts have mostly come from governmental archives such as the English chirograph offices or the so-called *Judenschreinsbuch* of Cologne. Important documents have also reached us from Vienna, and the Spanish archives. An excellent general selection from both historically authenticated documents and the various theoretical books of deeds of older and more recent vintage is given, with good comments, in A. Gulak's *Oṣar ha-sheṭarot* (Thesaurus of Deeds Current among Jews). But Gulak's fine introduction has merely scratched the surface. Among recent publications we need mention here only S. Assaf's edition of "Ancient Deeds from Palestine and Egypt" (Hebrew), *Yerushalayim* (annual), I, 104–17; and Z. Karl's analysis of deeds as parts of "The Types of Evidence in Jewish Law" (Hebrew), *Ha-Mishpaṭ ha-'ibri,* V, 105–88. An intensive study of Jewish deeds from their paleographic and chancery, as well as legal, aspects still is a major desideratum. See also *supra,* Chaps. XX, n. 38, and XXII, nn. 71, 81.

75. Saadiah's *K. al-Mawarit* (Book of Inheritance), ed. by J. Müller in Saadiah's *Oeuvres,* IX, 1–53, esp. pp. 9 f., 18 ff., 35 ff.; Naḥmanides' *Ḥiddushim* (Novellae) on the tractate Qiddushin (cf. M. Steinschneider's *Arabische Literatur,* p. 48 Nos. 3–4); Sherira Gaon's resp. in *Sha'are Ṣedeq,* III.3,11, fol. 17b (with the corrections

by E. E. Hildesheimer in his Hebrew essay, "Geonic Responsa," *Ozar Hachaim,* III, 97 ff.); and S. Abramson's ed. of "A Fragment of the Arabic Original of R. Hai Gaon's *Sefer ha-Meqaḥ ve-ha-Mimkar*" (Hebrew), *Tarbiz,* XX, 297 f., 305 f., 311 n. 50. Cf., however, the lengthy marginal note in *Sha'are Ṣedeq, loc. cit.,* showing that some later medieval jurists agreed with Saadiah's view, disputed by Sherira. We have no reason to doubt Hai's assertion that at the end of his "Book of Inheritance" Saadiah had a section dealing with the laws of sales. Hai himself merely objected to some statements as insufficiently clear and detailed. That Saadiah had undertaken to write a comprehensive treatise on all three methods of transfer of property is evident from his introduction to the "Book of Inheritance," the first section of that trilogy. We perhaps owe the preservation of the "Book of Inheritance" to its geometrical computations of how land was to be subdivided and other practical hints for busy judges. See *infra,* Chap. XXXV. The other two sections were more readily superseded by later juridical monographs and codes, and hence were less frequently copied.

76. See the bibliographical data furnished by Malter and Werfel (see n. 73); and the interesting quotation from Saadiah's Treatise on Pledges in a responsum by Alfasi reproduced in *Teshubot ha-geonim,* ed. by Harkavy, No. 454, pp. 238 (Arabic), 322 (Hebrew). See also Müller's brief comment in Saadiah's *Oeuvres,* IX, 146 f. No. 8; my remarks in *Essays on Maimonides,* pp. 205 f.; and *supra,* Chap. XXII, n. 77. We know nothing further about the "distinguished book" in which, according to Abraham ibn Ezra, Saadiah had written "decisive answers to the Sadducees [Karaites] who outlawed the Sabbath light." See Ibn Ezra's *Commentary* on Exod. 35:3, fuller recension, ed. by L. Fleischer, p. 337. Although B. Klar made a valiant effort to prove the existence of such a special semijuridical and semipolemical tract, the weight of evidence still favors the inclusion by the gaon of some such polemical excursus in one or another of his commentaries on the Bible, Mishnah, or Talmud. Cf. the arguments presented by Klar himself in his meritorious Hebrew essay on "R. Saadiah Gaon's Treatise *Ner Shabbat* [Sabbath Light]," reprinted in his *Meḥqarim ve-'Iyyunim,* pp. 242–58. This subject was so close to the gaon's heart that he reverted to it on many occasions. Cf. Zucker's observations and other data cited *supra,* Chap. XXVI, nn. 80–81. Perhaps one might resolve some of these difficulties by assuming that Saadiah's extensive commentary on the Mishnah, or his partial commentary on the Talmud, bore the title *K. As-Siraj* (Book of Light), similar to those by Ibn Gayyat and Maimonides (see *supra,* nn. 65, 69), and that this title was translated into Hebrew as *Sefer ha-Ner.* Subsequently someone confused the title of this work with an excerpt therefrom relating to the prohibition of kindling lights on Sabbath. Such an excerpt from the commentary on the tractate Shabbat might have circulated in a separate pamphlet, similar to Saadiah's *Tafsir abot mel'akhot* (Interpretation of the Main Kinds of Prohibited Work), mentioned in the Genizah book list published by W. Bacher in "Une Vielle liste des livres," *REJ,* XXXIX, 200 No. 28, 206; and Malter's *Saadia,* p. 162, and n. 366. Be this as it may, it seems more prudent to omit, for the time being, that tract from the list of Saadiah's juridical monographs.

77. See the relatively few fragments published by S. Assaf in his "Three Newly Detected Works by Samuel ben Ḥofni" (Hebrew), *Zikkaron* (Abraham Isaac Kuk Memorial Volume), ed. by J. L. Fishman, pp. 117–59 (giving excerpts from the books

on the Duties of Judges, Alimonies, and Guaranties); his *Mi-Sifrut ha-geonim,* pp. 1–16 (from the Book of Gifts); S. Abramson's "From R. Samuel ben Ḥofni's Books, I–II" (Hebrew), *Tarbiz,* XVII, 139–64; XVIII, 34–45 (from the Books on Writs of Divorce and on Laws of Acquistion of Property; with an additional fragment of the former, ed. by Assaf, *ibid.,* XVIII, 28–33); and other data furnished by Samuel's "Fihrist" (Booklist), published by G. Margoliouth in *JQR,* [o.s.] XIV, 311; and other lists in Mann's *Texts and Studies,* I, 643 ff.; and Assaf's essay in *KS,* XVIII, 272 ff.; all briefly summarized by Assaf in his *Tequfat,* pp. 194 ff. See also S. Abramson's bibliographical references, including some to manuscript photostats in his possession, in his comments on the list of books once owned by Joseph ben Jacob, in the essay, "R. Joseph Rosh ha-Seder [Head of an Order in the Academy]" (Hebrew), *KS,* XXVI, 72–95; with additional notes by N. Allony, *ibid.,* XXX, 445–46; and *supra,* Chap. XXII, n. 81. As pointed out by Assaf (in *Zikkaron,* p. 140), Chap. IV of Samuel's Book of Guaranties reveals the author's familiarity with Muslim law and his understanding also of the differences between the two legal systems.

78. Samuel ben Ḥofni's *Sha'are Berakhot* (Chapters on Prayers), reproduced from an Adler MS in Lewin's *Otzar ha-gaonim,* I, Part 2, pp. 65 ff.; and his *Sha'are Sheḥitah* (Chapters on Ritual Slaughtering), cited from the unpublished portions of Eliezer bar Joel's *Sefer Rabiah* in Aptowitzer's "From the Geonic Literature" (Hebrew), *Krauss Jub. Vol.,* pp. 104 ff., with two additional excerpts in the latter's *Mabo,* p. 256. Samuel's *Chapters on Prayers* greatly suffered from copyists. On occasion a marginal note indicating other geonim's opposition to Samuel's opinions crept into the text itself. For instance, his view that a single benediction sufficed for the performance of several successive acts of slaughtering was controverted by such an early gloss which misled Isaac Or Zaru'a into believing that it was Samuel who had insisted on separate benedictions for each act. See Lewin's ed., pp. 72 f. and his notes thereon. On the other hand, the "Remnants of R. Samuel ben Ḥofni's Book of Partnerships," published by I. Friedlaender in the *Festschrift David Hoffman,* Hebrew section, pp. 83–97 (in Arabic with a Hebrew trans.), are of questionable authenticity. The editor himself admits that the author's name is nowhere mentioned, while his arguments from other sources are quite inconclusive. Cf., however, the fragment, ed. by B. M. Lewin in *GK,* VI, 41–73. Samuel seems to have written in considerable haste (as is reflected in the aforementioned invitation to inquirers that he be asked to prepare for them extensive comments on talmudic tractates; see *supra,* n. 45), and often repeated himself. It is, therefore, doubly uncertain as to whether some of his works mentioned in later literature really were independent treatises or merely sections of more comprehensive works. For example, the excerpt from his "Book of Alimonies," reproduced in Lewin's *Otzar ha-gaonim,* VIII, Part 3, pp. 87 f., deals mainly with testamentary dispositions; it may be identical with his "Book of Wills," known by name only.

79. See S. Assaf's editions of fragments of Hai's *Sefer ha-Sheṭarot* (Book of Deeds); of his "Book of the Conduct of Judges" in *Madda'e ha-yahadut* (of the Hebrew University), II, 18 f., 90 f. No. 84, 104 ff. No. 108 (excerpts from a British Museum fragment of Yehudah bar Barzillai's *Sefer ha-Din* [Book of Law] compiled, according to the editor's hypothesis, by Abraham ben Isaac of Narbonne); his "Book of Loans" in *Tarbiz,* XVII, 28–31; and *supra,* n. 7. Some excerpts from the gaon's "Laws of Phylacteries" have been recovered from late transcripts, now in New York and

Oxford, and published by B. M. Lewin in *GK,* III, 72–75; IV, 10. Hai's *Mishpeṭe ha-Shebu'ot* (Laws of Oaths) has long been known in an anonymous Hebrew translation first published in Venice in 1602, and twice paraphrased and recast in poetic form (the passage quoted in the text is found in Part I, end). Equally prominent has been his *Sefer Meqaḥ u-mimkar* (Book of Purchase and Sale), published at the same time in the Hebrew translation by Isaac ben Reuben al-Barceloni (the quotation in the text relating to "fortified cities" is taken from Chap. xviii). But its nature has become far clearer through the publication of "A Fragment of the Arabic Original" by Abramson in *Tarbiz,* XX, 303 ff. See also M. Steinschneider's *Arabische Literatur,* pp. 38 ff.; and H. Hirschfeld's review thereof in *JQR,* [o.s.] XVI, 411.

Certain significant omissions in Hai's text, such as the laws governing the responsibility of guardians or depositaries, are now understandable in the light of Hai's own remark, "I do not need to explain these, for the Fayyumite, head of the academy may his soul rest in bliss [Saadiah], did it in a book he wrote on the laws governing pledges, which every interested reader should find satisfactory" (Abramson, p. 298). One may, indeed, look forward to the publication of further fragments by Abramson covering fully a third of the book and assembled from some thirty-three diverse manscripts. On the other hand, Abramson is convinced that the three small tracts (on Pledges, Conditions and Loans) appended to Hai's *Meqaḥ u-mimkar* in the Venice edition are not authentic, although they are based on some of the gaon's genuine statements. See his detailed examination of the first of these in his "*Sefer ha-Mashkon* [Book of Pledges] Attributed to R. Hai Gaon" (Hebrew), *Talpioth,* V, 773–80. See also other sources cited by Assaf in *Tequfat,* pp. 198 ff.; and more generally, A. Karlin's "R. Hai Gaon's Works and His Teachings in Civil Law" (Hebrew), *Sinai,* I, Nos. 12–13 (special 1000th anniversary issue in Hai's honor), pp. 677–92; and M. A. Amiel's analysis of "R. Hai Gaon's Juridical Method" (Hebrew), *ibid.,* pp. 495–506. Some additional information about Hai's halakhic monographs may be derived from his responsa, since he was often asked about the meaning of certain passages which appeared questionable to some inquirers. See S. Assaf's "On the Study of Hai Gaon's Halakhic Works" (Hebrew), *Ha-Zofeh,* VII, 277 f.

In passing we may mention here also a geonic monograph on Sabbath laws, fragments of which were published by J. N. Epstein in his "Geonic Halakhot" (Hebrew), *Tarbiz,* X, 119–34, 240. By closely following the sequence of the talmudic tractate Shabbat, however, this work may have belonged to the class of legal codes represented by Yehudai Gaon's and Simon Qayyara's works to be discussed presently. Obviously there were many easy transitions from one of these literary branches to another.

80. See S. Assaf's ed. of "Another Fragment of Samuel ha-Nagid's *Hilkhata Gibrata*" (Hebrew), *Tarbiz,* VI, 230–33, simultaneously denying Samuel's authorship of a similar fragment, ed. by J. Mann in his "Varia," *ibid.,* pp. 69–72. Both editors, however, had to resort to emendation of crucial phrases. Margulies's edition will also shed new light on the connection of this work with the Nagid's famous Introduction to the Talmud. See *supra,* n. 29. Only some sections of Isaac ibn Gayyat's *Halakhot kelulot* appeared under the title *Sha'are simḥah* or *Me'ah She'arim* (Chapters of Joy, or A Hundred Chapters), ed. with a detailed commentary, *Yiṣḥaq yerannen* (Isaac's Recital) by I. D. Bamberger. The former title has but recently become known from a booklist prepared by Joseph ben Jacob ben 'Ali, a twelfth-

century official of the Baghdad academy, himself a noted author and bibliophile. This list was published from an Adler MS by S. Abramson in his very informative essay on "R. Joseph Rosh ha-Seder" in *KS,* XXVI, 83 f., 87 nn. 47–48. Since Ibn Gayyat was frequently quoted in the later juristic literature, many of his statements in that work, as well as in his responsa, can be recovered from such later quotations. A valiant endeavor in this direction has been made by Z. Taubes in his *Lekutay* (Miscellany) by Ibn Gayyat, arranged in the sequence of the talmudic tractates. Thus far only one volume to the tractate Berakhot has appeared; it is provided by Taubes with an extensive commentary, *Eeyoon tsvee.*

Among other Spanish Jewish juridical monographs of the period was the aforementioned early "Book of Deeds," written in Lucena in 1021 and ed. by Assaf in *Meqorot,* pp. 100 ff. Cf. *supra,* Chap. XXII, n. 12. Another Spanish savant, Moses ben Jacob of Cordova, wrote a treatise on *Tefillin* (Phylacteries) which is no longer extant. Although rather ungraciously referring to it as a book which had "misled me and all the western people before me," Maimonides really explained R. Moses' error by a divergent reading of a talmudic source. Cf. his interesting reply to the scholars of Lunel in his *Resp.,* pp. 7 ff. No. 7, reporting also a noteworthy incident concerning the difference between the western and eastern phylacteries. Upon his arrival in Palestine, we are told, Moses Dare'i was "shown the statements of the ancient geonim and their proofs, whereupon he threw away his phylacteries and obtained others according to the order indicated here." On this misguided pseudo-Messiah, see *supra,* Chap. XXV, n. 66.

81. Yehudah bar Barzillai's *Sefer ha-'Ittim* (Book of Times), ed. in part with an extensive commentary by J. Schor, and his *Sefer ha-Sheṭarot* (Book of Deeds), ed. by S. J. Halberstam, have been quoted here in various contexts. See also the "Two Fragments Supplementing the *Sefer ha-'Ittim* by R. Yehudah bar Barzillai al-Barceloni," ed. from MS by J. L. Zlotnik in *Sinai,* VIII, Nos. 96–97, pp. 116–38. The extent to which Abraham ben Isaac of Narbonne's *Sefer ha-Eshkol* was indebted to Al-Barceloni's *Sefer ha-'Ittim,* is reviewed in some detail by S. Albeck in the introduction to his edition of the former work, I, 36 ff., 51 ff. On Abraham's unusual title *Ab bet din* (Father of the Court), see B. Z. Benedikt's observations in *Tarbiz,* XVII, 21 n. 19. Incidentally, while Albeck's edition offers an indubitably better text than the older edition by B. H. Auerbach, Auerbach's extensive commentary *Naḥal ha-Eshkol* has retained independent value. Albeck's accusation that Auerbach had committed many forgeries by inserting passages of his own making has been effectively disproved by H. Ehrentreu and J. Schor in their pamphlet, *Zidkath ha-Zaddik* (Correctness of the Righteous; includes a "Gutachten" by D. Hoffmann, exonerating the accused editor). See also *infra,* n. 130. H. Gross's older but still very useful biographical sketch of "R. Abraham b. Isaak, Ab-bet-din aus Narbonne," *MGWJ,* XVII, 241–55, 281–94; Abraham's *Resp.,* published in S. Assaf's *Sifran shel rishonim,* pp. 1–50; and, on the custumals written in the Provence, *infra,* n. 99.

82. Abraham ben David's *Ba'ale ha-nefesh* (Masters of the Soul), first published in 1602; Aaron ben Jacob ha-Kohen's *Orḥot ḥayyim* (Ways of Life; a legal manual), Part II, ed. by M. Schlesinger, p. 72. On Abraham ben David and his significant works in the fields of both jurisprudence and mysticism one may expect much new light from I. Twersky's forthcoming full-length biography. See *infra,* n. 106. Isaac ben Abba Mari of Marseilles, though consistently exploited by medieval and modern

students, has not yet received his deserved scholarly treatment. Only the first part of his *Sefer ha-'Iṭṭur* (Book of Word Separation of Scribes; a juridical manual), dealing with civil law appeared as early as 1608 in Venice. Parts II–III, devoted to ritual laws and holidays, which include also Isaac's youthful halakhic monographs on slaughtering and showfringes, appeared in 1860 with notes by S. Schönblum but without the necessary critical apparatus. Numerous lacunae could be filled in from extant manuscripts and quotations in later writings. See, e.g., the fragment published, on the basis of two manscripts, by A. H. Freimann in his "Supplement to the *'Iṭṭur* and the *Manhig*," *Festschrift Jakob Freimann,* Hebrew section, pp. 105–15. A mere listing of citations from geonic letters contained in this voluminous work (cf. S. Assaf's Hebrew "Index to the Geonic Responsa Cited in the Book *'Iṭṭur* by R. Isaac ben Abba Mari" in *Ha-Zofeh,* VI, 289–309) suffices to demonstrate the need of both a critical edition and a biographical investigation of the author's contribution to Jewish learning.

83. *Ma'aseh ha-Geonim* (Responsa and Decisions of Early Rhenish Rabbis), ed. by A. Epstein, pp. 52 ff. No. 61; and Epstein's general introduction, revised by J. Freimann, pp. x ff. Epstein expatiates here on his previous suggestion (in *MGWJ,* XLI, 298 ff.), that there had existed an earlier collection entitled *Ma'aseh ha-Makhir* of the Mayence school, contemporary with Rashi (it is so quoted, for instance, by Eliezer bar Nathan). See also the debate on this score between Epstein and S. Poznanski, in *MGWJ,* XLI, 456–60, 564–71. While Makhir, Gershom's brother, was personally more concerned with talmudic lexicography—his *Alpha Beta,* quoted by Rashi and the Tosafists, seems to have consisted mainly of a glossary of difficult talmudic terms with occasional translations into the current French idiom—his sons were strongly preoccupied with the juridical aspects of talmudic learning and geonic traditions. See, e.g., Rashi's reply to Nathan bar Makhir in his *Teshubot,* pp. 9 No. 15, 293 ff. No. 251; and the data discussed by A. Epstein in "Der Gerschom Meor ha-Golah zugeschriebene Talmud-Commentar," *Festschrift Steinschneider,* p. 136 n. 3.

84. The interrelations between the works from Rashi's school have long intrigued scholars. See esp. S. Buber's lengthy introduction to his edition of *Sefer ha-Orah* (Book of Light); H. J. Ehrenreich's briefer introduction to the *Sefer ha-Pardes,* reedited by him; J. Freimann's introduction to his edition of Rashi's *Siddur;* and more recently, I. Elfenbein's essays and textual editions relating to the theretofore unpublished *Sefer ha-Sedarim* (Book of Liturgical Orders)—all attributed to Rashi. See esp. Elfenbein's Hebrew essay in *Horeb,* XI, 123–56. Yehudah bar Barzillai's influence on the *Sefer ha-Orah* has long been recognized; it has even given rise to the theory that this work, too, had been compiled in Spain. More plausibly, B. Z. Benedikt suggested that its compiler lived in the Provence and was familiar with the works of both schools, as was, for instance, Abraham ben Isaac of Narbonne. Cf. Benedikt's "On the History of the Provençal-Jewish Center of Learning" (Hebrew), *Tarbiz,* XXII, 106 (cf. also his excursus, "Had Abraham ben Isaac of Narbonne Studied with Yehudah bar Barzillai in Barcelona?" probably to be answered in the negative, p. 109). On Simḥah of Vitry, see the analysis by S. Hurwitz accompanying his edition of the *Maḥzor Vitry* (Vitry Prayer Book for Holidays), mainly useful through its lengthy lists of authorities quoted in that large volume; and A. Epstein's rather negative critique of that edition in his review in *REJ,* XXXV, 308–13. Despite the great progress in our knowledge of the geonic and North African

writings of the period, to which these Western schools were deeply indebted, many extremely knotty literary problems still await solution. But, from the standpoint of legal evolution, there emerges the distinct picture of a ramified legal doctrine and practice cultivated by generations of competent and dedicated Western students, who even before the main schools of Tosafists had transplanted much of the Eastern lore to the shores of the Rhine and the Seine. Cf. also Tchernowitz's *Toledoth ha-Poskim,* II, 14 ff.; and *infra,* Chap. XXXI, nn. 82–84.

85. *Teshubot ha-geonim,* Lyck ed., fol. 30 f. No. 98, attributed to Hai Gaon (sometimes wrongly ascribed to Nissim bar Jacob, see *ibid.,* fol. 44a; on the general attitude of the geonim to Aggadah, see *infra,* Chap. XXVIII, n. 29); Sherira's responsum in *Ḥemdah genuzah,* fol. 1a, and in other geonic collections; Ibn Sa'd's *Biographien,* II, Part 2, p. 117, 1; and Jephet ben 'Ali's *Commentary* on Daniel 3:2, ed. by D. S. Margoliouth, p. 33. The authenticity of Sherira's resp. was impugned by Harkavy in the intro. to his ed. of *Teshubot,* pp. x ff.; and defended by Tchernowitz in his *Toledoth ha-Poskim,* I, 23 n. 4. For similar utterances of other geonim see the passages cited *supra,* Chap. XXIII, nn. 19–20. The glorification of rabbinic studies included in the introduction to Simon Qayyara's *Halakhot gedolot* appears in a longer and a shorter version in the usual editions of that work (in the "Spanish" version, ed. by Hildesheimer, pp. 3 ff.). It was reedited from Oxford and Leningrad MSS and provided with a detailed commentary by A. (V.) Aptowitzer in his *Derashah bi-shebaḥ ha-torah* (A Homily in Praise of the Torah; reprinted from *Sinai,* IV, Nos. 41–42, pp. 178–220). The homily on Deut. 17:11 is fully documented here from tannaitic and midrashic sources (p. 8 n. 44). It may also be mentioned that Bukhari's "scientific" method of selection, often questioned by Western scholars, has found an ardent defender in the Muslim convert, Muḥammad Asad (formerly Leopold Weiss). See the intro. to his English trans. of Bukhari's *Ṣaḥiḥ,* Vol. V. On the role of tradition within the general development of Muslim law, see the illuminating chapters in I. Goldziher's *Vorlesungen über den Islam,* 2d ed., pp. 30 ff.; Lammens's *Islam,* pp. 65 ff., 82 ff.; and esp. J. Schacht's critical exposition of the *Origins of Muslim Jurisprudence.* See also E. J. Jurji's "Islamic Law in Operation," *AJSL,* LVII, 32–49, and other literature mentioned *supra,* n. 4.

86. Cf. *supra,* Chap. XXVI. Perhaps it is no mere coincidence that the oldest code of Muslim jurisprudence extant today, namely the *Madjmu'a* by Zaid ben 'Ali (d. 740) is attributed to the founder of the Shi'ite sect of Zaidites. Cf. E. Griffini's ed. of the *Corpus juris di Zaîd ibn 'Ali;* available also in a partial French trans. by G. H. Bousquet and J. Berque entitled *Recueil de la loi musulmane de Zaîd ben 'Ali.* Not that the sectarians of either faith necessarily had chronological priority. There were Sunni juridical summaries before Zaid, although these are no longer extant, just as in their diverse ways Aḥai of Shabḥa and Yehudai Gaon preceded 'Anan. Yet the flow of "Books of Commandments," written by almost each and every Karaite leader, certainly had no parallel among the Rabbanites.

87. *Teshubot,* Lyck ed., fol. 17 f. No. 45 (here is assembled an entire series of queries submitted to Yehudai together with his brief answers; of course, we do not possess the original texts of these replies which may have been slightly more wordy); Pirqoi ben Baboi's statement in Ginzberg's *Ginze Schechter,* II, 558 f. Ben Baboi's high appreciation of Yehudai's personality and good judgment was also

shared by later geonim. Even Western inquirers once mentioned a custom "from the days of our master, light of the world [perhaps intended to underscore the contrast with his physical blindness], R. Yehudai, the saintly and pure teacher." Cf. *Ḥemdah genuzah,* fol. 3a No. 15. According to one of Sherira's responsa, Yehudai's successors had stated "We must not do what R. Yehudai had not done." See *Teshubot,* Lyck ed., fol. 16b No. 43. The frequent contention, however, that Yehudai vigorously combated 'Anan's propaganda (see, e.g., B. M. Lewin's "Genizah Fragments" [Hebrew], *Tarbiz,* II, 391 ff.) is chronologically impossible, if the gaon died in 763 and 'Anan's schism did not begin until 767. See *supra,* Chap. XXVI, n. 1. But neither date is absolutely certain, and Yehudai may well have combated similar sectarian trends antedating 'Anan.

88. See S. Sassoon's edition, from a private MS discovered by his father in Yemen, of Yehudai Gaon's *Sefer Halachot pesuqot* (Book of Legal Decisions); and A. L. Schlossberg's edition, from an Oxford MS, of *Hilkhot Re'u* (Laws of "See") together with the editors' introductions. The "Palestinian Laws concerning Maimed Animals" have all the earmarks of a later interpolation. To begin with, they are often at variance with the Babylonian Talmud, as may be seen from the parallels drawn by the editor in his notes, pp. 193 ff. They show, on the other hand, some striking similarities with the laws reported by Eldad ha-Dani, whose deviations from the Babylonian law had startled his North African hosts. Cf. M. Schloessinger's observations in *The Ritual of Eldad ha-Dani,* pp. 50 ff., and those by J. N. Epstein in his "Palestinian Lore" (Hebrew), *Tarbiz,* II, 308 ff. Not surprisingly, some of the regulations reported by Eldad appeared in the later Western literature with the curious attribution to *Hilkhot Ereṣ Yisrael* (Laws of Palestine).

89. Hai's responsum in *Teshubot ha-geonim,* ed. by Harkavy, p. 111 No. 232. In another responsum Hai declared that R. Simon "did not comprehend the motivations of R. Yehudai" and other masters. Cf. the text published by S. Assaf in his ed. of *Teshubot ha-geonim,* 1942, p. 44. Incidentally, here was found the first authentic confirmation that Simon was a native, or resident, of Baṣra, on whose importance as an intellectual as well as commercial center for Jews and Arabs alike, see *supra,* Chap. XVII, n. 21; and Assaf's introductory note, pp. 38 f. Otherwise, we know practically nothing about Simon and his early training or the reasons which had prompted him to undertake his major compilation.

90. Almost from the very outset there seems to have existed much confusion concerning the authorship and text of *Halakhot gedolot.* While the Pumbedita geonim correctly attributed them to Simon Qayyara, many of their colleagues of Sura not only viewed the work written in their own bailiwick (Baṣra was under Sura's jurisdiction) with much greater favor, but actually attributed it to Yehudai Gaon and ascribed the *Pesuqot* to Simon. Cf. A. Aptowitzer's, at times overingenious, arguments in his "Responsa Wrongly Attributed to R. Hai" (Hebrew), *Tarbiz,* I, Part 4, pp. 75 ff. This confusion greatly increased in the later Middle Ages, when the French and German scholars almost invariably quoted from a shorter version of the *Halakhot gedolot,* roughly comparable to the first printed edition, Venice, 1548 (since reprinted several times and provided with detailed commentaries), whereas the Spaniards seemed to know only the enlarged version, greatly altered by numerous interpolations and emendations. The latter largely resembled the

text more recently edited from a Vatican MS by J. Hildesheimer. Nor was this division quite sharp and consistent. For instance, Isaac ben Abraham of Narbonne, who in his *Sefer ha-Eshkol* leans heavily on the geonic materials accumulated by the Barcelona erudite Yehudah bar Barzillai, quotes almost exclusively from the shorter version, whereas Jacob Tam and others know of the existence of the enlarged "Spanish" recension as well. At the same time the copy of the "German" version used by the careful Eliezer bar Joel ha-Levi was quite different from that of our printed editions; many of his quotations are indeed known from none of our texts. Cf. the extensive list in Aptowitzer's *Mabo,* pp. 230 ff. To make that confusion even more confounded, Abraham ibn Daud, in this case deprived of the reliable guidance by Sherira's *Epistle,* dates the composition of Simon's *Halakhot gedolot* in 740–41 by both the Seleucidan era and that of Creation. He therefore considers Yehudai the borrower from Simon's work. See his Chronicle in *MJC,* I, 63.

It is small wonder, then, that modern scholars, too, have all through the nineteenth century conducted a rather inconclusive debate about the respective priority of Yehudai and Simon, and about the nature of their works. The last two generations, however, have been greatly impressed by the arguments advanced by A. Epstein in his penetrating Hebrew "Essay on the Book *Halakhot Gedolot,*" *Ha-Goren,* III, 46–81, according to which Yehudai composed his shorter volume of *Pesuqot* about 760 while Simon, greatly indebted to him, followed with his compilation of *Gedolot* about 825. This theory received additional, though as yet not quite decisive support, from the more recent publications by Sassoon and Margulies. See *supra,* n. 88; *infra,* n. 91. Further progress may now be expected only from additional finds, such as the Genizah fragments whose readings are found in neither version. See for instance, B. Lewy's succinct dissertation, *Halakot Gedolot, Genizah Fragmente;* and the text included in the Kaufmann collection and analyzed by A. N. Z. Roth in *Sura,* II, 280 ff.

In any case, there is great need for a truly critical edition of both versions, which would not only utilize the existing MSS and prints, but also reexamine critically the innumerable quotations from Simon's work scattered in the writings of the great jurists from the tenth to the thirteenth centuries. See the examples given in Ginzberg's *Ginze Schechter,* II, 101, 109. In the meantime, we must bear in mind that, despite the numerous interpolations, our texts also reveal important gaps. For it is unlikely that an author attempting to summarize the entire legal system should have omitted from consideration such basic legal problems as those affecting the marriage contract (the absence of its pertinent formula was already noted by Eliezer bar Joel), vows, the *nazirate,* and the separation of the priestly portion of dough (*ḥallah*), all of which are included in the introductory enumeration of biblical commandments. See *infra,* n. 104. On the other hand, Simon's apparent or real indebtedness to various statements in younger sources need not stem from later interpolations. For example, his enumeration of prophets who had appeared to the nations before the revelation of the Torah, which Hildesheimer found only in the *Seder tanna'im* (p. 632) composed about half a century after Simon's work, was probably known to him from older traditions, both written and oral. But he doubtless used Aḥai's *She'eltot* quite extensively. While mentioning Aḥai's name only on four or five occasions, he apparently cited the latter's work more than a hundred times. See the list appended to Epstein's study in *Ha-Goren,* III, 55, 74 f.; Hildesheimer's ed. of *Halakhot gedolot,* p. 140; Ginzberg's *Geonica,* I, 106 f.; and Aptowitzer's strictures thereon in his "Untersuchungen zur gaonäischen

Literatur," *HUCA,* VIII–IX, 374 ff. Similarly, Simon seems to have made more extensive use of the Palestinian Talmud than any other Babylonian teacher, even from among the pro-Palestinian scholars of Sura, although in his *'Inyanim,* pp. 19 ff., S. Poznanski was able to identify only nine certain quotations from that source—a figure, but slightly raised by subsequent researchers. On Simon's likely use of the Palestinian *Sefer ha-Ma'asim,* see Hai's aforementioned (n. 71) suggestion with its fairly derogatory undertone.

91. See M. Margulies's edition of the *Halakhot qeṣubot* (Adjudicated Laws). Because of the frequent divergences here from the Babylonian law, both talmudic and geonic, the reflection of certain local customs, and some peculiar linguistic forms, the editor suggested its composition during the ninth century in southern Italy. Dismissing all but its strictly legal deviations, E. E. Hildesheimer has argued for its outright Palestinian origin, while C. Tchernowitz has altogether explained away at least some of these deviations from the Babylonian Talmud. Cf. Hildesheimer's "Introduction to *Halakhot qeṣubot* Attributed to R. Yehudai Gaon" (Hebrew), *Sinai,* VII, Nos. 80–81, pp. 271–87; and Tchernowitz's *Toledoth ha-Poskim,* I, 112 ff. Perhaps some of the difficulties might be obviated if we assume that the author lived in tenth-century Byzantium. Although we know very little about the intellectual pursuits of Byzantine Jewry in that early period, it appears that, long before the great twelfth-century revival of Jewish learning among both Balkan Rabbanites and Karaites, both communities had lived a rich cultural life. With respect to the Karaites, see esp. Z. Ankori's pertinent observations in *Baron Jub. Vol.,* pp. 1–35, and his dissertation, *Karaites in Byzantium,* Chaps. III and VIII. The very rise of a powerful Karaite movement is testimony of an intellectual fermentation in the general community as well, even if its documentation, like that of most other contemporary Jewish centers, was totally ignored by the Palestinians and Babylonians, and hence has since disappeared. The presence of Byzantine students at least at Hai's academy is attested by the gaon himself. See his responsum sent to Kairuwan, in *Teshubot ha-geonim,* ed. by Harkavy, pp. 105 f. No. 225; another addressed to Abraham bar Moses ibn Jama' and published by B. M. Lewin in *GK,* II, 20 f. (here, too, *Romi* probably refers to Constantinople); and, more generally, J. Starr's data in *The Jews in the Byzantine Empire,* pp. 60 f., 180 f. No. 122. Of course, southern Italy too was within the general Byzantine cultural sphere.

92. Yeshu'a ben Yehudah's *Sefer ha-'Arayot* in D. B. Markon's *Texte und Untersuchungen,* p. 149; Isaac ben Abba Mari's *Sefer ha-'Iṭṭur, passim;* and, more generally, B. M. Lewin's introduction to his compilation of excerpts from *Metibot* (Subjects). The discussion on the use of a mortgaged object is to be found *ibid.,* pp. 69 f. No. 49, with reference to B. M. 67b, and the geonic sources analyzed in Assaf's *Tequfat,* pp. 271 f. While probably the large bulk of *Metibot* is irretrievably lost, it appears that it originally followed the sequence of the Talmud, rather than any independent system. According to Lewin, at least its earlier version had originated from the academy of Sura; it may even have been written by a son of Sar Shalom Gaon (848–53). However, Lewin's main argument from a responsum by Sar Shalom (in A. Marx's revised version) and a quotation by Isaac ben Abba Mari (pp. xvii, 24 No. 16, 49 f. No. 17) has been effectively controverted by Assaf in his review of Lewin's ed. in *KS,* XI, 163 f. Cf. also Lewin's comparison between "Metibot and Alfasi" (Hebrew), *Alummah,* I, 105–13. There has also been much confusion, still

far from dissipated, between that work and the so-called *Sefer Ḥefeṣ* (Book of Satisfaction, rather than Book by Ḥefeṣ), on which see *infra,* n. 105.

93. The *Sefer ha-Miqṣo'ot* (Book of Legal Decisions) has more recently also emerged from age-old obscurity owing to S. Assaf's compilation of all known excerpts. This comprehensive code of laws has been preserved mainly in scattered quotations by medieval German rabbis. Hence the deadlock among modern investigators as to the identity of its author (its attribution to Ḥananel having long been rejected) and the place of its origin, although there is generally little doubt about its mid-eleventh-century composition. Most scholars have argued for either North Africa or Germany, but the difficulties in either case are staggering. Perhaps it is not too venturesome to suggest again that this book, too, was written somewhere in the Byzantine Empire. This environment would best explain the author's relative unfamiliarity with Babylonian and, to some extent, also with Palestinian law, and its availability to the rabbis of both Egypt (as attested by the Genizah fragments) and Germany, with both of which countries the Byzantines maintained direct contacts, but not to those of Spain. Also the requirement of special mourning for martyrs for the faith (p. 10 No. 16 on M.Q. 25a) would seem quite appropriate to a country which so frequently had forced the Jews to adopt Christianity. The very glorification of martyrdom was germane to a Byzantine background even more than to that of medieval Germany before 1096. See also, more generally, Tchernowitz's *Toledoth ha-Poskim,* I, 78 ff., 112 ff.

94. Yehudah Halevi's elegy, *Harim ke-yom Sinai,* in his *Diwan,* ed. by Brody, II, 100; in his *Shire,* ed. by Zemorah, IV, 114 No. 6 (also in the forewords to many editions of Alfasi). B. M. Lewin has suggested that the "wisest men" in the last two stanzas referred to Joseph ibn Megas, the poet's colleague in Alfasi's academy, now its head. Joseph was, indeed, called a wise man by Alfasi himself, according to Ibn Daud's Chronicle. See *MJC,* I, 76, and Lewin's note on Jawitz's *Toledot,* XI, 240. Moses ibn Ezra, too, glowingly extolled Alfasi's piety, intelligence, and literary gifts. See esp. his *K. al-Muḥadhara,* v (*Shirat Yisrael,* trans. by B. Z. Halper, p. 73). The sudden impact of Alfasi's personality may perhaps best be understood by his transmission, to the eager Spaniards, of the best fruits of Kairuwanese learning (he may have himself studied under Ḥananel) and through it also of much geonic lore. We know little about Alfasi's birthplace, but it seems to have been identical with the Kalla of the Beni-Ḥammad in the province of Constantine, Algeria. Although the city was really important only during the years 1014–68, it may have embraced a Jewish community in the preceding century as well. See V. de Saint Martin, *Nouveau dictionnaire de géographie universelle,* III, 16. Whatever pride Spanish Jewry took in its native land—and Moses ibn Ezra was a most ardent local patriot also in the intellectual sense—did not militate against their welcoming with open arms new arrivals from older seats of learning. See *infra,* Chap. XXX, n. 19.

95. See Alfasi's *Halakhot* on Ketubot, x (fol. 93ab), No. 359, in the Vilna ed., fol. 51b. Here, as well as fols. 36b f., 54a f., are also reproduced the Arabic excursuses in two Hebrew translations. One, first published in Abraham ben David's *Temim de'im,* may have been prepared by Yehudah ibn Gayyat or Abraham bar Isaac the Physician, both of whom are recorded as translators of Alfasi's Arabic texts in the

Hamburg MS reproduced in H. Brody's introduction to Meshullam bar Moses' *Sefer ha-Hashlamah,* pp. xv f. See *infra,* n. 101. The other was produced by one Maṣliaḥ of Galilee and Solomon ha-Ma'arabi (of Morocco) and first included in the *Resp.* by Menahem Azariah da Fano. On Alfasi's and his contemporaries' general attitude toward the Palestinian Talmud and the geonim, see *supra,* nn. 25–26; and the numerous examples assembled in Tchernowitz's *Toledoth ha-Poskim,* I, 131 ff., which is, however, corrected in many significant details in B. Z. Benedikt's unduly sharp review in *KS,* XXV, 164–76. At times Alfasi dared even to depart from the ordinary meaning of a talmudic text and to reach a different legal decision. Such instances caused his medieval admirers to strain their ingenuity in seeking to harmonize both statements. Cf., however, I. H. Weiss's defense of some of Alfasi's teachings impugned on this score, in his *Dor dor,* p. 251; and Tchernowitz, p. 143 n. 4.

96. See Alfasi's *Halakhot* on Shebu'ot, II, in the Vilna ed., fols. 1b–7a. The designation of "Little Talmud" was given Alfasi's code already by such early successors as Ibn Daud in his Chronicle (*MJC,* I, 76), and Aaron bar Joseph ha-Levi in his Commentary on Alfasi, Berakhot, and Ta'anit entitled *Pequdat ha-leviim* (Numbering of Levites), ed. with a commentary by S. and N. Bamberger, p. 11. Cf. B. Z. Benedikt's remarks in his "Notes on the Biography of R. Isaac Alfasi" (Hebrew), *KS,* XXVII, 119–20. Except for responsa, no other work by Alfasi is extant or even definitely established. Apart from a questionable Prayer Book for the Day of Atonement, only a volume of "Chapters on Oaths" (*Sha'are Shebu'ot*) is mentioned by Eliezer bar Joel and, probably from him, by later medieval authorities. However, this was very likely but a case of mistaken identity, that book having been written by another Spaniard, Isaac bar Reuben al-Barceloni, who, on his part, merely paraphrased here in Hebrew a similar Arabic work by David ben Saadiah of the earlier eleventh century. Cf. the text in the Vilna ed. of Alfasi on Shebu'ot, Appendix, fol. 9b ff.; and Aptowitzer's *Mabo,* pp. 286, 373.

97. The existence of many variants in manuscripts of Alfasi's work during the twelfth century is well attested by Abraham ben David, Abraham ben Isaac, and especially Naḥmanides. On one occasion the latter gleefully reported that he had been able to consult a copy written in Cordova in 1123, that is only twenty years after the author's death. See his *Milḥamot Adonai* (Wars of the Lord) on Alfasi, Yebamot xv (fol. 118a), No. 152, in the Vilna ed., fol. 44b. On Alfasi's pupil Ephraim, see esp. B. Z. Benedikt's review of Tchernowitz's *Toledoth* in *KS,* XXV, 164 ff.; also his additional note on the "Birth Place and Surname of R. Ephraim, Alfasi's Pupil" (Hebrew), *ibid.,* pp. 229–30, suggesting that Ephraim was born in Alfasi's native place of Kalat al-Ḥammad and that his family name was Ibn Abi al-Ragan; he was also named after his birth place, Ephraim ha-Kal'i. See also *infra,* n. 98.

98. See the introduction by Zeraḥiah ha-Levi, together with an Aramaic poem, reprinted in the Vilna and other editions of Alfasi at the beginning of Berakhot. Zeraḥiah's *Ma'or* appeared in two parts, respectively called the "Great Book of Light" on the third and fourth orders of the Mishnah, and the "Small Book of Light" on Berakhot and the second order. Zeraḥiah mentions that he had used the earlier comments by Ephraim, but had found them totally unsystematic and disjointed.

He had incorporated, therefore, Ephraim's relatively few correct observations in the proper places of his own work, with due acknowledgement. That these were not quite so few has been shown by B. Z. Benedikt in his "R. Ephraim's Book of Supplementation to Alfasi's *Halakhot*" (Hebrew), *KS,* XXVI, 331 n. 39. Despite a number of rather forced arguments, Benedikt has made a case for Ephraim's intention to write not a series of polemics against his teacher, but rather to fill in many gaps in the master's presentation. Benedikt overstresses, however, Zeraḥiah's provincial bias in his approval or disapproval of Ephraim's opinions and his dependence on decisions current in the French scholarly circles which had long taken deep roots in his native Provence. See the detailed documentation, *ibid.,* p. 329 n. 38.

99. Naḥmanides' *Milḥamot Adonai* (Wars of the Lord), reprinted in the Vilna and other editions of Alfasi's *Halakhot;* Isaac ben Abba Mari's *Me'ah she'arim* (Hundred Chapters) on Alfasi's third and fourth order; Jonathan ben David's *Commentary* on Alfasi, 'Erubin, both likewise in the Vilna edition; and his similar *Commentary* on the tractate Berakhot, ed. by M. Y. Blau. It should also be noted that much of that polemical material had only become known in recent decades. Even Abraham ben David's important reply to Zeraḥiah's "Great Book of Light" (published under the title of its recurrent *incipit, Katub sham,* It is Written There) is still available only in a rather unsatisfactory mimeographed reproduction of a single MS in M. Z. Ḥasidah's (Bocian's) *Hassegullah,* I–V, Nos. 1–46 (on most tractates of the fourth, third, and second orders; often refers to his earlier writings of thirty or forty years before). Similarly, the more outwardly than intrinsically acrimonious exchange of the *Dibre ha-ribot* (Matters of Controversy) was published from another unique MS by B. Drachman. Incidentally, Abraham did not hesitate to attack outright a commentary on Zebaḥim written by Rashi (perhaps in an earlier recension), or by one of his disciples. "He who will examine the matter will find many mistakes in his statements." Cf. the small fragment of both the commentary and Abraham's strictures in Ḥasidah's *Hassegullah,* V, No. 47. On his part, Naḥmanides admitted that he had been unduly harsh in his comments on the "Great Book of Light," and promised to be more objective in his forthcoming comments on the "Small Book." Evidently Zeraḥiah's own change of tone had its effect. See also the older but still very informative biographical studies by J. Reifmann, *Toledot Rabbenu Zeraḥiah ha-Levi;* H. Gross, "R. Abraham b. David aus Posquières," *MGWJ,* XXII, 337–44, 398–407, 446–59, 536–46; XXIII, 19–29, 76–85, 164–82, 275–76; and in *Gallia judaica,* pp. 447 ff.; A. Marx in "R. Abraham b. David et R. Zerahya ha-Lévi," *REJ,* LIX, 200–224; LXI, 133–35; I. Bergman in "R. Abraham ben David, Author of *Hassagot*" (Hebrew), *Talpioth,* III, 470–74; IV, 810–27 (unfamiliar with the work of his predecessors); and esp. I. Twersky's forthcoming full-length biography of *Abraham ben David.* Naḥmanides' replies to both men will be treated more fully in connection with similar other works of the thirteenth century.

Rather than discouraging other scholars, these sharp exchanges greatly stimulated their interest in Alfasi's Code and gave impetus to ever renewed efforts to explore its ramifications and refine its results. Only a small segment of Jonathan of Lunel's commentary on Alfasi has thus far appeared in print. See S. K. Mirsky's sketch, "R. Jonathan of Lunel, Defender of Maimonides and His Commentary on the Mishnah and Alfasi" (Hebrew), *Sura,* II, 242–66; and A. Freimann's aforementioned "List of the Early Commentaries" (n. 48), often referring to Jonathan's works which, although frequently quoted in the later Middle Ages, still are extant only in manuscript. See also S. Assaf's "R. Jonathan ha-Kohen of Lunel and the First Recension of Rashi" (Hebrew), *Tarbiz,* III, 27–32. Various "Fragments of Commentaries and Books of Supplements of Alfasi's Halakhot" are discussed in B. Z. Benedikt's Hebrew essay in *Tarbiz,* XXI, 165–84. The author argues here plausibly that the fragments, respectively published by Assaf in *Abhandlungen Chajes,* Hebrew section, pp. 29 ff.; and by Ginzberg in *Ginze Schechter,* II, 382–94, were not, as their editors thought, commentaries on talmudic tractates, but rather on their paraphrases by Alfasi. On Ginzberg, II, 371–74, see, however, *supra,* n. 38. See also, more generally, Benedikt's informative Hebrew studies on "The History of the Provençal Center of Jewish Learning," *Tarbiz,* XXII, 85–109; and "Contributions to a Compendium of Provençal Scholars," *KS,* XXVII, 237–48 (with special reference to Samuel ben David of Lunel).

100. See Maimonides' *Resp.,* pp. 318 f. No. 353; and his *Hilkhot ha-Yerushalmi* (The Laws of the Palestinian Talmud), ed. by S. Lieberman. This responsum was written after the completion of the Code, Maimonides referring to his older epitome of the Palestinian Talmud to which he wished to add an extensive "explanation." That epitome itself must have been written, at least in part, during the early period of his work on the *Commentary* on the Mishnah or soon after, as is assumed by both Lieberman, in his very informative introduction, and M. Lutsky in his comments on the MS which he considers an autograph, despite certain differences between it and the other known Maimonidean autographs (p. 69). See also B. Z. Benedikt's review of Lieberman's volume in *KS,* XXVII, 329–49, which, however, reads more like a lawyer's brief marshaling arguments against the positive attribution of this work to Maimonides than a dispassionate airing of reasons for and against it. This review has not shaken the present writer's conviction that the weight of evidence favors Maimonidean authorship, although the jurist-philosopher clearly did not consider this work ready for circulation. There is no question that, as in the case of his *Commentary* on the Mishnah and his Code, Maimonides continued revising his *Hilkhot ha-Yerushalmi* in later years. From that responsum it would appear that he did not wish to divulge it to the public until he would also complete his accompanying "explanation"—a task he evidently never accomplished. On the generally far greater utilization of the Palestinian Talmud by Maimonides than by Alfasi, see Tchernowitz's *Toledoth ha-Poskim,* I, 140 ff. (by no means invalidated by Benedikt's strictures in *KS,* XXV, 174); as against the data analyzed by J. L. Fishman in his "Maimonides' Life, Works and Activities" (Hebrew), in *Rabbenu Mosheh ben Maimon,* ed. by him, Part 1, pp. 150 ff. This difference did not escape Abraham ben David's eagle eye. In his stricture, for instance, on Maimonides' rule concerning the prohibition of reciting *Shema'* in odoriferous places, Abraham observed: "This teacher usually relies on the Palestinian Talmud, but here he refrains from doing so." See his "objection" to *M.T.,* Qeri'at shema' III.6. See also the related controversy between Abraham, Zeraḥiah, Naḥmanides, and other scholiasts on Alfasi, Berakhot III, No. 77, Vilna ed., fols. 15b f.; and Jakob Horovitz's plausible denial of an alleged Maimonidean attack on Alfasi in his "Zum Mischne Thora und dem Mischnakommentar des Maimonides," *MGWJ,* LXXXIII, 356 ff., part of an as yet unpublished work, *Streifzüge durch den Mischne Thora und den Mischnakommentar des Maimonides.*

101. Meshullam bar Moses' *Sefer ha-Hashlamah* (Book of Supplementation). Only the following parts have thus far appeared in print: on Neziqin, ed. with a commentary *Torat ha-hashlamah* by J. Lubetzki; on Ta'anit and Megillah, ed. by M. Grossberg, in the appendix to his edition of Jacob of Vienna's (or Vienne's) *Sefer Peshaṭṭim u-perushim* (Erklärungen zum Pentateuch), pp. 235–72; and on Berakhot, ed. by M. Schochor (from Grossberg's copy of a Hamburg MS), and provided with an introduction, notes, and corrections by H. Brody. Lubetzki's introduction and comments are relatively the fullest and most informative. In his judiciously restrained admiration for Alfasi, Meshullam may have followed Ephraim, whose very work of supplementation he probably emulated, if B. Z. Benedikt's aforementioned suggestion should be borne out by further researches. See *supra*, n. 98. A close comparison of the extant fragments of, and quotations from, Ephraim's work with the extant portions of Meshullam's book may, indeed, shed new light on both authors.

102. Isaac ben Samuel's comment cited in Azulai's *Shem ha-gedolim*, ed. by Benjacob, fol. 43c No. 287 (following Conforte); and Samuel bar Meir's *Tosafot* on Alfasi, only partially extant in MS. See M. Steinschneider's *Verzeichnis der hebräischen Handschriften . . . Berlin*, p. 3 No. 6. An interesting critical comment on Alfasi's summary of the lengthy discussion in Giṭṭin IX, No. 563 (Vilna ed., fols. 47a ff.) is quoted from Eliezer bar Joel's MS in Aptowitzer's *Mabo*, p. 289. Aptowitzer also points out that, except for two brief references to Alfasi in Eliezer bar Nathan's *Sefer Eben ha-'Ezer* (Nos. 450, 681; cf. S. Albeck's intro. to his ed. of that work, p. xx), the first German scholar to mention Alfasi was the latter's grandson, Eliezer bar Joel. This relative aloofness of German scholars, contrasting not only with the Provençals but also with the northern Frenchmen, was probably owing more to difficulties of communication than to any aversion on principle.

103. Makkot 23b–24a. In his introduction to *A Volume of the Book of Precepts by Ḥefeṣ b. Yaṣliaḥ*, pp. 1 ff., B. Halper has correctly pointed to several tannaitic sources, showing that the figure of six hundred and thirteen commandments was much older than R. Simlai. A similar conclusion was independently reached by Y. M. Guttmann in his searching *Beḥinnat ha-miṣvot* (Examination of the Commandments according to Their Number, Order, and Subdivisions), mainly referring to Maimonides' *Book of Commandments* and his critique of Simon Qayyara's enumeration. See *infra*, nn. 104, 109, 111. But the tannaitic sources, too, date only from the second century, when Judaism was confronted by the Pauline and gnostic challenges. See the aforementioned study by B. W. Helfgott, *The Doctrine of Election in Tannaitic Literature*. For apologetic purposes it sufficed to emphasize the general immutability of Jewish law by symbolically attaching it to equally immutable astronomic and physiological laws. Had that division, however, been principally used for internal pedagogic purposes, as suggested by L. Blau in *Soncino-Blätter*, III, 113–28 (see *supra*, Vol. II, p. 421 n. 51), it would have been impossible for teachers to leave open the specific enumeration of these commandments. Once such an enumeration had been introduced into schools in the second or third century, it would never have been dislodged in later generations, and there would have been no room for the medieval uncertainties. Cf. also S. Greenberg, "The Multiplication of the Mitzvot," *M. M. Kaplan Jubilee Volume*, pp. 381–97,

which includes (p. 387 n. 37) an interesting communication by L. Ginzberg analyzing some earlier researches in this field; and the Hebrew essays by A. Kaminka in his *Kitbe biqqoret historit* (Writings on Historical Criticism: Selected Essays), pp. 139 ff.; and D. Margolith, "The Number of Commandments and that of Limbs and Veins in the Body" (Hebrew), *Sinai,* XX, No. 239, pp. 96–102.

104. Simon Qayyara's *Halakhot gedolot,* Introduction, Warsaw ed., 1874, pp. 9 ff. (with A. S. Traub's comments); ed. by Hildesheimer, pp. 8 ff.; Saadiah's *Siddur,* pp. 156 ff. (poem, *Et Adonai Elohekha tira,* Fear the Lord Thy God), 184 ff. (*Azharot,* beginning *Aṣal yom ha-lazeh,* God Has Reserved This Day); Ibn Gabirol's *Shemor libbi ma'aneh* (Guard Thy Speech, My Heart) in his *Shire,* ed. by Bialik and Rawnitzky, III, 135 ff. No. 99; IV, 72 ff.; Maimonides' *Book of Commandments,* Introduction, ed. by Bloch, p. 5; in the Hebrew trans., ed. by C. Heller, p. 2a. See *infra* n. 105. The fifteenth-century jurist David ibn abi Zimra suggested that, in his attack on the authors of poems of "warnings," Maimonides had Ibn Gabirol in mind. See his *Resp.,* III, fol. 53a No. 645. However, there must have existed many others, in fact many more than are extant today or were extant in twelfth-century Egypt, who to Maimonides' taste followed Simon's pattern too closely. In fact, the sage of Fusṭaṭ was indubitably mistaken when he assumed that the authors of these poetic creations necessarily followed Simon's computation, rather than the other way around. Although adhering to the regnant misconception that, unlike the rabbinic homilists, "the authors of liturgical poems did not invent such data but merely reproduced them from some other sources," Y. M. Guttmann has seen clearly that some of these "poems of warning" antedated Simon. See his *Beḥinnat ha-miṣvot,* pp. 8 ff.; and, on the greater credit owing to the independent hermeneutic creativity of the liturgical poets, *infra,* Chap. XXXI.

Maimonides was not alone, however, in objecting to these poetic enumerations. In fact, some scholars, especially Bible commentators, often voiced their resentment over the violent forcing of Scripture into the straitjacket of one or another computation. See, e.g., Yehudah ibn Bal'am's *Commentary* on Deut. 30:2, ed. by S. Fuchs, p. xxii. Abraham ibn Ezra, himself a poet of distinction, likewise objected to the exegetical recklessness of the composers of *azharot.* Cf. his *Yesod Mora* (Grundlage der Gottesverehrung), II, end, in M. Creizenach's ed., pp. 17 ff. (Hebrew), 42 ff. (German). Cf. also Naḥmanides' Introduction to his *Hassagot* (Strictures) on Maimonides' *Book of Commandments* (see *infra,* n. 112); and, more generally, I. Elbogen's summary, "Asharot," *EJ,* III, 508–12.

These poetic enumerations so impressed even the Samaritans that they, too, began writing poems of that genre. See M. Gaster's textual ed. and analysis of "Die 613 Gebote und Verbote der Samaritaner," *Festschrift . . . des Jüdisch-Theologischen Seminars Fraenckelscher Stiftung,* II, 393–404, Hebrew section, pp. 35–67; and M. Haran's "Maimonides' Computation of the Commandments in a Samaritan Poem" (Hebrew), *Eretz Yisrael,* IV, 160–69. This entire problem of the liturgical use of the poetic enumerations of commandments will be discussed *infra,* Chap. XXXI nn. 70 f.

105. Saadiah's *Siddur,* pp. 157 ff., 165; Simon Qayyara's *Halakhot gedolot,* ed. by Hildesheimer, p. 9; the list of the twenty-one (of a total of twenty-five, or twenty-four) categories, published from an Arabic MS by A. Neubauer in his "Miscellanea liturgica, II: Azharot on the 613 Precepts," *JQR,* [o.s.] VI, 705 ff. (in another version

by S. Schechter in *Saadyana,* pp. 42 f.), and reproduced in Hebrew translation with corrections in D. Z. Baneth, "The Beginning of R. Saadiah's Book of Commandments" (Hebrew), in *Rav Saadya Gaon,* ed. by Fishman, pp. 378 ff. Saadiah's philosophic classification is attributed, in the heading of Schechter's *Saadyana,* to Samuel ben Ḥofni's explanation of his predecessor's *Reshut* (Prayer for Permission) introducing liturgical poems. See A. Marx's remark in Ginzberg's *Geonica,* I, 179. Denied by Halper (in the intro. to his ed. of Ḥefeṣ, pp. 20 f.), it has largely been upheld by Baneth, p. 371 n. 33. Admittedly, however, Samuel ben Ḥofni himself had a different enumeration. On the other hand, the fragment of Saadiah's own introduction to his work (Baneth, pp. 372 ff., in Arabic and Hebrew) is less explicit. One may merely guess that Saadiah expatiated here on the general principles of the commandments along lines later fully developed in his great philosophic work (*Beliefs,* Book III). Throughout the book he also probably supplied reasons for his grouping of commandments and even for his decisions in controversial cases. But one can hardly gain therefrom any real inkling of the contents of the work. Fuller illumination may be expected only from the publication of the text itself. In his *Tequfat,* p. 193, S. Assaf stated that he had located in Oxford, Cambridge, and New York many Genizah fragments, "adding up to a large portion of the book." It is to be hoped that these will soon be edited by a competent student of geonic law.

Such publication would mark a substantial advance in the grand debate on Saadiah's enumeration of commandments which has been carried on for several generations. In fact, the aforementioned didactic poem (in Saadiah's *Siddur,* pp. 156 ff.) has so intrigued scholars that, in the very midst of the First World War, a Warsaw admirer of Saadiah's work, J. F. Perl (Perla), found the necessary leisure to publish an exhaustive commentary on it in four huge volumes, covering a total of 2,060 folio pages, under the somewhat misleading title of *Sefer ha-Miṣvot le-R. Saadiah Gaon* (Saadiah Gaon's Book of Commandments). Although the two poems give us a fair idea of Saadiah's classification, only the fuller text of his Book of Commandments might reveal many as yet unsuspected connections with Ḥefeṣ' and Maimonides' similar works. Saadiah probably wrote it in the same period (before 928) as the two poems, in which, by an intricate device, he revealed his title of *alluf* of the academy. See also Tchernowitz's brief analysis of Saadiah's classification in *Toledoth ha-Poskim,* I, 90 f.; A. Karlin's rather sketchy review of "The Law in the Teachings of R. Saadiah Gaon" (Hebrew) in *Rav Saadya Gaon,* pp. 428–41 (showing the comparatively slight influence exerted by Saadiah on later geonim and jurists); and other literature cited *infra,* n. 170; and Chap. XXXI, n. 71. Nor can one expect much help from a comparison with contemporary Muslim law codes which followed a standardized traditional, rather than logical, order paralleling the conservative Jewish codifiers' preference for the order of talmudic tractates. See the interesting table in W. Heffening's "Zum Aufbau der islamischen Rechtswerke," *Kahle Jub. Vol.,* pp. 102 f.

106. Ḥefeṣ ben Yaṣliaḥ's date of 980–85 is based on J. Mann's suggestion in *Tarbiz,* V, 280. B. M. Lewin, who succeeded in assembling sixty-three quotations from the "Book Ḥefeṣ" in later medieval works, attributed them glibly to Ḥefeṣ ben Yaṣliaḥ, the only prominent scholar bearing that name. See his edition of *Metibot,* pp. 119 ff., and the introduction thereto, pp. xxxi ff. Even more vigorously he denied here that *Metibot* stemmed from the same pen, rather postulating, in consonance with his general theory of Suranic pro-Palestinism, that the latter

was written by some member of the academy of Sura. See *supra,* n. 92. He has not, however, invalidated Aptowitzer's penetrating, if at times overspeculative, arguments in favor of the identity of both books. More questionable is their composition by Ḥefeṣ ben Yaṣliaḥ during his sojourn as Ḥushiel's pupil in Kairuwan. See Aptowitzer, "The Book Ḥefeṣ and the Book Metibot" (Hebrew), *Tarbiz,* IV, 127–52; and *R. Chuschiel und R. Chananel.* In fact, a closer examination of Ḥefeṣ ben Yaṣliaḥ's *Book of Precepts* reveals many basic differences in approach and methods from those in either treatise. Perhaps an Eastern book endeavoring to conciliate the divergent Babylonian and Palestinian traditions circulated for a time under some other name in the Franco-German schools, and, when its title had been forgotten, it was renamed the "Book of Satisfaction" in a way appealing to local tastes. Certainly it is noteworthy that, while Ḥefeṣ' *Book of Precepts* is cited exclusively by Spanish scholars, the "Book Ḥefeṣ" seems to have been known only north of the Pyrenees.

107. Ḥefeṣ, cited in Yehudah bar Barzillai's *Commentary on Yeṣirah,* ed. by Halberstam, pp. 55 f., and reproduced with an English trans. by Halper in his ed. of Ḥefeṣ, pp. 31 ff.; Baḥya's *Duties of the Heart,* Introduction, ed. by Yahudah, p. 7; in the Hebrew trans. by Yehudah ibn Tibbon, ed. by Zifroni, p. 8; in Hyamson's English version, I, 7 f.; Ibn Bal'am's *Commentary* on Judges 20:28, ed. by Poznanski, p. 24. Remarkably, unlike Maimonides, Ḥefeṣ does not quote Hamnuna's statement in support of his selection of the two first commandments. Of course, such a reference might have been omitted by Yehudah bar Barzillai in his summation (*toref debarav*) of Ḥefeṣ' evidently long and involved argument. But it is also possible that the Deuteronomic passage he quoted, "Know this day, and lay it to thy heart, that the Lord, He is God in heaven above and upon the earth beneath; there is none else" (4:39), suited Ḥefeṣ' philosophic purposes much better.

108. Ḥefeṣ' *Book of Precepts,* ed. by Halper, pp. 180 f. (Arabic), 255 f. (Hebrew), with reference to M. Niddah v.6; b. 45b; and Halper's introductory observations, pp. 53 ff. The passage here quoted rumbles on, adding few new ideas. Incidentally, as a fine linguist and lexicographer, Ḥefeṣ frequently offered explanations of talmudic terms which were subsequently quoted by such experts as Ibn Janaḥ and Ibn Bal'am. See the passages cited in full by Halper, pp. 103 ff.

109. Maimonides' *Book of Commandments,* Introduction, ed. by Bloch, p. 5; ed. by Heller, p. 2a. See also his aforementioned *Resp.,* pp. 225 f. No. 240. On the strong similarities between Maimonides' and Ḥefeṣ' treatment of numerous commandments, see the detailed comparison in Halper's introduction, pp. 59 ff. Of course, our knowledge of contemporary letters available to both jurists is so limited that we can confidently speak of indebtedness only in the case of direct verbal borrowings. Even then each might have unperturbedly lifted the same phrase or sentence from some common source. These problems may remain unresolved even if some day Ḥefeṣ' own introduction should turn up. Ever since Halper, it is generally assumed that this introduction was very lengthy, Halper postulating some two hundred pages, or about one fifth of the book. But the only supporting evidence consists in a brief reference to it in the text and the assumption that Ḥefeṣ' criticism of Simon Qayyara, mentioned by both Ibn Bal'am and Maimonides, must have been included in that introduction. See Halper's ed., pp. 50 ff., 170 (Arabic), 249 (Hebrew). All this is possible. However, in quoting Ḥefeṣ' exposition of the first two commandments, Yehu-

dah bar Barzillai writes as if they had appeared "at the beginning of his work." This would imply that only a brief introduction preceded that exposition, unless the Barcelona rabbi referred here to the book of his informant rather than to that by Ḥefeṣ. On the unsatisfactory state of the MS underlying the edition of Yehudah's own *Commentary,* see the editor's observations, pp. ix f.; his text, pp. 55 f.; and Halper's trans. of Ḥefeṣ, pp. 30 ff.

110. Maimonides' *Book of Commandments,* end (Prohibition No. 365), ed. by Bloch, p. 334; ed. by Heller, p. 136ab; and *passim.* Maimonides did not really reverse himself when, in his Code, he urged the reader to try to understand the reasons of each precept. "Wherever you can find a reason for it, do so" (*M.T.* Temurah IV.13). Once again Solomon is adduced as the example of a wise man who really understood most of the reasons underlying the biblical precepts. Ultimately, Maimonides himself allotted the final section of his philosophic work to an investigation into the reasons underlying the main commandments. There is no real contradiction in these statements. The Bible may indeed have abstained from furnishing the reasons, because it did not wish to encourage circumvention. But every thoughtful person could, indeed should, in Maimonides' opinion, speculate on the divine intentions and satisfy his own craving for knowledge and intelligent behavior. This distinction should have been clearer to the modern authors mentioned in the next note.

Nor is it at all surprising that Maimonides' exclusion of certain hermeneutic derivatives from Scripture from his total of six hundred and thirteen commandments did not enjoy unanimous acceptance among his successors. See Y. J. Neubauer's detailed analysis in his *Ha-Rambam 'al dibre soferim* (Maimonides on Rabbinic Enactments). This volume includes also a Hebrew translation of his German essay to be mentioned presently.

The Arabic edition of Maimonides' *Book of Commandments* from three MSS by Bloch is fairly adequate, but the available texts of the Hebrew trans., far more popular and historically effective, are not altogether satisfactory. Already in the Middle Ages no less than three independent Hebrew versions, by Abraham ben Ḥisdai ha-Levi, Moses ibn Tibbon, and Solomon ben Joseph ibn Ayyub, were circulating. Copyists and early printers, moreover, handled these texts with even greater freedom than usual, and sometimes corrected one through the other. See M. Steinschneider's data in *Die hebräischen Uebersetzungen des Mittelalters,* pp. 926 ff. C. Heller used the Munich MS of Ibn Tibbon's translation as a basis for his critical edition, but he also took cognizance of a MS of Ibn Ayyub's version and other materials. See the intro. to his ed., pp. 4 ff. Some variants from the Arabic text may be owing to Ibn Tibbon's use of a copy of the original sent to him by Abraham Maimonides, who, at times, had corrected the text in the light of subsequent inquiries. Cf. Ibn Tibbon's foreword, *ibid.,* p. 19; and Abraham's *Resp.,* p. 70 No. 64. The very title has not reliably been transmitted to posterity, even the Hebrew designations appearing in the two forms mentioned in the text. Cf. J. Neubauer's "Zum ursprünglichen Titel von Maimunis Buch der Gebote und seiner Geschichte," *MGWJ,* LXXXI, 105–19, 242. But this was not altogether unusual. Saadiah's similar work is quoted in later literature under four sufficiently different titles to give rise to a debate whether they referred to the same book. See D. Z. Baneth's observations in *Rav Saadya Gaon,* ed. by Fishman, pp. 365 f. Similarly, Maimonides (ed. by Bloch, pp. 5, 55) quotes Ḥefeṣ' work consistently as the *K. al-Shara'i',* but Ibn Bal'am cites it under slightly different designations in his *Commentaries* on Deuteronomy (30:20) and Judges

(20:28), respectively. See the citations in Halper's ed., pp. 104 f.; and *supra,* nn. 104, 107.

111. Maimonides' *M.T.* Ishshut 1.2, and Joseph Karo's and other exegetes' comments thereon; his *Resp.,* pp. 161 ff. No. 166, with Freimann's notes. Abraham Maimuni's report is not included in his own *Resp.,* however. These and other methodological difficulties underlying the Maimonidean classification have long been noticed by students of rabbinic law. They are also clearly illustrated by A. Hillwitz's more recent well-intentioned, but rather desperate, attempt to define seven basic principles in "The Order of the Commandments according to Maimonides" (Hebrew), *Sinai,* X, Nos. 114–15, pp. 258–67; or that by J. L. Moinester to reconcile the differing enumerations in the Book of Commandments and the Code in his *Seder ha-miṣvot le-Rambam* (Maimonides' Classification of the Mitzvoth) by showing that basically the former followed the sequence of the biblical books, whereas the Code was organized in accordance with the tractates of the Mishnah. See also J. K. Mikliszanski's analysis of "The Motives of the Commandments in Maimonides' Teachings," in *Maimonides: His Teachings and Personality,* ed. by S. Federbush, Hebrew section, pp. 85–97.

112. Maimonides' *Book of Commandments,* Introduction, Roots I–II, ed. by Bloch, pp. 9 ff.; ed. by Heller, pp. 3 ff. (with the editor's notes); and Naḥmanides' lengthy stricture thereon in his *Hassagot* (Objections) on the former, printed with many editions of the Maimonidean work. Cf. also the comprehensive commentary thereon, *Margenita taba* (Good Pearl) by Aryeh Leb Zisel Horowitz, largely devoted to the defense of the Maimonidean position; Simon bar Ṣemaḥ Duran's mediating efforts in his *Sefer Zohar ha-raqi'a* (Splendor of the Skies; on the 613 Commandments according to Ibn Gabirol), fols. 6 f.; and, more generally, I. Herzog's "Maimonides as Halachist," in *Moses Maimonides,* ed. by I. Epstein, pp. 144 ff. Herzog's promise to deal monographically with this significant controversy has, to the present writer's knowledge, not yet been implemented. Incidentally, Naḥmanides' work, too, often appeared in medieval letters under different titles. See Neubauer's observations in his *Ha-Rambam, passim.* Understandably, some of Naḥmanides' objections depended on different readings in either the original sources or the Hebrew version of the Maimonidean treatise at his disposal. That his copy did not simply follow Ibn Tibbon's or Ben Ḥisdai's translation, but rather substantially differed from all the Hebrew recensions now known, has been demonstrated by Heller, esp. pp. 8 f. See also, in general, F. Rosenthal's detailed analysis of "Die Kritik des Maimonidischen 'Buches der Gesetze' durch Nachmanides," in *Moses ben Maimon,* ed. by J. Guttmann *et al.,* I, 475–95.

113. Maimonides' *Resp.,* pp. 334 f. No. 368. Maimonides insisted that the very sequence of his enumeration, for instance with respect to positive commandments Nos. 134 and 141, "is just so." Even such a great admirer of Maimonides as Joseph ibn Kaspi, however, cryptically pointed out that the master's aforementioned contention that only sixty positive commandments obligated everybody at all times should be reduced further. See his *Sefer ha-Musar* (Guide to Knowledge), reproduced with an English trans. in I. Abrahams's collection of *Hebrew Ethical Wills,* I, 136 f.

114. Remarkably, though many lesser halakhic works, including Maimonides' own *Book of Commandments* and *Responsa,* have appeared in critical editions, his *M.T.,*

that climactic achievement of medieval Jewish jurisprudence, still circulates in long accepted rather than critically edited texts. The task is, of course, aggravated not only by the great popularity of the work and the ensuing availability of many manuscripts and early editions, but also by the author's constant revisions. If we accept S. Gandz's "Date of the Composition of Maimonides' Code" (*PAAJR,* XVII, 1–7), the first recension of the first part of *M.T.* was completed in 1176. But in numerous letters, particularly those addressed to the sages of Lunel, France, in 1199, the author protested that the original text had since been revised by him, or else that it had been despoiled by copyists. See esp. his *Resp.,* pp. xliii ff., lviii ff., 2 No. 2, 306 No. 340. Hence even an autograph text need not be the author's last word. See also M. M. Kasher's remarks in his "Rambam [Maimonides] in Print and in Manuscripts" (Hebrew), *Sinai,* IX, Nos. 104–9; supplemented by J. L. Zlotnik's brief illustrations in his "Toward a Critical Edition of Maimonides' Mishneh Torah" (Hebrew), *ibid.,* X, No. 111, pp. 76–81; and those supplied by P. Birnbaum in the introduction to his abridged and vocalized ed. of *M.T.,* p. xliv. See also the bibliographical studies by I. Joel, "The Usual and the Correct Text of Maimonides' *Mishneh Torah*" (Hebrew), *KS,* XIX, 140–43; supplemented by his brief remarks "On the Yemenite Version of Maimonides' *Mishneh Torah*" (Hebrew), *ibid.,* XX, 52; R. Wischnitzer, "Les Manuscrits à miniatures de Maïmonide," *Gazette des Beaux-Arts,* LXXVII, 47–52; and J. Avida (Zlotnik), "The History of Jewish Printing and the Prints of Maimonides' *Mishneh Torah*" (Hebrew), *Sinai,* XVII, No. 205, pp. 307–10.

Among more recent attempts to utilize manuscript resources for obtaining better texts, one may mention S. Rawidowicz's edition of the *Sefer ha-Madda',* the first book of *M.T.* (a second volume containing a detailed commentary has not appeared); M. Hyamson's edition of the first two books from a Bodleian manuscript with an English trans.; and S. Atlas's edition from a Bodleian autograph of *Qeṭa'im* (A Section from Yad ha-Ḥazakah). See S. Assaf's Hebrew review of the latter work (most copies of which were destroyed in the bombing of London on October 10, 1940), in *KS,* XVIII, 150–55. Very useful also are the briefly annotated English translations of the *Yale Judaica Series* of Yale University of which J. J. Obermann served as chief editor. The eight volumes hitherto published include the translation of the last book, dealing with the laws of "Kings," by A. M. Hershman who, having utilized the Oxford MS, expatiated on the "Textual Problems of Book Fourteen of the *Mishne Torah,*" in an essay under this title in *JQR,* XL, 401–12. Some of these problems may now be reexamined in the light of data pertaining to that book in the Stockholm and Budapest MSS reviewed in Hebrew essays by J. D. Wilhelm and A. Scheiber, respectively, in *KS,* XXIX, 145–48; XXXI, 152 (citing in full the anti-Christian passage untouched by censors). Somewhat less helpful have been the variants from the Trivulzio MS (in J. Hamburger's possession), ed. by J. Feigenbaum under the title, *Shinnuye nusḥa'ot* (Abweichungen des gedruckten Textes der Jad Hachasaka . . . von einer Handschrift aus Anfang des XIV. Jahrhunderts).

There is a plethora of secondary literature, some of genuinely high quality. Of the older writings various essays in *Moses ben Maimon,* ed. by Jakob Guttmann *et al.,* still stand out. See L. Blau, "Das Gesetzbuch des Maimonides historisch betrachtet," *ibid.,* II, 331–58. The octocentennial celebrations of Maimonides' birth in 1935, and the more recent 750th anniversary of his death in 1955, also gave rise to a number of significant publications. See in particular, the American *Maimonides Octocentennial Series* (with more popular contributions by Ahad Haam, A. Marx, C. Tchernowitz, and I. Husik); *Essays on Maimonides,* ed. by S. W. Baron; the

Anglo-Jewish papers on *Moses Maimonides,* ed. by I. Epstein; the Palestinian memorial volume *Rabbenu Moshe ben Maimon,* ed. by J. L. Fishman; the collection of Hebrew and English essays on *Maimonides,* ed. by S. Federbush; and the special issues of numerous periodicals, such as *JQR,* XXV, No. 4; *MGWJ,* LXXIX, No. 2; *REJ,* XCIX; *Tarbiz,* VI, No. 2; *M'oznayim,* III, Nos. 4–5; *Yearbook CCAR,* XLV, 355–418; and *Sinai,* XVIII, No. 217, pp. 201–434. An important Spanish collection of essays on Maimonides, including H. V. Besso's extensive bibliography of works by and on Maimonides, was to have been issued by the Instituto de las Españas of Columbia University, but this volume fell victim first to the Spanish Civil War and then to the Second World War and never saw the light of day. Cf. also the numerous additional entries, principally concerned with Maimonides as a philosopher and scientist, *infra,* Chaps. XXXIV–XXXVI; and some recent essays on the contemporary significance of Maimonides' work, such as those by S. Atlas, "The Contemporary Relevance of the Philosophy of Maimonides," *Yearbook CCAR,* LXIV, 186–213; and E. Mihaly, "Reform Judaism and Halacha," *ibid.*, pp. 214–26; as well as the numerous systematic investigations during many generations, such as M. Minkowich's recent *Meḥqarim ba-mishpaṭ ha-talmudi* (Studies in Talmudic Law Based on the Code of Maimonides).

115. Maimonides' *M.T.*, Introduction. In "Das Verhältnis Maimuni's zu den Geonen," in *Moses ben Maimon,* ed. by Guttmann *et al.*, I, 332–410, A. Schwarz has analyzed sixty-eight passages in *M.T.* containing express references to geonic views. In no less than twenty-two of these Maimonides disagreed with his predecessors. That many of these disagreements arose in the area of civil law is fully understandable in the light of the constant adjustments imposed upon the Jewish communities by the new economic transformations. Many similar instances could be quoted from Maimonides' other works and particularly from his *Resp.* which show that in some cases (for instance, No. 240), he had changed his mind and, after first subscribing to the older views, found sufficient reasons to reject them. Even more frequent were the cases of both agreement and disagreement in Maimonides' innumerable tacit borrowings from the older literature. See some additional data in my study of "The Historical Outlook of Maimonides" in *PAAJR,* VI, 86 n. 168.

116. The much-debated introductory section of *M.T.* has been illuminatingly reexamined in S. Rawidowicz's " 'Mishneh Tora' Studies (I–III)" (Hebrew), *Metsudah,* VII, 125–95. In a previous Hebrew essay, "Maimonides Studies, I," Rawidowicz had also analyzed the term *'Madda'* in the first book of the Maimonidean Code, *ibid.*, II, 132–43. In his opinion, this term is not to be translated by "knowledge," but by something more akin to the Arabic *I'tiqad* (religious conviction), just as Saadiah's *K. al-Amanat wal-i'tiqadat* is rendered in Hebrew by *Emunot ve-de'ot* (Beliefs and Opinions). On the complexities of this Arabic term, however, see D. B. Macdonald's "I'tiḳad," *Shorter EI,* p. 189; and the numerous discussions of Saadiah's title mentioned *infra,* Chap. XXXIV, n. 6.

117. Maimonides' *Commentary* on the Mishnah, Introduction, ed. by Hamburger, pp. 30 ff. In his *Book of Commandments* he had, in fact, already announced the general outline of his Code. Among modern scholars, A. Schwarz devoted the bulk of his monograph *Der Mischneh Thorah. Ein System der mosaisch-talmudischen Gesetzeslehre,* to the analysis of structure. More briefly, B. Ziemlich reviewed anew the "Plan

und Anlage des Mischne Thora," in *Moses ben Maimon,* ed. by Guttmann *et al.,* I, 248–318; while I. E. Herzog did the same in his Hebrew essay on "The Sequence of Books in the *M.T.,*" in *Rabbenu Mosheh ben Maimon,* ed. by Fishman, pp. 257–64. Even "The Number of Chapters in the 'Mishneh Torah' of Maimonides" followed the author's design, according to J. Avida (Zlotnik) in his recent Hebrew essay under this title in *Sura,* II, 267–75. Very pertinent observations on these problems are also included in Tchernowitz's *Toledoth ha-Poskim,* I, 222 ff., which show, however, that on many occasions even this radical innovator failed to depart from the biblical or talmudic sequence.

118. *M.T.* Sheḥitah x.12–13; 'Akum xi.16, and other passages. On Maimonides' astronomic studies and their impact on his views concerning the calendar, see *infra,* Chap. XXXV. See also L. Nemoy's data on "Maimonides' Opposition to Occultism" (Hebrew) in *Harofé Haivri,* cited *infra,* Chap. XXXVI, n. 17. To be sure, behind his decision not to amplify the *ṭerefot* on medical grounds may have loomed his personal experience that some patients given up by doctors had nevertheless recovered. Hence, scientific findings about an animal's impending death did not appear to him certain enough to overrule tradition. But in less obvious cases he gave serious consideration to the physiological effects of death-causing blemishes, as in some of his replies to the sages of Lunel and Montpellier, and to others. See his *Resp.,* pp. 85 ff. Nos. 88–91; in the latter he actually disregarded an overt Mishnah. In other contexts, too, he approached medical problems pragmatically. In the same chapter ('Akum xi.11) in which he so sharply denounced all forms of sorcery and demonology, he admitted that even on a Sabbath one was allowed to apply verbal charms to a patient bitten by a scorpion or a snake, "in order to give him peace of mind and to strengthen his heart, although it [such a remedy] is quite useless." None of these decisions, however, despite their external scientific motivations, shocked Western scholars so much as the rigid application to legal problems of his opposition to corporeal conceptions of God or the human soul. These teachings seemed to many readers to imply outright denial of the possibility of physical resurrection—an implication which not only aroused the ire of Abraham ben David, but, notwithstanding the inclusion of the belief in resurrection in the Maimonidean credo, was also to play a major role in the protracted anti-Maimonidean controversy of the following century.

119. See the interesting anonymous letter recently published by A. S. Halkin in "In Defense of Maimonides' Code" (Hebrew), *Tarbiz,* XXV, 418 (Hebrew), 424 f. (Arabic). The originality of Maimonides' interpretation of scriptural passages quoted in support of his legal decisions is evident in almost any chapter. Cf. the full list in S. A. (H. S.) Neuhausen's *Torah or le-ha-Rambam* (Bible Quotations in the Code of Maimonides).

120. See especially J. N. Epstein's searching investigation of "Mekhilta and Sifre in Maimonides' Works" (Hebrew), *Tarbiz,* VI, 99–138; L. Finkelstein's "Maimonides and the Tannaitic Midrashim," *JQR,* XXV, 469–517; M. M. Kasher's *Me'ah halakhot be-Mishneh Torah* (Hundred Laws in the *Mishneh Torah* Derived from R. Simon ben Yoḥai's *Mekhilta* on Exodus Unavailable to Us); and from another angle, B. M. Lewin's "Halakhic Midrashim and Maimonidean Decisions Arranged in the Sequence of the Bible" (Hebrew), *Rabbenu Mosheh ben Maimon,* Part 1, pp. 101–45

(publishing from New York, Jerusalem, and Leningrad MSS three fragments pertaining to parts of Leviticus). See also A. I. Bromberg's *Meqorot le-pisqe ha-Rambam* (Sources of Maimonides' Decisions), Vol. I, which offers data on both the talmudic sources of selected laws in *M.T.* and quotations therefrom in later medieval letters. But very much more remains to be accomplished.

121. Maimonides' unfamiliarity with Rashi's *Commentary* has long been noted. Remarkably, even his son Abraham seems to have known about it only through inquiries addressed to him by outsiders. See the latter's *Resp.*, ed. by Freimann, p. 9 No. 3 (dated in 1208). Moses Maimonides had frequent occasion to complain of the malevolent objections raised by the Baghdad scholars, for whose learning he evinced little admiration. In one of his replies to the sages of Lunel, he stated that the passage of his Code incriminated by them had also been questioned by the heads of the Babylonian academy "with slight arguments which could not possibly be doubtful to you, but they had no perception of your penetrating queries." See his *Resp.*, p. 54 No. 57. More generally, the jurist-philosopher complained to another correspondent, Joseph ha-Ma'arabi, that all his opponents seemed "to suffer from the same disease, namely whenever one of them finds some of my statements, whether general or specific, at variance with a statement by a gaon or commentator, he takes it for granted that I have erred." See "Maimonides' Responsum to His Pupil Joseph ha-Ma'arabi," ed. by A. H. Freimann with a Hebrew trans. by D. Z. Baneth, in *Lewin Jub. Vol.*, pp. 36 ff. Even more sharply, Maimonides denounced the majority of his detractors in a letter to his beloved disciple, Joseph ibn Shime'on, as envious evil men, confused, fantasy-loving tyros, or narrow-minded, ultraconservative pietists. See that famous letter, in Baneth's ed. of his *Iggerot*, pp. 49 ff., and Baneth's remarks thereon, pp. 31 ff.

122. Benjamin's *Massa'ot*, pp. 3 f. (Hebrew), 3 f. (English); Maimonides' Epistle to Phinehas ben Meshullam of Alexandria in his *Qobeṣ*, ed. by Lichtenberg, I, fol. 26ab No. 140. In this letter written toward the end of his life, the sage of Fusṭaṭ admitted that, on several occasions when challenged by an inquirer, he himself had been unable speedily to locate the source of his decision. "What should other people do?" In his contemplated revision he wished to supply at least the less obvious sources not easily identified by the treatment of that subject in a particular talmudic tractate. More detailed errors which he had interveningly corrected are mentioned in his letters to Lunel reproduced in his *Resp.*, pp. 2 No. 2, 87 No. 90, 306 No. 340, and elsewhere. As a matter of record Maimonides kept on revising statements in all his works to the end of his life. According to Abraham Maimuni, he and his father had discussed one of the propositions formulated in the *Guide*. "I have already asked my father of blessed memory that question, but at that time received no answer. He delayed it until further detailed reflection, but there was not enough time." Cf. Abraham's *Resp.*, p. 141 No. 96; and *supra*, n. 100.

Obviously, Abraham ben David belonged to none of the three categories of carping critics denounced by Maimonides. The codifier himself unwittingly expressed his admiration for the keenness of his opponent's strictures, when he so highly praised the quality of the Lunel inquiries, many of which had verbatim reproduced Abraham's objections. Cf. the sixteen passages listed by Freimann in his introduction to Maimonides' *Resp.*, p. xliv. Probably Jonathan ben David and his associates, torn between their loyalty to their teacher Abraham and their admiration for the new Code, tried to ascertain Maimonides' reaction to some of these objections known to them from oral or written exchanges with the Provençal master. Unfortunately, just as Maimonides was unaware of the ultimate source of some of these queries, so was Abraham unable to take a stand on the codifier's defense of his views. It took four letters from Lunel spread over as many years to induce the sage of Fusṭaṭ to reply to these searching questions. Cf. the notation, probably by Maimonides himself, published by S. M. Stern in his "Maimonides' Correspondence with the Scholars of Provence" (Hebrew), *Zion,* XVI, 18–29. His reply, apparently dated in 1199, arrived about a year after Abraham's death. Otherwise we might have had a repetition here, on a higher plane, of the *Dibre ha-ribot,* that remarkable exchange of juridical views between him and Zeraḥiah. Certainly, the area of disagreement between the two men, though not as large as it often appeared to the popular mind, was far more extensive than is admitted by the subsequent efforts to harmonize their teachings. See, e.g., R. Margulies's brief comments on "Maimonides and Abraham ben David" (Hebrew), *Sinai,* XVIII, No. 217, pp. 387–90.

On the other hand, despite his strictures, Abraham ben David could not always withhold his admiration from the younger scholar's accomplishments. Apart from a number of complimentary observations in his "Objections," he quoted Maimonides' interpretation with full approval at least in one of his own decisions. See the brief fragment, ed. from a Jerusalem MS by S. Assaf in "A Note on Abraham ben David's Attitude Toward Maimonides" (Hebrew), in *Rabbenu Mosheh ben Maimon,* pp. 276–78. See also the literature listed *supra,* n. 114; I. D. (B.) Bergman's brief biographical sketch of "R. Abraham ben David, Author of *Hassagot*" (Hebrew), *Talpioth,* III, 470–74; IV, 810–27; and I. Twersky's forthcoming biography of the latter.

123. See the related Hebrew studies by J. Ratzaby, "Maimonides in Yemenite Legend," *Yeda ha-'am,* II, 191–97; and J. Itiel, "Maimonides in the Popular Parlance of Morocco," *ibid.,* pp. 197–200. See also A. Mentsher's "Maimonides' Burial Place" (Hebrew), *Sinai,* XIX, No. 222, pp. 215–19.

124. Abu Ḥanifa, cited by C. C. Adams in his "Abu Ḥanifah," *MW,* XXXVI, 221; Soṭah 22a; Palṭoi's and Ṣemaḥ's replies in Müller's *Mafteaḥ,* pp. 92, 144; *Ḥemdah genuzah,* fol. 19a No. 110; Ḥananel's *Commentary* cited *supra,* n. 50. Palṭoi's responsum is doubly noteworthy inasmuch as the inquirers themselves had already expressed deep concern that "the majority of the people follow the adjudicated *halakhot* and say, 'Why should we bother with the talmudic debates?' " See also the text in Assaf's ed. of *Teshubot ha-geonim,* 1928, p. 81 No. 158. The *ḥadith* invoked by Caliph Harun, already considered "weak" by Ghazzali, has long since been declared unhistorical by scholars. See S. D. Goitein's remarks in "A Turning Point in the History of the Muslim State (A propos of Ibn al-Muqaffa'''s Kitāb aṣ-Ṣaḥāba)," *IC,* XXIII, 120–35.

125. The Nineveh inquiry is recorded under this name, rather than the more customary rabbinic designation of Ashshur, in Ta'anit 14b. That this happened almost eight centuries after the destruction of the former Assyrian capital is characteristic of the tenacity with which ancient Jewry clung to historically hallowed names. Jews still used it in Muslim times for a locality opposite Mosul, the former "Jews' castle," although it is possible that the Talmud had referred to the

Transjordanian town of Neva. See J. Obermeyer's *Landschaft Babylonien,* pp. 136 f., 139. On the early development of written juridical exchanges, see J. Müller's *Briefe und Responsen in der vorgeonäischen jüdischen Literatur,* pp. 8 f.; and Z. Frankel's *Mebo ha-Yerushalmi* (Introduction to the Palestinian Talmud), fol. 40b. Both these scholars also pioneered in the general field of geonic and early postgeonic responsa. See especially Frankel's *Entwurf einer Geschichte der Literatur der nachtalmudischen Responsen* which, almost a century ago, called the attention of scholars to this vital source of historical information; and J. Müller's *Mafteaḥ li-teshubot ha-geonim* (Einleitung in die Responsen der babylonischen Geonen). Müller also edited several collections of early responsa frequently referred to in our notes. *Die arabischen Glossen in den Schriften der Geonim* are treated in M. Wald's dissertation under this title.

126. Cassel's ed. of *Teshubot geonim qadmonim,* fol. 9a No. 46 (Sar Shalom); *Ḥemdah genuzah,* fol. 19b No. 113 (Ṣemaḥ). Of course, the fault often lay with the questioners who failed to state their cases with the necessary juristic precision. They thereby forced the scholars to give "iffy" answers, or else to reply by mentioning various alternatives. Some geonim of a more dialectical bent of mind, like Samuel ben Ḥofni, actually enjoyed exploring such alternate possibilities inherent even in purely theoretical problems. See, e.g., Samuel's replies to a series of exegetical questions in Assaf's ed. of *Teshubot,* 1942, pp. 11 ff.

127. See Saadiah Gaon's letter, ed. by Ginzberg in *Geonica,* II, 86 ff., and in a revised ed. by B. M. Lewin in his "Letter by the Fayyumite, Head of the Academy" (Hebrew), *GK,* II, 33 ff.; and *supra,* Chap. XXIII, n. 34. Discussing problems of mourning, Naṭronai Gaon observed that in "a distant place like Spain or France or any other place where the news does not come until after twelve months one need not eulogize" a deceased Eastern leader. See *Sha'are teshubah,* fol. 20b No. 12. Such duration of the journey seems not to have differed greatly between a sea voyage through the Mediterranean, the perils of which are so graphically depicted in Halevi's poems, and land travel across North Africa and western Asia, as described by Ibn Khurdadhbah and others. Cf. Mez, *Renaissance,* pp. 492 ff., 497 f., 505 ff.; *supra,* Chap. XXII, nn. 39, 42, 47; and *infra,* Chap. XXXII, n. 39.

128. See Maimonides' *Ueber die Lebensdauer,* ed. by G. Weil; and *infra,* Chap. XXXVI, n. 38. An interesting example of questioners submitting to a gaon several connected problems and receiving a series of replies in return is found in Ginzberg's *Geonica,* II, 301 ff., 326 ff. While the Genizah copy before us evidently deviates in many details from the original reply by Amram Gaon and his associates, it does show how many unrelated or loosely connected questions were combined in a single comprehensive answer. Of the fifty-one numbers nineteen deal with showfringes (Nos. 3–21), and nine with Passover laws (Nos. 24–32), some brought in merely because the original debate occurs in the talmudic tractate Pesaḥim. Incidentally, this lengthy responsum serves also as a commentary on various passages in the two tractates of Menaḥot and Pesaḥim.

Some other responsa offer comments on a single talmudic tractate. In his correspondence with Spanish communities, Naṭronai was twice approached by different questioners there to explain to them the meaning of certain terms and institutions recorded in the tractate Shabbat. The gaon's replies amounted to two commentaries on parts of that tractate. Curiously, Naṭronai referred the later questioners to his earlier reply, a copy of which they were evidently supposed to get from the earlier recipients. This procedure was often followed by other geonim. Cf. the texts published and commented upon in Ginzberg's *Geonica,* II, 293 ff., 318 ff.; and Assaf's *Teshubot,* 1928, pp. 147 ff., 155 ff. Neither fragment is complete. They have to be supplemented by other responsa from Naṭronai's pen, including another reply exclusively dealing with explanations relating to the same tractate which seems to antedate both. See the "Responsa by R. Naṭronai Gaon" (Hebrew), ed. by B. M. Lewin in *GK,* IV, 22–30. As pointed out by Lewin, his text, reproduced from an Oxford MS, seems to be the fullest of the three. But probably it, too, suffered not only from the usual scribal errors, but also from conscious abridgments by copyists. On the other hand, it seems not to have been addressed to any Spanish or Kairuwanese community. Otherwise it probably would have come to the attention of Nathan ben Yeḥiel, who, according to Assaf, quoted Naṭronai's interpretations in the other two replies no less than seventy-five times, expressly or without mentioning the author. This example ought to suffice to show both the sketchy preservation of geonic fragments and the tenuous nature of the distinction between geonic responsa and commentaries.

129. The evidence for the regular preservation of copies of dispatches in the academies' archives is rather inconclusive. In the case mentioned in the last note, Naṭronai must have had before him a transcript of his earlier communication to which he referred in his later reply. See Ginzberg's observations in *Geonica,* I, 184; II, 310. Similarly, Ṣemaḥ bar Palṭoi once merely copied a previous responsum by his father (see Cowley's text in *JQR,* [o.s.] XVIII, 401 f.). But this procedure may not have been typical, since Naṭronai may have remembered his earlier dispatch and Ṣemaḥ had long been his father's close collaborator. On the other hand, Hai Gaon who, on one occasion, referred Moses ben Isaac ha-Ma'arabi to a similar answer he had given to Egyptian correspondents, in another instance had to concede, "We do not remember what we have written, nor what our father of blessed memory had stated, but we shall tell you what appears to us right and what ought to be done." This admission was the more poignant as it came in answer to a Kairuwanese inquiry which had quoted that previous correspondence. See *Teshubot,* ed. by Harkavy, p. 20 No. 45; *Sha'are Ṣedeq,* fol. 94b No. 6. Certainly, Hai's or Sherira's replies written to great scholars (one had been addressed to Jacob bar Nissim) and relating to the ever complex problems of division of profits among partners did not fall into the category of those simple questions which the geonim briefly answered and then destroyed—a procedure which, though logically probable, is nowhere documented. The proof adduced by Ginzberg from Naṭronai's responsum No. 38 (*Geonica,* II, 310, 324) is inconclusive in the light of Assaf's reading in his *Teshubot,* 1928, pp. 157 f. No. 24. In any case, this important problem of geonic archives ought to be carefully reexamined.

130. See Ginzberg, *Geonica,* I, 182 ff.; Assaf, *Tequfat,* pp. 218 f., 297 f. As early as 1891, J. Müller registered some 2,400 individual replies then known, of which fully 855 were ascribed to Hai, in addition to 252 attributed to Sherira, but for the most part written with Hai's cooperation. See Müller's *Mafteaḥ,* pp. 62, 183 ff., 204 ff.; and the next note. This number has increased greatly since the discovery of the Fusṭaṭ Genizah. To the more recent finds belong those which appeared in L. Ginz-

berg's *Geonica* and *Ginze Schechter;* S. Assaf's *Teshubot ha-geonim,* 1928 and 1942; his *Mi-Sifrut ha-geonim* (Selections from Geonic Literature), Vol. I; and in the numerous periodicals, especially *Ginze Kedem,* ed. by B. M. Lewin. A brief list of nineteen collections published between 1516 and 1942, all of them including responsa by Western writers, is found in Assaf's *Tequfat,* pp. 219 f. A fuller description of the six earliest collections, as well as of several extant MSS, is given by E. E. Hildesheimer in *Die Komposition der Sammlungen von Responsen der Gaonen,* also suggesting a classification and analyzing the mutual relationships between the collections of printed and manuscript responsa in so far as they were extant in 1927. Some additional aspects connected with the collection, *Sha'are teshubah* and Abraham ben Isaac's *Eshkol* have been clarified in the acrimonious debate between Hildesheimer and C. Albeck in *Jeschurun,* XIV, 698–716. See *supra,* n. 81. See also J. Mann's topical survey of "The Responsa of the Babylonian Geonim as a Source of Jewish History," *JQR,* VII–XI.

A much-needed rearrangement of the vast and scattered material was undertaken by B. M. Lewin. In the thirteen (of the projected twenty) volumes of his *Otzar ha-gaonim* he reproduced the whole legal matter of the geonic age now extant by placing each geonic decision in its connection with one or another talmudic passage and thus transforming it into a sort of running halakhic commentary on the Babylonian Talmud. The editor was, of course, fully cognizant of the frequently arbitrary nature of his selection of passages, since the Talmud often reverts to the same themes in other contexts. See Lewin's introduction, I, ii. Its value will, of course, be greatly enhanced by the publication, now under way, of Kasovski's Talmudic Concordance. See *supra,* n. 46.

131. *Sha'are Ṣedeq,* fol. 18a No. 11; Ibn Megas' *Resp.,* Warsaw ed., fol. 17bc No. 114; Ginzberg's *Geonica,* I, 183 n. 2. While some first names of Eastern geonim, like Naṭronai, Palṭoi, or Sherira, had no counterparts in the West, others like Joseph or Jacob were quite common. It is often difficult, therefore, to identify the very country of origin of such replies. Somewhat indiscriminately, J. Müller edited a collection under the revealing title, "Responsa of Eastern and Western Geonim." In Harkavy's collection are included some hundred and sixty replies by Alfasi alone. Nor were the Western collectors always aware of the difference between replies received from Babylonia or Palestine. Although Babylonia's overwhelming preponderance in this field cannot be doubted, some responsa of Palestinian vintage are still identifiable in such collections as *Sha'are Ṣedeq,* or are quoted in the *Pardes* emanating from the school of Rashi. S. Assaf was able to add to our stock of Palestinian replies in both his *Mi-Sifrut ha-Geonim,* pp. 90 ff., and his edition of *Teshubot,* 1942, pp. 116 ff. In the former he also listed the older debates on this score, while in the latter (Intro., pp. xi f.) he mentioned additional fragments in his possession. Because of their bad state of preservation he was awaiting further discoveries before using them for publication. In his *Meḥqarim,* pp. 31 ff., to be sure, A. Aptowitzer endeavored to deny the Palestinian provenance of most of these responsa and claimed that they really had been Babylonian replies sent *to* Palestine. But his arguments were effectively countered in Assaf's review of that volume in *KS,* XVIII, 321 ff. See also the aforementioned "Responsum of a Palestinian gaon," ed. by A. I. Agus in *Sura,* I, 23 ff., although the failure of other sources to mention a Shalom Gaon in Jerusalem makes its origin somewhat doubtful. See *supra,* Chap. XXIII, nn. 37 ff. No more certain is the Palestinian provenance of several of the "Responsa by Palestinian

and Babylonian Geonim," published by Agus even more recently in an otherwise interesting Hebrew essay in *Horeb,* XII, 194–216. Here one responsum (pp. 198, 207 No. 10) is again attributed to the Palestinian Shalom Gaon, Agus apparently being unfamiliar with that debate between Aptowitzer and Assaf.

More successfully, Aptowitzer impugned the authenticity of many responsa attributed to Babylonian authors, including the last great gaon of Pumbedita. See his "Responsa Wrongly Attributed to R. Hai" (Hebrew), *Tarbiz,* I, Part 4, pp. 63–105; his "Responsa Wrongly Attributed to R. Ḥananiah," *Abhandlungen Chajes,* Hebrew section, pp. 49–59; and his *Meḥqarim,* pp. 135 ff. (showing that genuine responsa by the Sura gaon Moses were attributed to other teachers). Certainly, a great deal of detailed criticism is still needed to establish the literary contributions of each gaon. In any case, even today L. Ginzberg's assertion of a half a century ago (*loc. cit.*) may not be considered unduly pessimistic. "Barely a third of all Responsa known," Ginzberg declared, "can be assigned to authors with any degree of certainty."

132. *She'elot u-teshubot me-ha-geonim* (Questions and Replies from the Geonim; on this Constantinople ed. of 1575 and its variants in subsequent impressions, see Müller's *Mafteaḥ,* pp. 10 ff.); Lewin's *Otzar ha-gaonim,* I, pp. iii, 50 ff. No. 127, 130 ff. No. 357; Part 2, pp. 91 ff. Here we cannot tell, of course, whether Hai's responsum or commentary was written first. Similarly some of the Palestinian responsa quoted in "Rashi's" *Pardes* were not replies to questions at all, but rather decisions excerpted from the *Sefer ha-Ma'asim* and other Palestinian sources. Cf. J. N. Epstein's observations on the latter in *Tarbiz,* I, Part 2, pp. 34 f.; and, on a specific responsum, A. Epstein's analysis in "A Jerusalem Responsum in Rashi's *Pardes*" (Hebrew), *Ha-Goren,* VI, 69–73. Neither of these essays is entirely invalidated by A. Aptowitzer's strictures in his *Meḥqarim,* pp. 52 ff., 87 ff. See *supra,* n. 131.

133. Despite his enormous reputation, Alfasi's responsa have never yet been assembled in a comprehensive critical edition. A first collection from texts current in a Hebrew trans. was published by Yehudah Aryeh Leb Ashkenazi in Leghorn, 1781. As we recollect, more than one hundred and sixty of his Arabic responsa, provided with a Hebrew trans. by Harkavy, appeared in the latter's ed. of *Teshubot ha-geonim,* pp. 235 ff., 318 ff. Another twenty-seven responsa were published in Lichtenberg's edition of Maimonides' *Qobeṣ,* I, 38d ff. Nos. 182–208 (in the heading read: [Isaac ben] Jacob). Further replies from Alfasi's pen are included in *Temim de'im,* attributed to Abraham ben David, while many others are quoted by later medieval authorities or are known to exist in various manuscripts. The more recent collection, published from a Jewish Theological Seminary MS by Z. Biednowitz, claims on the title page that "the vast majority had never been printed before." This claim is decidedly untrue, for there is much duplication in all these compilations. The main advantage of Biednowitz's volume consists in the few comments by A. I. Kuk and I. Z. Meltzer, as well as in five new geonic responsa. The collection edited by Harkavy is relatively the best preserved and most carefully edited. The most recent edition (Pittsburgh, 1954) of Alfasi's *Resp.,* though equally incomplete, is at least provided with several commentaries by Ephraim Zalman Margulies, Zeeb ben Aryeh, and Wolf Leiter. Apart from its significance for the history of Jewish law, Alfasi's correspondence includes important data on the socioeconomic and political history of the Jews in Muslim Spain, as may be seen from the illustrations cited, esp. *supra,*

Chap. XXII. A good critical edition would, therefore, prove helpful to both the social and the legal historian.

To a lesser extent this also holds true for Ibn Megas' *Resp.*, part of which, in anonymous early Hebrew translations, was published in Salonica in 1786. On other Spanish writers, see, e.g., A. I. Laredo, "Las 'Šĕelot u-tĕšubot' como fuente par la historia de los judios españoles," *Sefarad,* V, 441–56, which also includes a bibliography (pp. 453 ff.), though incomplete, of such responsa by centuries. More comprehensive, though limited to the collection at that time (1930) accumulated at the Jewish Theological Seminary of America, is B. Cohen's *Quntres ha-teshubot* (Bibliography of Responsa).

134. See J. Müller's edition of, and detailed introduction to, *Die Responsen des R. Meschullam, Sohn des R. Kalonymus.* Nine additional responsa were reproduced from a Vatican MS by A. Freimann in his "Meschullam b. Kalonymos' Polemik gegen die Karäer" in *Judaica: Festschrift Hermann Cohen,* pp. 569–78. Either the Vatican collection is incomplete, or Meshullam took a stand on the Karaite problem also on some other occasion. For, as pointed out by Freimann, an argument reiteratedly quoted by Yehudah the Pious, once expressly in Meshullam's name, is not included in the Vatican copy under No. 5. See also S. Assaf's observations on "The Teachings of the Early Italian Rabbis" (Hebrew), *Sinai,* XVII, No. 201, pp. 15–40.

135. See esp. the recent text editions frequently mentioned in our previous notes: S. Eidelberg, *Teshubot Rabbenu Gershom Me'or ha-Golah;* I. Elfenbein, *Teshubot Rashi;* and A. I. Agus, *Teshubot ba'ale ha-tosafot.* The latter volume is largely derived from quotations in a single manuscript by Mordecai bar Hillel ha-Kohen, now at the Jewish Theological Seminary in New York; other parts, including excerpts from the curious geonic work *Basar 'al gabe geḥalim* (Meat on Coals; a halakhic treatise), had already been published by A. Sulzbach in his two essays in *JJLG,* III, Hebrew section, pp. 1–30; V, Hebrew section, pp. 61–68. The other two volumes are compiled from numerous sources, printed as well as in manuscript, although many responsa by Gershom had already been included in Müller's edition of *Teshubot ḥakhme Ṣarefat ve-Lotar,* and some are of dubious authenticity. The difference between an original responsum and brief summaries in later compilations stating but the gist of the author's arguments is quite obvious. It is illustrated in Eidelberg's volume (pp. 147 ff. No. 63) by Gershom's lengthy reply to two inquirers concerning a testamentary disposition, first edited by E. Hildesheimer from a Halberstam MS; and to a lesser extent by the "Five Responsa by R. Gershom Light of the Exile" published in a Hebrew essay by S. Assaf in *Ṣiyyunim (J. N. Simḥoni Memorial Volume),* pp. 116–21, mainly from an Oxford MS of Zedekiah Anav's *Shibbole ha-Leqeṭ.* We are better off in Rashi's case. The compiler of his *Teshubot,* I. Elfenbein, was able to consult not only more than a score of MSS, but also editions of several early rabbinic works emanating from Rashi's school. Hence quotations from the master's answers were probably subjected to fewer conscious or unconscious alterations. However, here, too, a number of critical problems raised by Elfenbein's predecessors are still unresolved. See esp. A. H. Freimann's "Rashi's Responsa" (Hebrew), *Sefer Rashi,* ed. by Fishman, pp. 140–52, and the related essays by S. H. Kuk, B. M. Lewin, and I. Werfel in the same volume.

136. See Abraham ben David's *Temim de'im,* No. 113 (*supra,* n. 63); Azriel Trabotto's *Seder ḥakhamim,* ed. by D. Kaufmann in his "Liste de rabbins dressée par Azriel Trabotto: une des sources de Guedalya ibn Yahya," *REJ,* IV, 212, 215, 223 n. 87 (mentioning the legend about Abraham's visit in Rameru); all cited by Urbach in *Ba'ale ha-tosafot,* pp. 60 ff. The main collection of Tam's responsa is available in F. Rosenthal's ed. from an Epstein-Halberstam MS (originally owned by Azulai and now at the Hebrew University), of the pertinent portion of Tam's *Sefer ha-Yashar.* Rosenthal also used MS comments by Ephraim Zalman Margulies, which he had found in the latter's copy of the printed Vienna edition of that book. Although far superior to that edition, Rosenthal's text leaves much to be desired. It does not even include numerous responsa which had appeared in other sections of the Vienna publication. Some additional texts, were available to both S. D. Luzzatto and J. Müller, who published ten and eleven responsa, respectively, in *Kerem Chemed,* VII, 19–53; and *Teshubot ḥakhme Ṣarefat ve-Lotar,* fols. 23a ff. Nos. 35–39, 41a ff. Nos. 64–69 (some of these may have been written by one of Tam's contemporaries). Further responsa by Tam were quoted by later medieval authorities, such as Eliezer bar Joel and Mordecai bar Hillel. See the texts, reproduced from the latter by Agus in his *Teshubot ba'ale ha-tosafot,* pp. 53 ff. Unfortunately almost all these texts are in a very unsatisfactory state of preservation. From the outset Tam himself seems to have assembled them without any rigorous method. Subsequently he made numerous changes in his manuscript. Pupils, too, later added or deleted a great deal on the basis of what they had heard from their master on other occasions. All that happened even before the copyists laid their hands on the MSS and altered them with their customary insouciance. See the illuminating analysis in E. Urbach's *Ba'ale ha-tosafot,* pp. 80 ff., also listing and correcting the older literature, and J. Feliks's even more recent Hebrew study of "R. Jacob Tam's *Sefer ha-Yashar,*" *Sinai,* XIX, Nos. 232, pp. 52–61; 233, pp. 106–15; 234, pp. 172–82; 235, pp. 224–39; 236, pp. 284–97; 237, pp. 363–73.

A host of other responsa by Franco-German scholars of the period is available in both manuscripts and prints. Among recent publications one might mention especially S. Assaf's *Sifran shel rishonim* (Book of Early Teachers) which includes a collection of forty-eight responsa by Abraham ben Isaac of Narbonne, supplemented by Assaf's study of "The Responsa by R. Abraham ben Isaac Head of the Court and Author of *Eshkol*" (Hebrew), *Sinai,* XI, Nos. 124–25, pp. 157–65. Also I. Z. Kahan's ed. of "The Responsa by Isaac Or Zaru'a and Meir bar Baruch" (Hebrew), *ibid.,* VII, Nos. 76–81, pp. 12–20, 88–95, 287–94; and those included in Agus's collection. On the latter, see also the important observations by E. Urbach in his review of that volume in *KS,* XXX, 200–205; and more generally his data in *Ba'ale ha-tosafot, passim.*

137. Maimonides' *Resp., passim,* and esp. pp. li ff., 62 ff. Nos. 67–69, 363 ff.; Abraham Maimuni's *Resp.,* ed. by Freimann, pp. xvi f. The controversy over the doctrine of resurrection is discussed *supra,* Chap. XXIII, n. 22; and *infra,* Chap. XXXIV. According to the editor's general plan, Moses' correspondence with Jonathan and his associates, one of the most important of all Maimonidean exchanges, is dispersed in his *Resp.* according to their subject matter in the sequence of Joseph Karo's code. However, it can easily be reassembled with the aid of the table included in Freimann's introduction, p. xliv, and by consulting especially A. Marx's essay "The Cor-

respondence between the Rabbis of Southern France and Maimonides about Astrology," in *HUCA,* III, 325 ff., 338 ff. Freimann's excellent edition includes only the Hebrew version of these responsa, although most of them had been written in Arabic. The projected edition of all extant Arabic texts, independently planned by B. Z. Halper and J. N. Simḥoni, was never carried out because of the premature death of both these scholars. This is doubly regrettable as Maimonides is one of the few medieval Jewish authors from whom we possess some answers in his own handwriting. See his *Resp.,* pp. 271 No. 301, 351 ff. Nos. 384–86, given here in the Hebrew trans. by Halper and B. Z. Baneth, respectively, but with indications where the originals had been published. Western inquirers received their answers in a Hebrew which, even if not always quite so punctilious as the style of the Code, bears many earmarks of the Maimonidean combination of elegance with lucidity and precision. Freimann's collection is by no means exhaustive, however, for new Maimonidean responsa are constantly coming to light. See the texts, ed. by M. Lutsky in his "Five Autograph Responsa by Maimonides (From the Cairo Genizah Collection in the Jewish Theological Seminary in New York)" (Hebrew), *Hatekufah,* XXX–XXXI, 679–704, also listing the autographs previously published; S. Assaf in "A Hitherto Unpublished Responsum by Maimonides" (Hebrew), *Melilah,* III–IV, 224–29; and *supra,* nn. 65, 97. These and other materials are now included in the new edition of Maimonides' *Resp.* in Arabic and Hebrew, published in Jerusalem by the Mekize Nirdamim Society.

Most Maimonidean responsa no longer include dates. But if the suggested date of 1166–67 for responsum No. 371 be correct (see the data given in Freimann's note, p. 342 n. 15), it would show that the then young scholar of thirty-one was considered sufficiently learned to pass judgment on such a crucial problem as the Rabbanite relations with the Karaite sectarians. Perhaps the questioners considered him, a newcomer to the Egyptian community, a more impartial judge in matters which had become deeply enmeshed in local communal politics. More certain is the date of 1176 indicated in another important responsum related to an Egyptian ordinance. See *infra* n. 155; Freimann's note to *Resp.,* No. 111, p. 106 n. 10; and, more generally his list, pp. xlviii f.

138. Cf. the passages indicated by Eidelberg in the intro. to his ed. of Gershom's *Teshubot,* pp. 46 f.; and Jacob Tam's *Sefer ha-Yashar,* ed. by Rosenthal, p. 38 No. 23. There were, of course, stylistic variations dependent on individual temperaments, momentary moods, and particularly the scholarly rank of recipients. We must also bear in mind that most of Gershom's and other responsa are known to us only in the abbreviated form cited by later authorities.

139. Maimonides' *Resp.,* p. 68 No. 69; Tam's *Sefer ha-Yashar,* ed. by Rosenthal, p. 75 No. 44, 1. Even in addressing a pupil, Joseph bar Isaac of Orléans whom he assured of his burning love, Tam informed him "You are mistaken in the interpretation of my statement . . . and what you have said is ignorance and stupidity." See Agus's *Teshubot ba'ale ha-tosafot,* p. 57 No. 11. Other examples of such inconsistencies on the part of the sage of Rameru are quoted by Aptowitzer in his *Mabo,* pp. 359, 363. Tam's violent outbursts were not frequently duplicated in the rabbinic responsa of the postgeonic age. Yet differences of personal interpretation or varying local traditions were often to lead to protracted quarrels embroiling many communities.

140. Lewin, *Otzar ha-gaonim,* VIII, 1 f. No. 2, 18 f. No. 60; *supra,* Vols. I, pp. 80 f., 328 n. 21; II, pp. 7 f., 431 f. n. 13; and Chap. XXIII, n. 27. In addition to the literature quoted there, see also the older analysis, especially of the cases where "custom abrogates law," by A. Perls in "Der Minhag im Talmud," *Festschrift Israel Lewy,* pp. 66–75.

141. Aḥai's *She'eltot,* on Va-yaqhel (Vilna ed., p. 208 No. 67, with reference to Pesaḥim 50b); Lewin, *Otzar ha-gaonim,* I, Part 1, pp. 23 No. 41, 117 f. Nos. 329, 334; II, Part 1, p. 111 No. 340. Some leaders were disturbed by certain customs which apparently infringed on general laws. Eleazar ben Samuel, a native of Spanish Lucena who had attained the high post of *alluf* at a Babylonian academy, inquired from Naṭronai whether the custom of placing Sabbath light wicks in oil floating in glasses of water was not contrary to law, inasmuch as one thus helped extinguish the candles when the oil burned out and the wicks dropped into the water. The gaon reassured his correspondent that there was no violation of the law, "and the whole people does it." According to another version, he specified that "we are in the habit of thus kindling the lights in Babylonian synagogues, schools, the house of our master [Rab's old synagogue at Sura] and the two academies." See *Otzar,* II, Part 1, p. 49 No. 150; and, on the identification of Rab's synagogue, Ginzberg, *Geonica,* I, 41 n. 2; Mann, *Texts and Studies,* I, 69 n. 16; and *infra,* Chap. XXXI, n. 61.

142. M. Ketubot IV.12; b. 54a; Lewin, *Otzar ha-gaonim,* VIII, Part 1, pp. 149 ff. Nos. 385–87; and S. Assaf's brief analysis in his *Tequfat,* pp. 272 f. In this essay on "The Differences in Customs and Legal Teachings between the Academies of Sura and Pumbedita," Assaf examined nine other major divergences between the two schools. At times, however, a powerful gaon like Hai rode roughshod over what other heads of academies had designated as observances of both academies. See the questions raised on this score by A. Marmorstein in his "Hai Gaon et les usages des deux écoles," *REJ,* LXXIII, 97–100. Similar problems were faced by Muslim jurists. Interesting examples of the insinuation of local customs into Muslim law are adduced in M. Morand's detailed *Etudes de droit musulman et de droit coutumier berbère,* esp. pp. 295 ff. See also the aforementioned (n. 9) distinction between "Droit de l'Islam et droit islamique," drawn by J. H. Kramers. Only the latter represents universal Islamic law, and as such an integral part of the Muslim faith, whereas the "law of Islam" consists of laws and institutions developed in the course of time in various Muslim countries.

143. See the geonic responsa and other sources assembled by Lewin in his *Otzar ha-gaonim,* VI, Part 1, 62 ff. Nos. 215–20 (*kapparot*), II, Part 1, pp. 20 No. 53, 82 No. 267 (wrappers); Naṭronai's responsum relating to "heretical" Passover rituals, *ibid.,* III, Part 2, pp. 89 f. No. 220; and that referring to *Kol Nidre,* cited in Isaac ibn Gayyat's *Sha'are simḥah,* I, 60b (here also an interesting early formula of that prayer). See also I. D. Bamberger's comments *ad loc.* Naṭronai was doubly handicapped in discouraging the *Kol Nidre* prayer because he did not wish to appear as yielding to the constant Karaite assaults on that liturgical custom. See Mann, *Texts and Studies,* II, 51 ff. Here Mann incidentally suggests that the reference to that prayer in a responsum by Palṭoi of Sura, cited by Eliezer bar Joel in his *Sefer Rabiah,* II, 189, is a later interpolation. However, this reading seems to be confirmed by the sources cited in Aptowitzer's note 18 thereon, except that some of these

attribute the responsum to Naṭronai. Of course, both these ninth-century geonim may have been equally impressed by the growing Karaite attacks on that prayer.

The *kapparot* ceremony, too, has been the subject of extensive debates in medieval and modern letters. That it does not go back to ancient times appears very likely. Even the attribution of one pertinent responsum to the early gaon of Sura, Sheshna, is denied by Ginzberg in his *Ginze Schechter,* II, 2 f., 18, 122 f. Here are also listed other geonic and postgeonic sources, including those by such opponents of that ceremony as Ibn Adret. From that Barcelona rabbi, the objection was taken over into the first edition of Joseph Karo's law code, although it was subsequently deleted by some pious practitioners of a custom which by the 1600's had already been hallowed by centuries of uninterrupted usage. A. Aptowitzer has suggested that that ceremony had originated from the "redemption of first-born sons," Israel being considered God's first-born. See his "Gleanings" (Hebrew), *Ha-Zofeh,* VII, 92 ff.; and J. Z. Lauterbach's more general observations on "The Ritual for the Kapparot Ceremony" (1935), reprinted in his *Rabbinic Essays,* pp. 354 ff. Cf. also *infra,* Chap. XXXI, n. 20.

144. Saadiah's pamphlet, ed. by H. Y. Bornstein in *Sefer ha-Yobel . . . Nahum Sokolow,* p. 75; Saadiah's *Siddur,* pp. 10 f., 37 n. 6; Lewin's *Otzar ha-gaonim,* I, Part 1, pp. 32 f.; and *infra,* Chap. XXXI, n. 74. Sherira made short shrift of Saadiah's argument against the phrasing "New Light" by stating that "from time immemorial it has been recited at the two academies." Not surprisingly, Saadiah's name rarely occurs among the geonim invoking custom as a major argument. See the large accumulation of data in J. L. Fishman's Hebrew study on "'Custom' in Geonic Literature," *Lewin Jub. Vol.,* pp. 132–59. The indubitable merits of this essay are diminished, however, by the absence of any recognition of the historic evolution which took place in this respect during the long geonic period. See *infra,* n. 145.

145. Ibn Gayyat's *Sha'are simḥah,* I, 22 ff., 114. Ibn Gayyat reported still another interesting responsum by Hai, *ibid.,* pp. 63 f. See also Lewin, *Otzar ha-gaonim,* I, Part 1, pp. 32 f.; VI, Part 1, p. 41 No. 121. Asked about a local custom to recite the story of the ancient Temple worship (the so-called *'Abodah*) during both the morning and *musaf* services of the Day of Atonement, Hai admitted that at both academies it was customary to recite it only during *musaf.* But he added that Baghdadian Jewry had early introduced the double recitation, because it had taken such delight in this description. Hai ben David, the first of the geonim to move to Baghdad (in 890), had in vain "tried to dissuade them from this custom." Since the later geonim had quietly tolerated that ritual, "you, too, ought not to depart from the custom of your forefathers." Evidently in their own home town the geonim, as usual, could not uproot a cherished custom, the younger Hai simply bowing to the inevitable.

146. Maimonides' *M.T.* Introduction; his *Resp.,* pp. 46 f. No. 46, 64 No. 67, 366; Abraham Maimuni's *Resp.,* pp. 119 f. Nos. 82–83, 126 No. 83 end, 133 f. Nos. 87, 89; and *infra,* n. 155. Occasionally the very absence of custom could be adduced as a legal argument. Asked whether one ought to seize the working tools of a man unable to pay the marriage settlement to his divorced wife, Maimonides declared with abandon that it was against the law to allow such divorces altogether, "for otherwise no daughter of Israel would stay married to her husband." In another context he emphasized again that "a custom has been established in most countries that one

cannot divorce a wife without paying her the marriage settlement." But he admitted that courts were not obliged to sell the husband's clothing or the tools on which his livelihood depended, to satisfy his wife's financial claims. See his *Resp.*, pp. 172 No. 176, 198 f. No. 203.

147. Rashi's *Teshubot,* pp. 301 No. 258, 337 No. 327. Rashi's information about the customs of other countries was rather sketchy. His sweeping assertion, for example, that the non-recitation of the "seven blessings" during the betrothal ceremonies was "universal practice," was soon controverted by Isaiah ben Mali of Trani with respect to the Byzantine possessions. *Ibid.*, pp. 212 No. 191, 387 (note by L. Ginzberg). Really cognizant only of the customs in the Rhinelands, which he expressly quotes, and of his own country, Rashi was familiar with only those Eastern observances which were recorded in the literary sources accessible to him. The Babylonian-Palestinian background of his assertion is indeed confirmed by the *Hilkhot re'u* or *Halakhot pesuqot* which had emerged from the school of Yehudai Gaon (see *supra,* n. 88). See the text, ed. by A. L. Schlossberg, XIII, p. 84. On the other hand, living in southern Italy, Isaiah frequently quoted "Romanian" (Byzantine) usages.

148. Tam's responsum in his *Sefer ha-Yashar,* ed. by Rosenthal, pp. 82 ff. No. 45, 5–6. See Urbach's *Ba'ale ha-tosafot,* pp. 62 ff., 69 ff. This ambivalent quest also characterized Tam's disciples. Ephraim bar Isaac of Ratisbon, who on one occasion had received a severe scolding from Tam, in turn administered a sharp rebuke to his own pupil, Joel bar Isaac ha-Levi of Bonn, for too readily rationalizing a custom running counter to talmudic law. Accusing his pupil of excessive timidity, he exclaimed, "You must see for yourself whether the custom of your forefathers is good or bad." Somewhat inconsistently, however, Ephraim not only rejected Joel's argument that in that particular case the law appeared uncertain, but himself invoked the customs practiced "in France, Rome, Lombardy and our states [Germany]" as opposing that accepted by Joel. "Your own forefathers have gone against you." Cf. the interesting exchange between these rabbis quoted by Isaac bar Moses in *Or zaru'a,* I, fols. 58cd f. No. 413; Urbach, pp. 171 ff.

149. Abraham bar Nathan ha-Yarḥi's *Sefer ha-Manhig* (Guide), ed. by J. M. Goldberg, Introduction. This publication is but a new impression of the Constantinople printing of 1519, and ought to be replaced by a more critical edition. That our text is incomplete is shown, for example, by the missing lengthy quotations from its *Hilkhot me'un* (Laws relating to a minor girl's refusal to stay married) in Solomon ibn Adret's *Resp.,* I, No. 1108, Vienna ed., fol. 127d f. Another fragment was published by A. H. Freimann, on the basis of two Vatican manuscripts, in his Hebrew essay cited *supra,* n. 82. About the author's life and other works we know little more than is recorded in his own volume. See D. Cassel's "Ueber Abraham b. Natan aus Lunel, Verfasser des Manhig," *Jubelschrift . . . Leopold Zunz,* pp. 122–37; and other literature listed by S. Bialoblocki in *EJ, s.v.,* I, 524–28.

150. Abraham's *Sefer ha-Manhig,* fols. 7ab, 15b, 39b, 91ab, 95b. Saadiah's responsum is also recorded in other sources with considerable variants. Cf. J. Müller's note on Saadiah's *Oeuvres,* IX, 157 f. No. 73. On the abstention from marriage during the interval between Passover and the Festival of Weeks, see *supra,* Chap. XXI, n. 67. Some of Abraham's inaccuracies have been pointed out by J. Reifmann in his suc-

cinct notes on "Abraham ibn Jarchi," *MWJ,* V, 60–67. Nonetheless the *Manhig* has long served as a major source for the social life and folklore of twelfth- and thirteenth-century Jewry. It has been used to particularly good advantage by such early Jewish social historians as M. Güdemann and A. Berliner.

151. Ibn Daud's Chronicle in *MJC,* I, 47; Abraham Maimuni's *Resp.,* p. 134 No. 89 with the editor's note thereon; Lewin's *Otzar ha-gaonim,* I, Part 1, p. 11 No. 19; VIII, Part 1, p. 99 No. 260. Probably most customs had originated from some such immediate impulses. This was particularly true in the realm of synagogue rites, which were constantly elaborated by an untold number of synagogue readers. Abraham Maimuni was not alone in disparaging such "an innovation by precentors who do not distinguish between the permitted and the forbidden." See his *Resp.,* p. 134 No. 90; and, more generally, *infra,* Chap. XXXI.

152. Naṭronai's responsum briefly reproduced by Isaac ben Abba Mari in his *Sefer ha-'Iṭṭur,* Warsaw ed., Vol. II, fol. 34a; and more briefly in his *Me'ah She'arim* on Alfasi, xxv, on Ketubot 45a (Vilna ed., Appendix, fol. 13a); Maimonides' *M.T.* Ishshut xvi.7, Nizqe mamon viii.12, and especially Malveh ve-loveh xi.11. Although Isaac's report, citing Samuel ibn Nagrela, attributes that responsum to Sar Shalom Gaon, as well as to his successor in office, Naṭronai, H. Tykocinski has plausibly argued that the extant text must have been written by Naṭronai. The latter merely referred to an eighty-two-year-old practice also mentioned in an earlier responsum by Sar Shalom. Its approximate date of 787 is largely based on three complementary statements by Sherira. See *Die gaonäischen Verordnungen,* pp. 37 ff. Here Tykocinski also quotes extensively other pertinent geonic and postgeonic sources, translates them into German, and analyzes them with great care. Cf. some variants in Lewin's *Otzar ha-gaonim,* VIII, Part 1, pp. 210 ff. Nos. 527–37, 260 No. 622; and Alfasi's decision on Ketubot 69b Nos. 305–6, in the Vilna ed., fol. 30b, with the commentaries thereon. Since Maimonides never drew a sharp line of demarcation between Saboraim, geonim, and the teachers of the eleventh century, his designation of the originators of our ordinance as "late geonim" is the less surprising, as he wished to emphasize their lack of authority to overrule talmudic law. Jacob Tam, on the other hand, tried to justify this enactment as but a dialectical derivation from talmudic law. See Meir ha-Kohen's *Haggahot Maimoniot on M.T.* Ishshut xvi.7; and more generally A. Schwarz's observations in *Moses ben Maimon,* ed. by Guttmann *et al.,* I, 345 f., 372 ff., 391 ff. Maimonides was technically right, but he failed to take cognizance of the economic needs which had dictated the extraordinary solemnity of the original proclamation. The very necessity to threaten judges resisting that innovation with removal from office showed the strength of the conservative opposition which could only be broken by drastic action. See *supra,* Chap. XXII, n. 2.

153. The fullest information on this ordinance is available in a responsum by Sherira Gaon in *Sha'are Ṣedeq,* fol. 56a No. 15. But there are numerous earlier and later sources, both complementary and slightly contradictory, which are reproduced and carefully analyzed by Tykocinski, pp. 4 ff. See also Lewin, *Otzar ha-gaonim,* VIII, Part 1, pp. 192 ff. Nos. 478, 484, 486. Most of these sources are somewhat vague with respect to the date of that enactment, only Isaac ben Abba Mari mentioning the exact year of 962 Sel. era, or 651 C.E. Other data seem to indicate that it was not issued until a decade or two later. In any case, it took about a generation

until the aftereffects of the Muslim conquest were fully felt in Babylonia, and the newly revived authority of exilarchate and academies could be used to institute such a far-reaching reform. The strong objections raised by Jacob Tam are found in his *Sefer ha-Yashar,* ed. by Rosenthal, p. 40 No. 24; those by Maimonides in *M.T.* Ishshut XIV.14. Although formally wrong, Zeraḥiah ha-Levi was not historically incorrect when he designated that geonic ordinance as a "temporary measure" (*hora'at sha'ah*). Cf. his *Sefer ha-Ma'or* on Alfasi Ketubot, Nos. 283–85, Vilna ed., fol. 27a (on b. fol. 63a); and Naḥmanides' stricture *ibid.*

154. See the texts cited and analyzed by Tykocinski, pp. 117 ff., 153 ff.; and *supra,* Chap. XXIII, n. 15. In addition to the four geonic ordinances here mentioned, Tykocinski discusses in considerable detail fifteen other regulations attributed in the sources to such "geonic" innovations. In some cases, however, this term is used rather loosely, since these enactments owed their origin to teachers of the eleventh and twelfth centuries.

155. Maimonides' *Resp.,* pp. 91 ff. No. 97, 152 f. No. 158, with the editor's comments thereon. On the historical background see S. Eppenstein's observations in *Moses ben Maimon,* ed. by Guttmann *et al.,* II, 40 ff. (also quoting from a Simonsen MS the clause pertaining to the penalties to be imposed upon husbands), 56 f.; and *supra,* Chap. XXVI, n. 67. In both cases Maimonides and his associates made it clear that they were not abrogating any established law, but merely reinforcing its administration.

156. See the data cited by L. Finkelstein in his *Jewish Self-Government,* pp. 23 ff., 139 ff.; and by S. Eidelberg in the intro. to his ed. of Gershom's *Teshubot,* pp. 19 ff. In "Einiges über die Tekanot des Rabbi Gerschom b. Jehuda, der 'Leuchte des Exils,'" *Hildesheimer Jub. Vol.,* pp. 37–53, F. Rosenthal argued that the original ordinance was issued only for the three communities of Mayence, Worms, and Spires. Except in so far as it refers to the latter community, established in 1084, fifty-six years after Gershom's death, this suggestion is not controverted by Finkelstein's contention that "it is intrinsically improbable that a Takkanah intended only for a few communities would have been so generally accepted." There is no evidence whatsoever that Gershom or any other scholar of that generation exercised direct authority beyond his own community, and could issue ordinances for other localities without the direct cooperation of local elders. On the contrary, communities of that period generally observed the principle of noninterference in each other's inner affairs, except in cases affecting the fundamentals of the Jewish faith. In an interesting responsum Joseph Bonfils (Tob 'Elem) clearly formulated that principle, at least with respect to monetary matters: "When a community elects trustees who enact an ordinance in consultation with, and the approval of experts, no other community is empowered to overrule it on account of its superiority in wisdom or numbers." Quoted in Meir bar Baruch's *Resp.,* Lwów ed., fol. 43c No. 423. In this respect an ordinance clearly differed from a legal decision in a commentary, code or even responsum which, even if addressed to specific individuals, was supposed to settle a problem of general Jewish law with the view toward universal acceptance. A *taqqanah,* on the other hand, was an avowed innovation, enjoying validity only for those groups which lawfully adopted it, or else later voluntarily submitted to it. Of course, it is possible that Gershom

had consulted the communal leaders of a larger area, but there is no intimation of such concerted action in the sources. See also S. Schwarzfuchs, "A propos des Takkanôt de Rabbenu Gershom et Rabbenu Tam," *REJ*, CXV, 109–16.

157. Ibn Adret, quoted in Joseph ben Solomon Colon's *Resp.*, No. 101, Sudzilkov ed., 1834, fol. 45a; Samuel ben Moses di Medina's *Resp.*, on *Eben ha-'ezer*, No. 120, Salonica ed., 1797, fol. 90b. Ibn Adret himself is reported to have learned of that time limit only from hearsay. That to an eleventh-century scholar the sixth millennium might have appeared as the beginning of the messianic era is quite plausible in itself, and is further borne out by the matter-of-fact tone with which Rashi discussed the various dates for the expected redemption, all of which belonged to the period after 5000 A.M. See *supra*, Chap. XXV, n. 19.

158. Gershom's *Teshubot*, pp. 113 f. No. 42; Finkelstein, *Jewish Self-Government*, p. 28. Eidelberg's suggestion that this responsum was written before the ordinance is supported by no other evidence. Certainly even after its enactment Gershom might have suggested that the husband be placed under a ban, but he hardly would have declared the second marriage null and void.

159. Aptowitzer, *Mabo*, pp. 330 ff. Aptowitzer suggests here that Eliezer was unaware of any regulation allowing a hundred men or rabbis to dissolve Gershom's ban, a practice which was to degenerate into the modern factory-like procedures which Aptowitzer so eloquently denounces. However, the substance of that provision occurs already in the oldest reports such as Simḥah of Vitry, *Maḥzor*, p. 798; and the Munich MS of the Babylonian Talmud, written in 1369. More probably, that remedial measure had been included as an escape clause in Gershom's original proclamation itself, but rather than being relaxed, the ordinance was sharpened in time, as European Jewry grew larger and more self-confident. The very redundancy of the provision that the hundred men stem from three countries and three communities indicates that originally one needed but to secure a dispensation by popular action in three neighboring communities. This provision was later sharpened by the requirement that the hundred men reside in three provinces, although in their typical conservatism the rabbis retained the phrase relating to three communities. This change seems to have come in the twelfth century when Anjou and Poitou became distinct feudal units, and were counted as three "countries" in a synodal resolution. See Baer's observations in his "Nachwort zu dem Aufsatz von Finkelstein," *MGWJ*, LXXIV, 32. Later jurists broadened the scope still further, and at least in one version the hundred men were required to reside in three such diverse regions as Aragon, Lombardy, and France. See the different texts cited by Finkelstein, p. 140, in the variants to lines 7–8.

160. I. Abrahams's ed. of "A Formula and a Responsum," *Jews' College Jubilee Vol.*, pp. 101–8 (reprinted in A. Gulak's *Oṣar ha-sheṭarot*, pp. 34 f. No. 30; cf. also p. 23); Maimonides' *Resp.*, p. 152 No. 155. The Maimonidean ordinance was aimed exclusively at foreigners. It did not protect Egyptian women against lengthy absences of their native spouses. True, talmudic law had already provided that husbands must not absent themselves from home beyond certain stated periods related to their respective occupations. Asked about a woman's demand that, before embarking on a lengthy journey, her husband leave her a writ of divorce with a time

limit, Hai had advised the inquirers to help persuade the husband to do so, but not to force him unless his absence exceeded the limits set by talmudic law. See Lewin's *Otzar ha-gaonim,* VIII, Part 1, p. 186 No. 463. In practice apparently the majority of wives accepted their husbands' long business journeys to India and elsewhere, which had become a major feature of international trade.

161. See Finkelstein, *Jewish Self-Government,* pp. 111 ff.; M. Z. Weiss, "Genizah Fragments" (Hebrew), *Ha-Zofeh,* V, 4 (citing the geonic provisions for the secrecy of letters); j. Megillah IV.4, 75a (threatening worshipers depleting a quorum with the verse, "And they that forsake the Lord shall be consumed"; Isa. 1:28); Eliezer bar Joel's *Resp.,* No. 1006, cited from MS in Aptowitzer's *Mabo,* p. 55. Like the ordinance against plural marriages, that protecting the letter writers' privacy is nowhere recorded in full. It appears first in a list of ordinances enacted by a synod presided over by Jacob Tam. See Finkelstein, pp. 171 ff., 178, 189.

162. The Baghdad ordinance, first published by D. S. Sassoon, is excerpted in Lewin's *Otzar ha-gaonim,* VIII, Part 4, p. 93. The elders claim to have sought merely to "renew an agreement" of long standing. As pointed out by Lewin, this ordinance ran counter to the ceremony demanded from the Khorasanians by Yehudah Gaon, mentioned *supra,* n. 140. Probably Yehudah was aware of the local Baghdad provisions, but paid them no attention in dealing with a distant community, especially since no gaon had participated in their original promulgation.

163. *Ḥuqqe ha-torah* (Laws of the Torah), first published by M. Güdemann and republished in S. Assaf's *Meqorot le-toledot ha-ḥinnukh,* I, 6 ff. Since in the only extant text (a Bodleian MS of 1309) the original preamble was replaced by a pietistic introduction, we know nothing about the origins of this remarkable document. Even the guesses concerning the country of its origin have ranged from France and Germany to Spain and Babylonia. Assaf argued for Bohemia or Moravia, and suggested that it was formulated before the end of the twelfth century. More recently B. Z. Benedikt (following a suggestion by B. Z. Dinur) stated his preference for the Provence. See his remarks "On the History of the Provençal-Jewish Center of Learning" (Hebrew), *Tarbiz,* XXII, 98. While most scholars assumed that these rules were carried out in practice in some region or other, I. Loeb somewhat timidly suggested that we have here but a work of fancy, or rather a proposal emanating from a pietistic circle, perhaps a single individual. See his review of M. Güdemann's *Geschichte des Erziehungswesens* in *REJ,* II, 159 ff. One may add that the absence of any direct reference to it in the subsequent rabbinic literature militates very strongly against its being a reflection of communal practice, or even an official proclamation demanding such reforms. Neither its inclusion in a collection of rabbinic tracts, nor the rather faint echo of some such rules in a work by one Moses bar Aaron, a seventeenth-century Moravian teacher living in Lublin (cf. Assaf's remarks, pp. 8, 85 ff.), prove anything beyond the influence such idealistic postulates exercised on the minds of a few pious individuals. Nevertheless, they have been included here as an example of a potential, if not actual, communal ordinance. See also my *Jewish Community,* I, 356 f.; III, 92 n. 10; and *infra,* Chap. XXXIII, nn. 47 ff.

164. Maimonides' *Guide,* III.27 (in Friedländer's English trans., p. 312); Halevi's *K. al-Khazari,* II.48, ed. by Hirschfeld, pp. 106 ff. (English, pp. 111 f.); Ibn Daud's

Emunah ramah, pp. 102 f. (Hebrew), 191 ff. (German). Even in the asocial mood in which he wrote his major philosophic work (see *infra,* Chap. XXXIV), Maimonides could not escape the impact of the social aims of Jewish law. He indicated his own preference, however, by disparaging the law's social objectives as aimed only at the welfare of the body. Even more sharply Halevi argued against the philosopher's ideal *regimen solitarii,* for the necessity of rational laws, as a preamble to the divine laws, although he admitted, as we shall presently see, that the former, too, required further specification by the revealed will of God. See L. Strauss's observations in his *Persecution and the Art of Writing,* pp. 126 f.; and, on the contrast with Platonic teachings in their Arab reinterpretation, E. I. J. Rosenthal's "Politische Gedanken bei Ibn Bajja," *MGWJ,* LXXXI, 153–68, 185–86. Incidentally, the Arabic text of Ibn Bajja's *Tadbīru'l-mutawaḥḥid* (Rule of the Solitary), previously known only from Hebrew extracts analyzed in Munk's *Mélanges,* pp. 383 ff., was, in part, published from a Bodleian MS by D. M. Dunlop in *JRAS,* 1945, pp. 61–81; and more fully by Asín Palacio in *El Regimen de Solitario de Avempace.* See also some pertinent remarks included in G. Horowitz's comprehensive analysis of *The Spirit of Jewish Law.*

165. Ibn Daud, *loc. cit.;* Maimonides' *Commentary* on M. Sanhedrin x, Introduction, especially Principle VIII, ed. by J. Holzer, pp. 26 ff.; his *Guide,* III.31 (English, p. 322); Baḥya's *Duties,* Introduction and VIII.3, pp. 20, 340 f. (Zifroni, pp. 16, 233 f.; Hyamson, I, 12); Abraham Maimuni's *High Ways,* II, 44 f. The story about Al-Haitham ibn 'Adi is cited by D. S. Margoliouth in his *Lectures on Arabic Historians,* p. 95. Maimonides' insistence on the basic equality of all commandments is also reflected in his repeated restatement of the entire Jewish law in terms of the six hundred and thirteen commandments, together with their ramifications, despite arguments to the contrary voiced by such enlightened critics of this entire concept as Abraham ibn Ezra. The latter contended that, after all, many a positive law presupposes a negation, and vice versa; for instance, the Sabbath rest commandment clearly involves a prohibition to work. Cf. his *Yesod mora,* II, VII, ed. by M. Creizenach, pp. 12 f., 34 f.; D. Rosin's remarks thereon in "Die Religionsphilosophie Abraham Ibn Esra's," *MGWJ,* XLIII, 84 f.; my recent address, "Maimonides' Significance to Our Generation," printed in *Maimonides,* ed. by S. Federbush, pp. 11 f.; and *supra,* n. 111.

166. Halevi's *K. al-Khazari,* I.79; III.23, 53, ed. by Hirschfeld, pp. 32 f., 176 f., 202 ff. (English, pp. 56, 162, 180 ff.); Saadiah's *Beliefs,* III.1, pp. 113f. (Hebrew, p. 59; English, pp. 139 f.); Maimonides' *Guide,* II.40; III.17, 31, 35 (English, pp. 233, 288, 321, 329 f.). Maimonides disliked the very term "rational" laws, so called by "some of our later sages, who were infected with the unsound principles of the Mutakallimun." See his *Eight Chapters,* VI, ed. by Gorfinkle, pp. 36 (Hebrew), 77 (English). On occasion he used instead the term *al-mashhurat* (*mefursamot*), corresponding to the scholastic term *ius conventionale.* See his *Guide,* I.2 (English, p. 15 incorrectly rendered); his *Treatise on Logic,* VIII, ed. by I. Efros, pp. 17 (Arabic), 39 f. (Ibn Tibbon), 47 (English); and, more generally, Efros's *Philosophical Terms,* p. 77; and J. Klatzkin's *Oṣar ha-munaḥim,* II, 248 f. S. Munk and C. Neuburger have correctly pointed out the connection between this term and the Aristotelian concept *endoxa* utilized by Maimonides in his insistence on the autonomous nature of human ethics. Cf. Munk's note on his translation of the *Guide,* I, 39 n. 1, and Neuburger's dissertation, *Das Wesen des Gesetzes in der Philosophie des Maimonides,* p. 18. Some inconsistencies in "R. Saadiah Gaon's Division of Commandments" were pointed out in a

Hebrew essay under this title by S. Z. (A.) Altmann in *Rav Saadya Gaon,* ed. by Fishman, pp. 658–73 (in the first book of his *Beliefs* the gaon followed the Kalam, whereas in Books II–IV he evidently was under more direct Platonic-Aristotelian influence). Such inconsistencies are, however, neither fundamental nor at all surprising in a book compiled from independent monographs written over a period of years. See also Altmann's "Saadya's Conception of the Law," *BJRL,* XXVIII, 320–39.

167. Maimonides' *Guide,* II.40, III.17 (English, pp. 233, 288); Munk's note on his trans. of that work, III, 127 n. 1; Isaac Abravanel's *Commentary* on it, I.2; and Halevi's statements quoted in n. 168. On the ancient Greek versus the Judeo-Christian background of the doctrine of natural law, see Wolfson, *Philo,* II, 170 ff., 310 ff.; and *supra,* Vol. II, pp. 136, 381 n. 10, 432 n. 14. The reason why Hugo Grotius could so wholly misinterpret Maimonides as to make him an exponent of the doctrine of natural law is explained by L. Strauss in *Persecution,* p. 96 n. 4. See also my comments in *Essays on Maimonides,* p. 138 n. 25; and, more generally, L. Strauss's *Philosophie und Gesetz;* M. Lazerson's observations on "La Philosophie du droit de Maïmonide," *Archives de philosophie du droit,* VII, 191–219, somewhat expanded in his *Ha-Pilosofiah ha-mishpaṭit shel ha-Rambam* (The Maimonidean Philosophy of Law); L. Gardet's "Philosophie et loi religieuse en Islam et dans le Judaïsme médiéval," *Revue thomiste,* LI (LIX), 671–84 (a review article); and especially with reference to the thirteen articles of faith, M. Waxman's "Maimonides as Dogmatist," *Yearbook CCAR,* XLV, 397–418.

168. Halevi's *K. al-Khazari,* I.83 (pp. 36 f. Arabic and Hebrew; p. 59 English); Maimonides' *M.T.* Melakhim VIII, end. In his "Maïmonide sur l'universalité de la morale religieuse," *REJ,* XCIX, 34–43, M. Guttmann has pointed to Maimonides' source in *The Mishnah of Rabbi Eliezer,* ed. by Enelow, p. 121. However, the differences here are as significant as the similarities. Maimonides not only omitted "R. Eliezer's" disqualification of a Gentile who "associates" the seven commandments with an idol, and thus breaks the most important commandment, but he also insisted on the specific recognition, by the Gentile, of the Mosaic revelation. In fact, to reconcile the contradictory enumeration of six or seven Noahide commandments in the talmudic sources, Maimonides taught that the prohibition of consuming the limb of a living animal was added to the earlier six commandments by a divine order to Noah. However, all these commandments, as well as those added in the days of the patriarchs, such as circumcision and the three daily orders of prayers, had to be validated again in the great Mosaic theophany. See the sources cited by me in "The Historical Outlook of Maimonides," *PAAJR,* VI, 13 nn. 12–13. In other words, all commandments depended equally on the announced will of God. Of course, some divine commandments may have been intended to operate only for a limited time; Maimonides found in the Bible more than three hundred such temporary regulations. See his *Book of Commandments,* Intro., Root 3 (ed. by Bloch, p. 17; by Heller, p. 8), offering a number of interesting illustrations but not a complete list. On the use made of the Noahide commandments by early advocates of separation of state and church, see Hermann Cohen's observations in "Die Nächstenliebe im Talmud," reprinted in his *Jüdische Schriften,* I, 145–74. This problem will be more fully discussed in its modern context.

169. Ibn Daud's *Emunah,* pp. 75 f. (Hebrew), 95 (German); Saadiah's *Beliefs,* III.7–9, pp. 128 ff. (Hebrew, pp. 66 ff.; English, pp. 157 ff.). Ibn Daud's historical outlook is

discussed *infra,* Chap. XXVIII. The seventh argument in favor of abrogation mentioned by Saadiah was, in many ways, the most relevant to the Judeo-Muslim controversy. "Just as it was permissible," the proponents of abrogation argued, "for the Law of Moses to be different from that of Abraham, so should it be permissible for a later Law to be different from that of Moses." In reply Saadiah, Halevi, and Maimonides insisted that Moses had only increased the laws binding on Abraham and his successors, but had not abrogated any of them.

170. Saadiah's *Beliefs, loc. cit.;* Maimonides' *Guide,* II.29 (English, pp. 208, 210); the Maimonidean credo, articles VIII–IX, derived from his *Commentary* on M. Sanhedrin x, ed. by J. Holzer, pp. 26 f. On the role of the doctrine of abrogation in the Judeo-Muslim religious controversy, see *supra,* Chap. XXIV, n. 9.

171. Maimonides' *Guide,* III.41 (English, p. 345); *M.T.* Genebah I.3; Shekhenim XIV.1, 5, with reference to B.M. 108b. See Alfasi's, Rashi's, and the Tosafists' comments thereon. See also my observations in *Essays on Maimonides,* pp. 168 ff.; those by S. Albeck in *Zion,* XIX, 104 ff.; and *supra,* Chap. XXII, *passim.* On the parallel evolution in Muslim law, see R. Brunschvig's pioneering essay, "Urbanisme médiéval et droit musulman," *Revue des études islamiques,* XV, 127–55 (chiefly from the standpoint of Malikite law). Brunschvig's appeal for further investigations in this field may readily be echoed by students interested in the sociohistorical evolution of Jewish law.

172. Maimonides' *Guide,* III.32, 46 (English, pp. 322 ff., 359 ff.); his *M.T.* sections on 'Abodah and Qorbanot, *passim;* Saadiah's *Beliefs,* III.10, pp. 141 ff. (Hebrew, pp. 72 f.; English, pp. 175 ff.); Baḥya's *Duties,* III.3, IV.4, VII.5–6, pp. 138 f., 213, 289 ff. (Zifroni, pp. 88, 141 f., 198 ff.; Hyamson, II, 42 f.; III, 36 f.); Naḥmanides' *Commentary* on Lev. 1:9; Halevi's *K. al-Khazari,* II.26, pp. 96 f. (English, pp. 101 ff., 104). See Cassel's note in his edition of the latter, p. 132 n. 1. It may be noted that Maimonides, whether or not familiar with Baḥya's reasoning, offered a similar interpretation of the traditional depictions of the material rewards in the Hereafter, without stressing, however, their historical limitations. See his *Commentary* on M. Sanhedrin x, ed. by J. Holzer, Text, pp. 4 ff. Perhaps he was led to invoke the historical explanation of sacrifices by a homily recorded in Lev. r., XXII.8, ed. by Margulies, pp. 517 f. See also G. Vajda's analysis of some Muslim sources of Baḥya's doctrine of repentance in *La Théologie ascétique,* pp. 99 ff.; and, more generally, G. Golinski's dissertation, *Das Wesen des Religionsgesetzes in der Philosophie des Bachja Ibn Pakuda.*

CHAPTER XXVIII: HOMILIES AND HISTORIES

1. Trullan Synod, canon 19, in Mansi's *Sacrorum conciliorum collectio,* XI, 951 f. (greatly abridged in Hefele's *Histoire,* III, Part 1, p. 566; and his *History,* trans. by Clark, V, 227); Leo the Philosopher's *Homiliae et panegyrici* in *PG,* CVII, 1–298 (uses frequently such terms as "perverse," "ingrate," or "formerly malevolent" synagogue; pp. 72, 89, etc.). On the story of Yannai and the peddler, see J. Mann's "Some Midrashic Genizah Fragments," *HUCA,* XIV, 304 f., 327; and Lev. r. XVI.2, ed. by M. Margulies, Vol. II, pp. 349 ff., with both editors' notes thereon. While the history of ancient rhetoric and Christian preaching has been the subject of extensive investigations for many decades, there is a dearth of information concerning early Jewish and Muslim homiletics. The ancient Jewish preachers and the methods used by them are discussed in the scanty literature listed *supra,* Vols. I, pp. 389 f. n. 51; II, pp. 382 n. 12, 422 f. n. 55, 429 n. 7. On the Muslim art of preaching and soapbox oratory, see the brief remarks by I. Goldziher in his *Muhammedanische Studien,* II, 161 ff.; and, somewhat more fully, J. Pedersen's studies of the "Islamic Preacher" in *Goldziher Mem. Vol.,* I, 226–51; and "The Criticism of the Islamic Preacher," *Welt des Islams,* n.s. II, 215–31. These brief analyses reveal many similarities, but also many differences, between the Muslim and Jewish preachers and storytellers.

Far more intensively cultivated has been the field of Byzantine homiletical research. See the still useful older survey by A. Ehrhard in K. Krumbacher's *Geschichte der byzantinischen Literatur,* 2d ed., pp. 160 ff., and his more recent comprehensive bibliographical and analytical work, *Ueberlieferung und Bestand der hagiographischen und homiletischen Literatur der griechischen Kirche von den Anfängen bis zum Ende des 16. Jahrhunderts.* Yet certain basic shortcomings were pointed out by modern students. Scholars "have often debated," observes J. List, "the problems concerning literary history, such as the authorship and genuineness of individual homilies; they have often taken cognizance of the sermons' content in so far as it served to characterize their authors' position in the history of Church and dogma. The sermons have also been treated philologically, and have furnished materials relevant to the history of language. But their literary form has seldom and but incidentally aroused the interest of students." See List's careful *Studien zur Homiletik Germanos I. von Konstantinopel und seiner Zeit,* p. iv. In the case of the Jewish homily, on the contrary, it was, for example, the literary form of the *petiḥah* (characteristic opening section) which attracted the greatest attention. See *infra,* n. 13. Considerable work has also been done on the methodological and theological-ethical aspects of the rabbinic homilies. See esp. I. Heinemann's searching analysis of the *Darkhe ha-Aggadah* (Methods of the Aggadah). But no effort has as yet been made to reconstruct ancient or early medieval sermons in all pertinent details, and we know even less about the informal addresses of Jewish leaders at communal assemblies. Equally neglected thus far have been the social aspects of the preacher's calling, his required training and economic status, the frequency of his public appearances, the size and reactions of average audiences, or even the attitude to sermons—in contradistinction to the Aggadah as a discipline—on the part of communal leaders. Of course, the extant sources take only incidental note of these aspects. It will require, therefore, considerable perseverance in assembling the stray bits of evidence, and much ingenuity in interpreting them, before any satisfactory answer to these questions can be supplied.

2. Abot de-R. Nathan, IV (first version; ed. by Schechter, p. 18); Maimonides' *Iggeret Qiddush ha-shem* (or *ha-Shemad;* Epistle on Martyrdom) in his *Qobeṣ teshubot,* ed. by Lichtenberg, II, fol. 12c; Cant. r. I.1.9; 15.2; IV.1.2. The date of the latter midrash is uncertain. But we may accept C. Albeck's suggestion (in his notes on Zunz's *Ha-Derashot,* p. 129) that the three midrashim on the Song of Songs, now known, are all excerpts from a much older compilation. In its present form, Cant. r. may, therefore, be as late as the parallel *Aggadah,* compiled toward the end of the tenth century, according to S. Schechter. See the latter's concluding remarks in his edition of the *Agadath Shir Hashirim,* pp. 100 ff.

A number of interesting aggadic statements scattered through the *She'eltot* of R. Aḥai are listed in I. H. Weiss's *Dor dor,* I, 23 n. 8. However, most of these clearly belong to the realm of ethics, on the borderline between Aggadah and Halakhah. Weiss has also pointed out that quite a few of these homiletical interpretations are not attested elsewhere and, hence, may be original with R. Aḥai. Of course, such an argument *a silentio* is always precarious, and doubly so in this area, in which only a small fraction of the written sources, and probably but an infinitesimal sampling of the oral traditions circulating in Aḥai's day, have come down to us. See *supra,* Chap. XXVII, nn. 38–42.

3. *Chronicle of Ahimaaz,* ed. by Salzman, pp. 5 f. (Hebrew), 67 ff. (English); ed. by B. Klar, pp. 18 f., 161 f. The words placed between parentheses in our quotation are a gratuitous addition of the English translator. Similarly Silano's reported erasure of two lines did not take place in the "scriptural portion" itself, which would have been easily detected, but rather in the text of "the midrash on the scriptural portion," as the original has it. This term suggests that a draft of the visitor's forthcoming address had been entrusted to Silano for the preparation of his Italian paraphrase, a procedure very likely adopted by many other preachers as well. It is generally assumed that our visitor was a messenger and fund raiser for the Jerusalem academy. See Mann, *Jews in Egypt,* I, 57; J. Marcus, "Studies in the Chronicle of Ahimaaz," *PAAJR,* V, 86; and A. Yaari, *Sheluḥe Ereṣ Yisrael* (Palestinian Messengers), p. 198. However, our text does not mention this fact. This silence is doubly remarkable, as a century earlier a brief epitaph erected in Venosa for a fourteen-year-old girl emphasized that she had been eulogized by *duo apostuli et duo rabbites* (two messengers and two rabbis; see Frey's *Corpus,* No. 611). Nor is it likely that a fund raiser would have spent several weeks in the relatively minor community of Venosa, and that Silano would have played his trick had it interfered with the visitor's charitable mission. More probably he was merely an itinerant preacher who, at least in the Muslim world, was considered a legitimate object of derision.

4. See Gen. r. XXXIII.3, ed. by Theodor and Albeck, p. 307; j. Shabbat XVI.1, 15c; *Massekhet Soferim* XVI.2, 8, 10 (ed. by Higger, pp. 284, 291 ff., 296 f.; see also the introduction, pp. 24 ff.); b. Temurah 14b; Giṭṭin 60a. These objections to the written Aggadah had nothing to do, of course, with any rationalist compunctions about its veracity and practical validity, on which see *infra,* n. 29.

5. Gen. r. IX.5, p. 70; C. Rabin's "Notes on the Habakkuk Scroll and the Zadokite Documents" (with a Note by J. W. B. Barns), *VT,* V, 148–62. So popular did R. Meir's marginal note become that it elicited a considerable number of variations on the same theme by later rabbis, and seems even to have displaced the masoretic text in some copies. David Qimḥi read about the existence of that version, *tob mot,* in an ancient Torah preserved in the "synagogue of Severus" in Rome. See his *Commentary* on Gen. 1:31; the comments thereon in M. M. Kasher's *Torah schelemah* (Complete Torah: Talmudic-Midrashic Encyclopedia of the Pentateuch), I, 174 No. 817; and *supra,* Vol. II, pp. 187, 400 n. 19.

6. See esp. the apocalyptic midrashim discussed *supra,* Chap. XXV. Many such apocryphal works became known only in recent generations. With untiring effort A. Jellinek published many smaller writings in the six successive volumes of his *Bet ha-Midrasch* (reprinted in Jerusalem in 1938). Another indefatigable researcher in this area was S. A. Wertheimer. See esp. his *Bate midrashot* (a midrashic anthology) in the posthumous edition revised by his grandson, A. J. Wertheimer. Some further manuscript material was brought to light by Ḥasidah in his periodical *Hasseggulah;* and by others, listed *supra,* Vol. II, pp. 427 ff. n. 6. J. D. Eisenstein's *Ozar Midrashim: A Library of Two Hundred Minor Midrashim,* in alphabetical order, is very comprehensive, but its introductions and notes are keyed to a more popular audience and are not free from significant factual errors.

Midrashic creativity continued, especially in Yemen, down to the modern period. Among the Yemenite midrashim one must assign the first place to the *Midrash Hagadol* (see the editions listed Vol. II, *loc. cit.*), compiled by David al-Adeni in the thirteenth century, although S. Fish claims that David merely translated an earlier Arabic compilation by Abraham Maimonides. See Fish's Hebrew essay on the "Midrash Haggadol: Its Author, Its Date and Place, and Its Importance in Rabbinic Literature," *Melilah,* I, 129–41. Actually, some biblical commentaries written in that southern land between the thirteenth and the fifteenth centuries appeared under the name of midrashim. Occasionally, Arabic-speaking authors would produce a mixed Arabic-Hebrew midrash such as was written by a fourteenth-century philosophically minded homilist and published in part by M. Friedländer in the *Steinschneider Festschrift,* Hebrew section, pp. 49–59; and in the *Gedenkbuch Kaufmann,* Hebrew section, pp. 1–7. Cf. Steinschneider's *Arabische Literatur,* pp. 286 No. 90c, 292 No. 125. Curiously, we even find an obscure midrash explaining a verse in the Qur'an (20:95). See in general S. Lieberman's lecture on *Midreshe Teman* (Yemenite Midrashim), esp. pp. 10 ff., 18, 39. This plethora of midrashim, partly quoting older traditions, both genuine and spurious, and partly adding hermeneutic interpretations of their own, has aggravated the difficulties of dating. The most useful guide still remains Zunz's *Ha-Derashot,* with the more up-to-date comments by Albeck.

7. Ketubot 106a; Pesaḥim 94a, 112a; 'A.Z. 9a; *Seder Eliyahu, rabba* and *zuṭa,* ed. by Friedmann, II, VI, XXIX, pp. 6 f., 163, and n. 52. On the much-debated date of *Seder Eliyahu,* its relation to the earlier work cited by this name in the Talmud, and the authenticity of the chronological passages, see the older literature reviewed in M. Kadushin's *Theology of Seder Eliahu,* pp. 3 ff.; V. Aptowitzer's "Seder Elia" in *Kohut Mem. Vol.,* pp. 5 ff.; and Albeck's critical comments in Zunz's *Ha-Derashot,* pp. 55 ff., 292 ff. This century-old debate received a new impetus with the publica-

tion in 1928 of a responsum by the ninth-century gaon, Naṭronai bar Hilai, which had described the then current version of *Seder Eliyahu, rabbah* and *zuṭa,* as consisting of thirty and twelve chapters respectively, and asserted that "what the Talmud quotes in the name of the *Debe-Eliyahu* is all found in that work." See the text published by S. Assaf in his *Teshubot ha-geonim,* 1928, p. 176 No. 163; and his comments thereon in the intro. to that fragment, pp. 153 f.

More recently, M. Margulies subjected this work to a renewed critical analysis. In his ingenious study, "On the Problem of the Antiquity of *Seder Eliyahu*" (Hebrew), *Sefer Assaf,* pp. 370–90, he demonstrated the weaknesses of the older negativistic arguments, and identified an early third-century Palestinian sage, Abba Eliyahu as the author of our Midrash. A native of Yabneh, the preacher lived for a time in Jerusalem but subsequently moved to Babylonia. Witnessing there the profound effects of the transition from Parthian to Persian rule under Ardashir, he saw in them forebodings of the coming of the Messiah. He traveled from place to place, delivering discourses and inspiring his audiences with the moral teachings of Judaism, citing statements by no less than twenty-four tannaitic authorities (but none of later date) and opening vistas for the speedy redemption of the people. One need not accept all of Margulies's arguments. For instance, his assumption of Abba Eliyahu's prolonged residence in Jerusalem in the face of the strict Hadrianic prohibition still appears rather dubious. Moreover, like other similar literary products of antiquity, this work was subject to interpolations and other changes by later scribes and interpreters. But its core may indeed have come down from ancient times, preserving for us at least some semblance of this oldest full-length midrashic compilation. Needless to say, much detailed and painstaking work will still be needed before the original version is more fully recovered and isolated from the later layers. See also R. J. Z. Werblowsky, "A Note on the Text of *Seder Eliyahu,*" *JJS,* VI, 201–11.

8. *Midrash Agur* in Menahem de Lonzano's *Shete Yadot* (Two Hands; a collection of midrashim, see the title page); H. G. Enelow's edition of the *Mishnah of Rabbi Eliezer,* pp. 56 ff. (English), 57, 65 ff., 184 lines 10 ff. (Hebrew). Although toying with other strange etymologies to justify the identification of Agur with Solomon, Saadiah admitted the possibility that Agur was an even earlier author and that the last two chapters in Proverbs may have been quoted by the king from him. See Saadiah's trans. of Prov. 30:1 and his comment thereon in his *Oeuvres,* V, 183. The date of that midrash is no less controversial than that of *Seder Eliyahu.* While its recent editor, H. G. Enelow, as well as L. Ginzberg and M. Gifter, without entirely agreeing among themselves, attributed it to the fourth or fifth century, J. N. Epstein saw it as a product of the late seventh and H. Albeck as that of the eighth century. Disputing these theories which he briefly enumerated, M. Zucker compared that midrash with some extant parts, published and unpublished, of Saadiah's *Commentary* on the Bible, and he concluded that its author had heavily borrowed from the gaon in both content and phraseology. See the second section of his stimulating essay "On the Solution of the Problem of the Thirty-Two Modes of Interpretation and the 'Mishnah of Rabbi Eliezer,'" *PAAJR,* XXIII, Hebrew section, pp. 20 ff. On the *Midrash Agur,* its nature and name, as well as the complex bibliographical problems of its first printings, see also S. Lieberman, "Midrash of the Thirty-Two Modes—Midrash Agur" (Hebrew), *GK,* V, 186–90 (with special reference to an intriguing text published by L. Ginzberg in his Hebrew essay, "Three Fragmentary Homilies

from an Unknown Midrash," *Tarbiz,* IV, 297–342); and S. H. Kook, "Midrash Agur" (Hebrew), *KS,* XXVIII, 206–9.

In any case, P. Maas's deprecatory observation on the Christian sermons of the fourth century for which even testimony furnished by old manuscripts "has no more weight than a feather" (cf. his "Kontakion," *BZ,* XIX, 291 n. 1), applies with equal force to the somewhat more reputable midrashic records. On the Midrash *Ve-Eleh ezkerah* (And These I Shall Remember) and the story of the Ten Martyrs, see *supra,* Vols. I, p. 231; II, p. 370 n. 9. In regard to numerous later Yemenite compilations, Lieberman has rightly noted that many names of ancient sages recorded in them were but figments of a fertile imagination, and expressed amazement that modern scholars had treated them seriously. See his *Midreshe Teman,* p. 39.

9. Despite their basic similarity in method and general approach, the Palestinian Targumim differed greatly from the midrashim on the same books precisely because they had to reproduce the biblical text verse by verse. Suffice it to compare the Targum on the Song of Songs with either the *Shir ha-shirim rabbah* or the *Agadat Shir ha-Shirim* (often erroneously called *zuṭa*). The former (also called *ḥazita,* because of its *incipit* borrowed from Prov. 22:29) is available in many editions, including a greatly divergent recension published by L. Grünhut in 1897. Cf. also the additional significant variants (from a MS Landau) in S. A. Wertheimer's *Bate midrashot,* I, 347 ff. The shorter midrash was published, almost simultaneously, by S. Schechter (*Agadath Shir Hashirim*) and S. Buber (in his collection *Midrasch suta* which includes also junior compilations for the books of Ruth, Lamentations, and Ecclesiastes and other midrashic fragments). On the question of priority, see Schechter's review of Buber's ed. in *MGWJ,* XXXIX, 562–66. This collection is also available in a German translation with a brief introduction and notes by R. Brasch, who rightly gives preference to the Schechter edition (pp. 4 f.). The influence of the Targum of the Song of Songs on later medieval aggadists is well illustrated in the case of the Byzantine author, Tobiah ben Eliezer. See L. J. Liebreich's "Midrash Lekah Tob's Dependence upon the Targum to the Song of Songs 8, 11–12," *JQR,* XXXVIII, 63–66. See also, more generally, P. Vulliaud, *Le Cantique des cantiques d'après la tradition juive; supra,* Vol. II, p. 386 n. 23; Mann's "Some Midrashic Genizah Fragments," *HUCA,* XIV, 333 ff.; and Zunz's *Ha-Derashot,* pp. 128 f., 404 f. Similarly the so-called *Targum sheni* (Second Aramaic Version) of Esther is rightly called the "Aggadah of the Scroll of Esther" by Rashi, the first commentator to mention it (on I Kings 10:19), and some older editions. On its date about 650–700, see Zunz's *Ha-Derashot,* pp. 264 f. n. 87; and M. David's intro. to his critical ed. of this text, entitled *Das Targum scheni zum Buche Esther,* p. vii n. 3.

10. Origen's *In Canticum Canticorum Homilia Prima,* Prologue, in *PG,* XIII, 63 f. (in Rufinus' Latin trans.); and M. Friedländer's aforementioned ed. of the Arabic-Hebrew midrash in the *Steinschneider Festschrift,* Hebrew section, p. 53, with the comments thereon by A. Marmorstein in his "Deux renseignements d'Origène concernant les Juifs," *REJ,* LXXI, 195 f.; and esp. by S. Lieberman in his *Midreshe Teman,* pp. 12 ff. The Judeo-Arabic midrash concludes with the majority opinion holding that "one is allowed to read the Song of Songs in its ordinary meaning, but one does not reveal its matters of wisdom [mysteries] except to a judge or elder of the city." Cf. the related statement in the minor tractate *Kallah* (1.4) that "he who reads a verse in the Song of Songs and turns it into a sort of song . . . brings a

deluge upon the world," in Higger's ed. p. 127, with the other sources listed there. See also, from another angle, J. P. Smith, "Hebrew Christian Midrash in Irenaeus, Epid. 43," *Biblica,* XXXVIII, 24–34.

11. On Simon Qara, see the scanty biographical data assembled by M. Horovitz in his *Frankfurter Rabbinen,* pp. vi f., 2 f. The *Yalquṭ Shime'oni* seems to have been written not long before its oldest manuscript now extant (in the Bodleian Library), which is dated 1307. See A. Neubauer and A. E. Cowley, *Catalogue of the Hebrew Manuscripts in the Bodleian Library,* II, 34 f. No. 2637. The colophon seems to indicate that already at that time the copyist had found the compiler's annotations relating to his sources in an appendix, rather than in the text itself. Another manuscript consulted by Azariah de' Rossi had been written in 1310. See De' Rossi's *Me'or 'Einayim* (Light of the Eyes; historical studies), XIX, ed. by D. Cassel, p. 230. Of modern investigations, see esp. A. Epstein, "R. Simon Kara and the Yalquṭ ha-shime'oni" (Hebrew), *Ha-Ḥoqer,* I, 85–93 (denying Qara's authorship); E. (L.) Grünhut, "The Author of the *Yalquṭ Shime'oni* and the *Mekhilta* of R. Simon bar Yoḥai" (Hebrew), *Sokolow Jub. Vol.,* pp. 232–40; and Zunz and Albeck, *Ha-Derashot,* pp. 146 ff., 443 ff.

In consonance with his general "lachrymose" conception of Jewish history, Zunz explains the early neglect of the *Yalquṭ* by the general persecutions and impoverishment of German Jewry during that period. Such impoverishment might indeed have accounted for the absence of customers for a weighty and expensive volume. But, as we have just seen, at least two manuscripts were copied within two or three years of one another at the beginning of the fourteenth century. Certainly, as R. Isaac had long before observed, poverty was generally conducive to the spread of aggadic interests. It is more likely, therefore, that the author's failure to cater to the pietistic and folkloristic predilections of those generations militated against his popularity, when compared, for example, with that of Yehudah he-Ḥasid's "Book of the Pious." Perhaps for the same reason the later *Yalquṭ ha-Makhiri,* written by Makhir bar Abba Mari in the latter part of the fourteenth century, likewise suffered from widespread neglect, notwithstanding its considerable scholarly and literary merits. It was so totally ignored, in fact, during the following three centuries, that only a few fragments could be pieced together by modern scholars, and the first author to mention it was the distinguished bibliographer Shabbetai Bass (1648–1718). See J. Z. Lauterbach's "Unpublished Parts of the Yalkut ha-Makiri on Hosea and Micah," *Gaster Anniversary Volume,* pp. 363–73, which also includes a comparison between the two *yalquṭim.*

12. *Pesiqta de-R. Kahana* (Pesikta, die älteste Hagada redigirt in Palästina von Rab Kahana), ed. by S. Buber, fol. 1b, with the editor's comment thereon. A new critical edition is now being prepared on the basis of seven known MSS by D. (B.) Mandelbaum. See the sample published in his "Pesiqta de-R. Kahana, Sheqalim" in *M. M. Kaplan Jubilee Volume,* Hebrew section, pp. 123–48. On the recitation of the chapter relating to the Tabernacle on the Sabbath of Ḥanukkah, see *Massekhet Soferim,* XX.8, ed. by Higger, p. 349; and the literature listed there. That the original compilation of the *Pesiqta* probably began with a New Year's sermon, rather than with one on Ḥanukkah as now given in both texts, is rightly stressed in H. L. Strack's *Introduction to the Talmud and Midrash,* English trans. from the German, pp. 210 ff., 334 ff. Although the reading *Pesiqta* is generally accepted, M. Friedmann,

the editor of the *Pesiqta rabbati,* suggested that the original reading was *Pisqata* (Chapters). See the introduction to his edition, pp. 25 f. Accepting Friedmann's contention that it was a plural form, L. Blau proposed the reading, *Pesiqata* (Sections). See "The Names of Works in Oral Law," *Poznanski Mem. Vol.,* Hebrew section, pp. 12 f. Neither scholar insisted, however, on changing the now accepted pronunciation. The date of the compilation of these two midrashim is likewise controversial, but the weight of scholarly opinion leans toward dating the *Pesiqta de-R. Kahana* in the seventh century and *Pesiqta rabbati* in the ninth century. Cf. C. Albeck's arguments in *Ginzberg Jub. Vol.,* Hebrew section, pp. 36 ff.; his and Zunz's *Ha-Derashot,* pp. 81 ff., 107, 117 ff., 121, and the notes thereon.

13. See List's *Studien;* D. Gerson's analysis of "Die Commentarien des Ephraem Syrus im Verhältniss zur jüdischen Exegese," *MGWJ,* XVII, 16–33, 64–72, 98–109, 141–49; and *infra,* Chap. XXIX, n. 66. As pointed out by S. Buber, the present text of Lam. r. contains the full thirty-six proems, two each being included in Nos. 2 and 31. See the intro. to his ed. of *Midrash Ekhah rabbati,* p. 4. Possibly, however, these were later interpolations by a copyist who wished to round out the number to thirty-six. All but five of the proems in Lam. r. lead up to an express quotation of the first word or words of that biblical book. These five (Nos. 16, 24, 25, 28 and 34), too, end with a clear intimation of mourning for the destruction of the sanctuary, which easily led to the subsequent elaboration of the main theme of the book. The date of the compilation of that midrash still is uncertain. Zunz's suggestion that it was completed in the seventh century was based on the reading "Yishmael" instead of "Se'ir" in the homily on Lam. 1:14 (ed. by Buber, p. 77). But even the former version might have referred to the pre-Islamic rule of Nabataeans or Lakhmids. Cf. Buber's observation, p. 9; and *infra,* n. 15. Cf. also the monographs listed in Strack's *Introduction,* p. 341 n. 4.

The general problems of the *petiḥah* have been discussed frequently and with considerable attention to detail. See esp. W. Bacher's *Proömien der alten jüdischen Homilie,* supplemented by several specialized monographs by D. Künstlinger (e.g., *Die Petichot des Midrasch Rabba zu Leviticus*), and others; I. Heinemann's terminological remarks in his Hebrew essay, "On the Development of Technical Terms in Bible Exegesis," *Leshonenu,* XVI, 23 ff.; and C. Albeck's intro. to his and Theodor's edition of Gen. r., pp. 11 ff. Bacher (pp. 19 ff.) has shown, though perhaps not quite so conclusively as one might wish, that the proem was used by R. Eliezer ben Hyrcanus and R. Joshua ben Ḥananiah soon after the fall of Jerusalem. In his *Bible as Read* (I, 11 ff.), J. Mann vigorously argued in favor of a constant nexus between the theme of the proem and the extrapentateuchal readings appended to the weekly and holiday lessons, the so-called *hafṭarot.* So convinced was Mann of this essential combination that he even attempted, without other evidence, to reconstruct from some themes of introductory remarks the underlying *hafṭarot*—indubitably an act of daring. As a matter of fashion, it appears, rather than for any intrinsic reasons, Zechariah's prophecy, "The residue of My people shall spoil them, and the remnant of My nation shall inherit them" (2:9), was found to offer a particularly expressive finale for an epilogue and was widely used by medieval preachers. Cf. the instances quoted in Ginzberg's *Ginze Schechter,* I, 136. Cf. also, from other angles, E. Stein, "Die homiletische Peroratio im Midrasch," *HUCA,* VIII–IX, 353–71 (chiefly concerned with the sermon's messianic conclusions); A. Marmorstein's remarks on "The Background of the Haggadah," *ibid.,* VI, 183 ff.;

and more generally, I. L. Seeligmann's "Voraussetzungen der Midraschexegese," *VT*, Supplement I, 150–81, pointing out the dynamic nature of the midrashic exegesis which, with all its reverence for the accepted text, felt free to treat it as if its formulations still were in the process of evolution.

14. Jaḥiẓ, cited in Goldziher's *Muhammedanische Studien,* II, 162 f.; Suyuti's *K. Tabaqat* (Liber de interpretibus Korani), ed. by A. Meursinge, p. 22. The various midrashim, in particular those known under the name of Midrash rabbah, although compiled by various authors over a period of several centuries (from Gen. r., which is generally dated in the fifth or sixth century, down to Num. r., the first part of which apparently quotes the distinguished eleventh-century French preacher, R. Moses ha-Darshan; see Zunz's *Ha-Derashot,* pp. 76 ff., 122 ff., and the literature cited in the notes thereon), seem to have originated from such primarily exegetical discourses. Strack's distinction among the midrashim bearing the name of *rabbot,* some of which, including Gen. r. and Lam. r., he calls "expositional" whereas the four midrashim on Exodus to Deuteronomy, including the admittedly old Lev. r., are styled "homiletic" (cf. his *Introduction,* pp. 210 ff., 217 ff.), is decidedly artificial. Both groups had originated in part from sermons delivered in the synagogues, and in part from exegetical efforts at academies or private studies. As epitomes of sermons grew more lengthy, such excerpts occupied relatively more space and were more fully included in the later compilations. See also M. Margulies's critical edition of *Midrash Wayyikra Rabbah.* The differences, as well as similarities, between the attitude of the ancient Jewish homilists, even including Philo, toward their Scripture and that of their Hellenistic confreres toward Homer are succinctly discussed in Heinemann's *Darkhe ha-Aggadah,* esp. pp. 182 f.

15. Origen's *De principiis* (*Peri archon*), IV.11 (*PG,* XI, 364 f.). See *supra,* Vol. II, pp. 137 f., 144, 382 ff.; and Chap. XXV, n. 21. In his aforementioned essay (n. 8), M. Zucker attacked the accepted notions concerning the antiquity of the system of the special thirty-two modes of aggadic interpretation, contrasted with the thirteen modes long accepted for halakhic hermeneutics and formulated in the so-called *Mishnah of R. Eliezer.* Cf. the Hebrew text, ed. by Enelow, pp. 11, 36 ff. (the elaboration follows a slightly different order); the introduction to the *Midrash Haggadol* on Genesis, ed. by M. Margulies, pp. 22 f. (here are also listed the numerous previous eds. of the Midrash of the Thirty-Two Modes, and the commentaries thereon); and the older debate on this score between L. Bardowicz (in *Die Abfassungszeit der Baraita der 32 Normen*); and V. Aptowitzer (in "Das Alter der Baraita der 32 Normen," *Schwarz Festschrift,* pp. 121–32). With great assurance Enelow dates the *Mishnah of Rabbi Eliezer* in the fourth century. An early date is also advocated by M. Gifter, notwithstanding his own demonstration that the work contains ingredients from both the Palestinian and Babylonian traditions recorded in the two Talmudim. Cf. his "Halakhah in the Midrash of R. Eliezer son of R. Jose ha-Gelili" (Hebrew), *Talpioth,* I, Part 2, pp. 314–35; II, 132–38; VI, 674–85. Other scholars, and particularly C. Albeck, have proved, however, that the bulk of the midrash, esp. beginning with Chapter III, was compiled much later; Albeck thought that it had been done in the eighth century. See Albeck's note on Zunz's *Ha-Derashot,* pp 142 f., 436 nn. 73–74; and J. N. Epstein's Hebrew notes "On the Mishnah of R. Eliezer, Son of R. Jose the Galilean" in *Tarbiz,* IV, 343–53. On the basis of Genizah fragments which he publishes, Zucker goes further and postulates the emergence of this entire enumeration in the late geonic age. He contends that the thirty-two

modes are but a selection from forty-nine modes systematized by Samuel ben Ḥofni Gaon for the study of the nonlegal parts of Scripture. But Zucker himself quotes (pp. 5 f.) Samuel's assertion that he had collected these modes from earlier writings. With his well-known penchant for systematization (see *supra,* Chap. XXVII, n. 78), the gaon may indeed have collected stray items from many writings and built them into a logical system. Independently there may have existed the earlier collection of the *"Mishnah,"* even if its occasional Arabisms should be accepted as decisive evidence for its compilation in the Muslim era. For the time being it will be more prudent, therefore, to suspend final judgment about both the origin of the list of thirty-two modes and the date of its formulation by "R. Eliezer." But no matter to what date we ascribe their initial compilation, the thirty-two modes are essentially a heritage of the Hellenistic-talmudic approaches to the hermeneutic interpretation of ancient sources. Cf. also *infra,* n. 30; and the studies listed *supra,* Vol. II, p. 427 n. 4.

16. See esp. such mystical midrashim as the *Otiot de-R. 'Aqiba* (Letters of R. 'Aqiba) which will be discussed more fully *infra,* Chap. XXXIII. The overwhelming majority of foreign etymologies are derived from Greek and, to a lesser extent, from Latin. See, e.g., the list in Lam. r., ed. by Buber, pp. 55 ff.; and that prepared by M. Güdemann for Friedmann's ed. of the Pesiqta r., fols. 203b ff. This fact by itself testifies to the origin of most midrashim from a Graeco-Roman, especially Byzantine environment. Even the occasional Arabic words need not date from the Muslim period. For example, the two Arabic etymologies suggested in Lam. r. on 1:15 and 2:13 (ed. by Buber, pp. 78, 118) are not only quoted in the name of a third-century sage, R. Levi (bar Ḥamma), but they refer specifically to the dialect spoken "in Arabia," and not the Arabic spoken by Jews or their Arab neighbors in Palestine.

Incidentally, debates on such casual utterances point up the difficulties of dating midrashic works, since not even direct references to Arabs are really conclusive. For example, the same midrash discusses, with reference to Lam. 1:14 (ed. by Buber, p. 77), the reigns "of Edom and Ishmael." Apart from the possibility that the homilist had some pre-Islamic Arabs in mind, the original MS has *Se'ir,* instead of Ishmael. Because it seems to be but a duplication of *Edom,* this evidently is the *lectio difficilior,* and as such more likely to be authentic. The preacher may have wished to contrast the earlier, milder domination of pagan Rome (Se'ir) with the outspokenly anti-Jewish regime of Christian Rome (the usual equivalent of Edom). Certainly a copyist of the Muslim period could easily substitute the word *Ishmael* for *Se'ir.* See also Buber's intro., p. 9. It is indeed so cited, though in the reverse order, by the later author of *Midrash Tehillim,* on Ps. 6:1 (ed. by Buber, p. 59). Later copyists and paraphrasts, understandably, replaced also many Greek loan words, no longer familiar to their communities, by Hebrew equivalents. That this happened, for example, in the case of homilies included in the "original" *Midrash Tanḥuma* was shown by Ginzberg in *Ginze Schechter,* I, 107 f.

17. Lam. r. II, ed. by Buber, p. 100; j. Ta'aniot IV.8, 68d. Cf. C. Albeck's plausible arguments (in *Ginzberg Jub. Vol.,* pp. 34, 42) in favor of dating Lam. r. *after* Lev. r., that is at the end of the sixth century or later; and N. Wieder's introduction to his German translation of that midrash, p. 15.

18. See Giṭṭin 57b; Lam. r. on 1:16, ed. by Buber, pp. 84 ff.; *Seder Eliyahu r.* XXIX (XXX), ed. by Friedmann, pp. 151 ff. (apparently a later interpolation, cf. Friedmann's

note 17). The reasons for the switch from the Maccabean heroes to the Maccabean martyrs, were discussed *supra,* Vols. I, p. 400 n. 30; II, pp. 383 f. n. 15. On the liturgical role of the Scroll of the Hasmoneans (or of Antiochus), cf. Isaiah of Trani's *Tosefot ReYaD* (Halakhic Comments on the Talmud), on Sukkah 42b. The peculiarities of that Scroll and its mixture of history and legend will be more fully analyzed *infra,* n. 44.

19. See, e.g., J. Barth, "Midraschische Elemente in der muslimischen Tradition," *Festschrift A. Berliner,* pp. 33–40. The tale of the impoverished widow's sudden affluence was published from a Cambridge Genizah fragment by Ginzberg in his *Ginze Schechter,* I, 298, 302 ff., while the "Story of R. Meir," extant in Oxford MSS in both Arabic and Hebrew, is included in the latter version in Wertheimer's *Bate midrashot,* I, 184 ff. This narrative need not refer to the well-known Tanna, although popular imagination liked to weave many a legend around him and his wife, Beruriah. To illustrate, for example, the behavior of a "woman of valour," a homilist described at some length Beruriah's fortitude in concealing the death of their two sons from R. Meir until after the Sabbath. See *Midrash Mishle* on Prov. 31:10, ed. by S. Buber, pp. 108 f.; and on its likely influence on somewhat similar Arabic stories, M. Goldmann's "Geschichte von Rabbi Meir und Beruria in arabischer Fassung," *MGWJ,* LXXXI, 81–85. See also *infra,* n. 39.

The fact that many of these midrashic compositions have come to light only in recent years does not necessarily militate against their original popularity. Quite likely they were disparaged by the intellectual leaders and kept out of permanent use in communal libraries and archives. Hence each discovery of such a midrash in a genizah may be considered a lucky find. Even the great popularity of the *Pirqe de-R. Eliezer,* did not prevent its concluding chapter from long lying dormant in a manuscript. It was first published by Wertheimer and reprinted in his *Bate,* I, 225 ff. On the *isra'liyat* see S. D. Goitein's analysis, with special reference to Malik ibn Dinar, in *Tarbiz,* VI, 89–101, 510–22; and, more generally, the literature cited *supra,* Chap. XVII, nn. 12, 15. The fundamental similarities, notwithstanding certain interesting differences in detail, of the approach to great biblical figures in Jewish, Christian, and Muslim letters are well illustrated by a series of essays on "Moïse, l'homme de l'alliance" by R. Bloch *et al.* in a special issue of *Cahiers sioniens,* VIII, 93–402. See also A. Rosmarin's older study of *Moses im Lichte der Agada;* and the vast materials accumulated in L. Ginzberg's *Legends of the Jews,* Vols. V–VI; or in the shorter version entitled *Legends of the Bible.*

20. Maimonides' *Commentary* on M. Sanhedrin x.1, in J. Holzer's *Zur Geschichte der Dogmenlehre,* p. 20; Peter of Cluny's *Tractatus adversus Judaeorum inveteratam duritiem,* v end, in *PL,* CLXXXIX, 645 ff. Two different recensions of the *Alfa beta de-Ben Sira* (Alphabet of Ben Sira) are available in critical and well-annotated eds. by M. Steinschneider and, on the basis of a Budapest MS, by D. Z. Friedmann and D. S. Löwinger in *Blau Jub. Vol.,* pp. 250–81. Friedmann and Löwinger reject the accepted notion that this concoction originated in a Muslim environment after the eighth century (see, e.g., Israel Lévi, "La Nativité de Ben Sira," *REJ,* XXIX, 197–205) and point out that several talmudic quotations of sayings by Sirach, too, are missing from the ancient collections. This argument is only partially valid. There undoubtedly circulated among the ancient Palestinians numerous epigrams ascribed to Sirach; some of these were accepted by the rabbis and quoted as gems of true

wisdom; others were rejected. All existing collections were, therefore, under a cloud of suspicion. But apparently it was only in the Muslim period that a few epigrams would be picked out by a fiction writer in order to attach to them stories whose theme remotely resembled their content. One of these more ancient epigrams (not the subsequent yarn on it) relating to the psychological effects of a thin or a thick beard, may well have been quoted by a Muslim student of the Qur'an via Ka'b al-Aḥbar. See E. Marmorstein's "Note on the 'Alphabet of Ben Sira,'" *JQR,* XLI, 303–6.

21. The extremely complicated problems of the literary provenance and form of the *Yelamdenu* midrashim and their relation to *Midrash Tanḥuma,* which is extant in two widely divergent forms (available, respectively, in the older editions and in the more critical edition by S. Buber), have been the subject of heated controversies over many decades. See the literature listed by L. Ginzberg in his *Ginze Schechter,* I, 32. The debate entered a new phase with the discovery of new fragments from the Genizah and their publication by Ginzberg (*ibid.,* pp. 23 ff.; see also his lengthy excursus, pp. 449–513) and, later, by Mann in his *Bible as Read,* Vol. I, Hebrew section, pp. 7 f., 69 ff., 112 ff., 149 ff. See also the latter's collection of *Yelamdenu* excerpts from the so-called *Yalquṭ talmud torah, ibid.,* pp. 270 ff.

Rather prematurely, Ginzberg thought that the new documents had contributed to the ultimate solution of the problem. He postulated the existence of a very old, almost tannaitic midrash, which began with a brief legal discussion, was followed by a succinct homily on an aggadic subject, and then took up more fully topics specifically suggested by the weekly lesson. While some quotations from that early midrash penetrated the various versions of *Tanḥuma,* as well as other midrashic works, the *Tanḥuma* was nevertheless an independent work using newer homilies as well. This theory was repudiated by Mann (*loc. cit.*), who attributed the fragments published by him to the *Tanḥuma.* Regrettably, the fuller discussion promised for Vol. III never appeared. Other students of the Aggadah also voiced dissent. In his "Zur Erforschung des Jelamdenu-Problems," *MGWJ,* LXXIV, 266–84, A. Marmorstein not only published additional fragments of that midrash, but also argued that, because of its constant use of the divine name *Elohim,* it must have been compiled some time after Gen. r., but before Exod. r. or Num. r. This criterion was questioned by K. Wilhelm in his introductory remarks to another "Jelamdenu-Fragment," *ibid.,* LXXV, 137; and rather lamely defended by Marmorstein, *ibid.,* pp. 377–79. It was further weakened by the frequency with which the divine name El, rather than the Tetragrammaton, had been used already by the Qumran sectarians in their Dead Sea Scrolls. Finally, disregarding this new midrashic "Elohist" and using other linguistic criteria, Aptowitzer came to the "heretical" conclusion that there never existed an original *Yelamdenu* or *Tanḥuma,* but that all the pertinent midrashim depended on Aḥai's *She'eltot.* See his "Scheeltoth und Jelamdenu," *MGWJ,* LXXVI, 558–75; and *supra,* Chap. XXVII, nn. 39 ff. See also M. Stein's methodologically significant Hebrew essay "On the Study of the Yelamdenu Midrashim," *Księga jubileuszowa . . . Moses Schorr* (M. Schorr Jubilee Volume), pp. 85–112; and Albeck's notes on Zunz's *Ha-Derashot,* pp. 112 ff., 373 ff. These problems must, therefore, be left open for the present.

22. See Goldziher's *Muhammedanische Studien,* II, 167 (quoting Ibn al-Jauzi); his *Richtungen der islamischen Koranauslegung,* pp. 91, 289 ff.; Ginzberg's *Ginze*

Schechter, I, 310 ff.; and particularly B. Heller's interesting data on "Die Scheu vor Unbekanntem, Unbenanntem in Agada und Apokryphen," *MGWJ*, LXXXIII, 170–84. This "shyness" may readily be explained by the fear of many preachers and storytellers that they might lose prestige or money, or both. See also *supra* Chap. XXV; and Aptowitzer's detailed analysis of the legends concerning "Asenath, the Wife of Joseph," *HUCA*, I, 239–306.

23. On R. Moses ha-Darshan, his likely authorship of the *Midrash Tadshe* (so called because it begins with a comment on Gen. 1:11), and the latter's indebtedness to either the book of Jubilees or Philo, see the texts and introductions in A. Epstein's *Mi-Qadmoniyot ha-Yehudim* (Beiträge zur jüdischen Alterthumskunde), I, 139 ff. (finding influences of Jubilees even where our texts of that apocryphal book fail to supply a parallel); his monograph, *R. Mosheh ha-Darshan mi-Narbona* (R. Moses the Preacher of Narbonne), reproduced in his *Kitbe*, ed. by Habermann, I, 213–44 (incidentally pointing out the occasional confusion between the preacher of Narbonne and Moses the Preacher of Coucy who lived two centuries later and produced a distinguished law code); J.-J. Brierre-Narbonne's *Commentaire de la Genèse de R. Moïse le Prédicateur* (defending the authenticity of the midrashic quotations in Raymond Martini's *Pugio fidei*); C. Albeck's introduction to his ed. of *Midrash Bereshit Rabbati*, pp. 16 f.; and S. Belkin's "Midrash Tadshe or the Midrash of R. Pinḥas ben Yair: an Ancient Hellenistic Midrash" (Hebrew), *Horeb*, XI, 1–52 (showing that Midrash's great dependence on certain Philonian doctrines). Belkin takes an extreme "either-or" position in denying the influences of Jubilees altogether. More probably, our author compiled sayings based upon a variety of doctrines circulating in his immediate environment, which must have preserved traditions less familiar, or more effectively suppressed, in the Eastern centers. Even in the East, we recall, some residua of Philo's works were known in the ninth and tenth centuries, probably even in Hebrew translation. See *supra*, Chap. XXV, n. 50. In any case, the peripheral areas of Jewish life in France and the Yemen may well have had access to sources which had interveningly disappeared from the main intellectual centers of geonic learning. See also other examples analyzed by C. Albeck in his "Agadot im Lichte der Pseudepigraphen," *MGWJ*, LXXXIII, 162–69.

24. A fuller analysis of Martini's work and the extent to which his quotations may be helpful in reconstructing older Jewish midrashim must be deferred until our treatment of the Judeo-Christian controversies in the later Middle Ages. Here we need but mention some major studies in this field in addition to those listed in the last note; and *supra*, Chap. XXV, n. 8. Among the Jewish defenders of the essential authenticity of Martini's quotations are especially Abraham Epstein in his "Bereshit-rabbati . . . Dessen Verhältnis zu Rabba-Rabbati, Moses ha-Darschan und Pugio fidei," *MWJ*, XV, esp. pp. 85 ff.; and S. Lieberman in his *Shkiin* (Sheqi'in); and, more fully, in his "Raymund Martini and His Alleged Forgeries," *HJ*, V, 87–102. On the other side accusers of Martini's forgeries beginning with Abravanel's *Yeshu'ot meshiḥo* (The Salvation of His Anointed) found strong support in Y. Baer's detailed study of "The Forged Midrashim of Raymond Martini and Their Place in the Religious Controversy during the Middle Ages" (Hebrew), *Gulak-Klein Mem. Vol.*, pp. 28 f. (includes a number of comments by H. Albeck). See also A. Diez Macho's review of these debates in his "Acerca de los midrašim falsificados de Raimundo Martini," *Sefarad*, IX, 165–96. Little cognizance has thus far been taken,

however, of the impact on Martini of the earlier Christian controversial literature. For one example, the curious midrashic pun concerning the pork (*ḥazir,* also a symbol for Rome), which God would decide to restore (*le-haḥzir*) during the messianic age, is discussed already in the anonymous tractate ed. by J. M. Millás Vallicrosa which, according to the editor, dates from the early thirteenth century, or several decades before the *Pugio.* See *Sefarad,* XIII, 8, 32 f.; the texts quoted by Baer in his aforementioned essay, p. 40 n. 1, and by M. Margulies in his notes on his ed. of Lev. r. XIII.5 end, p. 295; and *supra,* Vol. II, pp. 152, 388 f. n. 31.

25. See the anonymous text and Ginzberg's introductory comments thereon in *Ginze Schechter,* I, 18 ff.; Wertheimer's *Bate,* pp. 222 ff., 234. A most striking illustration of the new anti-intellectual attitude is found in the relatively late Yemenite *Midrash ha-Ḥefeṣ,* written about 1427 by Zechariah ben Solomon (Yaḥya ibn Suleiman). Cf. the fragments communicated by D. S. Sassoon in his "Ancient Legends from the Yemen," *JJLG,* XVI, Hebrew section, pp. 1–30; and his *Ohel Dawid: Descriptive Catalogue of the Hebrew and Samaritan Manuscripts in the Sassoon Library, London,* I, 50 ff.; as well as the comments thereon in Lieberman's *Midreshe Teman,* pp. 22 ff. These anti-intellectual trends had made themselves felt in earlier periods, too. On the generally derogatory views of the mental equipment and morals of elementary teachers held by Jewish and Muslim leaders alike, see my *Jewish Community,* II, 182 f., III, 163 n. 11.

26. See *supra,* Chaps. XXI, nn. 24, 65; XXV, nn. 55 ff.; and Tobiah's comments esp. on Cant. 1:6. Z. Ankori is right in giving preference here to the version included in Jellinek's over that of Greenup's edition of that portion of Tobiah's *Leqaḥ ṭob.* See his comments on "Some Aspects of Karaite-Rabbanite Relations in Byzantium," *PAAJR,* XXIV, 36 ff. Ankori also points out how the same verse in the Song of Songs was used by a contemporary Karaite exegete for an anti-Rabbanite attack, and quite rightly urges further detailed exploration of the interrelations between Tobiah's works and the Karaite Bible exegesis of that time.

27. Tobiah ben Eliezer's *Midrash Leqaḥ ṭob,* on Exod. 2:5, ed. by S. Buber, p. 9. See esp. the data assembled in Buber's introduction; as well as the introductions by the editors of his lesser commentaries, such as J. Nacht in Tobiah's *Commentar zu Threni;* S. Bamberger in *Ein aggadischer Kommentar zu Megillat Ruth;* and A. W. Greenup in *The Commentary of Tobia ben Elieser on Canticles.* See the list, together with some significant reviews of these editions, compiled by J. Starr in *The Jews in the Byzantine Empire,* p. 216. Several passages in the book referring to the dates of 1096 and 1106 C.E. (Buber, pp. 23 ff.) give us an approximation of the period of Tobiah's literary creativity. His letter of introduction for the Russian pilgrim was published by A. Marmorstein in "Nouveaux renseignements sur Tobiya ben Eliezer," *REJ,* LXXIII, 92–97, and frequently commented on by J. Mann and others. See *supra,* n. 9 and Chap. XXII, n. 34. The respective chronologies of Job and Jeremiah are evidently based on Tobiah's acceptance of the assumption by the author of *Seder 'olam rabbah,* that Job had been a non-Jewish prophet living before Moses in whose time Gentile prophecy had drawn to an abrupt end. See the chronological computations in *MJC,* II, 34, 43 ff. This standard work in rabbinic chronology (see *supra,* Vol. II, p. 384 n. 17) is indeed frequently quoted by Tobiah. Cf. the passages listed by Buber in his intro., p. 37.

28. See Abraham ibn Ezra's introduction to his Bible *Commentary,* with W. Bacher's remarks thereon in his "Abraham ibn Esra's Einleitung zu seinem Pentateuch-Commentar als Beitrag zur Geschichte der Bibelexegese," *SB* Vienna, LXXXI, 428 ff. (showing that Ibn Ezra himself could not quite escape the impact of the Aggadah); the impressive list of forty-five authorities citing Tobiah's work assembled by Buber in his intro., pp. 45 ff., 58 f.; and the additions thereto in Bamberger's and Nacht's introductions. The fact that Rashi's French disciples had already quoted Tobiah's work (Buber, p. 46) is a clear indication not only of the author's instantaneous popularity but also of the speed with which works of this kind spread to other countries as a result of the awakened intellectual curiosity in the twelfth century. On the anthropomorphic views of the *Hekhalot* literature and their spirited defense by Tobiah, see *infra,* Chap. XXXIII. In his own exegesis, however, Tobiah tried to steer clear of anthropomorphisms. See, e.g., his lengthy explanation of the crucial terms "our" or "His image" in Gen. 1:26–27, ed. by Buber, pp. 14 f.

29. Sherira and Hai, cited by Abraham ben Isaac of Narbonne in his *Sefer ha-Eshkol,* ed. by B. H. Auerbach, II, 47; and Hai's responsum in *Teshubot ha-geonim,* Lyck ed., No. 99, with reference to Ḥagigah 14b. The views of these and other geonim were reviewed on the basis of thirty pertinent excerpts in E. E. Hildesheimer's "Mystik und Agada im Urteile der Gaonen R. Scherira und R. Hai," *Festschrift für Jacob Rosenheim,* pp. 259–86. Cf. also Mann's observations in his *Texts and Studies,* I, 579 ff. On the geonim's ambivalent attitude to mysticism, see also *infra,* Chap. XXXIII.

30. Cf. the excerpts from Samuel ben Ḥofni's exegetical writings published in Arabic with a Hebrew translation by M. Zucker in his aforementioned essay in *PAAJR,* XXIII, Hebrew section, pp. 2 ff.; *supra,* nn. 8 and 15; Chap. XXVII, nn. 31, 35; and *infra,* Chap. XXIX, n. 67. Zucker quotes (pp. 9 f.) several contemporary sources referring to a system of thirty-six or thirty-three aggadic modes of interpretation as contrasted with the more standardized list of thirty-two in the *Mishnah of R. Eliezer.* This very difference of opinion merely underscores the far greater freedom in the treatment of the Aggadah, as opposed to the fairly uniform and disciplined approaches to the traditional legal sources.

31. Maimonides' *Resp.,* p. 343 No. 373 with the literature listed there; his *M.T.* Shabbat XIX.13, with reference to Shabbat 61a; *ibid.,* Tefillah XIV.7 with reference to Ḥagigah 16a and j. Megillah IV.8, 75c (here mentioned to mitigate the prohibition). Cf. other examples cited by I. H. Weiss in his *Toledot Rabbenu Mosheh ben Maimon,* pp. 20 ff.; and I. Epstein in his "Maimonides' Conception of the Law and the Ethical Trend of his Halachah" in *Moses Maimonides,* ed. by him, pp. 59–82.

32. Maimonides' *M.T.* De'ot V.11, quoting Deut. 20:5–7, 28:30, with reference to Soṭah 44a; *ibid.,* Tume'at ṣara'at XVI.10, with reference to the brief allusion in T. Nega'im VI.7, 625; his *Commentary* on M. Sanhedrin X. Intro., ed. by J. Holzer in his *Zur Geschichte,* pp. 7 ff., 19; and Abraham Maimuni's "Essay on the Homilies of the Ancient Sages" (part of his *Kifayat al-'abadin*), published in Hebrew trans. in Maimonides' *Qobeṣ,* II, fols. 40d ff. See W. Bacher's detailed analysis of "Die Agada in Maimunis Werken," in *Moses ben Maimon,* ed. by Guttmann *et al.,* II, 131–97;

and, on Abraham Maimuni's own equally free attitude toward the Aggadah, Rosenblatt's introduction to his ed. of *Kifayat,* I, 115 ff. Not surprisingly, Maimonides, far less critical in the domain of history, accepted without demurrer the numerous legends about biblical and talmudic events and personalities. He did not hesitate to build on them most of his historic reconstructions, including the famous chain of tradition with which he prefaced both his *Commentary* on the Mishnah and his Code. See *supra,* Chap. XXVII, n. 115; and, more generally, the data analyzed by me in "The Historical Outlook of Maimonides," *PAAJR,* VI, 5–113.

33. Sometimes Maimonides seems to have chosen alternate talmudic readings. In his enumeration, for example, of persons who had no share in the world to come he counted "those who deny resurrection." Most versions of the Mishnah (Sanhedrin x.1) and the Babylonian Talmud (90a) add two words converting the meaning to read: "those who deny that resurrection was revealed in the Torah." Cf. Rashi's emphasis on that point in his *Commentary, ad loc.* Yet Maimonides preferred the shorter version which did not threaten transgressors with eternal damnation for the mere denial of the Pentateuchal source of that dogma, in the quest of which many ancient sages had to sharpen their hermeneutic wits. See A. I. Bromberg's *Meqorot le-pisqe ha-Rambam,* p. 5.

34. Abu Manṣur adh-Dhamari's midrash *Siraj al-ʿaql* (Lamp of Wisdom), in the excerpt cited from a Deinard MS by A. Kohut in his *Notes on a Hitherto Unknown Exegetical, Theological and Philosophical Commentary to the Pentateuch,* p. 47; *Baraita de-Niddah* (Tannaitic Work on the Menstruating Woman) in C. M. Horowitz's ed. of the collection *Tosefta ʿatiqata* (Ancient Toseftas), Part IV (on pp. 48 ff. the editor argues strenuously, but unconvincingly, for its ancient origin); with the comments thereon in S. Lieberman's *Midreshe Teman,* esp. p. 39; and in A. Aptowitzer's *Meḥqarim be-sifrut ha-geonim,* pp. 166 ff. On the use of such aggadic data by medieval Western jurists, see also the numerous examples cited by E. E. Urbach in his *Baʿale ha-tosafot,* pp. 551 ff.; and, with respect to Eldad ha-Dani, *supra,* Chap. XVII, n. 53.

35. See Aptowitzer's quotations from *Sefer Rabiah* which had, in fact, whetted his interest in that entire compilation. Nor was the ambitious term *Baraita* necessarily selected in order willfully to mislead the readers, although such less disinterested motivations often determined the attribution of works to ancient authors. See *supra,* n. 5. Once a writer invoked the authority of a first- or second-century sage, he unhesitatingly called that tannaitic statement a *baraita.* Such *baraitot,* both genuine and spurious, were indeed frequently cited in older and newer midrashim. See the numerous examples assembled by M. Higger in his "Baraitot in Midrash Samuel and Midrash Mishle" (Hebrew), *Talpioth,* V, 669–82. Undoubtedly more pretentious was the use of the term *Mishnah* in the collection to be discussed presently. But even that usage seems not to have caused serious misgivings to medieval readers.

36. *Baraita de-Niddah, loc. cit.; Mishnat Massekhet Kallah* (Mishnah of the Tractate Kallah) in Wertheimer's *Bate midrashot,* I, 221, 227 ff.; allegedly supplementing the well known "minor" tractates *Kallah* and *Kallah rabbati,* which largely were likewise of geonic provenance. See the texts, ed. by M. Higger; the latter's

introduction, esp. pp. 36 ff., 106 ff.; and, more generally, the data assembled by L. M. Epstein in his *Sex Laws and Customs in Judaism,* which, however, is primarily concerned with the legal aspects.

37. *Ma'aseh R. Kahana* (The Story of R. Kahana and His Son Saliq) in Wertheimer's *Bate midrashot,* I, 292 f., 301 ff. This story begins, and is interspersed, with a few hermeneutical interpretations of biblical verses, but these have little bearing on the main events or characters. While the story of that mythical creature, half-cow and half-dog, is not limited to any particular civilization, it was given here a Judaistic turn by the halakhic debate on the potential use of its meat after ritual slaughtering. Written in pure Hebrew, this Yemenite midrash may have originated, therefore, in almost any country, but perhaps particularly in Palestine, Italy, or some other area in the Byzantine sphere of influence. The only hint to its original locale, namely the coin *qasqas* (mentioned several times, p. 303), cannot readily be identified. But certainly the general overtones of women wishing to deny their sons Jewish education and the masses' deprecation of scholars would seem to fit a Byzantine environment much more than those of either the Muslim Near East or western Europe. In any case such stories may serve as partial correctives to the prevailing opinion, nurtured on the rabbinic propaganda, that all Jewish communities evinced deep and unwavering reverence for learning. On the latter, see *supra,* Vol. II, pp. 276 ff., 422 f.; and the data collected by H. W. Reines in his "Public Support for the Students of Torah in the Past" (Yiddish), *Yivo Bleter,* XXVIII, 291–316 (with an English summary, p. 423). See also *supra,* n. 25.

38. Nissim bar Jacob ibn Shahin, *Ḥibbur yafeh me-ha-yeshu'ah* (Worthy Book of Comfort) has long been known in a Hebrew trans. published in Constantinople, 1519, and in at least fifteen editions thereafter. Its Arabic original, however, lay dormant for centuries until it was first discovered in a manuscript and briefly described by A. E. Harkavy in 1896. It was fully edited from the New York MS about a quarter century ago by J. Obermann under the title, *Studies in Islam and Judaism, the Arabic Original of Ibn Shâhîn's Book of Comfort Known as the Ḥibbûr Yaphê of R. Nissim b. Ya'aqobh.* The text is given here in facsimile reproductions of the MS in Hebrew letters with a printed transcript in the Arabic alphabet. See also Obermann's somewhat exaggerating analysis, "Ein Werk agadisch-islamischen Synkretismus," *Zeitschrift für Semitistik,* V, 43–69; and D. Z. Baneth's important corrections and general observations in his principally philological Hebrew review of Obermann's edition in *KS,* XI, 349–57. The Arabic text was newly translated into Hebrew and accompanied with an illuminating introduction and notes by H. Z. Hirschberg under the traditional title of *Ḥibbur yafeh me-ha-yeshu'ah.* See also E. Ashtor's Hebrew review of that rendition in *KS,* XXIX, 313–14. The introductory Hebrew statement referring to the friend's mourning is missing in the single extant Arabic MS. But there is no reason to doubt its authenticity, although the content of the book has little bearing on death and mourning. Nissim's intention evidently was to supply his friend with amusing stories so as to divert his mind and lighten his grief.

39. Nissim's *Book of Comfort,* IV, XXV, XXVII, ed. by Obermann, pp. 19 ff., 120 ff., 129 ff.; in Hirschberg's Hebrew trans., pp. 12 ff., 68 ff., 73 ff. Of course, Meir was a fairly common Hebrew name in the Middle Ages. Yet it must always have evoked

in the minds of Jewish readers the image of the great second-century sage, as well as of his learned wife, Beruriah. From Jewish circles the story of that remarkable couple also penetrated Arabic letters, appearing in works such as those of Ibn Sa'd. See *supra,* n. 19.

40. See Nissim's *Book of Comfort,* VII, XIX, XXI, ed. by Obermann, pp. 25 ff., 93 ff., 100 f.; in Hirschberg's trans., pp. 15 ff., 54 ff., 58 ff.; the latter's introduction, pp. 51, 59, 69 ff.; M. Gaster's ed. and English trans. of "An Unknown Hebrew Version of the Story of Judith" (1894), reprinted in his *Studies and Texts,* I, 86–91 (English), III, 31–32 (Hebrew); and Obermann's "Two Elijah Stories in Judeo-Arabic Transmission," *HUCA,* XXIII, Part 1, pp. 387–404. See also the older studies by I. Friedlaender, *Die Chadhirlegende und der Alexander-Roman,* esp. pp. 42 ff.; and by B. Heller, "Chadhir und der Prophet Elijahu als wundertätige Baumeister," *MGWJ,* LXXXI, 76–80. On medieval France, see *supra,* Chap. XVI, n. 38. The improbability that Nissim knew the Qur'an from first hand is evidenced by the general ignorance of that book even among outright Jewish apologists other than Saadiah. See *supra,* Chap. XXIV, n. 4. Nissim's almost exclusive dependence on Jewish homiletical and folkloristic sources has rightly been postulated by Harkavy, Hirschberg, and others. Their quest for these sources has in part been vitiated, however, by their customary concentration on literary materials, of which admittedly but a small part has been preserved. It stands to reason that in that domain of uncontrolled popular narratives and beliefs, transmission by word of mouth had played an even greater role than it did in the more orderly transfer of halakhic doctrines. Nissim, too, had undoubtedly learned much from listening to the numerous storytellers in a community regularly visited by a multitude of commercial and intellectual travelers.

41. See Obermann's aforementioned essay in *Zeitschrift für Semitistik,* V, esp. pp. 51 ff. In his more recent study of the "Two Elijah Stories," to be sure, Obermann did take cognizance of the oral transmission, stressing particularly its significance for the spread of legends in pre-Islamic Arabia. Cf. *HUCA,* XXIII, Part 1, pp. 387 n. 1, 401 n. 28. But this factor was no less important in the folklore of medieval Jews despite their higher degree of literacy. Even today, in our age of newspapers and radios, one can learn much from tales current among the Near Eastern peoples, both Muslim and Jewish. Z. Vilnai tells, for example, about another reputed intervention by Elijah which he had heard among the Palestinian Arabs. Appearing in the guise of an itinerant beggar, the prophet allegedly asked a farmer for a melon from his field. When the farmer put off the mendicant by pretending that his field was covered by stones, not melons, Elijah made the melons turn into stones. See I. Löw, *Die Flora der Juden,* IV, 333 f. For a sample of interesting variants, folkloristic as well as linguistic, of biblical legends among the Jews of North Africa, see C. Pellat's primarily philological analysis of "Nemrod et Abraham dans le parler des Juif de Debdou," *Hespéris,* XXXIX, 121–45.

42. See *infra,* Chap. XXXII, esp. nn. 66 ff. The borderline between the folk tales and those written or rewritten by individual authors often is extremely tenuous. It sometimes merely depends on our chance familiarity with the names of these later authors. To the category of the anonymous, and hence largely "folk," narratives belong also those assembled by Israel Lévi in "Un Recueil de contes juifs inédits,"

REJ, XXXIII, 47–63, 233–54; XXXV, 65–83; XLVII, 205–13. Near Eastern Jewish folklore still awaits careful exploration, despite the significant contributions made to it by a few workers, particularly the indefatigable Bernhard Heller. See the rich bibliography of his writings compiled by A. Scheiber and published in the *Bernhard Heller Jubilee Volume,* pp. 22–51, 325–26. Heller also made a valiant effort to correlate the Jewish with the Arab folk traditions of the early Islamic period. On the latter, see J. Sauvaget's concise remarks and bibliographical references in his *Introduction à l'histoire de l'Orient musulman,* pp. 26 ff., 39 ff. The relevance of these materials for the historical understanding of that period is succinctly reviewed in R. Paret's lecture, *Die Geschichte des Islams im Spiegel der arabischen Volksliteratur.* See also the more general considerations, though exclusively focused on western Europe, in H. Schauerte's "Entwicklung und gegenwärtiger Stand der religiösen Volkskundeforschung," *Historisches Jahrbuch,* LXXII, 516–34.

43. *Midrash Va-Yosha'* (Thus the Lord Saved Israel), in E. Ashkenazi's collection, *Dibre ḥakhamim* (Words of the Sages), fols. 2–16, and in Jellinek's *Bet ha-Midrasch,* I, pp. xvii, 35–57; *Midrash Abba Gorion, ibid.,* pp. xiv f., 1–18, and in S. Buber's ed. of *Sifre de-Agadeta* (Sammlung agadischer Commentare zum Buche Ester), pp. i ff., 1–42; M. David's ed. of *Das Targum scheni.* On the dates of these three relatively late aggadic works, of which the second is particularly controversial, see the data analyzed by Zunz and Albeck in *Ha-Derashot,* pp. 141 f., 423 ff.; and *supra,* n. 9. Among the numerous dramatizations of the book of Esther, see especially the two other midrashim, ed. by Buber in the same collection, the small fragments of "Mordecai's Dream" (including Mordecai's and Esther's prayers), and a "Jerusalem Midrash on the Scroll of Esther," both published in Wertheimer's *Bate midrashot,* I, 316 ff., 331 ff.

44. *Megillat Antiochus* (Scroll of Antiochus), reedited in Aramaic and in Arabic from a Yemenite MS in Wertheimer's *Bate midrashot,* I, 309 ff., 319 ff. (also listing previous editions and scholarly debates); S. Atlas and M. Perlmann's "Saadia on the Scroll of the Hasmonaeans," *PAAJR,* XIV, 1–23, quoting Deut. 33:11, Daniel 2:32, 38–39, Joel 4:6–8, and Zech. 9:13–16, with the variant trans. suggested by F. Rosenthal in his "Saadyah's Introduction to the Scroll of Hasmoneans," *JQR,* XXXVI, 299. An earlier edition was published with an English translation by M. Gaster in the *Transactions* of the Ninth International Congress of Orientalists, II, 3–32; and reprinted in his *Studies and Texts,* I, 165–83 (English), III, 33–43 (vocalized Hebrew). See also L. Nemoy's facsimile reproduction of *The Scroll of Antiochus* in a fully vocalized Yale MS of 1558, handwritten by the well-known historian, Joseph ha-Kohen. As pointed out by Atlas (*PAAJR,* XIV, 22 f.), the quest for biblical hints of the future Maccabean victory goes back to Talmud and Midrash. Rashi, too, saw in Deut. 33:11 a prayer for, if not a prediction of, that victory.

The widely accepted dating of the Scroll in the early Muslim period is based in part on such tenuous arguments as that the fort of Bagras, recorded at the beginning of the Scroll as built by Antiochus' general bearing that name (Bacchides), was thus called only because of the Arabic misspelling of the place name of Pagras. See esp. Israel Lévi's note, "Un Indice sur la date et le lieu de la composition de la Meguillat Antiochos (Rouleau d'Antiochus)," *REJ,* XLV, 172–75. On the other hand, despite the skepticism of Saadiah's contemporaries, the gaon himself and his early successors evinced no doubt as to the Scroll's antiquity. Nissim ibn Shahin, perhaps under Saadiah's influence, actually placed it on a par with the Scroll of Esther, as generally known records of miracles which required no restatement in his book, although he felt impelled to retell the story of Hannah and her seven sons. In this connection he repeated a tradition, known also from Christian reports, that, after executing the martyrs, Antiochus had caused them to be buried in Antioch and "built upon it [their grave] the synagogue *sheminit* [evidently a variant from *ḥashmonait*]. This was the first synagogue built after the erection of the Second Temple." See his *Book of Comfort,* Intro. and Chap. VI, ed. by Obermann, pp. 4, 28; in Hirschberg's Hebrew translation, pp. 3, 17, with his introductory remarks, *ibid.,* pp. 58 f. The identification of the Antioch *sheminit* synagogue with the Hasmonean family, suggested by A. Schlatter in his *Geschichte Israels von Alexander dem Grossen bis Hadrian,* 3d ed., p. 411 n. 111, was elaborated by Obermann in "The Sepulchre of the Maccabean Martyrs," *JBL,* L, 250–65. See also G. D. Cohen's more comprehensive review of "The Story of Hannah and her Seven Sons in Hebrew Literature," *M. M. Kaplan Jubilee Volume,* Hebrew section, pp. 109–22. It may be noted that in the brief allusion to the Maccabean martyrs in Solomon bar Simson's chronicle (see *supra,* Chap. XXI, n. 7) the mother's name Hannah is absent, reinforcing Cohen's suggestion (pp. 118 ff.) that that name was first widely adopted in Spain.

45. A. Hatem, *Les Poèmes épiques des croisades,* p. ix. It made little difference in this respect whether the work was written in ordinary or rhymed prose, although the latter underscored its semifictional character.

46. D. Flusser, who for several years past has been preparing a critical edition of Yosephon, believes that only a few MSS, especially that of Rothschild, come close to the oldest version, while the Vatican MS is related to the much inferior text used by Conat for his edition of Version II. Version III, represented by the Constantinople edition and subsequent reprints, is based upon another old recension which had been available to Ibn Daud in 1160–61 (see *infra,* n. 73). Even the oldest texts now available, however, include numerous alterations by copyists. See Flusser's preliminary Hebrew study, "The Author of the Book of Josiphon: His Personality and His Age" (Hebrew), *Zion,* XVIII, 109–26. That the Constantinople edition, too, deserves more serious consideration than had been accorded to it by scholars since the days of Zunz has also been argued by Y. Baer in his searching analysis of "The Hebrew Book Yosephon" (Hebrew), *Sefer Dinaburg,* pp. 178–205. The Arabic translation was probably prepared by a Jew, though its main copy now available was apparently written by a Copt. See J. Wellhausen, *Der arabische Josippus.* The Ethiopic text, a translation from the Arabic dating from about 1300, was more recently edited by Murad Kamil under the German title, *Des Josef ben Gurion (Josippon) Geschichte der Juden; Zena Aihud,* where the underlying Arabic text is likewise discussed. See also A. Z. Aeshcoly's and J. Simon's comprehensive reviews of that edition in *REJ,* CIV, 133–38, and in *Orientalia,* IX, 378–87.

47. In view of the numerous uncertainties, textual as well as chronological, which have plagued modern investigators, the discovery, German translation, and subsequent publication of the Slavonic Josephus was hailed as opening new vistas on its Hebrew counterpart as well, since both works had originated from approximately the same period in an area under Byzantine influence. But the discussion

soon became deeply entangled in the textually minor, though theologically significant, problem of the so-called *testimonium Flavianum.* See esp. the heated debate between S. Zeitlin and R. Eisler in the former's several essays, particularly "The Slavonic Josephus and the Relation to Josippon and Hegesippus," *JQR,* XX, 1–50; and *Josephus on Jesus, with Particular Reference to the Slavonic Josephus and the Hebrew Josippon;* Eisler's comprehensive German volume, *Iesous basileus,* and its abridged English translation, *The Messiah Jesus and John the Baptist;* and his "Flavius Josephus on Jesus Called the Christ," *JQR,* XXI, 1–60. Whatever one thinks of Eisler's general theories (see *supra,* Vol. II, p. 379 n. 2) his analysis of the existing Yosephon MSS is particularly valuable. See also Israel's Lévi's "Jésus, Caligula et Claude dans une interpolation de Yosiphon," *REJ,* XCI, 135–54.

Even the subsequent publication of the full Slavonic text and the ensuing more fruitful debate (see *supra,* Vols. I, p. 378 n. 24; II, p. 379 n. 2) has shed little light on its interrelations with the Hebrew paraphrase. It has merely reinforced the conviction that even obvious medieval interpolations need not be entirely devoid of historical value for the reconstruction of ancient developments. See, e.g., F. Scheidweiler's negative answer to his own query, "Sind die Interpolationen im altrussischen Josephus wertlos?" *ZNW,* XLIII, 155–76. They are doubly valuable for the understanding of the historical outlook of the medieval paraphrasts themselves and of its impact on contemporary readers. Yosephon's influence on Arab historians, at least from the time when the Arabic translation became available, is well illustrated by W. J. Fischel's "Ibn Khaldun and Josippon," *Homenaje a Millás Vallicrosa,* I, 587–98. Even most earlier Arab historians were generally indebted to the biblical tradition concerning the early days of humanity, which had long percolated into the broad masses of the population. Cf., for instance, Count Du Mesnil du Buisson's "Trois histoires d'Arabes sur Abraham et Moïse," *REJ,* XCIX, 119–22 (heard from Bedouins on the Syrian-Iraqi frontier); and the literature listed *supra,* n. 41; and Chap. XXIV, n. 4.

48. *Yosephon,* ed. by D. Günzburg and A. Kahana (a reedition of the Conat text), cols. 1 ff., 60 ff., 405 ff., 409 f. The Alexander Romance had undergone many changes even before it was echoed in talmudic literature. As retold by Yosephon it has striking similarities with, but also divergences from, the then current Western versions. Cf. the detailed older but still useful analysis by P. Rieger in Vogelstein and Rieger, *Geschichte der Juden in Rom,* I, 185 ff., 483 ff. (includes also a reexamination of the whole book); and the complementary studies by L. I. Wallach, "Quellenkritische Studien zum hebräischen Josippon, I–II," *MGWJ,* LXXXII, 190–98; LXXXIII, 288–301; "Alexander the Great and the Indian Gymnosophists in Hebrew Tradition," *PAAJR,* XI, 47–83; and "Yosippon and the Alexander Romance," *JQR,* XXXVII, 407–22 (a trans. from *MGWJ,* LXXXIII). According to Wallach, the first part of the Romance (ed. by Günzburg, cols. 65–87) is a twelfth-century interpolation based on a tradition which underlay the younger version of the *Historia de Proeliis Alexandri,* and is indirectly connected with a similar work by the tenth-century presbyter Leo of Naples. However, our knowledge of the popular tales then circulating in oral form is too incomplete for us to rule out the possibility that Yosephon was independently familiar with the ultimate sources of Leo or his interpolators. Moreover, Hegesippus, the major Latin source used by Yosephon, circulated in the Middle Ages in greatly differing recensions, enabling any student to choose between variants, or else to make harmonizations and other

modifications of his own. See, e.g., V. Bulhart's pertinent observations in his twin essays, "Textkritische Studien zum lateinischen Flavius Josephus," *Mnemosyne,* 4th ser. VI, 140–57; and "Textkritisches und Exegetisches zum Hegesippus," *ibid.,* pp. 314–17.

49. *Yosephon,* ed. by Günzburg and Kahana, cols. 116, 206 f. On Nicolaus' probably fabricated genealogy, see *supra,* Vol. I, p. 397 n. 19. The messianic and apologetic implications of Yosephon's historical outlook, briefly referred to in Baer's essay in *Sefer Dinaburg,* would bear further detailed examination.

50. *Yosephon,* ed. by Günzburg and Kahana, cols. 405 ff. Josephus' speech to his fellow survivors from the siege of Jotapata is of course recorded in the ancient historian's own story. See *War,* III.4.362 ff., ed. by Thackeray and Marcus, II, 676 ff. But the Hebrew paraphrast eliminated many peculiarly Greek ideas and phrases and clothed the oration in a fine, genuinely Hebraic and pietistic garb.

51. See Mann's *Texts and Studies,* I, 24; and, more fully, *infra,* n. 54; L. Nemoy's English trans. and analysis of Qirqisani's "Disquisition on Suicide," *JBL,* LVII, 411–20; Baer's observations in *Sefer Dinaburg,* pp. 193 ff.; and those by Flusser in *Zion,* XVIII, 17 f. These authors, however, adduce records of Jewish self-sacrificing tendencies only from the German environment, whereas the Genizah letter and other documents clearly show the deeper roots of these trends in all Christian lands. See also *supra,* Vol. I, pp. 297 n. 7, 400 n. 29; Chaps. XXI, n. 66; XXVI, n. 37.

52. In *M. M. Kaplan Jubilee Volume,* pp. 118 ff., G. D. Cohen has plausibly argued for Yosephon as the originator of the name Hannah. However, even he admits that only some versions of the book known in Spain, and none in the Franco-German communities, included that name. It is doubly remarkable, therefore, that despite the occurrence of the name Miriam in several midrashic sources Hannah so speedily became the generally accepted name of the exalted martyr.

53. See the crucial passage quoted from the Rothschild MS and analyzed by Flusser in *Zion,* XVIII, 113 f.; and *infra,* n. 92. In the perennial debates on the date of Yosephon the problem of sources has loomed very large. In his noteworthy article, "Zur Kritik des Gurionides," *Nachrichten der königlichen Gesellschaft der Wissenschaften zu Göttingen,* 1895, pp. 381–409, K. Trieber tried to prove that the Hebrew author had used only older patristic sources. He suggested, therefore, somewhat timidly, that the book was written as early as the fourth century. S. Zeitlin, on the other hand, stressed principally the fact "that the author of Josippon knew of Tannaitic sources and incorporated them in his work, while apparently he was unaware of the Talmud." See *JQR,* XX, 33 ff. But, rather than accepting Trieber's date, Zeitlin argued in favor of the "fifth century, or certainly not later than the beginning of the sixth." More recently, A. A. Neuman, in his twin essays on "Josippon: History and Pietism" and "Josippon and the Apocrypha," reprinted in his *Landmarks and Goals: Historical Studies and Addresses,* pp. 1–34, 35–57, drew certain interesting parallels between stories narrated by Yosephon and the ancient apocryphal literature. He concluded, therefore, with respect to Yosephon's date that "this analysis . . . definitely points to the early centuries of the common era when

Jewish sources different from and, in some instances, older than the Apocrypha and Josephus were still available" (p. 57).

Apart from the obvious precariousness of all such arguments, one must bear in mind that the tannaitic sources allegedly reflected in Yosephon are for the most part *baraitot* recorded in the Babylonian Talmud. The availability of these sources from some extratalmudic collections to a Byzantine Jew of the fifth or sixth century is yet to be proved. Moreover, a closer examination of certain passages reveals similarities, both substantive and linguistic, with stories recorded in later Hebraic letters, although one need not postulate Yosephon's direct familiarity with them. Similarly, many apocryphal narratives doubtless had long been preserved in oral form, and their mention in a particular book does not necessarily prove its early provenance. Applying the same criteria to the stories of Judith and the Maccabean martyrs, as retold in Nissim's *Book of Comfort,* vi, xix (ed. by Obermann, pp. 25 ff., 93 ff.; in Hirschberg's trans., pp. 15 ff., 54 ff.), one could argue with equal force for its early date, too. It certainly contains ingredients which are at variance with both the apocryphal and the early rabbinic traditions, but which doubtless were perpetuated by word of mouth for countless generations. See *supra,* n. 41. Moreover, in this area of uncontrolled fancy, Yosephon, Nissim, and even copyists transcribing their works, felt free to alter existing versions and to add to and subtract from them so as to suit their own moralistic or literary purposes. On the other hand, the numerous positive indications, particularly of a linguistic and literary nature (the use of many Latin and Italian words, even Latinized forms of Italian, the knowledge of medieval institutions, and the apparent familiarity with works of Western Christian writers) point to a mid-tenth century author. He apparently lived in southern Italy at the crossroads of the Western and Byzantine civilizations, where both Greek and Latin were still much alive, but before the impact of the Muslim domination over Sicily and parts of the Italian mainland was deeply felt.

At the same time, Yosephon's description of Vespasian's coronation, which ever since Basnage had been associated with Otto I's coronation in Rome in 962, is decidedly inconclusive. It appears only in the Constantinople edition and in the MSS attributed by Flusser to the same group III. In its present form, it probably is a later interpolation, using a nomenclature which had become current only in the eleventh century. See Rieger's observations in Vogelstein and Rieger, *Geschichte,* I, 196 ff.; and P. E. Schramm's *Kaiser, Rom und Renovatio,* I, 217 ff., II, 112–19 (excursus), despite Baer's serious reservations in *Sefer Dinaburg,* pp. 186 f. nn. 11–12. Moreover, Yosephon may have embellished here with picturesque details what he had read about the coronation of Charlemagne, or some Byzantine emperor. Unfortunately, we do not possess complete descriptions of these elaborate ceremonies, but in all of them, at least beginning in the fifth century, the leading churchmen of Rome or Constantinople played an active role. See esp. Constantine Prophyrogenitus' description of the installation ceremonies of emperors Anastasios, Justin I, and others in his *De ceremoniis aulae byzantinae,* I.91–96, ed. by J. J. Reisk, I, 410 ff. (with the critical analyses thereof by G. Ostrogorsky and E. Stein in "Die Krönungsurkunden des Zeremonienbuches," *Byzantion,* VII, 185–233; and by F. Dölger in his review of that essay in *BZ,* XXXVI, 145–57); and the Western data assembled by F. L. Ganshof in *The Imperial Coronation of Charlemagne.* See also W. Ensslin, "Zur Frage nach der ersten Kaiserkrönung durch den Patriarchen und zur Bedeutung dieses Aktes im Wahlzeremoniell," *BZ,* XLII, 101–15, 369–72.

54. H. Malter's *Saadia Gaon,* p. 51 n. 84 (promising fuller elucidation in his then projected but unrealized critical edition of Saadiah's *Beliefs and Opinions* in Ibn Tibbon's Hebrew translation, VIII end); and Yehudah ben Jacob's letter, first published by E. N. Adler in "Un Document sur l'histoire des Juifs en Italie," *REJ,* LXVII, 40–43 (with part of the MS reproduced in facsimile in Adler's *Catalogue of Hebrew Manuscripts* in his collection, Plate IV); and revised with a good commentary by Mann in his *Texts and Studies,* I, 12 ff., 23 ff. Although the writer of that epistle is called "from Rome," he probably wrote it from some other Italian community, perhaps Bari. The crucial point in dating this document is the name Ḥisdai, recorded in the superscription, and identified by Adler and Mann with Ḥisdai ibn Shapruṭ. However, this identification is quite questionable, particularly if we believe that the letter immediately following (Mann, pp. 16 ff., 27 ff.) was written to the Jewish "king" of Narbonne, rather than to the Jewish statesman of Cordova. See *supra,* Chap. XX, n. 59. See also U. Cassuto's ingenious attempt at identification of the various local scholars mentioned there in "Una Lettera ebraica del secolo X," *GSAI,* XXIX, 97–110. But even if the letter had been written not long after 952, it would not necessarily controvert Yosephon's tenth-century date, but rather show an astounding interest of the Spanish patrons of learning in securing copies of Hebrew writings, old and new. On Ḥisdai's and Samuel ibn Nagrela's major efforts in this direction, see *supra,* Chap. XVIII, nn. 40, 42.

55. *The Chronicles of Jeraḥmeel,* English trans. from a unique Hebrew MS by M. Gaster; A. Neubauer, "Yeraḥmeel ben Shelomoh," *JQR,* [o.s.] XI, 364–86, 697–99 (with notes by S. J. Halberstam), esp. pp. 370, 374 ff. Gaster's text brings the story down only to Judah Maccabee but other sections of the same manuscript, possibly part of Yeraḥmeel's chronicle, continue to the fall of Jerusalem or even to the composition of the Mishnah at the end of the second century. See *infra,* n. 57. Neither the date nor the locality of Yeraḥmeel have thus far been established. With his usual penchant for early dating, Gaster postulates a date close to the sixth or seventh century, and because of the inclusion of Hebrew translations of the Aramaic portions of the book of Daniel, he places the compiler in Spain, where we have some evidence of the popular neglect of the Aramaic Targum. See Gaster's rather equivocal introduction, esp. pp. xlii ff. These extravagant claims have been rejected by almost all other scholars, who have preferred Neubauer's hypothesis that Yeraḥmeel lived in southern Italy not long after 1100 and that he knew both Rashi and the latter's grandson Samuel bar Meir. None of them questioned the priority of Yosephon, which Gaster also admitted, or that of Moses ha-Darshan. See Albeck's intro. to his ed. of Moses' *Bereshit Rabbati,* pp. 5 ff., 30 ff.; and his note on Zunz's *Ha-Derashot,* pp. 324 f. n. 172.

56. Of the vast literature on the subject of pseudo-Philo, see esp. L. Cohn's pioneering study of "An Apocryphal Work Ascribed to Philo of Alexandria," *JQR,* [o.s.] X, 277–332; M. R. James's English trans. of *The Biblical Antiquities of Philo;* and G. Kisch's more recent revised edition of the Latin text on the basis of the Admont and Melk MSS, entitled *Pseudo-Philo's Liber Antiquitatum Biblicarum.* The latter two volumes are provided with extensive introductions and rich bibliographical references, to which one might also add O. Eissfeldt's recent essay, "Zur Kompositionstechnik des pseudo-philonischen Liber Antiquitatum Biblicarum,"

Interpretationes . . . Sigmundo Mowinckel . . . missae, pp. 53–71. Pseudo-Philo's manifold relationships with, though not influences on, the Aggadah are illustrated by the references included in the notes of L. Ginzberg's *Legends of the Jews,* V–VI, as listed in the Index, Vol. VII, pp. 537 ff. See also *supra,* Chap. XXV, n. 56. True, some Renaissance scholars, including Azariah de' Rossi, doubted Philo's authorship of that work. De' Rossi merely argued that if it, or a related work, were written by another Philo, it would doubly prove the authenticity of some midrashic tales. See his *Me'or 'Einayim,* IV, XXXII, ed. by Cassel, pp. 103 ff., 281 ff. (includes Azariah's Hebrew trans. of a lengthy passage); my observations in "La Méthode historique d'Azaria de' Rossi," *REJ,* LXXXVII, 43 ff., 49; and R. Marcus's more recent analysis of "A 16th Century Hebrew Critique of Philo," *HUCA,* XXI, 42 ff. But no such doubts were heard in the twelfth century.

Yeraḥmeel's great indebtedness to this work may, therefore, shed some new light on the intellectual interests of northern European Jewry. As pointed out by Kisch (p. 29), "a German or Austrian origin is established for all of" the twenty Latin manuscripts of that text now known. Since the fourteenth-century Hebrew copyist was also a German Jew, there seems to be no valid reason to place Yeraḥmeel in either Spain or southern Italy. Certainly, the absence of any Greek and Arabic loanwords or other Graeco-Arabic influences in his works, unless it be in the Hebrew meter of one or another poem, seems to controvert that locale. By the twelfth century the Spanish Hebrew meters had gained many adherents in Ashkenazic communities as well. On the other hand, Yeraḥmeel's strong interest, even greater than that of Yosephon, in synchronizing Roman with Jewish history points toward his connection with the Holy Roman Empire. Certainly, numerous unsuspected midrashic sources were available also to German students of Aggadah, as is fully attested by the vast documentation of the *Yalquṭ Shime'oni.* See *supra,* n. 11. For example, the oft-neglected *Midrash Abkir* (I Shall Bear the First Fruit) was available to Germanic readers; this work, or its source, was on one occasion quoted almost verbatim by Yeraḥmeel (Gaster's trans., pp. 48 f.). See A. Marmorstein's "Midrash Abkir" (Hebrew), *Debir,* I, 114 ff., 138 f., 144; and Zunz and Albeck's *Ha-Derashot,* pp. 142, 430 f. At the same time, Yeraḥmeel's knowledge of astronomy and his interest in the scientific interpretation of ancient traditions probably arose from his sojourn in such communities as Rome or Lucca, rather than in Germany proper. These communities in the 1140's encouraged the Spanish visitor, Abraham ibn Ezra, to compose some of his scientific tracts in their midst. See *infra,* Chap. XXXV. However, more definitive answers must await a further critical reexamination of Yeraḥmeel's Hebrew text in its relation to the other texts included in that unique Bodleian manuscript.

57. See the two excerpts from Eleazar ben Asher ha-Levi's MS published by Neubauer in *MJC,* I, 163–75 and 176–78. The "Book of Adam" mentioned in the Talmud and accepted at its face value by Sherira Gaon and others, was discussed *supra,* Chap. XXVII, n. 17. Neubauer's attribution (pp. xix f.) of both excerpts to the Chronicle of Yeraḥmeel, however, appears rather dubious. Neither excerpt contains any allusions to Yeraḥmeel, although his own *Chronicle* is replete with such personal references. He inserted his name twice even into a simple quotation from Yosephon and wrote "I Yeraḥmeel have found in the book by Strabo" or "in the book by Nicolaus of Damascus," where he had obviously borrowed these quotations from Josephus via Yosephon. Cf. the passages listed by Neubauer himself in

JQR, [o.s.] XI, 364 ff.; and by Flusser in *Zion,* XVIII, 111 nn. 7–8. It appears, therefore, that Eleazar unconcernedly juxtaposed here excerpts from various authors, according to his introductory announcement, "For I saw many books scattered and dispersed here and there. I then resolved to collect them and unite them in one book" (Gaster's trans., p. 1). We may merely assume that, having evinced interest in older writings exclusively, he included our two excerpts from books written in the twelfth century or earlier. Their tenor resembles, in fact, that of similar Eastern works more closely than the blend of history and folklore characteristic of Yosephon and the Chronicle of Yeraḥmeel, the two typical products of Western Jewish folklore.

58. Joseph ben Samuel's Preface to his edition of the *Sefer ha-Yashar* (Book of the Just), Venice, 1525, reproduced in L. Goldschmidt's new impression in his *Sepher hajaschar* (*Das Heldenbuch Sagen, Berichte und Erzählungen aus der israelitischen Urzeit*). Except for a brief introduction restating the long-regnant scholarly view, the Goldschmidt edition is only the most attractive of numerous reprints, since it is also provided with lovely woodcuts by Leo Michelson. The solution of critical problems of the book, however, has made little advance since the first edition of *Die gottesdienstlichen Vorträge* by Zunz in 1832. In fact, in his recent Hebrew revision H. Albeck had little to add even on the basis of more recent researches. See their *Ha-Derashot,* pp. 69 f., 323 ff. In his effort to secure an early dating for the Book of the Just, too, which may indeed be cited twice in the Chronicle of Yeraḥmeel, M. Gaster raised a legitimate objection against Zunz's purely stylistic criteria. See his trans. of that Chronicle, pp. xvii, 116, 130. But many other arguments, too, such as the use of Spanish terms and the mention of Seville, seem to favor the regnant position. A consultation of the relatively few extant MSS, although mostly of recent origin, might help to establish some better readings. For example, the Adler MS, now at the Jewish Theological Seminary in New York, written in Herat in 1773, may have preserved some different Middle Eastern traditions. See E. N. Adler's *Catalogue,* p. 150 No. 67.

59. 'Abd Allah ibn Muslim Ibn Qutaiba's *K. al-Ma'arif* (Handbuch der Geschichte), ed. by F. Wüstenfeld, p. 3; Maimonides' *Commentary* on M. Sanhedrin x.1, ed. by Holzer, p. 20 (Arabic and Hebrew). See K. Ayad, "Die Anfänge der arabischen Geschichtsschreibung," in *Geist und Gesellschaft* (Kurt Breysig Festschrift), III, 35–48; and my observations in "The Historical Outlook of Maimonides," *PAAJR,* VI, 7 ff.

60. See *supra,* Chaps. XXIII, nn. 5, 24 (Bustanai's and Saadiah's ancestry); XXVI, n. 17 (Karaite *nesiim*). One of the Bustanai versions actually refers to a "Book of Memoirs of the House of David," which must have contained such official genealogical records of the exilarchic family. See the excerpt and analysis in Tykocinski's Hebrew essay, "Bustanai the Exilarch," *Debir,* I, 158 ff., listing the earlier editions. Of course, such official genealogies could also be doctored, but on the whole their authors abstained at least from wild guesses.

61. The episodes relating to Mar Zuṭra II and III are fully treated in the "Smaller World Order," revealing clearly the author's purpose in justifying the claims of the Palestinian branch. But rather than having a polemical intent against the Baby-

lonian exilarchs, as suggested by Zunz and Graetz, the chronicler probably wished to defend the leading Tiberian family against local opponents. In any case, the dating of these events is crucial not only for the understanding of our author's historical method and aims, but also for much of Jewish history of that obscure period. The date of Mar Zuṭra III's emigration to Palestine, namely 4280 A.M. (520 C.E.), in particular, has been the subject of extended debates. While Graetz assumed that Mar Zuṭra II's execution had taken place in 518, only two years before his son's emigration at the age of two, Halevi argued for 557 as the date of the execution, while M. Auerbach spoke more vaguely of the middle of the sixth century as the period of Mar Zuṭra III's settlement in the Holy Land. See Graetz's excursus I in his *Geschichte,* 4th ed., V, 394 ff.; I. Halevy's *Dorot ha-rishonim* (Die Geschichte und Literatur Israels), III, 38 ff.; and M. Auerbach's more recent excursus in "Die jüdische Geschichtsschreibung im Mittelalter, I," *Jeschurun,* XIV, 158 ff. It is highly improbable, however, that all this occurred during the strong regime of Khosroe I, either as coregent after 513 or as sole "king of kings" from 531 on. For this and other reasons, we ought to accept the following as the more plausible dates: Mar Zuṭra II's revolt in 471, his execution in 491, and his son's subsequent emigration, perhaps indeed in 520 at the age of twenty-nine—all that as a result of the Mazdakite upheaval. See *supra,* Vol. II, pp. 182 f., 399 n. 15; and Chap. XVI, nn. 69–70. The priority of the Mar Zuṭra story, as told in our chronicle, over the related Bustanai legends has rightly been postulated by Tykocinski in *Debir,* I, 171 ff. See also O. Klima's recent study of "Mazdak und die Juden," *Archiv Orientálni,* XXIV, 420–31, which reaches the conclusion that the episode of Mar Zuṭra II's independence is to be placed in 494–500. Klima's arguments are in part vitiated, however, by his unfamiliarity with the more recent literature after Funk.

The text of the *Seder 'olam zuṭa* is available in various recensions, none of them satisfactory. See the two versions reproduced in Neubauer's *MJC,* II, 68–77; and M. Grossberg's edition, together with that of *Seder tannaim va-amoraim.* See *infra,* n. 62. Earlier printings, beginning with that of Mantua, 1513, are listed in Steinschneider's *Geschichtsliteratur der Juden,* pp. 11 f. Numerous changes were introduced into the text by partisan considerations connected with the Karaite claims, which, as late as the tenth century, caused difficulties to the Rabbanite leader Aaron ben Meir. See *supra,* Chap. XXVI, n. 17; and the various genealogical lists published and analyzed by Mann in his *Texts and Studies,* II, 128 ff. The main permanent value of our "World Order" as an historical, not historiographic, source probably consists in the brief concluding section, which has been used to good advantage also for the reconstruction of the early generations of Masorites and liturgical poets in the Holy Land. See *infra,* Chap. XXIX, n. 14. Even this part, however, as well as the preceding (incomplete) genealogy of the Babylonian line to the days of Mar Zuṭra III, would merit critical reexamination in the light of present-day knowledge. In fact, no comprehensive study of our document, except for its bearing on the Bustanai episode, has been made since F. Lazarus's essay *Die Häupter der Vertriebenen,* published some seventy years ago. Lazarus's plan to publish a critical edition of the text has likewise remained unfulfilled.

62. See the various editions of the *Seder tannaim va-amoraim* (Order of Tannaitic and Amoraic Sages) and the modern literature thereon, listed *supra,* Chap. XXVII, n. 32. The passages cited in our text are found in Grossberg's ed., pp. 62 ff.; in Kahan's ed., pp. 5, 8 (Hebrew), 2, 4 (German), with Kahan's comments, pp. 23 ff.

In trying to make a careful recension of that work available to his French compatriots, Tob 'Elem may have evinced certain historical interests similar in nature to those of Gershom bar Yehudah when the latter copied the Yosephon. On his general activity as a compiler and copyist of more ancient letters, see the sources carefully analyzed by S. J. L. Rapoport in his introduction to the *Teshubot geonim qadmonim,* ed. by Cassel, fols. 3a ff.; and *supra,* Chap. XXVII, nn. 37, 130. Rapoport's arguments remain valid, especially with respect to the *Seder,* notwithstanding the strictures by J. H. Schorr and J. Müller against certain details. See the latter's *Mafteaḥ,* p. 23. In any case, Rapoport has shown that there existed in the Middle Ages two major versions of the *Seder* (a Spanish and a French) which differed in many details. None of the existing versions is correct, however. See the further examples cited by a modern student of rabbinic chronology, A. Hyman, in the introduction to his *Toldoth Tannaim ve'Amoraim* (Comprising the Biographies of All the Rabbis and Other Persons Mentioned in Rabbinic Literature), I, pp. viii ff. See also Kahan's general introduction to his edition, in which he reaches the conclusion that "we must assume that the author of the Seder was not quite familiar with the history of the Amoraim and that he had taken over some clearly fallacious statements" from his sources (p. ix).

In the perennial debate on this important historical and methodological work, the very year of its composition indicated in the text (the various recensions vacillate but slightly between 4644–47 or 884–87; the first figure seems the best attested) has been impugned—for no good reason. Similarly, the author often betrays his decided preference for the academy of Sura, whose latter-day heads are more or less fully enumerated while those of Pumbedita are hardly mentioned. He even cites a passage from Sura's nearly contemporary gaon Amram (869–81). Perhaps he was living in Sura or its bailiwick, though he was not Naḥshon Gaon himself (882–89), as suggested by Graetz. A gaon certainly would not have committed so many factual blunders, some of which arose only from the author's timidity in deciding between controversial traditions. See Kahan's introduction, pp. x ff.

63. Cf. the fragment of Saadiah's *Sefer ha-Galui,* recovered from a quotation by an unnamed Karaite opponent and published in Arabic with a Hebrew trans. by Harkavy in his *Zikhron la-rishonim,* V, 194 f.; and the fragment of the Mosul letter in Schechter's *Saadyana,* p. 135 No. L. In neither text is Saadiah mentioned by name, but the editors' arguments in favor of his authorship appear quite cogent. The future gaon was apparently asked to explain both Judah's genealogy back to Hillel and the work carried on by Judah's disciples, Ḥiyya and Rab. The inquiry thus seems to have combined questions relating to the redaction of the Mishnah with a special interest in the contributions of the Babylonians, Hillel, Ḥiyya, and Rab. It possibly reflects the first rumblings of the Palestino-Babylonian conflict. On the likely date of Saadiah's sojourn in Mosul, see my remarks in *Saadiah Anniv. Vol.,* pp. 23 f. Nothing new about Saadiah's alleged study entitled *Seder tannaim va-amoraim* has transpired to dispel Malter's skeptical discussion in his *Saadia Gaon,* pp. 173, 354.

64. Jacob bar Nissim's inquiry in Sherira's *Iggeret,* pp. 1 ff. There are but minor variants in this text between the "Spanish" and the "French" versions. The query took the literary composition of Mishnah and Tosefta for granted, although in the gaon's reply there is a decided difference between the two versions on this score.

Cf. *infra,* n. 65. As in many legal inquiries, the questioner did not pretend to be wholly uninformed about these "elementary" questions. Even if Sherira had not known that Jacob was a scholar in his own right (he was to serve as the academy's official representative in Kairuwan), the question betrayed his familiarity with the official story of rabbinic succession of the Saboraim following Rabina, not R. Ashi. Cf. *supra,* Chap. XXVII, nn. 18, 20. Jacob wrote, moreover, in behalf of the community of Kairuwan, which for a century or longer had established its reputation in the field of rabbinic learning. Perhaps in order not to offend Sherira's sensitivities, he omitted the related problem of the literary origins of the Palestinian Talmud, which was appreciated as a major legal source in the scholarly circles of the North African community.

65. Sherira's *Iggeret, passim.* In his introduction, B. M. Lewin rightly stresses the fundamental difference between the Babylonian leaders and such outsiders as Saadiah and the Kairuwan scholars. Saadiah's emphasis on the Mishnah's literary composition was echoed in Jacob's inquiry. But in his answer Sherira underscored above all the reliability of oral transmission even after the days of Judah and Ashi. In one passage, referring to a tannaitic tradition in the school of Mar Samuel, he stated bluntly that "if we now find different versions of that *baraita,* we need not rely on them because they had not been so recorded by the memorizers. We do not know which of them are truthful, except for those which had been formulated by our teachers [at the academy]" (*Iggeret,* p. 47 in the "French" version, with but one important variant in the "Spanish" recension). To be sure, the "Spanish" version frequently disregards this basic theory and on various occasions speaks of the Mishnah and other rabbinic compilations having been "written" by their redactors. However, Lewin and others have seen in this discrepancy but a reflection of the differences between the northern European believers in oral transmission and the overwhelmingly literary-minded Spaniards. As early as 1887, in fact, in the introduction to his edition of the "Epistle," Neubauer had cited as long-accepted parallels the *Halakhot gedolot* and several other widely used rabbinic texts which had likewise come down in such twofold Spanish and French recensions. See *MJC,* I, pp. viii f.

This theory was successfully challenged, however, by I. Elbogen in his "Wie steht es um die zwei Rezensionen des Scherira-Briefes?" *Festschrift . . . des Jüdisch-Theologischen Seminars Fraenckelscher Stiftung* (Breslau), II, 61–84. Pointing out that the best MS underlying Lewin's edition of the "French" text was found not in France or Germany but in Aleppo, that many Genizah fragments belong to that recension, and that it had been used extensively by the Spaniard Abraham ibn Daud, Elbogen rightly questioned the separation of these two recensions along geographic lines. Going further and carefully analyzing certain crucial passages, he concluded that the "Spanish" version was but a later copyist's "softened, paraphrasing text intended to facilitate the reader's comprehension" (p. 70). As is frequently the case elsewhere, Elbogen's criticism of earlier views was stronger than his attempts at novel reconstruction. Apart from his dubious assumption that Ibn Daud used Sherira's "Epistle" (see *infra,* n. 72), he too glibly glossed over, especially, the recurrent "insertions" by the "Spanish" reviser of references to the written redaction of Mishnah, *baraitot,* and Talmud. These variants decidedly are neither accidental nor merely pedagogic.

Perhaps we may come closer to a solution by assuming that these divergent interpretations originated immediately after Sherira's reply. The Babylonians, who had long insisted on the primacy of their academies as guardians of ancient traditions, adhered to Sherira's original emphasis on the preponderant role of reliable memorizers. The Kairuwanese recipients, however, bent upon the development of a more independent provincial center, preferred the contrary views held by the Palestinian geonim, with whom they likewise were in regular communication. They, and their like-minded Western followers, did not hesitate to insert into Sherira's text phrases relating to the literary composition of ancient sources, doubly so as their highly articulate environment had generated serious doubts in the reliability of purely oral traditions. Such alterations in support of the Kairuwanese independence are not at all controverted by Ḥananel's statement quoted to this effect by Lewin, p. xiii. In the divine injunction to Abraham and his children "that they may keep the way of the Lord" (Gen. 18:18), the Kairuwanese jurist saw an adumbration of the ultimate equality of oral and written laws. The very Ten Commandments, he argued, had first been heard by the people, and only subsequently were they written down by Moses. Similarly, the Mishnah was equally binding before and after its literary composition. Nowhere does Ḥananel indicate that the Mishnah was written after Judah's time, Lewin himself noting his affinity with Saadiah. From Kairuwan this modified version of Sherira's "Epistle" made its way to Spain, where it was undoubtedly hailed by Samuel ibn Nagrela and other "autonomist" leaders. At the same time, copies of the original version, with less significant modifications, were still circulating throughout the Mediterranean world, including Spain. Its underlying view of Babylonian hegemony soon appeared as an innocuous antiquarian reminiscence. It appealed especially to the Franco-German rabbis, whose academies continued to cultivate oral traditions, particularly those relating to local customs. Its general outlook, if not necessarily its text, also impressed such a student of history as Abraham ibn Daud, who was mainly interested in combating the Karaite denial of the authenticity of the oral tradition. But even Abraham stated distinctly that Judah had "composed" (*ḥibber*) the Mishnah, and that Judah's early disciples had "written" the Tosefta and other *baraitot* (*MJC*, I, 57).

66. See the significant supplementary material, including another inquiry addressed by Jacob to Sherira himself, republished by Lewin in his appendix to the *Iggeret*, pp. 123 ff. Relying principally on archival records and oral traditions, Sherira felt little need to quote sources, except when he reported an anecdote or legend likely to raise doubts in the readers' minds. For instance, discussing the anti-Jewish persecutions at the end of the talmudic period, he stated, "We have heard from our predecessors and seen it written in their memoirs that they [R. Sama and Mar bar R. Ashi] had prayed for divine mercy and a sea monster swallowed King Yazdegerd in his sleep, whereupon the persecution ceased." *Iggeret*, p. 96 (in both versions). Otherwise, as we recall, Sherira was quite certain that he knew in precise detail some happenings at least at his own academy over a period of a century or more. See *supra*, Chap. XXVII, n. 23.

67. Hai Gaon's methodological work is obliquely cited in a letter sent to Kairuwan and published by A. Marx in his "Studies in Gaonic History and Literature," *JQR*, I, 101 (reprinted by Lewin in the Appendix to Sherira's *Iggeret*, pp. xxxi f.); that by Nissim bar Jacob is mentioned as but a projected work in the introduction to his *Mafteaḥ*. But, from Menaḥem ha-Meiri's brief reference to a *Seder ha-Qabbalah*

(Order of the Tradition) by Nissim, S. Poznanski concluded that such a book had indeed been written, although Meiri may only have had in mind some fuller extract from Nissim's encyclopedic "Key." See Poznanski's "Men of Kairuwan," *Festschrift Harkavy,* Hebrew section, p. 212. Incidentally, in the passage here quoted, Nissim gives as the date of Rab's arrival in Babylonia 530 Sel. era (219 C.E.), which is in accordance with all the extant MSS of Sherira's *Iggeret,* p. 78. Hence the suggestion, first advanced by Rapoport and supported by A. Epstein and others, that Rab had first come to Pumbedita thirty years earlier, and that the date of 530 represents only a Sura tradition, has little support from Sherira, as loyal a Pumbeditan as any. Certainly, the assumption that here, as well as in most copies of the *Seder tannaim,* that date is a mere "Schreibfehler" is too facile an evasion. See Epstein's "Sources for the History of the Geonim and the Babylonian Academies," *Festschrift Harkavy,* Hebrew section, p. 167; K. Kahan's introduction to his edition of the *Seder tannaim,* pp. xiv ff.; and *supra,* Vol. II, pp. 207, 405 n. 39.

68. Ibn Daud's *Sefer ha-Qabbalah,* in *MJC,* I, 79, 81; and *supra,* Chaps. XX, n. 47; XXVI, n. 72. We have neither the text of Ibn Daud's anti-Karaite pamphlet, nor any quotation therefrom in subsequent letters, which indicates that the issue appeared far less burning to his Spanish successors. As a thinker rather than communal leader, Ibn Daud may have been seriously perturbed by the intellectual challenge offered by Abu'l Faraj's book. He probably had the jurist-philosopher Abu'l Faraj Furqan ibn Asad or Yeshu'a ben Yehudah in mind, rather than the grammarian Abu'l Faraj Harun. That the Bible commentaries of Yeshu'a were well known and appreciated in twelfth-century Spain is evidenced by Abraham ibn Ezra's criticisms in the introduction to his Bible commentary. See also I. Markon's introduction to his ed. of *Sefer ha-'Arayot* (see *supra,* Chap. XXVI, n. 26); and esp. Poznanski, *The Karaite Literary Opponents of Saadia,* pp. 48 ff.

69. Ibn Daud's Chronicle, in *MJC,* I, 51. Equally remote was the nexus between Ibn Daud's attack on Qirqisani and 'Anan, in that order, and his account of the great prestige enjoyed by R. Gamaliel. *Ibid.,* p. 54. Ibn Daud was evidently aroused by the theologico-historical theories of Qirqisani, the most historically minded Karaite thinker. Regrettably, the pertinent portions of the latter's comprehensive Bible commentary are no longer extant. See *infra,* n. 75.

70. Ibn Daud's Chronicle, in *MJC,* I, 53, 60 f., 62, 82; his *Zikhron dibre Romi* (History of Rome), *infra,* n. 73. The conflict concerning the date of Jesus goes back to ancient times. See *supra,* Vol. II, pp. 387 f. n. 27. By naming Shabur, rather than Bahram I, as Mani's deadly foe, Ibn Daud did not necessarily betray ignorance of Persian history. "Shabur" had long before become among Jewish writers a generic title for any Persian "king of kings."

71. Ibn Daud's Chronicle, in *MJC,* I, 60. Of course, even the purely legendary portions are not wholly without merit. In his "Mythology in Spanish Historiography of the Middle Ages and the Renaissance," *Hispanic Review,* XXII, 1–18, R. B. Tate has rightly argued that "these chapters of mythological history were not composed in a purely imitative fashion, that there were definite factors at work controlling the selection of material and composing it, that they are useful from a literary point of view in determining the attitude of the age towards its classical heritage, and finally

that the advent of the Renaissance brought no abatement of effort in this particular field." See also *infra,* n. 73.

72. See the long list of editions of Ibn Daud's Chronicle in Steinschneider's *Geschichtsliteratur,* pp. 47 f., and the more recent Spanish rendition, with an extensive introduction, by J. Bages Tarrida. Ibn Ṣaddiq's epitome and Abraham ben Solomon's continuation appeared in *MJC,* I, 85–100, 101–14. Both have been translated into Spanish and analyzed by F. Cantera Burgos, under the title *El Libro de la cabala de Abraham ben Salomón de Torrutiel y Un fragmento histórico de José ben Zaddic de Arévalo.* Cf. also J. M. Millás Vallicrosa's earlier comments on a previous trans. by J. Bages in his "Al margen de la traducción del 'Séfer ha-Kabbalah' de Abraham ben Salomón de Torrutiel," *Boletín* of the R. Academía de la Historia, Madrid, LXXXVIII, 424–37 (also reprint).

It is doubly astonishing, therefore, that the work has not yet received that fully critical examination which it so amply deserves. Neubauer's edition, while better than the others, still leaves much to be desired. The critical notes accompanying full or partial translations, such as those by Bages Tarrida or M. Katz's Bern dissertation, *Abraham Ibn Dauds Sepher Hak-Kabbala. Uebersetzung, Quellennachweis nebst kritischen Bemerkungen,* are, of course, not satisfactory substitutes. We may look forward, therefore, with keen interest to the critical edition of Ibn Daud's text now being prepared by G. D. Cohen. Among scholarly analyses one need mention only I. Elbogen's "Abraham ibn Daud als Geschichtsschreiber," *Festschrift Jakob Guttmann,* pp. 186–205; and the Hebrew essay by M. Klein and E. Molnar, "R. Abraham ibn Daud as a Student of History," *Ha-Zofeh,* V, 93–108, 165–75; VIII, 24–35; IX, 85–88. The latter authors have concentrated particularly on Ibn Daud's sources, arguing, for example, that he was unfamiliar with Sherira's "Epistle," but knew of its main findings through such derivative treatments as Nissim's *Mafteaḥ.* Ibn Daud could, of course, also use the vast geonic materials assembled by Samuel ibn Nagrela and Yehudah bar Barzillai. See *supra,* Chap. XXVII, nn. 36, 80.

73. Ibn Daud's brief *Zikhron dibre malkhe Yisrael ba-bayit ha-sheni* (Memoir on the History of the Jewish Kings during the Second Temple); and his *Zikhron dibre Romi* (Memoir on the History of Rome) were first published, together with his *Book of Tradition,* in Mantua, 1513; they were frequently reprinted thereafter. But none of these editions approximates the relative care extended to the "Book of Tradition" in Neubauer's collection; they are full of ugly mispellings, particularly of names and places less familiar to the Hebrew copyists and printers. In his main work the Toledan thinker had already announced his intention to relegate certain parts of his narrative to the two appendixes so as not to interrupt the flow of his story (*MJC,* I, 53, 81 f.). We may assume, therefore, that he wrote them immediately after the completion of his main essay in 1160–61, and not in 1166–67 as suggested without further proof by Klein and Molnar in *Ha-Zofeh,* IX, 85. Closely scrutinizing Ibn Daud's sources, these scholars have shown that until the days of Augustus our chronicler unhesitatingly summarized Yosephon. From there on to the end of the fourth century, he followed closely Paulus Orosius' *Historiae adversus paganos,* whereas for the third section, dealing with the barbarian migrations and the conquest of Spain by the Vandals, he made extensive use of the chronicle by Hydatius and the writings of Isidore of Seville. Of course many mistakes had crept into the original sources available to him, to which he added many errors of his

own—all compounded by the carelessness of later copyists. Although as a Toledan he was undoubtedly trilingual, he may have preferred to use even Orosius in one of the existing Arabic paraphrases. See G. Levi della Vida, "Le Traduzioni arabe delle storie di Orosio," *Al-Andalus,* XIX, 257–93 (previously published in *Miscellanea G. Galbiati,* III, 185–203), esp. p. 290, on the basis of an Arabic MS at Columbia University. Della Vida admits, however, that Ibn Daud may have had at his disposal a better Arabic text. Some mistakes doubtless originated from Ibn Daud's own faulty combinations. For one example, in his enumeration of the second-century Roman emperors, he counts two Hadrians, instead of Trajan and Hadrian. Probably overlooking the talmudic references to a *polemos Trachianus* (Trajan's war), he thus wished to explain the nexus between the Hadrianic persecutions, frequently mentioned in the rabbinic literature, and the earlier Jewish uprising in Egypt and adjoining areas. Because of that confusion he ventured to assert that Koziba (Bar Kocheba) and his troops "waged great wars against all nations and they overran the land of Egypt," cited by Klein and Molnar in *Ha-Zafeh,* VIII, 30. See *supra,* Vol. II, pp. 94 ff.

74. Saadiah's *K. at-Ta'rikh* (Book of Chronology), including additions by a later chronicler, was published from two rather unsatisfactory Bodleian MSS by Neubauer in *MJC,* II, 89–110. See his introduction, pp. x f.; and an additional fragment, ed. by A. Marx in his "Sur le 'Kitab al-Tarikh' de Saadia," *REJ,* LVIII, 299–301. After a prolonged debate among scholars, the gaon's authorship was definitely established with the aid of other MSS quotations. See the data reviewed by H. Malter in his *Saadia Gaon,* pp. 172 f., 353 f., with additional references by I. Werfel in *Rav Saadya Gaon,* ed. by Fishman, p. 652; *supra,* n. 63; and *infra,* Chap. XXXV, n. 75. Saadiah's source is the Bible. As often elsewhere, he views the biblical stories through the eyes of the Aggadah in its more moderate hermeneutic interpretations, but not in its colorful legendary embellishments. One may merely surmise that the gaon's historical curiosity was fully aroused only after his arrival in Baghdad. The controversy with Ben Meir, in particular, which involved many fine points in Jewish chronology, both mathematical and historical, may have whetted his appetite. But in the main this tract is merely a counterpart of his biblical studies, which accounts for the almost identical transliteration of biblical names here and in his translation of Scripture.

75. Yehudah bar Barzillai cited by Samuel ben Sirillo in his *Kelale Shemu'el* (Rules of Samuel; on talmudic methods) in the collection *Tummat yesharim* (Equanimity of the Just), ed. by Benjamin ben Abraham Moṭal, fol. 109; Qirqisani's brief chronological excursus at the end of his hitherto unpublished *Commentary* on the Bible, reproduced from a Leningrad MS in *MJC,* II, 249–51; and the equally brief Byzantine list, *ibid.,* I, 185–86. See also Nicetas Choniates' *Historia,* ed. by I. Bekker, pp. 767 f.; H. Hirschfeld's *Qirqisani Studies,* pp. 29 f.; and *supra,* Chaps. XIX, n. 12; XXV, n. 3; *infra,* Chap. XXIX, n. 71. On the Samaritan chronicles, see esp. the texts and studies thereon listed *supra,* Chap. XXV.

76. Nathan ben Isaac the Babylonion's "Report" is intermingled in Neubauer's edition (*MJC,* II, 77–88) with another account which, after a rapid survey of world history from Adam to Saadiah, expatiates on the superiority of the Sura academy over that of Pumbedita. Similarly, only a small part of "The Arabic Original of the Report of R. Nathan Hababli" has been recovered and published by I. Fried-

laender in *JQR,* [o.s.] XVII, 747–61. See also n. 77. Since practically no autobiographical data are included in these excerpts, Nathan's personality and even the date and place of composition of his significant "Report" have been the subject of lengthy and inconclusive debates. The sharp discrepancies, particularly between Nathan's and Sherira's accounts, have not yet been satisfactorily resolved. Among the main contributions to this discussion were H. Graetz's *Geschichte der Juden,* V, Note XII, pp. 446 ff.; I. Halevy's *Dorot ha-rishonim,* III, 249 ff.; L. Ginzberg's *Geonica,* I, 55 ff.; A. Marx's specific analysis of "Der arabische Bustanai-Bericht und Nathan ha-Babli," *Poznanski Mem. Vol.,* pp. 76–81; and Mann's "Varia," *Tarbiz,* V, 148 ff. See *supra,* Chaps. XXIII, n. 5; and XXVII, n. 31. Having to rely on memory, or at best on notes he may have brought with him, concerning events transpiring some thirty or more years before, Nathan confused the names of some important personalities and committed other blunders concerning secondary issues. But he has proved a fairly reliable recorder of those places, events, and persons that made a lasting impression upon him. Cf. my "Saadia's Communal Activities," *Saadia Anniv. Vol.,* pp. 25 ff., 62 ff.

77. "Neṭira and His Sons," ed. in Arabic with a Hebrew trans. by A. E. Harkavy in *Festschrift Berliner,* Hebrew section, pp. 34–43, may have formed a part of Nathan's original "Report," if we accept I. Friedlaender's plausible suggestion in *JQR,* [o.s.] XVII, 749 n. 2. It is probably based on a family chronicle which had circulated in Baghdad during Nathan's stay there in the 930's and 940's. Such indebtedness to diverse sources may help to explain the slight differences in the Arabic style of that fragment and Nathan's main chronicle. See also S. Fraenkel's "Jüdisch-Arabisches," *JQR,* [o.s.] XVII, 386 ff.; and *supra,* Chaps. XVIII, n. 36; XXIII, n. 7. On the crucial point of Nathan's likely presence at the installation of the son and successor of David ben Zakkai in 940, rather than at David's own installation in 916–17, as is generally assumed, see my arguments in *Saadia Anniv. Vol.,* pp. 28 f. Most decisive in that description was the participation of both geonim in the election of the new exilarch and the ensuing ceremonies, whereas, according to Nathan himself, David's election had been boycotted by the Pumbedita representatives for three years.

78. Abiathar ben Joseph ha-Kohen, *Megillat Abiathar* (Scroll of Abiathar), in S. Schechter, *Saadyana,* No. xxxviii, pp. 80 ff.; Abraham ben Hillel's *Megillat Zuṭṭa* (Scroll of [Concerning] Zuṭṭa), in A. Neubauer, "Egyptian Fragments: Scrolls Analogous to that of Purim," *JQR,* [o.s.] VIII, 541–61; with additional fragments in Neubauer's "Note" thereon, *ibid.,* IX, 721; and A. Cowley's "Megillath Zuṭa: Note on *JQR,* VIII, 541 and IX, 721," *ibid.,* XI, 532. Here Cowley points out that the extant five fragments, differing in shape, size, and writing, represent five different manuscripts and show that the controversy over Zuṭṭa's leadership had aroused widespread interest. It is more likely, however, that from the outset both "scrolls" were but circular letters sent out in numerous copies to various communities and then preserved in the latter's archives either in their originals or in local transcripts. There is no way of ascertaining now whether Abraham ben Hillel saw fulfilled his hope that his rhymed chronicle "might forever be ready for male and female singers" to be recited in the manner of the Scroll of Esther. See *JQR,* [o.s.] VIII, 551. A fuller analysis of the issues involved in the conflicts recorded in both scrolls, as well as some additional letters addressed to Abiathar, are found in J. Mann's *Jews in Egypt,*

I, 185 ff., 234 ff.; II, 222 ff., 292 ff.; his *Texts and Studies,* I, 234 ff., 346 ff.; E. Ashtor-Strauss's "Saladin and the Jews," *HUCA,* XXVII, 313 ff.; and *supra,* Chaps. XXIII, n. 50; and XXVII, n. 155.

79. Schechter, *Saadyana,* pp. 87, 92 ff. We also possess a brief presentation of David's side in the conflict. Here stress is laid on the Babylonian Talmud's championship of the world supremacy of the Babylonian exilarchs from whom "the scepter shall not depart." *Ibid.,* No. XL, pp. 106 ff., with some textual corrections by Mann in *Jews in Egypt,* I, 190 n. 1. This letter, anticipatory of many general objections but not of the specific strictures by David's leading opponent, seems to have been written before the "Scroll of Abiathar."

In contrast to this exchange which related to the broad problems of relations between the royal house of David and the priesthood, the "Scroll of Zuṭṭa" limits itself to the deflation of the "pretender's" scholarship in both Jewish and general subjects, derides his public addresses, and expatiates at length on his high-handed and treasonable acts against the best interests of Egyptian Jewry. Regrettably, in this case we have no statement from the defense. Since Maimonides, soon after his arrival in Egypt, joined the opposition and the pressure of public opinion finally forced the despotic *nagid* out of office, we may perhaps accept the veracity of these accusations, even if we discount the predilection of medieval and modern scholars to assume that a man of Maimonides' superlative scholarly attainments could do no wrong even in a communal conflict.

80. When the *Chronicle of Aḥimaaz* was first published from a Toledo MS by Neubauer (in *MJC,* II, 111–32, with brief introductory remarks, pp. xi f.), it caused a great stir in the Jewish scholarly world. Although the debate has largely exhausted itself in the following two decades, the two reeditions of the text by Salzman and Klar have not only helped to summarize the earlier researches but also added significant new observations. In his English translation Salzman was able to avoid most of the pitfalls of rhymed Hebrew prose and to present a wholly readable account. He added to it a careful analysis of the chronicle's contributions to our historical knowledge. Klar, on the other hand, effectively supplemented Aḥimaaz' text by reprinting poems written by southern Italian poets of the period, including several ancestors of Aḥimaaz himself. Klar's extensive notes, offering a careful textual and substantive analysis, are likewise very helpful. Both these editions have been, and will be, cited frequently in our notes.

81. See esp. Salzman's lengthy introduction; and the numerous observations on excerpts from this chronicle included in J. Starr's *Jews in the Byzantine Empire, passim.* Many crucial problems, including that of the intriguing personality of Palṭiel, the alleged *nagid,* still await elucidation. See *supra,* Chaps. XIX, n. 7; XX, nn. 20 ff.; XXIII, n. 48. Perhaps not by mere chance the sole manuscript of Aḥimaaz' chronicle survived in Spain, where book collectors always evinced interest in Jewish letters of all kinds, including Yosephon. See *supra,* n. 54.

82. Cf. the two editions of these chronicles by Neubauer and Stern (with the somewhat inadequate German trans. by S. Baer), and by Habermann, together with the comments thereon by H. Bresslau and others mentioned *supra,* Chap. XXI, esp. nn. 7 and 9. Here again Habermann's edition is greatly enhanced by the addition

of many contemporary poems, some published for the first time. As pointed out in Baer's penetrating Hebrew essay on the "Persecutions of 1096" (in *Sefer Assaf,* pp. 126 ff.), the early source underlying the three Hebrew chronicles of the First Crusade may merely have pursued the practical objective of warning other communities and exhorting them to emulate the great martyrs. It used for that purpose the data accumulated in letters previously sent out by the various communities with the same objective in mind. Baer has also made it plausible that the Jewish and Christian writers of the period borrowed freely from one another and at least tangentially referred to statements they wished to correct.

Baer and his predecessors have underestimated, however, the overwhelming impact of the oral traditions. In his childhood Eliezer bar Nathan had probably himself witnessed the Mayence tragedy. Solomon or the Mayence Anonymus, too, very likely remembered certain episodes from their own experience or had learned about them from their elders. Certainly, in 1140, if that be the date of Solomon's account, there still were many survivors of the massacres around to transmit the heroic record by word of mouth. Of course, stories about dramatic events are apt to be constantly elaborated in oral transmission, but they are not necessarily less reliable than written accounts composed under the immediate impact of an overpowering personal tragedy. Certainly, oral exchanges between Jews and Christians are more credible than direct borrowings from each other's literature, the Hebrew accounts, in particular, being inaccessible to Christian writers. But whatever their sources, the Hebrew chroniclers were able to integrate them into smoothly flowing narratives, whose very simplicity and avoidance of rhetorical artifices rendered them so eloquent and moving.

83. See *supra,* Chaps. XVIII, n. 39; XXI, nn. 2 and 60. In the case of the Egyptian official's autobiographical record we must necessarily discount the inherent bias. Yet it offers so many interesting insights that we must regret the Jews' general failure to follow the example of their Arab neighbors in composing autobiographical accounts. See F. Rosenthal's analysis of "Die arabische Autobiographie," *Analecta Orientalia,* XIV, 1–40. L. W. Schwarz's popular anthology, *Memoirs of My People Through a Thousand Years,* necessarily reproduces such Jewish writings chiefly from the modern period. See also, more generally, G. Misch's *Geschichte der Autobiographie,* Vol. II, Part 1 (covers the High Middle Ages to Bishop Rather).

84. Ḥisdai's letter to the king of the Khazars in P. K. Kokovtsov's *Evreisko-khazarskaya perepiska,* pp. 16 (Hebrew), 66 (Russian); and in the English trans. by E. N. Adler in his *Jewish Travellers,* p. 29; Eginhard's (Einhard) *Annales, ad* 801 and 802; and his *Vita Caroli Magni,* XVI, in *MGH,* Scriptores, I, 190; II, 451. On the authenticity of these reports and the extensive literature thereon, cf. *supra,* Chaps. XIX, n. 30; XX, n. 57.

85. See A. Epstein's introduction to his edition of the various Hebrew texts of *Eldad ha-Dani;* and M. Schloessinger's observations on "The Eldad Legend" in the Appendix to *The Ritual of Eldad ha-Dani,* pp. 105 ff. (otherwise chiefly concerned with the halakhic aspects). L. Rabinowitz's questionable theory that, before going West, Eldad had reached China, was mentioned *supra,* Chap. XVII, n. 53, where additional literature is cited. At the conclusion of his letter to Spain of [56]43 (883; in Epstein's ed., pp. 29, 52 f.), Eldad enumerated his thirty-eight ancestors up

to Dan, son of Jacob. This genealogical tree has, of course, little historic merit, except for confirming Eldad's acceptance of the usual medieval foreshortening of ancient Jewish chronology.

86. Epstein, pp. xxiii ff.; he also quotes, however, negative remarks by Abraham ibn Ezra and Meir of Rottenburg, the latter apparently in the name of Jacob Tam. Eldad's influence on the Christian world and his contribution to the legend of a mighty Christian kingdom of "Prester John" in the Orient, still remains in the realm of speculation. The origin of that legend, apparently first appearing in Otto of Freising's chronicle, has been plausibly traced to the first news about the victory of Yeluatshi, ruler of the Kerait (the Black Kitai) and possibly a Nestorian Christian, over a large Muslim army near Samarkand (1143). Apparently magnified by the wishful thinking of the rulers of the then hard-pressed Latin Kingdom of Jerusalem, these reports spread through Christendom and gave rise to both a forged epistle of Prester John to Emperor Manuel I Comnenus of Byzantium and an authentic letter of Pope Alexander III of 1177 to the Prester. There evidently is no direct connection between this mixture of diplomacy and utopia and Eldad's narrative, but when in the subsequent four centuries European nations increasingly viewed Ethiopia, rather than India, as Prester John's real country, this identification was doubtless facilitated by Jewish, as well as by Ethiopian, legends concerning that country's ancient connections with the biblical Holy Land. The confusion of India and Ethiopia is not surprising, since in ancient and medieval minds "India" embraced a wide, never clearly defined area. Had not many Byzantine writers (for instance, Theophanes), as well as numerous Jewish homilists and *Targum Jonathan,* looked at the inhabitants of Axum (Ethiopia) or the country south of it, as "Indians"? See Theophanes' *Chronographia,* VI.13, ed. by De Boor, I, 222 f. (Greek), II, 142 (Latin); and the numerous rabbinic and other sources assembled by Epstein in his notes on Eldad's narrative, II, 33 ff. n. 19. Here Eldad may indeed have further confounded that confusion. Subsequently, Benjamin's reports about the Ten Tribes must have deepened the mystery. Of the vast and still growing literature on Prester John, see the more recent additions, by R. Hennig, "Neue Forschungen zur Sage des Priesterkönigs," *Universitas,* IV, 1261–65; his *Terrae incognitae,* III, 2d ed., *passim;* and C. E. Nowell, "The Historical Prester John," *Speculum,* XXVIII, 435–45.

87. Abu 'Ubaid 'Abd Allah ibn 'Abd al-Aziz al-Bakri's *K. al-Mamalik w'al-masalik* (Book of Routes). This hitherto unpublished work, extant in an Istambul MS of 1337 and some subsequent copies thereof, contains excerpts from Ibrahim's itinerary, now available in T. Kowalski's critical edition, with a Latin and Polish translation and Polish notes, entitled *Relatio Ibrahim ibn Ja'ḳub de Itinere slavico.* Also of considerable value is the earlier, extensively annotated German translation by G. Jacob in his *Arabische Berichte von Gesandten an germanische Fürstenhöfe,* pp. 11 ff. See the additional literature listed in Kowalski's introduction; in G. Labuda's Polish study of "The Oldest Report on Poland in a New Edition," *Roczniki historyczne,* VI, 100–183; W. Maas's review of Kowalski's edition in "La 'Relación eslava' del judío-español Ibrahim b. Ya'qub al-Turṭuši," *Al-Andalus,* XVIII, 212–14; B. Hospodar's more popular essay, *An Early Traveler in Prague;* and *supra,* Chaps. XVIII, n. 40; XIX, n. 57.

The section preserved by Al-Bakri deals only with Ibrahim's journey from the vicinity of Magdeburg to the Baltic and with his return trip from Magdeburg to Prague. Very likely the Arab geographer found only that part sufficiently novel, and reproduced it more or less faithfully. Ibrahim's identity with the diplomatic envoy who traversed Christian Spain and France and whose data were quoted by Al-Qazwini and Al-Ḥimyari, is now more or less definitely established, despite the objections still raised by G. Jacob (pp. 3 ff.). However, Ḥisdai ibn Shapruṭ's role in this mission is nowhere stated. We do not even know for certain that he was still alive in 965, although Graetz's arguments that he lived until about 970 are quite convincing. See Graetz, *Geschichte der Juden,* V, Note XXI.1 pp. 538 f. As mentioned above, the Jewish statesman played an active role in receiving Otto I's ambassadors in Cordova in 956, and he may well have had a share in the selection of the Moorish envoys to Germany nine years later. Professionally, Ibrahim may have been a practicing physician, if we may take a clue from his numerous, more than casual observations of hygienic practices among the central Europeans. However, interest in medical matters was not limited to professional physicians among Arabic-speaking Jews at that time. On the location of the Jewish salt mine (*mallaḥa* which may, however, relate only to a Jewish quarter, similar to the Moroccan *mellaḥ*) at Dürrenberg or Halle on the Saale, see Kowalski's note, p. 87 n. 59.

88. More than a century ago, A. Asher, in preparing his edition and English translation of Benjamin's *Itinerary,* was able to list twenty-three previous editions (I, 1 ff.). He had no access, however, to manuscript materials. Hence the critical edition by M. N. Adler, reproducing the text of a British Museum MS with variants from two other complete and two incomplete MSS, is our only reliable guide. Asher's edition has retained its value mainly through its extensive notes, in which the translator was ably assisted by several scholars, including L. Zunz. Independently valuable is also L. Grünhut's edition with a German translation, while I. Gonzalez Llubera's Spanish version entitled *Viajes de Benjamin de Tudela 1160–1173* is largely based upon the work of these predecessors. The date given in this title is doubtless too broad. Only Benjamin's return to Spain in 1173 is attested by the original editor's introductory statement (see n. 89). His departure, however, and his individual stops can be but partially reconstructed from the few names mentioned by him. He seems to have left Spain about 1165, since his early visit to Rome occurred during Alexander III's effective reign, that is between the end of 1165 and 1167. See Adler's note on his translation of that introductory passage. Benjamin's arrival in Baghdad in 1168 is plausibly argued by J. Obermeyer in *Die Landschaft Babylonien,* p. 128.

The duration of some eight years for Benjamin's extended journey represented a fair average for that period. His difficulties have been analyzed, on the basis of much personal experience, by P. Borchardt in several interesting essays. See especially his attempted reconstruction of "Der Reiseweg des Rabbi Benjamin von Tudela und des Petachia aus Regensburg in Mesopotamien und Persien," *JJLG,* XVI, 137–62 (listing also several earlier studies). Borchardt was also preparing a new, as yet unpublished, critical edition, with an extensive "geographical commentary." See "The Sculpture in Front of the Lateran as Described by Benjamin of Tudela and Magister Gregorius," *Journal of Roman Studies,* XXVI, 68–70. The need for such a commentary is well illustrated by the numerous emendations, for the most part quite convincing, offered by J. Obermeyer in regard to the Babylonian sections in *Die Landschaft Babylonien, passim.* See also A. M. Andreades's "Sur

Benjamin de Tudèle," *BZ,* XXX, 457–62 (showing Benjamin's route from Corfù to Leucade-Lecatto, rather than Arta in Greece).

89. The contemporary character of this attestation was long obscured by the past tense used in the earlier editions, but, as shown by Adler, both the British Museum and the Casanatense MSS reproduced it in its indubitably original present tense. This attestation was probably issued in Benjamin's lifetime—even the *nishmato 'eden* (may his soul rest in Eden) and *ha-nizkar* (aforementioned) of the British Museum MS evidently are later accretions—to answer scoffers who attacked the veracity of the great traveler. His overall trustworthiness, generally accepted also by modern scholars, was again emphasized by Borchardt in the *Journal of Roman Studies,* XXVI, 68 ff.

90. Benjamin's failure to mention the names of leading citizens in the more distant communities is not surprising, as these regions could boast of relatively few leaders of high repute. Even on his visit to the ancient centers of Sura, Pumbedita, and Shaf ve-Yatib, the traveler mentioned ancient synagogues and tombs, but no contemporary leaders. In contrast thereto he spoke in the immediate sequel of R. Ḥanan the Nasi (Prince), the "ruler" of the Jews of Teima in northern Arabia. On the value of Benjamin's population figures, see *supra,* Chap. XVII, n. 48.

91. Petaḥiah's travelogue, best available in L. (E.) Grünhut's edition with a German translation and in A. Benisch's older edition with a fully annotated English translation, is extant in a far less satisfactory form than that of his Spanish contemporary. Possibly he himself was less methodical. In any case, he seems to have brought back with him to Germany only disjointed notes, which he may have handed over to the famous mystic, Yehudah the Pious. On one occasion, we are told, he left behind some notes in Bohemia; for instance, the important list of tombs of Amoraim, handed him after his visit to the grave of Rab (see Grünhut, pp. 19 [Hebrew], 26 [German]; Benisch, pp. 36 f.). Yehudah edited these notes according to his own lights, omitting some rather significant details. For example, after reporting Petaḥiah's visit to Nisibis, with its old Ezra synagogue, the editor simply remarked, "From thence he [Petaḥiah] went to Ḥamath. He named all the cities; and stated how many days it took him to travel from city to city. However, there is no occasion to write it down"; Grünhut, pp. 28 (Hebrew), 38 (German); Benisch, pp. 52 f. Similarly, we are told by a later epitomizer, that a prominent Nineveh astrologer, R. Solomon, had divulged to Petaḥiah the date of the advent of the Redeemer, "but R. Yehudah the Pious would not write it down, lest he should be suspected of being a believer in the words of R. Solomon"; Grünhut, pp. 7 (Hebrew), 8 (German); Benisch, pp. 12 f.

Sometimes our traveler was hampered by personal mishaps. On that very occasion, we learn, Petaḥiah had fallen ill, but he could not linger in Nineveh because his wealth had aroused the cupidity of the local governor. Although most Muslim laws provided that "heirless" Jewish estates should be taken over by the local Jewish communities, Petaḥiah was informed that Nineveh's local custom demanded "that when a travelling Jew dies, the sultan takes half of his property; and because R. Petaḥiah was dressed in beautiful clothes they thought that he was rich" (Benisch, p. 11). Under these circumstances his account does not lend itself so well to close critical examination as does that of Benjamin. Cf. for example, the aforementioned analytical effort by P. Borchardt in *JJLG,* XVI. We must be grateful, however, that at least such incidental references as enable us to establish the chronological framework of Petaḥiah's journey have not been eliminated by either R. Yehudah or the later epitomizer. The fact, for example, that Petaḥiah arrived in Damascus after, and in Jerusalem before, the conquests by Saladin gives us at least the general chronological framework of the years between 1174 and 1187 for his visits to these communities.

92. *Yosephon,* ed. by Günzburg and Kahana, pp. 3 ff.; the comments thereon by Baer in *Sefer Dinaburg,* pp. 180 f.; and by D. (G.) Flusser in *Zion,* XVIII, 112 f. Cf. also Flusser's more detailed examination of "The Report on the Slavs in a Hebrew Chronicle of the Tenth Century" (Czech), *Česky Časopis Historický,* XLVIII–XLIX, 238–41. As often elsewhere, the Hebrew historian-folklorist follows here the lead of Hegesippus, but brings the facts more nearly up to date. The fairly universal use of the Bible's historical data is illustrated by the Austrian chroniclers of the sixteenth century who in all seriousness reported events in their country which had supposedly taken place so and so many generations "after the Flood." The alleged "Canaanite" ancestry of both the North African and the Slavonic populations had a direct bearing even on the medieval Jewish status. So did the ever recurrent assertions by both Jews and Christians that Jews of Spain, France, the Rhinelands, and other areas had settled there before the second fall of Jerusalem. To the data mentioned *supra,* Chap. XVI, nn. 3, 58, and XIX, n. 53, add I. Elbogen's *Geschichte der Juden in Deutschland,* pp. 11 ff. Even the distinguished Muslim savant Al-Biruni did not hesitate to explain the etymology of the then still important "Sabian" sect by their founders' descent from Sabi, son of Methuselah. He also reported that scholars distinguished between Sabians and Harranians, the latter designation stemming from Haran ben Teraḥ, Abraham's brother who "among their chiefs was the most deeply imbued with their religion." See *The Chronology of Ancient Nations,* English trans. by E. Sachau, pp. 186 ff. Mas'udi, too, unquestioningly accepted the Jewish identification of Esau as Rome's ancestor and believed that Job had been Esau's great-grandson.

At times such historical reminiscences were colored by dogmatic preconceptions, as when the Shi'ites saw in Enosh a prophet who had received the hereditary prophetic soul from his father, Seth, and bequeathed it to an *imam* of each subsequent generation down to Mohammed. This assertion was reported by Mas'udi as an historical fact, although it had specifically been denied by the historian Ṭabari. Curiously, Mas'udi saw no difficulty in reconciling such biblical derivations with the findings of Greek science. See his *K. Muruj adh-dhahab* (Les Prairies d'or) in the text, ed. with a French trans. by Barbier de Meynard and Pavet de Courteille, I, 69 ff., 89 ff. (in A. Sprenger's English trans. pp. 68 f., 88 f.); my remarks in "The Historical Outlook of Maimonides," *PAAJR,* VI, 14 n. 16, 16 n. 20; and, on Mas'udi's extensive documentation from Greek and Arabic astronomic and geographic sources, S. Maqbul Ahmad's "Al-Mas'udi's Contributions to Medieval Arab Geography," *IC,* XXVII, 61–77. The interesting geographic data scattered through the medieval rabbinic letters were briefly reviewed as early as 1841 in L. Zunz's twin essays "On the Geographical Literature of the Jews from the Remotest Times to the Year 1841," and "On the Geography of Palestine from Jewish Sources," appended to Asher's ed. of Benjamin's *Massa'ot,* II, 230–317, 393–448 (the German original of the former appeared thirty-four years later in Zunz's *Gesammelte Schriften,*

I, 146–216). The Jewish studies in physical geography will be discussed *infra,* Chap. XXXV.

93. Maimonides, *M.T.* Bet ha-beḥirah II.2; Halevi, K. *al-Khazari,* I.95, ed. by Hirschfeld, pp. 44 f.; in Hirschfeld's English trans., pp. 64 f. Maimonides derived the historical background of the Temple from a combination of homiletical sources, cited in my "Historical Outlook of Maimonides," *PAAJR,* VI, 13 n. 12. Although the codifier frequently used aggadic data to reinforce juridical doctrines, he felt here the necessity of stressing the universal agreement on this score. One wonders whether this reference to the *idjma'*-like quality of this legendary concept was intended pointedly to reemphasize the exclusive Jewish claim to the Temple site then occupied by the Mosque of 'Umar. See also *infra,* Chap. XXXV, n. 77.

94. Halevi's *K. al-Khazari,* I.4; III.63, and many other passages in Hirschfeld's ed., pp. 8 ff., 208 ff.; in his English trans., pp. 39 ff., 185 f.; Maimonides' *Guide,* II.32 ff., in Friedländer's English trans., pp. 219 ff.; his *M.T.* Yesode ha-torah VII.6; his *Commentary* on M. Sanhedrin X, Intro., Principles VI–VII, ed. by Holzer, pp. 23 ff.; and *Seder Eliyahu r.* X, ed. by Friedmann, p. 48. On the latter, see M. Kadushin, *The Theology of Seder Eliahu,* pp. 125, 167 f. The ramified doctrines of the nature and historical manifestations of prophecy as expounded by Maimonides, Halevi, and other medieval thinkers will be more fully discussed *infra,* Chap. XXXIV.

95. See my remarks in *PAAJR,* VI, 25 ff., 96 ff., together with the sources cited there; and *supra,* Chap. XXVII, n. 155. The doctrine of an intervening decline in Jewish intellectual creativity and the disappearance of ancient writings had venerable antecedents. Nurtured in part by the gnostic teachings of cyclical changes in history, a similar rationalization had also been used by Zoroastrian thinkers to explain the absence of any written Zoroastrian Scriptures from the Achaemenid period. See H. S. Nyberg, *Die Religionen des alten Iran,* German trans. by H. H. Schaeder, pp. 427 f. Although the Zoroastrians must have felt an even more urgent need to justify the total "disappearance" of their sacred writings, Jewish priority in developing that rationale appears likely. It may well have developed already in the crucible of the Pharisaic defense of the Oral Law, the Hellenistic Jewish apologias repudiating the supremacy of Greek culture, and the quest of the ancient apocalyptic writers to date some of their fantastic outpourings back to the earliest generations of man. See also *supra,* Chap. XXVII, n. 19.

The enormous impact of Gentile hostility and the sufferings during the Exile also on all other phases of the thinking of medieval Jewry has been mentioned here in various connections, esp. in Chaps. XXIV and XXV. It was subjected to a keen analysis in Y. F. Baer's "Palestine and the Exile in the Eyes of the Medieval Generations" (Hebrew), *Ṣiyyon,* VI, 149–71, esp. pp. 157 ff.; and his *Galut,* pp. 16 ff. Remarkably, neither Maimonides nor Halevi, nor for that matter any other medieval Jewish thinker except those immediately concerned with messianic speculations, paid much attention to the doctrine of the four monarchies. Its very nexus with the messianic idea and the "computation of the end" must have discouraged the more rationalist thinkers. For other reasons, opinions on this score differed also among the medieval Christian interpreters. See the data assembled by J. Adam in his dissertation *Vom römischen Weltreich in der mittelalterlichen Bibelerklärung.*

96. See Saadiah's *Beliefs and Opinions,* III.7, ed. by Landauer, pp. 128 ff.; in Ibn Tibbon's Hebrew trans., pp. 66 f.; in Rosenblatt's English trans., pp. 157 ff.; and *supra,* Chap. XXIV, n. 13. On the "seven climates" and their relevance for Palestine, see A. Altman, "The Climatological Factors in Yehudah Halevi's Theory of Prophecy" (Hebrew), *Melilah,* I, 1–17; and *infra,* Chap. XXXV. Such emphasis on intellectual life also enabled the Jewish thinkers to minimize the importance of Jewish powerlessness, Yehudah Halevi greatly stressing the supreme role of martyrs and scholars in all human history. On one occasion, Saadiah even argued that Jewish sufferings were part of God's design to persuade the world that Jews had adhered to their belief in Him not because they had prospered on account of their faith, but despite all the sacrifices it had entailed. See his *Beliefs and Opinions,* III.10 end, pp. 145 (Arabic), 74 (Hebrew), 179 (English).

These few examples of various medieval Jewish approaches to history must suffice here. A comprehensive analysis of the rabbinic views on the processes of history still is in the realm of desiderata, despite N. N. Glatzer's and others' monographs mentioned *supra,* Vol. II, pp. 363 f. n. 35, 381 ff. See also the more recent, rather cursory discussion of "Das Geschichtsbild des Talmud" by R. R. Geis in *Saeculum,* VI, 119–24. Among medieval Jewish writers only Halevi and Maimonides have been subjected to somewhat closer examination in I. Heinemann's penetrating study of "The Historical Picture of R. Yehudah Halevi" (Hebrew), *Zion,* IX, 147–77; and my essays in *JSS,* III, 243–72; and in *PAAJR,* VI, 5–113. But much more detailed work of this kind will yet have to be done before we may secure an adequate picture of the historical thinking, approaches, and methods of the medieval Jewish historians, homilists, philosophers, and jurists. This task will be facilitated by further progress in our knowledge of the Muslim historiographic evolution, which in some areas rather closely converges with, but in many others just as sharply diverges from, that of medieval Jewry. The studies now available include D. S. Margoliouth, *Lectures on Arabic Historians;* G. Richter, *Das Geschichtsbild der arabischen Historiker des Mittelalters* (in *Philosophie und Geschichte,* Vol. XLIII); and F. Rosenthal, *A History of Muslim Historiography;* as well as the numerous studies pertaining especially to Ibn Khaldun, in part quoted in my aforementioned essays. Of considerable interest is also G. E. von Grunebaum's "Firdausi's Concept of History" (1953), reprinted in his *Islam,* pp. 168–84, which shows the conflicts created in the great poet's mind by his Persian ancestry and national feeling versus his Muslim faith. On the other hand, the much better cultivated fields of Byzantine and especially Western historiography, while productive of some insights concerning European Jewish historians like Yosephon, Ibn Daud, and Abraham bar Ḥiyya, become really significant only for the understanding of the dominant Jewish historical outlook during the later Middle Ages when the center of the Jewish people had moved to the West.

97. Abraham bar Ḥiyya's *Megillat ha-megalleh (*Scroll of Disclosure), esp. IV and V, ed. by A. Poznanski, pp. 84 ff. Cf. also *supra,* Chap. XXV, n. 23; and *infra,* Chaps. XXXIV and XXXV. Abraham expatiated on his crucial interpretation of the talmudic passage that "Israel has no lucky star" (p. 115, quoting the well-known statement in Shabbat 156a) in his apologetic letter to Yehudah bar Barzillai. Alluding to other rabbinic statements, he asked the rhetorical question of how stars could have dominion over Israel, if all of them had been created only for Israel's

sake and if Israel's refusal to accept the Torah would have caused the entire universe to return to chaos. Hence "the pious men of Israel are able, through their righteousness and prayers, to nullify the decrees indicated by the stellar movements, which is not the case with the nations of the world." See the text, ed. by A. Z. Schwarz in *Festschrift Schwarz,* Hebrew section, p. 27. Curiously, as pointed out by Julius Guttmann (in his introduction to Poznanski's ed., pp. xii f.), Yehudah himself had likewise used mathematical, if not astrological arguments, in seeking to ascertain the date of the coming of the Messiah. Three passages in his *Perush Sefer Yeṣirah* (Commentary on the book *Yeṣirah,* ed. by Halberstam, pp. 238 f.), are actually so much akin to those of Bar Ḥiyya that one wonders which of the two scholars borrowed from the other. Perhaps both merely rephrased some older source, since Abraham clearly indicates his indebtedness to numerous unnamed predecessors, whose works are no longer available today.

98. As pointed out by Guttmann (in his introduction, pp. xiii f.), the important computation of a seven-day cosmic week totaling 6,000 years is to be found in the works of Isidore of Seville (*Quaestiones in Vetus Testamentum:* in Genesin, II; and his *Chronicon, passim,* in *PL,* LXXXIII, 213 ff. and 1017–58). A close examination of the Isidorian and pseudo-Isidorian historical concepts will reveal further affinities between this seventh-century Spanish scholar and his Jewish compatriot half a millennium later. See esp. J. L. Romero's interesting summary of "San Isidoro de Sevilla; su pensamiento histórico-político y su relaciones con la historia visigoda," *Cuadernos de historia de España,* VIII, 41 ff., 48 ff. But in the absence of direct quotations it is impossible to ascertain whether Bar Ḥiyya had first-hand acquaintance with the works of the Spanish churchman. See also J. M. Millás Vallicrosa's Catalan trans. of Bar Ḥiyya's *Llibre revelador.*

99. See M. Krammer's stimulating suggestions in "Die Legende als Form geschichtlicher Gestaltung," in *Geist und Gesellschaft* (Kurt Breysig Jubilee Volume), III, 22–34 (quoting Goethe). See also the pertinent observations in I. Wolfsberg's "Aggadah and History" (Hebrew), *Zlotnik Jub. Vol.,* pp. 31–39. On the other hand, A. Marmorstein's analysis of "The Historical Relevance of the Aggadah" in his *Studies in Jewish Theology,* Hebrew section, pp. 77–91, merely pursues the customary line of culling from rabbinic homilies certain vestiges of the past, for instance, testimony of the widespread observance of Jewish rituals by Gentiles. The deeper interrelations between theologically colored legend and factual history ought to appear the less surprising, as many of our own overtly secular conceptions of history unwittingly hearken back to theological preconceptions. See K. Löwith's suggestive recent study of *Meaning in History, the Theological Implications of the Philosophy of History,* even more clearly expressed in its German title, *Weltgeschichte und Heilsgeschehen;* and R. Mehl's "Philosophie de l'histoire ou Théologie de l'histoire," *Revue d'histoire et de philosophie religieuses,* XXX, 93–120. Much work indeed must yet be done before the complex task of unraveling the folkloristic from the factual strains in the medieval Jewish conceptions of history and their impact on our modern philosophies of Jewish history is accomplished.

CHAPTER XXIX: RESTUDY OF THE BIBLE

1. Qiddushin 30a; Naṭronai Gaon's responsum in *Teshubot ha-geonim,* Lyck ed., No. 90, with reference to Eccles. 1:7, and the homily in Midrash Ḥazita, v. On the different meaning of "Talmud" in the tannaitic period, see *supra,* Chap. XXVII, n. 37. The impact of Naṭronai's statement on the later Middle Ages will be discussed in connection with the general history of Jewish education of that period. We must bear in mind, however, that in the ninth century, when Naṭronai's responsum was written, only relatively few copies of the Babylonian Talmud were in circulation outside the main academic centers in Babylonia and Palestine. The majority of educated Jews certainly had easier access to the Bible and the Mishnah. For this reason, too, the exclusive concentration on talmudic studies became a regular feature in the Franco-German communities only in the twelfth century and after.

2. Ketubot 106a; Josephus, *Against Apion,* I.8.42–43. Although not expressly stated, the tradition, recorded by the well-informed R. Johanan, implied that the Temple scribes corrected copies for general use by checking them against a standard exemplar kept at the Temple. Later rabbis, too, tried to discourage the circulation of unrevised copies. Applying to it Job's warning, "Let not unrighteousness dwell in thy tents" (11:14), R. Ammi forbade keeping uncorrected copies at one's home for more than thirty days (Ketubot 19b). This prohibition was understood by Maimonides to refer only to the Torah scroll (*M.T.* Tefillin VIII.2), but it could apply also to other parts of Scripture, according to Rashi (Ketubot 19b). Rab, too, tried to encourage both the purchase and constant revision of scriptural texts, assuring the corrector, in particular, that if he merely corrected a single letter, he would earn the heavenly reward of one who copied the whole book (Menaḥot 30a).

3. 'Erubin 13a. Rashi illustrates R. Ishmael's saying by apposite examples: If a scribe omits but the letter *alif* in the third word of the phrase *Va-YHWH Elohim emet* (But the Lord God is the *true* God; Jer. 10:10) he alters the meaning to say that the Lord is *dead* (*met*). Similarly by adding a *vav* to any of the numerous words, *va-yedabber Elohim* (And God spoke; Gen. 8:15 and many other verses) he makes Scripture say: And gods spoke (*va-yedabberu*). Ironically, the more distinguished readers of the talmudic era were designated *qara'im,* the very term which later came to be used for the principal opponents of talmudic Judaism. See Qiddushin 49a, and other illustrations given by Z. Jawitz in his *Toledot,* IX, 123 f. In this section Jawitz graphically, though not altogether critically, summarizes the talmudic sources showing the rabbis' deep concern for the preservation of accurate scriptural texts. On the origin and evolution of Hebrew accents, see the various theories discussed by A. Spanier in *Die masoretischen Akzente.* These are not quite so mutually exclusive as Spanier contends. More recently S. Lieberman has carefully reexamined the rabbinic data on the text-critical marks and related problems, and pointed out especially their similarities with, as well as divergences from, the parallel editorial work performed by the Alexandrian schools on ancient Greek classics. See his *Hellenism in Jewish Palestine,* pp. 28 ff.

We need but mention here in passing the intriguing old problem of the relation between the "original" scriptural readings circulating during the Second Commonwealth and the *textus receptus* as it emerged from the careful recension of the Pharisaic and tannaitic schools. This long and inconclusive debate has received new impetus from the discovery of the Dead Sea Scrolls. Some tentative results, succinctly summarized by J. P. Hyatt, seem to show that "at present we can distinguish at least three pre-Masoretic recensions or text types: 1) One is a proto-Masoretic type represented particularly in the Isaiah scrolls. 2) Another may be described as corresponding to the *Vorlage* of LXX; it is represented particularly by the fragments of Samuel and other historical books. 3) The third is like the Samaritan recension of the Pentateuch. In time other text-types may be identified." See Hyatt's address on "The Dead Sea Discoveries: Retrospect and Challenge," *JBL,* LXXVI, 5 f. It is generally conceded, however, that a sectarian group like that residing in the vicinity of Qumran is far from typical of the Jewish majority. In fact, the few biblical fragments found in Wadi Murabba'at, reflecting the "normative Judaism" of Bar Kocheba's revolutionary army, invariably agree with our accepted text. See M. Greenberg, "The Stabilization of the Text of the Hebrew Bible, Reviewed in the Light of the Biblical Materials from the Judean Desert," *JAOS,* LXXVI, 157–67, and the literature listed there as well as that quoted by Hyatt. We may assume, therefore, that from the second century on the consonantal text of the Old Testament was fully canonized, leaving room only for minor disagreements in regard to details among the large majority of Jews and their rabbinic leaders. See esp. M. H. Segal, "The Promulgation of the Authoritative Text of the Hebrew Bible," *JBL,* LXXII, 35–47. Certainly, in the period here under review, all Jews, including sectarians other than the Samaritans, invoked the testimony of the same scriptural readings.

4. Qiddushin 30a. See *Massekhet Soferim,* IX, ed. by M. Higger, pp. 200 ff. The date and geographic provenance of this important compilation still is conjectural. See Higger's introduction, pp. 78 ff.; and *supra,* Chap. XXVII, n. 70. But there is no doubt that much of its material is pre-Islamic and at times goes back to tannaitic traditions. The ramified problems of the division of letters, words, and verses in Scripture and its historical evolution have frequently been discussed. See, e.g., L. Blau's "Masoretic Studies," *JQR,* [o.s.] VIII, 343–59; IX, 122–44, 471–90. R. Aḥa bar Adda seems, like his father, to have been a prominent student of the biblical text. Both are recorded in connection with R. Hamnuna, a key figure in the masoretic tradition. R. Adda appears in the oft-quoted chain of tradition recorded by Aaron ben Moses Ben Asher in his basic masoretic treatise, *Diqduqe ha-ṭe'amim* (ed. by S. Baer and H. L. Strack, p. 56), while R. Aḥa is mentioned together with R. Hamnuna in a brief note in *Ein Commentar zur Chronik aus dem 10. Jahrhundert* (attributed to a pupil of Saadiah Gaon), ed. by R. Kirchheim, p. 56.

5. Aaron Ben Asher, *Diqduqe,* p. 56; Ḥagigah 6b; Spanier, *Akzente,* pp. 112 ff. Through a slight emendation of Ben Asher's text, the name Naqqai was recovered by A. Berliner and W. Bacher more than sixty years ago and has since been universally accepted. The much-debated question of Syriac and Byzantine influences on the Hebrew system of vocalization and accentuation is still awaiting a more definitive solution. Some aspects of Hebrew pronunciation, and especially the Palestino-Babylonian differences on this score, soon became the subject of heated

sectarian debates. See, for instance, the debate between Qirqisani and Jacob ben Ephraim mentioned *infra,* Chap. XXX, n. 11. See also, more generally, W. Chomsky, "The History of Our Vowel-System in Hebrew," *JQR,* XXXII, 27–49; and *infra,* Chap. XXXI, n. 4.

6. Ḥagigah 24b; 'Erubin 53b. A contemporary homilist added another telling illustration. By mispronouncing *teḥallel* instead of *tehallel* in the concluding verse of the book of Psalms, one changed the meaning of "Let every thing that hath breath praise the Lord" into "desecrate the Lord" (Cant. r. v.51). The Israel phoneticist Y. P. (F.) Gumpertz has devoted several interesting essays to the development of these mispronunciations and the work of the masoretic schools in reestablishing a more disciplined and stable pronunciation. See esp. his "Phonetical Notes on the Grammar of Tiberian Punctuators" (Hebrew), reprinted in his *Mivta'e sefatenu* (Studies in Historical Phonetics of the Hebrew Language), pp. 87 ff. These dialectal differences persisted, with some modifications, in the later Middle Ages. They will be more fully discussed *infra,* Chap. XXX.

7. Marcus Aurelius Cassiodorus, *De institutione divinarum literarum,* Preface, *PL,* LXX, 1105. Although the Bamberg MS lacks the important preposition *ab* before *Hebraeis,* P. Kahle, who called attention to this passage, and A. Baumstark interpreted it to refer clearly to a Jewish academy in Nisibis. See Kahle, *Masoreten des Westens,* I, 52 ff. Both scholars accepted this fact despite their belief that after its destruction by Trajan Nisibis had ceased for a long time to be a center of Jewish learning. This is not borne out by the talmudic and posttalmudic references. Especially after its conquest by the Persians in 363, the city became a center of both trade and culture, of which Arab writers speak in glowing terms. According to Nathan the Babylonian, a man of the "sons of Heman" (I Chron. 25:4 ff.) was called from Nisibis to Baghdad to assume the exilarchic office. See *MJC,* II, 82 f.; my remarks in *Saadia Anniv. Vol.,* pp. 72 f.; and, more generally, J. Obermeyer's observations in *Die Landschaft Babylonien,* pp. 129 f. Cf. also H. R. Nelz's dissertation, *Die theologischen Schulen der morgenländischen Kirchen während der sieben ersten christlichen Jahrhunderte,* pp. 77 ff.

8. Syriac influences on the masoretic punctuation and accentuation have long been postulated by specialists, especially A. Merx. These scholars readily overlooked the fact, however, that the Nestorians, whose fifth-century school in Nisibis laid the foundations for the Syriac Masorah, had themselves been greatly influenced by Jews, with whom they were equated outright by emperors and Church councils. See *supra,* Vol. II, pp. 190 f.; and Chap. XVI, n. 1. On the other hand, F. Praetorius pointed out certain similarities between the Hebrew accents and the Byzantine ekphonetic symbols. See Spanier, *Akzente,* pp. 112 ff. See also J. B. Segal, *The Diacritical Point and the Accents in Syriac.* Nevertheless, as in the field of law, we may rather assume a basically independent, and only occasionally *mutually* influenced evolution. See *supra,* Vol. II, pp. 299 ff., 429 ff.; and Chap. XXVII, nn. 1 ff. On the close social relations between the Jews and the eastern Christians, see Vol. II, pp. 149, 191, 399 n. 16; and *supra,* Chaps. XVIII, nn. 45–46; XXIV, nn. 1, 35.

9. Like many other passages of the *Book of Creation,* this introductory paragraph is obscure and subject to a variety of interpretations. L. Goldschmidt, for example,

reads the crucial words *bi-sefar, ve-sofer, ve-safur,* and translates them by "Zahl, Zähler und Gezähltes." See his vocalized ed. of *Sepher Jeṣirah,* p. 49. In his English trans. I. Kalisch reproduces the three words as *s'for, sippur,* and *safer,* and translates them as "number or idea, word and the writing of the words." See his trans., pp. 11, 47. Reading and interpretation, given here, are more widely accepted, however. See, e.g., M. Lambert's ed. and trans. of Saadiah's *Commentary on Sefer Yeṣirah,* pp. 22 ff. (Arabic), 42 ff. (French); and Moses ben Jacob's *Oṣar Adonai* (Commentary on Yeṣirah), *ad loc.* Cf. also *Teshubot ha-geonim,* ed. by Harkavy, pp. 11 f. No. 29.

10. Mez, *Renaissance of Islam,* p. 195; I. Goldziher, *Richtungen der islamischen Koranauslegung,* pp. 1 ff., 20 ff., 44, 47. The complexities of the Arabic diacritical marks in the seventh century are well illustrated by G. C. Miles's data in his "Early Islamic Inscriptions near Ta'if in the Ḥijaz," *JNES,* VIII, 240 f. The influence of these Muslim controversies on the development of Masorah was stressed, even somewhat overstressed, by P. Kahle in his *Cairo Geniza,* pp. 78 ff., 115, and in "The Qur'ān and the 'Arabīya," *Goldziher Mem. Vol.,* I, 163–82. One must not overlook, however, the essential difference between the main Muslim objective of imposing a single Bedouin-oriented type of language and pronunciation upon a multitude of living and ever changing dialects, and the masoretic effort to achieve consistency in a text no longer reflecting a spoken, dynamically evolving language. Even the Aramaic of the Targum was, as we shall see, gradually dying out. Jewish students merely had to salvage and to review carefully the debris of their own traditional texts to achieve conformity. Not only was their task greatly facilitated; they also could, like Harun ibn Musa, set the pace for their neighbors. In fact, during the first decisive century of the Muslim era, Jewish influence was so great that, according to Bukhari, Ibn 'Abbas (distinguished by tradition as the recipient of Mohammed's last blessing, "O God, teach him the Qur'an!") urgently warned his coreligionists not to keep on consulting the "people of the book," and added, "We have never seen any one of them inquiring from you what had been revealed to you." See *Les Traditions islamiques,* trans. by Houdas and Marçais, II, 622; and G. Vajda, "Juifs et Musulmans selon le hadiṭ," *JA,* CCXXIX, 118.

11. Harkavy, *Zikhron,* VIII, 31; Maqrizi's *Khiṭaṭ* in the excerpts long known from A. I. Sylvestre de Sacy's ed. and trans. in his *Chrestomathie arabe,* I, 161 (Arabic), II, 176 (French; the mention in this text of a Mishnah in Moses' autograph can refer only to *Mishneh torah,* or the book of Deuteronomy); Naṭronai Gaon's responsum cited by the eleventh-century compiler Simḥah ben Samuel of Vitry in his liturgical work, *Maḥzor Vitry,* ed. by S. Hurwitz, p. 91 No. 120; S. Poznanski's "Aus Qirqisani's Kitab al-'anwâr w'al-marâqib," *Semitic Studies in Memory of Alexander Kohut,* p. 455; and *supra,* Chap. XXVI, nn. 4 ff. On the liturgical use of punctuated texts by the Karaites, see Hadassi's *Eshkol,* fols. 60cd, 70a; and R. Hoerning's *British Museum Karaite MSS. Descriptions and Collation of Six Karaite Manuscripts of Portions of the Hebrew Bible in Arabic Characters.* Fourteen other such MSS in the same collection, "for the most part provided with the Hebrew vowel-points and accents (in red ink), and accompanied by the Arabic translations and Commentaries of Yefeth and other Karaite authors" are briefly described *ibid.,* pp. v ff.

12. Qirqisani's *K. al-Anwar,* 1.3, p. 50 (*HUCA,* VII, 350); the anonymous anti-Karaite Bible exegete in the text published by S. Schechter in *JQR,* [o.s.] XIII, 358,

364. On this author see *infra,* n. 98. The Rabbanite appropriation of the term *maskilim,* long a favorite vehicle of self-glorification for Karaite leadership, must have been a doubly bitter pill for Qirqisani and his associates to swallow. In fact, Saadiah censured both 'Anan and Benjamin for erroneously interpreting scriptural passages, accusing the latter specifically of "lack of acquaintance with the language of Scripture." Cf. his *Beliefs and Opinions,* vi.1, 5, ed. by Landauer, pp. 190 f., 201 f.; in Ibn Tibbon's Hebrew trans., pp. 96, 100 f.; in Rosenblatt's English trans., pp. 238, 250 ff. In 'Anan's case Saadiah was certainly wrong in attributing to him a view he did not hold. See Harkavy, *Zikhron,* VIII, 67, 128 n. 2. Moreover, the intensive Karaite preoccupation with Scripture grew during the generations following Benjamin and reached its apogee in the tenth and eleventh centuries. Another Rabbanite author, more directly concerned with masoretic problems, inquired about a difficult point in Aaron ben Asher's punctuation and sarcastically added, "If you, my brethren the Karaites, have an answer, please give it to me, for Scripture is your main preoccupation and specialty and you assert, 'We are extremely conversant with the holy tongue and are expert teachers of vowel points and accents.' " See the excerpt from a Leningrad fragment cited by A. Neubauer in *Aus der Petersburger Bibliothek,* p. 104; and, with minor corrections, by Baer and Strack in their introduction to Ben Asher's *Diqduqe,* pp. xxxviii f. On the other hand, the Karaites alone made of the study of Hebrew and Scripture an article of faith. See Hadassi's *Eshkol,* fol. 21cd. On Abu'l Faraj Harun see *infra,* n. 76; and Chap. XXX, n. 45.

13. See Strack's photographic reproduction of *Prophetarum posteriorum codex Babylonicus Petropolitanus,* with P. Kahle's comments thereon in his *Masoreten des Ostens,* pp. 124 ff., 157 ff.; Saadiah's *Commentary on Sefer Yeṣirah,* ed. by M. Lambert, pp. 28 ff. (Arabic), 64 ff. (French); and the colophons of the famous Aleppo MS and that of Leningrad dated 943, in Kahle's *Masoreten des Westens,* I, 4, 59. See also the latter's more complete listing and excellent reproductions of *Die hebräischen Bibelhandschriften aus Babylonien* (reprinted from *ZAW,* XLVI, 113–37).

14. Cf. the lists published by Baer and Strack in their edition of Ben Asher's *Diqduqe,* pp. 78 f.; and by J. Mann in *The Jews in Egypt,* II, 43 ff. Mann's reconstruction (*ibid.,* p. 47), placing all the Masorites here named in the first two generations between 775 and 825 and leaving the entire subsequent century to the four members of the Ben Asher family alone, has been rejected by Kahle in his *Masoreten des Westens,* p. 40 n. 2. But see below. Mann is also right in placing Phineas at the head of the academy of Jerusalem (despite Kahle's objections, *ibid.,* p. 39) and connecting him with the Phineas mentioned among the latest descendants of Mar Zuṭra by the eighth-century author of *Seder 'olam zuṭa* (*MJC,* II, 76 f.). See his *Jews in Egypt,* I, 58 f. See also Harkavy, *Zikhron,* V, 112 ff.; and *supra,* Chap. XXVIII, n. 61. Similarly, Aḥiyahu ha-Kohen, "the *ḥaber* from the city of Ma'aziah [Tiberias]," was very likely a Rabbanite. Needless to say that neither the provenance of that list from the Rabbanite Genizah in Cairo nor its author's express reference to the "genuine tradition from the Men of the Great Synagogue" precludes pro-Karaite sympathies of some of those listed. See also the still useful "Bemerkungen über die Vocalisation der Targume" by A. Merx in the *Verhandlungen* of the Fifth International Congress of Orientalists, Berlin, 1881, II, Part 1, pp. 142–225.

We must bear in mind, however, that the chronology adopted by both Mann and Kahle is rather mechanical. The *terminus ad quem* is given by Moses Ben Asher's colophon of 895 and by the fact that his son, Aaron, must have had a well-established reputation before 920, for Saadiah to attack him in a major poem. See *infra,* n. 15. But the five generations of Asherites—there may have been six—need not have averaged 25 or 30 years as is assumed respectively by Mann and Kahle. We certainly ought to use the comparative data available in contemporary lists of Rabbanite and Karaite heads of academies and exilarchs. True, the aforementioned genealogy of *Seder 'olam zuṭa* suggests eleven generations from Mar Zuṭra to Phineas, or a period of some two hundred and eighty years according to Mann, or well over three hundred years if we accept the approximate date of 491, or not long after, for Mar Zuṭra III's emigration to Palestine, given *supra,* Vol. II, pp. 182, 196, 399 n. 15; and Chap. XXVIII, n. 61. If correct, this succession would indeed confirm an average range of 25–30 years for a generation. On the other hand, Hilai bar Naṭronai seems to have ascended the gaonate of Sura in 896, exactly 119 years after the assumption of the same office by his great-grandfather, Mari ha-Levi (777). Though unlikely, it is not impossible that the latter's father, Mesharsheya, was identical with the gaon of Sura, Sheshna, also known by the name Mesharsheya, before 689. After all, we definitely know that Saadiah's posthumous son, Dosa, became gaon of that academy in 913, fully seventy-one years after the accession of his father. If so, the five generations from Mesharsheya to Hilai covered a period of well over two centuries. More reliably, the six generations from 'Anan to David ben Boaz extended over a period of some two hundred and thirty years or more (from 767 to 993 [?] when David wrote his commentary on Kohelet; see Mann's *Texts and Studies,* II, 128 ff.). It is quite possible, therefore, that the Masorites, too, averaged nearly 40 years of leadership and that Asher himself began his activity some time early in the eighth century. That is perhaps why no manuscripts provided with the primitive "Palestinian" punctuation seem to date after the seventh century. Of the six biblical fragments of this kind known to Kahle, one of Psalms is dated by him in the sixth century, and that of Ezekiel in the seventh century. See his *Masoreten des Westens,* I, 86; II, 66 ff., 16* ff., and his *Cairo Geniza,* pp. 50 ff.

15. See Graetz's arguments in "Die beiden Ben Ascher und die Masora," *MGWJ,* XX, 1–12, 49–59, and, more succinctly, in his *Geschichte der Juden,* V, 548 ff.; supplemented by B. Klar's fine Hebrew essay on "Ben-Asher," reprinted in his *Meḥqarim ve-'iyyunim,* pp. 276–319. Klar has plausibly reconstructed the Arabic heading on the Cambridge MS of Saadiah's polemical poem, *Essa meshali* (various fragments of this significant poem have been reassembled with a detailed introduction by B. M. Lewin in J. L. Fishman's collection, *Rav Saadya Gaon,* pp. 481–532) to mean "A Reply to Ben Asher, Hebrew." He also compared Saadiah's anti-Karaite arguments with the views expressed by Ben Asher in his own *Diqduqe,* illustrating the true relevance of the gaon's attack. It is, of course, possible that Saadiah did not assail Aaron Ben Asher, but rather his father, Moses, whose colophon in the Cairo MS of Prophets dated in 895 has decidedly Karaite overtones. His praise, in particular, of the scholars of Tiberias who "have not concealed anything of what was given to them, and they have not added a word to what was transmitted to them" sounded like Karaite fighting words professing the completeness of the written Torah without supplementation by Oral Law. See the text reproduced by Kahle in his *Cairo Geniza,* pp. 111 f. Moses' poem, too, on the old theme of the parallel between Israel and the vine, completed by Klar from a Cambridge MS, has many distinctly Karaite allusions. See his *Meḥqarim,* pp. 309 ff. On the other hand, it is clearly against Aaron that Saadiah consistently denied the existence of twelve "servile" letters (including

ṭet) in the Hebrew alphabet, as asserted by Ben Asher. See the latter's *Diqduqe*, p. xi n. 11; and *infra*, Chap. XXX, n. 37.

These lines were written before M. Zucker informed the present writer that he had found strong evidence showing that Aaron Ben Asher was an undeviating Rabbanite. While such official adherence would not necessarily militate against an author's pro-Karaite sympathies, at least in the area of biblical research, we ought to suspend final judgment until the publication of Zucker's forthcoming essay. The twilight position of the Ben Ashers seems to have been shared by such other outstanding Tiberian scholars as Abu Kathir, Saadiah's teacher. This Bible translator (see *infra*, n. 40) could be claimed later by Hadassi (*Eshkol*, fol. 98c) as a fellow Karaite. See also A. Dothan's more recent negative answer to his query, "Was Ben Asher a Karaite?" (Hebrew), *Sinai*, 1957, pp. 280–312, 350–62.

16. See the colophons reproduced and translated into German by Kahle in his *Masoreten des Westens*, I, 3 ff.; Maimonides' *M.T.* Sefer torah VIII.4; and Saadiah ben David ha-'Adeni's commentary thereon cited by Kahle from a Bodleian MS in his *Cairo Geniza*, p. 58. In "The Ben Asher Bible Manuscripts" (*JJS*, II, 20 ff.), J. L. Teicher has marshaled weighty arguments against Kahle's interpretation of these annotations in the Aleppo MS. He considers in particular the lengthy colophon a "dedication" of the eleventh or twelfth century reconstructed by a copyist from an earlier MS. Stronger in negative than in positive reconstructions, Teicher's critique has not altogether replaced Kahle's hypothesis, which still seems best to integrate the diverse elements into a unified whole. See Kahle's on the whole persuasive reply in "The Hebrew Ben Asher Bible Manuscripts," *VT*, I, 161–67, and his additional study, including a defense of his theories against strictures by Ḥanokh Yalon, in "The Ben Asher Text of the Hebrew Bible," *Donum natalicum H. S. Nyberg*, pp. 161–70. One may sympathize, therefore, with Kahle's deep regret at not having been able to utilize the Aleppo MS for his recension of the Hebrew text in R. Kittel's edition of *Biblia hebraica*. See his English foreword in the *Prolegomena* to the 8th ed. of that standard Bible, pp. xxix f.

Kahle's explanation, however, of a brief note mentioning the possession of the Aleppo MS by the Rabbanite Jews living in Jerusalem is very questionable. According to Kahle, the Rabbanites owned the manuscript until it was acquired by Israel ben Simḥah under the condition that it remain accessible to Rabbanite students as well. However, the Rabbanite community would surely not have called itself *Yisrael ha-rabbanim*, a term used in contradistinction to Karaites only. It seems more likely that this annotation stemmed from a Karaite hand. It was followed by another note (on the bottom of the same page) mentioning the transfer of the manuscript after its liberation from the hand of the Crusaders to the "Jerusalem" congregation in Egypt. If, as it appears, Egyptian Jewry of both persuasions contributed funds for the indiscriminate release of the Jewish victims and their sacred possessions in Jerusalem, we may understand why the Karaites, who celebrated the release of that manuscript together with other precious religious objects in a special thanksgiving service on Ab 10, 1037, after the destruction of the Second Temple (July 23, 1105), delivered it to the Cairo Rabbanites rather than to their fellow sectarians of that city. Cf. the colophon on a Karaite Torah scroll reprinted by Mann in his *Jews in Egypt*, I, 200 n. 1; Kahle's comments in his *Masoreten des Westens*, I, 10 f.; and our interpretation of the new documents published by Goitein *supra*, Chap. XXI, nn. 29–30. In any case, sacred books readily changed hands from one group to the other. Even the Rabbanite owners did not care to expunge Israel ben Simḥah's original dedication which was supposed to vouchsafe eternal possession of the manuscript by the Jerusalem Karaites.

17. Mann, *Texts and Studies,* II, 32 f.; L. Lipschütz's ed. of Mishael ben 'Uzziel's *Ḥillufim* in his dissertation, *Ben Ašer-Ben Naftali* (used to good advantage, in its more complete typewritten form, by Lipschütz's teacher, P. Kahle, in the preparation of the masoretic text and the Masorah in Kittel's *Biblia hebraica;* see Kahle's English foreword, pp. xxix f.); F. Pérez Castro's recent reexamination of the readings of Num. 13–15 in five Hebrew MSS in his "Ben Ašer-Ben Naftali?" *Homenaje a Millás,* II, 141–48; and A. Díez Macho's study of a New York MS in "Un Manuscrito hebreo protomasorético y nueva teoría de los llamados MSS. Ben Naftali," *Estudios biblicos,* XV, 187–222. Neither Mishael's date nor his sectarian allegiance is known. S. Poznanski assumes that he lived in the twelfth century. See *Karaite Literary Opponents of Saadia,* p. 30 n. 3, and his comments (in "Miscelle," *ZHB,* IV, 186) on the letter written by a Mishael ben 'Uzziel and published by J. Horovitz in "Ein arabischer Brief an R. Chananel," *ZHB,* IV, 155–58 The colophon of the Cairo Pentateuch, published by R. Gottheil in his "Some Hebrew Manuscripts in Cairo," *JQR,* [o.s.] XVII, 632 f., contains an addition from a later hand which begins "I, Mishael ben 'Uzziel ben Joseph ben Hilleli have examined this holy Torah. . . . " If authentic, this statement might indicate Mishael's Karaite allegiance. However, the genuineness of this note has rightly been impugned; it was perhaps but an unabashed attempt to connect this text with the famous "Hilleli" codex, which, according to the historian Abraham Zacuto, was some six hundred years old in 1504, when Zacuto wrote his chronicle. See his oft-quoted *Sefer Yuḥasin,* p. 220a; and Mann's comments in his *Texts and Studies,* II, 29, 134 f. (Zacuto may rather have had in mind the codex, now in Leningrad, written in 994 by "Moses, the scribe, son of Hillel"; see Kahle, *Masoreten des Westens,* I, 65 ff., and Plate 22/6). On the other hand, if our author of *Ḥillufim* is identical with the Mishael, "master of hidden matters, celebrated above all praise," to whom greetings were sent by a letter-writer of 1194 or 1197, then he almost certainly was a Rabbanite. Otherwise, he would not have been enumerated together with Maimonides and other Rabbanite scholars. See Mann, *Jews in Egypt,* I, 245 f.; II, 321 f. Knowledge of this fact would not, in any case, have deterred the Karaite student of Masorah, Joseph ha-Qonstandini (of Constantinople) from speedily incorporating in 1060 a Hebrew translation of Mishael's treatise into his own *'Adat deborim,* a copy of which was prepared as early as 1207, probably by other Karaites in the Black Sea port of Gagri. See the colophon cited by Mann in his *Texts and Studies,* II, 291 n. 13, and Kahle's *Cairo Geniza,* p. 67 (referring also to Harry Levy who had made a special study of the *'Adat* in preparation of his unpublished Berne dissertation). See also A. Ben David's recent Hebrew study of "The Differences between Ben Asher and Ben Naftali," *Tarbiz,* XXVI, 384–409 ("involve not grammatical principles, but only the musicological aspects of the accents").

18. J. Halévy, "Origine de la transcription du texte hébreu en caractères grecs dans les *Hexaples* d'Origène," *JA,* 9th ser. XVII, 335–41; F. Wutz, *Die Transkiptionen von der Septuaginta bis Hieronymus;* P. Kahle's aforementioned works and his essay "Die überlieferte Aussprache des Hebräischen und die Punktation der Masoreten," *ZAW,* XXXIX, 230–39; A. Sperber's "Hebrew Based on Greek and

Latin Transliterations," *HUCA*, XII–XIII, 103–274; his "Hebrew Phonology," *ibid.*, XVI, 415–82; and E. Brønno's *Studien über hebräische Morphologie und Vokalismus auf Grund der Mercatischen Fragmente der zweiten Kolumne der Hexapla des Origines.* See also I. Davidson's *Maḥzor Yannai,* pp. xlii f. In view of the great variations in the Yannai MSS, however, one cannot speak with any assurance about the genuineness of the original readings. Cf. M. Zulay's remarks in his ed. of *Piyyuṭe Yannai,* pp. xviii f.; Y. F. Gumpertz's observations in his *Mivta'e sefatenu* (*supra,* n. 6); his other essays briefly criticized by Kahle in *Cairo Geniza,* p. 231; Kahle's more detailed, often doctrinaire criticisms of Brønno's work, *ibid.*, pp. 231–34; and *infra,* Chap. XXXI, nn. 37, 42. To be sure, some of the conclusions drawn from Origen and Jerome seem to go too far. Apart from the evident double pronunciation of most gutterals in these texts, even the chief culprit, *pe,* was evidently known to Jerome also in the pronunciation of *p.* In explaining his transcription *apedno* (Dan. 11:45), he writes that although generally the Hebrew language has no letter *p,* "in this place the Hebrew texts writes *phe,* but is read *pe*" (*PL,* XXV, 601). Certainly unfamiliar with the Accadian origin of this word, he must have echoed only the pronunciation on the tongues of contemporary Jews. It may not be too venturesome to suggest that his informants read *p* where the Masorah put a *dagesh forte,* but pronounced every other *pe* as *f.* See also N. H. Torczyner's serious reservations concerning the use of Graeco-Latin transliterations for the reconstruction of biblical phonetics in "Die Aussprache des Begad-Kefat in der Geschichte der hebräischen Sprache," *MGWJ,* LXXXI, 340–51 (also in a Hebrew essay, reprinted in *Ha-Lashon ve-ha-sefer,* I, 143 ff.). See also *infra,* n. 20.

For other reasons the Jews' Semitic-speaking neighbors mispronounced Hebrew words and particularly names. The biblical Enoch, important also for Mohammed's genealogy, is called in some Muslim traditions *Ḥanuḥ* (akin to the Hebrew *Ḥanokh*) and in some others *Aḥnuḥ.* K. Levy has, therefore, rightly urged closer examination of the phonetic transcriptions in the vast *ḥadith* literature. See his *Zur masoretischen Grammatik,* p. 9. As is well known, Semitic linguistic feeling rebelled against any word beginning with a double consonant and hence provided, for example, the name Plato with a preliminary vowel: Aplatun. Similarly, according to Solomon ibn Parḥon, Jews from Palestine to Morocco were still pronouncing the word *shetayim* (two), *eshtayim*—a usage which startled such Spanish visitors as Halevi and Ibn Ezra. See Ibn Parḥon's *Maḥberet he-'arukh* (Lexicon hebraicum), ed. by S. G. Stern, fol. 4b.

19. Ḥullin 137b; 'A.Z. 58b; M. 'Eduyot 1.3, and Maimonides' *Commentary* thereon (contrasted with Rashi's frank supplement in his comments on b. Shabbat 15a); b. Nedarim 37b with the geonic comment thereon in *Teshubot ha-geonim,* ed. by Harkavy, No. 217; and the geonic responsum quoted in *Toratan shel rishonim,* ed. by H. Hurwitz, I, 55. How open to misspelling and mispronunciation was the very Tetragrammaton may be illustrated by N. Walker's note, "The Writing of the Divine Name in Aquila and the Ben Asher Text," *VT,* III, 103–4. According to Walker, the vocalization of that name in the Bible, which from the thirteenth century on was to give rise to the widespread mispronunciation *Jehovah,* did not stem from the Masorites' desire to accentuate its substitute reading, *Adonai,* but rather an original pronunciation *Yehya.* But apart from the difficulty of explaining how the *o* sound (*ḥolam*) subsequently crept into the masoretic texts, Walker's theory presupposes widespread pronunciation and, hence, also mispronunciation of

the divine name. In fact, however, even in antiquity many conscientious Jews had been reluctant to use the very circumlocutions of *Adonai* or *Kyrios* without some compelling reason. See *supra,* Vol. II, pp. 18, 335 n. 20. Cf. also Joseph Karo's later warning (in his commentary on *Ṭur* O.Ḥ., LXI) against the "swallowing" of *yod* in *ve-hayu* (in Gen. 1:14; "let them be," etc.); and other illustrations given in B. M. Lewin's introduction to Sherira's *Iggeret,* pp. lx ff. On the Qumran sectarians see *supra,* Chap. XXVIII, n. 21.

In support of his thesis, Kahle constantly invokes the testimony of a tannaitic source (cited with minor variations in b. Berakhot 15b; and j. II.4, 4d) which warned the worshipers to pause between like-sounding consonants in the *Shema'*. This warning included the words *'esev be-sadekha* (Deut. 11:15) and *ha-kanaf petil* (Num. 15:38), indicating a current pronunciation of *ve-sadekha* and *fetil,* which could easily be confused with the preceding words, *'esev* and *kanaf.* Of course, we deal here once again only with a *b* and *p* provided by the Masorah with a *dagesh lene.* Moreover, the rabbis were obviously concerned here only with the private devotions of countless individuals expected to recite the *Shema'* three times daily. They certainly had to take cognizance of widely used forms, even if they themselves did not approve of them. In fact, their emphasis on the *Shema'* alone would seem to indicate that they feared less confusion in other prayers which, usually recited in the synagogue, could be more effectively controlled. See also Maimonides' *M.T.* Qeri'at shema' II.9; the strictures thereon by Ibn Daud; and Abraham Maimuni's *Resp.,* No. 79, p. 103, showing that some questioners were disturbed even by the proximity in one verse of *Shema'* of the two *yods* of *bene Yisrael* (Num. 15:38). Interesting archaeological evidence as to the importance for gnostic speculations of the single letter *vav* was presented by A. Dupont-Sommer in *La Doctrine gnostique de la lettre wāw d'après une lamelle araméenne inédite,* esp. pp. 35 ff.

20. For this reason the two forms of *sheva* became a cornerstone of Hebrew phonetics and a subject of many special monographs. Two early manuscripts, probably dating from the tenth or eleventh century, were published (with a German trans. and extensive comments) by K. Levy in his *Zur masoretischen Grammatik;* and, with some use of the latter's materials, by N. Allony in his *Mi-Sifrut yeme ha-benayim* (From Medieval Letters), pp. 1–12. See also, more generally, Allony's Hebrew study of "The Mobile and Quiescent Sheva" in his *Mi-Torat ha-lashon ve-ha-shirah bi-yeme ha-benayim* (on Grammar and Poetry in the Middle Ages), pp. 69–84; and the further defense of his thesis, against competent opponents, in his *Mi-Sifrut,* pp. 25–42. This recent controversy demonstrates how important the issues connected with the use of *sheva* can still be for modern philology. See also H. Hirschfeld's observations on "The Dot in Semitic Palaeography," *JQR,* X, 159–83. The double pronunciation of *BGDKPT* is analyzed in H. Torczyner's aforementioned essays in *MGWJ,* LXXXI, 340–51; and *Ha-Lashon ve-ha-sefer,* I, 143 ff. His conclusion, however, that in the preexilic period all six letters were pronounced as nonspirants, in the postexilic and tannaitic times the latter three became aspirate *Kh, Ph,* and *Th,* while only in the Middle Ages did they all receive their double pronunciation, will hardly receive unanimous acceptance.

Perhaps under the impact of Arabic, the Masorites also restored to universal usage the double pronunciation of *shin* (*Sh-S*), which had evidently been sloughed off in popular parlance, though probably not in the academic reading of Scripture. See Y. P. Gumpertz's "Shin and Its Metamorphoses" (Hebrew), reprinted in his

Mivta'e sefatenu, pp. 33 ff. On the other hand, the Tiberian scholars refused to go along with the author of *Sefer Yeṣirah* and Saadiah in maintaining a double pronunciation of *r*. See *Yeṣirah,* IV.2 (in Goldschmidt's ed., p. 59; English trans. by Kalisch, pp. 24 f.), and Saadiah's comments thereon, ed. by Lambert, pp. 78 f. (Arabic), 102 (French). Needless to say, this Tiberian decision did not assure uniform pronunciation of the *r* sound, which, in general, most readily betrays the speaker's linguistic antecedents. Environmental influences on this phase of modern Hebrew speech are well illustrated in M. Gottstein's "On the Pronunciation of the *Resh* in Hebrew" (Hebrew), *Leshonenu,* XVI, 209–11. See also L. Koehler's more general "Bemerkungen zur Schreibung und Aussprache der tiberischen Masora," *HUCA,* XXIII, Part 1, 137–55. The musical aspects of the biblical accents will be discussed *infra,* Chap. XXXI, n. 87.

21. Kahle's theories in this complex subject, formulated over a lifetime of intensive and penetrating research, are well summarized in his *Cairo Geniza,* esp. pp. 94 f. Cf., however, the legitimate reservations made, among others, by M. Kober in his review of Kahle's earlier book, *Masoreten des Westens,* Vol. I, in *Jeschurun,* XVII, 147–52.

22. Exod. 15:6, 11, 17, and the masoretic notes thereon. The daily recitation of the Song of Moses by the community of Rome and all Spanish communities "from the days of the exile from Jerusalem until now" is attested by R. Simḥah bar Samuel in his *Maḥzor Vitry,* p. 226. Since Spain largely followed the Babylonian, and Rome the Palestinian ritual, we have here a remarkable confluence of both traditions. See also Gumpertz's related observations in his *Mivta'e sefatenu,* pp. 34 ff.

23. See Abraham ibn Ezra's *Sefer Ṣahot* (Zachot oder Das Buch der Eleganz der hebräischen Sprache), ed. by G. H. Lippmann, fol. 2ab; and Ben Asher's *Diqduqe,* pp. 60 ff. with the editors' notes thereon. Curiously, Ibn Ezra, though himself a Spaniard, seems to have admired the å pronunciation of the men from Tiberias, Egypt, and Ifriqiya. See Kahle's interpretation in his *Masoreten des Ostens,* p. 159, a modification of the view held by W. Bacher in his *Abraham ibn Esra als Grammatiker,* p. 37. Cf., however, the reservations suggested by Joseph ha-Kohen in his Hebrew "Comments on Grammatical and Masoretic Problems," *Leshonenu,* XIII, 209 f. In his "Hebrew Grammar: A New Approach," *JBL,* LXII, 137–262, A. Sperber has assembled many illustrations of masoretic inconsistencies. He went too far, however, in denying for that reason the authenticity of the "medieval Masoretic schematization." In many cases, it appears, the Masorites willfully conformed with a hallowed tradition even when it was inconsistent with their rules or within itself. See also Y. P. (F.) Gumpertz's remarks on "An Old *Deḥiq,* Not Approved by the Punctuators" (Hebrew), reprinted in his *Mivta'e sefatenu,* pp. 262 ff.; and, more generally, B. J. Roberts's discussion of recent views in "The Divergencies in the Pre-Tiberian Masoretic Text," *JJS,* I, 147–55; and F. Pérez Castro's review article, "Problemas de las fuentes de conocimiento del hebreo premasorético," *Sefarad,* VIII, 145–87. See also note 24.

24. David ben Abraham al-Fasi's *Kitāb Jāmi' al-alfāẓ* (The Hebrew-Arabic Dictionary of the Bible), ed. by S. L. Skoss, II, 684; and the editor's introduction *ibid.,* I, lxxxi f. The texts of both Masorahs, with their innumerable variants, have long

been known through detailed compilations by Jacob ben Ḥayyim (1524–25), supplemented by Elijah Levita's *Massoreth ha-Massoreth* (1538; ed. with an English trans. and notes by C. D. Ginsburg); and the more modern works by S. Baer and C. D. Ginsburg. See esp. the latter's four-volume work, *The Massorah. Compiled from Manuscripts.* All these works have been severely, perhaps too severely, criticized by Kahle, particularly on the basis of newly utilized biblical manuscripts representing the "eastern" tradition (he was able to muster an imposing array of some one hundred and twenty manuscripts representing that tradition, although his own *Masoreten des Ostens* is based on only the best fourteen). Unfortunately, his preparation of a new critical edition of the Masorah, nearing completion in 1939, was interrupted by the Second World War. Cf. his *Cairo Geniza,* pp. 50 f., 74 n. 1. Cf. also A. Ramirez's study of "Un Texto puntuado y masora de la escuela de Ahron ben Mošéh ben Ašer," *Biblica,* X, 200–213; XI, 108–21; XIV, 303–29 (on MS Or. 4445 of the British Museum Library); F. Díaz Estaban's "Notas sobre la Masora," *Sefarad,* XIV, 315–21; and especially the comprehensive studies by A. Sperber including his "Problems of the Masora," *HUCA,* XVII, 293–394; and his "Masoretic Hebrew," a general introduction to the *Codex Reuchlinianus* which forms the first of four volumes of *The Pre-Masoretic Bible* in the *Corpus codicum hebraicorum medii aevi,* ed. by R. Edelmann, Part II.

25. Ibn Janaḥ's *Kitab al-Uṣul* (The Book of Hebrew Roots), ed. by A. Neubauer, col. 228 (in the Hebrew trans. by Yehudah ibn Tibbon entitled *Sefer ha-Shorashim,* ed. by W. Bacher, p. 155; cf. also *ibid.,* p. 265 n. 2); and his *Kitab al-Luma'* (Grammar), ed. by J. Derenbourg, pp. vi ff. (in the Hebrew trans. by Ibn Tibbon entitled *Sefer ha-Riqmah,* ed. by M. Wilensky, I, 15 f.). Cf. Baer and Strack's ed. of Ben Asher's *Diqduqe;* and S. Frensdorff's ed. of *Das Buch Ochlah W'Ochlah* (on the basis of a Paris MS). Both editions have been severely criticized by Kahle, but his call for new critical editions has thus far remained unheeded, except for the statement in a 1954 article (*Sefarad,* XIV, 317) by Díaz Estaban that the latter was preparing such an edition of *Okhlah ve-Okhlah.* A modified and enlarged version of that work, called by early grammarians "The Great Masorah," is also extant; it is fully analyzed on the basis of a Halle MS by H. Hupfeld in his "Ueber eine bisher unbekannt gebliebene Handschrift der Masorah," *ZDMG,* XXI, 201–20. Other early masoretic monographs include the so-called *Midrash ḥaserot vi-yeterot* (On Full and Defective Spellings), ed. by S. A. Wertheimer (reprinted in J. D. Eisenstein's *Ozar Midrashim,* pp. 194 ff.), with additional fragments in Ginzberg's *Ginze Schechter,* I, 206 ff. (dating from a period close to that of Hai Gaon who quotes it); *Sefer Tagin* (Book of Crownlets) in Eisenstein's *Ozar,* pp. 563 ff.; those ed. by J. Derenbourg under the title "Manuel du lecteur," *JA,* 6th ser. XVI, 309–550; by A. Neubauer under the title *Petite grammaire hébraïque;* as well as those more recently edited by Lipschütz, Levy, and Allony, mentioned *supra,* nn. 17, 20.

26. See the photographic reproduction mentioned *supra,* n. 13. Another related Leningrad fragment of Job in four folios was described in detail by J. Weerts in his "Über die babylonisch punktierte Handschrift No. 1546 der II Firkowitschen Sammlung," *ZAW,* XXVI, 49–84. See also Kahle's *Masoreten des Ostens,* pp. 141 ff., and Plate I. According to Kahle, the Babylonian punctuation at the height of its

evolution is best represented by two Cambridge fragments, described *ibid.*, pp. 113 ff., 123 ff., and in part reproduced there on Plates VI and VII. Seventy additional facsimiles were published by him in *Die hebräischen Bibelhandschriften aus Babylonien* cited *supra,* n. 13. He considered, on the other hand, another Leningrad MS, written in 1008, the relatively best representative of the Tiberian school. This MS became, therefore, the mainstay of the latest edition of R. Kittel's *Biblia hebraica.* See Kahle's analysis in the *Prolegomena* to that ed., English foreword, pp. xxix ff.; and *supra,* n. 16. See also R. Meyer's brief observations, "Die Bedeutung der linearen Vokalisation für die hebräische Sprachgeschichte," *Wissenschaftliche Zeitschrift der Karl-Marx Universität Leipzig,* III, 85–94 (referring to Ugaritic, Phoenician, and Qumram texts).

27. Maimonides' *M.T.* Sefer torah VII.8; VIII.4; Abraham ibn Daud's *Emunah ramah* (Exalted Faith), ed. by S. Weil, pp. 80 (Hebrew), 101 (German; somewhat mistranslated); B. Kennicott's *Vetus Testamentum;* and G. B. de Rossi's *Variae lectiones veteris Testamenti.* On the three small-sized letters *nun* (in Jer. 39:13, Isa. 44:14, Prov. 16:28), see *Ochlah W'Ochlah,* ed. by Frensdorff, p. 117 No. 178. Although in his apologetic fervor Ibn Daud often indulged in sweeping generalizations, as in his total disparagement of Karaite contributions to learning (see *supra,* Chap. XXVIII, n. 68), his harangue here did not overshoot the mark too widely. Only in Yemen did some minor variants retain wide circulation. For example, the psalmist's exclamation, "I will cry unto God Most High; unto God that accomplisheth [*gomer*] it for me" (57:3), appears in some Yemenite manuscripts of both Psalms and the *Midrash ha-gadol* as the equivalent of "unto God that does me good [*gomel*]." Cf. the *Midrash Haggadol* on Genesis, ed. by M. Margulies, p. 865 line 10; and the editor's note thereon. On the sharp partisan controversies concerning the Qur'anic text, see I. Goldziher's *Richtungen der islamischen Koranauslegung,* pp. 270 ff.; and, in contrast thereto, the relatively moderate emendations suggested by Isma'il al-'Ukbari, according to Qirqisani's *K. al-Anwar,* I.15, ed. by Nemoy, I, 56; in his English trans. in *HUCA,* VII, 388.

28. *Teshubot ha-geonim,* ed. by Harkavy, pp. 13 No. 33, 188 f. No. 373, 230 No. 437; Hai's *Resp.* published by Harkavy in his "Old and New" (Hebrew), *Hakedem,* II, 82; Mann, *Texts and Studies,* I, 446 n. 2, 554 n. 1; Ginzberg, *Ginze Schechter,* II, 375, 378 (twice gives the date of 1092–93). Hai's statement is essentially confirmed by the observations of Al-Mas'udi. Writing several decades before Hai, the Arab historian and world traveler minimized the differences between the Hebrew and the Arabic languages. He remarked that the Jews of Iraq "speak a Syriac idiom called Tarjum, into which they had translated the Torah from ancient Hebrew because the latter idiom is familiar and clear to them, whereas their majority finds it difficult to understand and pronounce Hebrew properly." Cf. his *K. at-Tanbiḥ* (Book of Recollection and Revision), ed. by M. J. de Goeje, p. 79 (in the French trans. by B. Carra de Vaux, p. 115). This formulation is extremely revealing. The former world language of Aramaic was reduced in the eyes of this well-informed Arab historian to little more than the lingo of the Jewish translation of Scripture. Hai's contention may, in some respects, have been but an exaggerating rationalization of his own academy's conservative adherence to the Aramaic language. We shall see that practically all prayers composed by geonim other than Saadiah were

written in Aramaic, out of conservatism rather than actual need. In most of his other works, including his halakhic monographs, Hai himself no longer hesitated to make use of the Arabic medium. See also *infra,* Chap. XXX, n. 4.

29. Megillah 3a, with reference to Neh. 8:8; T. Meg. IV.41, p. 228; b. Qiddushin 49a. Perhaps to preserve a measure of uniformity the Tannaim had forbidden the confiding of any of these Aramaic versions to writing. Yielding to popular pressure, the later rabbis had to allow written recensions, but they still forbade their recitation in the synagogue from manuscript. Cf. Berakhot 8ab; Giṭṭin 60b; j. Megillah IV.1, 74d. Even this limitation had ultimately to be abandoned. Cf. Ginzberg's *Ginze Schechter,* I, 459.

30. Kahle, *Cairo Geniza,* pp. 117 ff., 179 ff. The complex origins of both Targum and Peshiṭṭa have been the subject of numerous investigations for several generations. The problem of the Jewish, indeed talmudic, background of the Peshiṭṭa was the subject of extensive debates already in the mid-nineteenth century between S. J. L. Rapoport and J. Perles, arguing in the affirmative, and Gesenius and T. Nöldeke, supporting the negative. The former position was reinforced, though not conclusively proved, on the basis of a reexamination of the entire Syriac translation by C. Heller in his *Untersuchungen über die Peschittâ,* I. The medium ground, crediting strong Jewish antecedents to what in time was to become an essentially Christian reworking, is taken by A. Baumstark in his "Pešiṭṭā und palästinensisches Targum," *Biblische Zeitschrift,* XIX, 257–70; and most other recent scholars in the studies listed *supra,* Vol. II, pp. 386 f. n. 25. To these monographs add some of the more recent researches in this field, esp. by A. Vööbus, whose brief study of "Der Einfluss des altpalästinischen Targums in der Textgeschichte der Peschitta des Alten Testaments," *Muséon,* LXVIII, 215–18, reinforces Baumstark's views. In "The Oldest Extant Traces of the Syriac Peshitta," *Muséon,* LXIII, 191–204, Vööbus has also plausibly argued against Burkitt's long-accepted theory that this Syriac translation was first introduced by Rabbula after he became bishop of Edessa in 411. Vööbus pointed out that a British Museum MS of that version was actually written in 411, showing that at that time it had already been widely recognized. He reinforced his arguments for the existence of such a version in the fourth century in "Das Alter der Peschitta," *Oriens christianus,* XXXVIII, 1–10 (also listing his additional earlier publications, of which those published in the *Contributions* of Baltic University, Nos. 59, 64–65, are particularly relevant); and, more broadly, in his comprehensive "manuscript studies" of the *Early Versions of the New Testament.* Similar investigations of the existing manuscript resources have been published also by M. H. Gottstein in "Eine Cambridger Syrohexaplarhandschrift," *Muséon,* LXVII, 291–96; and "A List of Some Uncatalogued Syriac Biblical Manuscripts," *BJRL,* XXXVII, 429–45. See also such detailed researches into individual books as those by D. M. C. Englert, *The Peshitto of Second Samuel* (the introduction includes a concise review of the older publications); and A. Vogel, "Studien zum Pešitta-Psalter," *Biblica,* XXXII, 32–56, 198–231, 336–63, 481–502. It is doubly remarkable, therefore, that we do not as yet possess truly satisfactory critical editions of either the Syriac or the Aramaic versions. Some three decades ago A. Sperber began to prepare, under the sponsorship of the Jewish Academy of Berlin, a critical edition of both the Targum "Onkelos" to the Torah and the Targum "Jonathan" to Prophets. Although near-

ing completion before 1933, this work is only now (1957) scheduled for publication in Leiden. See also L. Delekat, "Die Peschitta zu Jesaja zwischen Targum und Septuaginta, I–II," *Biblica,* XXVIII, 185–99, 321–35 (part of a Heidelberg dissertation).

31. *Pesiqta rabbati,* ed. by M. Friedmann, fol. 14ab, compared with j. Megillah IV.1, 74d; b. Giṭṭin 60ab; and other sources listed by Friedmann. His suggested correction, "*We are* Israel," is unnecessary.

32. See A. Sperber's brief illustrations in his "Peschitta und Onkelos," *Kohut Mem. Vol.,* pp. 561 f.; and, in contrast thereto, S. Wohl's analysis of *Das Palästinische Pentateuch-Targum.* N. H. Torczyner is certainly right in stressing the dependence of "Onkelos," too, on the theological and aggadic preconceptions of rabbinic hermeneutics, but he goes too far in understating, for this reason, the difference between it and the preponderantly aggadic "Targum Jonathan." See his Hebrew essay, "Toward an Understanding of the Aramaic Translation of the Torah" in *Magnes Anniversary Book,* pp. 143–51; and *infra,* n. 35. Cf. also L. H. Brockington's analysis of the respective theological attitudes of the authors of "Septuagint and Targum," largely explainable by the different audiences to which they were addressed, in his essay in *ZNW,* LXVI, 80–86. Even those who still adhere to the traditional view of the origin of Onkelos' version in the early centuries of the Christian era (see, e.g., A. E. Silverstone's *Aquila and Onkelos*), need not deny that the final recension was made in the Babylonian academies late in the talmudic period and after. Kahle seems right in assuming that it was this Babylonian revision which established a fairly uniform text from a variety of readings in manuscripts circulating throughout the Near East. Originally the multiplicity of traditions must have resembled that of the Samaritan Targum, which, never having undergone such a thorough official recension, retained its innumerable variants. See Kahle's criticisms of H. Petermann's ed. of the *Pentateuchus Samaritanum* in his "Zu den in Nāblus befindlichen Handschriften des Samaritanischen Pentateuchtargums," *ZDMG,* LXI, 909–12; his *Cairo Geniza,* pp. 37 f.; and J. R. Diaz's brief comments on "Ediciones del Targum Samaritano," *Estudios biblicos,* XV, 105–8.

33. The Masorah to Onkelos is available in two editions: by A. Berliner, *Die Massorah zum Targum Onkelos* (see also notes to his ed. of *Targum Onkelos*), and by S. Landauer, *Die Mâsôrâh zum Onkelos.* Cf. also J. Wood's comparative data in "A Syriac Masorah," *Transactions* of the Glasgow University Oriental Society, XV, 35–42. Of considerable use is also C. J. Kasovski, *Oṣar ha-millim* (A Concordance to Targum Onkelos). Despite P. de Lagarde's adverse criticisms of Berliner's general work on the Targum and Kahle's equally sharp strictures on the latter's and Landauer's editions in his *Masoreten des Ostens,* pp. 208 ff., these texts clearly reveal the numerous disagreements between the schools of Nehardea and Sura. None of the extant manuscripts, however, clearly follow either of the two schools. According to Kahle, the Nehardea recension is best reflected in an Oxford MS described by him *ibid.,* pp. 110 ff., together with a sample thereof on Plate III. The Sabionetta ed., on the other hand, and the Yemenite ed. of the Pentateuch in Hebrew, Aramaic, and Arabic, entitled *Keter torah* (published in Jerusalem, 1894–1901, it is based on numerous Yemenite MSS which, although revised in the light of the Tiberian punctuation, reflected Babylonian traditions), largely follow the school of Sura. It

is provided with a commentary *Ḥeleq ha-diqduq* (Grammatical Section) by Yaḥya ben Joseph Ṣalaḥ. Cf. Kahle, pp. 203 ff.

In any case, considerable new source material has been accumulating over the years to justify a new critical edition. See esp. A. Díez Macho, "Un Importante manuscrito targúmico de la Biblioteca Vaticana," *Homenaje a Millás,* I, 375–463; his "Un Nuevo Targum a los Profetas," *Estudios bíblicos,* XV, 287–95 (from a Cambridge and a New York MS); his essay cited *infra,* n. 37; the bibliographically significant list of 64 manuscripts extant in various libraries in his "Nuevos manuscritos importantes, bíblicos ó litúrgicos, en hebreo arameo," *Sefarad,* XV, 1–22; and R. Fuste Ara, "El Fragmento targúmico T. S. B3 de la Biblioteca Universitaria de Cambridge," *Estudios bíblicos,* XV, 85–94. On the other hand, substantive and broadly analytical investigations have largely been neglected in recent years. See, e.g., M. Herskovics's unpublished dissertation, *Halakah and Agadah in Onkelos* (Yeshiva University, 1950). J. Weinberg, who more than a quarter of a century ago had announced the preparation of a comprehensive survey of the targumic literature, published but a brief summary, "Zur Geschichte der Targumim. Eine Darstellung der Entstehung und Entwicklung der aramäischen Targumim," *Festschrift Jacob Rosenheim,* pp. 237–58. See also P. Kahle's brief Hebrew study of "The Targums," *Melilah,* III–IV, 70–76, with reference also to some Genizah fragments.

34. Harkavy, *Zikhron,* V, 150 ff., 160 ff., 200 ff.; A. Spanier, *Akzente,* pp. 12 f.; Kahle, *Cairo Geniza,* pp. 51 f.; and *supra,* Chap. XXIII, n. 21. That the Babylonians likewise occasionally used their vocalization for the punctuation of the Mishnah is evident from three fragments extant in St. Petersburg's Firkovitch collection, one item of which was published by I. D. Markon in "A Fragment of the Mishnah" (Hebrew), *Hakedem,* I, 41–48 (with four reproductions); and from other fragments published by Kahle in "The Mishnah Text in Babylonia, I–II," *HUCA,* X, 185 ff. (with T. Weinberg), and XII–XIII, 275 ff. See also *supra,* Vol. II, pp. 427 ff., n. 6.

35. *Sha'are teshubah,* No. 330, ed. by Leiter, fol. 29c; Targum of Eccles. 3:21 (with Ibn Ezra's speculative elaboration), and Gen. 21:21 (the Bible speaks of Ishmael's wife in the singular); Hai's responsum in *Teshubot ha-geonim,* Lyck ed., fol. 29a No. 93, with reference to Megillah 3a. Cf. S. D. Luzzatto, "Nachträgliches über die Targumim," *Wissenschaftliche Zeitschrift für jüdische Theologie,* V, 124–37; and Z. Y. (W.) Gottlieb, "The Translation of Jonathan b. 'Uzziel on the Pentateuch" (Hebrew), *Melilah,* I, 26–34. Gottlieb rightly emphasizes that Targum's lack of stylistic unity which clearly indicates the multiple authorship of its underlying versions. It is also fundamentally dependent on Onkelos which it often merely elaborates on the basis of rabbinic traditions. Less plausible are Gottlieb's arguments in favor of an eighth-century date for its ultimate compilation merely because of the possibly interpolated reference to Ayesha and Faṭima in Gen. 21:21.

36. Close examination of 345 verses containing statistically relevant figures in the historical writings of the Old Testament has shown that only eight revealed minor variants in the Peshiṭṭa and none whatsoever in the Targum. See my Hebrew essay on "The Israelitic Population under the Kings," *Abhandlungen Chajes,* pp. 78 ff., 87. On the various forms in which the Targum of prophets and Hagiographa appears in the later midrashim, see Ginzberg's *Ginze Schechter,* I, 172 ff., 180 f., 326.

37. Hai's responsum in *Teshubot ha-geonim,* ed. by Harkavy, pp. 6 f. No. 15, 124 ff. No. 248, with the editor's comments thereon, p. 345. The dates of the original composition and final redaction of the two forms of the Palestinian Targum cannot be ascertained. Even such a reference as is found in the translation of Num. 24:19, which hints at the forthcoming destruction of Constantinople and hence may have been written in the critical years of 717–18, may be a later interpolation. A number of important manuscripts of the Palestinian Targum are reproduced and carefully analyzed by Kahle in his *Masoreten des Westens,* II, 1–65, and more briefly, in his *Cairo Geniza,* pp. 120 ff. This "Palestinian" version, sometimes called *Targum Yerushalmi I,* is to be distinguished from the related purely aggadic *Targum Yerushalmi II* (extant only in disjointed homiletical notes on individual verses and, hence, often called also the Fragmentary Targum), as well as from the so-called Pseudo-Jonathan on the Pentateuch. See M. Ginsburger's editions of *Das Fragmententhargum* and *Pseudo-Jonathan.* The latter works are midrashic commentaries on the Bible rather than translations, and belong to the literature discussed *supra,* Chap. XXVIII. In addition to the numerous textual and analytical studies listed *supra,* Vol. II, pp. 386 f. n. 25, see the more recent essays by J. L. Teicher, "A Sixth Century Fragment of the Palestinian Targum?" *VT,* I, 125–29 (denying Kahle's early dating of that Genizah fragment); A. Díez Macho, "Nuevos fragmentos del Targum palestinense," *Sefarad,* XV, 31–39 (from an Adler MS, with facsimiles); his brief identification of "Una Copia del todo el Targum jerosolomitano en la Vaticana," *Estudios bíblicos,* XV, 446–47 (also in *Sefarad,* XVII, 119–21); M. Brayer, *Pseudo-Jonathan on Genesis* (unpublished diss. Yeshiva University). R. Bloch's "Note sur l'utilisation des fragments de la Geniza du Caire pour l'étude du Targum Palestinien," *REJ,* CXIV, 5–35 (with two facsimiles; argues for the more primitive form of the "Fragmentary Targum"); and the illustrations of ancient residua offered in P. Winter's comparison of "Lc 2^{49} and Targum Yerushalmi," *ZNW,* XLV, 145–79; XLVI, 140–41 present interesting sidelights.

38. Yehudah bar Barzillai's *Sefer ha-'Ittim,* CLXXV, CLXXIX, ed. by Schor, pp. 258, 267 f. See also B. M. Lewin, *Otzar ha-gaonim,* I, Part 1, pp. 18 f.; M. Ginsburger, "Les Introductions araméennes à la lecture du Targum," *REJ,* LXXIII, 14–26, 186–94 (continuing an earlier study of "Aramäische Introduktionen zum Thargumvortrag an Festtagen," in *ZDMG,* LIV, 113–24); and L. J. Liebreich's elucidation of "The Benedictory Formula in the Targum to the Song of Songs," *HUCA,* XVIII, 177–97; and *infra,* nn. 40 and 47. On the problem of the Aramaic Gospels and their relations to the ancient Aramaic liturgy, see the theories advanced by Torrey, Wensinck, and others in the studies listed *supra,* Vol. II, pp. 354 f. n. 12. Wensinck's hypothesis has since been criticized by Kahle in his aforementioned study of "The Targums" in *Melilah,* Vols. III–IV. The broader implications of the Targumim for the development of Jewish liturgy and linguistic studies in the High Middle Ages will be discussed *infra,* Chaps. XXX, nn. 4, 17; and XXXI, n. 11.

39. Michael Syrus, *Chronique,* ed. by Chabot, II, 422 (Syriac), 431 f. (French); the Vatican MS discussed in A. Mingana's introduction to 'Ali aṭ-Ṭabari's *Book of Religion and Empire,* pp. vi, xix f., and the text, pp. 78, 95, 98. Here Ṭabari quotes Isa. 24:16–18 according to the Syriac translation by "Marcus" and adds that "the Hebrew, which is the original, says, 'We have heard from the ends of the earth

the voice of Muḥammad.' " Of course, there is nothing of the kind in the Hebrew Bible. On Marcus, the translator, see Mingana's simple identification with Mark the Evangelist who, according to legend, had first initiated the Syriac version (*ibid.*, pp. xx f.), and C. Peters's denial of this equation in *RSO,* XX, 140. On closer examination of Ṭabari's Old Testament citations, F. Taeschner noticed that they resembled the Masoretic text (and hence the Targum) much more than the Peshiṭṭa. He concluded therefrom that the Arab apologist must have used an earlier version. See his remarks in *Oriens christianus,* XXXI, 27 ff., 37 f. The vast Jewish and Christian literature on Bible translations into Arabic and the quotations therefrom in Muslim letters, sectarian as well as orthodox, was noted *supra,* Chaps. XVII, nn. 12, 15; and XXIV, n. 4. See also P. Kahle's older, but still worth-while, study of *Die arabischen Bibelübersetzungen.*

40. Ibn Daud's Chronicle, in *MJC,* I, 69 ff.; *Seder Rab Amram,* ed. by A. L. Frumkin, II, 68; Hai's responsum quoted *supra,* n. 37; Yehudah ibn Quraish's *Risala* (Missive to the Jews of Fez), ed. by J. J. L. Bargès and D. B. Goldberg, p. 1; in the Hebrew version by M. Katz, p. 1. If we were to accept Katz's dating of Ibn Quraish between 770 and 800, we would here have reliable testimony for the neglect of the Aramaic version some two centuries before Yehudah bar Barzillai. However, we probably have to place this North African linguistic pioneer some time after 820, or perhaps even late in the ninth century. Cf. the arguments presented by G. Vajda in "La Chronologie de Juda ibn Quraysh," *Sefarad,* XIV, 385–87; and *infra,* Chap. XXX, n. 17.

41. Qirqisani's *K. al-Anwar,* II.18, 11, in Nemoy's ed., I, 145; Mas'udi's *K. at-Tanbiḥ,* in M. J. de Goeje's ed., pp. 112 ff. (in Carra de Vaux's trans., pp. 159 ff.); Ibn an-Nadim's *Fihrist,* ed. by G. Flügel, I, 22. Steinschneider's query (in his *Arabische Literatur,* p. 36) as to whether Mas'udi confused Abu Kathir with his pupil Saadiah, is answered by the Arab historian's explicit independent reference (*loc. cit.*) to Saadiah's translation among several Jewish versions, almost all of which he had "seen." According to Mas'udi, Saadiah's rendition had already become "the most highly esteemed among many of his coreligionists." Curiously, Mas'udi reports that Ḥunayn ibn Isḥaq's Bible translation was "generally considered the most exact," although he admitted that it had been made from the Greek version. This was doubtless owing to Christian propaganda (had not the Byzantine Georgius Syncellus actually declared in 806 that the Septuagint was superior to the Hebrew Bible itself?; see *supra,* Chap. XXIV, n. 50), as well as to the great reputation of Ḥunayn and his school as translators of ancient classics. On the latter see esp. the several studies by G. Bergsträsser listed *infra,* Chap. XXXV; with M. Meyerhof's enlightening comments thereon in his "New Light on Ḥunayn ibn Isḥâq and His Period," *Isis,* VIII, 685–724. The relation of Saadiah's version to that of Ḥunayn would bear further examination, especially since the gaon is known to have used the Syriac writer's *Apothegms.* See Malter's *Saadia Gaon,* p. 250 n. 532.

42. See Joseph Kafih's testimony in his recent essay, "A Fragment of Saadiah's Commentary on Proverbs" (Hebrew), *Tarbiz,* XXVI, 292–96. Only the following portions of Saadiah's translation are now extant:

1. Pentateuch. Originally translated twice, once with a long, detailed commentary and the second time in simplified language for popular use, it is now available in

the latter form in J. Derenbourg's ed. of Saadiah's *Oeuvres complètes,* I (with J. Mieses's corrections on the basis of the Polyglots printed in Constantinople, 1546, and London, 1656, in his "Textkritische Bemerkungen zu R. Saadja Gaons arabischer Pentateuchübersetzung," *MGWJ,* LXIII, 269–90), and in the aforementioned Yemenite triglot, *Keter torah* (both these editions are unfortunately based on the same Yemenite MS); see also R. Edelmann's recent comments in his aforementioned essay in *Johannes Pedersen . . . dicata,* pp. 71–75 (in Hebrew, *Melilah,* V, 45 ff.).

2. Earlier Prophets. Long known through quotations of later authors, this section is largely lost. Only a small fragment of the book of Samuel (I, 30:6–21) has been plausibly identified and published by N. Allony in his *Mi-Sifrut,* pp. 52 ff., while Y. Ratzaby's publication of "Fragments from an Arabic Translation of the Former Prophets" (Hebrew), *Sinai,* XIII, Nos. 149–50, pp. 168–78 (covering portions of three weekly pericopes from Judges 4:23–25; I Kings 1:1–31; II Kings 4:1–37) is attributed by the editor only to the "School of Saadiah."

3. Later Prophets. (a) Isaiah, in Saadiah's *Oeuvres,* III; (b) Jeremiah, known only from subsequent quotations; (c) Ezekiel, only a small fragment (Ez. 41:18–44:25) was published by Allony in *Mi-Sifrut,* pp. 57 ff.; (d) Minor Prophets, known only from later quotations.

4. Hagiographa. (a) Psalms, in consecutive partial editions by S. H. Margulies (1–20), S. Lehmann (21–41), T. Hofmann (42–49, etc.), S. Baron (50–72), S. Galliner (73–89), E. Eisen (90–106), J. Z. Lauterbach (107–24), B. Schreier (125–50); (b) Proverbs, ed. by J. Derenbourg and M. Lambert in Saadiah's *Oeuvres,* VI, with corrections by J. Kafih in *Tarbiz,* XXVI, 293 ff.; (c) Job, ed. by W. Bacher *et al.* in *Oeuvres,* V; (d) Canticles, in the very dubious, though well annotated, ed. by A. Merx; (e) Ruth nowhere documented, see *infra,* n. 48; (f) Lamentations, ed. by Y. Ratzaby in *Tarbiz,* XIII, 92–106, XIV, 77–78 (with notes by E. Eisen); (g) Ecclesiastes, only the commentary is mentioned by Ibn Janaḥ; (h) Esther, in the Yemenite prayer book published in Vienna, 1896 (see S. Poznanski's analysis in his "Miscellen über Saadja, IV," *MGWJ,* XLVI, 364–72); (i) Daniel, ed. by H. Spiegel; (j) Ezra, Nehemiah, and Chronicles, none documented in our sources.

See the comprehensive and careful, though no longer up-to-date, bibliographical surveys by H. Malter in his *Saadia Gaon,* pp. 307 ff. (with brief supplements by I. Werfel in *Rav Saadya Gaon,* ed. by Fishman, pp. 645 ff.); and S. Poznanski in "A Fihrist of Saadya's Works," *JQR,* XIII, 374 ff. See also M. Katten's *Untersuchungen zu Saadja's arabischer Pentateuchübersetzung;* his "Sur quelques discordances dans la version du Pentateuque de Saadia," *REJ,* CII, 115–19; and E. Algermissen's interesting comparison of the Ibn Ḥazm quotations with Saadiah's version in his *Pentateuchzitate Ibn Ḥazms,* pp. 34 ff. Further search through the world's libraries and a comprehensive new critical edition are clearly indicated.

43. See Saadiah's trans. of Gen. 2:11 in his *Oeuvres,* I, 7 (confirmed by Ibn Ezra); many other examples assembled by J. Fürst in his *Librorum sacrorum veteris Testamenti Concordantiae,* p. 1235, *s.v. Tarshish;* S. A. Wertheimer's annotated ed. of Saadiah's *Be'ur tish'im millot bodedot ba-tenaḥ* (Explanation of Ninety Hapax Legomena in the Bible); and B. Klar's analysis, at the hand of two newly identified fragments, of "The Original Text of the 'Solution for Seventy Hapax Legomena'" (Hebrew) in J. L. Fishman's ed. of *Rav Saadya Gaon,* pp. 275–90. The difference between the title, *Seventy Hapax Legomena,* attested by the older sources, and the actual presence of *ninety* (or even one or two more)

words in this list, is plausibly explained by Klar (pp. 280 f. n. 26) through later accretions. See also S. Krauss's detailed analysis of "Saadya's *Tafsir* of the Seventy *Hapax Legomena*" in E. I. J. Rosenthal's *Saadya Studies,* pp. 47–77. The Karaite reaction to the gaon's strictures concerning the dependence on tradition of all interpreters of the Bible is well illustrated by Jephet's remark cited in Pinsker's *Lickute kadmoniot,* II, 71 n. 1; and particularly by Qirqisani's summary of Saadiah's seven "roots" bearing on this subject, together with an attempted refutation, in his *K. al-Anwar,* II.14, 2 ff. (in Nemoy's ed., I, 124 ff.). See also Klar's notes thereon in his essay, pp. 277 f. We must also bear in mind that the investigation of rare and difficult words in the Qur'an had long been a well-established branch of Muslim exegesis (Ibn an-Nadim's *Fihrist,* ed. by Flügel, p. 35 lists no less than fourteen prominent authorities in this field). See J. Feilchenfeld's dissertation, *Ein einleitender Beitrag zum qarīb-al-Kur'an.* The penchant to substitute names for anonyms likewise had an age-old tradition. See *supra,* Chap. XXVIII, n. 22. Curiously, the Christian versions used by 'Ali aṭ-Ṭabari had left the name Pishon or Pison untranslated, whereas they, like Saadiah and the Targum, seemed to be sure of the equation of Ḥiddeqel with the Tigris. Cf. his *Book of Religion,* p. 90.

44. Saadiah's *Oeuvres,* I, 7, 179. The gaon's dogmatically colored interpretations are particularly noticeable in his translation of, and comments on the book of Job (*Oeuvres,* Vol. V). See the telling illustrations cited by E. I. J. Rosenthal in his "Saadya's Exegesis of the Book of Job," in *Saadya Studies,* ed. by him, pp. 177–205. Saadiah's frequent agreement with ancient versions other than the Targum, which so greatly puzzled Rosenthal (pp. 187 ff.), is not so astonishing when one realizes the gaon's likely familiarity with these versions through Ḥunayn (if the Syriac translator had rendered the whole Old Testament and not only the Pentateuch) or his other predecessors, both Jewish and Christian. Very interesting results were obtained by J. Rivlin in his detailed reconstruction of "Saadia's Commentary on the Torah Deduced from His Translation" (Hebrew), *Tarbiz,* XX, 133–60. See also, more generally, E. Eisen's introduction to his ed. of Saadiah's trans. of Ps. 90–106; A. S. Halkin's "Saadia's Exegesis and Polemics" in *Rab Saadia Gaon,* ed. by L. Finkelstein, pp. 117–41; M. Waxman's Hebrew essay on "Saadiah as Biblical Exegete" (1942), reprinted in his *Ketabim nibḥarim* (Selected Writings), II, 177–200; P. R. Weis's somewhat overstated review of "The Anti-Karaite Tendency of R. Saadya Gaon's Arabic Version of the Pentateuch" in *Saadya Studies,* ed. by Rosenthal, pp. 227–44; and *supra,* Chap. XXVI, n. 80.

45. See Saadiah's translations of the passages mentioned in the text, in his *Oeuvres,* I, 8, 10; VI, 51 ff. Many other writers, too, tried to reproduce Hebrew words by phonetically similar Arabic terms. Cf. the examples assembled in Malter's *Saadia Gaon,* p. 145 n. 315. It may also be noted that in his translation the gaon usually rendered only the biblical words as read by the Masorah (*qeri*), although in his commentaries he often tried to detect the reasons why the Bible had also preserved the written form (*ketib*), thereby evidently wishing to convey some other, more hidden meaning. Cf. Ibn Ezra's *Commentary* on Isa. 49:5, ed. by M. Friedlaender, p. 84 (in Friedlaender's English trans., p. 223); and *infra,* n. 59.

46. Saadiah's *Beliefs and Opinions,* Intro., VI, pp. 23 (Arabic), 12 (Hebrew), 29 (English); his responsa, cited in *Oeuvres,* IX, 141 f., 169 No. 130; *supra,* Chaps.

XXVI, n. 81; XXVIII, n. 74; and *infra,* Chap. XXXV. Although most of Saadiah's historical works are known to us by name only, their apologetic import is also self-evident.

47. Mubashshir ha-Levi's *K. Istidrak,* ed. by M. Zucker (cited *supra,* Chap. XXIII, n. 21); Dunash ben Labraṭ's *Teshubot* (Criticisms of Saadiah), ed. by A. Schröter, p. 2 (a spirited defense of Dunash's much-disputed authorship of this "Polemic Treatise against Saadya" is offered by D. Herzog in Rosenthal's *Saadya Studies,* pp. 26–46); and the reply thereto in Abraham ibn Ezra's *Sefat Yeter* (Overbearing Speech; defense of Saadiah), ed. by G. H. Lippmann, fol. 4b, repudiating Dunash's critique, "for we have found all vowels to be interchangeable." See Isaac ben Yehudah ibn Gayyat's trans. of Eccles., ed. by J. Loewy; J. Saphir's interesting account of his travels in Yemen in 1848 and 1854, in his *Eben Sapir,* I, 53b; and Yehudah ibn Tibbon's "Testament," in I. Abrahams's *Hebrew Ethical Wills,* I, 65 f. C. Heller rightly emphasized the fact that it had entered "the mind of neither of those who attacked him [Saadiah], nor of his defenders, both of whom lived shortly after him, to attribute to Saadja a different text" than that established by the Masorah. Heller, *The Samaritan Pentateuch: An Adaptation of the Masoretic Text,* pp. 18 ff., 28 ff. Cf. also *infra,* n. 105.

48. Joseph ibn Nuḥ's translation is known to us only through a few subsequent quotations, but that of Jephet is extant in considerable fragments. So are many of his Bible commentaries. In the introduction to his edition of Jephet's commentary on Hosea, pp. l–lvii, P. Birnbaum has made a strong case even for Jephet's authorship of the anonymous translation (with brief explanatory notes) of the later Prophets, extant in a much-debated Bodleian MS (Codex Huntington 206), parts of which have also appeared in print. That the Rabbanites did not hesitate to make use of Jephet's translation, wherever that by Saadiah was unavailable (for instance, of the book of Ruth), was pointed out by S. Poznanski in his review of N. Schorstein's ed. of *Der Commentar des Karäers Jephet ben 'Ali zum Buche Ruth,* in *ZHB,* VII, 134. Curiously, we also possess Karaite manuscripts in which the biblical Hebrew is transliterated into Arabic script, just as there are Qur'anic *surahs* transliterated into Hebrew. Cf. *supra,* n. 10; and Chap. XXIV, n. 2.

49. See Kahle's *Cairo Geniza,* pp. 37 ff., and E. Robertson's analysis of "The Relationship of the Arabic Translation of the Samaritan Pentateuch to that of Saadya" in E. I. J. Rosenthal's *Saadya Studies,* pp. 166–76. Various theories have been advanced on the authorship of the Samaritan Arabic translation. They are summarized by J. Bloch in his ed. of *Die samaritanisch-arabische Bibelübersetzung, Deuteronomium I–XI,* pp. 4 ff. Bloch's own identification of the author with Abu'l Ḥasan aṣ-Ṣuri is very dubious, however. Cf. A. S. Halkin's remarks in *PAAJR,* VII, 20 ff., 59. Cf. also Halkin's analysis of "The Relations of the Samaritans to Saadia Gaon," in *Saadia Anniv. Vol.,* pp. 274 ff.; his "Scholia to Numbers and Deuteronomy in the Samaritan-Arabic Pentateuch," *JQR,* XXXIV, 41–59; C. Heller's *Samaritan Pentateuch,* pp. 18–185; and, more generally, Jacob ben 'Uzzi ha-Kohen's aforementioned Hebrew essay on "Old-Time Samaritans and the Arabic Works of their Scholars" in *Keneset,* IV, 321–27. See also *supra,* n. 47. Saadiah's influence on Christians and Muslims is but slightly less apparent.

50. Maimonides' *Epistle to Yemen,* ed. by Halkin, pp. 38 f. (Arabic and Hebrew), viii (English), with Halkin's notes 55–56 thereon; and *supra,* Chaps. XXIV, nn. 31–32; XXVIII, n. 96. On the connections between Mardan Farukh and Ḥivi ha-Balkhi, see *infra,* n. 93. See also M. Schwab, "Une version persane de la Bible," *REJ,* LVIII, 303–6 (describing a Paris MS containing a translation of Prov., Cant. and Eccles.); and W. J. Fischel, "The Bible in Persian Translation: a Contribution to the History of Bible Translations in Persia and India," *HTR,* XLV–XLVI, 3–45, largely offering materials from the later periods. In all such considerations of indebtedness to biblical prototypes in the later Islamic period we must take cognizance of the vast Arabic literature accessible to the Empire's non-Arab intelligentsia as well. See the older studies by M. Grünbaum, "Zu Jussuf and Suleicha," *ZDMG,* XLIII, 1–29, reprinted in his *Gesammelte Aufsätze zur Sprach- und Sagenkunde,* ed. by F. Perles, pp. 515–51 (showing biblical and aggadic influences on Firdausi); and more broadly, by W. Bacher, "Bibel und biblische Geschichte in der muhammedanischen Literatur," *Jeschurun,* ed. by Kobak, VIII, 1–29.

51. Peter Abelard's *Dialogus inter philosophum, Judaeum et Christianum, passim;* and his *Heloisae Problemata cum . . . solutionibus,* xxxvi, in *PL,* CLXXVIII, 718, 1609 ff.; A. M. Landgraf's ed. of *Ecrits théologiques de l'école d'Abélard* (in *Spicilegium sacrum lovaniense,* XIV), pp. xl ff. (see *infra,* n. 52); his excerpt from "Ein frühscholastischer Traktat zur Bibelexegese der Juden," *Biblica,* XXXVII, 403–9 (from an Einsiedeln MS); A. Wilmart's "Nicolas Manjacoria Cistercien à Trois-Fontaines," *Revue bénédictine,* XXXIII, 136–43 ("this man of the twelfth century, stimulated by the memory of the works of the recluse of Bethlehem, did not hesitate to become a student of the rabbis and to undertake a new edition of the Old Testament in accordance with the Hebrew text"); all also quoted by B. Smalley in *The Study of the Bible in the Middle Ages,* 2d ed., pp. 77 ff.; her study of "A Commentary on the *Hebraica* by Herbert of Bosham," *Recherches de Théologie ancienne et médiévale,* XVIII, 29–65; and R. Loewe "Herbert of Bosham's Commentary on Jerome's Hebrew Psalter," *Biblica,* XXXIV, 44–77, 159–92, 275–98. On the enormous literature relating to the Latin versions of the Bible and to some extent also to their Jewish connections, see *supra,* Vol. II, pp. 143 f., 385 f. n. 21. Those entries are in part even more relevant for the High Middle Ages than for ancient times.

More recent publications include the significant new edition of Vols. I–II (covering the book of Genesis and the symbols used for the vast documentation) of the *Vetus Latina,* sponsored by the Abbey of Beuron, with the comments thereon esp. by F. König, "Die Bedeutung der Vetus Latina," *Saeculum,* IV, 267–73 and such monographs as the following: F. J. Carmody, "Quotations in the Latin *Physiologus* from Latin Bibles Earlier than the Vulgate," *University of California Publications in Classical Philology,* XIII, 1–7; B. Bischoff, "Neue Materialien zum Bestand und zur Geschichte der altlateinischen Bibelübersetzungen," *Miscellanea Giovanni Mercati,* I, 407–36; M. Stenzel, "Altlateinische Canticatexte im Dodekapropheton," *ZNW,* XLVI, 31–60; and his "Zur Frühgeschichte der lateinischen Bibel," *Theologische Revue,* XLIX, 97–103. Of interest also are B. Fischer's observations on "Der Vulgata Text des NT," *ZNW,* XLVI, 178–96 on the occasion of the completion, in 1954, of *The Oxford Critical Edition of the Vulgate New Testament,* initiated by John Wordsworth in 1877. See also, more broadly, R. Weber's *Problèmes d'édition des ancients Psautiers latins;* and the bibliographical works by H. Rost,

Die Bibel im Mittelalter; and esp. F. Stegmüller's comprehensive *Repertorium biblicum medii aevi.* O. Paret, *Die Bibel, ihre Überlieferung in Druck und Schrift,* 2d ed., though geared to a wider audience, likewise offers many interesting observations and facsimiles. On Alcuin, Raban Maur, and Abelard, see also *supra,* Chaps. XX, n. 56; XXIV, n. 42.

Some Jews undoubtedly knew of the existence of such Latin versions. But on the whole they were on the giving, rather than the receiving, end in the process of translation. None of these versions is mentioned in any detail in medieval Jewish letters. At the most we have some such cryptic references as that by Maimonides to a Latin rendition, probably the Vulgate, among other pre-Islamic versions. See D. S. Blondheim's still fundamental study of *Les Parlers judéo-romans et la Vetus Latina;* U. Cassuto's interrelated essays on "La Vetus Latina e le traduzioni giudaiche medioevali della Bibbia," *Studi e materiali di storia delle religioni,* II, 145–62; and "Jewish Bible Translation into Latin and Its Importance for the Study of the Greek and Aramaic Versions" (Hebrew), *Sefer Johanan Lewy,* pp. 161–72. On the Jewish influences on the medieval Christian Bible exegesis, see *infra,* n. 58.

52. John Scotus Erigena in his *Expositiones* on Pseudo-Dionysius and the Gospel of John, in *PL,* CXXII, 243, 283 ff.; M. Cappuyns, *Jean Scot Érigène: sa vie, son oeuvre, sa pensée,* pp. 225 f.; B. Smalley, *The Study of the Bible,* pp. 43 f. See also H. Steinecker, "Die römische Kirche und die griechischen Sprachkenntnisse des Frühmittelalters," *Mitteilungen des Instituts für österreichische Geschichtsforschung,* LXII, 28–66 (showing how the decline in the knowledge of Greek forced the Western students to rely on their own resources). The unusual Hebrew quotations in Odo have been the subject of extended debates ever since the publication of Odo's tract, from a Cambridge MS written *ca.* 1200, by A. M. Landgraf in his aforementioned essay on the school of Abelard and the comments thereon by J. Fischer in "Die hebräischen Bibelzitate des Scholastikers Odo. Ein bedeutsamer Fund für die Geschichte des hebräischen Bibeltextes," *Biblica,* XV, 50–93. These citations, however, appear to be written in such a faulty Hebrew that C. Peters has suggested that they merely were retranslations into Hebrew from some non-Hebraic version. See his "Aussermasoretische Überlieferung in den Zitaten des Scholastikers Odo?" *Muséon,* LI, 137–49. This venturesome suggestion was rather effectively rejected by Fischer in his "Ist das Rätsel 'Odo' schon gelöst?" *Biblica,* XXV, 167–95. It still appears more prudent, nevertheless, to heed M. Sister's warning against too far-reaching conclusions, in view of the obvious insufficiencies of the writer who had inserted these Hebrew phrases. See his review of Fischer's first study in *MGWJ,* LXXXII, 65–67.

53. Ibn Ezra's intro. to his larger *Commentary* on Genesis in M. Friedlaender's *Essays,* IV; Maimonides' *Resp.,* pp. 331 f. No. 364 with reference to Sanhedrin 59a. On the whole, Jewish exegetes agreed with Ṭabari and most other Muslim commentators that one must follow the ordinary meaning of Scripture, except when there are strong reasons against it. See Goldziher's *Richtungen,* pp. 88 f. On the other hand, Jewish literalists did not separate themselves from the majority of the more naive followers of the Aggadah, as did the Muslim Zahirites. The very Karaites, notwithstanding their professions of literalism, not only applied most Rabbanite modes of interpretation in order to secure scriptural support for their legal doctrines and observances, but they also often resorted to allegorical interpre-

tation to justify certain philosophic ideas. See S. Poznanski's data on the "Allegorische Gesetzesauslegung bei den älteren Karäern" (*Studies . . . Kaufmann Kohler,* pp. 237–59) which could readily be amplified by more recent materials. We shall see (*infra,* n. 71) how tenuous was often the borderline between the avowed adherence to simple meanings and the no less deeply ingrained respect for hermeneutic meanings. Moreover, the very midrash often supplied useful simple explanations of biblical terms and phrases. Cf. the examples adduced by A. Preiss in "The Interpretation of Biblical Verses by the Midrash" (Hebrew), *Sinai,* XIX, No. 229, pp. 247–53. On the other hand, Jewish scholars did not have to overcome serious objections in principle such as were raised by the *Old Muslim Opposition against Interpretation of the Koran.* See H. Birkeland's pertinent monograph under this title.

54. In "Die Bibelexegese vom Anfange des 10. bis zum Ende des 15. Jahrhunderts" in J. Winter and A. Wünsche, *Die jüdische Literatur seit Abschluss des Kanons,* II, 237–339; *Die Bibelexegese der jüdischen Religionsphilosophen des Mittelalters vor Maimuni;* and in numerous monographs cited below, W. Bacher rendered yeoman service to the history of medieval Jewish exegesis. Even today, more than half a century after their publication, these studies still offer the most comprehensive summaries. See also the more popular surveys of *Toledot biqqoret ha-miqra* (The History of Bible Criticism) by M. Soloveitchik and S. Rubasheff; and *Parshanut ha-miqra* (The Exegesis of the Bible: a Sketch of Its History and Development) by M. H. (Z.) Segal. Bacher's researches must be supplemented, however, not only by more recently discovered texts, especially of Karaite authors, but also by greater utilization of comparative materials from the contemporary Muslim and Christian exegetical literatures. The few extant fragments of Benjamin's commentaries are listed in Mann's *Texts and Studies,* II, 17 n. 32; those by Daniel and his school, *ibid.,* pp. 9 ff. See also I. D. Markon's "Daniel al-Kumisi, ein karäischer Schrifterklärer des IX. Jahrhunderts," *Korrespondenzblatt . . . Akademie für die Wissenschaft des Judentums,* VIII, 18–30; and "The Karaite Daniel al-Kumisi and his Commentary on the Minor Prophets" (Hebrew), *Melilah,* II, 188–206. On Saadiah's commentaries, likewise lost for the most part, see the literature listed *supra,* nn. 39–42, in connection with his translations. Of more recent writings, see esp. S. Abramson's Hebrew essay "On Saadiah Gaon's *Tafsir* on the Bible," *Sinai,* XI, Nos. 126–27, pp. 334–36; Y. Ratzaby's, "Supplements to Saadiah Gaon's Commentary on Job" (Hebrew), *Sinai,* XVIII, No. 224, pp. 316–63; the reconstructions of Saadiah's comments from quotations in later writings by J. Leveen in his "Saadya's Lost Commentary on Leviticus" in Rosenthal's *Saadya Studies,* pp. 78–96; and by B. Cohen in his "Quotations from Saadia's Arabic Commentary on the Bible from Two Manuscripts of Abraham ben Solomon," *Saadia Anniv. Vol.,* pp. 75–139; as well as the additional bibliographical data mentioned by A. Freimann in his "Saadia Bibliography 1920–1942," *ibid.,* pp. 327 ff.; and by I. Werfel in *Rav Saadya Gaon,* ed. by Fishman, pp. 645 ff. That utmost care must be exercised, however, in attributing to Saadiah subsequent quotations bearing his name is rightly stressed by S. Poznanski in his "Citations de Saadia ou attribuées à Saadiah chez les exegètes de la France septentrionale," *REJ,* LXXII, 113–34; and, with some variations, "Who is R. Saadiah Mentioned by the French Bible Commentators?" (Hebrew), *Hagoren,* IX, 69–89. Much of this material may soon be superseded by M. Zucker's prospective critical editions of Saadiah's commentaries, on which see, e.g., his "From Saadiah Gaon's Commentary on the Pentateuch" (Hebrew), *Sura,* II, 313–55, and his other essays cited *supra,* esp. Chap. XXVI.

55. Ibn Bal'am's comment on Isa. 1:8 in J. Derenbourg's ed. of his *Gloses sur Isaïe,* p. 16; and J. Galliner's *Abraham ibn Esras Hiobkommentar,* pp. 18 f. On the general Jewish exegetical literature of the tenth and eleventh centuries, both Karaite and Rabbanite, see especially Tobiah ben Eliezer's old-fashioned midrashic commentary, *Leqaḥ tob,* ed. by S. Buber *et al.* (cf. the texts listed *supra,* Chap. XXVIII, n. 27). See also S. L. Skoss's intro. to his ed. of *The Arabic Commentary of 'Ali ben Suleiman the Karaite on the Book of Genesis,* pp. 1 ff.; S. Poznanski's *Moses b. Samuel Hakkohen Ibn Chiquitilla nebst den Fragmenten seiner Schriften;* his "Aus Mose ibn Chiquitilla's arabischem Psalmenkommentar," *Zeitschrift für Assyriologie,* XXVI, 38–60; W. Bacher's ed. of Ibn Chiquitilla's Arabic trans. of and commentary on Job in *Festschrift Harkavy,* Hebrew section, pp. 221–72; J. Finkel's ed. of parts of his commentary on Psalms in *Horeb,* III, 153–62 (Chaps. 3, 4, 8); Ibn Bal'am's "Commentary on Jeremiah," ed. in Arabic with a Hebrew introduction and notes by J. Israelsohn, *Festschrift Harkavy,* pp. 273–308, and his "Arabic Commentary" on the Minor Prophets, ed. by S. Poznanski in *JQR,* XV, 1–53. The editor lists here Ibn Bal'am's known commentaries, whether published (on Lev., Num., Deut., Joshua, Judg., Isa.), cited in later writings, or as yet unpublished (Ps., Job, Cant., Ruth, Eccles., Esther, Daniel), together with the literature thereon. Moses ibn Ezra had already noted the sharpness of that Sevillan author's comments with respect to the slightest faults of his predecessors and ascribed it to his general irascibility. See Moses ibn Ezra's *Kitab al-Muḥadhara wal-mudhakhara* (Treatise on the Hebrew Ars Poetica), cited by Derenbourg in his ed. of the *Gloses,* pp. 7 f.; and in the Hebrew trans. by B. Z. Halper, entitled *Shirat Yisrael,* p. 73.

56. Because of their very popularity, Rashi's commentaries were often disfigured by additions and alterations, conscious as well as unconscious, by a host of coypists. It required arduous labors of examining and collating the numerous extant manuscripts for Abraham Berliner to restore, however incompletely, Rashi's original *Commentary* on the Pentateuch. See his *Rashi 'al ha-torah* and his *Beiträge zur Geschichte der Raschi-Commentare.* Equally satisfactory in their diverse ways are the critical editions of the commentaries on Isaiah, the Minor Prophets, and Psalms by I. Maarsen, and of Ezekiel 40–48 by A. J. Levy. The tremendous difficulties of selection and classification can easily be gauged from D. S. Blondheim's enumeration of 160 MSS of Rashi's *Commentary* on the Pentateuch and almost 200 MSS relating to other biblical books—without counting Genizah fragments. See his "Liste des manuscrits des Commentaires bibliques de Raschi" in *REJ,* XCI. On Rashi's Talmud commentaries, see *supra,* Chap. XXVII; and on the philological aspects of his work, *infra,* Chap. XXX, n. 33. Cf. also I. Sonne's "On the Textual Criticism of Rashi's Commentary on the Pentateuch," *HUCA,* XV, Hebrew section, pp. 37–56 (offering a brief review of the earlier transmission of Rashi texts and showing the difference between the pertinent Sephardic and Ashkenazic traditions); J. H. Lowe's annotated English translation of *"Rashi" on the Pentateuch;* and A. M. Silberman's ed. of the *Pentateuch with Targum Onkelos, Haphtaroth and Prayers for Sabbath—Rashi's Commentary;* as well as A. Scheiber's recent edition of "A New Rashi Fragment," *Studies in Bibliography and Booklore,* II, 37–39 (I Kings 20:33–II Kings 4:1).

With respect to the large secondary literature we need refer here only to the biographies and anniversary volumes quoted *supra,* Chap. XXVII, n. 58. An analysis of Rashi's method and his place in the history of Jewish Bible exegesis is offered by the older but still useful study of *Raschi als Exeget* by N. Kronberg; *Rashi mefaresh ha-torah* (Rashi the Bible Commentator: A Literary Survey) by P. Ne'eman;

the monographic studies included in *Sefer Rashi,* ed. by Fishman; Poznanski's essays mentioned in the next note; and, on a more popular level, M. Waxman's Hebrew article on "Rashi the Bible Exegete" reprinted in his *Ketabim nibḥarim,* II, 201–36. See also S. M. Blumenfield, *Master of Troyes,* mainly concerned with the educational aspects of Rashi's commentaries; and, on their influence on non-Jews, E. I. J. Rosenthal's "Rashi and the English Bible," *BJRL,* XXIV, 138–67; and H. Hailperin's articles cited *infra,* n. 58.

57. See I. Schapiro's bibliography of *Parshane Rashi 'al ha-torah* (A Bibliography of Supercommentaries on Rashi's Pentateuch Commentary), supplemented by A. Freimann's list of manuscript supercommentaries in *Rashi Anniv. Vol.,* pp. 73–114; S. Poznanski's compilation of R. Menaḥem bar Ḥelbo's *Pitrone* (Fragments de l'exégèse biblique); and his comprehensive study of the northern French Bible exegetes in the intro. to his ed. of Eliezer of Beaugency's *Perush* (Commentary on Ezekiel and the Minor Prophets). See also *infra,* nn. 81–82.

58. Bede's Prologue to his *In Samuelem prophetam allegorica expositio,* in *PL,* XCI, 499 f. Bede was one of the relatively few Western churchmen of his time who had a smattering of Hebrew, at least through what "he was able to glean from the writings of St. Jerome." See E. F. Sutcliffe's largely negative data in "The Venerable Bede's Knowledge of Hebrew," *Biblica,* XVI, 300–306; and, more generally, the mutually complementary analyses of *The Study of the Bible in the Middle Ages* by B. Smalley and the chronological *Esquisse d'une histoire de l'exégèse latine au moyen âge* by C. Spicq. Although primarily concerned with the later Middle Ages, the following brief studies also shed some light on Judeo-Christian interrelations in the field of Bible exegesis before 1200: A. Berliner, *Persönliche Beziehungen zwischen Christen und Judem im Mittelalter;* H. Hailperin, "Intellectual Relations between Jews and Christians in Europe before 1500 A.D. Described Mainly According to the Evidences of Biblical Exegesis," *Bulletin* of the University of Pittsburgh, Abstract of Theses, IX, 128–45; his "Nicholas de Lyra and Rashi: The Minor Prophets," *Rashi Anniv. Vol.,* pp. 115–47; and his more general survey of "The Hebrew Heritage of Mediaeval Christian Biblical Scholarship," *HJ,* V, 133–54. Here (pp. 150 f.) Hailperin testifies to the general reliability of the Christian quotations from rabbinic writings, which is the less surprising as copyists of biblical texts in all languages had been taught to be painstakingly faithful in transcribing or translating texts of, or relating to, Scripture. See B. Blumenkranz's succinct remarks on the "Fidelitè du scribe. Les citations bibliques," *RMAL,* VIII, 323–26. Of interest also are such more recent monographic studies as M. L. W. Laistner, "Some Early Medieval Commentaries on the Old Testament," *HTR,* XLVI, 27–42, chiefly analyzing the work of the ninth-century commentator Angelomus, but incidentally (p. 30) questioning the aforementioned references of Raban Maur to the assistance of a Jewish scholar (see *supra,* Chap. XXIV, n. 41); and S. R. Daly, "Peter Comestor: Master of Histories," *Speculum,* XXXII, 62–73, which, however, contributes little to our knowledge of the indebtedness of that influential twelfth-century historian and exegete to Rashi and his school. See also such general observations as B. Bischoff's "Wendepunkte in der Geschichte der lateinischen Exegese im Frühmittelalter," *Sacris erudiri,* Jaarboek voor Godsdienstwetenschappen, VI, 189–281; and J. Leclerq's "Ecrits monastiques sur la Bible aux 11ᵉ–13ᵉ siècles," *Mediaeval Studies,* XV, 95–106 (includes an interesting excerpt from a Paris MS of the *Hexameron* by Arnaud, Abbot of Bonneval,

debating the existence of a pre-Mosaic Hebrew literature, pp. 96 ff.); and the comprehensive, though unsystematic and rather uncritical, accumulation of interesting data by L. R. E. Froom in *The Prophetic Faith of Our Fathers: The Historical Development of Prophetic Interpretation,* Vol. I.

59. Ibn Ezra's *Sefat Yeter* his *Commentary* on Isa. 52:13, ed. by Friedlaender, p. 90 (in Friedlaender's English trans., p. 240); Profiat Duran's (Efodi's) *Ma'ase efod* (Introduction to Hebrew Grammar), ed. by J. Friedländer and J. Kohn, p. 44. See N. Ben-Menahem's *Abraham ibn Ezra—Siḥot ve-aggadot 'am* (Stories and Popular Legends); and his "Popular Legends about R. Abraham ibn Ezra" (Hebrew), *Zlotnik Jub. Vol.,* pp. 141–61. Ibn Ezra's great popularity is evidenced also by the numerous editions of the Pentateuch and other biblical books which included his commentaries. A story circulating in many variants reported a biblical student as saying, "Rashi wrote with the view of being understood, and I really understand him. R. Samuel bar Meir [Rashbam] also wrote in order to be understood, but I do not understand him. Ibn Ezra wrote so as not to be understood, and I really fail to understand him." See Ben-Menahem's collection in *Zlotnik Jub. Vol.,* pp. 155 f.; and, more broadly, J. L. Fleischer's comprehensive Hebrew study of these "Supercommentaries on Abraham ibn Ezra's Commentary" (Hebrew), *Ozar Hachaim,* Vols. XI–XII, XIV. It is doubly remarkable, therefore, that we do not yet possess complete critical editions of Ibn Ezra's exegetical works, based on the numerous extant manuscripts. Only the "short" commentary on Exodus, ed. by Fleischer, that on Isaiah, ed. by Friedlaender, and that on Canticles, ed. by H. Mathews, more or less meet the requirements of scholarly texts. See also such detailed monographs as L. Levy's *Reconstruction des Commentars Ibn Esras zu den Ersten Propheten.* In recent years interest in Ibn Ezra's exegesis has generally abated, and we still depend largely on the nineteenth-century investigations, notably those by M. Friedlaender and W. Bacher. See the former's *Essays on the Writings of Abraham ibn Ezra;* Bacher's "Abraham ibn Esra's Einleitung zu seinem Pentateuch-Commentar," *SB,* Vienna, LXXXI, 361–444; and J. L. Fleischer's "Abraham ibn Ezra and His Literary Creativity in Lucca, III" (Hebrew) *Ha-Soqer* (*Blau Mem. Vol.*), IV, pp. 186–94. On his cognate philological studies, see *infra,* Chap. XXX, nn. 59 ff. See also S. Ochs's sketch of *Ibn Esras Leben und Werke.*

60. More fortunate than most of his fellow commentators, David Qimḥi and his work were subjected to closer examination by modern scholars. See esp. the critical editions of his commentaries on Isaiah by L. Finkelstein (Hebrew intro., p. vii; Appendix IV, pp. xciv ff., reviewing the chronological order of Qimḥi's commentaries); on Hosea by H. Cohen; on Amos by S. Berkowitz (unpublished two-volume Cambridge diss., 1938–39); on Nahum by W. Windfuhr; on Psalms Parts I (Chaps. 1–41), ed. by S. M. Schiller-Szinessy; II (Chaps. 42–73) by S. I. Esterson in *HUCA,* X, 309–443; and V (Chaps. 107–50) by J. Bosniak (see also the latter's English intro. in *Conservative Judaism,* VI, Nos. 2–3, pp. 1–19). Despite his occasional excursuses into the homiletical field, it was Qimḥi's predominantly rationalist approach which had prompted him to undertake his exegetical work. He began with the book of Chronicles, otherwise of little interest to medieval commentators, because he had been dissatisfied with all existing commentaries as overlaid with homiletics. He seems to have tackled the Pentateuch at the very end, never progressing beyond the book of Genesis. At least only that much of his Pentateuchal commentary is extant today. See also *supra,*

Chap. XXIV, n. 38; *infra,* Chap. XXX, n. 62; and G. Caló's analysis of "Una Traduzione italiana del commento di R.D.Q. ai Salmi" in the *Miscellanea di studi ebraici in memoria di H. P. Chajes,* pp. 10–18 (from a Mantuan MS of a trans. by Giovanni Eustacchio di Mantova of 1766).

Among Qimḥi's Provençal compatriots one need but mention his father, Joseph, who had set the pace for the son through his exegetical as well as philological and apologetic writings (his commentaries on Proverbs and Job have appeared in print), and Menaḥem ben Simon, on whom see M. Barol's study, *Menachem ben Simon aus Posquières und sein Commentar zu Jeremia und Ezechiel,* together with S. Poznanski's review thereof in *REJ,* LIV, 302–5. Both these writers agree that this commentary, completed in 1191, resembles those of Ibn Bal'am more than those of Ibn Ezra, to supplement which they were seemingly intended.

61. Ibn Ezra's *Commentary* on Gen. 2:11. Cf. *supra,* n. 43; B.B. 91a; and Gershom's comment thereon. Very dubious even in ancient times, this explanation has little support in the sectarian controversies of the Muslim era. In fact, Saadiah's identification of Pishon with the Nile not only underlay the interpretation of Gen. r. (xvi.2, p. 142) followed by Rashi (on Gen. 2:11), but was unhesitatingly accepted also by Samaritans and such Karaites as David al-Fasi and 'Ali ben Suleiman. See their respective dictionaries (*Agronot*), ed. by S. L. Skoss, II, 460; and by Pinsker in *Lickute kadmoniot,* I, 213. The real motivation may be found in man's perennial dread of the unknown and his quest to fill, if need be, with phantoms the gaping vacua in his otherwise familiar outlook. Cf. *supra,* n. 43; and Chap. XXVIII, n. 22.

62. Ibn Ezra's Intro. to his *Commentary* on Genesis. See Bacher's observations thereon in *SB* Vienna, LXXXI, esp. p. 376. Despite the considerable increase in our knowledge of the medieval exegetical literature during the last eighty years, some of Ibn Ezra's references, unexplained by Bacher, are still obscure.

63. Ṭabari's *Djami al-bayan fi tafsir al-Qur'an* (Commentary on the Qur'an); C. Brockelmann's *Geschichte der arabischen Literatur,* rev. ed., I, 205. Later generations further exaggerated this penchant toward prolixity. They attributed to Ibn Shahin a *tafsir* of a thousand volumes, and to Ghazali one of, more precisely, 999 volumes. No less an authority than Suyuti, to whose history of Qur'anic exegesis modern scholarship owes a great debt of gratitude, claimed that even in his day the Nizamiya Academy in Baghdad owned a 600-volume commentary by Al-Ashari. See Goldziher's *Richtungen,* p. 113 n. 4.

64. Brockelmann, *loc. cit.;* Derenbourg in his intro. to Ibn Bal'am's *Gloses,* pp. 10 f. The eclectic character of Ibn Bal'am's work is borne out by the few fragments attached by S. Fuchs to his analytical *Studien über Jehuda ibn Bal'am.* Because of this intentional selectivity, there is no good reason to postulate, for example, a lacuna in Ibn Bal'am's *Commentary* on Isaiah 1:9–12 simply because these verses "should have offered the author an opportunity for manifold comments" (Derenbourg in *Gloses,* p. 16 n. 3). As a matter of fact, our author frequently refrained from commenting even on the beginnings of chapters (9, 14, 15, etc.). In Chapter 4 he found only one verse requiring comment, while he passed over in silence the entire twelfth chapter. This was a rare restraint, indeed, in contemporary letters. Similarly, in the introduction to his *Commentary* on Jeremiah, David Qimḥi announced

his intention to write "in the exposition of this book only on verses requiring explanation and on words in need of identification, but not on each and every verse, as I have done in the book of Isaiah." Evidently in the latter case he had found so many passages in need of elucidation that he wrote what amounted to a running commentary on the entire book. See L. Finkelstein's intro. to his ed. of Qimḥi's *Commentary on Isaiah,* pp. xxiii ff.

65. Mann, "Early Karaite Bible Commentaries," *JQR,* XII, 439, 441 f. (Fragment E). Another commentator on Gen. 1:28 (in the fragment published in Ginzberg's *Ginze Schechter,* I, 10 ff.) stressed, in particular, the injunction, "and replenish the earth." In his opinion, the Bible wished thereby to enjoin man not to dwell anywhere except on earth. This is a rather odd injunction and, if it meant anything at all, it would merely outlaw dwelling on ships. Be this as it may, the fact that both fragments deal with this verse in terms of an injunction to multiply and replenish the earth is truly significant. This view had long been accepted in Rabbanite circles (cf. Yebamot 63b–65b), but later Karaites saw therein merely a blessing. Cf. Aaron ben Elijah's *Keter torah,* fol. 19b.: "For how can He [the Lord] impose an obligation beyond man's control?" Benjamin Nahawendi even followed the Rabbanite interpretation to the extent of forcing a man to divorce his childless wife after ten years. See his *Mas'at Binyamin,* fol. 4d. It is quite possible, therefore, that both fragments represent excerpts from Benjamin's, rather than from Daniel's, commentary on the Torah. That possibility is heightened by the author's unusual emphasis upon the creation of time itself. This doctrine, introduced into Jewish philosophy by Philo, may well have influenced Benjamin, as did other Philonic teachings. See *supra,* Vol. II, pp. 158, 391 n. 37; and *infra,* Chap. XXXIV. Along with other views of the Alexandrian philosopher it also seems to have impressed the author of *Midrash Tadshe,* who in this way explained the creation of the celestial bodies on the fourth, rather than the first day. See the text, ed. by A. Epstein, in his *Mi-Qadmoniyot ha-Yehudim,* p. xv; and Belkin's comments thereon in *Horeb,* XI, 7 f. There is no evidence that Daniel, or any member of his school, ever evinced interest in such fine philosophical distinctions.

66. See Mann's edition of Fragment F, *JQR,* XII, 453; of Fragment G, *ibid.,* pp. 454 f.; and the pertinent observations in his *Texts and Studies,* II, 11 f. Mann argues here for Benjamin's authorship of Fragment G, and ascribes the aforementioned Fragment E (XII, 439 ff.) to Daniel. He finds less reason to attribute Fragments F (XII, 451 ff.) and F′ (*ibid.,* pp. 456 ff.) to Benjamin, although his chief argument from the fact that F essentially goes over the same ground as Fragment G, and that F′ substitutes the Ark for the angel who led the Jews out of Egypt, is rather inconclusive. We know next to nothing about Benjamin's astronomic views, but he or one of his pupils may well have advanced some such alternate explanations of the biblical story of Creation. Nor does acceptance of a divine intermediary in Philonic terms necessarily lead to a literal interpretation of biblical narratives concerning the intervention of angels. In general relying much too frequently on such negative considerations, Mann also denied Benjamin's authorship of the Arabic commentary on Ecclesiastes (cited in part in Pinsker's *Lickute kadmoniot,* II, 109 ff.) and, for that matter, of any Arabic commentary. See his *Texts and Studies,* II, 12 n. 21. Certainly, the misspelling "Ha-Awendi" (instead of Ha-Nahawendi) in the manuscript entry of a later purchaser does not conclusively prove the spuriousness of Benjamin's

authorship. Mann's positive arguments in favor of Benjamin as the author of Fragment G are equally unconvincing. As against some remote similarities (also serious dissimilarities) with the passage cited by Harkavy (*Zikhron,* VIII, 175) and the author's occasional use of simple talmudic words, one may point to his application of such philological criteria as the meaning of crucial Hebrew terms in their different biblical contexts. This new emphasis is more characteristic of the period of awakened philological curiosity in the early days of Saadiah. The very elaborateness of the fragment is also indicative of its relatively later date, although one might argue that any philosophically oriented commentary on the first verses of Genesis is likely to be far more extensive than one dealing with less perplexing sections. For interesting comparative data, see A. Levene, *The Early Syrian Fathers on Genesis,* which includes the text and annotated trans. of the first eighteen chapters of a Mingana MS containing a detailed commentary on that biblical book. See esp. the editor's excursus on "The Exegesis of the MS. Compared with the Contemporary Rabbinic Exegesis in Midrashim and Talmud" (pp. 315–32; also *ibid.,* pp. 333 ff.). This entire problem would merit careful reexamination by a competent student of early Jewish Bible exegesis.

As a matter of fact, the cryptic statements in the story of Creation so deeply preoccupied the minds of exegetes, philosophers, and mystics alike that it is not easy to draw a sharp line of demarcation between a purely expository and a primarily philosophical tract. Not long after the author or authors of the fragments here discussed, Shabbetai Donnolo, the tenth-century southern Italian Jewish scientist, tried to come to grips with the meaning and implications of the famous divine pronunciamento, "Let us make man in our image" (Gen. 1:26). When first published by Jellinek, Donnolo's exposition appeared as part of a biblical commentary, although it soon turned out to be but part of the introduction to his *Taḥkemoni* or *Ḥakmoni,* a commentary on *Yeṣirah* (Book of Creation), ed. by D. Castelli. See the text revised by S. Muntner in his critical edition of Donnolo's *Kitbe ha-Refu'ah* (Medical Works), I, 24 ff.; together with "A New Fragment" (Hebrew) thereof published by A. Scheiber from a Genizah fragment in the Kaufmann collection in *Sinai,* XV, Nos. 177–79, pp. 62–64. See also *infra,* Chaps. XXXIII and XXXV.

67. See Ibn Ezra's *Commentary,* Introduction. We possess no fragment of Israeli's commentary, unless it be the brief comment on Gen. 1:20, ed. from an incomplete Hebrew trans. by S. Sachs in "The Beginning of a Discourse on 'Let the waters swarm' by Isaac Israeli" (Hebrew), *Ha-Techijjah,* 1850, pp. 39–41. Similarly, only small parts of Samuel ben Ḥofni's exegetical work on the Bible have reached us. See esp. J. Israelsohn's ed. of Samuel's commentary on the last three chapters of Genesis; and, chiefly on that basis, W. Bacher's analysis of "Le Commentaire de Samuel ibn Hofni sur le Pentateuch," *REJ,* XV, 277–88; XVI, 106–23. See also the strenuous reconstruction of portions of Samuel's commentary from quotations by Abraham Maimuni in S. Poznanski's "Mitteilungen aus handschriftlichen Bibel-Commentaren, III," *ZHB,* II, 55–60. These scanty materials bear out Ibn Ezra's critique.

68. Saadiah's *Oeuvres,* I, 1, with Derenbourg's n. 1; Jephet's sarcastic comment quoted by S. Munk in his "Notice sur Abou'l-Walid, Merwan ibn-Djana'h," *JA,* 4th ser. XV, 336 n. 1; Ibn Ezra, *ad loc.* Cf. also S. L. Skoss's intro. to his ed. of *The Arabic Commentary of 'Ali ben Suleiman,* pp. 42 ff. We need not be astonished by the gaon's stress on the parallelism of biblical verses. Although systematically developed by

later grammarians, particularly Menaḥem ben Saruq, this significant characteristic of the Bible's poetic prose could not possibly have escaped so sensitive an interpreter as Saadiah.

69. Saadiah's *Oeuvres,* VI, 1 ff., 51 ff. (Arabic), 14 f. (French). See B. Heller's detailed analysis of "La Version arabe et le commentaire des Proverbes du Gaon Saadia," *REJ,* XXXVII, 72–85, 226–51; and other literature listed *supra,* nn. 42, 44. Regrettably, Bacher's promise to prepare for Saadiah's collected works a comprehensive monograph on the gaon's work on the Bible (see J. Derenbourg and M. Lambert's preface to Saadiah's *Oeuvres,* VI, p. vii) never materialized.

70. Saadiah's *Beliefs and Opinions,* VII.2, in the variant version published by Bacher in *Festschrift Steinschneider,* pp. 219–26, and Hebrew section, pp. 98–112; and in S. Rosenblatt's English trans., p. 415. See also *ibid.,* pp. 265 ff. Saadiah was particularly vehement with respect to persons who allegorized precepts of the Torah or speculated on the divine attributes in a way fostering heresy. Such people, in his opinion, bordered on the category of false prophets and to them applied Ezekiel's condemnation of persons "that follow their own spirit, and things which they have not seen" (13:3). *Beliefs,* V.8, 186 (Arabic), 93 (Hebrew), 232 (English). Such opposition to individualistic "excesses" was also widely shared by conservative Muslim exegetes who quoted an alleged saying of Mohammed: "Whosoever interprets the Qur'an according to his own light will go to hell" (Ṭabari's *Tafsir,* I, 28). In fact, avowed originality was generally discouraged in the Middle Ages. The Muslims spoke disparagingly of their seventh-century exegete, Shureiḥ because he had allegedly greatly "admired his own knowledge." Goldziher, *Richtungen,* pp. 20 f. Jews likewise used increasingly the Isaianic phrase of "them that are wise in their own eyes" (5:21) to condemn such reliance on one's personal judgment. See, e.g., "The Oldest Collection of Bible Difficulties," ed. by Schechter in *JQR,* [o.s.] XIII, 358 line 14, 366 line 22 (ed. by Rosenthal under the title "Old Questions on the Bible," in *HUCA,* XXI, Hebrew section, pp. 38 line 15, 46 line 21). Ultimately, Samuel ibn Nagrela quoted a popular saying, "A man 'wise in his own eyes' is a fool," evidently referring to Prov. 26:5. See the additional data cited by S. Abramson in his "Schoolmen's Sayings and Popular Proverbs" (Hebrew), *Zlotnik Jub. Vol.,* pp. 26 f. Of course, heretics were the most obvious culprits relying on their own lights in challenging firmly rooted traditions. While rarely quoting predecessors other than the talmudic sages, Saadiah occasionally went out of his way to attack 'Anan's legal interpretations. Two such attacks are cited from Saadiah's *Commentary* on Leviticus by Abu'l-Faraj Harun, who remarked that "as usual, he [Saadiah] trounces 'Anan and calls him an ignorant fellow and attributes stupidity to him." See the texts cited by Leveen in Rosenthal's *Saadya Studies,* pp. 81 (English), 86, 88 (Arabic).

71. See Hirschfeld's *Qirqisāni Studies,* pp. 22 ff.; and Cant. r. II.4 (on 2:4). This old Jewish acceptance of concurrent and even contradictory interpretations was fundamental to all rabbinic exegesis. The school of R. Ishmael had already cited Jeremiah's simile, "Is not My word like a fire, saith the Lord; and like a hammer that breaketh the rock in pieces?" (23:29) to teach that "just as a hammer generates many sparks, so does one verse produce many meanings" (Sanhedrin 34a). This fundamental approach unavoidably colored Muslim exegetical literature, too, and as early as the eighth century it was sharply formulated by the

philosopher 'Ubaid Allah al-Anbari. Citing a number of contradictory doctrines which could equally well be supported by Qur'anic quotations, Al-Anbari declared, "At times one may derive two mutually exclusive doctrines from the same verse." Goldziher, *Richtungen*, pp. 178 f.

72. Hirschfeld's *Qirqisāni Studies*, p. 9; Skoss's *'Ali ben Suleiman*, pp. 36 f. Skoss rightly points out that, although occasionally voicing independent opinions, 'Ali was essentially a compiler of earlier views. The very title page (*ibid.*, p. 33) speaks of 'Ali having "compiled [this commentary] for himself from the abridgment of the venerable Sheikh 'Abu'l-Faraj Harūn ibn al-Faraj . . . from the commentary on the Pentateuch by the Sheikh Abu Yakub [Joseph] ben Nuḥ. . . ." See also Skoss's remarks on "The Date of 'Ali ben Suleiman the Karaite" (Hebrew), *Tarbiz*, II, 510–13 (insisting against D. Z. Baneth on 1072/3–1103 as the most probable date). On Ibn Ezra see *supra*, n. 63.

73. See Pinsker's *Lickute kadmoniot*, I, 158, II, 130 ff.; Mann's *Texts and Studies*, II, 18 ff., 85. It is to be regretted that this extensive commentary by Salmon (according to Pinsker, one MS consisted of two large volumes totaling 604 folios) has never been fully published. Only that on Chaps. 42–72 has recently been ed. by L. Marwick, regrettably without introduction, translation, or notes. Mann seems to have consulted another Leningrad manuscript covering only Psalms 90–150 in 247 folios. In fact, of all of Salmon's recorded exegetical works (on the Pentateuch, Psalms, Proverbs, Job, Daniel, and the five "Scrolls") only those on Lamentations and Ruth have appeared in full. The former in the Arabic original, ed. by S. Feuerstein, and the latter in the Hebrew trans. by Tobiah ben Moses, ed. by Markon in *Poznanski Mem. Vol.*, Hebrew section, pp. 78–96 (see *supra*, Chap. XXVI, n. 7), Markon, who lists here also additional literature on Salmon the exegete, points out that the Hebrew translation contains many Grecisms and thus betrays its Byzantine origin. Salmon's authorship of that commentary is very dubious, however. In his review of P. Birnbaum's ed. of Jephet's commentary on Hosea, L. Marwick attributed it to Jephet, rather than Salmon (*JBL*, LXII, 39). The same conclusion was reached, it seems independently, by L. Nemoy in his note "Did Salmon ben Jeroham Compose a Commentary on Ruth?" *JQR*, XXXIX, 215 f. Its relative brevity contrasts, indeed, with Salmon's frequent lengthy digressions in his genuine commentaries on Psalms and the other "Scrolls." The Firkovitch and British Museum MSS of his commentary on Ecclesiastes cover 101 and 107 folios, while the three Paris and London MSS of his commentary on Lamentations number 123, 198, and 244 folios, respectively. See Mann, *Texts and Studies*, II, 20 n. 36; H. Zotenberg, *Catalogue des manuscrits hébreux et samaritains de la Bibliothèque Impériale* [*Paris*], p. 39 No. 295; and G. Margoliouth, *Catalogue of the Hebrew and Samaritan Manuscripts in the British Museum*, I, 191 ff. Nos. 252–54. See also *ibid.*, pp. 256 f. In Feuerstein's partial edition Salmon's observations on the first chapter of Lamentations alone extend over 46 printed pages. There was little to choose between the longwindedness of the tenth-century Rabbanite and Karaite exegetes. Such attempts of either group at exhaustive treatment certainly proved self-defeating.

74. Jephet's *Commentary* on Hos. 3:3, 14:3, ed. by P. Birnbaum, pp. xxvii ff. (English), 52, 215 ff. (Arabic). The tenor of these comments is quite in line with

the then prevailing Karaite standards. In fact, despite many divergences in detail, their general approach greatly resembles that of the earlier Karaite commentary on Hosea which had apparently emanated from Qumisi's circle. Cf. Fragment I published by Mann in his "Early Karaite Bible Commentaries," *JQR,* XII, 483 ff. Jephet himself readily admitted that his observations were partly derived from other "scholars." See Schorstein's ed. of *Der Commentar des Karäers Jephet ben 'Alī zum Buche Rûth,* p. 7 (the British Museum MS underlying this edition was copied in 1004–5, that is in Jephet's lifetime; see also the numerous corrections suggested in S. Poznanski's review of that edition in *ZHB,* VII, 133–35); and by Birnbaum, pp. viii f. Jephet doubtless had in mind here his Karaite predecessors, rather than the much-maligned Saadiah. This is particularly true when he specifically referred to "one of our colleagues," probably his contemporary, Sahl ben Maṣliaḥ. See I. Günzig's introduction to his ed. of *Der Commentar des Karäers Jephet ben 'Ali Halêvi zu den Proverbien,* pp. 25 f. (only the first three chapters are edited here). See also P. Jung's Göttingen dissertation, *Ueber des Karäers Jephet arabische Erklärung des Hohenliedes.* Jephet's other published works are conveniently listed by S. L. Skoss in his "Jefet ben Ali ha-Levi," *EJ,* VIII, 757 ff.

75. See Günzig's ed., pp. vi ff. and the introduction, pp. 22 ff.; D. S. Margoliouth's ed. and trans. of *A Commentary on the Book of Daniel by Jephet ben Ali the Karaite,* pp. vii f.; Birnbaum, pp. xx ff.; and Ibn Ezra's oft-quoted introduction with Bacher's comments thereon in *SB* Vienna, LXXXI, 398 ff. On Jephet's condemnation of Saadiah's exegetical methods, see, e.g., the passage from his *Commentary* on Daniel, cited *infra,* n. 105. And yet he imitated Saadiah in writing explanatory introductions on the objectives of each book commented upon. For example, he explained that the book of Ruth was composed to show that even heathens could, by conversion and deep piety, reach the highest ranks of Jewish nobility. See Schorstein ed., pp. iii f., and Intro., p. 8. Jephet unhesitatingly adopted even some of Saadiah's mannerisms such as using phonetically, rather than substantively related Arabic words. On one occasion he specifically apologized for repeating an earlier statement, but cited in excuse a similar repetition by Saadiah. See the excerpt from his *Commentary* on Exod. 12:1, cited by Günzig, p. 22 n. 31. In many respects, however, Jephet's work marked a distinct advance over Saadiah, and D. S. Margoliouth's generally low appraisal of its quality (pp. viii f.) is decidedly an underestimate. See also E. L. Marwick, "The Order of the Books in Yefet's Bible Codex," *JQR,* XXXIII, 445–60.

76. Abraham ibn Ezra's *Sefer Mo'znayim* (Scales of the Hebrew Language; a Grammatical Treatise), ed. by W. Heidenheim, fol. 1b. Cf. W. Bacher's *Abraham ibn Esra als Grammatiker,* p. 174; J. Galliner's observation on Ibn Ezra's *Commentary* on Job, pp. 30 ff.; S. L. Skoss's analysis of Abu'l Faraj Harun's exegetical contributions in his *'Ali ben Suleiman,* pp. 11 ff.; Poznanski's *Moses ibn Chiquitilla,* pp. 34 ff.; the introduction and comments in his edition of Ibn Bal'am's *Commentary* on Joshua; and S. Fuchs's *Studien über . . . Juda ibn Bal'am.* On Ibn Janaḥ, see n. 77. Needless to say, like the other commentators of the period, all the last-named exegetes were under the influence of Saadiah. In a notable controversy on the meaning of Jacob's wish that "unto their assembly let my glory not be united" (Gen. 49:6), Ibn Chiquitilla followed Saadiah in equating glory with "soul" and postulating an exact parallelism with the preceding phrase, whereas

Ibn Bal'am translated it (with Saadiah's opponent, Dunash ben Labraṭ) by "body." See Ibn Ezra's comment *ad loc.* (in favor of Ibn Chiquitilla's rendering); and Poznanski's *Ibn Chiquitilla,* p. 127. Even Saadiah's simple identification of biblical plants could become the subject of extended debates in the subsequent exegetical literature. See the data cited by I. Markon in his "*Mar deror* (Exodus XXX. 23) Explained by Saadya and His Successors" in *Saadya Studies,* ed. by Rosenthal, pp. 97–102. Here Saadiah's rendition by the equivalent of "pure musc," reproducing a tradition shared also by Syriac Christians, was repudiated by Hai Gaon, Ḥananel, Ibn Janaḥ, and others, but accepted by Maimonides. Unfortunately, Poznanski never completed his intended edition of all extant exegetical works of Ibn Bal'am. We shall see that in the famous controversy between Samuel ibn Nagrela and Ibn Janaḥ, which was to last beyond the lifespan of both protagonists, this sharp-witted, though often ungenerous, scholar of Seville took sides against his fellow townsman, the *nagid,* while his much-hated opponent Ibn Chiquitilla fought on the *nagid's* side against his fellow Saragossan, Ibn Janaḥ. See *infra,* n. 109; and Chap. XXX, n. 52.

77. See M. B. Alavi's "Inimitability of the Qur'ān," *IC,* XXIV, 1–15; H. Singer's ed. of *Die Summa decretorum des Magister Rufinus,* p. 23 ("hence the Hebrew text is more corrupt than the Greek, the Greek more than the Latin"); Spicq's *Esquisse,* pp. 90 ff.; *supra,* Chap. XXIV, n. 12; Ibn Chiquitilla's trans. of *Two Treatises on Verbs containing Feeble and Double Letters,* by Yehudah Ḥayyuj, ed. and trans. into English by J. W. Nutt, p. 1; B. Klar's "Bible Exegesis in the Language of Spanish Hebrew Poetry" (Hebrew), reprinted in his *Meḥqarim ve-'iyyunim,* pp. 174–79; W. Bacher's *Aus der Schrifterklärung des Abulwalîd Merwân Ibn Ǧanâḥ (R. Jona)*; and A. Z. Rabinowitz's compilation (partly based on Bacher) of a *Perush le-kitbe ha-qodesh* (Commentary on the Bible) by R. Jonah ibn Janaḥ, with additions and corrections in Rabinowitz's trans. of Bacher's *Anfänge,* entitled *Niṣṣane ha-diqduq,* Appendix. Cf. also *infra,* Chap. XXX, n. 51. On Augustine's views (*De doctrina christiana,* II.14 in *PL,* XXXIV, 45 f.), and on the linguistic impact of the Latin liturgy, see F. König's observations in "Die Bedeutung der Vetus Latina," *Saeculum,* IV, 267–73.

78. See Saadiah's comments on II Sam. 23:18 and II Kings 8:10, as reconstructed by B. Cohen in *Saadiah Anniv. Vol.,* pp. 124, 132; Ibn Ezra's reference thereto in his *Commentary* on Isa. 49:5, ed. by Friedlaender, p. 84 (in Friedlaender's trans., p. 223); B. Heller's observations in *REJ,* XXXVII, 227, 247; Ibn Yashush cited by Ibn Ezra on Gen. 36:33; and Abraham Maimonides' *Resp.,* ed. by Freimann, p. 31 No. 16. Even 'Ali ben Suleiman's suggestion that "it is said" that in lieu of "he planteth an ash" (*Oren;* Isa. 44:14) one should read "cedar" (*erez*) was hardly an emendation. The very Masorah distinguishes here the "n" by a small letter. Cf. Pinsker's *Lickute kadmoniot,* I, 177 f. In his defense of the biblical tradition, Saadiah went to great lengths in answering twelve different criticisms voiced by opponents but none of these related to alleged corruptions in the text or the need of emendations. Even where the Bible seems to contradict figures previously quoted, as in the two versions of David's census (II Sam. 24:9 and I Chron. 21:5), or of Ahaziah's age (II Kings 8:26 and II Chron. 22:2), both the critics and the apologist resorted to logical arguments, not to textual expedients. See the gaon's *Beliefs and Opinions,* III.10, pp. 140 ff. (Arabic), 72 ff. (Hebrew), 173 ff. (English).

Yehudah Halevi, too, strongly argued against the alteration of a single letter even if, because of it, a biblical phrase appears to be "in contrast to common sense." See his *K. al-Khazari,* III.27 ff., ed. by Hirschfeld, pp. 180 ff.; in Hirschfeld's trans., pp. 164 ff.

79. Ibn Janaḥ's *Kitab al-Luma'* (Grammatical Treatise), XXVIII (XXVII, p. 295; in the Hebrew trans. by Yehudah ibn Tibbon, entitled *Sefer ha-Riqmah,* ed. by M. Wilensky, II, 308 f., with the editor's notes thereon, *ibid.,* and p. 544; and in the French trans. by M. Metzger, p. 287); Ibn Parḥon's *Maḥberet he-'Arukh,* fol. 7a; and Ibn Ezra's views on these and other linguistic anomalies in the Bible analyzed by W. Bacher in his *Abraham ibn Esra als Grammatiker,* pp. 40 ff., 115 f. Many grammatical rules were specifically devised to justify a biblical form which ran counter to accepted usage. These and other philological techniques utilized for reducing textual difficulties, such as the transposition of words, phrases, or sentences and the elliptic omission of words, will be more fully discussed in the next chapter.

80. In his comment on the first verse of Genesis, Rashi insisted that "This verse calls for hermeneutic interpretation." Three verses later he added, "Here, too, we require the aid of the Aggadah." On another occasion, however, he declared, "There are many aggadic expositions [of that verse], and the sages have already arranged them properly in Bereshit rabbah and other midrashim. But I am only after the simple meaning, and [use only] an Aggadah removing the obstacles from the proper understanding of Scripture" (on Gen. 3:8). Cf. also other examples cited by Lipschütz in his aforementioned Hebrew biography of Rashi, pp. 164 ff. Qara's statement, quoted in our text from his *Commentary* on Judg. 5:4 (ed. by S. Eppenstein in his "Studien über Joseph ben Simon Kara als Exeget," *JJLG,* IV, Hebrew section, p. 6) is repeated by him in many other formulations in his other commentaries. But the editors of extant fragments, as well as Poznanski in his general introduction to Eliezer of Beaugency's *Commentary* (pp. xxxi f.) have pointed out Qara's numerous inconsistencies. Some of these, especially in his early works, may readily be explained by his indebtedness to his teacher, Rashi, although at times he indulged in courageous, even sharp dissent. See H. Englander's "Joseph Kara's Commentary on Micah in Relation to Rashi's Commentary," *HUCA,* XVI, 157–62 (showing total indebtedness); and, more generally, Eppenstein's analysis in *JJLG,* IV, 238 ff. Qara also frequently quotes his paternal uncle, Menaḥem bar Ḥelbo. See the data assembled by Poznanski in his ed. of Menaḥem's *Pitrone* (Fragments de l'éxegèse biblique), pp. 9 f., 19 ff.

81. Samuel bar Meir's *Perush ha-torah* (Commentary on the Pentateuch), on Gen. 1:5, 37:2; Exod. 13:9, in D. Rosin's ed., pp. 5 f., 49, 98. See also Rosin's still indispensable monograph, *R. Samuel ben Meir als Schrifterklärer;* and S. Neuhausen's "Strokes in a Profile of Rashbam" (Hebrew), *Ha-Zofeh,* XV, 194–201. There is no evidence that Samuel knew that Karaites had interpreted away the commandment of phylacteries on exactly the same grounds, and that his contemporary, Benjamin of Tudela, was to find in the Orient sectarians who "profane the eve of the Sabbath, and observe the first night of the week, which is the termination of the Sabbath." Cf. his *Massa'ot,* ed. by Adler, fol. 18ab (Hebrew), p. 15 (English). Even Abraham ibn Ezra, world traveler though he was, need not have known of these surviving vestiges of the 'Ukbarite sect, about which see *supra,* Chap. XXV,

nn. 59–60. That is why his polemical *Iggeret Shabbat* (Epistle on the Sabbath), in which he repudiated Samuel's interpretation, may well have had a purely literary rather than empirical origin. Certainly, during his sojourn in France he could have learned of either Rashbam's comment or its underlying source, Poznanski's arguments (in his "Meswi al-Okbari," *REJ*, XXXIV, 176 ff.) to the contrary. On the other hand, Ibn Ezra's may have been a doubled-pronged attack on both the "French Commentary," to which he alludes as brought to him in a dream, and some distant sectarians possibly known to him from hearsay. See also *infra*, n. 86.

82. How little influence Samuel bar Meir's brilliant and penetrating exegesis had on subsequent generations may be gauged from survival of only one fairly adequate, though incomplete, manuscript of his Pentateuch commentary, while his comments on other biblical books have totally disappeared. Similarly, Joseph Bekhor Shor's *Commentary* on the Pentateuch is extant only in one manuscript, from which it was published in slow driblets since 1856. See the list of earlier publication in M. A. Bamberger's ed. of the section on Num. 16–36 in *Ha-Zofeh*, XI, 98 n. 7. See also M. Abraham's ed. and analytical treatment of the section on Leviticus, *ibid.*, VIII, 209–67; and in *REJ*, LXXVII, 41–60, respectively. To such an extent has Rashi's commentary overshadowed those of all his northern French successors. Of some interest is also "A Commentary to the Pentateuch à la Rashi's," probably dating from the thirteenth century, and ed. by J. Mann in *HUCA*, XV, 497–527. Anonymity, as we recall, was an integral part of the midrashic tradition, since the more ancient a homily was purported to be, the more authority it carried with the public. See *supra*, Chap. XXVIII, nn. 6 ff. See also, more generally, M. Ginsburger's review of "L'Exegèse biblique des Juifs d'Allemagne au Moyen âge," *HUCA*, VII, 439–56 (on the basis of a Reuchlin MS at Karlsruhe); and the even broader recent survey of "The Mediaeval Jewish Exegetes of the Old Testament" by S. B. Gurewicz in the *Australian Biblical Review*, I, 23–43.

83. See J. J. Rivlin's "R. Saadiah Gaon's Prefaces as an Introduction to the Bible" (Hebrew), *Rav Saadya Gaon*, ed. by Fishman, pp. 382–427 (includes a Hebrew trans. of the gaon's two introductions to the book of Psalms); A. S. Halkin's ed. of "A Fragment of Saadiah's Introduction to His Commentary on the Pentateuch," *Ginzberg Jub. Vol.*, Hebrew section, pp. 129–57; W. Eisenstädter's ed. of Saadiah's *Tafsir* (Arabischer Midrasch zu den *Zehn Geboten;* with his Hebrew and German trans.); Isaac Morali's French trans., entitled *Dissertation homilétique sur le Décalogue récitée dans les synagogues d'Algérie;* and Freimann's bibliographical additions in *Saadia Anniversary Volume*, p. 331 Nos. 15–18. A genuine *Tafsir* on the Ten Commandments seems to be attributed to Saadiah in the old book list published in Schechter's *Saadyana*, pp. 78 f. Its main ideas were undoubtedly reflected in the gaon's composition on the Ten Commandments, ed. by A. Neubauer in "Some Unpublished Liturgica Attributed to R. Sa'âdya Gaon," *Semitic Studies in Memory of Alexander Kohut*, pp. 392 ff. Cf. Malter's *Saadia*, pp. 336, 406 ff.; and Saadiah's *Siddur*.

84. Baḥya's *Duties of the Heart*, IV.7; VI.2, ed. by Yahuda, pp. 225, 261; the former also in M. Hyamson's English trans., III, 51; Abraham bar Ḥiyya's *Sefer Hegyon ha-nefesh* (Ethical Treatise), ed. by Y. E. Freimann, fol. 23b f. Cf. *infra*, Chap. XXXIV. An interesting combination of simple interpretation, linguistic semantics, and homi-

letical elaboration is offered by a typical Eastern commentator, Samuel ben Nissim Masnut of twelfth-century Aleppo, in his commentary on Job entitled *Ma'ayan gannim* (Spring of Gardens). See the text, ed. by S. Buber.

85. *Guide,* III.41; in Friedländer's trans., p. 347. In his "Beiträge zur Pentateuchexegese Maimuni's" (in *Moses ben Maimon,* ed. by J. Guttmann *et al.,* I, 411–20), S. Eppenstein culled eighteen interpretations communicated, in the father's name, by Abraham Maimonides. See also Eppenstein's biography of *Abraham Maimuni,* pp. 29 f., 33 ff.; and, more generally, W. Bacher's *Bibelexegese Moses Maimûni's;* I. Friedlaender's "Maimonides as an Exegete" in his *Past and Present,* pp. 193–216; and *supra,* Chap. XXVII, n. 119.

86. Ibn Ezra on Gen. 28:12; Saadiah's aforementioned passages in the two versions in his *Beliefs,* VII.2, in Rosenblatt's English trans., pp. 265 ff., 414 ff.; Maimonides' *Guide,* I.5, pp. 18 f. (on Exod. 3:6) and many other passages. Cf. I. Heinemann, "Die wissenschaftliche Allegoristik des jüdischen Mittelalters," *HUCA,* XXIII, Part 1, pp. 611–43; and *supra,* Chap. XXVIII, nn. 31–32. The term "mysteries of the Torah" is frequently used by Maimonides even in the Arabic context of his *Guide* (see esp. I.35; in Friedländer's trans., pp. 49 f.) or his *Maqala fi teḥiyyat ha-metim* (Treatise on Resurrection), ed. by J. Finkel, p. 10; see the editor's introduction in *PAAJR,* IX, 83. Needless to say, the sage of Fusṭaṭ merely wished to refer here to some allegorical, rather than to more specifically kabbalistic, meanings which these words came to denote in the later Middle Ages. See Bacher's *Bibelexegese Maimûni's,* pp. 12 ff. On the legend of Maimonides' ultimate conversion to the secret lore of Kabbalah, see *infra,* Chap. XXXIII. Of considerable interest, in this connection, is also the Commentary on the book of Ecclesiastes written in 1143 by Abu'l-Barakat Ḥibbat Allah of Baghdad. This distinguished thinker, styled *Awḥad az-zaman* (the only one of his time), who after his conversion to Islam at an advanced age, was often considered one of the five greatest Muslim philosophers of all times, used this commentary as a vehicle for the formulation of many daring ideas. See the introduction and two passages published from a Bodleian MS by S. Poznanski in his "Mitteilungen aus handschriftlichen Bibelkommentaren, VIII," *ZHB,* XVI, 32–36; and, more generally, S. Pines's "Etudes sur Awḥad al-Zaman Abu'l Barakat al-Baghdâdi," *REJ,* CIII, 3–64; CIV, 1–33. Unfortunately, Pines's intention to publish this entire commentary as well as Abu'l Barakat's comprehensive philosophic work has not yet materialized.

Biases often were so insidious that unwary students at times cited statements by predecessors without realizing their full doctrinal implications. This happened, for example, to Ibn Ezra, who in his *Commentary* on Hos. 5:11, took over an interpretation by Jephet ben 'Ali without noticing the peculiar Karaite coloring of the phrase that Ephraim had willingly "walked after the man-made commandment." Cf. P. Birnbaum's *Arabic Commentary of Yephet,* p. xliv.

87. See H. Ritter's "Philologica, VI: Ibn al-Ǵauzīs Bericht über Ibn ar-Rewendī?" *Der Islam,* XIX, 1–17; and P. Kraus's ed. of the *"Kitāb Az-Zumurruḏ* [The Emerald] des Ibn Ar-Rāwandī," *RSO,* XIV, 93–129, 335–79. The name of Ibn ar-Rawandi's Jewish host is given as Abu 'Isa ben Levi by S. Poznanski in his Hebrew essay on "Ḥivi ha-Balkhi," *Hagoren,* VII, 128 f. On the "pagan counter offensive" in antiquity, and particularly on Porphyry's penetrating criticism of the Bible, see *supra,* Vol. II,

pp. 156 ff., 390 f. To the literature listed there add P. Frassinatti's more recent analysis of "Porfirio esegeta del profeta Daniele," *Rendiconti* of the Istituto lombardo di scienze, Classe di lettere, LXXXVI, 194–210.

88. On Isma'il's Bible criticisms, see Qirqisani's *K. al-Anwar,* I.15, ed. by Nemoy, I, 56 f. (in Nemoy's English trans. in *HUCA,* VII, 388). The date of Ḥivi's literary activity (about 873) has long ago been reconstructed from a remark in Saadiah's *Sefer ha-Galui.* In this pamphlet, written in 933, the gaon mentioned that the critic's questions had circulated among Jews for sixty years (Harkavy's *Zikhron,* V, 147, 176 f.). This date of *ca.* 873 is roughly confirmed by Qirqisani's reference to Abu-'Imran's reply. See his *K. al-Anwar,* I.16, p. 57 (*HUCA,* VII, 389); and *supra,* Chap. XXV, n. 60. However, the crucial Arabic word *aqam* (Harkavy, p. 177) may mean that Ḥivi's work had circulated for sixty years before the composition of Saadiah's reply, probably in 926–27, or even, according to Wertheimer, many years earlier. See below in this note; and my remarks in *Saadia Anniv. Vol.,* p. 48. On the community of Balkh, recorded by Ibn Khurdadhbah as situated on a route traversed by the "Radanite" Jewish merchants, cf. *supra,* Chap. XXII, n. 39; and P. Schwarz's "Bemerkungen zu den arabischen Nachrichten über Balkh," *Oriental Studies . . . Pavry,* pp. 434–43.

Ḥivi's *She'elot* (Questions), or *Ṭa'anot* (Arguments; both titles are mentioned in the sources, the former being more widely accepted), have intrigued scholars ever since S. J. L. Rapoport, more than a century ago, analyzed with great penetration the few extant references to them in later medieval letters. Little further progress was made until 1915, when I. Davidson published a substantial Genizah fragment of *Saadia's Polemic against Ḥiwi al-Balkhi.* Apart from adding an English translation and notes, Davidson reproduced here also all known references to Ḥivi in the later Hebrew and Arabic literatures. Saadiah's polemical tract was soon thereafter republished, with additional comments, by S. Poznanski in his *Teshubot Rab Saadiah Gaon* (Ein Fragment der polemischen Schrift Saadja Gaons gegen Chiwi al-Balchi); and by S. A. Wertheimer under a similar title. Among the analytical studies one must mention especially M. Stein's "Ḥivi al-Balkhi, the Jewish Marcion" (Hebrew), *Sefer Klausner,* pp. 210–25; and J. Rosenthal's "Ḥiwi al-Balkhi: a Comparative Study," *JQR,* XXXVIII, 317–42, 419–30; XXXIX, 79–94. In his observations on "The Sources of Ḥivi al-Balkhi," *Marx Jub. Vol.,* Hebrew section, pp. 95–102, J. Guttmann completely overlooked Stein's essay while raising essentially the same problems.

Notwithstanding these arduous efforts, many fundamental literary and ideological questions still await elucidation. It is generally assumed, for example, that Ḥivi wrote his tract in rhymed Arabic prose. The only evidence adduced in support of this assumption is one of Saadiah's censures of Ḥivi. The future gaon blamed his opponent for having "roared before strangers" (stanza 37, in Davidson's ed., pp. 58 f.). However, shouting, or rather declaring something "in a loud, undignified voice" (see C. Rabin's "Saadya Gaon's Hebrew Prose Style" in Rosenthal's *Saadya Studies,* p. 120), "before" (*lifne*) strangers does not necessarily imply the use of Arabic, and still less of rhymed prose. Even more flimsy is the argument based on Pseudo-Baḥya's eleventh-century ethical treatise, *Kitab Ma'ani al-nafs* (Buch vom Wesen der Seele, ed. by I. Goldziher, p. 16; reproduced by Davidson, p. 99) stating that "the reason which prompted him [Saadiah] to answer in Hebrew was that Ḥiwi was a follower of the Magi and he began to undermine the Torah, so in answering him R. Saadiah could not make his reply public in Arabic." The unknown Spanish author of this treatise was evidently completely uninformed. Certainly, writing as a high-ranking official (*alluf*) of the academy of Sura, or, if Wertheimer's suggestion (in his ed., pp. 2 ff.) is correct, drafting the first version of his reply as a young man in Egypt or Palestine while Ḥivi was still alive (some phrases resemble indeed exhortations to a living contemporary), Saadiah had very little to fear of Zoroastrian reprisals. As far as Islam and, for that matter, Zoroastrianism were concerned, there is nothing in Saadiah's reply which could not have been published in Arabic, even in the Arabic alphabet, in which the gaon's main philosophic treatise was soon to appear.

Equally questionable is the general assumption that the twelve anti-traditionalist criticisms, to which Saadiah replied at the end of the third section of his *Beliefs and Opinions,* had likewise for the most part stemmed from Ḥivi. Davidson added the queries underlying nine of these replies to the thirty-one he had reconstructed from the new fragment, and to seven others known from outside sources. He thus obtained a total of forty-seven recorded strictures by Ḥivi. Poznanski reduced this total to forty-four, while Rosenthal subdivided some questions and thus reached a total of sixty-five. These and other scholars agreed, therefore, that only one fifth to one third of the two hundred criticisms formulated by Ḥivi (this figure is cited in Saadiah's name by Yehudah bar Barzillai in his *Commentary* on *Yeṣirah,* ed. by Halberstam, p. 21; Davidson, pp. 83 f.) have so far been recovered.

This matter requires careful reconsideration, however. Evidently, Saadiah's fragment is incomplete in the beginning, where it starts abruptly with a reply to Ḥivi's stricture on Gen. 3:22. Very likely the earlier portions of the story of Creation, highly intriguing to other exegetes, also exerted their great fascination on Ḥivi's inquiring mind. Only two of these early questions relating to the *tohu va-bohu* (Gen. 1:2), which Ḥivi allegedly tried to twist in a dualistic vein, and to God's apparent ignorance of Adam's whereabouts (Gen. 3:9) have been reconstructed from Pseudo-Baḥya (*loc. cit.*) and Ibn Ezra (in his longer *Commentary* on Gen., ed. by Friedlaender, p. 39; Davidson, pp. 100 f.). On the other hand, the conclusion of Saadiah's "Replies" definitely bears the earmarks of a finale of the whole work. Perhaps the gaon answered only the section of Ḥivi's book dealing with Genesis. If so, that may be why he mentions no strictures on the story of Moses, a few of which are answered, with the accompaniment of customary curse words, by Ibn Ezra. Since Moses' personality and work were in the very center of the then raging religious controversies, Ḥivi, too, must have devoted considerable space to them. The detailed ritualistic regulations of the book of Leviticus and the narratives of the book of Numbers, on the other hand, offered fewer targets for Ḥivi's anti-biblical bias. Possibly he limited his comments altogether to the first two books of Moses, the critique of Num. 14:23 (Davidson, pp. 95 f.) being, like that mentioned before on Deut. 32:9, but incidental to an earlier animadversion.

For this reason Davidson's and Poznanski's hypotheses that only about a quarter of Ḥivi's criticisms had been reconstructed is far too mechanical. Ḥivi apparently followed the sequence of the Pentateuch, but commented only on what aroused his special interest. In the book of Genesis, his queries are almost wholly concentrated on the first twenty-two chapters, while he had little to say about anything that followed the sacrifice of Isaac. Nor must we forget that, while he seems to have indulged in occasional excursuses on related subjects, he also liked to harp on basically the same themes in different questions. "Thou hast asked," Saadiah commented, "further concerning the kinds of suffering; hunger and sickness, fear and [robbery] and destruction, and [excessive] heat and cold, why they are not kept from men. All these are but one question and thou hast multiplied words" (stanza 10; Davidson, pp. 42 f.). It is not improbable, therefore, that we now know the majority of Ḥivi's significant points and that nothing startingly new may be expected from the further discoveries of Saadiah's replies. The main portion of Ḥivi's critique, now missing, which probably referred to the biblical cosmogony and the doctrine of prophecy, was doubtless covered in the gaon's comprehensive reply to all opponents of the traditional lore. See his *Beliefs,* I and III, *passim.*

89. Joseph al-Baṣir's *Sefer Maḥkimat peti* (Making Wise the Simple; a philosophic treatise) cited from a Leyden MS by P. Frankl in "Die Stellung Joseph al-Basir's in der jüdischen Religionsphilosophie," *MGWJ,* XX, 156 f.; and Ibn Ezra's comments on Exod. 16:13, 34:29, ed. by L. Fleischer, pp. 108, 334 f.—all reproduced by Davidson, pp. 98 f., 101 f. See Rosenthal's notes 78–80. On the *tarnjabin* (or *tarnjakhin* in Fleischer's ed. of Ibn Ezra, p. 108); and various other identifications of manna, see I. Löw's *Flora der Juden,* I, 25 f.; and F. S. Bodenheimer, "The Manna of Sinai," *Biblical Archaeologist,* X, 2–6.

90. Saadiah's *Polemic,* stanzas 43, 61–62 (Davidson, pp. 62 f., 72 f.); *Beliefs and Opinions,* III.10, p. 140 (in Rosenblatt's trans., pp. 173 f.). The problem of Isaac's age (on which see the various midrashic traditions cited by Theodor in his comments on Gen. r. LV.5, p. 587, and by L. Ginzberg in his *Legends of the Jews,* V, 249 n. 229, 254 n. 255; cf. also S. Spiegel's data in the *Marx Jub. Vol.,* Hebrew section, p. 472) disturbed also such moderate rationalists as Maimonides. According to Abraham Maimuni, his father had objected to Isaac's alleged age of thirty-seven on the ground that in this case the son's merit in accepting the sacrifice would far have exceeded that of Abraham. Cf. S. Eppenstein's remarks in *Moses ben Maimon,* ed. by J. Guttmann *et al.,* I, 414. Maimonides may have heard of similar objections by Ibn Ezra who, at the same time, rejected Isaac's alleged age of five and suggested thirteen instead. See Ibn Ezra's *Commentary* on Gen. 22:4.

In the reconstruction of Ḥivi's questions, Saadiah's major philosophic work was used here with considerable misgivings. This procedure, originally adopted by Graetz, has been applied with a fair degree of unanimity in recent decades. The fact that Ḥivi's name is nowhere mentioned could still be explained away by Saadiah's, as well as other contemporaries', general reticence in mentioning names of either friends or adversaries. This general practice obviates Wertheimer's untenable suggestion that Ḥivi's name was forgotten during the few years between the circulation of Saadiah's rhymed replies and the composition of his comprehensive apologia (p. 3 n. 2). More serious is the fact, pointed out by Poznanski (in his ed., pp. 12 f.), that Saadiah himself introduced the second of the twelve crucial objections as that of "someone else who would question . . ." (*Beliefs,* III, *loc. cit.*), thus drawing a distinction between the exponents of the first two questions. Such phrases may perhaps be dismissed as mere figures of speech, but there is no evidence whatsoever that Saadiah necessarily intended to single out Ḥivi from among the numerous contemporary Jewish rationalists or "separatists," as they were called by the author of the "Early Theologico-Polemical Work," published by Mann in *HUCA,* XII–XIII, 411 ff.

91. Saadiah's *Polemic,* stanzas 7, 28–29; and the Arabic *Commentary* on Num. 14–23 (first published by Harkavy) in Davidson's ed. pp. 40 ff., 52 ff., 95 f. The various

explanations suggested for the obscure passage in stanza 7 are summarized by Rosenthal in *JQR,* XXXVIII, 329 n. 57. But that B. M. Lewin was right (against Davidson) in relating the crucial words to Cain, rather than Abel, is evident from the sequel in which Saadiah obviously referred to the world to come as a place for ultimate judgment and "reproof" (*tokhaḥat*) of criminals who may have escaped their due penalty in this world. One is reminded in this connection of the ancient gnostic sect of Cainites, Cain's role in the perennial Judeo-Christian religious controversies, and the ultimately kindlier attitude of the rabbis to this first criminal whom they were prepared to treat on a par with an accidental slayer. See *supra,* Vol. II, p. 137.

92. See Davidson, Poznanski, Wertheimer, and Rosenthal, *passim.* The last question is doubly remarkable as it came from an inhabitant of the eastern parts of the Caliphate, who normally would have thought of his people living in the captivity of Ishmael rather than Esau-Edom-Se'ir. Of course, it was easy enough for Saadiah to deny that long-accepted rabbinic genealogy and to point out that the Se'ir region of Palestine was no longer under Christian domination, and that Christians or Romans were not really descendants of Esau. See also his *Beliefs,* III.8, pp. 133 f. (Arabic), 68 f. (Hebrew), 165 (English). This did not prevent Saadiah himself in another context from predicting that, upon the arrival of the Messiah, Jerusalem would be held by Armilus (clearly a corruption from Romulus) or someone else who "would also be of Edom." *Ibid.,* VIII.6, pp. 241 (Arabic), 123 (Hebrew), 305 (English).

93. See Baḥya's *Duties of the Heart,* Intro., pp. 28 f. (Arabic; in M. Hyamson's English trans., I, 18); and *supra,* Chap. XXIV, nn. 31–32. Ever since Mardan Farukh's critique of the Old Testament was called to their attention by J. Darmesteter's annotated French translation of parts of Chapters XIII–XIV (in *REJ,* XVIII, 1–15; XIX, 41–56), Jewish scholars, beginning with D. Kaufmann, often connected that late ninth-century Zoroastrian attack on Judaism with Ḥivi's questions. Incidentally, Massignon's quotation from Al-Baghdadi (in "La Legende 'De tribus impostoribus,'" *RHR,* LXXXII, 74 ff.) betrays considerable similarity with some of Mardan Farukh's arguments, especially with respect to Jesus' unfulfilled promise not to abrogate the law of Moses. On the *zindiqs* and other skeptics, see *supra,* Chap. XXIV, n. 29.

94. Ibn Daud's *Chronicle* in *MJC,* I, 66; and Mann's ed. of "An Early Theologico-Polemical Work," *HUCA,* XII–XIII, 450. S. Schechter's suggestion (in *JQR,* [o.s.] XIII, 354 f.) that Ibn Daud referred to Ḥivi's expurgated Bible has rightly been accepted by more recent scholars. Whatever one thinks of the general reliability of Ibn Daud's chronicle (see *supra,* Chap. XXVIII, n. 71), this historian-philosopher was rather careful in the choice of his terms. Discussing, for instance, 'Anan's work, he used exactly the same words *badah mi-libbo* (invented) as he did in Ḥivi's case, but he made clear that the heriesiarch's invention consisted in "laws that are not good," not in a new "Torah." In this way he doubtless paraphrased an inquiry to Naṭronai Gaon which quoted 'Anan as asserting "I shall prepare for you a Talmud of my own." See *supra,* Chap. XXVI, n. 79. Here, too, Ibn Daud must have rephrased some older source. The term *luḥot* (tablets or blackboards), however, may have been but a literary reminiscence of the story told about R. 'Aqiba in *Abot de-R. Natan,* VI, ed. by Schechter, p. 29. In any case, it seems likely that Ibn Daud never saw Ḥivi's work, which rapidly lost its popularity. Even the *Kitab Ḥivi Balkhi,* allegedly found

by Poznanski in an old book list, turned out to be a simple misreading. Cf. Poznanski's "Einige Bemerkungen zu einem alten Bücher-Catalog," *JQR,* [o.s.] XIII, 329; and S. Abramson's "R. Joseph Rosh ha-Seder," *KS,* XXVI, 80.

95. Mardan Farukh's *Decisive Solution,* XIII.148–49; XIV.40–50; ed. by Menasce, pp. 192 f., 198 f.; in West's trans., pp. 220 f.; Saadiah's *Polemic,* stanzas 47 ff., 59, ed. by Davidson, pp. 66 ff., 70 ff. True, our fragment of Saadiah's reply begins slightly later in Gen. 3, and hence we are in no position to reconstruct Ḥivi's query with any degree of precision. But it seems unlikely that Ḥivi should have passed over in silence the question of Adam's punishment, whether on the basis of morals or as an illustration of God's alleged changeability. Neither could Saadiah dismiss this criticism curtly, as he did in the case of Ḥivi's stricture on the punishment of Sodom, as being none of the critic's business (stanzas 57–68, Davidson, pp. 70 f.). Remarkably, however, the gaon addressed himself only to the question of changeability, related also to Ḥivi's attack on God's instability, concerning the Jewish possession of Palestine, for which Saadiah offered an explanation in a slightly different vein. Cf. his *Beliefs,* III.9, pp. 138 (Arabic), 70 (Hebrew), 170 (English), which is mainly aimed at the general Christian and Muslim contentions that the divine will was subject to abrogation. Although Ḥivi had apparently made a major issue of the ethical justification of hereditary penalties as well as rewards, this problem is totally ignored in Saadiah's chief apologetical work. This fact ought to give additional pause to those who single out Ḥivi as the main target of Saadiah's twelve-point analysis. See *supra,* nn. 88 and 90.

96. Saadiah's *Polemic,* stanzas 50–51, 54, ed. by Davidson, pp. 66 ff. See esp. Stein's data in *Sefer Klausner,* pp. 213 ff.; and Rosenthal's observations in *JQR,* XXXVIII, 335 n. 81, 419 ff. Neither Salmon nor Ibn Ezra hints in any way at Ḥivi's apostasy, although they let no mention of his name pass without appending to it some curse word or other. We must, therefore, go no farther than G. Vajda, who declared Ḥivi merely a *zindiq,* a radical freethinker, although he exaggerates somewhat the parallel with Ar-Rawandi. See his "Judaeo-Arabica," *REJ,* XCIX, 81 ff., 90. See also Menasce's introduction to Mardan Farukh's Chapters XIII–XIV, pp. 180 f.

97. The *Baraita* of the school of R. Ishmael at the beginning of *Sifra* on Lev., ed. by Weiss, fol. 3a; Abraham ben David's comment thereon *(ibid.)*; Saadiah's *Perush shelosh esreh middot* (Commentary on the Thirteen Modes) in Nahum ha-Ma'rabi's Hebrew trans. in Saadiah's *Oeuvres,* IX, 82 f. (see also J. Müller's intro., *ibid.,* pp. xxiii ff.; and H. J. Ehrenreich's introduction to his new ed. of the same work); the *Midrash Shene ketubim* (Midrash on the Two Contradictory Verses) in S. A. Wertheimer's *Bate midrashot,* I, 247 ff.; and another midrashic fragment, published from a Cambridge MS by Ginzberg in his *Ginze Schechter,* I, 230 ff. On the Christian exegetical literature of a related type, see, e.g., Theodoret of Cyrrhus' *In loca difficilia scripturae sacrae quaestiones selectae* (in *PG,* LXXX); Maximus Confessor's *Quaestiones, interrogationes et responsiones diversorumque difficiliorum capitum electa* (*ibid.,* XC, 785–856); Anastasios Sinaites' *Interrogationes et responsiones de diversis capitibus a diversis propositae* (*ibid.,* LXXXIX, 311–824); and on their relation to Ḥivi and other Jewish critics, see Rosenthal's observations in *JQR,* XXXIX, 80 ff. See also the brief MS notes from geonic replies in Wertheimer's *Qehillat Shelomoh* (Fragments of Geonic Responsa), p. 69; Ginzberg's *Ginze*

Schechter, I, 216 ff.; B. M. Lewin's and J. Mann's editions of still other fragments of a midrash *Shene ketubim* in *GK,* V, 145–46; and in J. Mann's "Some Midrashic Genizah Fragments," *HUCA,* XIV, 338 ff.

98. "The Oldest Collection," beginning, lines 10–11, with reference to Micah 7:3 and I Sam. 3:13. S. Schechter's ed. of that tract (in *JQR,* [o.s.] XIII, 358–69) was corrected by subsequent scholars, especially Bacher, Poznanski, and Porges, and supplemented by a fragment published in Ginzberg's *Ginze Schechter,* II, 491 ff. (its connection with the "Oldest Collection" was demonstrated by Mann in his *Texts and Studies,* II, 60 n. 111); and another, more lengthy piece reproduced in A. Scheiber's "Unknown Leaves from *She'elot 'atiqot* [Old Questions]," *HUCA,* XXVII, 291–303. The former two texts, together with their revisions, were fully reproduced and subjected to a careful scrutiny by J. Rosenthal in his Hebrew essay on "Old Questions on the Bible" in *HUCA,* XXI, 29–91. The censure of Bible students, quoted in our text appears in both eds. in the author's introductory statement, lines 10–11. It appears that the approximately 240 stanzas now known are only a fraction of the poem, which must have contained at least 506 stanzas. The various theories concerning its authorship and date are discussed by Rosenthal, pp. 32 ff.; and Scheiber, pp. 292 ff. It may be noted that Schechter himself recognized his error and admitted that, rather than being anti-Rabbanite, our author "demonstrated the necessity of Oral Law." See his letter to Poznanski of November 11, 1908, in his *Iggerot* (Letters to S. A. Poznanski), ed. by A. Yaari, p. 73. Mann's timid attribution of the poem to 'Ali ben Israel (*Texts,* II, 98) is disproved by the likely four-letter name in the acrostic, which, in Scheiber's reconstruction, seems to indicate the name of Yiṣḥaq (Isaac). The date was plausibly derived by N. Porges from the mention of a gaon, Joseph, apparently alluded to in the reference to Deut. 33:17 (Rosenthal, p. 51 line 5). The description of that gaon's authority as extending over the whole dispersion makes it unlikely that it concerned the head of a Palestinian academy, as is usually assumed. The author may well have had in mind the leader of Sura, Joseph ben Jacob surnamed Bar Satia, counter-gaon and successor of Saadiah (about 942–44). See Sherira's *Iggeret,* ed. by Lewin, p. 118. His poem may thus reflect the same climate of opinion which had induced Saadiah to write both his poem *Essa meshali* (see *supra,* n. 15; and *infra,* Chap. XXXII, n. 12) and his polemic against Ḥivi, both of which it resembles in many ways.

99. Rosenthal's ed., pp. 38 f., contrasted, for example, with the commentary apparently emanating from Qumisi's school, published by Mann in *JQR,* XII, 455 (Fragment G). See *supra,* n. 66. In his reconstruction of our author's "Difficulties" (pp. 55 ff.), Rosenthal failed to recognize these four fundamental questions (p. 39, lines 5–12). Similarly, two stanzas relating to the prophet Haggai's question (2:11–13) addressed to the priests of Jerusalem (p. 43, lines 8–12) probably meant to emphasize the difficulty for reason alone to explain the phenomenon of the communicable nature of impurity, as opposed to holiness which cannot be transmitted through mere touch. Even the ancient priests, though inured to the handling of sacred objects and endowed with the holy spirit, were unable to supply any logical reason for this contrast and had to rely on tradition as its sole justification. On numerical inconsistencies, see Scheiber's essay, pp. 301 f. If one adds these and other questions to the 103 "difficulties" reconstructed by Rosenthal, it becomes evident that our author had assembled an impressive number of several hundred ingenious queries

of this kind. The questions raised by the aforementioned unknown midrashic author (in Ginzberg's *Ginze Schechter,* I, 230 ff.; see *supra,* n. 97) must likewise have been quite numerous. Fully ten queries relate to the simple narrative of Jacob's encounter with Esau (Gen. 32:8–33:18), only one being concerned with the theologically important problem of why the angel had to depart at daybreak (Gen. 32:27).

100. Richard Simon's *Histoire critique du Vieux Testament* immediately became popular among both Protestants and Catholics and, within four years of its publication, was issued in an English translation entitled *A Critical History of the Old Testament.* Even contemporaries sensed that, despite its title, its purpose was apologetic rather than critical, a view fully shared by modern historians of biblical criticism. See esp. F. Stummer, *Die Bedeutung Richard Simons für die Pentateuchkritik.* The impact of these Catholic-Protestant controversies on contemporary Jewish biblical studies will be more fully analyzed in their seventeenth-century connections.

101. *Pirqe de-R. Eliezer,* Chaps. VI–VII, ed. by Higger in *Horeb,* VIII, 101–11 (in Friedlander's trans. pp. 31–59), with S. Gandz's comments thereon in his careful analysis of "The Problem of the Molad," *PAAJR,* XX, 251 ff.; Saadiah's *Kitab at-Ta'rikh* (Book of Chronology) in *MJC,* II, 89–110 (see *supra,* Chap. XXVIII, n. 74). Maimonides' *M.T.* Shemiṭṭah ve-Yobel x.2–8; his *Resp.,* No. 234; M. Steinschneider's "Jüdische Chronik nach Hamza el Isfahani," *Zeitschrift für die religiösen Interessen des Judentums,* II, 271–78, 321–28. See also other works by and on Saadiah analyzed in Malter's *Saadia Gaon,* pp. 168 ff., 351 ff.; I. Werfel's supplement thereto in *Rav Saadya Gaon,* ed. by Fishman, p. 652; Gandz's "Saadia Gaon as a Mathematician" in *Saadia Anniv. Vol.,* pp. 141–95; E. Baneth's "Maimonides als Chronologe und Astronom" in *Moses ben Maimon,* ed. by J. Guttmann *et al.,* II, 243–79 (both indirectly relevant also for historical chronology); E. Frank's interpretation of "A Perplexing Passage from Maimonides; a Contribution to the Chronology of Sabbatical Cycles," *JQR,* XXXVII, 149–64; my remarks in *PAAJR,* VI, 93 ff.; and, more generally, *supra,* Chap. XXVIII, and *infra,* Chap. XXXV.

102. See *Sifre* on Deut. 37, ed. by Friedmann, fol. 76a (ed. by Finkelstein, p. 70, with the editor's note thereon); Gen. r. I.1, p. 7 (with Theodor's note thereon); *supra,* Vol. II, pp. 319 f.; and Maimonides' *Commentary* on M. Sanhedrin x, Intro., ed. by Holzer, p. 26. Of course, whatever they thought of their own Scriptures, Jews never doubted that the canonical works of other faiths were invented by man. That is why Aḥmad ibn Ḥanbal need not have been completely wrong when he attributed the origin of the debate on the createdness of the Qur'an to a Jew (Labid)—the usual scapegoat for orthodox Muslims wishing to discredit a particular doctrine. See W. M. Patton's *Aḥmed ibn Ḥanbal and The Miḥna,* p. 47; and, more generally, W. M. Watt's "Early Discussions about the Qur'an," *MW,* XL, 27–40, 96–105.

103. Saadiah's two introductions to his translation of the Psalms, ed. by S. Eppenstein in *Festschrift Harkavy,* Hebrew section, pp. 144 f., 151 f.; and in J. J. Rivlin's Hebrew trans. in Fishman's *Rav Saadya Gaon,* pp. 408 f., 418; David Qimḥi's *Commentary* on Psalms 1–41, ed. by Schiller-Szinessy, pp. 12, etc.; Abraham Maimuni's *Resp.,* No. 45; Ibn Ezra's *Commentary* on Job, Introduction and verses 1:1 and 2:11. On the talmudic views concerning Job, see B. B. 14b f. So gullible in historical matters was Saadiah that he appended his aforementioned translation of the "Scroll of the

Hasmoneans" to his commentary on Esther, in order to emphasize the biblical prediction of the Maccabean victory and thus the better to reform "most of the nations" who "do not fully realize the import" of the events narrated there. See the text published by S. Atlas and M. Perlmann in their "Saadia on the Scroll of the Hasmoneans," *PAAJR,* XIV, 6 f.; and *supra,* Chap. XXVIII, n. 44. On his part, Ibn Ezra insisted on the identity of Ezekiel's Job with the author of the biblical book, for otherwise the Bible would have indicated the distinguishing patronymic of the two namesakes. See additional illustrations in Galliner's *Abraham ibn Esra's Hiobkommentar,* pp. 9 f.; and, more generally, D. Herzog's negative appraisal in his "Bemerkungen zu ibn Esra dem 'Historiker,'" *MGWJ,* LXXXI, 422–38 (in opposition to D. Feuchtwang).

104. Jephet's *Commentary on Daniel,* ed. by Margoliouth, pp. 2, 64 ff. (English), 6 f., 123 ff. (Arabic); David al-Fasi's *K. Jāmi' al-alfāz,* ed. by Skoss, I, xxxix, 375. Cf. *supra,* Chap. XVII, n. 18. Although not going to such lengths, Qirqisani, too, formulated exegetical rules which, when closely adhered to, proved serious obstacles to any detached historical criticism of the Bible. One of his thirty-seven propositions emphasized that Scripture contained no untrue statements whatsoever, unless they be expressly designated as such, or attributed to an author responsible for them. To explain some obvious discrepancies, Qirqisani stated in another proposition that biblical narratives were not exhaustive and that omissions in one narrative must be filled in from other contexts. See Hirschfeld's *Qirqisani Studies,* pp. 26 f.

105. See Jephet's *Arabic Commentary on Nahum,* ed. by Hirschfeld, pp. 17 (Arabic), 34 (English); his comments on Dan. 12:9–10, 13, ed. by Margoliouth, pp. 82, 85 ff. (English), 147, 151 ff. (Arabic); Saadiah's computations discussed *supra,* Chap. XXV, n. 21. Not implausibly, H. Hirschfeld (pp. 8 ff.) connected Jephet's, and to a lesser extent Saadiah's, messianic expectations with the contemporary Qarmatian troubles. That some such computation had been included by the gaon already in his commentary on Genesis is implied in Salmon ben Yeruḥim's attack thereon in his *Milḥamot Adonai* (Wars of the Lord), ed. by Davidson, p. 49 lines 85 ff. On the general messianic speculations of the medieval Jewish thinkers, including Saadiah and Jephet, see also *supra,* Chap. XXV, esp. nn. 18 ff.

106. Ibn Ezra's *Commentary* on Gen. 36:31. The identity of Isaac with Ibn Yashush, here attacked, has long been generally accepted. See the literature cited by Poznanski in his *Ibn Chiquitilla,* p. 28 n. 6. Ibn Ezra, to whom the idea that this chapter had been dictated by God to Moses long before the event was equally repugnant, resorted to the expedient of explaining that the reference to the kings of Israel was really to the days of Moses, whose kingship, often asserted in the Aggadah, seemed evident from the biblical allusion, "And there was a king in Jeshurun" (Deut. 33:5). See also the numerous other explanations offered by the Midrash and medieval commentators in M. M. Kasher's *Torah shelemah,* V, 1379 f.

107. See the fragments recovered by Poznanski in his *Ibn Chiquitilla,* pp. 96, 100 f., 109, 113, 145 f.; his introductory remarks, pp. 26 ff.; and Ibn Bal'am's comments on Zech. 9:9 and Mal. 3:23, ed. by him in *JQR,* XV, 51 ff. Ibn Chiquitilla's views were sufficiently veiled even for his opponent, Ibn Bal'am, to misunderstand them completely. In his comment on Isa. 60:13. Ibn Bal'am actually attacked the

"false opinion" held by many persons, including Ibn Chiquitilla, that the following messianic prophecies (verses 19 ff.) related to Hezekiah. He could easily "demolish" this opinion by stressing the biblical record of Hezekiah's political weakness. See his *Gloses,* ed. by Derenbourg, pp. 137 f.

108. Poznanski's *Ibn Chiquitilla,* pp. 98, 103 ff.; Ibn Bal'am in a comment on the First Prophets, ed. and trans. by J. Derenbourg in his *Gloses,* pp. 9 f., 120 f. Compared with these radical views, the mildly critical opinions expressed by northern scholars like Joseph Qara were extremely tame. Qara's denial, for example, that the reference in the Song of Deborah (Judg. 5:4) to the Lord coming from Se'ir or Edom related to the days of the Sinaitic revelation as postulated by the Midrash was little more than the long-accepted facultative approach to aggadic interpretation. Qara merely argued that after carefully studying all biblical poems he had found none referring to a miracle from a distant past. Cf. his Commentary, *ad loc.,* ed. by S. Eppenstein in *JJLG,* IV, 6.

109. Ibn Bal'am, *Gloses,* pp. 9 f.; and his *Commentary* on Jer. 31:14, 49:25, ed. by Israelsohn, in *Festschrift Harkavy,* Hebrew section, pp. 297, 304 f. (cf. the editor's remarks, *ibid.* p. 276); Ibn Ezra on Isa. 40:1. In his *Commentary* on Zech. 9:9, Ibn Bal'am was particularly vehement in rejecting any relationship between that prophecy and the work of Nehemiah. He accused Ibn Chiquitilla of intentionally disregarding contradictory data merely "in order to weaken the hearts of those awaiting the coming of the Redeemer who is described here as the acme of humility, righteousness and helpfulness." See the excerpt published and translated by Poznanski in *Ibn Chiquitilla,* pp. 157 ff. On Ibn Chiquitilla's great influence on Ibn Ezra who, notwithstanding frequent criticisms, could not refrain from occasionally paying him homage as "one of the great exegetes," see *ibid.,* pp. 55 ff.